# FUNDAMENTALS OF
# BUSINESS COMMUNICATION

# FUNDAMENTALS OF BUSINESS COMMUNICATION

**FRANCES G. CHANDLER**
SANTA MONICA COLLEGE AND
CALIFORNIA STATE UNIVERSITY, LOS ANGELES

*IRWIN*

Chicago • Bogata • Boston • Buenos Aires • Caracas
London • Madrid • Mexico City • Sydney • Toronto

Senior sponsoring editor: *Craig Beytien*
Associate editor: *Karen Mellon*
Marketing manager: *Kurt Messersmith*
Project editor: *Stephanie M. Britt*
Production manager: *Bob Lange*
Designer: *Laurie Entringer/Annette Spadoni*
Art studio: *Electra Graphics, Inc.*
Art coordinator: *Heather D. Burbridge*
Compositor: *Weimer Graphics, Inc.*
Typeface: *10/12 Berkeley Book*
Printer: *Von Hoffman Press, Inc.*

**Library of Congress Cataloging-in-Publication Data**

Chandler, Frances G.
    Fundamentals of business communication / Frances G. Chandler.
      p.   cm.
    Includes index.
    ISBN 0-256-10699-1
    1. Business communication.   I. Title.
HF5718.C448   1995
651.7—dc20                           94–24777

*Printed in the United States of America*
1 2 3 4 5 6 7 8 9 0 VH 1 0 9 8 7 6 5 4

To my students for providing the reason.
To my husband Jim for the counseling.
To our children Stacey, Marcey, Alyssa, and Rachel for the motivation.

# MESSAGE TO STUDENTS AND PROFESSORS

*Fundamentals of Business Communication* was written for you. Students will find everything they need to know to produce effective letters, memos, reports, and business presentations. Professors will appreciate the inclusion of what used to be considered the extras (communication technology, diversity issues, ethics, collaborative writing, etc.) into key chapters. Whether you are a student or a professor, you will appreciate the sound learning theory that has gone into the development of this book. Specific, measurable learning objectives were the basis for every chapter—from chapter outlines to the discussion questions and exercises at the end and even the exam questions. Appearing at the beginning of every chapter, highlighted within the chapters, and reappearing with their corresponding questions and exercises—these objectives guide you, helping you focus on what is most important.

# PREFACE

Take a few minutes to read about a few of the unique features that make this book remarkably better than other business communication textbooks on the market today.

### Chapter 1: Communicating in Today's Business World

Nonverbal communication, oral communication, and written communication are introduced in terms of their importance to you and to the organization for which you work.

Rather than a separate chapter at the end of the book, communication technology is given the importance it deserves—at the front of the book where you can see how technology has become as much a part of effective communication as the words we speak.

You may have been using the telephone your entire life, but you'll discover a few tips that will improve your telephone and dictation skills.

A unique model of the communication process is presented to highlight the barriers and the stimuli that affect you when you speak and write.

### Chapter 2: Communicating with Diverse Cultures

You are a product of your culture. No one can communicate well without understanding that the cultures and subcultures of which we are a part make us who we are. You will enjoy this in-depth, unique, interesting, and entertaining treatment of communication differences between males and females and between business people of many other cultures.

### Chapter 3: Communicating Nonverbally

No other business textbook on the market provides such comprehensive coverage of body language. You'll learn how to use it to your advantage and how to interpret the body language of others. Lying behavior, compliance gaining, dominance, submissiveness, and more are revealed by the position of the hands and arms, the face and eyes, the legs, and the position of the body.

You will also find tips to improve your ability to listen and to determine if others are really listening to you.

### Chapter 4: Putting the You Attitude in Business Messages

Understanding motivational psychology can help you improve your ability to get others to do what you want them to do. Whether it's getting people to buy your products, agree with you, or hire you for a job, this chapter will make you more persuasive.

### Chapter 5: Choosing the Right Words

Skillful use of words can give you power; poor use of words can take it away. After reading this chapter, you will be able to avoid language that discriminates, is inappropriate, and has offensive connotations. You will be able to use the power of words to enhance the readability of your messages.

### Chapter 6: Planning Business Messages and Solving Problems with Critical Thinking

The most successful people in the world are problem solvers. You can improve your ability to solve problems by thinking critically. The simple, logical techniques practiced in this chapter show you how. Solving communication problems through effective planning, organizing, composing, and evaluating sets the stage for the rest of the chapters. These four steps in the message formulation process are broken down to guide you through every business message you will ever have to compose.

Ethical issues are presented as one of the most important considerations in any communication encounter.

In addition, you will learn how to freewrite, a fantastically easy technique to help you get over that disease known as *writer's block*.

### Chapter 7: Writing Direct Messages

Composing effective direct messages is simple when you put these easy-to-follow steps to use by writing letters and memos chosen from the 25 exercises at the end of this chapter. Take a look at the comprehensive checklist. There's one like it in almost every chapter.

### Chapter 8: Writing Indirect Messages

Have you ever wondered how to tell people no and make them like it? The tips in this chapter can help you improve your ability to convince your readers and listeners that a negative answer is fair and reasonable.

### Chapter 9: Writing Persuasive Messages

You will learn how to use Madison Avenue advertising techniques to get people to buy your products and your ideas. Need to collect money owed to you? No problem—good persuasive messages can do it for you.

### Chapter 10: Producing Visual Aids

In a society where people are bombarded with more visual stimulation than ever before, you must know how to capture their interest by incorporating graphics of all kinds into your written and oral presentations. Even if you're not an artist, you can follow these principles to construct visual aids that will add impact to your messages.

### Chapter 11: Writing Short Reports

Give your readers well-planned and well-written progress reports, feasibility studies, justification reports, problem-solving reports, and proposals. After reading this chapter, your ability to present information in a way that is interesting and informative and that satisfies your readers will be greatly improved.

### Chapter 12: Planning and Organizing Formal Reports

Where is it written that formal reports must be hard? When you understand exactly what is expected, they don't have to be difficult. This chapter describes in detail everything you need to know to plan and organize formal reports. Even the sample report is interesting—do people really interrupt women more often than men to gain control of conversation?

### Chapter 13: Researching and Documenting Formal Reports

Your own personal librarian to guide you through the stacks and a statistician of your own to prepare and administer your research—these are the only things that would make researching a formal report easier than this chapter. APA style, Chicago style, MLA style, and CBE style documentation are all covered at length.

### Chapter 14: Planning Business Presentations

It's not true that successful speakers are born, not made. You can learn to speak effectively. Giving good formal and informal business presentations is easier when you consider the probable reaction of your audience. Then, all you have to do is support your major points in an interesting way. Reaching an audience is just a matter of psychology and learned technique, not magic.

### Chapter 15: Delivering Business Presentations

No magic here either! Just lots of good commonsense techniques for delivering business presentations interestingly and competently. You'll appreciate the humorous examples as well as the advice on how to control anxiety and how to use body language to support a topic.

### Chapter 16: Researching Jobs and Writing Resumes and Application Letters

Once your communication skills have been perfected, you'll need a good job with a real future to show them off! Collecting information on the company and the job you want is merely the first step in your job-hunting campaign. You'll also learn how to write an ethical application letter that stresses what you can do for the company.

### Chapter 17: Interviewing for Jobs and Following Up

Picture this—you in a job interview: poised, confident, professional, and comfortable. Sound familiar? If not, this chapter will help you prepare for the interview by anticipating what is important to the employer. You'll have a chance to frame responses to all kinds of questions—even those that are legally questionable. What to do after the interview to continue the campaign is also included.

# THE LEARNING STRATEGY

In addition to the specific learning objectives mentioned in the first paragraph of this message, emphasis is placed on the process of writing in every chapter that teaches letters, memorandums, reports, and business presentations. Subheadings repeated in these chapters guide you through steps that will eventually become automatic:

Plan your message

Establish your purpose

Choose a medium and channel

Consider ethical and legal issues

Analyze your audience

Gather necessary resources

Organize your message

Freewrite major points

Choose an organizational strategy

Compose your message

Evaluate your message

In summary, by studying from this book, you will not just learn to produce specific kinds of letters and reports. More importantly, you will learn the thinking skills necessary to solve any communication-related problem.

Finally, professors, to make sure your students understand the concepts, you can choose from the large number of assignments at the end of each chapter. Look at Chapters 7 and 8, direct and indirect messages, to get an idea of the variety of assignments you will be able to give your students. The large number of exercises will allow you to pick and choose situations of interest to you and your students, and you will be able to change them from semester to semester.

## ORGANIZATIONAL FEATURES

Many features make this textbook a more effective way to learn to communicate competently in the field of business. A few of the organizational features that should appeal to you follow.

**OPENING VIGNETTES.** Every chapter begins with an opening vignette, consisting of typical communication incidents people face daily on almost any job. The heading, *What Would You Do If . . . ?* says it all. These cases require you to think about how you would handle each situation, thus involving you directly in the action. For each vignette, the information in the chapter gives clues to what went wrong and to how each situation should be handled. The vignettes go beyond the often-ignored case studies in other textbooks; they are an essential part of each chapter.

**MARGINAL NOTES.**   The notes included in the margins of every chapter summarize the chapter's key points. When you find yourself short of time or in need of review, skim these marginal notes and the headings and subheadings.

**CHECKLISTS.**   Included in all letter, memorandum, and report chapters as well as the chapters on business presentations and the job application letter are comprehensive checklists you should complete for every assignment. To see how detailed they are, take a minute to look at Exhibit 6.8 in the chapter on indirect messages. Then you'll see how helpful these will be in pulling together all the information in an entire chapter.

**EXAMPLES.**   In 22 years of teaching business communication, I have had to amass file cabinets full of examples for this class—for no other reason than there were no textbooks that explained or illustrated the concepts adequately. This book corrects that problem. As a student, you will be shown example after example of each principle as it is presented—not just the usual full-page examples of letters, memos, and so on, but also an enormous number of one-sentence examples within the paragraphs. These examples aren't simply presented complete or in perfect form; in most cases, you are asked to analyze them to determine whether they are good or bad. What makes them good or bad is discussed; and when appropriate, suggested revisions are provided. By involving you in the learning process as you read the chapter, you do not have to wait to do the assignments to find out if you really understand what you are reading.

**LEGAL AND ETHICAL ISSUES.**   Where did we get the idea that ethical issues and legal considerations could be covered once and then forgotten? The laws that govern each type of communication as well as the ethical considerations we face daily are covered in each chapter on letters, memos, reports, and business presentations. You can't just think about ethics and the law occasionally if you want to be an effective communicator. Logic requires you to consider the legal and ethical aspects of every message you produce at the time you are planning it. This book helps you do just that.

**MEMO AND LETTER COVERAGE.**   Many textbooks cover interoffice memorandums separate from business letters; and due to time constraints, many teachers forgo the teaching of memorandums. However, other than format, there are no substantive differences in how the two forms of communication are written. Therefore, since memorandums and business letters are covered in the same chapters of this book, you will not miss out on this vital component of business communication.

**TECHNOLOGY.**   Because computers, voice mail, networks, electronic mail, and so on are merely tools that make communication and research easier, they can no longer be kept separate. This book includes an overview of technology in Chapter 1, because technology is truly a major component of communication basics. However, technological aspects are also included where appropriate throughout. For example, software that enables groups to work together is discussed in the chapter on reports, presentation software is mentioned in the chapter on business presentations, and computerized screening is brought up in the chapter on job interviews. You should find this integration informative and interesting.

**COLLABORATIVE WRITING.**   In business, many letters, memorandums, and reports are the result of group effort. Therefore, tips for improving your collaborative writing experiences are covered in every chapter where they are pertinent. Collaborative writing is a major consideration in one of the most important steps in the communication process—*gather the necessary resources.* People are resources, and the benefits and drawbacks of *groupthink* must always be considered.

## SUPPLEMENTS

Professors, to assist you in teaching this course in business communication, please take advantage of these supplements available for your use. Consult the Instructor's Manual for further information on computerized testing services.

**INSTRUCTOR'S MANUAL.**   You will find this resource an invaluable timesaver. Included within it are

- Detailed chapter outlines indicating when to use transparencies and when to refer to text exhibits.
- Numerous transparencies and transparency masters to make your lecture/ discussions more effective.
- Suggested answers for the *What Would You Do If . . . ?* opening vignettes.
- Sample solutions to application exercises.
- Answers to the discussion questions at the end of every chapter.
- Evaluation sheets for grading written assignments and business presentations.
- Suggested reading for controversial and unusual topics.
- Grammar units with pre-tests, rules, and exercises ready for duplication.

**TEST BANK.**   Whether you prefer writing exams or objective exams, the test bank will make it simple for you to prepare tests to determine how well your students understand communication principles. Written by Rebecca Smith of San Diego, the test items are keyed to the specific learning objectives in the chapters. Therefore, none of the questions should surprise your students. A computerized version of the book's test bank (Computest 4) is also available.

**VIDEOS.**   Richard D. Irwin has made available a number of business communication videos. Tapes 1 and 2 consist of four self-contained, informative segments on writing correctly, concisely, clearly and interestingly. Tape 3 covers listening skills, and tape 4 shows examples of resumes and discusses self-assessment as a part of the job search.

## ACKNOWLEDGEMENTS

Writing this textbook was truly a collaborative effort, collaborative in the sense that hours of discussion with colleagues and business representatives helped to form my views on the subject and collaborative in the sense that some of them sacrificed to provide teaching schedules that would facilitate my writing. It is a pleasure to publicly thank these people for their help and their advice: Chuck Inacker, Darrell Clemmensen, Linda Beamer, Marguerite Shane Joyce, MaryLynn Knutsen, Gladys Robbins, Ralph Spanswick, Guyla Armstrong, David Dauwalder, Kenneth Zimmer, Patricia Garner-Hynes, Wanda Stitt-Gohdes, Janet McKay, Audrey Roche, Patricia Mantabe, Lynette Shishido, Leon Singleton, Jackie Harless-Chang, Espy Bolivar-Owen, Fran Manion, Judi Smith, Russell Colburn, and John Kelly. A special thanks goes to Rebecca Smith of San Diego who served as the book's developmental editor. Becky tirelessly read and edited the first draft of every chapter and gave me many suggestions for improvement. Her infusion of objectives into several of the chapters and reorganization of chapter material resulted in a much-improved final product.

It takes many people to put a book together; however, the primary work boils down to the relationship between the author and the publisher's representatives. This book would never have been finished without the gentle, but firm, guidance of two wonderful people: Craig Beytien and Karen Mellon of Richard D. Irwin. Their enthusiasm for the project and their expertise made them invaluable resources to me. Stephanie Britt also did a superb job of taking the book from its final draft through to its production.

Finally, gratitude must be expressed to my colleagues who reviewed parts of the manuscript. These reviewers include:

Beverly Amoroso, Kirkwood Community College

Melvona Boren, San Juan Community College

Jean Embree, Sawyer College of Business

Yolanda Foley, Watterson College

Marguerite Shane Joyce, California State University, Los Angeles

Carolyn Quantrille, Spokane Falls Community College

Joan Ryan, Lane Community College

Tim Saben, Portland Community College

Peggy Scheloski, Johnson County Community College

Opal Terbeek, Windward Community College

Sandy Thomas, Kansas City Kansas Community College

## FEEDBACK

You're going to like this book. However, no matter how good a textbook is, it can always be improved. Your suggestions will help make the next edition even better. Therefore, please write to me with suggestions for improvement as well as positive reinforcement. If something worked for you, I'd like to hear about it. If something didn't work, I need to hear about that, too. If you have original exercises you would like to see incorporated into the next edition, please send them to me (I'll see that you receive credit for your material). You can reach me at the following address:

Fran Chandler
Professor of Business and Office Information Systems
Santa Monica College
1900 Pico Boulevard
Santa Monica, CA 90405

Thank you for using my book. It was written with you in mind.

**Frances G. Chandler**

# CONTENTS IN BRIEF

# CONTENTS

## PART TWO   *Business Letters and Memos*

**PART FIVE**   *Employment Communication*

# FUNDAMENTALS OF
# BUSINESS COMMUNICATION

# Part **ONE**

# BUSINESS COMMUNICATION BASICS

# CHAPTER 1

# COMMUNICATING IN TODAY'S BUSINESS WORLD

## OBJECTIVES

When you finish studying this chapter, you will be able to:

- Define *communication* and list five of its dimensions.
- Explain why good communication is important to the organization and to the individual.
- Describe the three forms of communication in business.
- Identify the three goals of business communication.
- Describe the communication process.
- Identify seven types of barriers to communication.
- Describe the formal and informal communication channels within an organization.
- Explain how computer and telecommunications technology helps businesspeople work more efficiently.
- Use the telephone to conduct business efficiently and to maintain good relationships with others.
- Show how new technology can be used to communicate electronically with others in your workplace or at remote locations.
- Identify computer software that will help you write business documents more effectively.
- Discuss the major legal and ethical issues related to using the new information technology.

### WHAT WOULD YOU DO IF...?

**A PEEK INSIDE.**   Sometimes what is going on inside us prevents us from communicating effectively. Such is the case in the following conversation between Carter Halley, the owner of a small business that needs more money to continue its operations, and Bridgett Johansen, who has decided to give Carter the money he needs in return for a 50 percent share in the business. Bridgett and Carter have talked on the telephone about the deal many times, and a lot of paperwork has gone back and forth between them. Now, with their attorneys, they are meeting to work out the final details. The words in brackets show what their thoughts are as they speak.

Carter    Welcome, Ms. Johansen, I'm pleased to meet you in person at last. Please sit down. [*What's this Ms. business? Not another feminist who hates men! Gads, my head hurts; will this headache ever go away?!*]

Bridgett    Please call me Bridgett; after all, we might be partners soon. [*I was afraid of this; he's at least 60! This company really needs a young go-getter if it's going to survive.*]

Carter    Well, that's what we're here to talk about. We still have a lot of work to do to figure out who's going to run this place. [*Who does she think she is? My partner? With her fancy suit and heels, they'd laugh her out of the factory! She won't last long, that's for sure! Why, my men will think I've lost my mind!*]

Bridgett    A 50 percent share implies equal control. Did you have something else in mind? [*It's so hot in this room I can't even think! Not only is he old, he's also a rigid control freak. I've had enough of them in my life. Does he think I'm going to sit back and let him use my money to continue running this company into the ground?*]

Carter    Yes, I do have something else in mind. My employees are used to taking orders from me. We're like a family; they trust me to look out for them, and I do it. Why, Frieda, my girl in the outer office, has been with me for 20 years. I have a responsibility to these people. You'll probably understand this after you settle down with some nice man and have a family. [*Equal control? No woman young enough to be my daughter is capable of being my equal!*]

Bridgett    Mr. Halley, my personal life has nothing to do with your need for funds to continue your operations. These are the facts: For the last year you have failed to convince anyone to invest in your company, and the likelihood of finding anyone soon enough to save this sinking ship is slim! [*Girl? Settle down? How condescending can you get? Working with him would be like working with my father. Who needs it? I can't breathe in here; why is that heat turned up so high?*]

Carter    Sinking ship? I'll have you know, Ms. Johansen, that all this company needs is a one-time infusion of cash; then the profits will start rolling in! Then all of you will regret not being smart enough to place your confidence in me! [*Failed? Not me, I never failed at anything in my life! I didn't think my head could hurt any worse than it did an hour ago; now I know otherwise.*]

Bridgett    Well Mr. Halley, it seems that we are not as close to agreement as we thought we were. Perhaps you should spend your time now looking for another investor who is smarter than I am. [*Get me out of here! I can't work with such an insulting old coot!*]

As you read this chapter, you will learn about the barriers that are preventing Carter and Bridgett from communicating well. Think about how Carter and Bridgett might have used the basic concepts of business communication to reach their goal—a productive partnership without any control problems.

## A Definition of Communication

**Communication is used to build relationships.**

■ Define *communication* and list five of its dimensions.

Communication is something we all do, and we communicate in many different settings. It is a human activity so common that we seldom think about what it is—we just communicate. However, if you are to study communication, you need a more formal definition. In this book, **communication** is defined as the process of interchanging thoughts, feelings, and information. Take note: The word *process* indicates that communication changes constantly as interactions take place.

Many people assume that there is no need to study something they have been doing all their lives. Unfortunately, practice does not necessarily make perfect. These sentences are probably as familiar to you as they are to most people: "No, that's not what I meant," "I'm sorry; I misunderstood you," "I already told you that," and "Can't you hear?" We continue to study communication in the hope that we may eventually get it right.

One reason that communication is more difficult than we assume is that it has many dimensions:

**Communication has five dimensions.**

**Communication Can Be Intentional or Unintentional.**   The words you choose to express yourself are intended to have a particular meaning. Sometimes those words communicate something other than what you intended—they have an unintentional meaning. The word *girl* in the vignette at the beginning of this chapter is an excellent example of unintentional communication. Carter used the term affectionately, but Bridgett perceived it as a sexist term used to make women seem childish.

**Communication Can Be Verbal or Nonverbal.**   Our communication is often more **nonverbal**, involving our body and other objects and actions, than **verbal**, involving words alone. Even when we do not speak, the way we walk, stand, and sit communicates a message to others. Our body language reveals whether we are truly interested or bored. It can indicate when we lie and when we tell the truth. Other forms of nonverbal communication include the appearance of letters and memos, the arrangement of office furniture, and the style and condition of our clothing and accessories.

**Communication Can Be Internal or External.**   Internal, or **intrapersonal,** communication is the way we talk to ourselves, without putting thoughts into words. As you saw in the chapter-opening vignette, internal communication can influence the course of a conversation even more than external discussion. The words that are actually written and spoken are external communication. Nonverbal items chosen to given a certain impression—such as jewelry, cars, and art—are also examples of external communication.

**Communication Can Involve Humans, Machines, and Animals.**   Communication obviously involves humans. Less clearly, it also involves machines. Think about how computer scientists work to improve communication between one computer and another as well as between humans and computers. With the increasing reliance on computers in business, we need to learn how to use modern technology and electronic information more than ever. We also need to learn more about how animals communicate, because the nonverbal behavior of humans and animals is quite similar.

**C**OMMUNICATION **C**AN **T**AKE **P**LACE **BETWEEN** **T**WO **P**EOPLE **AS** **W**ELL **AS** **WITHIN** **G**ROUPS. A conversation between two people is called **interpersonal** communication. Communication within groups is classified as either small-group communication or mass communication. Researchers look at the ways groups include or exclude individuals, conduct small group activities, measure the effectiveness of small group communications, and so on. Communication within large groups is the concern of media communication experts because most large-group communication involves the use of microphones, television, movies, telecommunications, and other forms of media.

Explain why good communication is important to the organization and to the individual.

Communication is important in any human activity, but this book is particularly concerned with communication in the business world. This book's goal is to show you how to write and speak in a way that will help you and your organization achieve results. Good communication is important to the organization and to individuals within that organization.

### **I**MPORTANCE **TO THE** **O**RGANIZATION

Maintaining good communication has four main advantages for organizations:

- *It saves money.* Poor communication is costly. How many customers are lost when salespeople do not listen to their needs? How many unclear letters require follow up with a telephone call or another letter clarifying the first communication attempt? How many hours are wasted in negotiations between people who cannot or will not understand each other, as with Carter Halley and Bridgett Johansen? How many form letters go unread because they are unappealing to the reader? The list goes on. The costs of poor communication are indeed high.
- *It improves morale.* When employees and management feel free to discuss things and know that their ideas and feelings will be received with respect and given full consideration, they are better able to work together to achieve common goals. In such situations, people feel good about what they are doing and with whom they are working.
- *It increases productivity.* When given a number of employees or a given amount of other resources produces more goods or services, we say that productivity increases. Good communication increases productivity by reducing the time spent explaining issues, seeking information, and handling misunderstandings. It increases the efficiency of the organization's employees.
- *It promotes trust.* Good business communication also fosters an environment of honesty, sincerity, and respect. Employees are more likely to remain with a company that deals with them honestly and openly, thereby reducing the company's training costs. Customers, clients, suppliers, and the community are also more loyal to companies that treat them with respect.

*Effective communication saves money, improves morale, increases productivity, and promotes trust.*

## IMPORTANCE TO THE INDIVIDUAL

Your study of business communication will be invaluable to you and to the organization for which you work. The ability to communicate well is often cited by companies as one of the skills they desire most in employees. Poor communicators are not able to relate well to others and find their career paths blocked.

Effective communicators are well liked, have more power to influence change, and project an air of competence.

Good communicators have a better chance at success for several reasons. People who are good communicators are well liked by others. Think of the people you like most. Chances are you like them because you can trust them to tell the truth and you can depend on them to do what they say they will do. They are probably good listeners, too; you get to talk at least as much as they do. Even when these people disagree with you, they are probably tactful and courteous as they present logical and sound reasons for their disagreement.

Good communicators also have the power to influence events in an organization. Sound communication skills help you persuade other people to think and do what you want them to think or do. If you want your employer to purchase vans for employees to travel to and from work, you have to show the decision makers the benefits to themselves and the company. As an effective communicator, you would probably mention benefits such as: an increase in employee morale and, therefore, less turnover and use of sick leave; compliance with government ride-sharing guidelines; reduced harm to the environment; and the chance to look good to superiors in the company.

Good communicators are also good persuaders because they project an image of competence. They are able to coordinate body language, voices, and words to make themselves understood. Their arguments are logical, believable, and forceful. Other people listen to them and are more likely to carry out their orders with enthusiasm and commitment. Their exceptional ability to persuade others makes them influential leaders.

Your study of business communication will give you an opportunity to practice communicating in ways more likely to yield results, and your ability to communicate will have improved significantly. The principles and exercises within this book will help you capitalize on the communication skills in which you are already strong and will give you a chance to improve any weak areas.

## FORMS OF COMMUNICATION

Communication can be divided into three forms: oral, written, and nonverbal activities.

Describe the three forms of communication in business.
Communication activities take three forms: oral, written, and nonverbal. All three activities, covered in detail later, operate in both business and nonbusiness settings.

### ORAL COMMUNICATION

Oral communication involves speaking and listening. A great deal of your time in business will be spent speaking—for example, using the telephone, attending meetings, negotiating, and making presentations. All require good oral communication skills.

Good listening skills also enable you to communicate better with others. Simple actions such as leaning forward in your seat, opening your arms, and uncrossing your legs can let your listener know you value what he or she has to say. Through good listening, you will be able to help speakers improve the quality of what they say to you. (Chapter 3 provides more information on listening.)

Oral communication has some real benefits in the business world. Because of the feedback you receive immediately from your listener, you are able to tailor your message. If your listener indicates by his or her facial expressions and/or words that your message is not clear, you can revise or add more information and restate the message. Any questions that exist can be cleared up immediately. On the other hand, oral messages are usually not recorded for future reference. Careful wording of a sensitive message is more difficult with oral communication than it is with written communication.

### WRITTEN COMMUNICATION

Written communication—letters, memos, reports, and other types of documents—are essential to modern business. Managers spend approximately 45 percent of their time reading and writing. Employees at all levels must also be able to write to express their ideas and document their decisions and actions, and they must be able to read to communicate with others inside and outside the organization.

The main advantage of written communication in business is that it provides a permanent record. Others can read a document some time later and get the same message as the original, undistorted by time and faulty memory. Sending copies of a written message to many people in different locations is much easier than trying to speak with each of them face to face.

### NONVERBAL COMMUNICATION

**Nonverbal communication** encompasses all communication that occurs without the use of words. It exists in many forms. **Proxemics** is the study of our need for space and how we relate to the space we have. It explains why American executives typically require spacious offices and why Japanese executives do not. **Body language** is the study of behavior and how it reinforces or contradicts verbal communication. The way you gesture, the way you stand or sit, the way you walk, and the amount of eye contact you maintain with different people reveal a great deal about you. A third form of nonverbal communication is **object language,** the messages that are sent by the objects we choose to wear and keep around us. Consider the different messages that clothing sends. If you were to enter an investment firm with $300,000 to invest, how comfortable would you feel trusting your money to an investment counselor who was dressed in torn blue jeans and a sweatshirt? (In-depth coverage of nonverbal communication is provided in Chapter 3.)

## GOALS OF BUSINESS COMMUNICATION

To come to a common understanding is the primary goal of communication.

Identify the three goals of business communication.

Communication comes from the Latin *communis,* meaning "common." The primary goal of communication in general is to come to a common understanding. Within an organization, this goal of common understanding can be further broken down into the following goals:

**BUILDING RELATIONSHIPS.** Strong relationships are critical to business success. Companies place a high value on long-term relationships with clients and customers, and put much effort into building these relationships. Strong relationships among a company's employees are also necessary so people can work together effectively. If you practice good listening skills, you will be able to determine what is important to the people with whom you work. Sincere and tactful writing and speaking will then enable you to show how your products and your ideas will benefit your customers, co-workers, superiors, and subordinates. Meeting the needs of all parties is the best way to build long-term relationships.

**REDUCING CONFLICT.** When the people who are trying to communicate are aware of the things that might cause conflict, they can work around the problems. For example, say your company is negotiating with someone who you know has a strong bias against people from a certain region of the country. For the smoothest possible negotiations, you would probably avoid sending a company representative who has an accent that identifies him or her as being from that region. This is not to say that you must compromise your principles. After your company gets the deal and proves to be a reliable business partner, you might be able to help break down the other person's bias by assigning to that account someone who has the offending accent.

Good communicators also help reduce conflict by giving instructions clearly and concisely. They are open about what they expect of others but tactful in expressing it. They avoid both hurt feelings and protests such as these: "Why didn't you tell me?" "That's not what you said!" "How am I supposed to know what you want?" When people know the expectations they face and have clear instructions to follow, conflict is less likely and business proceeds more smoothly.

*The need to share information, ideas, and feelings is the reason for the development of verbal and nonverbal language.*

**SHARING INFORMATION, IDEAS, AND FEELINGS.** When most people think of communicating, they think of sharing information, ideas, and feelings, which is, of course, the main reason for the development of language. Words give meaning to information and ideas, but feelings are often transmitted nonverbally, as well. For example, a presenter may say that he's happy to be speaking at a meeting, but his true feelings are revealed by his trembling hands and quavery voice.

Powerful communicators structure their verbal and nonverbal messages so the content is understood as they intended it to be. Although it is unreasonable to expect perfect communication 100 percent of the time, by practicing the principles you will find your messages are less likely to be misunderstood.

## THE COMMUNICATION PROCESS

Describe the communication process.

Think about the definition of communication as a process, a changing flow of thoughts, feelings, and information between two or more people. There are many ways to represent this process. Most contain the features shown in Exhibit 1.1. A person sending a message goes through three active stages: stimulus, message formulation, and filtering.

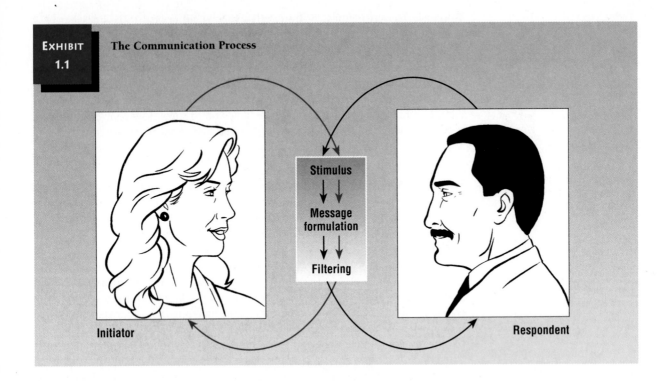

**EXHIBIT 1.1**   **The Communication Process**

Stimulus

↓   ↓

Message formulation

↓   ↓

Filtering

Initiator

Respondent

A need to communicate triggers the communication process.

Feedback triggers further communication.

1. *Finding a reason to communicate (stimulus).* The communication process begins when you discover a **stimulus,** or need to communicate. That need may be prompted by, for example, a letter that needs to be answered, a telephone call, a visit from someone, something you hear, or a cologne that reminds you of someone. The need to communicate may also come from within you—for example, a new idea about a project you have been working on, or a lonely feeling. **Feedback** from a listener may also lead you to communicate further. If the listener shakes his or her head, cocks an ear toward you, wrinkles the brow, and opens his or her mouth slightly, you know the listener does not understand. This nonverbal feedback then leads you to restate the message or to provide more information.

Formation of the message includes selection of the medium by which the message will be sent.

2. *Forming the message (formulation).* Once you have a reason to communicate, you proceed to **formulation,** in which you form a message—a verbal message (written or spoken), a nonverbal message, or a combination of the two. Often, a large part of the nonverbal message comes from your subconscious, and that nonverbal message sometimes contradicts the intended verbal message. For example, a job applicant preparing to lie to an interviewer might subconsciously give such nonverbal cues as shaking hands weakly, touching his or her face over and over, and maintaining eye contact poorly. At this stage, you also choose the method of delivery—whether in person, during a staff meeting, on the telephone, by letter, by press release, by sign language, by teleconferencing, through a policies and procedures manual, or through any number of other media.

Barriers block or distort communication by preventing the message from being interpreted as the sender intended.

3. *Overcoming barriers (filtering).* Any message must overcome a series of obstacles before it can be interpreted by the receiver of the message. Such **filtering** prevents the message from being received as it was intended. Some communication barriers affect both parties, such as intense heat, traffic noise, and microphone feedback. Other barriers are more personal, such as the prejudices and biases through which each individual interprets events. Carter Halley and Bridgett Johansen's ill-fated deal was the victim of some of these personal barriers. Barriers will be discussed in more detail.

A response is formed in reaction to the verbal and nonverbal messages of the sender, which provide a need for the receiver to communicate.

Following these three stages, the receiver responds—and in doing so, becomes the sender and repeats the communication process. For example, the person who receives a letter asking questions about products might respond with a letter answering the questions. The original letter, of course, provided the stimulus. In writing the response, the receiver formulated a message. In sending it, the receiver must overcome a variety of psychological and physical barriers that filter the message.

However, responses do not occur only after the three stages of the communication process are completed. In most cases, responses are actually being formed even before the message has been completely received. What goes through your mind when someone you dislike approaches you and starts speaking? You probably react with a defensive nonverbal message—arms crossed in front of you, little eye contact, an insincere smile or even a frown, or a clenched jaw. These responses to the other person probably begin even before he or she speaks, because of your previous experience with the individual. Such feedback lets the speaker know if his or her message is being received. Feedback also prompts further communication.

In short, most acts of communication are far more complex than this simple three-step model implies. One person's message stimulates a response that, in turn, provides the reason for another message. As a result, all three stages may occur at the same time. The communication process is dynamic, not linear or static. It does not proceed in an orderly fashion. For the respondent, the stimulus is the message or the person who initiated the conversation. The respondent filters that person's message through common and personal barriers at the same time he or she formulates a verbal response and determines a method of delivery. While all this is occurring, the respondent is already communicating nonverbally.

## BARRIERS TO COMMUNICATION

Identify seven types of barriers to communication.

Misunderstandings arise because of communication barriers.

**Communication barriers** distort a message so the message received is different from the one sent. Have you ever said something to someone only to have that person misunderstand? If so, you have dealt with communication barriers. Even communication experts frequently find themselves saying, "No, that's not what I meant." Hundreds of different types of barriers can cause communication to go astray. Among these are physical barriers, language barriers, body language barriers, cultural barriers, motivational barriers, perceptual barriers, and organizational barriers.

## PHYSICAL BARRIERS

Physical barriers are a common problem in communicating. Consider the physical barriers that might prevent you from receiving some of my message as you read this chapter. Are you sitting in an uncomfortable chair? Is the temperature of the room you are in too hot or too cold? Is traffic noise or a nearby conversation distracting you? Do you have enough time to read this chapter, or are you concerned about something else you also need to do?

Although physical barriers have a big effect, they are relatively easy to overcome. For example, good speakers arrange ahead of time for a portable microphone, which lets them overcome physical barriers between them and the audience such as tables or lecterns. Good speakers know that moving toward the audience, even slightly, makes the audience feel that the speaker is one of them and more worthy of their attention.

Another example of a physical barrier is the way a book is printed. A lot of white space on a page (wide margins, more space between the lines) as well as frequent use of headings and pictures make a page look easier to read. Things that look easier to read actually are easier to read because of the psychological lift that the reader receives. You know the sinking feeling you get when you turn the page of a textbook and there are no pictures and no headings—nothing but tiny printed characters from one edge of the paper to the other.

## LANGUAGE BARRIERS

Obviously, communication is more difficult when people do not speak the same language. If you conduct business in another country, you should probably have a trustworthy interpreter unless you are fluent in the language and have lived in that country long enough to know the subtle meanings of words.

A related barrier is slang. We tend to judge people by the way they speak. Imagine your reaction if an attorney greeted you with this statement: "Yo, Baby, wha's hap'nin?" Because it would be unprofessional for someone in business to use such slang, you would probably decide that this attorney is not one you should use. Slang should be used only with other people who use such language; you should never risk using it outside your immediate group.

**The words you use and the way you carry on conversations determine, to a great extent, the value others place on what you have to say.**

The way in which people put words together and carry on conversations can also be a barrier. For example, some people use tag questions and unnecessary qualifiers that weaken what they say. Compare the impact of these two statements: "I believe the best way to increase our market share is to advertise more heavily, don't you?" versus "The best way to increase our market share is to advertise more heavily." Two parts of the first sentence ("I believe" and "don't you") give the impression that the speaker is unsure and seeking reassurance from the audience. In the business world, a direct, forceful style is more likely to get the desired response.

Repetitive phrases also draw attention away from the message. Have you ever found your attention wandering while you counted the number of times someone said "uh," "in fact," or "you know?" Although there is nothing wrong with using any of these phrases occasionally, they are distracting when used often.

**Ambiguity,** the lack of specificity, can be a language-related barrier to communication as well. Beware of ambiguity; unless you are sharp, you may end up with an idea of a message's meaning completely different from what was actually expressed. Confusion may, in fact, be the intended result. These are some ambiguous words and phrases that are used commonly:

| Ambiguous Expressions | Unanswered Questions |
|---|---|
| I'll do it soon. | When? |
| It's important we take action. | Who? When? What action? |
| I'll try to do that. | Try? What does that mean? |
| I'll get that done for you. | When? Who will do it? |

In short, what you have to say is judged by the words you use, the way you string them together, and how well you speak the appropriate language. Some people won't listen to anyone who speaks with a particular accent; people from Brooklyn, Texas, the South, and foreign countries complain frequently of this prejudice. Some people "tune out" when the speaker or writer uses words that they do not understand. Therefore, communicate to express meaning, not to impress your audience. When listening, move beyond personal prejudices and biases by concentrating on the content of the message.

## BODY LANGUAGE BARRIERS

Body language and other forms of nonverbal communication (described in detail in Chapter 3) can easily get in the way of effective communication. For instance, angry finger-pointing gestures may make people feel defensive and stop listening. Nervous habits such as ring twisting, fingernail biting, and hand wringing draw attention away from the message, especially when they are done repeatedly.

The way people use space, proxemics, is another form of nonverbal communication. We all need a certain amount of space around us, and we feel uncomfortable if people we don't know well invade that space. We don't receive the sales messages of salespeople who get too close; we are too busy backing away. People who are called into their bosses' offices to discuss problems feel uneasy and are, therefore, less likely to listen than if the meeting were held elsewhere. Different cultures have different ideas of the appropriate amount of space between people. In addition, men who share offices with other people tend to stake out larger areas for themselves than women do. Territorial needs such as these are the result of cultural background and learned behavior.

## CULTURAL BARRIERS

Every culture and subculture teach people to look at events in a special way. For example, if a person comes from a culture that looks up to older people, he or she would be more inclined to communicate well with an elderly person. A person who grows up in a culture in which the elderly are viewed as senile, out of date, and useless is unlikely to communicate effectively with older people.

Chapter 2 discusses the problems encountered by American businesspeople when communicating with people from other cultures and subcultures. For example, in some Middle Eastern cultures where women are not allowed to work with men, an American businesswoman would not be accorded the respect necessary to negotiate a business deal. Americans also encounter many cultural barriers when they try to do business in Japan. Because the Japanese value harmony, they rarely say "No" directly. Instead, they might say "I will do everything possible to see that this goes through." Appreciating cultural differences like these helps Americans compete more effectively on a global scale.

## MOTIVATIONAL BARRIERS

Unfortunately, no one has to listen to every word you say or read every word you write. Before people will listen to or read your communications, you must identify their **motivations,** the drives that influence what they do. Then you must convince them that what you have to say will be useful to them—in other words, you have to motivate them. As a student, for example, you are motivated to listen to teachers for a variety of reasons: The information might be on a test, it might be needed to complete an assignment, or it might be useful to you in your work or personal life.

An understanding of motivation and persuasion is essential to those preparing for business careers.

Motivation is a barrier when people do not understand how they will benefit from your message. Therefore, you are most likely to get people to do what you want them to by convincing them of how they will benefit personally. Whether you are selling goods or services, attempting to convince your boss to take a different course of action, buying a new car, or negotiating a contract, you must be aware of what will fulfill the needs of the other person.

## PERCEPTUAL BARRIERS

It is difficult to communicate with black-or-white thinkers.

Differences in **perception,** the way one views the world, can be an obstacle to communication. Have you ever known someone who is always negative or someone who always looks on the positive side of anything? Someone who sees the world as black or white, with no shades of gray? This sort of person labels everyone as either a friend or an enemy and every idea or opinion as right or wrong. Communicating with such thinkers takes time and patience. For any idea you want to promote or product you want to sell, you will have to mount an intensive campaign to convince them that they will benefit. You will also have to listen very carefully to what they say, because they tend to leave out anything that doesn't suit their perception of the world. A union leader reporting on the latest negotiations might announce only the information that makes management look arrogant and insensitive. A person who has been passed over for promotion might complain only of the good things he or she did that weren't recognized and neglect to mention any shortcomings. When you deal with such thinkers, avoid being trapped by their "either/or" logic.

Prejudices and biases are also perceptual barriers. Despite the laws against discrimination based on age, gender, race, nationality, and religion, these prejudices and more exist. However, they are a real drawback in a business environment. Imagine that there are only two kinds of people, Blues and Greens. If the Blues are in power, many of them probably believe that they are superior to Greens. Therefore, the Blues may tend to believe that most Greens do not have much to say that is worth listening to. As a result, very few Greens are promoted or paid as much as Blues. What is worse for a business, some very good ideas may never get a proper hearing—simply because Greens came up with them. On the other hand, Greens, who have to fight the assumption that they are inferior, are probably angry at the Blues. As a result, they tend to believe that all Blues are untrustworthy. Some Greens themselves might even believe that they are inferior to Blues and will believe anything a Blue tells them. Again, a business suffers from a failure to carefully examine all decisions and actions. Unfortunately, there will always be Blues and Greens or something similar in any organization.

One important task of managers is to ensure that prejudiced thinking does not block the flow of communication. They need to encourage teamwork and an appreciation of people's differences rather than separateness among employees.

## ORGANIZATIONAL BARRIERS

Organizations are like cultures; over time, they develop their own ways of doing things and their own beliefs. Any attempt to change things in an organization creates uncertainty and stress, both of which interfere with communication. New people in an organization often learn this lesson the hard way. Even the simplest change can be misunderstood. Consider the case of Quinn Lee, who, after years with a large multinational corporation, was hired to oversee the computerization of a small firm of 250 people. Following the custom of the company he used to work for, Quinn typed frequent memos to his supervisor. All requests and progress reports were sent to his immediate supervisor in writing. Unfortunately, his supervisor misunderstood Quinn's reasons for such documentation. Because the small firm was used to handling everything informally and in person, Quinn's supervisor felt threatened by the formality of Quinn's messages and considered him a troublemaker.

One type of communication barrier in organizations is the pattern in which communication travels (covered in the next section of this chapter). For example, in an organization with many levels, messages can become distorted by the time they travel from the top level through all the middle levels to the lowest level. Exhibit 1.2 illustrates how a message can become distorted as it passes through too many people. Modern technology, however, can help to solve this problem. When a message can be recorded once and sent at the same time to everyone who needs to see it, there is less likelihood that it will become distorted.

A person's status within an organization is another potential communication barrier. People with little authority sometimes do not communicate openly with those above them in the organization unless a nonthreatening climate has been established. To encourage such a climate, some executives eat regularly in the company lunchroom. Others have an open-door policy that allows any employee to come to their offices, even without an appointment. Many upper-level decision makers make a point of chatting informally with employees at all levels as they walk through the plant or offices, a practice referred to as management by walking around (MBWA).

Status within an organization is not always reflected in job titles. Some people get as much respect as top decision makers, either because of whom they work for (e.g., the president's secretary) or because of a personal relationship (e.g., the president's racquetball partner or the executive director's son). In some cases, however, others do not share information with this sort of high-status

A major task of management is to manage the flow of communication.

**EXHIBIT 1.2**

**How a Message Can Become Distorted in an Organization**

Company president: Buy 15 Macintosh computers for the design department right away. They've needed them for a long time.

Vice president: I want you to personally make sure 15 Macs are purchased for the design department right away. It's important to the president.

Telecommunications manager: The president says this is top priority and put me in charge. We need 15 Macintoshes ordered today. Design has the specs.

Design department head: Telecommunications has no need for Macs! If they think I'm going to help them out by writing up the specs, they're crazy!

Puchasing agent: I need specifications for 15 Macintoshes that have been approved for the telecommunications department. Can you get them to me today?

employee, because of either jealousy or the fear that they will reveal information that might be harmful.

Labor–management relations may also get in the way of communication. When those relations are strained, both workers and managers are suspicious of any messages that come from the other side and guard what they say for fear it will be used against them. However, in organizations where workers and management trust each other, communication is freer and, thus, more effective.

Job specialization can also be a barrier to communication. Highly trained workers, such as information systems specialists, accountants, attorneys, doctors, and engineers, are often unable to communicate well with those who do not have the same kind of knowledge. In addition, experts who might be brilliant in their own fields sometimes have trouble understanding and caring about the concerns of other departments or the company as a whole.

If you will look on any company as a culture in itself, you can begin to understand the types of communication problems that might occur. Many colleges now offer degrees in organizational communication and are producing specialists who can help businesses improve the effectiveness of their communication networks.

## COMMUNICATION CHANNELS IN AN ORGANIZATION

Describe the formal and informal communication channels within an organization.

Written and oral messages within any organization move in two basic patterns: through formally established channels and through informal channels. You can find out how communication flows formally in any organization by determining who can call or write to whom. Are all memos and phone calls supposed to be cleared by a supervisor before they can be sent to a higher level? Are employees allowed to communicate on business matters only with people on their own level or in their own departments? You can determine how communication flows informally by noting who goes to lunch with whom, who spends leisure time with whom, or who is related to whom.

### FORMAL COMMUNICATION PATTERNS

Information and the control of information are predictors of power in an organization.

Communication is a river, and gatekeepers have the power to control the flow of the river.

The formal paths by which messages flow in an organization are important because information and the control of information are predictors of power. Think of communication as a river. Wouldn't those people who could stop or divert the river's flow have a great deal of power over what got done? Those who have the power to control the flow of communication are called **gatekeepers.**

One powerful gatekeeper in an organization is the executive assistant to the chief executive officer (CEO). This person typically can read everything that is addressed to the CEO and probably channels all telephone calls to the CEO as well. Thus, the executive assistant often determines what matters should be handled by the CEO and who gets to speak or meet with the CEO. Such a gatekeeper takes much of the workload off the shoulders of the CEO, but the CEO may not be receiving important information about the organization.

Formal communication channels can be described in terms of the direction in which the communication flows. Exhibit 1.3 shows the three channels in the formal communication network: downward, upward, and lateral. Every organization contains elements of these three patterns; indeed, a healthy mix of all three patterns is good for organizations. Problems occur when an organization heavily favors one form over the others. However, each person in an organization may communicate using mostly or only one of the three patterns.

**UPWARD COMMUNICATION.**   Upward communication is the type that moves from lower levels to upper levels of the organization. Information needed to make decisions, such as sales data and employee surveys, is generated by

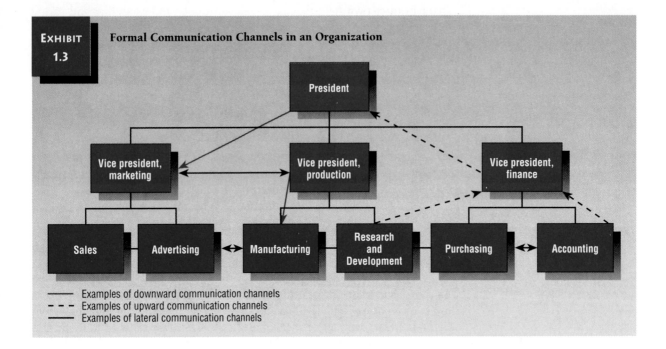

**EXHIBIT 1.3**   **Formal Communication Channels in an Organization**

—— Examples of downward communication channels
- - - Examples of upward communication channels
—— Examples of lateral communication channels

those at lower levels in the organization. This information is then fed to those at higher levels, where it is used to make decisions about future events. Exhibit 1.3, for example, the head of manufacturing might send a proposal to the vice president of production to buy three new computer numerical controlled milling machines. The vice president would then send that report, along with a recommendation to buy the machines, to the president, who would make the final decision. Upward communication also allows managers to keep informed about problems and the progress of projects under their direction.

Upward communication is not always channeled through each level of the hierarchy. It also occurs when, for example, the head of advertising bypasses his or her superior, the vice president of marketing, and goes straight to the president. Although there is not a formal hierarchical relationship between the two levels on the chart, this type of communication occurs in many organizations and is often encouraged.

Relying too much on the upward communication pattern has disadvantages. When they do not get feedback from the top, employees at lower levels feel cut off from the decision making; they lose sight of their own importance in the organization because they are not informed of how their information has been used. Too much upward communication can also overburden managers and supervisors, who find their time taken up by matters that could be handled more effectively by their subordinates.

**DOWNWARD COMMUNICATION.**   In most organizations, communication flows most often from upper levels to lower levels. Downward communication takes many forms, including company newsletters; memos about new policies, procedures, instructions, and announcements; performance evaluations; reports; telephone conversations; personal visits; meetings; and policy manuals.

Sharing information with lower-level employees boosts morale, especially when it is used to explain management's actions before they occur. When messages flow easily from top to bottom, employees feel that they matter and they appreciate knowing management's reasoning. For example, it would be better for management to explain ahead of time why an entire department is being moved to another building. The employees would be angry and frustrated if they were told only to pack up and move, without explanation, or if the explanation arrived on the same day as the movers. Another important example is telling employees ahead of time how their performance will be evaluated.

Downward communication is valuable for letting people know the results of management decisions that affect them in some way. For example, imagine how frustrated the head of manufacturing would be if he or she never got a response to a proposal for new machines. Whether the president responded through the vice president of production or directly to the head of manufacturing, with a photocopy to the vice president of production, at least those who had made the request would feel that they mattered.

Sharing information encourages people at all levels to participate in decision making. This, in turn, helps to promote team spirit, which is vital to productivity. In addition, most people operate best when they know their boundaries. Most employees like to know what the rules are and the information required to do their jobs. However, there is a danger that too many directives from upper-level management could make lower-level employees feel resentful.

Although downward communication is generally positive, sometimes it is not advised. Sensitive issues such as company buyouts, takeovers, plans for large-scale layoffs, termination of individuals, grievance information, and so on must sometimes be kept secret. Some information can only be released after critical management decisions have been made. Upper-level managers must weigh the benefits and pitfalls of having everyone in the organization know specific information before deciding to release information to lower-level employees.

**LATERAL COMMUNICATION.** Lateral communication occurs between people who appear on the same level of an organizational chart. Notes, memos, and phone conversations between people who work in the same department are examples of lateral, or sideways, communication, as are messages between different departments. For example, in Exhibit 1.3 an employee in the advertising department may send memos to people in his or her own department or to someone who works in the sales department.

Lateral communication increases productivity because everyone knows what everyone else is doing. Outsiders who call for information may not have to be passed from one office to another until the person who can answer their questions is finally found. Lateral communication also helps employees understand the problems of other departments and the way that the work of one department affects the work of another. People in the sales department, for example, will understand why they must turn in their weekly sales reports to the payroll department by 1 PM on Thursdays once they know what payroll clerks must do to compute and issue paychecks.

There are drawbacks to lateral communication, however. One is that it increases the amount of information shared with people who do not really want or need it. The result may be a lot of wasted paper (a problem for environmentally aware organizations) and a lot of useless messages in voice-mailboxes (a problem for time-conscious employees).

## INFORMAL COMMUNICATION PATTERNS

Rumors, which travel through what is commonly referred to as the **grapevine,** and personal relationships are two common types of informal communication channels. In many organizations, the informal channels have more impact on employees than the formal channels do. For instance, an employee of your firm who also serves on the board of a charitable organization with the president of your company might not be very high on your company's organization chart, but he or she has the ear of the most important person in the firm. If the director of research and development is dating the vice president of finance, another very powerful informal communication channel exists. Although other employees might have to run all their ideas through several levels before getting approval, those with informal access to key decision makers have the opportunity to be heard immediately.

The grapevine can be nurtured as a fruitful source of communication, or it can be battled like a weed.

The grapevine can be a good thing for an organization. It helps employees feel like a team, and it carries important information about employee morale. However, rumors are sometimes damaging to individuals and the organization. For example, Enrique Rodriquez, a middle-level manager, returned from his first vacation in two years to discover that people believed the president had forced him to check himself into a recovery center for alcoholics. Although the source of the rumor could not be pinpointed, Enrique believes it was started by someone who saw a brochure from the center on his desk. The brochure had been left there by someone who wanted Enrique to see if this type of service could be added to the employee benefits package.

Grapevines are dangerous because everyone who hears a rumor changes it slightly before passing it on. What starts out as a message about 15 Macintosh computers can easily become a message about 150 Big Mac hamburgers! What is more, rumors pass through the grapevine at breathtaking speed. Thus, they quickly reach many people, distorting messages dramatically. Exhibit 1.2 presents a good example of how grapevines work.

There is no way to prevent rumors. However, you will find that the grapevine is less damaging in organizations with the following characteristics:

- Upper-level management shares all need-to-know and nice-to-know information with lower-level employees.
- Managers and supervisors practice open-door policies so that questions, concerns, and ideas can be addressed immediately.
- Supervisors make a point of maintaining regular, casual contact with key people in the grapevine.
- Lower-level employees are given frequent feedback to let them know how the upward communication they provide is used to make decisions.
- All levels participate actively in decision making.
- Relationships between management and labor are open and honest and are based on mutual trust and respect.

Managing informal communication channels is a major responsibility of upper-level employees. Executives are the ones who have the power to put the above principles into action. By doing so, they make grapevines less damaging. Well-informed employees who are part of the decision-making process and can get trustworthy, timely information from managers are better able to resist false rumors.

## THE TECHNOLOGY OF BUSINESS COMMUNICATION

### COMMUNICATING MORE EFFICIENTLY WITH TECHNOLOGY

◣ Explain how computer and telecommunications technology helps businesspeople work more efficiently.

We read daily of new developments in communication technology. Technology is developing so rapidly that by the time you read this some of the information may be out of date. What is an exciting new development one day rapidly becomes commonplace.

To give you an idea of how fast technology is moving, take a look at how far we have come in a very short time. The first computer used outside the military in the United States was purchased in 1951 by the Census Bureau at a cost of $1.3 million. The computer took up an entire room and required special air-conditioning to keep from overheating. Today, however, a desktop computer has 2,500 times the memory of that first business computer, is 3,000 times faster, and costs less than $5,000.

Most developments in computer technology make us more productive, so we can perform our jobs more effectively with less effort. For the most part, the new technology also makes jobs more rewarding by freeing us from mundane, repetitive tasks. For example, accounting clerks no longer need to retype monthly or yearly balance sheets and profit and loss statements. After the statements are typed in and stored on computer once, updated figures can be inserted automatically. All the clerk has to do is print a copy or merely send the updated forms electronically to a printing firm for inclusion in the company's annual report.

The changes brought about by new technology are leading to an exciting new information age in which more people will have faster and broader access to data than ever before. This section describes some of the major technologies you will encounter in the near future, if you have not already: telephones and voice mail, computer networks, E-mail, fax machines, telecommuting and home offices, tele- and videoconferencing, and electronic bulletin boards.

*The most dramatic technological developments are in computers and telecommunications.*

## TELEPHONES AND VOICE MAIL

◼ Use the telephone to conduct business efficiently and to maintain good relationships with others.

Telephones are not new; you have probably been speaking into telephones your entire life. However, new technology extends the value of telephones. Voice mail is a computerized message system, a more sophisticated version of an answering machine. It allows people to communicate by phone even when they cannot connect directly. If you call a company with voice mail, you might even be asked to use your touch-tone phone to choose various options, bypassing the work that used to be done by a receptionist.

*Voice mail is like an advanced answering machine; it allows callers to choose among routine options.*

Given this development, it makes sense to examine telephones more carefully. Have you ever wondered if you are using the telephone effectively? Have you ever wondered how informal use of telephones and business use of telephones differs? Do you ever find yourself endlessly playing telephone tag?

Many companies have realized that each employee's telephone skills contribute to the company's image, thereby affecting its ability to sell its products and services. The first impression people receive of a firm comes from the telephone. Therefore, telephone skills are among the most important technological skills you can master.

*Learn to project a businesslike and considerate image when you use the telephone.*

Here are some recommendations that will also help improve your telephone image.

- Identify yourself immediately when you call someone. Say something such as "Hi, Terry, this is George Francka. Is Mary Farrell in?"
- Identify yourself immediately when you answer a call.
- Avoid giving callers the impression that you feel your time is more important than theirs by placing all your own phone calls; don't have someone else do it for you.
- Return all calls immediately, if possible, to create a positive impression in the mind of the person who called. However, if time management is a problem, develop a routine of returning all telephone calls at a specific time each day.

- Summarize what the caller told you when you transfer a call to someone else; don't force the caller to repeat the entire story.
- Ask permission before placing someone on hold to get information. Check back with the caller every 30–40 seconds unless you have told him or her that you need more time.
- Answer your telephone before or during the second ring.
- Tell callers whether the person they want to talk with is in the office without making callers identify themselves first. Asking for a name first sends a clear message that the called party is available only to certain people.
- Leave your name, phone number, company's name, and a brief overview of the problem as the message. If you are available for return calls only at specific times, leave that information, too, so you can avoid playing telephone tag.
- Make sure callers know exactly how to leave a message on phone mail or how to transfer to speak to a human being. It is very frustrating to go through an entire button-pushing exercise and end up in the wrong place with no way back to the right place.
- Take notes during the call to help support your memory.
- Follow up important telephone calls with memos or letters spelling out the understanding. It is important to put commitments in writing so they can be reviewed and verified by both parties. If your understanding of the commitments made by telephone is not correct, the other party can immediately write or call to clarify any misunderstanding.

## Computer Networks

Show how new technology can be used to communicate electronically with others in your workplace or at remote locations.

Only a few years ago, each desktop computer stood alone, and data were transferred on disks. However, today desktop computers can communicate directly via computer networks, allowing information to be shared effortlessly. There are two types of networks: the local area network (LAN) that links users in a single office; and the wide area network (WAN) that links remote users. Such networks now allow workers to share files easily among offices in nearby buildings and in some instances across the country. Advanced systems are being developed that will allow people around the world to work as if they were in the same room.

> Computer networks link desktop computers within a worksite (local area networks) or with remote locations (wide area networks).

The "information superhighways," which are such a popular topic these days, are huge computer networks. At present, the Internet is the only network big enough to be called an information superhighway. It consists of more than 10,000 smaller computer networks, informally linked, with 20 million users in 50 countries. Internet users can exchange messages with other Internet users, access electronic databases, and subscribe to electronic "newsletters" on thousands of topics. The system was originally developed to serve scientists and then it expanded to researchers, professors, and students. It is now expanding quickly into the business and public arenas.

> The Internet is a huge network of computer networks that originally developed haphazardly to serve scientists and academics.

Using the Internet is not yet easy; it can be daunting. However, many Internet guidebooks are available to help you translate the computerese. You may be able to borrow one from the library or from your company's telecommunications department.

On a smaller (but more accessible) scale, on-line subscription services such as CompuServe, Prodigy, and The Well are available to anyone with a computer and a modem. Typically, these services have a monthly fee plus a charge for the amount of time spent on the network. Many businesses are networked in the same way through commercial providers. Specialized networks are also being developed to serve specific interests, such as the entertainment industry and the computer industry. Many predict that computer access to information will eventually replace magazine and newspaper subscriptions, providing up-to-the-minute information at the user's leisure.

## ELECTRONIC MAIL (E-MAIL)

E-mail messages can be sent to anyone on your company's network or by modem to anyone else who has a modem.

Electronic mail (e-mail), the electronic transmission of messages from one person to another using computers, has become commonplace in business. If you work in a company with a local area network, you can send e-mail messages to other people on the network. Even if you are not part of a LAN, you can send e-mail messages via modem to anyone who also has a modem.

To send an e-mail message within a company, enter the message into your computer, address it with the receiver's special e-mail code (much like a telephone number), and send it. The message will be stored in the recipient's computer until she or he is ready to read it. If you are sending e-mail to someone outside your company, you have two options. You can call the recipient's computer to make sure it is on and ready to receive messages, set the baud rate and rate of transmission, and then push a few buttons on the telephone and the computer. If the recipient is a subscriber to one of the on-line services, you can send the message without calling first; the message will be stored by the service until the recipient is ready to read it.

Some e-mail systems, especially those that are part of a LAN, offer special mailing services. You can mark a message "urgent," and it will move to the top of a person's mailbox so the receiver will read it before the other messages. Another option would notify your computer once a person has opened the message you sent, thereby letting you know exactly when a message was received. To keep expenses down, many businesses program their computers to send external e-mail at night, when telephone rates are lower and most business telephones are not in use.

E-mail is eroding organizational hierarchies by encouraging direct communication among all levels. As a result, companies whose employees use e-mail often enjoy an advantage in new ideas for improving operations, services, and products.

E-mail seems to have an interesting effect on organizations that use it for communication among employees: Those employees tend to send more messages to their co-workers and superiors than do employees in organizations that do not use internal e-mail. The typical result is a noticeable leveling of the organizational hierarchy. In low-tech organizations, people tend to believe they are allowed to or able to communicate directly with only their immediate superiors, those on their level, and those underneath them on the organizational chart. However, in businesses with electronic-mail capabilities, employees are more likely to contact those at the top with their ideas and comments and bypass their immediate supervisors. Making those at the top more accessible has given many employees a greater feeling of involvement in their organization. In addition, the very impersonality of electronic mail makes it seem less threatening to initiate new ideas and suggestions electronically. The same people who would never think about speaking up at meetings or to their superiors apparently find it easy to communicate electronically. As a result, more new ideas and suggestions are coming to the attention of decision makers, resulting in improved operations, services, and products.

## ELECTRONIC BULLETIN BOARDS

Electronic bulletin boards disseminate information within a company or to a broader audience.

Electronic bulletin boards are computer systems that allow the posting of information so it may be accessed and read by many other people in the system. With a modem, someone with a computer can call up the bulletin board and see, for instance, the latest prices of all the products a company sells all over the world. Others who read the notices and questions may respond directly if a telephone number is included, or indirectly by using their own modem to post the information in the same space on the bulletin board, or by e-mail when an e-mail number was part of the bulletin board message.

Companies are using electronic bulletin boards to keep their employees informed about all kinds of things. Employees are also posting notices on these bulletin boards about everything from a car for sale to questions about a particularly vexing technical problem. Commercial bulletin boards are available by subscription. Prodigy, CompuServe, and America On-Line contain many bulletin boards.

## FAX MACHINES

Fax machines are common in business today; they save time when an exact replica of a document must be delivered.

Fax machines, short for facsimile, send a copy of a document over telephone lines. Faxes in offices are almost as common today as computers. They are an easy way to get exact copies of documents quickly to people anywhere in the world. Although copies can also be send by e-mail via modem, fax machines are sometimes preferable. They transmit an exact copy of your document, whereas computers are sometimes unable to reproduce formatting commands such as tabs, boldface, italics, tables, and other indents.

Sending a fax is simple. All you need is a fax machine, the hard copy of what you are sending, and the fax number of the machine that will receive the copy. The transmission time varies, depending on the density of the material on the page. On the other end, the recipient's fax machine decodes the signal from your machine and reproduces a duplicate of your document.

Many businesses send a separate cover sheet with all faxed documents, like the one in Exhibit 1.4. However, environmental sensitivity is causing many people to realize that fax cover sheets are often unnecessary. When possible, they are simply typing or handwriting the transmittal information at the top of the document being sent. Keep your faxes short, no more than five pages, to save the recipient paper and to avoid tying up the machine. Remove unnecessary graphics, shading, and fills to reduce transmission time; and sign your faxed letters and memos just as you would any other business message.

## TELECONFERENCING AND VIDEOCONFERENCING

Teleconferencing allows groups who are geographically separated to meet by telephone and discuss issues; videoconferencing (using video cameras) provides visual information as well, if only to provide nonverbal cues about participants' meaning.

Teleconferencing is substituting telephone conference calls for meetings. Since most executives spend at least half of each business day in meetings and more than that when traveling, anything that makes meetings more convenient decreases costs significantly.

Telephone conference calls can be set up quickly as long as you have scheduled the call with a telephone operator ahead of time. All you have to do is make sure all the parties are available, then the operator calls everyone until they are all on the line.

**EXHIBIT 1.4**   Sample Fax Cover Sheet

**Facsimile**

# CHANDLER &
### ASSOCIATES

To:            William Zimmerman
Fax No.:       708-325-4435
From:          Don Chandler
Date:          March 31, 1995
No. of pages:  3 (including this sheet)
Subject:       Progress of Communication Audit

Bill, please react to the following information concerning
the communication audit of your organization. I am
particularly interested in your feelings on the
breakdown between your Purchasing and Accounting
departments. Is our initial perception correct or is there
something we're missing? Please let me know.

From the desk of…
**Don Chandler**
**President**
**Chandler & Associates**
**2025 Milan Avenue**
**Homewood, IL 60430**

**708-798-5443**
**Fax: 708-798-1000**

The best way to handle a conference call is to let one person lead the discussion, much as one person usually leads a meeting. The leader has the same responsibilities as in a meeting—making sure the participants know the purpose of the conference, have received a brief overview of the agenda, and have received any materials needed ahead of time. The leader should also ensure that each participant is heard and should move the participants through the agenda skillfully and tactfully.

An obvious disadvantage is the inability to see the people with whom you are talking. The majority of the meaning we get from any face-to-face conversation comes from nonverbal communication. This problem is solved with videoconferencing, which uses video technology to show the participants on a screen while they speak.

Imagine yourself sitting around a meeting table with your co-workers in Baltimore as you listen to your company president speaking from the home office in Miami. At the end of her presentation, she asks for comments on preliminary plans to sell a division. As each person raises his or her hand, the president calls on that person and then responds to the comment. All of you can see the president and she can see all of you. Now imagine that she directs you to look at specific pages in a booklet sent to you ahead of time. For those who forgot to bring the booklets, the pages appear on the screen next to the president, where she can point to specific text and figures.

Videoconferencing is used for more than formal meetings, especially in companies that have their own facilities. For instance, companies use videoconferencing to interview a more diverse pool of applicants than they might be able to reach locally. Proposals for new ventures, consulting reports, performance appraisals of key executives in outlying areas, and so on lend themselves well to videoconferences. After an environmental disaster, one large company was able to get a solution to its cleanup problems by videoconferencing with an 84-year-old Swedish expert whose ill health made it impossible for him to come to them.

Videoconferences are a great deal more expensive than telephone conference calls, but the cost is dropping. Several years ago, it took two semitrailers full of satellite equipment to set up a videoconference between executives in three cities. Now that same conference requires half that equipment. Many businesses now have their own videoconferencing facilities with all the electronics built right in. Others use hotels or other facilities available for rent. Kinko's, a retail photocopy center, has expanded into videoconferencing. Many of its stores rent rooms and technically proficient personnel on an hourly basis.

Desktop videoconferencing is just around the corner.

Desktop videoconferencing is expected to revolutionize the way people communicate. With the right equipment and software, you can see the person with whom you are meeting—on your computer monitor—and he or she can see you. This technology is currently available and many computers can be upgraded for several thousand dollars. This cost is small compared to the cost of sending people to meetings, which usually involves hundreds or thousands of dollars for airfare, hotels, food, taxis, tips, telephone calls to the home office, and so on.

## TELECOMMUTING AND HOME OFFICES

As technology makes it easier to communicate with people in other locations, some employees have begun working at their homes. They may visit the home office periodically or send the products of their labors to their employers or clients electronically. Many companies are providing workers with computers and other equipment that enables them to work more efficiently at home. Companies that downsize may also contract with individuals who are not employees—home workers—to undertake projects that the company's remaining employees don't have time to do. This is often called "outsourcing" and using "freelancers."

Telecommuters and home workers are often regarded as essential, dependable members of the corporate world. One advantage is that widely dispersed employees can be called on to react quickly to emergencies or to reach clients around a large community or around the country, thereby making the company seem more responsive to its clients. Concerns about traffic congestion, parking, office space, and personal work preferences all contribute to the decision to allow telecommuting and home work.

> Telecommuters, employees who work at home and communicate with the main office electronically, give companies expanded reach and may relieve traffic and space problems.

## WRITING MORE EFFECTIVELY WITH COMPUTERS

▰ Identify computer software that will help you write business documents more effectively.

Whether you compose your business messages on paper or at a computer, the steps in formulating the message remain the same. However, modern computer technology can make many of these steps easier. Many different types of software programs—word processing software, grammar and style checkers, groupware, desktop publishing software, spreadsheet software, database software, and voice recognition software—are now available to help you write more effectively. While all these software packages are important, only those that impact the communication process are discussed here.

> Regardless of the technology you use to write, you must still plan, organize, compose, and evaluate your message.

### WORD PROCESSING SOFTWARE

Word processing software is used with computers to produce printed documents. Computers of all sizes can perform word processing as long as the software has been loaded into the computer. The capabilities of word processing software vary roughly with the price. The two most used word processing software programs are WordPerfect® and Microsoft Word®. Both programs possess a full range of sophisticated features and capabilities.

Once you start using a word processing program, your typewriter will probably be put away in the closet forever. Word processing programs make it easy for you to revise text easily and quickly without retying an entire paper. Report too long? With the touch of a key or two, delete what is least important or reformat the pages. Need to rearrange topics? Highlight what you want to move, "cut" it from the screen, and insert it where it should be. Need to place a footnote at the bottom of a report page? With a keystroke or two or a quick movement of the mouse, you can type a footnote that will always appear at the bottom of the page where reference is made to it—no matter how many additions or deletions you make later. Want to create a table of contents automatically without having to type the headings and subheadings with page numbers after a report is finished? Indicate the level of each heading and subheading as they are typed in the report. The program will pull all the headings and

> Word processing is the production of documents using electronic equipment and software.

subheadings together on a contents page and will even insert the correct page numbers.

Even people who pride themselves on their ability to spell appreciate the spell check feature of word processing programs. A spelling checker compares each word in a document with the words in its dictionary. It alerts the writer to any words that do not match; and, in most cases, the program suggests alternative spellings. For example, if you type the word *convinience,* a good program will suggest *convenience* as the alternative spelling and will give you the option of ignoring its suggestion or changing it automatically. Most programs have a dictionary of 80,000–100,000 words and you can usually create another dictionary containing words you use frequently. However, these programs are no substitute for proofreading because their ability to determine when plurals and singular nouns and verbs should used is limited. They also have trouble with homonyms, such as *too, to,* and *two* as well as *there* and *their.*

## GRAMMAR AND STYLE CHECKERS

Grammar and style checkers analyze documents created with standard word processing programs. They flag grammatical and punctuation errors and suggest alternatives. Many word processing programs come with grammar and style checking features built in. However, there are many inexpensive programs available for purchase as well. Some that are well known are *Grammatik, Electric Webster,* and *RightWriter.*

These programs, with varying degrees of effectiveness, are able to analyze your documents for such things as lengthy sentences; incomplete sentences; clichés; subject-verb agreement; spelling; overly long words, sentences, and paragraphs; missing end-of-sentence punctuation; overuse of effusive adjectives and adverbs (i.e., *very* or *really*); overused words; jargon; sexist words; imprecise words (i.e., *there are . . . , in addition to*); and commonly confused terms (such as *currently* and *presently*).

Exhibit 1.5 is an example of the kinds of reports grammar and style checkers provide. Look it over and decide how useful such reports would be to you. While these programs are helpful, grammar and style checkers are limited by their inability to understand context and logic. Consequently, they are fallible and are best employed by users with enough knowledge of grammar to sort accurate advice from misplaced assertions.

## GROUPWARE

Groupware is software designed to support cooperative and collaborative work between writers and other office workers.

Groupware, sometimes referred to as workflow software, is designed to improve the productivity of work groups. This software works on computers connected by a local area network. Groupware establishes a sort of repository for information contributed by various co-workers, each of whom can call up the material anytime. Some programs, such as Lotus Notes and Reach's Workman, orchestrate the flow of information from person to person and keep track of who contributed what and when. Groupware can also automate routing documents that require the approval of several managers—purchase orders, for instance. If a decision maker isn't around or procrastinates, the software can assign the task to someone else.

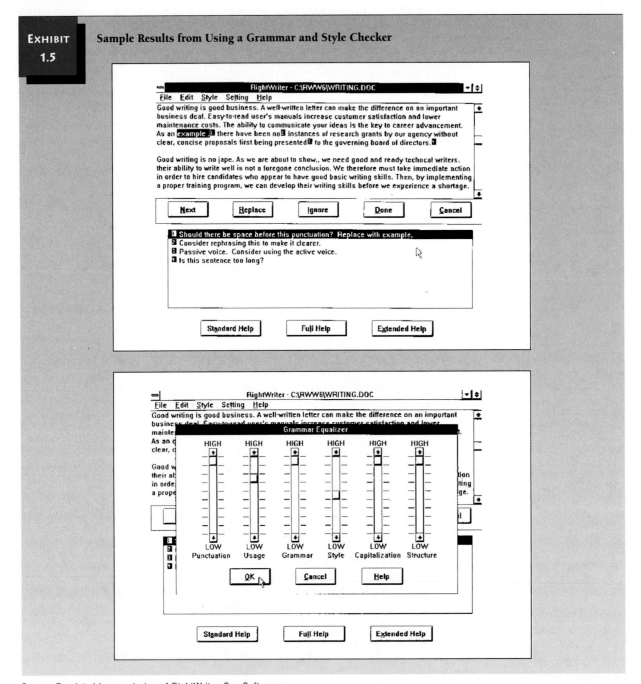

| EXHIBIT 1.5 | Sample Results from Using a Grammar and Style Checker |
| --- | --- |

Source: Reprinted by permission of RightWriter, Que Software.

To better understand groupware, note how it was used by a group collaborating on a feasibility study for a new product. The primary work group was made up of four people—Jason Hillips, from manufacturing; Ernst Shpilberg, from finance; Yool Ham, from research and development; and Peter Vargas, from marketing. An outline of the entire project with timelines for each segment was prepared at the conclusion of their first round of meetings, which took place over a two-week period. Each individual was assigned responsibility for writing the first draft of specific segments of the feasibility report. All members of the team, their supervisors, and upper-level company executives were able to access the report draft at any time. As they reviewed the drafts on screen, they were able to comment on the report, attach questions to be answered later by the writers, and even rewrite segments of the study. The groupware indicated the source of each comment. All the suggestions were available to any member of the team. However, each draft remained unchanged until the original writer revised it. This kind of interaction in the draft stage of important projects helps to ensure the final results are complete and meet expectations.

## Voice Recognition Software

**Documents can be composed on a computer using either a keyboard or voice recognition technology.**

The latest computers are able to recognize and respond to the spoken word. As the price of these computers comes down, they will become commonplace in business because they offer real convenience. With an audio-equipped computer and software that recognizes the voice, composing a business letter will go something like this:

> Computer, open Microsoft Word. Create a memo to Wilson Pietta in Purchasing. [The computer recognizes "memo," opens a template of the company's standard memo form, and automatically fills in Wilson Pietta's name on the "To" line and your own on the "From" line.] Subject: Procedure for Approval of Computer and Software Purchases. [You dictate the entire memo, perhaps making changes as you go along.] Take the sentence beginning "The third step . . . " and place it after the second sentence in the second paragraph.

Changes and additions can also be made by keyboard and mouse. When you are finished, sending the business letter will go something like this:

> Computer, send this memo to Wilson Pietta. Mark it "Urgent" so he opens it and reads it today. Wait for his response and send it to me immediately.

The computer will notify you that the message has been sent and whether it has been opened by Wilson (or someone at his end). If Wilson is not in today, your computer will read his electronic calendar and notify you that he cannot respond to your message today. If Wilson reads your memo but does not respond to it immediately, the computer will prompt him to answer the memo. However, if he chooses not to do so, the computer will notify you.

**Dictation skills are useful to anyone using voice recognition technology.**

Voice recognition software requires careful enunciation so the computer can understand what you want. Dictation skills are, therefore, once again important to anyone who plans a career in business. At one time, every key executive had a secretary to whom he or she dictated business correspondence. Less important executives dictated into machines, and those recordings were transcribed by clerk typists. Over time, however, more and more executives either turned their writing responsibilities over to executive assistants or began to compose and send their own correspondence on computers. This trend was due to the ease of composing, perfecting, and sending messages by computer as well as a shortage of trained secretaries. Now the technological wheel is turning

EXHIBIT
1.6

**Dictation Tips**

### ■ Before dictating

Organize your thoughts by preparing a brief outline.
Gather all reference material needed.
Identify yourself by name, title, and department.
Identify the type of document.
Give any special format instructions.
Indicate the number of copies required.
Give mailing, distribution, and filing instructions.

### ■ While dictating

Give instructions clearly, completely, and in sequence.
Differentiate clearly between instructions and text.
Speak slowly and directly into the microphone, computer, or telephone without turning
   away.
Specify the date to be typed on correspondence.
Announce paragraphs, capitalization, and special punctuation (parentheses, underscores,
   colons, apostrophes, semicolons, quotation marks, or exclamation points).
Spell unusual words and proper names.
Avoid mumbling, slurring, and clipping words.
Pronounce each syllable distinctly, emphasizing plural or past tense word endings.
De-emphasize any accent you might have (for example, "oil" pronounced by an East Texan
   sometimes sounds like "all").
Describe corrections and revisions clearly and completely.
Drop your voice slightly at the ends of sentences to indicate a period.
Indicate the type of heading when dictating headings and subheadings.
When dictating information for columnar and tabular formats, dictate from left to right
   across each line (state that you are dictating data horizontally), and identify a new line.
Avoid annoying habits such as clearing throat and saying "ah" and "er."
Don't chew gum, eat, or smoke while dictating.
Avoid interference from background noises such as squeaking chairs, tapping fingers,
   traffic, lip smacking, whistling, clicking pen, and so on.
Announce the end of the session.

### ■ When working with a human transcriptionist

Prioritize the document and identify a deadline.
Specify directions for returning transcripts for editing and signing.
Use his or her name if you know it.
Say "please" and "thank you" often.
Use the phonetic alphabet whenever a letter might be misunderstood (e.g., "Bismarck,—
   that's B as in boy, I as in Ida, S as in Sam, M as in Mary, A as in Adam, R as in Robert,
   C as in Charles, and K as in King."
Describe first your overall objective when giving instructions for tables, charts, or graphs.

again, and business writers will be able to compose documents without actually
writing.

Exhibit 1.6 is a list of helpful hints for anyone dictating to a person, a
transcription machine, or a computer. Good dictation skills combined with the
writing instruction found here should help to improve the effectiveness of your
dictated messages.

## COMMUNICATING ETHICALLY AND LEGALLY IN THE INFORMATION AGE

■ Discuss the major legal and ethical issues related to using the new information technology.

Electronic communication must meet the same ethical and legal standards as any other type of communication (explained in later chapters). However, two issues are particularly pertinent when using the new technology: privacy and sensitivity to others.

### PRIVACY

A person's right to a reasonable amount of privacy is protected by law. The Privacy Act, the Fair Credit Reporting Act, and many state and local laws are intended to prevent people from snooping into the lives of others. In addition, privacy laws prevent people who have legal access to private information, such as the credit files of an individual, from using that information for purposes other than it was intended. For example, it would be a violation of the Fair Credit Reporting Act for an accounts receivable clerk to sell to a credit counseling agency the names and addresses of people who are having trouble paying their bills.

*Whether employers have the right to access employees' electronic communications without permission is an unresolved issue.*

However, a gray area is what rights to privacy an employee has. How do you balance the rights of a company in accessing its electronic records against the rights of employees to expect privacy in their electronic communications? When an employee uses company equipment and company time to send and receive messages, do those messages and other computer records belong to the company or to the originator?

Employee privacy laws are still evolving and there are no clear answers to these questions. For example, electronic communications are protected from electronic eavesdropping by outside third parties; the Electronics Communications Privacy Act of 1986 protects electronic communications in the same way that wiretap laws protect telephone calls from third-party eavesdropping. However, court decisions have not made it clear whether an employer is an outside third party. Interpretation of the law is changing as more conflicts are brought to court for resolution.

Because routine business correspondence is normally filed in company files where it is accessible to all, the courts generally view company-related correspondence as belonging to both the writer and the employer. Such information sharing improves productivity, enhances decision making, and gets information out more quickly. It is essential in today's competitive environment. However, state courts have not clearly decided whether personal messages, such as love letters sent via company electronic mail, are protected by an individual's rights to privacy. Some states have ruled in favor of the individual; some have ruled in favor of the company. Therefore, you should investigate the laws of your state relating to an employee's rights to privacy.

Listening in on telephone calls is another matter that has not yet been clarified. In most instances, the courts have ruled that an employer has the right to supervise the work of employees, so when an employee does a substantial portion or all his or her work on the phone, listening in is merely supervising. However, in some cases, the courts have ruled in favor of the company only when employees were clearly informed in advance that their telephone conversations were subject to supervision.

Voice mail and e-mail are another area of concern. They are protected by federal law; it is a violation of the law for a person to access either without the "box holder's" permission. However, most voice mail and e-mail systems allow anyone who knows your password to collect your messages. Companies have reported the loss of highly secret information through illegal access to employee voice and electronic mail. It is a good idea to change your password frequently and use creative passwords that cannot be easily guessed by others.

In deciding what you can and cannot do, keep in mind that the laws are unclear and that what is legal is not always ethical. Companies show disrespect for their employees when they routinely review electronic messages, read employees' paper files, or search employees' desks. However, a company may be justified in looking at the following kinds of electronic information.

- Information that would be shared in the routine course of business (one employee covering for another employee who is out sick).
- Information that would verify that an employee suspected of stealing trade secrets or committing computer crimes is using the company's computer to do so.
- Records needed to cooperate with law enforcement agencies to investigate an employee's alleged part in criminal activity using the company's computers (gambling).

Without reasonable justification, a company's eavesdropping undermines employee loyalty and can cause embarrassment and the loss of good will.

At the very least, a company has an obligation to communicate clearly to all its employees what level of privacy they can expect when using the company's electronic communication system. Electronic records management policies should

- Encourage the sharing of electronic information.
- Prohibit supervisors from electronic snooping except when there is clear reason to expect abuse and when approved by a corporate officer.
- Reserve for the company its rights to control its electronic records.

The success of these policies hinges on whether employees and their supervisors know about them—and, moreover, whether all parties have been involved in establishing the policies. Therefore, electronic records policies should be written down, distributed, and discussed with all involved, as well as reviewed and updated frequently.

## SENSITIVITY TO OTHERS

Many people feel somewhat anonymous when writing electronically and tend to put things on a computer that they would not write or say anywhere else. This lack of inhibition can be useful and creative—but it can also be destructive when those messages are insensitive to the feelings of other people. Offensive visual and graphic jokes are far too common on computer networks, and some of those who send this type of humor electronically are people who would never tell racist, sexist, or otherwise insensitive jokes in the presence of casual acquaintances.

> Employers seem to have the right to access employees' electronic communications in certain situations.

> Cardinal rules of electronic communication: Think before you write. Think even harder before you send!

Research has also shown that a large number of people send angry messages via electronic mail and later regret it. Tales abound of business failures who put their mouths (and their fingers) ahead of their brains:

- The salesperson who lost her job after she wrote an angry computer message telling off an important client because he didn't keep their appointment earlier that day.
- Two police officers who were suspended without pay for six weeks for sending sexist jokes on a network after they had been warned to stop.
- The convicted engineer whose computer records proved he had infringed on a company patent.
- The executive whose husband found out about her affair with a co-worker by accessing her company computer from their home computer.
- The business owner who was fined by a government agency that subpoenaed his computer files to prove he had discriminated against applicants.

Apparently, it is easy to write and send something electronically without thinking of the consequences. Before computers and electronic mail, people had time to calm down before a U.S. Postal Service employee came to pick up the mail.

Do not store or send electronic remarks about religion, politics, gender, ethnicity, age, nationality, disabilities, sexual preference, and so on.

The words you store in a computer are often permanently recorded somewhere in the system, and they can slip beyond your grasp, particularly when you are on-line with an electronic mail service or when your computer is networked to others within your company. You might find your words copied and forwarded to hundreds of people without your consent. You should think before you write an electronic message and think again before you send it—especially when you are angry, upset, or simply feeling superior. People who express insensitive thoughts, opinions, or feelings electronically often find their careers and reputations irreparably damaged.

## DISCUSSION QUESTIONS

▪ Define *communication* and list five of its dimensions.

1. Define communication.
2. List the five dimensions of communication and give an example of each (use examples that were not used in the chapter).

▪ Explain why good communication is important to the organization and to the individual.

3. Identify four advantages of effective communication to business organizations.
4. Identify three advantages of effective communication skills to an individual within a business organization.

▪ Describe the three forms of communication in business.

5. List the three forms of communication. Give two original examples of each form.

6. What kinds of feedback are associated with each of the three forms of communication?

▪ Identify the three goals of business communication.

7. List the three goals of communication in business.

8. How does effective communication strengthen business relationships?

▪ Describe the communication process.

9. Explain each of the three stages of the communication process illustrated in Exhibit 1.1.

10. How does reception of a message trigger a repetition of the three stages in the communication process?

▪ Identify seven types of barriers to communication.

11. Give two examples of each of the seven types of barriers to effective communication.

▪ Describe the formal and informal communication channels within an organization.

12. Discuss how the formal and informal communication patterns within organizations affect workers and managers.

▪ Explain how computer and telecommunications technology helps businesspeople work more efficiently.

13. Identify six ways that new communication technology is affecting organizations.

14. How do computers and telecommunications technology help businesspeople work more efficiently?

▪ Use the telephone to conduct business efficiently and to maintain good relationships with others.

15. What is the main disadvantage of using voice mail?

▪ Show how new technology can be used to communicate electronically with others in your workplace or at remote locations.

16. Discuss how teleconferencing is or could be used in your company. If you are not currently working, you may use a former job as the basis for answering this question or you may discuss how teleconferencing is or could be used in the college you are attending.

▪ Identify computer software that will help you write business documents more effectively.

17. Why can't grammar checkers find all the grammar errors in documents?

18. Spelling checkers can't find all instances of misspelled or misused words. Name six words a typical spelling checker might not find.

🔳 Discuss the major legal and ethical issues related to using the new information technology.

19. Some information stored in computers must be accessible to many different people, not just to those who create the information. Identify three instances when electronically stored information should be readily available to others.

## APPLICATION EXERCISES

🔳 Define *communication* and list five of its dimensions.

1. Using business communication textbooks or books about communication theory, find three definitions of *communication* and compare them to the definition used in this chapter. How do they differ? Which definition do you believe best describes communication in a business setting? Answer these questions in a memo to your professor. Include the three definitions and cite your sources.

2. Find an article on one of the five dimensions of communication listed in this chapter (e.g., intentional, unintentional communication). What is the subject of the article? Is it based on research with people or animals, or is it based on library research? In summary, what does the author conclude about this dimension of communication? How does this information apply to the business world? What remaining questions do you have? Prepare a short (three- or four-page) informational report, citing your source. Your professor will inform you if you should be prepared to present a brief overview of your research to class.

🔳 Explain why good communication is important to the organization and to the individual.

3. Research the cost of communication in business. Using the four forms of communication activities as a guide, find figures and examples that justify the statement, "The cost of poor communication in business is immeasurable." For example, see if you can determine the latest figures concerning the cost of an average business letter and an average memorandum. Is there evidence to support the belief that its communication activities is an area a business should study and work to improve? Prepare a report for your instructor addressing this topic.

🔳 Describe the three forms of communication in business.

4. Analyze how you use oral, written, and nonverbal communication in your job. Which form of communication do you use most? Prepare a two-page memo report based on your analysis. If you are not working currently, you may use a prior job. If you have never worked, you may use a club or organization to which you belong or have belonged, or you may interview someone who is working currently (however, remember to cite your source).

🔳 Identify the three goals of business communication.

5. Observe your communication activities over a 24-hour period. Identify as many instances as you can of how you and the people you communicated

with pursued the three goals of communication in an organization (to impart feelings, information, and ideas; to strengthen relationships; and to reduce conflict). Note whether you or the people you communicated with were successful or unsuccessful. Submit this information in a memo report to your professor.

■ Identify the three goals of business communication.
■ Identify seven types of barriers to communication.

6. Watch a television show that is at least one hour long. The show you choose must be one that contains a great deal of conversation. Identify as many instances as you can of how the people in the show pursued the three goals of communication in an organization. Note whether they were successful or unsuccessful. For example, were there instances when it was clear that one character was not listening to another, which resulted in the blocking of information or the weakening of a relationship? Did you spot any examples in which the cultural barrier of prejudice promoted conflict? Submit this information in a memo report to your professor.

■ Describe the communication process.

7. Carry on conversations with three different people. For each conversation, analyze the kinds of feedback—verbal and nonverbal—the other person gave you. Was nonverbal or verbal feedback more common? How did this feedback affect you? What changes did you make in your conversation as a result of the feedback? Address these questions for each of the conversations, and submit the information in a two- or three-page informational report to your instructor.

■ Identify seven types of barriers to communication.

8. With your class, divide into groups of four. Within your group, assign the letter A, B, C, or D to each person. A and B should leave the room. C should read to D his or her report for one of the exercises in this chapter (your professor will tell you which one to use). D is responsible for summarizing what C is saying (D may take notes) but cannot interrupt C in any way. Then A should reenter the room. D should read his or her notes, and A should summarize without interrupting D. Then B should reenter the room to take notes while A reads his or her summary. At the end, C rereads the original report, comparing it to the final summary written by B. In discussion with your group, note the types of additions and omissions that occurred. How drastic were the changes? Did the grapevine become a barrier?

■ Describe the formal and informal communication channels within an organization.

9. Select an organization with which you are familiar. If you are not familiar with an organization, interview someone who is. Find out the following and summarize it in an informational report to your professor.
   a. What kinds of downward communication are used by management to inform or motivate employees? Which types of downward messages require a response from employees?
   b. What kind of upward communication is there between lower and higher levels of the organization? What kinds of information are

transferred? How does management let lower-level employees know that the information they feed to upper levels is being used?

    c.   What kinds of lateral communication occurs within the organization? About how much of the lateral communication is between people who work in the same department? About how much takes place between people from different departments?

    d.   Must upward or lateral communication be cleared by a department head before it can go outside the department?

■ Describe the formal and informal communication channels within an organization.

10. Read an article about informal communication in business. Write a one-page summary of the article, staple the article to your summary, and submit both to your instructor.

11. Give examples of the grapevine in action at your place of employment. What changes should management institute to reduce the likelihood of damaging rumors? Write a two-page memo report on this topic. (Be prepared to present it orally if the professor instructs you to do so.)

■ Explain how computer and telecommunications technology helps businesspeople work more efficiently.

12. Prepare voice mail messages for each situation. Write out the message you would record.

    a.   You are the general manager of a small local cable television company, which means you get many calls from people in the community. Usually, a receptionist answers the telephone and transfers the messages to the appropriate people—either Tom Harden for new orders and scheduled repairs and hookups; Casey Marlow for billing questions and problems (she is housed in another city); or you for everything else. When Midori Suma, the receptionist, is sick, your secretary, Terry Chozet, answers the telephone. However, a recent flu epidemic has hit the area and both Midori and Terry called in sick. You have been doing your best to answer the phone and do your own work, but you have to go to an important meeting, which should last from 2:30 to 4:30 or 5:00 PM. Since Tom is out in the field, the office will have to be locked up. You have placed a sign on the door explaining the problem and saying that the office will be open again at the usual time (8:30 AM to 5 PM) tomorrow.

    b.   You are now a customer of the cable television company. As the vice president of the local chamber of commerce, you are calling the general manager to discuss an idea for a one-hour television show featuring local business owners and managers and their involvement in charities, local youth events, and so on. However, when you call the cable company, you get the manager's voice mail. Leave a message asking the manager to call you tomorrow morning or afternoon between 4 and 5 PM. Give the manager a general idea of what you have in mind.

    c.   You work for a publishing company and are responsible for taking customer comments—the readers of the books you publish and the owners of bookstores who sell the product. You have to attend a two-day major publishing conference, so you are going to put a message on your answering machine. Let the bookstore owners know that they can call

Letitia Klemin at Ext. 2663 or they can leave a message for you. Other callers who want to comment on your books or have other questions may call Patrick Hong at Ext. 2870 or leave a message for you.

▪ Use the telephone to conduct business efficiently and to maintain good relationships with others.

13. Evaluate the following telephone conversations. What improvements or changes do you recommend?

   *a.* Participants: John Byerly, a salesperson; Sian Pierce, a secretary; and Beverly Villapondo, a client.

| | |
|---|---|
| John | Sian, get Beverly Villapondo on the phone for me, will you? |
| Sian | Hello, Beverly? Please hold for John Byerly. |
| Sian | John, Beverly is on the phone. |
| John | [Eating a doughnut, licking his fingers, and drinking coffee.] Hey, Beverly! How have you been? I just wanted to see if you've made your decision about the insurance policy we talked about. No? Well, you know, it was three weeks ago we talked. Why don't I come over and show you the figures again? Maybe if I present them to your boss, he'll go for it— sort of a man-to-man thing! |
| Beverly | [Summary: Don't call us; we'll call you!] |

   *b.* Participants: Oprah Freywin, a talent agent; David ManLetter, a casting director; and Patsy Fishency, an executive assistant.

| | |
|---|---|
| Patsy | Oprah, David ManLetter is on line four. |
| Oprah | What's he want? |
| Patsy | Oh, I don't remember exactly—something about a new film and Mel Gibson. |
| Oprah | Oh, hurry, find me those two files I gave you last week, those two new starlets we signed! |
| Oprah | David, baby, how's it going? Sewn up the money for your new film yet? Yeah, I've got two people you might want to test. Let me get their files. [She places David ManLetter on hold without waiting for a response.] |
| Oprah | Where's that file, Patsy? Let me help! |
| Oprah | [Two minutes later.] David, I finally found it! Hello? Hello? David? He hung up on me! What nerve! Patsy, try to get him on the line again! |

▪ Show how new technology can be used to communicate electronically with others in your workplace or at remote locations.

14. Imagine that you have been asked to prepare instructions on using some business communication technology for your company's training manual. (Your teacher may assign you one or more of these items.) Use numbered lists to make the steps easy to follow. Include enough detail to ensure the average person can use these step-by-step procedures without having to ask for help.

   *a.* How to send a document to another computer on a local area network (LAN).

    *b.* How to send a document to someone via a telephone modem attached to a personal computer.

    *c.* How to get on Internet and use at least two of the options.

    *d.* How to get on Prodigy, CompuServe or American On-line and use at least two of the options.

    *e.* How to post a message on an electronic bulletin board.

    *f.* How to send a document on a fax machine.

◼ Show how new technology can be used to communicate electronically with others in your workplace or at remote locations.

15. Select one of the letter or memo assignments from the application exercises at the ends of Chapters 7, 8, or 9. Using a tape recorder, dictate the letter or memo using the advice given in this chapter. You may organize your ideas beforehand, but do not write it out before you dictate it. (After all, anyone can read to a recorder.) Bring your tape to class for evaluation.

◼ Identify computer software that will help you write business documents more effectively.

16. Get information about one of the latest grammar and style checkers available for either WordPerfect or Microsoft Word. What are the major features of the program? How much does it cost? Locate reviews of this program, and determine what its weaknesses are. How helpful do you think such programs would be to the average college business student? Prepare a two-page summary of your findings for your instructor and include copies of the articles and advertising literature you used.

◼ Discuss the major legal and ethical issues related to using the new information technology.

17. Find an article that deals with a legal or ethical issue related to information technology. Write a two- or three-page summary discussing how the article relates to the legal and ethical issues presented in this chapter.

# Communicating with Diverse Cultures

## Objectives

When you finish studying this chapter, you should be able to:

- Define *culture, subculture,* and *ethnocentrism,* and identify examples of each.
- Explain why businesspeople need to understand cultural differences.
- Name the eight aspects of cultural differences that affect business communication.
- Describe differences in the ways two American subcultures—men and women—communicate.
- Describe seven areas in which business practices vary by culture.
- List seven principles for writing to businesspeople of other cultures.
- Describe cultural differences in nonverbal communication.
- List nine ways you can improve your ability to communicate with people of other cultures and subcultures.

## What Would You Do If...?

**CULTURE CLASH.**   Twenty-nine-year-old Rita Chacon, assistant coordinator of project management for Bildhauser, a large lumber firm, and 36-year-old James Carl, vice president of marketing, traveled to Japan to participate in three days of meetings with seven representatives of Sumitoro, a major Japanese construction firm. Rita and James had carefully prepared presentations and were confident no other company could offer such quality lumber at lower prices.

At a brief afternoon introductory meeting, the chief executive of Sumitoro, Tohuro Kawaguchi, invited James to have an evening of fun with him and the other executives. Excited about the prospect of getting to know their Japanese hosts better, James and Rita arrived at 9 PM, as instructed. They brought white roses and perfume for any wives who might be attending the gathering, and expensive, personally chosen gifts for each one of the executives (all male and over 45 years old). Because no women other than Rita were actually present at the gathering, James and Rita gave the roses and perfume to the executives to take home to their wives. James and Rita had been told Japanese businesspeople like to socialize until the early morning hours, so they were surprised when the Sumitoro president called for a chauffeur to take them home at 11 PM.

On the day of their second meeting with the Japanese representatives, Rita and James were determined to get results. To demonstrate how efficient Bildhauser was, James walked to the front of the room to begin his presentation right on time. To foster a feeling of friendship, he opened his presentation by welcoming each executive by his first name. He told them how profitable a relationship between Bildhauser and Sumitoro would be for both companies and stressed why Sumitoro should abandon the American lumber firm they were currently using. He assured the Sumitoro executives that he would personally make sure that they would receive from Bildhauser the service they deserved. In her presentation, Rita underscored James's promise by stating that he had a great deal of power in the organization because he held the company record for developing new accounts.

After the presentations were over, Rita took the Sumitoro chief executive aside to negotiate the details of the contract. During the negotiations, Rita was bothered by Mr. Kawaguchi's long periods of silence. As a result, she ended up giving more concessions than she had originally planned. Toward the end of the meeting, Mr. Kawaguchi said "Yes" frequently. Rita left the meeting thinking he had agreed to the contract she proposed.

The following day, Rita asked Mr. Kawaguchi to sign the finished contract, and he said he would do the best he could to get the other executives to agree. Reluctantly, Rita and James went back to the United States without a signed contract. Although over the next few weeks they made many follow-up telephone calls to Sumitoro, they never received a contract.

As you read this chapter, try to determine where Rita and James went wrong. How could they have improved the way they dealt with their Japanese counterparts? What types of miscommunication occurred during their three days of meetings?

## BASICS OF INTERCULTURAL BUSINESS COMMUNICATION

Differences in perception and language contribute to miscommunication among people of diverse cultures.

It is usually more difficult to communicate with people of diverse cultures than it is to communicate with people of your own culture. Miscommunication is more likely to occur because of the differences in the way people perceive events and how they use and interpret verbal and nonverbal messages. Many instances of intercultural miscommunication caused Rita and James to lose an important contract in the chapter-opening vignette. If Rita and James had been more sensitive to the customs and beliefs of Japanese people, they might have successfully negotiated a contract.

Define *culture, subculture,* and *ethnocentrism,* and identify examples of each.

**Culture** consists of the beliefs, attitudes, symbols, values, and behaviors that are acceptable within a given society and are passed from one generation to another. Anything made by people is considered a part of their culture—clothing, equipment, furniture, buildings, and so on. Intangibles are also part of a culture, such as attitudes toward education, aging, gender, and personal freedom.

The American culture consists of thousands of subcultures.

Within each culture are various **subcultures**—groups of people with the same overall beliefs and behaviors as the general culture but having some specific styles and attitudes of their own. Subcultures based on ethnicity, gender, religion, social status, political beliefs, and profession (as well as many other characteristics) exist within major cultures. African-Americans, entrepreneurs, fundamentalists, and women are only four of the thousands of subcultures that can be distinguished from other subcultures in the United States and Canada by their behaviors and beliefs. Each of these subcultures can also be broken down into additional subcategories.

Cultural diversity, like that in the United States, Canada, and the global economy, can stimulate many new ideas. Unfortunately, many of us don't reap the benefits of cultural diversity because we tend to judge others according to our own standards. **Ethnocentrism,** the belief that one's own cultural group is superior, prevents some people from appreciating cultural differences. Ethnocentrics also stereotype people from other cultures, stubbornly refusing to acknowledge that individuals in any group may be quite different from other group members. Some ethnocentrics let their biases about cultural groups guide their interpersonal relationships. However, failure to appreciate the impact of culture on business communication can cause much damage in a business environment.

◼ Explain why businesspeople need to understand cultural differences.

If you learn to appreciate cultural differences, you will be more valuable to companies that employ people of different cultures and subcultures or that do business in global markets.

Businesses need people who are appreciative of cultural differences. Everyone needs to be able to work harmoniously within a culturally diverse workforce, and companies need to expand into global markets for their products and services. Countries all over the world covet North American products; however, they want products designed to meet their needs. Determining how to show other cultures that North American products and services meet their needs is a major challenge facing businesses today.

The globalization of business is only one reason to appreciate cultural diversity; the dramatic change in the makeup of the workforce is another. Today, minorities, women, and older workers are entering the workforce in ever-increasing numbers. Motivating, training, and leading these workers will require more than a casual understanding of what makes them unique. In addition, businesses are placing new emphasis on teaching people to get along with people of other cultures. Making cultural diversity work is simply good business. In the future, there will be two kinds of businesses—those that appreciate cultural diversity and use it to their advantage, and those that are no longer in business.

## THE IMPACT OF CULTURAL DIFFERENCES

◼ Name the eight aspects of cultural differences that affect business communication.

The cultural differences that affect business communication fall into eight categories:

Language and linguistics.

Conversational style.

Individualism versus group orientation.

Interpersonal relationships.

Business practices.

Written communication.

Nonverbal communication.

Religious customs.

Because of the globalization of business and the dominance of North American companies, many people from diverse cultures have learned to observe Western business customs.

These categories are discussed in the following sections. As you read them, keep in mind the dangers of stereotyping. The qualities attributed to certain cultures are only generalizations—in no way can they be true for each individual who is a part of that culture. In fact, many businesspeople in other countries have become Westernized and no longer exhibit the behaviors normally ascribed to their compatriots. The information provided here should serve merely as guidelines, not hard and fast rules.

## LANGUAGE AND LINGUISTICS

It has often been said that English is the language of business, and there is some truth to that statement. For example, if someone from France and someone from Japan are conducting business, they will usually agree to speak English. However, you will be at a distinct disadvantage if you cannot speak and, more important, comprehend the language(s) of the culturally diverse people with whom you do business. Fortunately, even if you are not proficient in that language, you have three other viable options:

If you are doing business in a foreign country and are not proficient in the language, hire a reliable translator to avoid costly misinterpretations. Learn a few basic phrases in that language as a sign of respect.

- *Hire someone you trust to translate for you.* Make sure the translator you hire is thoroughly familiar with both languages, your company, and the contract you hope to negotiate. Regardless of the translator's skill, however, you must allow for differences in culture. For example, an American small business owner was using an interpreter to work out the details of an agreement with a company in Thailand to make custom-ordered rosewood doors. Through the interpreter, the Thai owner stated it would take 90 days after an order was received to make and ship a door to the United States. When the American asked whether the estimate was 90 calendar days (approximately three months) or 90 working days (approximately four months, assuming a five-day workweek), neither the Thai owner nor the Thai interpreter was able to answer without further clarification. They were not familiar with the concept of a five-day workweek.

- *Let a native speaker evaluate all written material before it is used.* Subtle differences in connotation may create expensive errors. A classic example was Pepsi-Cola's use of the slogan "Come Alive" in Germany and Asia. In Germany, the phrase translated as "Come out of the grave!" In Asia, it was interpreted as "Bring your ancestors back from the dead!" When Chevrolet marketed the Nova in Puerto Rico and Latin America, it failed to realize that *No va* in Spanish means "It does not go." How would you have felt if you were one of the marketing executives in charge of these failed promotions? Consulting a native speaker before plunging ahead would have saved a great deal of embarrassment, and, possibly, a career.

- *Honor your foreign business counterpart by learning and using a few basic phrases in that person's language.* If necessary, begin by saying that you will try your best to convey your message in the other language but you are still learning. By letting your listener know ahead of time that your use of his or her language is limited, you can avoid disastrous misinterpretations. For example, an American businessperson mistakenly used *tu,* one of the French translations for the American word *you,* when speaking to an executive. Because *tu* is used only for intimates, the French executive's first reaction was shock. Luckily, his second reaction was laughter! Exhibit 2.1 lists a few simple phrases often used when doing business in Spanish-speaking countries and Japan.

Even people who speak the same language often miscommunicate because of differences in terminology and word usage. Slang and clichés are major sources of miscommunication and should, therefore, be avoided when doing business. For example, a common way for young Americans to say someone is exceptionally good looking is to say, "He's hot!" You can imagine the cross-cultural confusion that expression has caused! Similarly, clichés such as "The ball's in your court now" and "Run with it" don't communicate well unless listeners are familiar with sporting events and are used to hearing these expressions used outside that context.

## CONVERSATIONAL STYLE

Describe differences in the ways two American subcultures—men and women—communicate.

Conversational style consists of the unconsciously applied rules by which people of a culture (or subculture) conduct conversations. This section discusses elements of conversational style, including qualifiers and tag questions, directness, turn taking, topic initiation and development, and tone of voice. Elements of conversational style dealing with international negotiations are covered later.

**QUALIFIERS AND TAG QUESTIONS.**  **Qualifiers** are words and phrases that soften a statement's impact. For example, the italicized phrases in the following sentences are qualifiers:

> "*Perhaps* we should find another way to fund the project. *It seems to me* that getting a federal grant is impossible in these hard times."

> "*I know this sounds silly,* but *I wonder* if we're doing the right thing by continuing to seek federal funding of the project."

> "*It probably won't work;* but *something tells me* we should find another way to fund the project."

> "*Well, you finance specialists are the experts,* but *why don't we* find another way to fund the project?"

> "*This is probably going to make you angry,* but *I think* we should find another way to fund the project."

This conversational style is common to both cultures that value harmony and the subculture of women. Some experts believe that women have not achieved equality in the business world because they use this sort of depowering language. In cultures that admire directness, the tentative nature of qualifiers makes people seem unsure of their opinions. A stronger, more assertive way to get across the idea expressed in the first statement above is "Government grants are

Qualifiers and tag questions soften statements. They are considered polite in some cultures and subcultures, but in others they indicate the speaker's weakness.

**EXHIBIT 2.1**

**Foreign Phrases Useful for Doing Business in Other Countries**

| ■ Types of Phrases | ■ English | ■ Spanish | ■ Japanese |
|---|---|---|---|
| Greetings | "Hello." | "Hola!" | "Kon-nichi-wa." |
| | "How are you?" | "Como esta usted?" | "O-shigoto-wa, doo desu ka?" (How is your business? "How are you" is not used in this sense in Japan.) |
| | "How may I help you?" | "En que puedo servirle(les)?" | "Kon-kahua, dono-yoo-na koto-de . . . ?" |
| | "It's so nice to meet you." | "Mucho gusto encantado" (said by a man). "Mucho gusto encantada" (said by a woman). | "O-ai dekite kooei desu?" |
| | "Good morning." | "Buenos dias!" | "Ohayoo gozai-masu." |
| | "Good afternoon." | "Buenos noches!" | "Kon-nichi-wa." |
| | "Good evening." | "Buenos tardes!" | "Kon-ban-wa." |
| Partings | "Goodbye." | "Adios!" | Levels of politeness from most polite to least: "Shitsu rei shi-masu." "Sayoonaara." "Deewa." |
| | "Please let me know when I once again can be of service to you." | "Por favor, aviseme cuando yo le pueda ayudar en algo." | "Wa tashi-domo-ni dekiru-koto-ga ari-mashitara mata, o-shirase kudasai." (Not used in Japan.) |
| | "Have a good day." | "Que tenga un buen dia." | |
| | "Please call me." | "Por favor, llameme por telefono." | "O-denwa-o o-machi shite i-masu." |
| | "See you later." | "Hasta luego." "Hasta pronto." "Hasta la vista." | "Ja, mata, nochi-hodo." |
| | "Take care." | "Que le vaya muy bien." | "O-ki-o tsuketa." |
| Others | "Please." | "Por favor." | "Doozo" (when you offer something). "O-ne-gai-shi-masu" (when you need help). |
| | "Thank you very much." | "Muchas gracias." | |
| | "It is an honor doing business with you." | "Es un placer trabajar con Ud." | "Issho-ni o-shigoto-ga dekite, hontoo-ni kooei-ni zonji-masu." |
| | "I'm very sorry." | "Lo siento mucho." | "Mooshi-wake ari-masen deshita." |
| | "You are very kind." | "Ud es muy amable." | "Go-shinsetsu-ni, arigatoo zozai-mashita." |
| | "Greetings to your wife (husband, children)." | "Saludos a su esposa (esposo, hijos)." | "Oku-sama-ni doozo yoroshiku." |
| | "Enjoy your vacation." | "Felices vacaciones!" | "Tanoshii Kyooka-ni nari-masu-yoo-ni." |

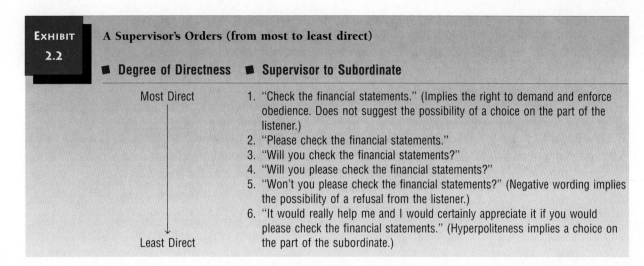

**Exhibit 2.2**

**A Supervisor's Orders (from most to least direct)**

■ **Degree of Directness**   ■ **Supervisor to Subordinate**

Most Direct

1. "Check the financial statements." (Implies the right to demand and enforce obedience. Does not suggest the possibility of a choice on the part of the listener.)
2. "Please check the financial statements."
3. "Will you check the financial statements?"
4. "Will you please check the financial statements?"
5. "Won't you please check the financial statements?" (Negative wording implies the possibility of a refusal from the listener.)
6. "It would really help me and I would certainly appreciate it if you would please check the financial statements." (Hyperpoliteness implies a choice on the part of the subordinate.)

Least Direct

impossible to get these days. Our stockholders are the best source of funding for this project." However, Americans who express themselves assertively are often considered rude by those from cultures (e.g., many Asian cultures) that place a stronger value on consensus and harmonious relationships.

Communication experts have also revealed that women use more **tag questions** than men, as in the following examples:

"I think we should seek funding from our investors, *don't you*?"

"If the government hasn't funded the project by now, they never will, *will they*?"

Tag questions almost beg listeners to disagree with the speaker, and thus weaken an argument. They can make speakers seem weak and unassertive. However, tag questions (as well as qualifiers) are sometimes desirable—for example, when you do not want to force your opinions or ideas on others, when you want to avoid conflict and confrontation, and when you want to encourage other people to speak up.

In the United States, directness is usually considered an asset in the business world; in other countries, however, it may be considered rude.

**Directness.**   Directness is considered a desirable quality in the United States, but it is seen as rude in many other countries. Indirect styles, such as qualifiers and tag questions, are considered more polite; but, in some cases, indirectness confuses and frustrates listeners. Wasting time by approaching topics too slowly is not a quality admired by people from direct cultures. The way questions are asked is another example of cultural differences in conversational style. For example, a direct, assertive American might ask, "How many people do we have working on the Swanson campaign?" An indirect way of asking the same question would be "I'd just like to ask how many people are working on the Swanson campaign." In the United States, this indirect type of question is more common to women than to men.

In an attempt to be polite, some people also tend to give orders to subordinates in a rather indirect fashion. Unfortunately, subordinates in the United States often interpret a polite order as an option and thus ignore it. Some experts have recommended that North American women learn to be less tentative so that they seem more authoritative and are therefore better able to progress in their careers. Exhibit 2.2 shows examples of a supervisor's orders arranged from most to least direct. As you read Exhibit 2.2, notice that the first, most direct option is the only one that does not suggest the possibility of choice. This is what makes it seem rude to some but authoritative to others.

**TURN TAKING.** When conversation occurs among people who communicate well together, somehow each person seems to know when it is his or her turn to speak. As soon as one person finishes speaking, another picks up the conversation and carries it forward until it is time for someone else to take over. Each person is able to introduce ideas and develop them fully without being interrupted by others. However, this is an ideal conversation, and there are few conversations that meet these standards. As you know, it is often very hard to maintain control of a conversation long enough to get your point across without being interrupted. These interruptions usually come from someone who wants to argue with you, someone who wants to change the topic of conversation, or someone who jumped to conclusions about what you were planning to say and wants to contribute his or her own experiences. Such interruptions violate the rules of turn taking.

In general, women and some minorities allow themselves to be interrupted more often than most North American men do. An **interruption** is a deliberate attempt by one person to take control of a conversation from a speaker who is in the act of speaking and not yet ready to relinquish control. Because the right to be heard without interruption is a privilege we give to those whose power over us we acknowledge and accept, it is easy to see how weak people seem when they allow subordinates and others to interrupt them successfully. To avoid seeming weak and ineffective, it is important that you not allow others to interrupt you when you are speaking. Say something to the interrupter, such as "Wait, let me finish my point"; then continue the conversation without a pause. If said in an assertive, yet unthreatening way, such a statement will result in reaffirming your right to control the conversation until you finish.

Do not confuse overlapping talk as an attempt to interrupt. Words and phrases, such as "Yes," "I know," and "That happens to me all the time," are meant to reinforce the speaker, not serve as interruptors.

**TOPIC INITIATION AND DEVELOPMENT.** Another cultural difference in communication style is a person's assertiveness in bringing a topic into group discussion. Again, this is a matter of power relationships and respect. For example, women in groups are generally more silent than men are and are less likely to initiate topics of discussion. In addition, topics initiated by women are less likely to be developed and favored by group members. It is interesting, however, that many women and others who wouldn't consider speaking up during a meeting are often far more assertive when communicating electronically. Electronic mail and teleconferencing seem to encourage assertiveness, perhaps because of the anonymity of these communication methods.

> Male and female subcultures in the United States have traditionally differed in their ability to initiate and develop topics in group discussion.

In our society, effective communicators, no matter what their gender, are expected to assert themselves by speaking up when they have something to say and by controlling the conversation to ensure that others have considered fully the topics and ideas they have presented. If you feel others have ignored or have not fully considered a topic you proposed, redirect the conversation with a statement such as "Wait a minute. Let's go back to the idea of a new stock offering. There is something that wasn't considered when it was discussed earlier. As you know . . . "

In other cultures, you may need to be more patient about returning to your topic. You would let the other person fully explain his or her topic, and then add your ideas.

**TONE OF VOICE.** The ideal voice volume, rate of speaking, and pitch vary from culture to culture. Within the United States, people who live in big cities are often stereotyped as being loud and vocally aggressive. That stereotype has been generalized to all Americans by cultures where loud voices and arguing are not acceptable, such as China, Japan, Korea, and the Middle East. When dealing with businesspeople from these areas, take care to speak softly and control your temper. However, in Germany, Spain, Mexico, Greece, Italy, and France, arguments and loud voices are viewed as normal during business negotiations. Make sure you understand where your foreign counterparts stand on this issue.

## INDIVIDUALISM VERSUS GROUP ORIENTATION

Cultural groups vary in the degree to which they admire individual initiative. Many cultures, such as that of the Japanese, believe the interests of society as a whole are always more important than the interests of the individual. When problems occur in a company, they are considered the responsibility of the entire organization. Successes and failures are not attributed to any one department, plant, or individual; they are considered to be shared by all. Individuals are seldom singled out for special praise or monetary reward. In the vignette at the beginning of the chapter, Rita's emphasis on James's, rather than the company's, expertise may well have had a negative connotation for the Japanese businesspeople to whom they were speaking.

In contrast, American heroes have always been individuals—the lone cowboy riding into a Western town to get rid of all the bad guys by himself without the help of the townspeople, the misunderstood police officer standing alone in his or her quest to fight crime in the streets, the executive who made it on his or her own without family or political connections, and the individual succeeding against all odds. These examples are symbolic of two of the most important of all American values: freedom and equality.

Americans and people of many other nationalities tend to rebel against anything that infringes on their freedom. Unfortunately, this constant striving to rule our own lives and resist attempts to dominate us sometimes works against the goals of the businesses for which we work. For instance, Americans change jobs far more often than do workers in many other cultures. In Japan, most people work for the same firm from the beginning of their working lives until retirement. Quitting a company is considered counter to the expectations of society, and anyone who does so is ostracized by others, who are shamed by the individual's failure. In addition, American workers are less likely than workers in other cultures to respect a company's formal lines of authority. It is not unusual for an American who does not like the boss's treatment to go to someone on the next hierarchical level. In more formal, group-oriented cultures, however, the individual does not challenge the hierarchy in this way. (The importance of rank in various cultures is considered in more detail in the section on business practices.)

American businesses have adopted some of the methods of group-oriented cultures, such as quality circles, but American individualism is beneficial in situations requiring quick action.

Despite the American emphasis on individualism, many American businesspeople have come to see value in the group orientation of other cultures. For example, Japan's group orientation has brought us **quality circles.** Decisions that guide company policy are made by groups that consist of all the key people involved, from labor to management. Everyone has an equal voice during discussions, and no changes are instituted until group consensus has been reached. Upper-level management almost always follows the recommendations of its quality circles. Although many American companies have also adopted quality circles, it has been difficult for some American managers to relinquish control, and in some cases it has not been efficient to spend the extra time it takes to have large groups arrive at decisions. Group decision making is changing the way many American companies work; however, this decision-making style is not yet common outside of large Japanese firms.

## INTERPERSONAL RELATIONSHIPS

Cultural groups differ in the way people relate to one another. Among the issues that sometimes cause problems for Americans doing business with other cultures are:

Some cultures still view women as inferior to men in business settings.

**GENDER.** In many Middle Eastern countries, men do not take orders from women, because to do so would make them seem weak and powerless to others of their culture. In Saudi Arabia, for example, women are considered weak and emotional, and men are considered strong and rational. Women are not allowed to interact with men outside of their families and are forbidden to drive cars or ride bicycles. Many of these laws also apply to female visitors. An American company would need to use caution in sending a female negotiator to Saudi Arabia. A similar caution applies in Japan. The social groundwork for most business dealings is laid at dinner or some other evening entertainment, and wives are not invited. Because most Japanese women work in low-level positions and traditionally quit working when they marry, it is hard for many Japanese men to negotiate with North American women.

Many cultures have more respect for older, more experienced workers than Americans do.

**AGE.** In many Asian and Middle Eastern cultures, older people are accorded more respect than is typically given to older Americans. In many Asian cultures, the elderly are considered wise, and employees honor the older executives by reacting immediately to every request. Older people are thought to have wisdom born of age and experience. In contrast, Americans have always admired the energy of youth more than the wisdom of the elderly. Many Americans tend to believe that older people are old-fashioned, unintelligent, and merely to be tolerated. Such attitudes must not be allowed to interfere with business negotiations.

**NAMES AND TITLES.** The use of names and titles in other cultures can be confusing. Thais, like Americans, address each other by first names and reserve last names for very formal occasions or for written communications. In Thailand, *khun* is often used with the first name, in the same way we use *Mr.* or *Ms.* (although we use these titles with the last name). In contrast, first names are seldom used in many European countries. In Germany, titles such as *Herr Direktor* or *Frau Direktor* are preferred to indicate honor and respect for the person and his or her position. In France, you will be expected to use *Monsieur* or *Madame* with the person's last name. In Mexico and Spain, use *Señor, Señora,* or *Señorita* with an individual's last name. Never use first names of Japanese businesspeople; use *Mr.* or *Ms.* and the last name instead.

## BUSINESS PRACTICES

Describe seven areas in which business practices vary by culture.

The way business is conducted varies considerably from one culture to the next. The major differences lie in the way business deals are negotiated and decisions are made, although many other smaller matters are also important. If you are planning to do business with someone from a different culture, it would be wide to study the business practices that he or she has learned to follow. Your demonstrated respect for the other person will help you achieve your goals.

**BUSINESS CARDS.**   When conducting business in a foreign country, it is important to have your business cards printed on both sides—one side in English and the other in that country's language. Because titles are important to some cultures (notably the Japanese and the Germans), your business card should specify the most impressive title you are qualified to claim.

In England, business cards are seldom exchanged unless someone's name might be unfamiliar or difficult to pronounce. In France, however, business cards are given to all business associates and often contain prestigious academic degrees in addition to business titles. Business cards are perhaps most important in Japan and South Korea. A card should be presented as soon as you are introduced, and it should be presented with both hands (foreign language side up). It is also appropriate, but not required, to bow slightly as the card is presented. A card you receive from another should be looked at carefully, and you should nod to indicate you understand the information on the card. During a meeting, spread the cards out in front of you according to where people are seated. At the end, gather them up carefully.

**GIFT GIVING.**   For people who do business internationally, gift giving can be a problem. In some countries (e.g., Germany, Belgium, the United Kingdom), gifts are seldom given to business acquaintances. In others, however, gift giving is not only expected but also complicated.

*The exchange of business gifts is a complicated practice. Cultures vary in the type of gift to be given, to whom it is given, and when.*

In some cultures, the timing of the gift is of crucial importance. Gifts given at a first encounter might be considered an attempt to influence business decisions unfairly. In other cultures, gifts given immediately after deals are made are interpreted as payments and are, therefore, insulting.

What to give is as complicated as when to give it. Many of the gifts we commonly give to one another in the United States are inappropriate in other countries. Avoid giving a gift of fragrance in France; it is considered far too personal for business purposes. Clothing is an inappropriate gift because of its personal nature for most Middle and Far Eastern countries, but the French love American T-shirts. Because cows are sacred in Hindu countries like India, leather gifts must be avoided there.

Even flowers can be dangerous if not chosen with sensitivity to customs. In Japan, white flowers are used only for funerals, and chrysanthemums are off limits because they are used in the Imperial family's crest. People in Eastern Europe use red flowers for funerals. In China, flowers are used to express hopes of a successful business venture. However, in China take care not to give flowers or any other gift in multiples of four (8, 12, 16, etc.) because these numbers represent death. In France, red roses are considered an intimate gift and would not be appropriate for business, but white roses in an uneven number *would* be appropriate (even numbers are unlucky).

Relatively safe gifts for an American company to give are uniquely American items, such as handmade quilts and Native American pottery and rugs. Products made by the company may also be appropriate. Gifts with the company logo or insignia on them (pen sets, clocks, etc.) are often well received. However, in China, clocks are associated with death and, therefore, the end of relationships. Gifts of liquor are sometimes acceptable (especially Scotch in Japan), but remember that liquor is illegal in most Islamic countries.

In some Middle Eastern countries, much business is done at home, so your host would be pleased if you brought inexpensive gifts for his children. However, because of the position of women in these cultures, you should not bring a gift for the wife—in fact, you should not even ask how she is. If you are invited to a German home, you might take flowers (not roses) or other simple gifts wrapped in brightly colored paper and ribbon (but do not use white, black, or brown paper).

Because of the complexity of gift giving, it is imperative that you thoroughly research local customs before selecting a gift for a business associate. The gift itself, the way it must be presented, and when it is presented differ from one culture to another.

**RANK AND DECISION MAKING.**   Rank is considered far more important in some societies than it is in the United States. In some societies, people of higher rank are not questioned openly by those of lower rank. In India, for example, teachers are not questioned by their students even when controversial or erroneous statements are made. (Your professor would probably like this custom!) In such societies, decision makers are seldom questioned by their subordinates. In many Latin American countries, for example, the person in charge is expected to be dogmatic and is viewed as weak if he or she allows questioning.

In Saudi Arabia, most of the large businesses are owned by families, and the paternalistic head of the family is the head of the business. Most of the management posts within these firms are held by family members and friends, but it is typical for the major decision-making responsibility to remain at the top. Therefore, vice presidents of Saudi Arabian firms usually have far less decision-making authority than American vice presidents do.

In the United States, Canada, France, and many other countries a fundamental belief is the equality of all people. Thus Americans and others do not hesitate to undertake tasks normally assigned to subordinates. For example, if you need a photocopy and a clerical worker is not available to do it for you, you would probably do it yourself. In some countries, however, this would be considered a major error. In the view of people from these cultures, your importance is diminished when you do work considered beneath your status.

Americans are far more egalitarian than people in many other cultures, who may look askance at our willingness to perform any task, no matter how lowly, to get a job done.

Participatory management, in which employees at all levels become involved in decision making, is a business practice borrowed from the group-oriented Japanese culture.

In Japan, rank is respected, but the belief in harmony has led to a participatory management style in which all employees' opinions are sought. For example, the decision to change the design of a car is not mandated by upper-level executives; it is discussed and agreed on by committees made up of people from all levels of the organization. The post-it notes sold in Japan reflect this management style. The notes are long and thin so that each person in the long management chain can write on them. Participatory management helps ensure that any new venture begins with the firm commitment of all involved.

**NEGOTIATIONS.** Negotiating styles vary dramatically from one country to another. When working on business deals, negotiators must be sensitive to a myriad of rules of protocol and etiquette, as well as many other cultural variables that can cause misunderstandings. It is in the negotiating arena that those who understand and respect cultural differences can best be of value to an organization.

> Intercultural negotiations require individuals who are well attuned to cultural sensitivities and communication styles.

All cultures have unique ways of working out agreement. Debate, conflict, compromise, and winning and losing are viewed differently by different cultures. For example, the French are fond of debate. The Japanese don't want to haggle over price, but Mexicans expect to do so. Australians want to hear both sides of an issue, and they won't feel you are being honest with them if you do not readily present each side. The Spanish believe compromise is the best way to solve conflict, and Mexicans will seldom say "no" directly.

Many nationalities value the personal relationships of people doing business together more than Americans do. In the United States, it is not considered essential to develop long-term trust before doing business. When representatives of two companies come together, Americans typically begin talking about the business issues immediately, and only later get to know one another personally. At the conclusion of a business deal, it is not unusual for the participants to meet socially for dinner or other entertainment. However, this direct negotiating style is undesirable in more subtle cultures. For example, the Japanese will typically spend several days socializing and getting to know their counterparts before they enter into discussions. Like the Japanese, many cultures believe that if they can trust you as a person, they can trust you as a businessperson. Negotiations with people from these countries usually take much more time than when two Americans or two Canadians conduct business.

> A major difference in negotiating style is whether participants build social relationships before negotiations begin or after they are concluded.

The Japanese negotiating style is most directly affected by the concept of saving face, which means that neither party in any communication encounter should be embarrassed or shamed. North Americans should be aware that the saving face philosophy causes a reluctance to say "no." Because of the value they place on peace and harmony, the Japanese will not openly disagree with or contradict you. As a result, you will have to listen carefully for implied negatives. For example, the statement "I'll do everything I can to do as you have asked" may be the closest you'll hear to "no."

> Americans tend to be direct and impatient. Directness may offend people from some cultures, and impatience may give those from more patient cultures an advantage.

When dealing with the Japanese, Westerners have also had to learn to tolerate long periods of silence. Silence is not a negative response; it could mean indecision or lack of understanding. Therefore, after a short period of silence, you might calmly restate your major points, stressing the quality or the benefit of your product to consumers. The Japanese know most Americans are uncomfortable with silence, and they often use this against Americans when negotiating business deals. American executives have also learned, the hard way, the meaning of "yes" in Japan: When a Japanese person says "Yes," it often means, "Yes, I understand what you mean," not "Yes, I agree with you."

Other cultures are equally challenging for direct, impatient Americans. Negotiations in France and in South America typically proceed much slower than in the United States. The French like to debate, study the consequences, and compare alternatives. They do not like to be rushed, and respond negatively to high-pressure tactics. They tend to place more importance on superior performance, longer life, and quality of products and services rather than on price. Most decision making in France is done by the top two or three executives of a company, and they do not make changes after contracts are signed. The French do not like to mix their social and business lives; therefore, even when entertaining as a part of doing business, you should discuss business, not personal topics. A visit to a French home is rare.

The English will expect you to have detailed material describing your company. Deliberation and decision making are slower in the United Kingdom as well, so be prepared for lengthy negotiations. Another important difference in British and American business meetings is worth noting—at the end of a business meeting, the visiting executive should initiate the departure, not the host.

Italians expect set prices and good-faith negotiations. They typically do not ask for expert opinions because they value their own judgment more. The people with whom they do business are important to most Italians, and you will find they want to get to know you personally.

Negotiations with Saudi Arabian companies will usually begin with a middleman, commonly referred to as a "Ten-Percenter." A Ten-Percenter is a Saudi Arabian whose job is to arrange business deals between companies, and he expects to be paid for his services (not necessarily 10 percent). It is often not possible to arrange even simple meetings with Saudi Arabians without using these entrepreneurial Ten-Percenters. Expect to have several meetings beforehand with minor, nonessential personnel before getting to meet the final decision makers. Avoid any show of impatience during the process; it will not be tolerated. Once a meeting has been arranged in Saudi Arabia, it will proceed at an informal, unhurried pace. Expect your host and other participants to be late. Saudi Arabians are similar to the Japanese in their dislike of directness. In Saudi Arabia, it is considered rude to discuss business right away. During business discussions with Saudi Arabians, do not be alarmed or insulted when others interrupt the meeting and converse with or whisper to your host; they do not consider this rude. Negotiations in Saudi Arabia require patience—business decisions are not made quickly.

**AMBIGUITY.**   Tolerance for ambiguity, the degree of doubt or uncertainty you feel comfortable with, is also a cultural variable. Lack of tolerance for ambiguity is characteristic of ethnocentrics. Because they cannot stand unpredictable situations, ethnocentrics avoid communicating with people of other cultures. It is easier to predict the outcome of a communication encounter with someone who has the same background, expectations, values, and beliefs you have.

Americans vary in the amount of ambiguity they can tolerate. Many Americans are willing to risk much for uncertain gain, but others avoid all risks. There are other cultures, however, that have learned to accept and expect uncertainty as a way of life. The people of many Chinese subcultures, for example, participate regularly in games of chance, even to the point where gambling is a lifestyle. Generally, people who believe their lives are governed by luck and fate rather than their own initiative are more willing to tolerate ambiguity.

Ambiguity is also characteristic of the French; many a business executive has been frustrated by the tendency of the French to change plans at the last moment. Therefore, you should confirm appointments with French executives and government officials two or three days ahead of time.

Although many Americans are willing to risk a great deal for uncertain returns, most expect no ambiguity in written contracts. However, many Middle Eastern cultures prefer not to discuss the minute details of a business deal, specifying only the overall agreement—the number of items to be delivered at an approximate time for an approximate amount of money. (This preference is discussed in greater detail in the section of this chapter dealing with written communication.) The way contracts are handled is probably more indicative of a culture's true view of ambiguity than any other business practice.

**TIME HORIZON.** The tendency of a cultural group to put its energy into projects that provide immediate gain distinguishes one culture from another. United States businesses have been criticized for years by other nations for their short-term views. American firms' lack of long-term planning, probably caused by the need for management to satisfy stockholders by paying immediate dividends, frustrates Japanese executives who participate in joint ventures with Americans. For example, a common criticism of the American auto industry is its reluctance to retool its plants. American auto executives, perhaps fearing for their jobs, seem to opt instead for short-term strategies, such as new car models, that will enable them to pay the expected dividends. The unwillingness of stockholders to wait years to realize the benefits of retooling is indicative of an American tendency to expect immediate results.

Long-term planning is as difficult for the French as it is for Americans. Asian cultures vary in their ability to deal with waiting. The Japanese seem to be very good at waiting, but people from Hong Kong expect immediate results.

When you deal in an international business environment, you must be aware of your own ability to see the short and the long term, the expectations of the companies and stockholders you represent, and the expectations of those with whom you are doing business. This knowledge will help you show your counterpart how your solution meets his or her expectations—the you attitude on an international scale.

**BRIBES AND FACILITATING PAYMENTS.** In some countries, if you expect to do business you might be expected to pay a bribe. Just getting a shipment unloaded on a dock will require facilitating payments, in addition to the under-the-table payments necessary to obtain government approvals and licensing agreements. Bribes are common in Italy, Korea, Japan, Germany, the Middle East, Mexico, and many African countries. In many countries (e.g., Britain and Germany), foreign bribes are legitimate tax deductions.

Compared with some cultures, the American culture is extremely intolerant of bribes.

Other countries are far less tolerant of bribes. In Saudi Arabia, where it is illegal to accept or give bribes, the practice reportedly still goes on, despite a three-year jail sentence for conviction. Americans have similar attitudes. Revelations of questionable payments by American companies to foreign officials prompted the passage in the 1970s of the Foreign Corrupt Practices Act (FCPA). The FCPA prohibits bribes intended to secure government contracts. However, it does not outlaw facilitating payments made solely to expedite official actions. For example, it would not be illegal to pay an accountant to ensure more prompt payment of a bill that would have eventually been paid anyway. However, it would be illegal to pay a foreign official to intervene on your company's behalf during negotiations with a foreign firm. Many U.S. companies have adopted formal codes of ethics to help their employees make decisions concerning payments for conducting international business.

The laws of the United States are clear, but U.S. ethics in this matter look like foolish prudery in some parts of the world. The question of whether or not to pay bribes to get business done remains one of the most difficult ethical decisions faced by all businesspeople dealing in an international environment.

## WRITTEN COMMUNICATION

Written communication between people of different cultures presents a special problem. If the reader misunderstands or is confused by what you have written, you seldom have another chance to explain what you meant. Therefore, it is very important to double-check written materials to minimize cultural confusion.

Differences in format can be expected when conducting business with people from other countries. In Germany, for example, letters are usually addressed to businesses, not individuals. If a person's name is included in the address, the letter is usually considered personal and confidential. Decisions explained in a German letter with two signatures were made by those two people, and the two signatures are intended to stress this point.

Additionally, the organization of the message must sometimes be adapted to suit the reader's expectations. The direct strategy of American letters (see Chapter 7) is considered rude in cultures (e.g., Japan and Mexico) that believe in establishing a social climate before jumping into business. The French are also less direct than Americans, and their letters are more eloquent. They prefer subtlety and tact to frankness. They will often talk around the point they wish to make, thereby increasing the importance of reading between the lines. However, the direct, indirect, and persuasive strategies are used in France much as they are in the United States.

Many other cultures believe all letters, whether they impart good news or bad, should begin with polite language that has little to do with the topic of the letter. For example, a typical Japanese letter might begin with a statement such as "It is hoped this letter finds you healthy and happy in this wondrous season of new growth and life. Spring brings forth the promise of renewal for all those who believe in its power to revive." Even English letters often contain a degree of politeness that seems excessive to Americans, who usually prefer to get to the point in the first sentence.

German and Austrian correspondence tends to be direct, much like American correspondence. However, Germans tend to be more direct with negative news (see Chapter 8) than Americans are. The Japanese are often so subtle about bad news that someone from a more direct culture may not even understand the message. Many Hispanics may choose to avoid the bad news entirely, so it is important to communicate with them in person or by telephone and ask very specific questions.

Malaysians select the degree of directness according to whom they are writing, not according to the message itself. For example, those in power tend to write short letters with the important information at the end of the letter. However, when writing to someone with far greater power (e.g., a citizen writing to a government official), an individual would be expected to show respect by writing long, convoluted messages. Long paragraphs praising the recipient are expected in countries such as China, Japan, Vietnam, and

> Because documents are permanent records and cannot be augmented by nonverbal communication, letters, memos, and reports to people from other cultures should be written with great care.

> You can get valuable information about other cultures' expectations of written messages by searching company files for previous correspondence with people from that country, asking people who have lived or worked there, or researching the subject at the library.

Malaysia. However, letters in these countries are usually more polite. Orders are usually phrased so politely that, to an American, they seem to be only suggestions. For example, a message from a Malaysian employer to an employee roughly translated as "I must ask you to consider the importance of consulting everyone involved before changing shipping policies." An American would be more likely to get the same idea across in this way: "Do not make any further changes in shipping policies without consulting everyone involved."

To prevent miscommunication with people from other cultures, educate yourself about their expectations before writing. Often, a search of your company's files will turn up letters and reports written by people from the country with which you are doing business. These can guide you in preparing correspondence that allows your reader to focus on the message rather than on practices and words that might seem rude or odd. Libraries also have information about written business communication in other countries. Additionally, it might be wise to ask people of that culture what they expect, especially in terms of report content.

List seven principles for writing to businesspeople of other cultures.

When writing letters to people of other cultures, follow these principles:

- Write in English, unless you are fluent in the other language.
- Use short, simple, and active words to improve clarity.
- Use short, simple sentences.
- Use short paragraphs.
- Use a tone slightly more formal than that used for American correspondence (less use of *you* and *your*).
- Use block or modified block format.
- Use visual aids (tables, charts, graphs, photographs, etc.) frequently to improve understanding.

Two particular types of documents—financial statements and contracts—require special attention.

**FINANCIAL STATEMENTS.**   The relative importance of major financial statements differs from one country to another. In the United States, the income statement is considered to be more important than the balance sheet in assessing a company's strength. Because earnings per share is of major importance to stockholders, generating income with which to increase payments to shareholders is the major emphasis of most American firms. However, the balance sheet is generally perceived to be more important than the income statement in Asian, European, and Latin American countries. In these countries, the ownership of wealth (assets and claims against those assets) is considered to be the most important factor in assessing the strength of a company.

Where the business time horizon is short, as in the United States, income statements showing income and expenses over a specific time period are considered more revealing. Where the business time horizon is long, balance sheets are valued for their "snapshot" of a company's assets and liabilities.

There are other differences in financial statements. Differences in the terms used and the location of information on the page can usually be dealt with quickly by a good accountant. However, the procedures used to arrive at certain figures, such as valuation and depreciation, are seldom disclosed in financial statements from other countries and should be investigated thoroughly.

Attitudes toward the importance and authority of contracts vary from culture to culture.

**CONTRACTS.**   The French and Germans view written contracts much as Americans do. However, they pay attention only to what is written and signed; oral commitments are not considered contracts. Because American contract law was derived from English law, the British view both oral and written statements with the same importance as Americans do.

Many businesspeople in the Middle East were educated in the United States, and others have done business with the United States for so long that they have become Westernized. However, traditional Middle Easterners do not consider a signed contract a moral commitment, and they often do not understand why Americans get upset when a contract's terms are not met. To many Middle Easterners, a signed contract is not "I promise to . . . "; it is merely "I hope to be able to . . . " American firms that have successfully done business in this part of the world are those that have learned to be flexible.

◼ Describe cultural differences in nonverbal communication.

## NONVERBAL COMMUNICATION

Nonverbal communication can cause problems when you deal with people from other cultures. This section highlights a few of the differences in nonverbal communication you will encounter when doing business with people from other countries. If you anticipate such contact, you should investigate further the nuances of body language and other forms of nonverbal communication that can cause miscommunication.

Gestures are notorious for meaning different things, so carefully research them before doing business with someone from a different culture.

**BODY LANGUAGE.**   Many gestures communicate different things to people from other cultures. For example, Mexicans touch others more frequently than people in some cultures are comfortable with. The American "okay" gesture (thumb and forefinger used to form a circle) means "zero" in France, "money" in Japan, and is an obscene gesture in some parts of South America. In 1992, President Bush made a critical error in Australia by using the victory sign (the first two fingers raised in the shape of a "V") with the back side of his hand toward the audience, a major insult to viewers.

The French use fewer hand gestures than most Americans. Thumbs up means good, but pounding a fist into your open palm is considered rude. When eating, your hands, not your elbows, should be on top of the table. The French also consider the American practice of eating some foods with the hands to be crude. Even fruit is peeled with a knife and eaten with a fork.

It is impolite to point at Saudi Arabians or signal them with your hand. Because the left hand is considered unclean, one should also avoid using it for gesturing, eating, or handling items in the presence of most Middle Easterners. Avoid crossing your legs or pointing the soles of your shoes toward Saudi Arabians, because both actions are considered insults. Also, avoid putting your hands on your hips when with Saudis, as this represents a challenging attitude. Many Middle Easterners consider coughing and sneezing to be extremely rude.

The body language for "yes" cannot be taken for granted in a multicultural business environment. Americans usually interpret the nodding of the head to mean "yes." However, in Italy, raising the chin means "no," and in Thailand, a side-to-side head movement means "maybe." In Japan, a subtle movement of the right hand can mean "no." In Greece and Bulgaria, shaking the head means "yes," and nodding the head means "no."

Greetings are another form of nonverbal communication. It is quite common for businesspeople in Mexico to hug one another, and women will exchange kisses. A handshake usually accompanies these affectionate

Greeting customs dictate the use of hugs and kisses, handshakes, and/or bows.

greetings. Handshakes are also important in France, but don't pump the other person's hand. As a visitor, you should not extend your hand first. Kissing on the cheek, even among men, is a common practice in much of Europe. In Eastern Europe, hand shaking is even more firm than in the United States, and might last for seven or eight pumps of the hand. People from Eastern Europe also tend to shake hands every time they see one another, and kissing both cheeks is a common greeting among men and women. Handshaking is also common in Saudi Arabia. In Japan, the bow is used for greetings and farewells, for expressing appreciation, when apologizing, and when asking a favor. The lower the bow, the stronger the show of respect. Among Japanese businesspeople who deal with Westerners, it is common to see a handshake combined with a bow.

Some cultures prefer direct eye contact, but others consider it disrespectful.

Eye contact is another important area of cultural differences. In the United States, most people are taught to maintain eye contact and interpret meanings by watching others' eyes. People who look away from us are considered to be either lying, untrustworthy, or shy and weak. However, eye contact in Asian countries, some Latin American countries, some African-American subcultures in the United States, and among the Navajo Indians of the American Southwest is avoided or is not as strong as in most Western cultures. In addition, American women often avert their eyes, especially when meeting men. Many of these cultures and subcultures consider it a sign of respect to avert the eyes when dealing with others. In some cases, aversion of eyes might be a subconscious way of avoiding contact and a possible misinterpretation of forwardness. In contrast, some Middle Easterners maintain even longer eye contact than Americans.

The importance a culture places on eye contact sometimes reveals itself in preferred seating arrangements during negotiations. The Japanese and the Chinese, for example, like to sit side by side when they are negotiating, whereas Americans like to sit opposite their counterparts. Middle Easterners often sit close enough to observe the changes in the other person's irises. The size of the iris (the black part of the eyes) increases when we are interested or excited, just as it increases when we enter a darkened room. Staring into someone's irises, however, makes most non-Middle Easterners extremely nervous.

When you consider the fact that most people do not even understand the subtleties of their own body language, you can understand how easy it is to misinterpret and ignore the body language clues of people from other cultures. However, when you go into an encounter with increased knowledge of all communication factors, your chances of achieving success are greatly increased.

Americans tend to be unrestrained in their use of space compared with people from more densely populated countries, and they do not like their personal space to be infringed on.

**SPACE.** The amount of space we require and how we use that space distinguishes us culturally. Generally speaking, those who come from countries that are very crowded require less space than those who come from less densely populated countries. For example, Americans, used to wide-open spaces, use expansive gestures and tend to move around a great deal. Physical distance is as important to the French as it is to Americans, although they tend to use fewer expansive gestures. In contrast, the Japanese use few hand and arm gestures when they are speaking, and they tend to stand in one place when speaking.

Requiring more space around them, Americans tend to be uncomfortable when speaking to Middle Easterners and some Asians. People from these cultures tend to stand and sit closer when speaking. Try to avoid backing away from them so you don't seem unfriendly and untrustworthy.

**Time-obsessed Americans tend to be more punctual than people from many other countries.**

**TIME.**    Cultures vary widely in their views toward the importance of time. It has been said that Americans are obsessed with time, and, in light of the casualness with which some cultures view deadlines and punctuality, there is some truth to that statement. Most Americans and English stress punctuality; business meetings usually begin on time, and it is considered rude to arrive late to an appointment. The French will expect you to be on time for appointments, but you should be prepared to wait to be received; the appointment will probably not begin on time. The French believe they are being more polite by clearing up any other business beforehand to prevent interruptions during your meeting. In Arab countries, as well as in Mexico and other Latin and South American countries, you can expect to start any business meeting 30 minutes to an hour late, because most of the participants will not show up on time. However, you should arrive for appointments on time to avoid offending others who are aware of the American expectation of punctuality.

**Standard business attire is appropriate almost everywhere in the world.**

**ATTIRE.**    With most cultures in the world, conservative business attire—suit and tie for men and skirted suit for women—is always appropriate. Resist the temptation to wear native costumes for business meetings. In some Middle Eastern countries, however, women are expected to cover their arms, legs, and faces. Observing these preferences while in the other person's country will show your respect and thereby improve your chances of completing your business successfully.

## RELIGIOUS CUSTOMS

**Religion often dictates a country's business schedules, attitudes toward work and success, and eating habits.**

Religious customs also often enter into business negotiations, more so in some countries than in others. Religion is responsible for many of the underlying attitudes and beliefs that guide our daily work lives. In addition, some of religion's influence is readily apparent. For example, most offices in the United States are closed on Saturday and Sunday (because, for most Americans, Sunday is a religious day of rest); however, in Islamic countries, Friday is the day of worship, and offices are closed on Thursday and Friday.

All countries have religious holidays that must be considered when scheduling appointments. In Canada and the United States, businesses usually close on Christmas and Easter, even though a large part of the population is not Christian. Canadians have Boxing Day. In Islamic countries, Ramadan, a religious observance, takes place over a one-month period (the dates change yearly), during which working hours are shortened considerably. During Ramadan, all Muslims abstain from food, drink, and smoking during daylight hours, and visitors are required by law to observe the fast of Ramadan while in public.

The way a culture views work is also a result of religion. In the United States and Europe, what is referred to as the "Protestant work ethic" has made hard work and thrift admirable. Most Asian countries that follow the teachings of Confucius, such as China, have a similar work ethic, as does Japan, where it is referred to as the "Shinto work ethic." Confucianism also emphasizes politeness, courtesy, and deference to the elderly.

The Hindu religion, practiced by more than 80 percent of India's population, has resulted in a caste system that directly affects the social division of labor. A person's caste is inherited, and it determines a person's job. Movement to a higher caste can take place only in another life. Although the government of India has outlawed discrimination based on a person's caste, little change has taken place in the business environment. Therefore, an American company must deal with the problem of caste when assigning individuals to supervise other Hindus.

Hindu and Buddhist religions stress that if their followers have no desires, they will not suffer in this life. The result is little need for achievement or material possessions. Because personal recognition and increased salaries are the two primary motivators used by American managers, it is easy to see how management techniques would have to change to motivate followers of Hindu and Buddhist religions.

In Hong Kong, centuries of Chinese myth and mystery infuse the business lives of its citizens. Buildings are planned with a *fung shui* man, who understands the balance between manufactured objects and nature. He sees that doors and windows are positioned to admit good spirits and prevent bad ones from entering. Real estate agents report the practice is still followed by many Chinese living in other countries.

Religion often determines what followers can and cannot eat and drink. Many Jewish people do not eat pork, and Orthodox Jews follow very specific rules of food preparation and serving. Because Hindus consider cows sacred, beef should not be served or eaten in their presence. In Islamic countries, alcohol is forbidden by religious law, and drinking is punishable. Therefore, it would not be appropriate for an American to offer alcohol to a Saudi Arabian visitor unless he or she asks for it. Americans traveling to Islamic countries should be careful not to pack alcohol in their luggage.

By understanding the basic tenets of the world's major religions, you will be able to determine what individuals who practice these religions are likely to value and how they might act in specific situations. Knowledge of the values and beliefs of others is as crucial to success in business negotiations as it is in the day-to-day operations of any business.

## TIPS FOR EFFECTIVE INTERCULTURAL COMMUNICATION

List nine ways you can improve your ability to communicate with people of other cultures and subcultures.

The following pointers will help you deal with anyone from a different culture or subculture. They will help you conduct business more effectively by improving your ability to communicate and by acknowledging the dignity and value of all individuals and their beliefs.

You can improve your ability to deal with people from diverse cultures by following these nine suggestions.

- *Recognize your own biases.* Acknowledging your biases and prejudices helps you deal with them. Admitting you have weaknesses is the first step toward correcting them.
- *Take responsibility for change.* Once you have acknowledged your biases, take active steps to change them. Because our biases and prejudices are deeply ingrained, such change will not come easily; however, with persistence you can open your mind.
- *Take advantage of your natural curiosity.* Human beings have an innate desire to learn. Most people will not be insulted if you ask them questions about their culture or subculture as long as they sense you are asking out of a

natural desire to learn and not as a prelude to criticism. In addition, you can research the cultures with whom you plan to do business by studying the many recent publications on multicultural differences in business. Ask people who have been to other countries. Go to embassies and consulates. Seek the help of groups such as the Intercultural Communications Network, 1860 19th Street NW, Washington, DC 20016.

- *Show respect.* You will be respected by others when you show respect for them and their culture. Learn all you can about other cultures, knowing that, no matter how silly some practices, values, and beliefs may seem to you, it is not your place to pass judgment. To people who practice them, these same practices, values, and beliefs are logical and accepted without question.
- *Look for common ground.* Instead of concentrating only on the differences between you and your business acquaintances from other cultures, try concentrating on areas of commonality. You might be surprised at how much like you they are.
- *Maintain formality.* In most international business environments, formality is preferred. Use titles and names correctly, practice etiquette appropriately, act with dignity, and convey an attitude of courtesy and respect.
- *Tolerate the cultural mistakes of others.* As a student of intercultural communication, you have become more sensitive to its importance than most people will be. When others make mistakes due to lack of cultural sensitivity, ignore their errors. If you can do so without causing embarrassment, tactfully explain how your culture views the actions or words. If you maintain a tactful and pleasant tone, they will appreciate your efforts and laugh with you.
- *Be patient.* Don't expect too much too fast—of yourself or of other people. The change from thinking about cultural sensitivity to actually being sensitive takes time.
- *Be persistent.* Don't give up—on yourself or your diverse counterparts. Changing basic values, beliefs, and practices normally requires continuing effort. Learning to accept the values, beliefs, and practices of other cultures without frustration also takes time. As you know, however, persistence often pays off in business dealings. If you don't succeed in your first efforts to do business in an international or diverse environment, analyze thoroughly all the possible reasons for the failure and then try again. Learn from your mistakes, and move on.

Today, Americans are more likely than ever to encounter people from other cultures—whether in a foreign country or in this country.

U.S. firms are major participants in international business. This country is now the second largest exporter of goods and services and the world's largest importer. However, many other countries are making rapid strides in the international marketplace. Maintaining U.S. competitiveness will require everyone in business to become more knowledgeable about other cultures. In addition, because of the favorable business climate in the United States, thousands of U.S. companies are now foreign owned. If you are not already doing so, you will soon find yourself working with people from another country. Finally, with the influx of immigrants from all over the world into the United States, and the notably diverse nature of the American workforce, you will be encountering many people from other cultures and subcultures. Multicultural sensitivity will enable you to deal effectively with all of them.

## DISCUSSION QUESTIONS

◼ Define *culture, subculture,* and *ethnocentrism,* and identify examples of each.

1. Define *culture, subculture,* and *ethnocentrism,* and list four examples of each (other than those specified in the chapter).

◼ Explain why businesspeople need to understand cultural differences.

2. Describe how an appreciation for cultural diversity can benefit employees, companies, and the U.S. economy.

◼ Name the eight aspects of cultural differences that affect business communication.

3. Briefly describe the impact of each of the eight areas of cultural differences that affect business communication.

◼ Name the eight aspects of cultural differences that affect business communication.
◼ Describe seven areas in which business practices vary by culture.
◼ List seven principles for writing to businesspeople of other cultures.

4. Describe how a culture's attitude toward directness affects its written communication, its conversational style, and its business practices.

◼ Describe differences in the ways two American subcultures—men and women—communicate.

5. Describe the differences in the ways men and women communicate.

◼ Describe cultural differences in nonverbal communication.

6. Provide three examples of how people from other cultures use gestures different from those of Americans.

◼ Describe cultural differences in nonverbal communication.

7. Provide three examples of other cultures' customs in greeting people.

◼ Describe cultural differences in nonverbal communication.

8. Why is eye contact culturally sensitive?

◼ List nine ways you can improve your ability to communicate with people of other cultures and subcultures.

9. List the nine tips for effective intercultural communication.

## APPLICATION EXERCISES

◼ Define *culture, subculture,* and *ethnocentrism,* and identify examples of each.

1. Divide a piece of paper into three vertical columns. On the left side of the page, write down at least four prejudices or beliefs you have concerning each of the following cultures and subcultures: men, women, Japanese, European-Americans, African-Americans, Hispanic-Americans, Asian-Americans, white (non-Hispanic) Americans, Western Europeans (French, English, etc.), and

Mexicans. In the middle column, write down how you acquired each prejudice or belief. In the last column, indicate whether this is a generalization
about the culture or subculture you could defend in class.

For example, this might be the entry about the subculture referred to as
*Texans*:

| | | |
|---|---|---|
| They're all rich. | Belief comes from a popu-lar television show. | No, I could not defend this misperception. |

🔳 Define *culture*, *subculture*, and *ethnocentrism*, and identify examples of each.
🔳 Explain why businesspeople need to understand cultural differences.

2.  Over the next several days, list five examples of ethnocentric statements
    you overhear. If you are currently working, listen for examples on the job.
    In a memo report to your professor, list the statements and describe how
    they reinforce or change your opinions of the persons uttering them.

🔳 Explain why businesspeople need to understand cultural differences.
🔳 Name the eight aspects of cultural differences that affect business
communication.
🔳 Describe seven areas in which business practices vary by culture.

3.  Identify two specific subcultures within your own city or region. Assume
    you work for a business that manufactures and sells wholesale clothing and
    food. Consider the differences between these subcultures that might influ-
    ence the way these products are sold. How would the advertising and the
    products have to be changed to appeal to each subculture? Would any
    changes in negotiating style be required to do business with retailers from
    each subculture? Because your employees also represent these subcultures,
    what changes will you have to make in your business practices to commu-
    nicate effectively with them and motivate them? Answer these questions in
    short report form. Include any other information that would help a man-
    ager understand the subcultures you have identified.

🔳 Explain why businesspeople need to understand cultural differences.
🔳 Describe seven areas in which business practices vary by culture.
🔳 List nine ways you can improve your ability to communicate with people of
other cultures and subcultures.

4.  Select a specific country you might like to do business with someday. Pay a
    visit to or write a letter to its consulate or embassy, asking for information
    concerning business practices, customs, and etiquette. Give a copy of the
    response to your professor; or, if you were able to visit in person, write a
    letter to your professor describing the visit.

🔳 Name the eight aspects of cultural differences that affect business
communication.
🔳 Describe differences in the ways two American subcultures—men and
women—communicate.

5.  Over the next several days, listen for examples of tag questions and quali-
    fiers. List at least 10 of each and, for each example, specify whether a
    male or a female uttered the statement. If you are currently working,
    specify the job title of the person uttering each statement. Submit the list

to your instructor, along with a brief memo on how the use of qualifiers and tag questions compared to the information contained in this chapter.

🔻 Name the eight aspects of cultural differences that affect business communication.

🔻 Describe seven areas in which business practices vary by culture.

🔻 List nine ways you can improve your ability to communicate with people of other cultures and subcultures.

6. Prepare a group presentation on cultural differences for the class, choosing people from one of these cultures:

Eastern Europe.

Western Europe (England, France).

Northern Europe (Finland, Sweden, Norway).

Southern Europe (Spain, Italy, Greece).

South America.

Mexico and Central America.

Northern Africa.

Southern Africa.

Middle East.

China and Hong Kong.

Japan.

Southeast Asia (Malaysia, Cambodia, Thailand, Vietnam).

Countries from the former Soviet Union.

Clear your choice with your professor, who will also specify the number of students in each group, the date of your presentation, and its length. If any group member is absent on the day of the presentation, other members of the group will be expected to give that person's part of the presentation.

*a.* Research specific information you would need to know to avoid cultural miscommunication when conducting business in this area of the world, organizing your search around the eight areas of cultural differences covered in this chapter. Use examples to clarify, and contrast your chosen culture with standard U.S. business culture.

*b.* Prepare at least one visual aid for use in the group's presentation that will clarify the topic.

*c.* Prepare a detailed group outline and a group bibliography. Meet briefly with your professor to make sure your group's approach will meet the requirements of this assignment. Submit a final version of the outline and bibliography before you actually give the presentation.

*d.* Following the presentation, evaluate the performance of each group member (including yourself). Use one sheet of paper for each group member and answer the following questions:

Did this group member participate in all planning and research sessions of the group?

Did this group member do everything he or she was supposed to do, as established by the group?

Aside from differences in personalities, would you be willing to work with this person again on another group project? (Obviously, you do not have to answer this question when you evaluate yourself!)

Give these confidential evaluations directly to your instructor on the day following your group presentation; they are not to be seen by others.

■ Name the eight aspects of cultural differences that affect business communication.

■ List nine ways you can improve your ability to communicate with people of other cultures and subcultures.

7. Find an article on the use of American advertising slogans and product names in other countries. In a short report to your instructor, explain whether the slogans and names translated well in the other country, and what the Americans did to increase their chances of success. Also explain how successful the advertising campaign was overall.

■ Name the eight aspects of cultural differences that affect business communication.

■ List nine ways you can improve your ability to communicate with people of other cultures and subcultures.

8. Interview someone who has done business in another country or who has worked for a foreign-owned company in the United States. Using the list of eight areas of cultural differences presented in this chapter as a guide, find out what someone in a similar situation would need to know to communicate effectively with people from that culture. How did this individual prepare for his or her assignment? What suggestions does he or she have to help students prepare for a similar assignment? Present this information, with specific examples, in a short report to your professor.

# CHAPTER 3

# COMMUNICATING NONVERBALLY

## OBJECTIVES

When you finish studying this chapter, you should be able to:

- Describe how nonverbal communication relates to verbal communication.
- Identify gender differences in nonverbal communication.
- Identify the four channels used to communicate meaning through body language.
- Describe how proxemics, objects, and time communicate nonverbally.
- Explain the role of metacommunication in business.
- Explain the importance of listening effectively in business.
- Identify the barriers to effective listening.
- Apply six active listening techniques in daily life.
- Apply three interactive listening techniques in daily life.

## WHAT WOULD YOU DO IF...?

**CAN'T YOU HEAR?**    Kristine Pearce, believing that her commissioned sales staff of seven had poor nonverbal and listening skills, arranged an exercise that she felt would both demonstrate the problems and motivate the salespeople to improve their skills. First she videotaped one of the monthly sales meetings. Then, at the next meeting, she showed the tape.

At the beginning of the meeting, Kristine handed out this list of nine types of poor nonverbal communicators, based on a list she found in the book *Effective Management Communications*, by Robert W. Rasberry and Laura F. Lemoine:

- *Faker.* Appears to listen intently, but in reality the person's thoughts are elsewhere.

- *Continual talker.* Always has something to say on everything; interrupts.

- *Rapid-writing note taker.* So intent on taking detailed notes that he or she misses important points.

- *Critic.* Finds fault with everything; personal biases arouse antagonistic feelings.

- *I'm-in-a-hurry communicator*. Too busy to stop and listen; tries to continue other work instead of listening and maintaining eye contact.

- *Hands-on-the-doorknob communicator*. Gives clear signals that he or she thinks the meeting should be over.

- *Make-sure-it-is-correct communicator*. Thrives on pointing out errors others make; seems to delight in making others look bad.

- *Finish-the-sentence-for-you communicator*. Impatient, interrupts when speakers pause momentarily; jumps to conclusions about what the speaker is going to say next.

- *I've-done-one-better communicator*. Responds to others by attempting to top everything, be it stories about difficult clients and product malfunctions or good results and product superiority.

Kristine told her employees to write down instances of these habits while they watched the videotaped sales meeting. At the end, she asked each salesperson to present his or her notes to the group.

Kristine had intended to end the exercise with an announcement about a series of voluntary seminars on listening that would begin the following week. Of course, she had hoped that all of them would be so motivated by seeing the kinds of problems they had that they would choose to attend the seminars. However, the meeting did not turn out the way Kristine hoped it would. Several of her employees were obviously hurt by their co-workers' criticism, and several reacted angrily to the other's characterizations. One person even stormed out of the meeting before it was concluded.

As you read the following chapter, consider two basic issues. First, was this exercise a good idea? What would you have done to handle the problem? Second, is this a complete list of the ways nonverbal communication can impede communication? What would you add to the list?

## NONVERBAL COMMUNICATION SKILLS

■ Describe how nonverbal communication relates to verbal communication.

**Nonverbal communication may reinforce, substitute for, or contradict verbal communication.**

As a human being, you communicate with far more than words; you use your whole body to express yourself, and you use your five senses to interpret meaning. Other people learn about you from your posture, your clothing and grooming, your facial expressions, your eye contact, your gestures, and many other things that have nothing to do with words. Between 60 and 90 percent of the meaning in two-person conversations comes not from what is said, but from the way it is said and the setting in which it is said. Those nonverbal elements usually support and reinforce the words, but they may also substitute for or contradict the words.

Communication experts have noted that we cannot avoid communicating. No matter how silent we are, communication still goes on. You can, therefore, think of nonverbal communication as a subconscious language, a mental activity just below the threshold of consciousness. We are usually not even aware of the signals we are transmitting or receiving.

A thorough understanding of nonverbal communication is very useful, because it enables you to interpret the behavior of those with whom you do business. You will be able to look beyond the written or spoken word to understand the true feelings of your clients, your co-workers, and your employers. For example, imagine that you are a car salesperson and a potential customer says, "I really can't afford this car." If the customer says it while smiling and staring at the car, signaling a real interest in buying it despite the cost, you would probably continue trying to convince the customer that the car meets his or her needs.

Identify gender differences in nonverbal communication.

> Nonverbal communication styles vary from culture to culture and between men and women.

Sensitivity to nonverbal behavior must also include an appreciation of cultural differences. In Chapter 2 you learned about the differences in nonverbal communication you will encounter as a member of a diverse society or as a business traveler in a global marketplace. You should also understand gender-based differences. In general, women are more accurate than men at reading nonverbal cues. Some have attributed this phenomenon to the lower status of women in primitive society. In other words, prehistoric women had to read the nonverbal cues of the more powerful and dangerous men as a survival technique. In today's business world, however, women in authority adopt dominant communication styles as needed. At the same time, male managers are learning to respond more sensitively to nonverbal cues to deal with an increasingly diverse workforce. More gender differences are covered throughout this chapter.

> The elements of nonverbal communication are body language; the use of space, objects, and time; and metacommunication.

Nonverbal communication is a combination of body language; the use of space, objects, and time; and the meaning behind words. Those five elements are discussed in the following sections. If you suspect your nonverbal behavior is detracting from your ability to achieve your goals, target two or three changes you would most like to make in these areas. Because every nonverbal action makes an imprint on the brain, any physical action that is practiced repeatedly should eventually become automatic. Once you have incorporated those changes into your communication style, you can turn your attention to a few others. Perhaps this is a lesson that Kristine Pearce, in the chapter-opening vignette, should incorporate into her sales training program.

## BODY LANGUAGE

Identify the four channels used to communicate meaning through body language.

**Channels** are the means by which we express meaning. The four body language channels are arms and hands; face and eyes; legs; and body angle and position. Some body movements have culturally specific meanings; others are used by humans everywhere. Some are even common throughout the animal kingdom. For example, one universal action used to express submission and shame is lowering the head and eyes. Have you ever noticed that dogs will lower their heads and avoid eye contact when they have been scolded by their masters? Test your understanding of human body language by matching the sketches in Exhibit 3.1 with the labels that are provided at the bottom of the exhibit.

> A specific instance of body language can be interpreted only in context: how it relates to other acts being performed at the same time and how the individual typically acts.

You should be careful in labeling nonverbal behavior, however. A little knowledge can be dangerous. The body language of domestic animals is useful to illustrate this point. Most people believe that a dog wagging its tail is a friendly dog. However, a dog that doesn't know you may be wagging its tail as a sign of indecision—it has not yet decided whether to bite you or lick you. Although you can rely on most people not to bite or lick when first meeting

EXHIBIT
3.1

**Reading Nonverbal Communication Clues**

See how good you are at reading nonverbal actions by matching the actions in the sketches below with the most appropriate descriptions listed below. Compare your answers with the correct answers in the fine print at the bottom.

**Labels: Sincerity • Dejection • Apprehension • Worried or closed mind • Frustration • Acceptance • Honesty • Discomfort • Critical evaluation • Defensive position • Indecisiveness • Gratitude**

Answers: 1. Evaluation (gaining time) 2. Dejection 3. Worried or closed mind, Defensive position, Disagreement 4. Dominance, Confidence 5. Confidence 6. Honesty, Sincerity 7. Frustration 8. Critical evaluation 9. Boredom 10. Openness, Honesty, Sincerity 11. Defensive position, Acceptance 12. Confidence 13. Worried or closed mind, Critical evaluation, Disagreement 14. Enthusiastic readiness.

you, people's actions are often as unpredictable as dogs'. Your analysis of the true meaning of people's actions is most accurate when you know them well. What you should look for are differences between how they usually act and how they are acting at the time.

The four channels of body language are the arms and hands, the face and eyes, the legs, and body angle and position.

**Kinesics,** another word for body language, is the systematic study of the relationship between body motions and communication. It is concerned with four channels of meaning—arms and hands, face and eyes, legs, and body angle and position—as well as the patterns of communication that incorporate all four channels.

**EXHIBIT 3.2** **Common Hand Signals**

Although many gestures are universal among human beings, many others vary with culture.

**ARMS AND HANDS.** Usually, emphatic arm movement indicates that a person feels strongly about the point he or she is making. People also tend to use more arm movements when they are expressing an opinion rather than stating a fact, and when they are dealing with the opposite sex. However, gender makes a difference: Males use more dominant gestures—such as closed fists, pointing, and sweeping gestures—than women do, which seem to signal aggressiveness and create an overall image of decisiveness.

Exhibit 3.2 shows some of the hand signals commonly used by human beings. Here are some others, along with typical interpretations:

- *Nervousness.* Rubbing the back of the neck or fidgeting with the hair.
- *Dishonesty.* Passing the hand across the mouth or rubbing the chin while speaking (almost a subconscious desire to "push" the lie back in).

- *Skepticism, defensiveness.* Crossing the arms in front of the body (a subconscious desire to shut out an unwanted message).
- *"Okay"* or *"Good job."* Raising the thumb ("thumbs up" sign).
- *"Great."* Making a circle by touching the thumb and forefinger.
- *"Come here."* Wiggling the fingers with the palm up.

Please note that these last three gestures, although common in our culture, are inappropriate in certain countries where they have offensive meanings. Chapter 2 discussed nonverbal signs you should avoid when doing business internationally.

Students know how to use arm movements to both attract and avoid attention. Students who really do not want the teacher to call on them know how to raise their hand tentatively in a way that almost screams, "Don't call on me because I'm not really sure!" Others know how to raise their hands so it appears they have been waiting forever to be called on.

**One of the most important gestures in the business world is the handshake.**

The handshake is one of the first nonverbal messages we use to judge those whom we meet. The handshake originated during a time when it was meant to signal "I come in friendship; I carry no weapon." It means much the same thing in today's business world. One indicator that someone might be getting ready to lie to you is a weak handshake, which sometimes results from the desire to avoid touching someone with whom we are going to be dishonest. Another interpretation of a limp handshake is arrogance the handshaker is trying to conceal. If you want to convey confidence, sincerity, and trustworthiness, you should develop a firm, no-nonsense handshake and deliver it while smiling and maintaining eye contact. Avoid the knuckle-crunching, power-displaying handshakes of the insecure bully. In days past, etiquette dictated who should present his or her hand first. However, today the only three rules to follow are

- When you meet someone, extend your hand.
- When someone extends his or her hand to you, shake it.
- When you leave a social or professional meeting, be prepared to shake hands again.

Hands can also reveal whether someone is married or not. In interactions between males and females in business situations, harmless flirting sometimes occurs. To indicate that no sexual advance is intended and to keep things on a business level, married people often subconsciously touch the ring fingers of their left hands. Nervousness also causes the same reaction in married people who are trying to pretend they are single (a useful bit of knowledge for your next dating experience).

**Touching behavior is culturally determined; in our culture, it can indicate either superiority or concern.**

The way people touch each other can also communicate a great deal. People in some cultures touch each other more than in other cultures, so you should become familiar with a culture's attitude toward touching when you do business internationally. Even in the United States, subcultures vary in the amount of touching they will allow. Typically, however, people in positions of power touch others more often than they are touched themselves. Because many feel that touching others is condescending and inappropriate, it should normally be avoided. However, there are times when a touch or the lack of it can be used effectively. For example, when you are criticizing a worker, you might touch the person on the arm or shoulder to let him or her know there are no hard feelings. Such a touch lets the person know you still care. In contrast, withholding a touch when praising a worker might deliver this message instead: "Don't get too excited about this; you still have some things to work on."

**FACE AND EYES.**    The face and eyes are capable of sending many messages. For example, tautness of the jawline and neck and narrowing of the eyes usually indicate anger. Narrowing of the eyes alone usually means the listener is suspicious of what is being said. Wrinkling of the forehead can mean tension, concern, or questioning. Our faces also reveal when we are happy, apprehensive, or bored.

The most important type of facial communication is eye contact, which indicates an interest in communicating.

Eye contact is the most important element of facial communication, and it is one of the hardest to learn to control. In most Western cultures, it is considered desirable to make eye contact with the other person at least half the time spent communicating face to face, so as to convey self-confidence and cooperation. Good eye contact is assumed to indicate a high level of commitment to sustaining a conversation. However, too much eye contact can project an air of superiority or intimidation and is considered rude. Notice how you tend to glare into the eyes of others when you are angry at them. We are normally comfortable with long periods of eye contact only when we are intimate with the other person.

When they are listening to women, their colleagues, or their subordinates, most men generally maintain less eye contact than women do—which sometimes makes men seem cold and disinterested. Men, however, are better than women at maintaining eye contact when they are listening to their superiors. Many women have found it hard to rid themselves of this submissive behavior, which leads others to believe they are uncertain and perhaps even flirtatious. Most women avert their gaze after a fleeting instance of mutual eye contact with most men—either those they don't know or those with whom they deal on a professional basis.

Head motions also communicate nonverbally. Shaking the head from side to side indicates "No," and nodding is used in Canada and the United States to indicate "Yes." (It is not this way all over the world, however.) Nodding to speakers indicates that you are listening, and it encourages them to either go on speaking or continue with a line of reasoning. Stiffening the neck and drawing the head back while cocking it to one side, usually with the eyebrows raised, can show doubt or derision. When you see people do this, you know instantly they don't agree with you or they doubt your statement's veracity.

Another indicator of true feelings is skin color. If someone's skin suddenly reddens, it usually means the person is embarrassed or angry. However, people with high blood pressure, those who are sensitive to temperature change, and those who have food and drink allergies sometimes turn red for other reasons.

A smile eases interpersonal relations but can easily be faked.

Smiles are revealing—but not as revealing for adults as for children. When we were children, a smile meant happiness and a frown meant sadness. However, as they grow older many people learn to mask their true feelings with smiles. Do you think beauty queens, politicians, and used-car salespeople are really as happy, friendly, and trustworthy as their smiles make them appear to be? Although adults' smiles can signal happiness, they may also indicate nervousness or an excessive need for affiliation or approval. Thus, the fact that women smile more often than men may have contributed to the perception of weakness in women. It is useful to remember, however, that a smile is a good way to put another person at ease.

**EXHIBIT 3.3**    **Common Leg and Arm Signals**

**Negative signals:** Man's crossed legs and arms; lack of eye contact; frown.
Woman's legs crossed away from man; arms clasped; frown.

**Positive signals:** Man's open arms and legs; eye contact; pleasant expression.
Woman's legs crossed toward man; open arms; pleasant expression.

You can sometimes tell if someone is listening to you by watching the position of his or her legs.

**LEGS.**    You can watch the position of someone's legs to determine if they are open and receptive to what is being said or whether they have closed their minds. Generally speaking, the more open the legs are, the more receptive to the ideas of the speaker the listener is. As Exhibit 3.3 shows, if the foot of the top leg is pointed in the direction of the other person, communication is probably open; legs that are crossed away from someone serve to block the other person and what he or she has to say. However, because people often cross their legs for comfort or out of habit, crossed legs do not always mean someone is shutting you out.

The leg positioning done by men and women is not the same. Women tend to cross their legs above the knees more than men do (see Exhibit 3.3). When sitting, males usually put both feet on the floor with their knees apart; however, when they deal with women, men tend to cross one ankle over the other knee. This gesture, when used primarily with the opposite sex, appears to be a barrier to communication.

Among people who are not good at covering up their emotions, fidgety, bouncy leg actions can indicate boredom, nervousness, and uncertainty. If a customer kicks his or her legs as you are attempting to sell products, you will have to look at other nonverbal and verbal cues the person is issuing to determine how to interpret the meaning of his or her leg motions. Fidgety legs might also be an indication of lying behavior; however, good liars can actually calm their leg movements when lying.

The way we walk also gives information to others about who we really are. For example, a hard walker is usually a determined person, while a fast walker is usually impatient and aggressive. A jaunty walker is probably a happy-go-lucky person without a care in the world. Many subcultures have developed their own way of walking; however, most of these trends are not practiced in the business world.

Body position can indicate interest, sincerity, dominance, and many other important attitudes.

**BODY ANGLE AND POSITION.** How someone's body is angled or positioned in relation to others reveals his or her actual or perceived relationship to the group. Here are some tips for using body angle and position to your advantage:

- *Dealing with your superiors in business.* Let them know your willingness to cooperate by leaning forward in your seat or by turning toward them when you are standing. Sitting far back in your chair with open arms and legs also indicates your cooperation and honesty.
- *Encouraging participation at a meeting.* Managers who want to foster increased dialogue among their subordinates will often sit down with the group to signal that no one in the group has any more authority to speak than does anyone else—everyone is equal. This technique is often used to encourage groups of employees to come up with their own unique solutions to problems faced by companies, rather than having them wait to be told what to do by the superior who is conducting the meeting.
- *Bringing a meeting to a close.* Start doing what you want the other person to do. First, tidy up the desk or table. Then move toward the edge of your seat and lean forward; this acts as a gentle body "push." Stand up while you are still talking and walk to the door. Usually the other person will imitate you, and no hard feelings will result.
- *Making a sale or negotiating a contract.* Copy the other person's body angle and movements. If you can do this without being obvious, the other person will be more comfortable with you. Do not loom over the person to avoid giving the impression you are trying to dominate. If possible, sit lower than the other person. These techniques also work well for counseling employees and colleagues.

In general, those who stand higher are perceived as being superior to or more powerful than those below them.

One important element of this particular nonverbal communication channel is height. Why do you think teachers stand up to lecture? Standing higher than students establishes a teacher's superior status. It tends to reinforce a speaker's right to be listened to by students. There is, indeed, a definite advantage to height. In presidential elections, the taller of the two candidates almost always wins. Even if you are not a tall person, you can stand straight to appear taller and give an impression of confidence. Slumping makes people appear to be secretive and submissive.

Another important element of body angle and position is the way a person joins a group. Imagine four men standing in a circle talking about the day's events. A typical man would walk up to the group with his chest forward and push his way in, thereby "taking over" a spot. A typical woman, on the other hand, would approach the group more tentatively—turning to the side, bending at the knees, and wriggling her way into the group sideways. Similar behavior occurs when women enter a meeting room after a meeting has already begun. They tend to bend over slightly, look sheepishly at the floor, and hurry to their seats. Most men, however, would walk into the same meeting without embarrassment, without apology, and without hurrying. Many people subconsciously interpret these behaviors that are typical of women as indicators of uncertainty and weakness. However, those who are sensitive to cultural differences know that women choose these behaviors out of a sense of politeness and concern for the group.

**PATTERNS OF BODY LANGUAGE.**   Understanding the significance of certain actions can help you interpret another person's true meaning. However, no action should be taken as proof by itself. Instead, you should examine each action in context with the person's other body language factors. You must look for *patterns*, or groups, of actions before you can decide whether a person's nonverbal behavior contradicts or reinforces his or her verbal statements.

For example, it would not be wise to surmise someone is telling the truth merely because he or she is looking you straight in the eyes and appears calm. If the person with whom you are speaking is a good liar, he or she will actually become calmer and will maintain better eye contact when lying than when speaking the truth. The change in behavior is the most important clue.

Exhibit 3.4 provides an overview of the patterns of behavior that characterize various conditions. As you can see, arms and hands, face and eyes, legs, and body angle and position work together to indicate how the person really feels.

> To detect deceptive body language, carefully observe the individual's pattern of nonverbal communication.

## PROXEMICS

Describe how proxemics, objects, and time communicate nonverbally.

**Proxemics** is the study of a person's spatial needs and people's interaction with that space. Each of us has several zones into which we allow other people, depending on their relationship to us (see Exhibit 3.5). The zones are listed below, from the closest, smallest zone to the widest:

- *Intimate zone.* The space around us into which no one is allowed except those to whom we are close. When other people enter this zone, we become uncomfortable or feel threatened and attempt to move away. Think of this space as a privacy bubble.
- *Personal zone.* The distance we maintain when chatting with friends or business associates in a social context.
- *Social zone.* The space between us and those we don't know well, such as a repair person, store clerk, customer, or negotiating partner.
- *Public zone.* The space we prefer to maintain between us and large groups.

> Most business is conducted in the personal zone or the social zone, which cover the space from 1½ to 12 feet around the individual.

In the United States, people with lower status are normally given less personal space; the more space over which you have control, the more power you are perceived to have. However, the amount of space people need is different in other cultures. Julius Fast, the author of *Body Language* and *The Body Language of Sex, Power and Aggression* says that the amount of space needed varies from six inches for an Arab to an entire room for a German. Because they apparently need relatively little personal space, executives in many other countries do not have huge offices with large desks, as do American business and political leaders.

Fast also says that drinking alters the amount of personal space a person requires, sometimes causing it to disappear completely and other times increasing it. He attributes many bar fights to an increase in personal space requirements. It has been shown that crowding brings out the undercurrent of violence we all have.

**EXHIBIT 3.4**

**Patterns of Body Language**

| ■ Channels | ■ Arms and Hands | ■ Face and Eyes | ■ Legs | ■ Body Angle and Position |
|---|---|---|---|---|
| | | **Nonverbal Patterns** | | |
| Lying behavior—poor liars | Tugging earlobes, hands covering mouth or approaching the face, chin, and cheek; nose rubbing; more fidgety than normal; nervous tapping of fingers; crossing arms over chest | Shifting eye contact—shifting eyes to floor and ceiling; superficial smile. | More fidgety than normal; tapping feet, kicking legs; feet pointing toward exits; crossing legs; crossing legs away from listener. | Fidgeting; moving body away. (Men—coat buttoned.) |
| Lying behavior—good liars | Calmer than he or she normally is; putting hands to chest. | Better eye contact than he or she normally maintains; wide, open smile. | Less fidgeting than normal. | Leaning forward in seat; sitting far back in seat. (Men—unbuttoning coat.) |
| Honesty, cooperation, acceptance | Putting hands to chest; hands and arms open; emulating gestures of counterpart. (Men—unbuttoning coat.) | Strong eye contact; smiling; nodding of head; some blinking—not excessive. | Legs uncrossed; feet flat on floor. (Females may also cross legs with foot on top, pointing toward other person.) | Leaning forward in seat; positioning buttocks far back in seat; sitting tall but not higher than others; shrugging shoulders. |
| Eagerness, readiness to take action | Hands and arms open; hand rubbing; hands on hips; fidgety movements of hands as readiness to take action increases. (Men—unbuttoning coat.) | Good eye contact; smiling; nodding of head; if action requires movement, eyes will glance repeatedly in that direction; tilted head. | Feet apart, sometimes on tip-toe; appears excited and eager to run or jump when standing. | Sitting on edge of seat; leaning forward in seat with hands on thighs; moving closer to signal acceptance. |
| Arrogance, intimidation | Pointing; hands on hips; elbows on desk; finger and/or thumb-pointing gestures toward objects of ridicule. | Smirking; little eye contact when listening, or maintaining piercing eye contact; no smiling; rolling eyes; raising eyebrows; lifting nose; cocking head to one side. | Feet on desk; leg over arm of chair; feet planted firmly when standing. | Crossed legs with top leg pointed away from listener; sitting sideways in seat; slumping in seat; standing—slumped when derisive, tall when intimidating; looming over other person. |

| | | *Nonverbal Patterns* | | |
| | | | | |
| ■ **Channels** | ■ **Arms and Hands** | ■ **Face and Eyes** | ■ **Legs** | ■ **Body Angle and Position** |
| --- | --- | --- | --- | --- |
| Dominance, superiority, power | Hands on hips; touching others; expansive gestures; spreading arms out on backs of other chairs; hand in coat pocket, thumb out; raised fist. | Increased eye contact (males—lack of eye contact when listening to females and subordinates); chin raised; raised eyebrow with slight twisting of head when listening. | Open (males—legs crossed one ankle over knee or legs apart); standing— legs apart and firmly planted (males—leg over arm of chair); feet on desk. | Physically elevating self; sitting with chairback as shield; leaning forward in chair; invading territory of others— within 13″; positioning self to get more space; staking out clearly defined territory. |
| Submissiveness, inferiority | Hands and arms close to body. | Minimal eye contact; submissive watching of superiors; smiling; crying; head down. | Feet flat on floor. (Women—knees together; men— knees slightly apart.) | Facing superiors directly; may turn sideways and cringe if fear is part of submissiveness; slumping, crouching; using as little space as possible—taking less personal space; moving out of the way of others. |
| Fear, apprehension, nervousness | Rubbing back of neck; hands fiddling with hair, jewelry, etc.; wringing hands; fingers clasping together; trembling; clearing throat; putting out cigarette or leaving it burning without smoking; tugging at pants and/or ears. | Minimal eye contact; increased blinking; head down; narrowing of the eyes; clearing of the throat. | Legs crossed; legs drawn into the body when lying down; nervous shifting from foot to foot when standing; fidgeting. | Cringing; slumping; crouching; shifting of weight and position; not sitting down immediately when entering room. |
| Boredom, inattention, information overload | Drumming fingers or pencil on desk; doodling; filing nails; clicking a ballpoint pen. | Yawning; resting head in hand on desk; little eye contact; looking at clock, door, paperwork, etc.; blank stares; drooping eyes; head erect; neck stiff. | Tapping feet; moving feet around in a circle. (Women— crossing legs with slight kicking motion.) | Slumping; body angled away from speaker; stretching; angling body toward exit. |

| | | ***Nonverbal Patterns*** | | |
| ■ Channels | ■ Arms and Hands | ■ Face and Eyes | ■ Legs | ■ Body Angle and Position |
|---|---|---|---|---|
| Thoughtful listening, evaluation | Hands calm; taking notes; hand and/or index finger brushing chin or cheek while thinking; index finger on bottom lip; putting glasses in mouth. | Good eye contact; increased eye blinking and squinting; raised eyebrows; nodding; tilted head, ear turned to speaker. | Open; calm; casual tapping of the foot. | Body parallel to speaker or turned toward speaker; leaning forward. |
| Anger, frustration, defensiveness | Tense, jerky movements; closed fists; flexing hands; arms crossed; pointing; hands gripping edge of desk; finger under collar; hiding hands in pockets; scratching back of head; tightly clenched hands; gripping the wrist. | Taut jaw line; squinting eyes; red skin; piercing eye contact (anger); dilation of pupils; frown or superficial smile; shaking head sideways; chin out; pursing lips; turning up nose; removing glasses; lip smacking. | Tense, jerky movements; crossed legs, top leg away from counterpart; kicking at the ground; locked ankles; knees held tightly together. | Tense, rigid posture; turning away from source of anger; staking out a fixed position when standing. |
| Closed mind, disagreement, suspicion, rejection, worry, disapproval | Arms crossed over chest or in lap; closed fists; hiding hands in pockets; hand-to-cheek gestures while leaning backwards; pinching bridge of nose while closing eyes; rubbing eyes; picking imaginary lint from clothing. | Squinting eyes; head cocked back or down; pursing lips; frown or superficial smile; nose touching or rubbing; peering over top of glasses; sideways glances at source of suspicion; eyebrows down. | Shuffling feet; feet pointed away; legs locked. | Positioning body toward exit and away from source of suspicion; presenting a silhouette to source of suspicion. |
| Confidence | Steepling of hands; subtle steepling (hand over hand); joining hands together behind back; hand in coat pocket, thumb out. | Frequent eye contact; less blinking; chin up; broad smiles. | Open. | Proud, erect stance; leaning back with both hands supporting head; blowing cigarette smoke upwards. |

**Gender differences in the use of space arise from the structure of prehistoric society; in today's business world, men's and women's styles may converge.**

Gender also makes a difference: Women do not seem to require as much personal territory as men and are often given less control over their territory. Some say that in primitive society women had no choice but to tolerate the approach of more dominant people. Today's women are still approached more closely by both sexes than are men. Men, in contrast, spread their things out over a wider area and take up more space when they sit, often spreading their arms over the backs of several chairs. At home, men are more likely to stake out chairs or rooms that are theirs and theirs alone. When men share offices with other people, they tend to arrange the furniture so their own territory is clearly

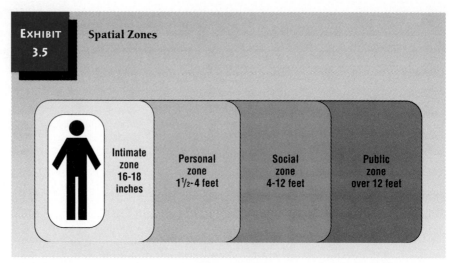

Source: A. Pease and D. Passalacqua (illustrator), "Signals," *How to Use Body Language for Power, Success and Love* (New York: Basic Books, 1984), p. 26.

defined, whereas women tend to move out of the way to accommodate others, as a polite gesture. In today's business world, perhaps women need to be a little more assertive about their personal space, and men need to be a little more considerate. Understanding cultural differences in and other implications of the use of space is critical to maintaining harmonious relationships.

## OBJECT LANGUAGE

*We display objects to fulfill personal needs, convey messages about who we are, and project the image desired by our employer.*

The objects with which we adorn ourselves and our surroundings serve two purposes: They fulfill personal needs, and they make a statement to others. Jewelry is an excellent example of object language. People purchase jewelry to meet their own belonging or esteem needs. However, jewelry also often reveals many things about its owner: social status, professional status (class rings, company watches), income level, artistic leanings, conservativism, rebellious nature (nose rings), age group, and self-concept.

Business clothing and accessories serve the same two purposes. In addition, they create an image for the individual's company. If the corporation wishes to project an image of conservatism and safety, such as a bank, you will find that most of its employees will wear conservative, sensible suits and ties. This image is translated by customers and clients in terms of the company itself—the firm is likely to be as sensible and trustworthy as its employees appear to be. The pressure to conform is strong, even when there is no formal, written statement of policy. People who do not dress properly either leave or change their style when they see promotions going only to people who meet the image. Job applicants are also screened to see how they fit into the company's perceived image of itself.

A number of people have condemned the clothing worn by many business-women for the statements of submissiveness such clothing makes. They believe the high heels, design, and soft fabric of many styles restrict movement and prevent females from competing with the same freedom as males. Therefore, most women executives adopt conservative dress: suits and blouses made of the same fabrics as men's clothing, and lower heels. These are still the standard for business, although there is a trend toward acceptance of dresses and lighter fabrics for women.

Office decoration, particularly the arrangement of desk and chairs, reveals the inhabitant's openness to communication.

The decoration and arrangement of offices is another way businesspeople use objects to express themselves. For insecure people, a desk can be a barrier. If chairs for visitors are placed on the opposite side of the desk, the office occupant remains separated and thereby safe from anyone seated in the chair. One salesperson tells of an executive who sought a height advantage by having visitors sit in low chairs and placing his own desk and chair on a raised platform. Swivel chairs with tall backs and arms are more authoritative than smaller chairs that are stationary. Self-confident, approachable managers may put a chair at the corner of the desk to facilitate visitors' feeling as equals, without a physical communication barrier. Many executive suites contain a sofa and chairs in a living room-type arrangement that fosters equality and encourages unthreatening conversation. Round conference tables also create a feeling of equality.

The way we use the objects in our vicinity also is a part of nonverbal communication. If you want someone to leave your office at the end of a meeting, you can close the desk drawer, push papers on the desk together, place papers in file folders, and line up pens and pencils. (These are the same gestures you use to hint to your professors that class is over.) Having attended to your objects, you can then stand up and walk to the door with your guest.

## TIME

How people use and view time is an important form of nonverbal communication. The ability to invest for the long term and wait for the monetary rewards, the degree of respect we have for the elderly, the way we negotiate business deals, and the way we conduct meetings are affected by our attitude toward time.

Americans have a distinctive attitude toward time: They try to squeeze as much possible activity into the shortest possible time.

Most Americans seem to suffer from a particularly stressful form of time disease, a frantic state of mind as we hurry through life. We maximize driving time by using our car phones, we fax our messages, and we try to outdo our co-workers by arriving at the office earlier and staying later—then we complain that we don't have a minute for ourselves! Most managers in US businesses are clock watchers; they try to micromanage every minute of their time, making every second count, and they expect their subordinates to do the same. They walk fast, they do three or four things at once, meetings begin and end punctually, and little time is wasted on small talk as everyone is anxious to get down to business. Even our "leisure" time is structured around business as we plan power breakfasts, golf dates, and dinners with clients.

Many people argue that the American obsession with time has been a driving force behind its economic success; others maintain that our emphasis on living only for today is harming our ability to compete in the world market. The second argument stems partly from a concern that our major industries make short-term decisions that enable them to pay immediate dividends to current stockholders, rather than updating their production equipment and investing in the long term. Retooling a plant requires a huge investment that would increase, in the long term, a company's ability to produce a quality product. However, some American executives fear that stockholders will not be willing to wait years to reap the increased profits.

The critical importance of time in Western business culture can best be seen in light of how other cultures view time. Chapter 2 contrasted the Western view with that of other cultures.

## METACOMMUNICATION

🔖 Explain the role of metacommunication in business.

Metacommunication is the message behind the overt message; it provides clues about how verbal and nonverbal messages are to be interpreted.

The fourth type of nonverbal communication, **metacommunication,** includes the intentional and unintentional implications of any communication act. The way we view colors is an example. In the United States and most Western cultures, black is associated with death. When a union negotiator wore a black dress and jacket to announce the details of a new contract, a colleague asked if her choice of outfit meant she was about to deliver bad news. The negotiator realized that she had perhaps unintentionally selected black as a way of expressing her negative feelings about the contract. The black outfit was, in other words, metacommunication that added meaning to the negotiator's announcement.

Because of the way different cultures perceive colors, businesses do a great deal of research before packaging products and designing advertisements for other countries. For example, purple is associated with death in much of Latin America, and white is the color of death in parts of the Far East. People are also superstitious about numbers, and in some countries people will avoid buying packages that contain even numbers of items or multiples of four.

Metacommunication takes many other forms as well. There are many connotations associated with the use of objects. The connotative meanings of words are also important (see Chapter 5). Metacommunication is also involved when selecting meeting locations. People are usually most comfortable in their own surroundings. Therefore, when you want to reassure someone, go to his or her office. However, when you want to make someone feel insecure, summon him or her to your office. It is known in sports as the "home court advantage." The implied message is "I have power, and I can use it whenever I want to." What do you think the implied message was in Kristine Pearce's choice of method for improving her sales staff's communication skills (described in the chapter-opening vignette)?

Acting confident when you may not be is one way of using metacommunication to your advantage.

It is especially important to be aware of metacommunication during periods of business stress. You unintentionally communicate far more than you may realize. When you find yourself in this situation, reassure your customers and your subordinates by giving the impression that it's "business as usual." They will tend to ignore any rumors they might hear if they see you walking around, greeting people in a relaxed and friendly manner, and remaining available. This intentional metacommunication may steady sales and production just enough to maintain business until the good times return.

## LISTENING SKILLS

🔖 Explain the importance of listening effectively in business.

A good listener is also good at interpreting body language and giving nonverbal feedback.

Closely tied to your ability to interpret nonverbal behavior is your ability to listen effectively. Good listeners read speakers' body language to gain insight into meaning, and they use effective body language to provide feedback.

Listening well encourages speakers to speak well. Furthermore, if you listen well, others will appreciate your interest in them and will in turn become more interested in you. Thus, listening is an essential part of both the two-way communication process and harmonious relationships.

As a student, you already know the importance of listening to the 2,000 or so lectures you will attend in your college career. You also know how easy it is to let your mind wander, focus on the mannerisms or delivery of the professors, or become impatient with them. You probably also know the consequences of not listening effectively—missing vital information needed to complete assignments and pass tests.

The consequences of poor listening in business are also costly. These costs include the loss of time and money as well as the loss of an individual's reputation. The results of poor listening are often poor service, repeat telephone calls, misunderstood instructions, incorrect orders, poor production, uncertainty, hurt feelings, embarrassment, and anger. Think of the costs in these terms: If every one of the 100 million or so workers in the United States made a mere $10 error only once a year due to poor listening, the resulting cost would be a billion dollars. Concern for the costs of bad listening habits is so great that firms such as IBM, Coca-Cola, AT&T, and General Motors, as well as many smaller companies, provide employee training in listening skills.

In many business careers, listening skills can make the difference between success and failure. People working in marketing and sales cannot sell products without listening to consumers to determine their needs. Individuals are not considered management material until they learn to listen to, meet, and exceed their superiors' expectations. Employees' morale and, hence, productivity often suffer if they do not feel someone is listening to them and their concerns.

> The most-used communication skill is listening—not speaking, writing, or reading.

In the business world and other realms, listening is the communication skill managers use the most; between 40 and 45 percent of an adult's time in a typical day is spent listening. Yet, if you are like most people, you have never had any formal training in how to listen. Most people seem to think that anyone who can hear can listen; however, hearing is not listening. If they were the same actions, people would not forget 50 percent of what they hear immediately after hearing it and, within two months, forget another 25 percent. Fortunately, listening skills can be learned. Learning to listen well, however, takes energy and attention. Practicing the listening skills discussed in this chapter will enable you to absorb and retain far more than 25 percent of what you hear.

## LISTENING BARRIERS

Identify the barriers to effective listening.

> Listening barriers include the external ones that affect the ability to hear and the internal ones that affect the ability to understand and appreciate information.

Chapter 1 discussed barriers that can interfere with the communication process. Many of those same barriers affect listening ability. Some barriers are external—for example, physical noise, odors, conversation, laughter, and so on. After all, even though hearing and listening are not the same, you must be able to hear before you can listen. Assuming external noise is not a problem, however, there are also internal obstacles within the listener that can be detrimental to effective listening. Among these obstacles are the following, which were listed in Norma Costner's chapter in the book *Facilitating Communication for Business*:

- Listening with a judgmental, prejudiced attitude—believing that it is necessary to approve or disapprove, [basing the] judging . . . on personal likes and dislikes.
- Thinking about oneself and giving a response as soon as the opportunity arises.
- Assuming what the speaker is going to say, that it is unimportant, and then tuning out.
- Hearing what one wants to hear, ignoring what one disagrees with or feels threatened by.
- Faking attentiveness and daydreaming.
- Prejudging the speaker or the content and closing one's mind to new ideas.
- Paying too much attention to the speaker's appearance, pronunciation, accent, voice, mannerisms, and grammar.

To overcome these barriers, you need to practice two types of listening techniques. Active listening techniques are those that require action only on the part of the listener; the speaker is not actively involved in improving the listening environment. Interactive listening techniques, however, require the interaction of both the speaker and the listener. Both were needed by Kristine Pearce's sales staff for them to sell effectively and work as a team.

### ACTIVE LISTENING TECHNIQUES

Apply six active listening techniques in daily life.

**Active listening techniques are used by listeners to concentrate on a spoken message.**

**Active listening** requires you to be prepared to listen, rather than simply to hear the message. It requires a commitment to evaluating the message instead of the speaker and allows no time for you to take your attention away from the message. The six techniques described here—focusing on content, listening with an open mind, listening for what the speaker doesn't say, listening without jumping to conclusions, controlling your emotions, and taking selective notes—will enable you to listen more effectively.

**FOCUS ON CONTENT.**   Clear your mind of other thoughts so you can focus on the message's content. Resist the temptation to think about things that have nothing to do with the situation, such as how hungry you are, whether you are making a good impression, what you have to do next, and so on. Avoid rushing the speaker so you can go on to other things. Recognize the fact that each individual with whom you deal will not always be able to express his or her message with perfect clarity, taking up as little of your time as possible.

It is easier to focus on content when you are patient and listen for the main ideas and supporting points. Doing so helps you filter out all the nonessential information. Consider the following conversation between a subordinate (Jim) who asked to meet with his supervisor (Wayne):

Wayne   How's it going, Jim? What would you like to see me about?
Jim         Well . . . as you know, Melvin Quantas is a customer service representative who's worked for us for a long time—at least 30 years, wouldn't you say? Maybe it has been more like 35 now that I think about it. He gets along well with almost everybody, but the other day he blew up at a customer—not the first time either. Now don't

get me wrong; he's a very nice guy and he does favors for people all the time. Why, a year ago, before we put in the computers, I was at least four days behind in tracking orders, and Melvin stayed late three nights to help me out. He was a great help, and he picked up quickly on the procedures. I'm sure he could figure out how to do the same thing on the computer. You know, putting in those computers was one of the smartest things we ever did. I'd sure hate to go back to the old days again, although we do still need someone else to do data entry. Well, anyway, Melvin can't seem to handle customers anymore. It takes someone like Jane Jackson; she's one of the best customer service representatives we've ever had. She's able to put up with customer demands, no matter how unreasonable, and she's kept up on all our latest products. If she doesn't know the answer to a question, she'll find out and follow up with a return phone call. Customers never have to telephone her twice. What do you think we should do?

Wayne    You're suggesting Melvin be transferred to your department where he would learn to track orders by computer? That would put him in a position he can handle and where someone is badly needed, and it would allow us to hire someone else who is better able to handle customer service. Is that correct?

As is typical in most conversations, a lot of the information in Jim's remarks can be viewed as filler. Filtering out the filler helped Wayne focus on the key ideas.

To understand what Wayne has done in this case, imagine being asked to briefly summarize the information in a chapter; you would look at the headings and subheadings as guides in preparing the summary. Speakers use implicit headings and subheadings to structure their messages. Focusing on these implicit guides will provide the majority of the information you need to grasp in any communication encounter.

**LISTEN WITH AN OPEN MIND.**    Resist the tendency to close your mind to the message because of who is delivering it. Unfortunately, we often use prior experience with individuals or groups as an indicator of the worth of what they have to say. Union leaders who refuse to open their minds to management's reasoning, racist students who dismiss what a professor of a different race has to say, adults who ignore all teenagers—all are examples of how personal prejudices get in the way of the message.

An alarming personal prejudice has been demonstrated repeatedly throughout the years. Both male and female members of audiences often pay more attention to male speakers than female speakers, and they recall more information from presentations given by males. Experiments have shown this phenomenon to occur even when male and female speakers make identical presentations. Make sure you give both female and male speakers your full attention so you do not miss important information.

You should also resist the tendency to make judgments about speakers because of their appearance, mannerisms, accents, and so on. Does an accent mean a person is stupid? Obviously, no. It is also dangerous to assume, for example, that someone in a cheap suit could not possibly know anything about running a successful business. Some people, no matter how successful they are,

Good listeners learn to set aside their biases about the "messenger" so they can focus on the message.

just don't care about their appearance. However, we often assume if someone doesn't look successful, they must not be successful. Too many people judge the speaker first, then decide whether they are going to listen. Judging a book by its cover, however, is dangerous. Move beyond factors that do not directly affect the message.

**LISTEN FOR WHAT THE SPEAKER DOESN'T SAY.**  Listening for what a speaker doesn't say has two major components. First, the listener should analyze whether the nonverbal messages reinforce or contradict what is being said. Exhibit 3.4 includes many examples of body language to watch for when analyzing the sincerity of a speaker's words. For example, if speakers repeatedly use hand-to-face gestures, maintain poor eye contact, cross their arms in front of their chests, and point their bodies toward the exit, you would be right to be suspicious of what they are telling you.

> *Good listeners learn to detect lying and evasion.*

The second component of critical listening is to listen for what the speaker leaves out. We all have a tendency to address only those areas of any subject that we choose to address. Many conversationalists, particularly dominant types and those who are avoiding lying, are particularly good at this. The following conversation illustrates this type of omission:

Supervisor   Fatima, when are you going to get the Nygren portfolio finished? It's three days overdue. Fax it to them as soon as it's done. By the way, you are including all the illustrations, text, and mock-ups we went over in our meeting, aren't you?

Fatima   Of course, I'm including everything I have in my notes. They're going to love it. It's my best work yet! You should see the ad for *TV Times;* no comparison! Don't worry; it's almost done. You can depend on me.

What Fatima didn't say, however, is more important than what she did. She has decided not to include everything they discussed in the meeting, but notice how she avoids the issue. She said she is including everything she has "in her notes," not everything they discussed in the meeting. She also avoided saying when the portfolio would be finished. Assurances of her dependability and her work's quality have nothing to do with the matter.

As you listen, be alert for the feelings, attitudes, and implied intent of the message. Avoid being sidetracked by manipulative people who substitute bluster and evasion for factual content.

**LISTEN WITHOUT JUMPING TO CONCLUSIONS.**  Although people can speak at a rate of only 130 to 160 words per minute, the brain can process over 700 words a minute. This leaves a great deal of time for the mind to jump to conclusions about what is being said based on scanty information. However, many important points and subtle nuances are missed when people do not listen to every word.

> *The brain can process words far faster than a person can speak; thus, it is difficult to listen to a speaker without jumping to conclusions or becoming sidetracked.*

People often jump to conclusions because they are too busy planning what they are going to say next. Even during speeches, many listeners concentrate more on their own replies or questions they want to ask during the discussion period than on what the speaker is saying. How many times have you heard someone ask a question that had already been answered clearly in a speech or class presentation? People who ask such careless questions are not good listeners.

People who are dominant personality types with strong opinions also have trouble in this area. Because they often feel they have more knowledge than anyone else, it is sometimes hard for them to listen to the comments and ideas of people they feel are less knowledgeable. Dominant personalities are used to having people pay attention to them. In groups of people, they speak up more and control the conversation more often. Their natural assertiveness does not always lead to effective listening skills.

Supervisors, managers, and business owners often have this problem. Their desire to control the conversation and their need to maximize every second of their time makes many people in positions of power jump to conclusions. They may interrupt or cut off subordinates who need to speak to them but who, because they are nervous, cannot quickly and concisely say what they mean. The result is frustration on both sides.

To avoid jumping to conclusions, use the extra time your mind has to process data to explore the message's content. Mentally summarize what the speaker is saying. Formulate challenges of your own and weigh them against the speaker's evidence. Anticipate where the speaker will head next, and evaluate your assumptions as the message proceeds.

**CONTROL YOUR EMOTIONS.** When speakers use terms or express ideas that anger you, avoid letting your feelings block communication. Most people, however, immediately stop listening to someone who angers them. Instead, they spend their time figuring out ways to show the speaker he or she is wrong. When you listen only for words and phrases you can refute, you are likely to miss the speaker's main points and the reasoning behind his or her conclusions.

Be particularly careful to avoid listening for **signal words**—emotion-laden words that sum up, in your mind, everything the speaker stands for. Words and phrases such as *exploitation, empowerment, manipulation, total lack of concern, hidden money*, and *creative accounting* act as barriers to communication when listeners allow them. The effective listener, however, recognizes that words such as these have a real meaning apart from the emotional content and tries to understand them without bias.

**TAKE SELECTIVE NOTES.** Every communication encounter does not provide an opportunity to take notes; however, when you are in a meeting or listening to a presentation, it has many advantages. For one thing, taking notes can help you concentrate on what the speaker is saying. If done correctly, note taking can help you listen for central themes and major ideas.

If done incorrectly, however, note taking can prevent you from listening effectively. When you concentrate on writing down everything that is said, you cannot observe the speaker for nonverbal signs. As a result, the speaker's feelings, moods, and nonverbal suggestions of intent, all of which are vital components of meaning, are lost.

As you take notes, jot down phrases, not complete sentences, that concisely describe each major point as it is made. Under each point, use phrases to note the supporting evidence the speaker provides. Use question marks in the margin to indicate areas you wish to ask the speaker about (areas that need further clarification). As you consider how the information will be useful to you, jot

Learn to take notes on a presentation or speech as a way of focusing on the important elements of the message; do not let your note taking distract you.

down in the margin one or two words that will remind you later how you plan to use that information. For example, the name of a client in the margin would be enough to trigger your thoughts later. This is perhaps the best way to ensure that you retain as much of what you hear as possible.

## INTERACTIVE LISTENING TECHNIQUES

▐▪ Apply three interactive listening techniques in daily life.

**Interactive listening** requires action on the parts of both the listener and the speaker to improve the transmission and retention of information. Interviews and almost all business conversations, meetings, and negotiations require interactive listening skills. This chapter concentrates on what the listener can do to promote interaction; Chapter 15 discusses interactive techniques for speakers that can help listeners listen more effectively. The three most important interactive listening techniques are using effective body language, giving effective verbal feedback, and avoiding interrupting and controlling.

> Interactive listening is used by listeners and speakers to ensure that they both understand the message.

**USE EFFECTIVE BODY LANGUAGE.**   Observing the body language cues of their listeners helps speakers in many ways. For example, professors will tell you that there are times when they can almost see large question marks superimposed on their students' faces. Whether or not students realize they are sending out nonverbal signals, they are helping to meet their own need for further clarification by using effective body language.

One section of Exhibit 3.4 details the body language patterns of a thoughtful listener. Thoughtful listeners maintain good eye contact with the speaker, thereby increasing the speaker's confidence and perhaps improving the quality of what is being said. Good listeners' legs, hands, and arms are open and calm. Their bodies are parallel to or turned toward the speaker. They lean forward in their seats and nod their heads to show agreement and understanding. When people are really listening, not just pretending, they often sit with a chin or a cheek in one hand. As a speaker, you will be able to tell when your listeners are bored, eager, frustrated, defensive, accepting, or disbelieving by learning and becoming sensitive to people's nonverbal patterns.

> Good listeners let the speaker know—through eye contact, posture, and so on—that they are participating in the communication act.

As a listener, you are responsible for developing good listening habits. This takes time because, for many people, it involves changing long-established bad habits. Awareness, however, is the first step; then comes practice. The more a behavior is practiced, the more likely it is to become automatic. For example, after attending a seminar on body language, one personnel interviewer vowed to work on his eye contact. To remind himself, he quickly drew one small eye on applicants' folders as he interviewed them. Each time he observed the eye, it reminded him of the behavior he was trying to improve. Within three months, he no longer needed the visual reminder.

**GIVE EFFECTIVE VERBAL FEEDBACK.**   Whether you are face-to-face with someone or communicating with him or her by telephone, verbal feedback improves communication. A simple "uh-huh" or "I know what you mean" lets the speaker know he or she is getting the point across. Try sometime to carry on a phone conversation without providing any of the normal reassuring verbal feedback.

You will probably find that the person on the other end of the line will begin asking you questions to elicit the same kind of information from you, such as "Are you still there?" "Do you understand?" "You know what I mean, don't you?" Feedback, positive and negative, lets speakers know when they need to restate or clarify as well as when their message is clear.

*Good listeners provide verbal feedback to ensure that they are understanding the speaker's message.*

Verbal feedback also elicits additional information the listener needs to understand messages. Listeners cannot depend on speakers to notice their confused expressions before asking for clarification. In most circumstances it is appropriate to ask speakers to clarify information as it is presented. For example, in any situation other than a formal oral presentation, you may tactfully indicate you have a question by raising your hand, signaling with your hand, or making eye contact. In many circumstances, however, it would be better to wait for a break between statements before asking the speaker to repeat something that was said before.

*Paraphrasing and probing are two forms of verbal feedback that listeners can use to check their understanding of a message's meaning.*

One of the most effective ways to find out if you understand a concept is to paraphrase what you think a speaker meant. The speaker can then correct any misconceptions you might have. Paraphrasing is particularly useful in business for making sure instructions are understood clearly. Paraphrases usually follow a pattern such as this: "Let me see if I have this straight. You want me to scrap the production schedule for the MR2 and replace it with . . . " If the listener is correct, the speaker says so and proceeds with the rest of the message. If the listener has misunderstood, it is now up to the speaker to go over the information again or to find another way to present the information to promote better understanding.

**Probing** is another interactive verbal technique that helps improve the quality of communication between two people or in a small group. There are two types of probing: prompting and nondirective questioning. Prompting consists of phrases such as "go on" and "tell me more" that let the speaker know you are paying attention but want more information. Nondirective questioning involves phrases such as "I'm not sure what you mean," which can be used to let the speaker know that the process of understanding is not complete and must be tackled again.

Supervisors and managers are often required to use effective listening skills in settling disagreements, misunderstandings, and conflicts. When you find yourself in such a situation, focus on the facts rather than the personalities of the individuals involved. Use effective body language and verbal feedback to show your willingness to listen. Show that you understand another person's positions by paraphrasing his or her viewpoint in your own words. Ask the other person how he or she would solve the problem. If there are better ways to handle the problem, point them out as possible alternatives, rather than concentrating on your objections to his or her solution. This type of verbal feedback can encourage inarticulate speakers to express themselves better, thus improving the quality of the communication.

*When two people converse, they are expected to take turns— without interrupting or trying to control the conversation.*

**AVOID INTERRUPTIONS AND CONTROLLING BEHAVIOR.**   In conversations, there are strong but unwritten rules for taking turns. An ideal conversation between two people would consist of person A speaking until finished (for a reasonable amount of time) while person B listens attentively. Then person B would speak while person A listens. However, ideal conversations, with all individuals respecting other people's rights, are probably few and far between.

Most of us will tolerate, to some degree, people who attempt to control conversations through interruptions. The degree to which we will allow other people to interrupt us, however, varies from one individual to the next. Most subordinates tend to allow their superiors to interrupt them; many women allow men to interrupt. However, interruptions are rude attempts to control the flow of conversation. The ability to control a conversation is power, and people who feel they are superior to others will use their power frequently. There are many specific reasons we interrupt when others are speaking, including

- We think we know more about the topic than the speaker does.
- We think we can say it better.
- We want to change the topic for various reasons.
- We do not respect the person speaking and dismiss whatever he or she has to say as unimportant.
- We think our story will be more interesting because it demonstrates how we have done it better, faced more difficulties, achieved better results, and so on.
- We believe the other person is inferior and will let us take over the conversation.

If someone interrupts you while you are speaking, say immediately in an insistent yet polite tone, "Wait a minute; let me finish my point." If a superior interrupts you, and you are in a position to refuse the interruption, say something such as this: "I'll be through here in about 15 minutes, Adena; will you be in your office?" As these words are spoken, a hand and arm raised in a "Wait a minute" gesture is also appropriate. Such a gesture and lack of eye contact can often be used in place of words to silence a would-be interrupter.

Good listeners do not interrupt in an attempt to wrest control of conversations away from speakers. They respect people with whom they are speaking and let the natural rules of turn taking guide their conversations with others. They realize that it isn't just the speaker who communicates—communication is a two-way street, and both listening and speaking are important to making it work.

## DISCUSSION QUESTIONS

◼ Describe how nonverbal communication relates to verbal communication.

1. How does nonverbal communication relate to verbal communication?

◼ Describe how nonverbal communication relates to verbal communication.

2. Why is nonverbal communication considered a subconscious language?

◼ Identify gender differences in nonverbal communication.

3. How should women change their style of nonverbal communication to make them more effective in the business world?

◼ Identify gender differences in nonverbal communication.

◣ Identify the four channels used to communicate meaning through body language.

4. Using the four communication channels, list three ways that men's and women's body language differs.

◣ Identify the four channels used to communicate meaning through body language.

5. Describe what is meant by a pattern of body language.

◣ Describe how proxemics, objects, and time communicate nonverbally.

6. Briefly describe and give examples of how proxemics, objects, and time communicate nonverbally. Use examples not used in this textbook.

◣ Explain the importance of listening effectively in business.

7. What percentage of an executive's time is spent listening? How does this relate to business communication?

◣ Identify the barriers to effective listening.

8. Name three barriers to effective listening.

◣ Apply six active listening techniques in daily life.
◣ Apply three interactive listening techniques in daily life.

9. What is the difference between active and interactive listening techniques?

◣ Apply six active listening techniques in daily life.

10. Describe three active listening techniques.

◣ Apply three interactive listening techniques in daily life.

11. Describe three interactive listening techniques.

## APPLICATION EXERCISES

◣ Describe how nonverbal communication relates to verbal communication.

1. Choose a speaker you listen to frequently (one of your professors might be a good choice). Without using names, analyze the speaker's use of nonverbal communication. How does his or her nonverbal behavior contradict or reinforce what he or she is saying? Give specific examples in a letter report to your teacher.

◣ Identify gender differences in nonverbal communication.

2. From the descriptions within this chapter, compile a list of typical male nonverbal communication behaviors and a list of typical female nonverbal communication behaviors. Present these lists in a memo report to your professor. Include in your report (*a*) a brief discussion of the dangers of stereotyping and generalizing about groups of individuals, (*b*) a discussion of the impact of these behaviors on perceptions of leadership ability, and (*c*) recommendations for change addressed to men and women in management. Your

recommendations for change should reflect an appreciation for the benefits of diversity as well as an understanding of the need for conformity.

◣ Identify gender differences in nonverbal communication.
◣ Apply three interactive listening techniques in daily life.

3. Attend a meeting or listen to a long conversation among a mixed group of men and women. Watch for instances of interruptive behavior. Did any of the participants interrupt others to gain control of the conversation? If so, were their interruptions successful? How did the person being interrupted handle the interruption? Did the females in the group allow more interruptions than the males? Were the males in the group the only ones who initiated interruptive behavior? When someone was successful in gaining control of the conversation through an interruption, how did the person who was interrupted behave? Did the interrupted person exhibit any signs of submissive behavior? Report on the meeting or conversation in a letter report to your professor.

◣ Identify the four channels used to communicate meaning through body language.

4. In teams of four, list as many specific examples of the four channels of body language as you can in five minutes—arm and hand movements, facial expressions, leg positions, and body angles and positions. If so instructed by your teacher, videotape them and then show the tape to the class; as an alternative, you can perform these gestures in front of the class. Ask other class members to identify the meaning of each. At the end of your presentation, give the correct answers to see how successful the audience was at interpreting your gestures.

◣ Identify the four channels used to communicate meaning through body language.

5. Observe a group of people in conversation for a minimum of 15 minutes. If you are currently working, use a work group. Identify three people in the group for observation. Block out their words and observe only their body language. For each of the three individuals, record the body language cues they are using in each of the four channels (arms and hands, face and eyes, legs, body angle and position). Afterwards, determine if the nonverbal cues you recorded for each individual can be grouped into patterns and labeled using the descriptors in Exhibit 3.4. For example, would you say an individual's behavior indicates he or she is honest and eager or, perhaps, arrogant and dominant? Present this information in a written or oral report to the class. Your professor will inform you of the preferred format.

◣ Describe how proxemics, objects, and time communicate nonverbally.
◣ Explain the role of metacommunication in business.

6. Spend some time in someone's office and analyze the objects there. What do they tell you about the person to whom the office belongs? Are there any other metacommunication elements, such as how the office is arranged, that give you clues to the occupant's personality? Summarize this information in a memo report to your professor.

◼ Describe how proxemics, objects, and time communicate nonverbally.
◼ Explain the role of metacommunication in business.

7. Compare the offices of an upper-level management employee to the office of someone else in an organization. Using your knowledge of proxemics, objects, time, and other metacommunication elements, reach conclusions about the occupants of these two offices. What "statements" do the objects within the offices and their arrangement make to you? Summarize this information in a memo report to your professor.

◼ Explain the importance of listening effectively in business.

8. Interview two or three managers or business owners about the importance of listening in business. Present your results in a short informative report.

◼ Explain the importance of listening effectively in business.
◼ Identify the barriers to effective listening.

9. The following communication situations are likely to be encumbered with many barriers. Identify possible listening barriers that might be encountered in these situations:
   a. Labor–management negotiations.
   b. A domineering supervisor meeting with his or her department staff.
   c. A new teacher meeting his or her first lecture class.
   d. A person who was turned down for a promotion meeting, for the first time, the person who was hired for that job.
   e. A teacher of a highly technical, required class greeting the students on the first day of the semester.
   f. A salesperson who is trying to sell a remote-controlled model airplane to a retired couple.

◼ Identify the barriers to effective listening.
◼ Apply six active listening techniques in daily life.
◼ Apply three interactive listening techniques in daily life.

10. Keep a journal of your own listening habits over the next two or three days. List occasions when you listened actively and interactively, as well as when you did not listen effectively. Identify the barriers you encountered. Present this journal with a memo report to your instructor. Your report should include the following:
    a. The changes you plan to make to improve your listening habits.
    b. Specific examples of listening errors you made that led to your conclusions.
    c. The steps you will take to improve your listening effectiveness.

◼ Identify the barriers to effective listening.
◼ Apply six active listening techniques in daily life.
◼ Apply three interactive listening techniques in daily life.

11. As a class, identify at least four controversial topics. For each of these topics, write down whether you personally agree or disagree. Your professor will then divide the class into teams of two (one who agrees and one who disagrees) to discuss the topics. Your professor will tell you which of

the following exercises your team is to do while he or she times the exercise (three minutes is suggested):

a.  As each team member presents his or her views on the subject, the other team member should use paraphrasing and other forms of inter- active listening techniques to be sure the person's reasoning is under- stood. No refuting or arguing about the topic is to take place.

b.  Each team member should present his or her views on the subject without using any hand or arm gestures.

c.  Each team member should present his or her views on the subject with his or her eyes closed.

d.  Each team member should present his or her views on the subject while the other team member completely ignores the speaker—no eye contact, no verbal feedback, and so on.

After the time is up, share your observations with the class. Did any of these exercises enlighten you about your own listening habits? As a speaker or as a listener, how did you feel during each exercise? How do you think the other person felt? Did any of the exercises improve communication? Did any of them detract from communication?

🔲 Apply six active listening techniques in daily life.

12.  Attend a speech or presentation (for a minimum of 15 minutes) and prac- tice the note-taking techniques presented in this chapter. Include your notes and the following information in a letter report to your professor:

a.  What problems did you encounter?

b.  Did your note taking ever prevent you from observing the nonverbal communication of the speaker?

c.  Did you find yourself trying to take too many notes?

d.  Are you able to summarize the key points and the supporting evidence from your notes?

e.  Were you able to identify instances where opinions or conclusions were stated strongly without supporting evidence?

f.  What kinds of questions were asked during the speech? At the end of the speech?

🔲 Apply six active listening techniques in daily life.
🔲 Apply three interactive listening techniques in daily life.

13.  Attend a speech or presentation (for a minimum of 15 minutes) and ob- serve the nonverbal communication of the audience. Write a memo report to your professor addressing the following points (as well as any others you feel are pertinent):

a.  What active and interactive techniques did the audience use?

b.  Describe specific instances of poor listening behavior and good listen- ing behavior.

c.  Did the speaker appear to react in any way to the nonverbal communi- cation of the audience?

# CHAPTER 4

# PUTTING THE YOU ATTITUDE IN BUSINESS MESSAGES

## OBJECTIVES

When you finish studying this chapter, you will be able to:

- Explain the link between psychology and communication.
- Define and explain the Six C's.
- Describe the five levels of the hierarchy of needs.
- Use the hierarchy of needs to determine which benefits to emphasize in a business message.
- Phrase messages so they are you oriented.

### WHAT WOULD YOU DO IF...?

**ANOTHER POINT OF VIEW.**   Good communicators understand other people and use this understanding to phrase messages that will bring about the desired results. For example, imagine that you work with Marcey Leonard, a receptionist. Marcey is consistently late to work. Your supervisor once spoke to Marcey about her tardiness, but Marcey could give no good reason for being late so often. In fact, Marcey continues to arrive 10 to 15 minutes late two or three days a week.

Marcey's tardiness has been hard on you. When she's late, you have to answer the phones and greet the clients, which makes you get behind in your own work. You would like to get Marcey to come to work on time, but you don't know exactly what to do. You're concerned that if you talk to Marcey yourself she'll be angry at you for interfering, and you're afraid that your supervisor won't be able to solve anything by talking to Marcey again. You need to either find a way to explain to Marcey why she should come to work on time in terms that she will understand and comply with, or get your supervisor to talk to Marcey in a way that will produce positive results.

This chapter explains how to form messages that other people can understand, accept, and act on. You will learn that before you can get your needs met, you have to consider the other person's needs. As you read, think about how you might use the ideas in this chapter to get through to Marcey.

## COMMUNICATION PSYCHOLOGY

Psychology is the science of mind and behavior.

■ Explain the link between psychology and communication.

To communicate well, you must first understand the basics of **psychology,** the science of mind and behavior. Researchers have been studying the human mind for centuries to determine why people behave as they do. If you are already good at dealing with people, you probably have some understanding of why people act in certain ways. In this chapter, however, you will learn about several psychological theories you can use to formulate even more effective messages.

In the business world, advertisers have a highly developed ability to link psychology and communication. They bombard us daily with reasons to buy their products. The best advertisers know why people do things, especially why they buy certain products. With this knowledge, they make us think that we can be more beautiful, more efficient, more intelligent, more loved, more everything that we want to be—if only we buy whatever it is they are selling. For example, if an advertiser can convince you that everyone of any importance is wearing its brand of designer jeans, you may be more likely to buy those jeans.

Advertising is not the only part of the business world in which an understanding of psychology pays off. For instance, because people often value prestige more than money, some employers give their employees lofty titles instead of pay raises. This is how people become sanitation engineers instead of janitors. Perhaps you have noticed in some banks that almost everyone you meet seems to be a vice president!

An understanding of psychology helps you get results when you communicate.

You can use this same knowledge of psychology to improve your chances of successful communication. Think back through your day. How many times today did you try to convince someone that your way of thinking or your ideas were correct? Weren't you most successful when you explained how your ideas would help the other person meet his or her needs? Some knowledge of what appeals to people is necessary for convincing them to do what you want—whether it be buy your product, hire you for a job, purchase new equipment for your office, let you out of class early, or simply convince them you are right about a particular point. This chapter shows how understanding three basic psychological concepts—the Six C's, the hierarchy of needs, and the "you" attitude—will help with all types of business communication.

## THE SIX C's

Your goal as a communicator is to answer the reader's or listener's question "What's in it for me?"

■ Define and explain the Six C's.

Before you can achieve a message's purpose, you must first satisfy the receiver's normal, automatic response: "What's in it for me?" Your goal as a communicator is to not only express your ideas but also answer this question. If the other person does not understand how your message will meet real needs, he or she is not likely to pay attention to it.

Communication experts know that the way a message is phrased is as important as the idea behind the message. Statements like the following don't work, because they are worded without regard for the other person:

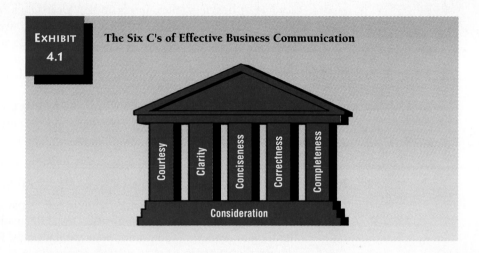

**EXHIBIT 4.1**   **The Six C's of Effective Business Communication**

Courtesy · Clarity · Conciseness · Correctness · Completeness

Consideration

"You failed to pay your account on time" (reminds the receiver of something that nobody likes—failure).

"Training Associates, Inc., wishes to announce its newest product" (emphasizes the writer, not the reader, and uses overly formal language).

"Send in the enclosed card without delay" (uses a discourteous tone and unnecessarily negative words).

Clearly, the phrasing of these messages does not take into account the other person's possible reaction to the words.

> The Six C's are the characteristics of a message that meet readers' and listeners' needs.

Good communicators use the Six C's—courtesy, clarity, conciseness, correctness, completeness, and consideration (the most important C)—to describe how a message can be phrased to meet readers' and listeners' needs. Messages that meet these requirements will produce results. Exhibit 4.1 shows how the Six C's interact. Notice that consideration is the basis for the other five.

## COURTESY

Standards of courtesy vary from one country to another, but all societies have customs that people observe to demonstrate basic respect for one another. In the United States and Canada, for example, polite terms like *please* and *thank you* are required in all forms of business communication. It does not matter whether you are communicating to your clients, customers, co-workers, supervisors, top management, or staff—all deserve equally courteous treatment.

> Courtesy is a matter of sincerity, tact, thoughtfulness, and appreciation.

There are several ways to make your messages more courteous. The most basic is to be sincerely tactful, thoughtful, and appreciative. You have probably seen many examples of insincere courtesy, such as the teacher who hands out a very hard test and tells the class to "Have a nice day." Although the words seem to indicate concern for the students, in this situation the statement seems insincere. Statements such as "I hope you do well on this exam" or even "This is the time that tries men's (and women's) souls" would be more sincere.

Another way to show courtesy is to take care in using other people's names in business messages. If you know the person well enough to use his or her first name in everyday situations, you may use that name in the salutation of a memo or business letter; for example, "Dear Louis." (See Appendix C for more on the format of business letters and memos.) However, if you don't know the person well or you are sending a formal message, always use the person's last name with the courtesy title *Dr., Mr., Miss, Ms., Mrs.,* or *M.* (for when you don't know if the person you are writing to is male or female). "Dear Mr. Armenta" is far more courteous than "Dear Armenta."

**Courtesy is required even in a command.**

Courtesy is expected even when you are in a position to give orders. When you give someone a command or suggestion, you are expected to do so politely. Note the difference in the following:

Discourteous: "Send a check today to bring your account up to date."

Courteous: "Please send a check today to bring your account up to date."

Even though your reader is legally obligated to pay regularly, and even though you have a right to expect payment on time, the reader is more likely to comply with your request if you ask for your money nicely. Remember that your goal is to get the payment—not to express your irritation about the delay.

**As a matter of courtesy, do not thank people in advance.**

Sometimes business communicators must show appreciation for some action that has not yet been performed. An attempt to show appreciation before the fact often sounds presumptuous, as if you are not allowing the other person to make his or her own decisions. Notice the subtle psychological difference between these two sentences:

Discourteous: "Thank you for sending your check today."

Courteous: "Sending your check today will bring your account up to date."

The first statement is presumptuous because it implies that the reader will do what you ask without question. Such an attitude belittles the reader. The second example is better because it leaves the decision about whether to mail the check up to the reader, which preserves his or her dignity; it encourages the reader to respond by mentioning the benefit.

Another aspect of courtesy is the apology. If you or your company makes a mistake that causes someone harm, you can usually restore goodwill only by making a sincere apology. However, you don't want to put too much emphasis on the apology; you want to move on to more positive things. Nor do you want to repeat the apology. Many ineffective letters begin with a negative statement, such as "We are sincerely sorry for the inconvenience we have caused you," and then end with another negative, such as "Again, we are sorry . . . " Dwelling on the apology in this way merely reminds the reader of the unpleasant event and does little to restore goodwill.

Many other types of expressions are likely to irritate or hurt the reader and should, therefore, be avoided, such as:

Discourteous: "We received your complaint of January 16."

Courteous: "We received your letter of January 16 in which you express concern about the performance of your Saxby 2311."

In this example, the words *your complaint* sound disrespectful. A person who writes a letter about a real problem does not want to be belittled. It is more courteous to think of everyone having justified concerns.

Discourteous: "You claim that the installation manual was not included with your computer."

Courteous: "Enclosed is a manual that will help you quickly and easily install your computer."

Courteous: "Your request for an installation manual was received today. Please check with your dealer for a replacement."

The words *you claim* imply that the writer does not believe the claim that the manual was missing. Obviously, the reader is going to react negatively. If you can meet the request, do so graciously. If you cannot, it is courteous to explain why not.

Discourteous: "Successful businessmen know the importance of a carefully written business plan."

Courteous: "Successful businesspeople know the importance of a carefully written business plan."

Watch out for words that belittle a whole group of people. The word *businessmen* implies that women do not know the importance of a carefully written business plan; in this case, it even implies that businesswomen are not successful.

Courtesy should be a top priority in your writing. You will find that your readers react positively to you and to your ideas if you are able to offer a good-natured apology when necessary, without dwelling on the negative; if you can choose words that show respect for your reader; and if you are sincerely tactful, thoughtful, and appreciative.

## CLARITY

The second of the Six C's, clarity, is another essential for those who want to communicate effectively. If your message is clear, it gets the meaning across so that the reader or audience understands what you have in mind.

To be clear, you must use correct sentence structure, punctuation, spelling, and so on in your business messages. The rules of grammar, word usage, and spelling enable us to communicate with others and be reasonably sure that our messages will be understood. Just as we can avoid traffic accidents by obeying the rules of the road, we can avoid miscommunication by obeying the rules of our language.

It is also true that others judge us by the quality of our messages. Poor language skills and carelessness give readers and listeners the impression that the communicator is either stupid or lacks respect. If you consider someone to be stupid or disrespectful, are you likely to believe what he or she says or writes? Probably not. The following examples illustrate the value of using language correctly:

As written: "The butler was ordered to stand by the door and call the guests names as they entered."

As intended: "The butler was ordered to stand by the door and call the guests' names as they entered."

As written: "We, the scholarship committe, would like to thank you for your application. We enjoy becoming acquaintee with you through your application. It sounds as if you have definely worked hard."

*Observing the rules of grammar, usage, spelling, and so on makes messages easier to understand.*

As intended: "We, the scholarship committee, would like to thank you for your application. We enjoyed becoming acquainted with you through your application. It sounds as though you have definitely worked hard."

Imagine how you would feel if you were the person who received the letter about the scholarship application. Being turned down is bad enough, but being told you're not worthy by someone who is incompetent and careless is even worse.

Many people make the mistake of trying to impress their readers or listeners instead of expressing meaning. Using fancy words when plain words will do, in an attempt to make the writing sound more professional, may only make other people feel stupid. Instead, use a conversational style that suits the educational level of your readers or listeners. Trendy jargon should also be avoided. Consider the following sentence taken from a business report:

> As written: "It is recommended that the finance department bottomline the action request and high-impact it by dedicating the efforts of all its staff members."

> As translated: "The finance department should make gathering the requested information its top priority and instruct all its staff to begin this task immediately."

The writer of the first version has created a monstrosity instead of communicating meaning.

Correct format—the way the message is laid out on the page—is also an important element for writing clear messages. Such messages should appear neat, attractive, and businesslike. Readers are confused when parts of memos or letters are left out or used incorrectly. Placing the dateline of a letter at the bottom of the page instead of at the top, for example, would focus attention on the format instead of the message.

Clarity may also require visuals, such as tables, graphs, pie charts, or other illustrations. Visuals aid understanding by clarifying meaning and allowing quick understanding of concepts. The drawing in Exhibit 4.2 illustrates how much easier it sometimes is to understand visual aids compared to the written word. If someone were to ask you what a Phillips screwdriver looks like, you might try to describe it like this: "It's like a regular screwdriver, but it has a cross on the end that comes to a point." If the person who asked is familiar with tools, this might be enough explanation. However, many people would still be confused.

## CONCISENESS

Effective messages use the fewest number of words possible. People are busy these days, and they become impatient when they have to work hard or spend a lot of time trying to figure out what something means. Here's an example of how conciseness helps the reader:

> Wordy: "The protracted appendage of the self-acting stimulus-response apparatus is immobilized, thus arresting its facility to move into an upraised state the automobile assembly components."

> Concise: "The robot's arm is stuck and won't pick up the car parts."

That's like calling ham and eggs the thigh of a hog's back leg, sliced and cured, with two oval masses encased in shells laid by a barnyard bird with female characteristics! Do you find such a lengthy description impressive, or just ridiculous?

*Use the writing style that will make your reader most comfortable.*

*Format, the way a written message is laid out on the page, contributes to clarity.*

*Use visuals to supplement your words whenever they will aid understanding.*

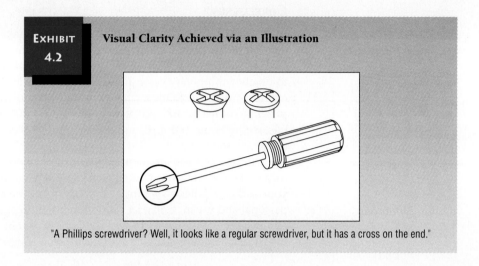

**EXHIBIT 4.2**

**Visual Clarity Achieved via an Illustration**

"A Phillips screwdriver? Well, it looks like a regular screwdriver, but it has a cross on the end."

**Effective communication is concise, getting to the point with the minimum number of words.**

If you want to communicate effectively, get to the point. Never use a long word when a short word will do. Omit excessive adjectives and adverbs. Use primarily short, simple sentences and active verbs. Consider the following example:

> Wordy: "We will be able to effectuate this plan as soon as we are cognizant of courses of action necessary to utilize its triple components in correlation with our current production line."

> Concise: "We can put this plan into effect as soon as we determine how to fit its three steps into our current production line."

The problem with the wordy version is that it is not specific; what are the components? In addition, *utilize* and *effectuate* can easily be replaced by simpler words.

> Wordy: "Notwithstanding its past position, the city will give its eager countenance to eradicate Hildegard Machinery's indefensible hindering of the enforcement of the new waste disposal ordinance; and this will enable, not just this city, but the entire country, to benefit from laws pertaining to illegal dumping of hazardous waste."

> Concise: "Although it ignored illegal dumping of hazardous waste in the past, the city will not allow Hildegard Machinery to block enforcement of the new waste disposal regulation. This decision should help in the nationwide effort to prevent illegal dumping."

The original version is too long and difficult to understand. Many of the words should be replaced by simpler words. Also, the original is too emotional for business writing.

**Try to use short paragraphs instead of long ones.**

In addition to using concise wording in sentences, you should compose concise paragraphs. Long paragraphs discourage the reader, because they look difficult or are tedious to read. Good goals for business letters and memos are to write paragraphs of no more than four or five typed lines, and never use two pages when one page will do.

## CORRECTNESS

Being correct is essential in business communication.

In business communication, you must always make sure that all details in the message are correct. For one thing, wrong information may cause confusion or lead to bad decisions. Wrong information could also bind you or your company to do something very costly, because a written document may be considered a contract. Michelle Johnson, for example, wanted to order 6,000 labels from a printing company. Instead of writing 6M (6,000) on the purchase order, she mistakenly wrote 6MM (6 million). Instead of $19, she had to pay $3,692 for the labels she ordered.

One of the most frequent errors in correspondence is incorrectly spelling names. People are very particular about their names, so it would be wise for you to double-check spelling. Correctly using names makes a message more personal and warm. Consider the following excerpt from a form letter soliciting money for a well-known charity. The letter was sent to Constance Martinez, the owner of a company named Colorado Plateau Mining and Logging Corporation:

| | |
|---|---|
| Inside address | Mr. Colo Plat Min Log |
| | P.O. Box 1938 |
| | Farmington, NM 87401 |
| Salutation | Dear Mr. Log: |

Constance Martinez, although amused, did not contribute to the charity. She reasoned that the mistake was probably just another case of a computer entry operator asleep at the keyboard. Nevertheless, the letter did not seem like the sincere plea for a worthwhile cause its writer intended it to be.

To achieve favorable reactions and avoid creating costly problems, your messages must be correct in every detail.

## COMPLETENESS

A business message must provide all the information that the other person wants or needs to know.

The fifth of the Six C's is completeness. Your messages, written and spoken, must be complete; they should leave no questions unanswered. Plan your messages to make sure your readers get all the information they want or need to know. Do you think the following message is complete?

> Please send me information about your resort and your cabins for rent. In addition, it would be appreciated if you would reserve a cabin for the next school vacation. Please include pictures. Thank you for sending this information as soon as possible.

Imagine the frustration of the reservations clerk attempting to meet this request. Dates of school vacations vary, so reserving a cabin for the right dates would be a lucky guess. Also, rates vary at most resorts, depending on the season. To be more complete, the letter should have specified arrival and departure dates, the number of people who would be staying in the cabin, the number of beds or rooms needed, the types of pictures and other information that should be sent, payment information (charge card number or a cash deposit), and the date by which the letter writer would like to receive a reply.

The business communicator who wants to show consideration for readers or listeners and their needs will provide all the information necessary for the readers or communicators to do their jobs. An incomplete request has a good chance of winding up in the round file we commonly call "the trashcan."

## CONSIDERATION

The most important of the Six C's is consideration.

Consideration means understanding the other person's motives and designing a message that meets his or her needs.

The sixth C—consideration of your reader's needs, beliefs, and values—is the most vital element for designing messages that get results. Of all the Six C's, this principle is the most complex and the most important. Abraham Lincoln expressed the importance of consideration best:

> Whatever men do, they do in response to motives. Discover the motives that cause them to act, and you can make them do your bidding.

Knowledge of the motives, or reasons, that cause people to act as they do is as important to personal success today as it was in Lincoln's time. Whether you are selling a good or service, influencing people to think and believe as you do, or persuading them to do things your way, you must first understand their motives and then convince them that your message will benefit them. People probably won't be convinced if you focus your message on your own needs.

Can you imagine someone deciding to buy a car just to help the salesperson meet a monthly sales quota? The buyer expects to get something out of the deal—save money, get better mileage, appear more successful to others, get reliable transportation, protect loved ones, or appease any one of a hundred other motives or combinations of motives. Good salespeople know they must point out these benefits to their customers; they don't make customers figure out these benefits for themselves.

In delivering your business messages, you must use many of the same techniques that good salespeople and advertisers employ. You must spend time considering the needs of the other person so you will be able to point out how buying your product, accepting and acting on your ideas, or simply hiring you for a job will satisfy the other person's needs.

## MASLOW'S HIERARCHY OF NEEDS

Maslow's hierarchy of needs is one way of identifying what motivates people.

Communication experts have been trying for decades to come up with easy ways to explain what motivates people to think and act as they do. One popular theory, proposed by Abraham Maslow, is the **hierarchy of needs.** At the simplest level, it suggests that everyone needs something and discovering that need will help you form a message that the other person will listen to and perhaps act on. The hierarchy of needs cannot explain everything that motivates people, but it has helped many communicators design messages that get results.

### UNDERSTANDING THE HIERARCHY OF NEEDS

Describe the five levels of the hierarchy of needs.

A person whose lower-level needs have not been met cannot concentrate on higher-level needs.

As stated earlier, people who are reading or listening to your message want an answer to the question "What's in it for me?" To answer this question, you must determine what they need or want. The hierarchy of needs, diagrammed in Exhibit 4.3, specifies five categories. The needs at the base are the strongest and must be satisfied before appeals to higher-level needs will work. For example, a thirsty person will search for water (a physiological need) and let his or her need for friendship (a belonging need) wait. It is only when that person is no longer thirsty that he or she will attempt to satisfy other needs. Have you ever

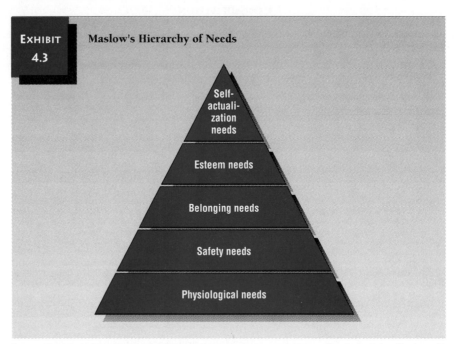

**Exhibit 4.3** — Maslow's Hierarchy of Needs

Self-actualization needs

Esteem needs

Belonging needs

Safety needs

Physiological needs

Source: Data based on Hierarchy of Needs from *Motivation and Personality*, 3rd ed. by Abraham H. Maslow. Revised by Robert Frager, James Fadiman, Cynthia McReynolds, and Ruth Cox. Copyright 1954, © 1987 by Harper & Row, Publishers, Inc. Copyright © 1970 by Abraham H. Maslow. Reprinted by permission of HarperCollins Publishers, Inc.

noticed that as you grow hungry, your attention in class wanders? Even though your education is important to you, a more basic need has taken over.

These are the five categories of needs in Maslow's hierarchy (listed here from most basic to most refined).

*Maslow's hierarchy of needs has five categories.*

**PHYSIOLOGICAL NEEDS.**   We are always trying to overcome our concern with these needs, which deal with basic survival. Physiological needs include hunger, thirst, comfort (shelter, some clothing), air to breathe, and reproduction.

**SAFETY NEEDS.**   Some of the safety needs that advertisers frequently appeal to are freedom from fear, danger, and illness; longer life; good health; and predictability. The desire for predictability is also often encountered in the business world, in the form of fear of change. New policies and procedures, the introduction of computers and robots into work sites, and new management all tend to seem especially threatening to employees with strong safety needs. In all these situations, management must "sell" the changes by showing that they do not threaten employees' safety and that they meet other needs of employees.

**BELONGING NEEDS.**   These needs include the desire for social approval, love/contact, affection, acceptance, sexual attraction, well being of loved ones, family closeness, camaraderie, friendship, and identity with certain groups. Many people are motivated to pay a lot of money for designer clothing just because other people important to them wear clothes by that designer. Such individuals fear that they will be rejected by the group to which they belong or wish to belong if they do not wear the right clothing. If you were attempting to sell another line of clothing to these individuals, you would have to convince them that the clothes would make them perhaps even more readily accepted by their peers. Another tactic would be to combine appeals, or to appeal to the next higher level on the hierarchy. Appealing to their desire to be a trend setter (an esteem need) rather than just to follow the crowd (a belonging need) might convince these individuals to buy your clothing.

**ESTEEM NEEDS.**    Examples of esteem needs include superiority over others, power over others, identifying with prestigious groups (as opposed to groups that satisfy our belonging needs), self-worth, self-indulgence, image-building motives, quality, and desire for the best or the most expensive. For example, expensive automobiles make some people feel superior to others, or they might satisfy a desire to possess something of quality or something that is the best or the most expensive. Advertisers and good salespeople are also aware that many individuals buy expensive cars because doing so makes them feel better about themselves (self-worth), giving them an "I work hard; I deserve it" attitude.

**SELF-ACTUALIZATION NEEDS.**    Examples of self-actualization needs include aesthetic needs, the desire to know and understand, things that promote health (as opposed to fear of illness), truth, beauty, goodness, perfection, simplicity, comprehensiveness, freedom, independence, being the best you can be, being in tune with nature and with yourself, going as far as you can go, doing things on your own, and the need for emotional or intellectual growth (as opposed to physical growth). You have undoubtedly experienced the motivational force provided by your own need for self-actualization. Have you ever walked along the beach at sundown just to see the beauty of the sun setting on the ocean? Have you ever continued to work on an assignment far beyond the effort needed to get a good grade—for no other reason than you wanted it to be perfect? Do you ever eat a salad just because you want to be healthy, not because you want to look better to others? If so, you understand the desire to satisfy self-actualization needs.

The first four levels of needs—physiological, safety, belonging, and esteem needs—motivate us when we are deprived of them. For example, when we feel that others don't respect us, we can be motivated by someone who appeals to our need for esteem. Conversely, when we feel that we have enough esteem, those same appeals lose their power over us. The need for self-actualization, however, is motivating whether or not we already feel self-actualized. These needs are continuous, neverending; we do not try to rid ourselves of these needs, because they make us feel good about ourselves. They tend to make us self-directed and independent, and we continually desire to fulfill them.

The first four levels of needs are most motivating when they are missing from our lives; the highest-level needs motivate whether they are missing or not.

## USING THE HIERARCHY OF NEEDS

Use the hierarchy of needs to determine which benefits to emphasize in a business message.

Maslow's hierarchy of needs includes only the most commonly recognized categories. Because motivators differ from one individual to another and from one culture to another, the groupings can be used only as a general guide to human motivation. For example, depending on the individual, education may be a safety need (a college degree will protect you from poverty and an uncertain future), a belonging need (everyone else who matters to you has a degree or is going to school), an esteem need (you want to feel superior to others who do not have a degree), or a self-actualization need (you want to know and understand the world around you, or you have the need to test yourself and your abilities).

**Most business messages require appeals to more than one need.**

Using the hierarchy of needs may seem simple: All you have to do is figure out at which level your reader or listener is operating. However, communication experts usually have to appeal to combinations of motives to convince message recipients of what's in it for them. Many messages are directed to groups of people, each of whom has her or his own motive. For example, someone writing a form letter to convince students it is valuable to complete a degree would have to appeal to the variety of motives that people have for going to college.

**An individual's needs often conflict.**

Another complication is that individuals often have conflicting motives. For example, when presented with a new, uncertain situation, one person may want to hang onto the past, out of the need for safety, but also want to explore new opportunities, out of the need for self-actualization. Examples of this conflict can be seen daily in the business world. Have you ever known anyone who turned down an offer of a better job or someone who did not apply for a promotion when there was a good chance of getting it? Very often these are the same people who complain that they are never given the chance they need to get ahead. Although they may believe the new position would help satisfy some of their personal needs, the risks involved in accepting or trying for the job are overpowering.

**Deciding which motivators to use in a business message is a three-step process.**

To use the hierarchy of needs in your own communication, follow these steps:

1. Determine the need level at which your readers or listeners are probably operating in regard to your particular idea or product.

2. Determine which motivators can be used to convince your readers or listeners, and consider conflicting motives.

3. Determine which of the motivators you will actually use in your message.

Imagine that you must write a memo to encourage employees to carpool or take the bus to work. Construction of a multilevel parking garage on a company-owned parking lot will soon begin. There are about 452 employee vehicles, but there will be only 264 parking spaces available during the construction, which is estimated to take 11 months. Once completed, the new parking garage will add 400 new spaces, so the problem is only temporary.

In the first step, you decide that you need to consider all five types of motivators in planning your memo, because it is directed to hundreds of people. The second step, determining which specific motivators you can possibly use, creates a sizable list:

- *Physiological needs:* Freedom from the stress of having to drive your own car in rush-hour traffic.
- *Safety needs:* Freedom from danger, because of the excellent safety record of city buses (caution: some readers may consider riding city buses and waiting at bus stops to be dangerous); predictability, because of the excellent time record of city buses (caution: some readers may feel that relying on others is always risky); and freedom from the risk of not finding a parking space and, therefore, being late to work and angering your boss (caution: an implied threat could make some readers resentful).

- *Belonging needs:* Social approval, friendship, acceptance, and "family" closeness.
- *Esteem needs:* Superiority over others, identity with certain groups.
- *Self-actualization needs:* Independence (caution: reliance on others for transportation may not appear to fulfill the need for independence); justice, through helping to reduce societal problems, such as pollution and traffic congestion; simplicity, through not having to worry about car expenses or deal with limited parking spaces; and fun and play, through rewards for all who carpool or take a bus.

In the third step, determining which of the motivators you will use, you might decide to focus on belonging, esteem, and self-actualization needs, which present fewer potential conflicts than physiological and safety needs do. These are the specific tactics you might choose to address each need:

- *Belonging:* To serve the need for social approval, friendship, and acceptance, you will get supervisors and groups of workers to endorse the campaign, reward the employees who carpool or ride the bus, and send thank-you notes to these employees. In your memo, you will stress the opportunity to meet new people by carpooling or taking the bus. To address the need for "family" closeness, your memo will stress that all the employees are facing this problem together and are working together to solve it.
- *Esteem:* To serve some employees' need to feel superior to others, you decide to give visible rewards to those who carpool or take the bus, such as pins or desk signs saying something like "I'm helping; I carpool"; another option is to publish their names in the company newsletter. To address the need to identify with prestigious groups, your memo will mention that those who carpool or take the bus are part of the group that is helping to solve the company's problems.
- *Self-actualization:* You decide that you can appeal to the need for simplicity by giving carpoolers special parking places. You can serve the need for fun and play by starting a license plate lottery among the cars parked in the carpool area, with cash rewards for winners.

The three-step process of applying Maslow's hierarchy of needs thus allows you to write a memo that answers the question "What's in it for me?" Once you determine the motives of the people with whom you deal, you can then phrase your message to show them you have considered their needs.

**Advertisers are good at analyzing people's needs and designing messages that use those needs as motivators.**

If you want more hints about using people's needs to make your messages more effective, study advertisements. Advertisers are good at using our needs, beliefs, and values to sell us products. You can adopt some of their techniques for motivating your own readers and listeners to "buy" your ideas or products. Take a few minutes now to read Exhibit 4.4, which shows numerous examples of how Maslow's hierarchy can be used to sell products and concepts.

## THE YOU ATTITUDE

**Good communicators adopt the "you" attitude and address the reader's or listener's needs in every message.**

▪ Phrase messages so they are you oriented.

The **"you" attitude** is the viewpoint that the reader's or listener's needs must be addressed in any business message. For example, a salesperson who has adopted the "you" attitude would not try to sell an expensive sports car to a couple who have stated they are looking for an inexpensive family car. A day

**EXHIBIT 4.4**

**Motivating Others by Assessing Their Needs**

| ■ Maslow's Levels | ■ Motivators | ■ Product and Concept Examples* |
|---|---|---|
| Physiological needs | Food and drink—the enjoyment of appetizing and satisfying food and drink | All food, drinks, snacks |
| | Comfort—the enjoyment of comfortable clothes, home, and surroundings | Clothes, shoes, homes, cars, furniture, mattresses, offices, theaters, room temperature, outdoor temperature, laxatives, decongestants |
| Safety needs | Freedom from fear and danger—elimination of fearful, painful, dangerous things | Burglar alarms, guns, self-defense lessons, pain relievers, well-constructed cars, self-inflating airbags in cars, motorcycle helmets, smoke alarms, personal medical and disability insurance, career selection, good grades, completion of courses/degrees, bargains, economy, profit |
| | Longer life and good health—the benefits of a long, healthy life; anything that prevents illness | Regular doctor and dentist visits, retirement homes, stress relievers, aerobics classes and gyms (if the motive is to prevent illness), vitamins, cleanliness, religion (for the purpose of preparing for life after death) |
| | Predictability—freedom from the threat of change | Job and financial security; stable investments; brand name, store and company name reliability and quality; stable family life; dependability. Needs are threatened by changes in supervisors, co-workers, and company policies and procedures; introduction of computers and other automated equipment; layoffs; rumors; company mergers and takeovers |
| Belonging needs | Social approval, friendship, and acceptance—the benefits of being part of a group or groups, acceptance by and affection of friends and associates, contact with others | Designer clothing, hair styles, cars favored by certain groups, alcohol sold with friendship appeal, soaps, shampoos, deodorants, country club memberships, some gym memberships (if not for safety or self-actualization), special-interest clubs (singles, model airplanes, political groups), participation in company social activities (happy hours, parties, bowling teams), records, plastic surgery, homes in certain areas, religious groups (if not for self-actualization or safety), grades, competitive sports |
| | Sexual attraction—the benefits of companionship, love, affection of and contact with desired mate, desirability | Cleanliness, perfumes, provocative clothing, some cars, some vacation resorts, restaurants with romantic settings, tobacco products, alcohol, diet and exercise programs, records, plastic surgery |
| | Welfare of loved ones and family closeness—provisions for the welfare of family and other loved ones | Life and medical insurance; some cars bought for family members; education; books; some games (those promoting family participation); purchases of some food, vitamins, and other products for one's family; funeral plots, caskets, and funerals; company attempts to promote a feeling of familylike closeness among employees; computers bought for children; family counseling; textbooks carefully chosen to help students |

| ■ Maslow's Levels | ■ Motivators | ■ Product and Concept Examples* |
|---|---|---|
| Esteem needs | Superiority over others—the advantages of being viewed as better than others | Designer clothing; some services (certain hairdressers, doctors, psychiatrists; limousines), college degrees (may also be self-actualization, belonging, or safety needs), grades, company programs that acknowledge special accomplishments of employees, some cars, expensive and/or exclusive jewelry, expensive weddings, college rings, products that have a reputation for unsurpassed quality and/or unsurpassed expense, status symbols of all kinds, homes in certain areas, some charitable contributions (if not for belonging or self-actualization needs), career selection |
| | Power over others—the advantages of being able to exercise power over others and to make others follow our orders | Job titles, office locations and furniture, number of employees under one's control, political office and some leadership positions (if not for self-actualization), career selection |
| | Identity with certain groups—the benefits of membership in groups that others look up to (as opposed to membership in groups that satisfy belonging needs) | Some sororities and fraternities; selective social organizations, being named to elite employee groups (employee of the month awards, sales awards determined by total dollar of sales), some country club memberships, participation in charitable organizations (if not for self-actualization), political office and some leadership positions (if not for self-actualization), some charitable contributions |
| | Desire for quality, the best, the most, or the most expensive—the esteem to be gained from possessing or producing a quality product, of having the best or the most of something, or having others know one possesses expensive items | Products or companies that have a reputation for quality or are reputed to be the best or the most expensive (quality may also be a self-actualization or a belonging need for some people), procedures that promote quality or accuracy, items that complete collections |
| | Image-building motives—the value of anything that fits into the image people have of themselves as well as the image they want others to have of them | Any product, idea, or concept that reinforces an individual's image of himself or herself (note: this image may not be realistic; it is often the person the individual would really like to be), luxury items, all esteem items, items sold with a self-actualization appeal that instead appeal to esteem needs, career selection |
| Self-actualization needs | Aesthetic needs—the benefits to oneself of being surrounded by beautiful things | Art, music, landscaping, homes, interior decorating, remodeling |
| | Independence—the benefits to oneself of being able to make personal decisions; to be self-directed, self-reliant, and separate from others; to do as one pleases | Cars, secluded retreats, divorce, separation from family, positions that allow for independence and personal control, courses teaching skills that once required reliance on others (automechanics, keyboarding) |

| ■ Maslow's Levels | ■ Motivators | ■ Product and Concept Examples* |
|---|---|---|
| | Desire to know and to understand—the advantages to oneself of knowing and understanding the nature of concepts and ideas, self-enlightenment | Many magazines and books, education, some television programs, religion, information, curiosity feedback (knowledge of how one is doing) |
| | Things that promote health—the value to oneself of eating right or doing things that promote personal health (as opposed to fear of illness) to allow one to enjoy all life has to offer | Health food, sports activities (if not for belonging needs), jogging, orthopedic shoes, company fitness programs (if not for belonging needs), regular medical care, vitamins, well-rounded diets |
| | Growth—the benefits of being the best you can be, being in tune with nature and yourself, going as far as you can go, the need to test oneself | Challenging activities or tasks [learning to operate a new piece of equipment or software (if not required for the job), wilderness camping, raft trips, scuba diving, high-powered sports cars], many personal goal-setting activities (jogging times, sales and production quotas, new work responsibilities, some job promotions) |
| | Justice—the benefits to oneself of doing what is just, of seeing that justice is done | Charitable contributions and causes, some political activities, career selection, letter-writing campaigns to influence change, petition-signing campaigns, investigative reporting, affirmative action and equal opportunity programs |
| | Perfection/comprehensiveness—the value to oneself of possessing or achieving perfection and comprehensive knowledge, abilities, or collections | Complete collections (stamps, coins, pottery), finishing (some people do not need to finish what they have started), editing written work, intensive and in-depth study of concepts beyond that needed to fulfill other needs |
| | Goodness and truth—the advantages to oneself of achieving a state of goodness, of finding and knowing the truth | Living in a state of harmony with one's beliefs and values, investigative reporting, comprehensive study of concepts beyond those needed to fulfill other needs, religious beliefs, scientific concepts not readily observable |
| | Simplicity—the benefits to oneself of living as simply as possible, of returning to nature, of making one's life simple and efficient | Return-to-nature items, home gardens, homemade crafts, home cooking, restructuring of complex company organizational structures, some interior decorating, some furniture, some art, some lifestyles, efficiency, convenience, textbooks with answer keys and transparencies |
| | Fun/play—the benefits to oneself of playing, of enjoying life by having fun | Games, certain cars, some sports activities, television sets, stereos, Disneyland, movies, vacations—anything an individual finds enjoyable or fun that does not fulfill other needs |

*People are motivated to buy products for different reasons; therefore, the categorization and concepts may differ from one individual to another. Because of this, some products and concepts appear in more than one need level.

care center operator who has the you attitude should, without waiting to be asked, assure working parents that they can pick up their children later than usual on days when they must work late.

The you attitude is not a difficult concept. If you are good at convincing people to buy your products, agree with your ideas, or stop arguing and start listening, you are probably already using the you attitude. You have learned that your messages get the best results when you are thinking in terms of other people's needs.

To polish your skills, you can adopt some specific techniques for phrasing business messages that will demonstrate your interest in your readers and listeners. One is to make good use of the words *you* and *your*. Another is to use positive words and phrases instead of negative ones. A third is to rely on confidence, not sarcasm, to send strong messages that are still you oriented.

Certain types of wording can demonstrate the you attitude.

### YOU AND YOUR

In general, use the second-person pronouns you and your instead of first-person pronouns like I and we.

In most situations, one of the easiest ways to show that you have the you attitude is to use more *you* and *your* pronouns and fewer *I, me, my, we,* and *our* pronouns. Here are some examples of how your choice of words can help you demonstrate the you attitude:

I oriented: "We shipped your order today." (Emphasizes the writer and the company by putting we" first; deemphasizes the reader and the good news by placing them at the end of the sentence.)

You oriented: "Your order No. 4845B was shipped today." (Focuses on what the reader wants to know—the good news and the order that the message refers to—and emphasizes *you*, the reader, by placing it at the beginning of the sentence.)

I oriented: "I want to take this opportunity to congratulate you on your promotion." (Places more emphasis on the writer than on the person being congratulated, even though it does use two you-oriented pronouns.)

You oriented: "Congratulations on your promotion."

Even more you oriented: "Congratulations! Your promotion is certainly well deserved." (Places more emphasis on the individual's need for esteem, to be looked up to by others.)

Use of the you attitude combines easily with use of Maslow's hierarchy of needs. For example, the management of one company had to compose a memo to 42 employees whose offices were being moved to another building because of overcrowding in the existing facilities. Many of these people did not want to move, but they had no choice. Management's job was to explain how the move might actually be to the employees' benefit. Management was aware that people are often afraid of change (Maslow's safety need) and that many employees might not want to be separated from their friends remaining in the old building (Maslow's belonging need). To address the safety need, management let the affected employees know that all policies, procedures, department supervisors, and so on would remain the same. However, management decided to bypass the belonging need and instead concentrate on the need for esteem. To serve that need, management would give something to the displaced employees that the other employees would envy: new furniture and a beautiful environment. Two sentences in the memo showed management's attention to the employees' needs:

Your new, spacious offices in the Cooper Building have been furnished with stylish new furniture. The desert sand, peach, and turquoise colors and the Southwestern decorating scheme used throughout the building have created an exciting, yet peaceful environment in which to spend your day.

Notice how the you-oriented phrasing complements the considerate planning behind the memo.

You have probably noticed that many messages place too much emphasis on the company instead of the reader or listener. The name of the company may be typed in capital letters and used over and over again:

I oriented: "HALFARE AND BRIMSTONE has expanded its inventory of home remodeling supplies." (Focuses on the company; forces readers to figure out for themselves how a larger inventory will benefit them; has a highly impersonal tone.)

You oriented: "You will be glad to know that Halfare and Brimstone now has all the material you need to make your remodeling job simple." (Gets to the point by telling readers specifically how they can use this good news; makes the company name secondary to the reader's interests; uses a more personal tone.)

Sometimes the you-oriented communicator must avoid *you* and *your* pronouns. What is said, not the way it is said, is the main consideration. If you ask a teacher how you did on the last test, she might gladly announce, "You got an A!" However, if you did not pass the test, the teacher would not say "You got an F!" Instead, a teacher who is good at using the you attitude would say something more neutral, such as "The grade was an F." Taking the word *you* out of the sentence makes the bad news easier to accept.

Here are some more examples of when avoiding *you* and *your* is actually the more tactful, you-oriented approach:

Insulting: "Your mistake in your checking account will cost you $15."

Tactful: "Returned checks result in a charge of $15."

Even when we have made a mistake, we don't like to be told that we have done so. It is also more tactful to leave out the pronoun when mentioning that the other person has to pay a fine. The tactful sentence is less personal and, therefore, easier for the other person to accept.

Insulting: "You must see why we cannot allow you to pay for this order on credit. You haven't been in business long enough to establish a credit record."

Tactful: "Credit terms are available for customers who have done business on a cash basis for at least six months. We would be happy to send this merchandise to you as soon as a check for the amount of the order is received. At the end of the six-month cash period, please resubmit your request for credit. We enjoy doing business with up-and-coming firms such as yours."

The sarcastic, lecturing tone of the first version will offend the reader, who would not have asked for credit if she or he had expected to be turned down. The less personal, passive tone in the tactful version gets the meaning across without insulting the reader. Obviously, the reader is not going to get credit

**Avoid using *you* and *your* when you are giving bad news or explaining the other person's mistake.**

terms now; however, the upbeat and eager tone lets the reader down easily without closing the door to future business.

## A POSITIVE OUTLOOK

A positive, pleasant approach is also an important part of the you attitude. It is human nature to avoid negatives. If you are like most people, you probably avoid people who complain about everything and try to surround yourself with positive people who make you feel good.

The following sales message was broadcast on a radio station. Imagine yourself as an employer listening to this sales appeal:

> Nobody needs to tell you that you are responsible for the employees who work for you. If you don't provide medical insurance for them, who will? Any sensible person knows what happens when people don't have medical insurance. They don't go to the doctor until it's too late to do much for them; their children are not taken care of properly; their average life span is 5 to 10 years less than the life span of employees whose companies provide a medical insurance plan. Don't do this to your employees! An American Insurance Co. employee medical plan takes the worry out of employer–employee relations and lets you sleep at night!

Although guilt might occasionally motivate people to take action, it usually is not an appropriate way to sell a product or an idea. Guilt is negative, and it makes people feel bad about themselves. People are more likely to stop listening to avoid guilt than they are to rush out to buy medical insurance for their employees.

People are more likely to pay attention to positive messages than to negative messages.

Here's another message from the same company that is more positive and, thus, more likely to bring results:

> Research reveals that you can cut the rate of absenteeism in your company by as much as 46 percent. Think of the thousands of dollars you could save and the increased production possible by doing nothing more than providing a low-cost American Insurance Co. medical plan for your employees. For pennies a day, you can have a healthier, more productive staff.

The promise of profit is not the only way to sell a medical insurance plan to employers, but it works much better than a negative, guilt-ridden sermon.

Replace negative words with positive ones.

By the same token, most of us prefer to read and hear positive words, such as *pleasant, encouraging, skilled, energetic, beautiful, meaningful, happy, kind, slender, good, bargain, value,* and *friendly*. We avoid negative words, such as *angry, hopeless, discouraging, stupid, ugly, meaningless, mean, cruel, fat, cheap, crook, liar,* and *unhappy*. It is wise, then, to avoid negative words when writing or speaking to others. Substitute positive words whenever possible to give your messages a tone to which people will respond positively.

The following examples show how easy it is to change a negative sentence into a positive one:

Negative: "It is not difficult to use the you attitude."

Positive: "It is easy to use the you attitude."

Negative: "Be sure not to miss the next issue of *The Insider*."

Positive: "Be sure to read the next issue of *The Insider*."

Positive and you oriented: "The next issue of *The Insider* includes an article on how to ask your employer for a raise."

Talk about what you can do rather than what you can't do.

Too often we emphasize what we cannot do rather than what we can. To make people more receptive to your messages, emphasize the positive:

Negative: "You won't ever say you're sorry you bank with Bank of America."

Positive: "You will receive friendlier service and more account options when you bank with Bank of America."

Negative: "We cannot send your home loan package to the loan officers for review until you complete all the information on the enclosed application form. You did not provide all the information requested on the form. Fill in all the blanks."

Positive: "Please provide the information marked by the red *X* on the enclosed application form. Once your completed home loan application is received, it will be rushed to the loan officers for immediate review."

## CONFIDENCE

An angry, abusive message is unlikely to get results.

It is easy to use *you, your,* and positive wording when you have a pleasant or neutral message; it is much harder when your message is unpleasant. Harder still is keeping up a you attitude when you are annoyed or angry with the other person. A message like the following is all too tempting:

Please let me know when I may expect to hear from you about the insurance information I requested three long months ago. It appears you do not want my business. Believe me, your company is not the *only* one that sells car insurance. If you can't bring yourself to send the information within ONE WEEK (that's seven days!!!) of the date of this letter, I will be forced to report your "excellent service" to the **State Department of Insurance.**

How would you like to receive this message? Would it make you feel motivated to help the writer? A person who is the target of sarcasm never appreciates it. Notice in this example how mechanical means of emphasis—such as underlining, capitalization, punctuation, and boldface—can impart a sarcastic tone to writing as easily as the words themselves can. Even if you were at fault for not getting the information to the letter writer sooner, it is unlikely that this sarcastic letter would make you react any faster. The offensive tone would probably only make you feel angry.

Confidence, assertiveness, and courtesy often succeed where sarcasm and hostility fail.

This revision would be more likely to produce the result the individual wants:

Please send the information requested in my June 14 letter. As you may recall, I would appreciate your sending me a price breakdown on the following for Policy No. 465-77-8430:

- Increased liability coverage—$50,000 per vehicle, $200,000 per accident.
- Decreased collision deductible—$100.

Your sending this information with one week of the date of this letter will give me time to add the better coverage when the policy is renewed. Please call me at (213) 555-4336 if you have questions.

Most people would react immediately to a request such as this. It is courteous, yet assertive, and it implies that the writer still intends to do business with the company despite the error. Confident, sincere wording makes the deadline easier to accept.

You can be direct and still be polite.

Sometimes, in an attempt to compose courteous, "you"-oriented messages, we try too hard to soften a tough message. It is better for the communication process, and for business, to confidently explain the problem and expect your reasonable needs to be met.

**Do not take the blame for the other person's mistakes; project confidence.**

Also, you are not required to make excuses when people fail to do what you asked of them. In the United States and many other countries, excusing someone else's mistakes is often interpreted as a sign of weakness. Consider this example:

> Please excuse my bothering you with this second request for information about increased coverage on my insurance policy. I probably did not make myself clear in the first letter I sent to you three months ago. If it isn't too much trouble, would you please send me as soon as possible a price breakdown on an increase to $50,000/$200,000 coverage for liability and a decreased deductible of $100?

Most people would not react positively to this letter, and they certainly would not react immediately. It conveys no sense of urgency; how soon is *as soon as possible?* The groveling tone makes the writer appear to be weak; and it is, unfortunately, human nature to take advantage of the weak. A positive, assertive, confident tone, combined with "you"-oriented statements, is more likely to get positive results.

## DISCUSSION QUESTIONS

⬛ Explain the link between psychology and communication.

1. Why is it important to understand the psychology of communication?

⬛ Define and explain the Six C's.

2. Name and briefly describe the Six C's.

⬛ Define and explain the Six C's.

3. Why is the sixth C, consideration, said to be the basis for the other five C's?

⬛ Define and explain the Six C's.

4. Name at least three ways in which you can show courtesy to the reader of your letter or memo.

⬛ Define and explain the Six C's.

5. How do correct grammar, spelling, and punctuation help the person who receives a message?

⬛ Define and explain the Six C's.

6. "Write not to impress, but to express." What does this statement mean, and how does it relate to the Six C's?

⬛ Define and explain the Six C's.

7. Why is it so important to spell your reader's name correctly? Name at least three sources for checking the spelling of a person's name.

⬛ Define and explain the Six C's.

8. How does knowledge of motives contribute to your ability to communicate successfully in business?

■ Describe the five levels of the hierarchy of needs.

9. Name and describe briefly the five levels of Maslow's hierarchy of needs.

■ Use the hierarchy of needs to determine which benefits to emphasize in a business message.

10. Which of Maslow's needs motivate best when people feel deprived of them? Why?

■ Use the hierarchy of needs to determine which benefits to emphasize in a business message.

11. Which of Maslow's needs are continuous (we do not try to rid ourselves of them)? Why?

■ Phrase messages so they are you oriented.

12. Define the you attitude.

■ Phrase messages so they are you oriented.

13. In most situations, which pronouns should you use to show that you have the you attitude? Which should you not use?

■ Phrase messages so they are you oriented.

14. Why is it better to use positive words instead of negative words?

■ Phrase messages so they are you oriented.

15. List 10 positive words and 10 negative words.

■ Phrase messages so they are you oriented.

16. How are sarcasm and anger revealed in business writing? Discuss the mechanical means of emphasis that should be avoided so as not to suggest sarcasm and anger.

## APPLICATION EXERCISES

■ Explain the link between psychology and communication.

1. At the library, look for information about a theory of motivation other than Maslow's hierarchy of needs. (Hint: Check psychology and introduction to business textbooks.) Write a two- to three-page paper describing the theory, explaining how it differs from Maslow's theory and explaining how it applies to your study of business communication. Be sure to document your sources.

■ Define and explain the Six C's.

2. Find a sales letter in your mail (or ask someone you know to find one for you). Analyze how the letter applies the Six C's, and evaluate its success in each category. For your instructor, write a memo report about the sales letter. Begin with a paragraph evaluating the letter's overall power to motivate you or the intended reader. Do you believe the writer had a good understanding of communication psychology? Then, to defend your

conclusion, write a paragraph about how the letter treats each of the Six C's. Attach the letter (or a copy) to your report. Your instructor will let you know if you will be asked to present your findings to the class.

◆ Describe the five levels of the hierarchy of needs.

3.  Choose three advertisements from magazines or newspapers. For each one, name the need or needs used to motivate the reader to buy the advertised product. Consider combinations of motives and conflicting motives. Bring the advertisements to class for discussion.

◆ Describe the five levels of the hierarchy of needs.

4.  Choose two form letters from junk mail you have received (or get two letters from someone you know). For each letter, name the need or needs used to motivate the reader. Consider combinations of motives and conflicting motives. Bring the letters to class for discussion.

◆ Use the hierarchy of needs to determine which benefits to emphasize in a business message.

5.  Follow the three steps for using Maslow's hierarchy and design a campaign to motivate people for each of the situations listed below. Step 1 is to determine the need level at which the reader or listener is probably operating in regard to your particular idea or product. Step 2 is to determine the motivators you can use to convince your reader or listener (be sure to consider combinations of motives and conflicting motives). Step 3 is to determine which of the motivators you will actually use in your message. Write two or three lines to explain how you would use each motivator.
    a.  Convince John Wilson, who has had a bill of $78.47 outstanding for two months, to pay or at least to tell you when he will pay. You have already sent him two reminders.
    b.  Convince the chief administrator of your school to buy five new computers for your classroom.
    c.  Persuade your state representative to support a bill that will more than triple the monies available for scholarships to students like you.
    d.  Convince your boss that you deserve a $2 per hour raise in pay.
    e.  Encourage all company employees to use the gym facilities that the company has made available. Research shows that people who are in good shape are absent from work less, use company-paid medical insurance less, and in general perform better on the job. However, very few of the company's employees have taken advantage of the gym facilities. The company has decided to extend gym privileges not only to employees but to their families as well.
    f.  Encourage your co-workers (or students) to donate blood in a company- (or school-) sponsored blood drive.
    g.  Convince a heavy smoker to stop smoking.
    h.  Ask an advertising agency to tell you which motivators or appeals they used in a successful advertisement or commercial. (Because most agencies do not want to reveal their secrets, you will probably have to convince the agency that you will use the information only for your own education.)

    *i.*  Ask a teacher whom you admire (or a former employer or co-worker) to write a letter of recommendation for you. You plan to use this letter to get a good job you just read about.

◣ Phrase messages so they are you oriented.

6.  Analyze what is wrong with each of the following sentences, and then rewrite it. Each violates one or more of the following principles: the you attitude, the positive approach, clarity, conciseness, spelling, or grammar. You may be creative in your rewriting as long as you retain the meaning of the original sentence.

  *a.*  We pay 5 3/4 percent on our passbook savings accounts.

  *b.*  We cannot quote you a price until we have seen the specifications.

  *c.*  I invite you to attend a special reception we are sponsoring.

  *d.*  I want to meet with you at 10 AM tomorrow if it is possible.

  *e.*  I am sending you a copy of our new brochure.

  *f.*  In reference to your letter of January 17, we must strongly request reconsideration of your intent to file a friend-of-the-court brief pursuant to the Supreme Court's in the *Findley* v. *California State University* tenure case.

  *g.*  I want you to be at your desk on time from now on.

  *h.*  Do not hesitate to call us if you have any questions.

  *i.*  It is against compny polcy to accept returns for merchandise purchased at our end-of-the-summer sale.

  *j.*  Don't waste money on overpriced brands.

  *k.*  We are in receipt of your order and letter of correspondence, which we received on Tuesday, November 27.

  *l.*  We're very sorry; but, as you know, mistakes are bound to occur.

  *m.*  We have it before us, its contents noted, and herewith enclosed are the prices you requested.

  *n.*  I specifically told you to prepare and mail *all* the 1099 forms *before* you did the billing! You *never* do what you're told!

  *o.*  We are sorry, but we must refuse your request.

  *p.*  I am pleased to announce that Marcia Bonottino, the president of the top training company in the business, has agreed to work with you to improve your ability to train new employees.

  *q.*  As an outstanding leader, I request that you speak to my department heads to improve their leadership skills.

  *r.*  I thank you in advance for sending your contribution to the election fund today.

  *s.*  A short word can be less readable than a long one.

  *t.*  I was reading the newspaper the other day and noticed your ad for a editor. I can do this work; I just know I can.

  *u.*  The picayune obfuscation must be eradicated posthaste.

# CHAPTER 5

# Choosing the Right Words

## Objectives

When you finish studying this chapter, you will be able to:

- Avoid words with offensive connotations.
- Choose specific words rather than vague words, except when vague words serve a purpose.
- Use familiar words in business correspondence.
- Avoid the use of jargon, slang, and colloquialisms.
- Avoid the use of out-of-date and trite expressions, foreign expressions, redundant expressions, and roundabout expressions.
- Recognize and avoid deliberate distortions and euphemisms.
- Use language that does not discriminate on the basis of gender, disability, age, race, religion, ethnicity, or nationality.
- Use positive words as much as possible to avoid negative reactions.
- Use active or passive words when each is most appropriate.
- Choose the writing style most suited to your purpose and your reader.
- Enhance the readability of business messages through attention to word choice, sentence and paragraph structure, and format.

## What Would You Do If...?

**Sticks and Stones.**    Derrick Stone, executive director of human resources for Stickley Construction, Inc., has to make an announcement tomorrow. He has the unpleasant job of telling the news media that 150 of the company's 550 employees will be laid off. The company has lost money for the last nine months, and it must make changes or go bankrupt. Derrick has three goals: to announce the layoffs, to keep up investor confidence by painting the company in a good light, and to raise the morale of the remaining employees. What do you think of his first draft?

Today represents a milestone for Stickley. To further enhance its inherent value, Stickley has undertaken a consolidation of its construction activities into an aggressive workforce management plan. This positive transaction will result in an increase in the market strength of this business segment. A brief period of deficit-based revenue necessitated thorough and in-depth research to identify surpluses and workforce imbalances. Stickley management is proud to announce its strategic plank of volume-related workforce adjustment. This restructuring will enable Stickley to concentrate on increased marketing with an emphasis on quality construction.

Stickley has made the positive decision to streamline by focusing on human resources as a priority area. To build its market share and competitive position, Stickley must disemploy 150 units of its 550-member workforce effective February 1. Identification of affected components is being announced privately today.

To enable an orderly and humane transition, Stickley will provide affected workers with outplacement counseling as a part of its Career Alternative Enhancement Program. A portion of the negative employment goal will be taken care of through early retirement encouragement. Generous separation packages will be provided.

While Stickley is sensitive to the effects of such involuntary leisuring, this step is necessary to enhance the long-term competitiveness of the firm. It will benefit two primary components of Stickley's strength—investors and long-term employees. This protective action of downsizing staff will enable remaining employees to benefit fully from a balanced program of growth and retraction. Stickley employees remain confident of company values that place high priority on the security of long-term employees. A resultant positive cash flow and increased market share will make this a positive termination experience for Stickley's investing public.

If you were Derrick Stone's supervisor, the firm's vice president, would you let him make this announcement? Is a public announcement for the media the best way to handle this news? How well has Derrick achieved his three goals? What evidence do you see of the Six C's (see Chapter 4)? How would you suggest that Derrick rephrase this announcement? Underline the words and phrases you believe will cause negative reactions. Circle the words and phrases that are confusing or misleading. Do you think the overall style of the announcement is a good one? What could Derrick do to make his message more understandable? This chapter will help you answer these questions.

## WORD CHOICE

Chapter 4 introduced you to ways of using your understanding of people to communicate more effectively. You learned that understanding what motivates people to act can help you design business messages that meet the needs of your readers and listeners. As a business communicator, you can do several things to transmit your understanding of people in messages that will achieve your goals. One of the most important is to choose your words carefully, especially when you're writing.

No matter what your message is—whether it is good news or bad news, simple or complex—the words you choose to express it can help you either hurdle over or crash into communication barriers. Good business communication, of course, seeks to overcome barriers. Therefore, you should try to choose words that meet the standards of the Six C's (courtesy, clarity, conciseness, correctness, completeness, and consideration). As you read this section,

| EXHIBIT 5.1 | **Denotations and Connotations** |

### How would you rather be described?

Competitive, fighting, opposing, contentious, combative, aggressive
Pigheaded, stubborn, unyielding, unbending, inflexible, obdurate, willful, insistent, contrary, firm
Antique, moth-eaten, out-of-date, obsolete
Co-worker, teammate, ally, associate, colleague, confederate, collaborator, co-conspirator
Mad, out of your mind, demented, not quite right, not all there, eccentric
Mad, angry, exasperated, foaming at the mouth, in a huff, ticked off
Serious, thoughtful, sober, sad, downcast, dangerous, perilous
Stupid, dull, unintelligent, ill advised, mistaken, inept

### With which would you prefer to be associated?

Cheap, inexpensive, reasonable, underpriced, low quality
Obsession, mania, neurotic conviction, fixation, all-encompassing desire, preoccupation
Money, loot, stash, currency, revenue, specie, dough, bread, medium of exchange

### Which would you rather do?

Check, verify, look over, investigate, probe, scrutinize
Plan, program, strategize, conspire, plot, scheme
Lie, fabricate, equivocate

consider which of the Six C's is addressed by each category of words: denotations, connotations, vague words, specific words, familiar words, jargon, slang, colloquialisms, out-of-date and trite expressions, foreign expressions, redundant expressions, roundabout expressions, deliberate distortions, euphemisms, discriminatory expressions, positive words, negative words, active words, and passive words.

## DENOTATIONS AND CONNOTATIONS

Avoid words with offensive connotations.
Most words have more than one dictionary meaning, or **denotation.** Consider the word *monkey*, which has seven definitions as a noun and four as a verb. The dictionary mentions, among other meanings, the tree-climbing animal, "a monkey on one's back," "don't monkey around with me," "a cute little monkey" (an active but endearing child), and even the monkey that is "the falling element of a pile driver."

Words also develop **connotations,** or the meanings that are not found in dictionaries. Connotative meanings include all the feelings and associations a word evokes. Experience with certain words causes us to react to them in ways that don't match their dictionary definitions. For example, some parents might be offended if you referred to their child as "a cute little monkey," because they do not want their child to be compared to an animal.

Read the lists of synonyms provided in Exhibit 5.1. Although the words in each group have the same denotation, their connotations are quite different. Because of these connotations, some of the synonyms would not be appropriate for business messages.

*Connotations result from our experience with certain words that provoke emotional reactions.*

## VAGUE WORDS AND SPECIFIC WORDS

■ Choose specific words rather than vague words, except when vague words serve a purpose.

Have you ever considered why people read business messages? They want information that they will find useful. Therefore, the words you choose should carry as much meaning as possible, and they should say exactly what you mean to say. Consider the following excerpt from a memo sent by a dean to the business faculty:

> Many of you have asked me about the possibility of the business department moving into new offices and of including personal computers in some of those offices upon completion of the new building. Consideration of this topic was of primary importance at the last meeting of the Dean's Council, when it met to consider this issue.
>
> Adoption of many of your suggestions was considered in depth, and all of them will continue to be discussed in subsequent meetings.

This excerpt suffers from the same lack of specificity as the *What Would You Do If . . . ?* vignette at the beginning of this chapter. Which offices are being considered for new computers? When did the Dean's Council meet? When will the subsequent meetings be held? The memo mentions two issues (the move and the computers), yet the second sentence says that the council considered one issue. Which one? What suggestions were considered? What decisions were made about these suggestions? Which issues are scheduled to be discussed at future meetings?

The memo is so vague that it essentially says nothing. This is what the dean really wanted to say:

> At the November 13 Dean's Council meeting, I presented the department's proposal that it move into new offices in the new building. However, the Council will make no decision until it has heard the proposals from other departments at Council meetings to be held on December 14 and January 12. The Council also discussed what offices will be provided with computer support. Again, no final decisions were made; but most deans seem to favor private computers only for those who teach computer classes, with two computers available in the main office for general faculty use. You may be sure that I will continue to support your proposal and will let you know how the proposal is progressing.

The revised memo is much more specific. It answers all the questions most readers would have; and, by meeting the needs of its readers, it also benefits the writer. Readers who would have confused by the first memo will not have to call or visit the dean for clarification if they receive the second memo.

Vague words confuse people because they are subject to many interpretations. Specific words express intended meaning better than vague words do.

The main drawback of vague, abstract words is that they leave too much room for interpretation. What you might consider "a sizable increase" in your mortgage, for example, might not seem sizable to a mortgage banker. A specific, concrete statement such as "an increase of $537" ensures that both the speaker or writer and the listener or reader have the same amount in mind. When you write or speak, use words that tell the other person exactly what you want him or her to know.

Another way to make sure the other person gets the right idea is to avoid using too many words that end in *-tion, -sion, -ness, -ance,* and *-ence.* These suffixes often make statements less specific. In the following examples, notice that the words ending in these suffixes can often be turned into meaningful, specific verbs; notice also that vague words like *immediately* and *preponderance* are replaced with more concrete terms:

> Vague: "The illustration causes confusion. Therefore, it is of utmost importance that a revision be made immediately."

> Specific: "The sketch confuses consumers and must be revised by December 2."

> Vague: "A preponderance of inventory exists in our Pittsburgh facility. A reduction is imperative to ensure the profitability of the plant."

> Specific: "Inventory in the Pittsburgh plant is $1 million over what it should be. It must be reduced to normal levels before the next quarter's figures are computed."

People sometimes start their sentences with **expletives,** or the words *there* or *it*. Rearranging sentences to avoid expletives makes the sentences more concise and direct—and hence more specific—because the most important words are at the beginning, as in the following examples:

> Vague: "It has been our experience that business and pleasure do not mix."

> Specific: "Business and pleasure do not mix."

> Vague: "There are no restrictions on prices in the current contract."

> Specific: "Price restrictions are not included in the current contract."

> Vague: "It was the county officials who prepared the bid package."

> Specific: "County officials prepared the bid package."

Unnecessary adverbs such as *very* and *really* may also confuse readers or listeners because they are vague. You will find that business messages contain fewer adverbs than informal messages do. People overuse adverbs for several reasons: They want to add a little extra punch to a word, they can't think of a more specific word, they are trying to cover up something, or they want to avoid being specific. If you replace words like *very* and *really* with more specific words, your sentences will become more meaningful. Look at the following examples:

> Vague: "The director of production services was really mad!"

> Specific: "The director of production services was furious!"

> Vague: "The chairperson is cognizant that completion of the order for Smith, Griego, and Barnes is very important."

> Specific: "The chairperson knows our market share will increase by 2.3 percent once we have completed the order for Smith, Griego, and Barnes."

> Vague: "I really don't know what the figures are. Are they really that important?"

> Specific: "I don't know what the figures are. Why are they important to you?"

In the third vague example, the use of *really* in the first sentence could indicate that the speaker is lying. People often overuse *really* and *actually* when they are lying. The more specific statement might not be truthful, but it is more specific.

In your messages, try to replace vague words with more specific ones, but realize that some vague words are useful. Abstract ideas such as productivity, morale, ethics, convictions, values, beliefs, love, hate, and progress all have their places in business writing. Sometimes you may want to evoke the feelings associated with abstract ideas like these. When you need to be sure the other person knows exactly what you mean, however, you should not use abstractions.

## FAMILIAR WORDS

Use familiar words in business correspondence.

Never use a long word where a short one will do; never use an unfamiliar word where a familiar one will do. Readers and listeners are not impressed by a large vocabulary when it gets in the way of understanding. Using unfamiliar words makes other people feel stupid, and hence resentful. When they feel resentful, they aren't likely to accept your message. Thus, choose words your audience will understand.

Notice the differences in understandability in the following examples:

| ■ **Unfamiliar** | ■ **Familiar** |
| --- | --- |
| surmise | guess |
| surreptitious | secret |
| perusal | reading, examination |
| inefficacious | unrewarding, fruitless |
| troika | group of three in a position of authority |
| subsequent | following |

Are you impressed by the "subsequent" sentence?

Unfamiliar: "The continuation of all existence as well as the twice-daily rise and fall of the oceans forgo a rest in expectation for mortal living bodies."

Familiar: "Time and tide wait for no one."

If you are like most people, you would probably rather read the more familiar version.

One benefit of your college education is a bigger vocabulary. However, you need to resist the temptation to get the maximum return from that education by loading your messages with multisyllabic words; most of your readers and listeners will prefer familiar words. Instead, use your education to choose from a much larger "dictionary" of words those that will match other people's vocabulary levels.

Go easy on your budget. Don't use complex words when simple words will express meaning more clearly.

## JARGON, SLANG, AND COLLOQUIALISMS

Avoid the use of jargon, slang, and colloquialisms.

**Jargon** is the language that develops around a profession. People in accounting, law, business, and other fields develop their own way of communicating with one another. For example, airlines use the term *spoilage* for empty seats, and they use *space controllers* to overbook seats as a part of their *capacity management program*. The simple bus that transports passengers from a departure gate to a plane is referred to as a *mobile lounge conveyance vehicle*.

The military is another rich source of jargon. Soldiers in the Gulf War used the phrase *high speed, low drag* to indicate that an operation went exactly as planned. They used the word *mick* as an abbreviated form of the word *minute*.

Jargon elicits negative reactions because it excludes those who do not understand it.

Buzz words such as these should be used only with people who are sure to understand; jargon should never be used to communicate with others outside your profession. Unfamiliar jargon, like unfamiliar vocabulary, excludes people and makes them feel ignorant. If you are lucky, your confused reader or listener will ask for an explanation. However, many people will not bother asking you to explain terms with which they are not familiar.

**Slang,** a vocabulary identified with specific groups, is a form of jargon. The only difference between slang and jargon is that slang is not related to a profession. However, it has all the characteristics of jargon—it consists of abbreviations, arbitrarily changed words, and elaborately coined phrases that streamline communication between group members. Age groups and ethnic groups typically develop a slang of their own to identify group members and to exclude outsiders. Any rap song on the radio provides numerous examples of slang that people who prefer other types of music would never understand. Similarly, surfers seem to speak a language all their own when they discuss surfing. Even yuppies (young urban professionals) have a slang that is unique. Can you think of any slang terms you and your friends use that your professor would probably not know?

Slang should not be used in business messages unless you are positive that the other person is also familiar with the terms. Because slang does not translate across wide groups of people, it should never be used in mass mailings. Furthermore, slang creates a tone of informality and, therefore, should be used sparingly, if at all. Business messages are not always formal, but they are supposed to be professional.

"Speechify like a broke-in John Deere with a new windshield in a three-acre plot." Translation: Use words like an expert—clearly and concisely.

**Colloquialisms,** another form of jargon, are words and phrases used by people in specific regions of a country. Like slang, colloquialisms do not translate well, although they are picturesque. Cowboys *shake a hoof at a watering hole* instead of dancing at a local bar. To them, *airin' the lungs* is swearing, and money is *dust, beans, chips,* or *rocks.* Colloquialisms are amusing, but they too should be avoided in business writing.

## OUT-OF-DATE AND TRITE EXPRESSIONS

Avoid the use of out-of-date and trite expressions, foreign expressions, redundant expressions, and roundabout expressions.

Certain "catch" phrases develop in every language. Some of them are jargon and some are slang, yet occasionally these words become so widely used they remain in the language for many years. Eventually, however, these phrases become **trite,** meaning stale from overuse. Sooner or later such phrases become outdated.

Unfortunately, because most business communicators learn by the apprenticeship method—under the direction of their bosses, who are often of an older generation—some of these words and phrases remain in written English much longer than they remain in spoken English. If you use them, your writing will sound pompous. Readers will feel you are speaking down to them, and they will resent you for being condescending.

Trim the fat from your writing. Avoid out-of-date and trite expressions.

Trite expressions, such as *the cutting edge, state-of-the-art, bottom line,* and *window of opportunity* should be avoided. They are effective when they are first used; however, they quickly become stale. The following expressions have been repeated so often they have lost their ability to communicate:

| ■ **Out-of-Date and Trite Expressions** | ■ **Suggested Revisions** |
|---|---|
| according to our records | the records show |
| acknowledge receipt of | thank you for . . . have |
| attached hereto | attached is . . . |
| enclosed please find | enclosed is . . . |
| enclosed herewith | enclosed is . . . |
| if I can be of further assistance | when you need help, please call |
| in due course | by June 15, soon |
| inasmuch as | since, because |
| kindly please advise | please let me know |
| of the opinion | think, believe |
| per your request | as you requested |
| please do not hesitate to write | please write |
| pursuant to our agreement | as agreed |
| take this opportunity to | (omit it completely; get to the point) |
| thank you in advance | your cooperation will be appreciated |
| under separate cover | separately |

Trim the fat (the out-of-date and trite expressions) from your writing so your messages will be lean and effective.

A **cliché** is another form of trite expression. Clichés are old sayings, and some of them are rules to live by. Clichés such as "Do unto others before they do unto you," "good as gold," and "a needle in a haystack" are recited to us so often that, by the time we reach adulthood, we think they are common knowledge. However, not all people who encounter them understand them, particularly people of other cultures.

> Clichés hinder readability because they are not universally understood.

One television news announcer learned firsthand how damaging clichés can be. He was swamped with angry telephone calls after describing the Reverend Jesse Jackson as a dark horse candidate for the Democratic presidential nomination. The announcer intended to compliment the Reverend Jackson on an exceptionally high number of votes for someone with no political experience. The cliché "dark horse" comes from horse racing. It refers to a horse not expected to do well who comes out of the shadows and wins or does well in a race. Many television viewers thought "dark horse" was a derogatory reference to Reverend Jackson's race.

As stated above, one problem with clichés is that they are often misunderstood by people from a different culture. The following phrases would be understood by most American-born people, but imagine how hard it would be for a person who grew up speaking a different language in a different culture to translate the true meaning:

■ **Clichés**

| | |
|---|---|
| a bird in the hand is worth two in the bush | jump to conclusions |
| a fly in the ointment | King Midas touch |
| a team player | knock it off |
| all work and no play make Jack a dull boy | lot of bull |
| almighty dollar | pay through the nose |
| bolt out of the blue | run with it |
| can of worms | security blanket |
| clip joint | sink or swim |
| clear as crystal | soft as silk |
| hard as nails | sticky fingers |
| in a nutshell | true blue |
| in hot water | white as snow |

Imagine trying to understand an expression like "I'm so happy I'm beside myself!" Someone unfamiliar with this cliché might picture you and a clone standing side by side and wonder why such a situation would make you happy. In business messages, you are better off using words that literally say what you mean.

## FOREIGN EXPRESSIONS

Foreign expressions are barriers to communication if the reader is unfamiliar with them.

Some foreign phrases are commonly used in law and some other professions, but they should be avoided in business. As with jargon, slang, and clichés, foreign words will not be understood by everyone. Here are some examples:

| ■ Foreign Expressions | ■ Meanings |
| --- | --- |
| per | a, an, each |
| ipso facto | by the fact, because of that |
| ex post facto | after the fact |
| ibid | in the same place (for bibliographies) |
| op cit | in the work cited previously |
| i.e. | that is, specifically |
| e.g. | for example |
| via | by, through, by means of |
| fait accompli | accomplished fact |
| pro forma | according to form |

Do not use foreign expressions like these unless you know your reader will understand them.

## REDUNDANT EXPRESSIONS

**Redundant** expressions are those that say the same thing twice. For example, phrases like *cooperate together, refer back,* and *basic fundamentals* contain too many words. Think about it: Can you cooperate apart? Doesn't *refer* mean to go back? Aren't the basics the same as the fundamentals?

Read the following list of redundant expressions and suggested revisions. Put an asterisk by any that you find yourself using so you can begin cutting them from your vocabulary.

| ■ Redundant Expressions | ■ Suggested Revisions |
| --- | --- |
| ask the question | ask, question |
| close proximity | close, in proximity |
| consensus of opinion | consensus, opinion of the group |
| each and every | each, every |
| end product | product |
| end result | result |
| exactly identical | exact, identical |
| first and foremost | first, foremost |
| necessary requirement | necessary, necessity, requirement |
| past experience | in the past, experience |
| visit with | visit |

## ROUNDABOUT EXPRESSIONS

Closely tied to both redundant expressions and out-of-date and trite expressions are roundabout expressions, phrases that use many pompous, stilted words when fewer and simpler words would do. Many roundabout expressions have been used for generations and have almost become clichés. They make your business messages seem wordy and old fashioned. You would never say to a friend, "Send me a check in the amount of $42," would you? Because we all know $42 is an amount, there is no need to say "in the amount of." Conversationally, the sentence reads best this way: "Send me a $42 check."

Do not attempt to make your writing more "businesslike" by using the overdone, imprecise statements in the following list. Instead, use the revisions on the right.

| ■ Roundabout Expressions | ■ Suggested Revisions |
| --- | --- |
| am in receipt of | have |
| at the present time | now, currently |
| due to the fact that | because |
| for your information | (omit it; it says nothing) |
| in order to | to, so, so that |
| in the near future | soon, (or specify a date) |
| must ask you to | (just ask) |
| regret to inform you | I am sorry . . . I regret . . . |
| wish to thank you for | thank you for . . . |

In the *What Would You Do If . . . ?* vignette at the beginning of the chapter, Derrick Stone's message would be much clearer if the roundabout expressions were eliminated. "Will result in an increase of" (in the third sentence) could easily be reduced to "will increase." See if you can identify some other places to simplify and clarify the language in Stone's announcement.

## DELIBERATE DISTORTIONS

Recognize and avoid deliberate distortions and euphemisms.
So far, you have been learning about words and phrases that are awkward and ineffective; using them is not sinister, just ignorant. Deliberate distortions, on the other hand, are words and phrases that are intended to hide the truth. They deliberately mislead, overwhelm, or confuse people because they can be interpreted in several ways. Deliberate distortions are also used to disguise unpleasant truths.

Officialese, the language of government, is full of examples of deliberate distortions. William Lutz, author of *Doublespeak*, a 1989 HarperCollins Publishers, Inc., bestseller on how people use language to deceive people, describes how, to avoid having to explain why a simple nut cost $2,043, the Pentagon refers to it as a "hexiform rotatable surface compression unit." The Navy referred to a couch, a love seat, and 20 dining room chairs as "habitability improvements"; perhaps that makes them worth the $31,672 price tag. To cover up an explosion that killed 3 and injured 16, the Air Force called it "an unplanned rapid ignition of solid fuel." For 15 years, the Pentagon was able to get funding for the neutron bomb (the bomb that kills people but leaves buildings intact) by calling it a "radiation enhancement weapon." To disguise an unpleasant truth, the Pentagon refers to the expected tens of millions of civilians who would die in a nuclear war as "collateral damage."

Advertising is also full of deliberate distortions. In fact, some experts believe that the public expects to be misled by advertisers. However, there is no evidence to prove this assertion, and most people resent being manipulated. William Lutz tells about one company's advertising that says its model DB-10

"Doublespeak is language that pretends to communicate but really doesn't. It is language that makes the bad seem good, the negative appear positive, the unpleasant appear attractive or at least tolerable. Doublespeak is language that avoids or shifts responsibility, language that is at variance with its real or purported meaning. It is language that conceals or prevents thought; rather than extending thought, doublespeak limits it."

William Lutz

electric window fan is manually reversible. If you believe that means you reverse it by manually flipping a switch, you are as wrong as all the people who purchased the fan. "Manually reversible" means you have to pick up the fan and turn it around. Anyone would be angered by such a deliberate distortion.

A government television advertisement cited by Lutz stated, "U.S. Savings Bonds are now tax free for college education." What the ad didn't say was that the bonds might be tax free only if they are used to pay for college, if the purchaser doesn't earn too much money, if they are bought in the names of the parents, and if those parents are at least 24 years old and file the correct IRS form.

Announcements about labor negotiations represent another type of message that is particularly susceptible to deliberate distortions. Each side phrases its messages in the most positive way as it vies for sympathy. The following sentence appeared in a company news release, which was sent to a local newspaper in an attempt to intimidate employees into voting against a strike. (The company name has been changed to protect the guilty.)

> Distortion: "Due to skyrocketing costs related to union demands, the Board of Directors of Nameless Industries met Wednesday to discuss the possibility of filing for reorganization under federal bankruptcy protection laws."

> Truth: The only thing discussed at the board meeting was that such a newspaper announcement might be an effective way of scaring employees into voting against going on strike. The company was in no danger of filing for bankruptcy.

The vignette at the beginning of this chapter contains many examples of deliberate distortions. Words such as these violate the ethical principles of sincerity and honesty, and destroy the audience's trust. Remember when you prepare business messages that people can usually buy what they want somewhere else if they feel uneasy about the source of a company's message. The American public votes with its dollars.

*Business communicators and their companies must value honest, sincere communication. They must respect their readers and listeners and have something worthwhile to offer.*

## EUPHEMISMS

Euphemisms are, in a sense, deliberate distortions. However, the purpose is not the same. Deliberate distortions are used to mislead and cover up, but **euphemisms** are terms chosen to soften harsh reality. Consider the abundance of words we use to avoid saying someone is dead. *Passed on, gone to the other side, kicked the bucket, bought the farm, bit the dust,* and *passed away* are only a few of the phrases we have invented. When we use such a euphemism, we know that everyone involved knows the real meaning of *dead,* but we use the euphemism because it is kinder and gentler. We use such words as *correctional institution* instead of *prison,* and *under the table, payoff,* or *campaign contribution* instead of *bribe.*

Euphemisms are fine if you are positive the person receiving the message will understand your true meaning. However, they should never be used for mass mailings or where cultural misrepresentation might occur.

## DISCRIMINATORY EXPRESSIONS

Use language that does not discriminate on the basis of gender, disability, age, race, religion, ethnicity, or nationality.

People are sensitive to words that seem to imply discrimination against them. Therefore, even a sensitive, unbiased person must take special care to use nondiscriminatory words. Becoming aware of the hurt caused by biased words is the first step. Then focusing on the purpose of your message will help you communicate with sensitivity. By ensuring that gender, disability, age, race, religion, ethnicity, and nationality never become communication barriers, you will preserve good relations with clients, co-workers, superiors, and subordinates.

**GENDER BIAS.**   In the 1960s and 1970s, Americans and Canadians became more aware of discrimination against women. Theorists proposed that bias in our language contributes to the lack of equality between men and women in terms of salary and promotions. Subtly sexist messages reduce society's expectations of women.

It is easy to avoid words and expressions that show insensitivity to gender.

Today, good business communicators avoid expressions that might be considered sexist:

> Sexist statement: "If we are to finish this project on time, we'll need more manpower."
>
> Interpretation: Only men should be hired. Only men are capable of getting us out of this dilemma.
>
> Revision: "If we are to finish this project on time, we'll need more people."

This revision required nothing more than substituting a commonly used word for the one that could be misinterpreted. Here's another example:

> Sexist statement: "The chairman of the committee must be selected because of his outstanding leadership qualities."
>
> Interpretation: A man must be selected to head the committee.
>
> Revision 1: "Outstanding leadership qualities should be the basis for selecting the committee's chairperson."
>
> Revision 2: "The chair of the committee must be selected because of his or her outstanding leadership qualities."

These two revisions were easy. Revision 1 required only the substitution of *chairperson* for *chairman* and the removal of the pronoun *his*. Revision 2 used *chair,* a word that has no gender. For the pronoun, *his or her* was used to indicate the leader could be either gender.

Repeating *his or her* or *her or his* several times in a paragraph may begin to sound awkward. A better way to solve the problem is to avoid the need for singular pronouns such as *his* or *her*:

> Sexist statement: "The secretary who anticipates her employer's needs knows the way to his heart."
>
> Interpretation: All secretaries are female, and all employers are male.
>
> Revision: "Secretaries who anticipate their employers' needs will find secure places in their employers' hearts."

This solution is better than using singular pronouns. Because the plural pronoun *they* is not gender specific, it can be used without bias.

Just as you avoid referring only to men, you should avoid always putting men first:

Sexist statement: "Men and women do not communicate in the same way. Communication experts have determined that men speak more directly and that women smile more frequently."

Interpretation: Men are always first; men are more important.

Revision: "Women and men do not communicate in the same way. Communication experts have determined that women smile more frequently and that men speak more directly.

You can also avoid the impression of putting men first by sometimes using *she or he* and *her or his* instead of *he or she* and *his or her*.

Editing for gender bias is a simple task, but it must still be taken seriously. Although some women will not be offended if you use terms such as those below, many will be. When you write or speak, your goal is to get your message across. Don't risk creating a communication barrier. Because it is difficult to tell when a word will offend and when it will not, it is best to avoid words and phrases such as those in the left column in the following list. You will find it best to use the suggested revisions in the column at the right.

| ■ Insensitive | ■ Sensitive |
|---|---|
| businessman, business woman | businessperson, business executive |
| lady lawyer | lawyer |
| man (as a verb) | staff |
| mankind | humanity, people, humankind, human race |
| manmade | artificial, manufactured, constructed |
| manpower | workforce, workers, human energy |
| manslaughter | accidental murder, unpremeditated killing |
| manhole cover | (This is an old joke! What do you think?) |
| my girl | my secretary, my assistant |
| salesman | salesperson, sales associate |
| tax man | accountant, tax person, IRS agent |
| the fairer sex | women |
| the girls/the ladies | women |
| the little woman, my old lady | wife, friend |
| the old man | husband, father |

People do not like words that indicate insensitivity to physical or mental disabilities.

**DISABILITY BIAS.** Most people who are impaired physically or mentally are offended by terms that were, at one time, considered acceptable. Today, they carry negative connotations.

| ■ Insensitive | ■ Sensitive |
|---|---|
| handicapped, crippled, lame | physically challenged, disabled |
| retarded, simple minded | mentally challenged |

Furthermore, avoid referring to any physical or mental impairment a person might have unless it is pertinent to the topic:

Insensitive: "Although she is crippled, Phyllis does a remarkable job."

Sensitive: "Phyllis is a remarkable purchasing agent."

If the disability is pertinent, as in the following example, be sensitive to the way it is introduced:

Insensitive: "Alvin Sheade is an epileptic, and he seems to manage just fine."

Sensitive: "Yes, I am familiar with epilepsy. Alvin Sheade's epilepsy has not interfered with his work in any way."

Avoid mentioning the ages of people and using terms that are attributed to certain age groups.

**AGE BIAS.**    Many people are sensitive about their age—perhaps because of the general lack of respect given to older people in the United States (see Chapter 2, which discusses diversity). However, even young people experience discrimination when they are not taken seriously. To avoid the appearance of discrimination, refrain from referring to people's ages, and do not use terms that are normally attributed to certain age groups. The following insensitive sentences can easily be revised:

> "Bette Milan, 55, was appointed to the position of vice president of international operations." (Leave out her age; who cares how old she is?)

> "Bette Milan, still spry and active, should make an excellent vice president of international operations." (Leave out *still spry and active*; these words say "old" to the reader.)

> "Thomas McKay is rather young to be holding such a responsible position." (Does youth really have anything to do with ability to handle responsibility? Perhaps this statement shouldn't be made at all.)

Avoiding references to race, religion, and nationality shows sensitivity to delicate topics.

**RACE, ETHNICITY, AND NATIONALITY BIAS.**    Another sensitive area concerns people's racial, ethnic, or national heritage. Avoid referring to a person in a way that does not relate to the matter under discussion:

> Insensitive: "Mushinskie? How do you feel about what is happening economically in Poland?"

> Sensitive: Avoid it completely; not everyone with a Polish-sounding name has a Polish background or is interested in Polish matters.

> Insensitive: "Takamoto? Oh, good, then you can do the math!"

> Sensitive: This job requires higher-level math skills. What is your background in math?"

> Insensitive: "I was introduced to two of their top people, Allan Baker and a Mexican-American named Arturo Griego."

> Sensitive: "I was introduced to two of their top people, Allan Baker and Arturo Griego."

### POSITIVE AND NEGATIVE WORDS

Use positive words as much as possible to avoid negative reactions.
Take a moment to read the list of positive words in Exhibit 5.2, and then read the list of negative words there. Did you notice any change in your attention span as you read the negative words? If you are like most people, you probably did not read as many of the negative words as you did the positive ones. Even your body language probably changed. Did you find your brow wrinkling and your teeth clenching as you skimmed the unpleasant words?

Negative words should not be used, because people avoid the unpleasant and negative words tend to evoke negative reactions.

Even when there are only a few negative words, people do not like to read or hear them. Consideration for your reader, which should be the underlying basis of the you attitude, requires the use of positive words. Your task is to find the negative words in your message and substitute positive words wherever you can without changing the meaning.

Obviously, you can't say "yes" when you really mean "no"; however, there are ways to lessen the negative impact when you must say "no." One, as explained in

**EXHIBIT 5.2**

**Positive Words versus Negative Words**

### Use Positive Words Such as These:

| | | |
|---|---|---|
| achievement | initiative | smile |
| accuracy | joy | success |
| advantage | judgment | thank you |
| agree | kind | think |
| benefit | lasting | thoughtfulness |
| character | level-headed | thrive |
| comprehensive | loyal | trust |
| cooperation | maximum | truth |
| confidence | music | understand |
| determined | neatness | willingness |
| diplomacy | opportunity | unity |
| excellence | pleasure | useful |
| generosity | productive | valuable |
| good | profit | victory |
| grateful | pure | warm |
| guarantee | reasonable | willingness |
| happiness | reliable | wonderful |
| helpful | satisfaction | you |
| honesty | save | your |
| ideal | security | |

### Avoid Negative Words Such as These:

| | | |
|---|---|---|
| absurd | disrepute | killing |
| alibi | egotism | lazy |
| allege | embezzle | liar |
| anger | enrage | meaningless |
| attack | error | mistake |
| avenge | failure | obstacle |
| awkward | fearful | obstinance |
| backward | fight | pain |
| blame | guilty | policy |
| careless | hopeless | politics |
| complain | humiliate | poor |
| condemn | hurt | ridicule |
| contrary | illicit | standstill |
| counterfeit | imperfect | suspicious |
| coward | inconvenient | threat |
| discouraging | insecurity | ugly |

Chapter 6, is to organize negative business messages to make them easier to accept. Another is to adopt a positive tone. The following examples show how to eliminate a negative tone (the negative words and phrases are italicized):

Negative: "Your Order No. 23777 will be sent *without delay*."

Evaluation: Why combine the mention of your product with a negative word? In addition, you can replace a vague expression with one that is both positive and specific.

Positive: "Your Order No. 23777 will be shipped to you by March 4."

Negative: "You *won't* care about gas mileage once you experience the smooth, calming ride of the 427E."

Evaluation: Why bring up a negative aspect of the product? Instead, emphasize positives and eliminate negatives.

Positive: "Picture yourself gliding on a magic carpet miles above the Earth, arriving at your destination with more energy than when you started. The 427E's powerful engine and its superior engineering can give you that magic carpet experience every day."

**Avoid the lecturing, "stern parent" tone; people don't like being made to feel like children.**

Negative: "*Don't waste* money on *overpriced* brands."

Evaluation: The lecturing tone makes the reader feel like a child. Avoid combining "You," the understood subject, with a negative.

Positive: "Take advantage of quality products at affordable prices."

**When you must tell people "no," don't use *we, I,* or the company name to deny permission.**

Negative: "*We never* make adjustments without seeing the *merchandise that failed* to satisfy."

Evaluation: The use of *we* does not reflect a you attitude, especially because *we* are wielding power. It is also bad form to combine references to your merchandise with the word *failed.*

Positive: "An adjustment decision will be made promptly at any of our convenient local outlets."

Concentrate on what you want people to do instead of what you don't want them to do, and use the "you" attitude to let them know how they will benefit.

Negative: "*Despite* your proposal, *we do not* see any reason for changing *our policy*."

Evaluation: *Policy,* when used as a reason for telling people they can't do or have what they want, is a negative word. People are far more receptive to explanations of the policy.

Positive: "Thank you for your proposal to change the vacation policy, It will be considered fully when the policy is reexamined."

Positive: "Thank you for your proposal to change the vacation policy. The current procedure for assignment of dates was recommended three years ago by a committee made up of employees from all levels of the company. After looking into alternatives, the committee decided that assignment by seniority would be the fairest way to resolve conflicts that cannot be settled by employees themselves. The committee has found that most conflicts can be resolved when employees work with one another informally."

When the policy cannot be explained, people should at least be reassured that their individual concerns have been taken into account.

Negative: "*No wonder* you are having *trouble* with the machine. *Obviously, you neglected* to read the operating instructions."

Evaluation: *Obviously* and *no wonder* add an inappropriate note of sarcasm. *You* should not be combined with a negative such as *neglected;* it's as personal as a slap in the face. Also, don't assume that the operating instructions were included or that they are easy to follow. Few operating instructions are written in a way that the average person can understand.

Positive: "The operating instructions are enclosed. Please read instruction No. 3b before operating the machine. If the switch is engaged before the gear has been changed, an error light will go on."

Negative: "*If* you think more of these posters would be helpful during your sale, indicate in the appropriate blank on the enclosed card the number of posters you want."

Evaluation: *If* can be a negative; it shows doubt, especially when it comes after an enthusiastic sales pitch designed to convince people they definitely need these posters to boost sales.

Positive: "Please indicate the number of posters you want in the appropriate blank on the enclosed card."

Negative: "*Why not* call this bulletin to the attention of your department staff?"

Evaluation: Asking *why not* might produce a negative answer, such as "Because I'm too busy" or "Because I don't want to." The negative statement also displays no you attitude.

Positive: "For your staff members to be able to complete the new forms correctly, please have them read the enclosed bulletin carefully."

**Emphasize what you can do, not what you can't do.**

Negative: "*We cannot* quote you a price until we have seen the specifications."

Evaluation: Don't dwell on what you can't do; concentrate on what you can do. Convince people that what you want will also benefit them.

Positive: "A price quote will be rushed to you as soon as your specifications for the parts arrive."

**Diplomacy requires skillful use of language to avoid arousing hostility.**

Negative: "What you are saying is a *bunch of garbage!*"

Evaluation: Even though this statement might be true, the same thing can be stated more diplomatically. Statements such as this do nothing but earn enemies.

Positive: "Perhaps a realistic look at the issue would help us pinpoint solutions."

**Justify your saying "no" by stating reasons that either benefit the other person or will seem reasonable to the other person.**

Negative: "The names of those on our mailing list *cannot* be released.

Evaluation: This statement concentrates on what can't be done, and it gives no reason to justify the policy.

Positive: "Giving you the names of people on our mailing list would violate their right to privacy, and they would lose confidence in our firm."

Negative: "*If you do not* send your payment by March 7, *we will be forced* to take *other action.*"

Evaluation: This example is so full of negative words that there is little chance of achieving the positive action desired—the payment. The threatening tone is likely to cause resentment. Concentrate on the benefit instead.

Positive: "Sending a payment by March 7 will ensure that you will continue enjoying the benefits of an excellent credit rating."

As you can see, positive language exerts a subtle psychological influence on people. It enables them to concentrate on your message and understand how it benefits them. Positive language makes it easier for readers and listeners to say "yes" to you.

However, don't try too hard to avoid ever saying anything negative. Substitute positives for negatives as long as the message is still clear, but don't use positive words to disguise true meaning. Terminate or fire employees, don't "select them out" or "dehire" them. If you use distortions such as these, you will end up with messages that don't communicate clearly. Sometimes negative language may be needed to get your point across forcefully. However, take care to choose words that do not reveal a negative attitude toward readers or listeners. Such a tone makes people feel resentful.

## ACTIVE AND PASSIVE WORDS

Use active or passive words when each is most appropriate.

*Active verbs make writing direct and clear.*

Generally, active words—specifically verbs—are more effective than passive words are. Not only do active verbs draw people into the sentence, they also are more direct than passive verbs. Sentences in which the subject acts on the object are easier to understand than are passive, roundabout sentences. Compare these two sentences:

Passive: "The effect of the takeover attempt was a depletion of assets."

Active: "The takeover attempt depleted assets."

In the passive sentence, the action is hidden in the word *depletion*. In the second sentence, the verb (*depleted*) describes the action, and the subject (*attempt*) acts on the object (*assets*).

Passive sentences often contain being verbs: *is, are, am, was,* and *were*. Notice how weak the passive pattern is and how strong the active pattern is:

Passive: "The price *was discounted* by the broker." (What was done by whom?)

Active: "The broker *discounted* the price." (Who did what to what?)

Passive: "The delegation of responsibilities *is* one of the hardest tasks *learned* by entrepreneurs." (What is done by whom?)

Active: "Entrepreneurs *must learn* to delegate responsibilities." (Who does what?)

*Watch out for passive verbs that enable the writer to mislead readers by not being specific.*

Another problem with passive sentences is that they can be used to mislead. Notice how the passive verb in the following sentence allows the writer to avoid saying exactly who or how many have criticized the president's leadership:

Passive: "The president's leadership *has been criticized* frequently."

Active: "Union leaders *criticized* the president's leadership."

The active version identifies the critics, but it still could be misleading. It does not say whether the union leaders who criticized the president are current or previous leaders, or how recent their criticism was.

The passive sentence below is similarly unethical. It was used to start the rumor that a lot of people were unhappy with a project leader. It avoids saying who has been talking or even when the talk occurred. In this case, all the talk came from the one person who uttered the sentence, and all his talk took place many months before this harmful statement was made to the project leader's supervisor:

Passive: "There *has been talk* of removing the project leader by petition."

Active: "I *talked* to several people about the project leader's performance and would like to remove her by petition."

If you look again at the vignette at the beginning of the chapter, you should be able to spot several passive sentences used to avoid taking responsibility for actions that will upset many people. How could Derrick Stone reword those sentences to make them more active and, hence, more ethical and understandable?

**The passive voice can be used when the content of the message is more important than who said it or did it.**

Despite the possible misuses of passive words, sometimes they are better than active words. When the content of the message is more important than who said it or did it, the passive voice is appropriate:

Passive: "The original copy of the document was destroyed."

Passive: "The total of your Invoice No. 11288 was added incorrectly."

In these examples, the use of passive words avoids assigning blame (which is not relevant) and softens the bad news.

**Passive verbs may be used to emphasize the "you" attitude.**

You can also use passive words to emphasize the message's recipient rather than you or your company. This is an important aspect of the you attitude (as explained in Chapter 4). The following passive example is actually more you oriented than the active alternative:

Passive: "Your request will be given top priority."

Active: "We will give your request top priority."

The active version emphasizes who is going to give the request top priority, not who will benefit. The passive version indicates that the reader or listener is more important than the person or organization sending the message.

## WRITING STYLE

**Style is the result of matching the words you use to your reader or listener, the situation, and the purpose.**

◤ Choose the writing style most suited to your purpose and your reader.

As you compose messages, you juggle the words you use to suit your reader or listener, the situation, and your purpose. The result of these considerations—sentences, paragraphs, and complete messages—is referred to as *writing style*. Writing style varies depending on how these three factors are handled.

You would use a casual, conversational style, for example, when writing a chatty letter to a friend. This casual style might include some slang, a few incomplete sentences, and emotional language, as in the following:

Thomas, I've spent this whole week running around, and don't have a rotten thing to show for it! Oh, well, what else is new, huh? Aren't many jobs out there for someone with my "superior" skills!! Tell that to my calculus teacher!

A more formal, scientific style would be used in a report. For a marketing class, for example, you might write something like the following. (Notice the difference in vocabulary and sentence structure.)

> It is a commonly accepted tenet of marketing that consideration of the reader is a primary concern in increasing sales volume. In general, without such consideration, mass-produced sales correspondence fails to reach intended targets. To maximize mass marketing expenditures, writers must account for every element in the marketing equation—with consideration of the reader's needs being paramount.

The casual style is used in business very rarely, except perhaps in short personal notes to close business associates. The formal style is more common, especially in published reports; it can also be used in selected sentences within letters and memos. Most business memos and letters, however, use a style called *informal business style*. It combines elements of the conversational style (which make your correspondence seem direct, clear, concise, positive, and you oriented) with elements of the formal style (which make your messages seem objective, controlled, powerful, and authoritative). The main differences between the formal and informal business writing styles are outlined in Exhibit 5.3.

Good writers know how to write both formally and informally, and they know when to use each writing style. Good writers know when a personal, informal tone is needed and when the authority and objectivity of the formal style is needed. Once you learn how to use the two styles, you will be able to switch from one to the other, depending on the tone you want.

To this point, this chapter has concentrated on informal business writing style. You can combine all the elements of word choice discussed so far to develop this style. Formal style, however, uses passive writing to seem objective and unbiased. To understand the difference, read carefully the following examples:

> Formal: "The comparison of the alternatives did not consider Option No. 5 in adequate detail."

> Informal: "Your comparison of the alternatives did not consider Option No. 5 in adequate detail."

> Evaluation: The formal example downplays the person who made the mistake. It is less personal than the informal example and concentrates on the message, not on who did it.

> Formal: "It is recommended that the costs of the project be investigated fully."

> Informal: "I recommend that the costs of the project be investigated fully."

> Evaluation: The formal example sounds as though the recommendation is based on scientific study. The informal example sounds as though the writer may be expressing a personal opinion. It implies that the recommendation is not based on objective study.

> Formal: "The impact of advanced technology on today's business curriculum must be considered."

> Informal: "Don't forget to consider the impact of 'high tech' on today's business curriculum."

> Evaluation: The informal example speaks directly to the reader. The subject of the sentence is the understood "you." The formal example does not use

| EXHIBIT 5.3 | A Comparison of Formal and Informal Business Writing Styles | |
|---|---|---|
| | **■ Formal Style** | **■ Informal Style** |
| | Is impersonal (uses no first or second person personal pronouns—I, me, my, you, your—and uses third person pronouns—one, we, our, their—sparingly) | Is personal (uses pronouns freely and emphasizes *you* and *your*) |
| | Does not speak directly to reader | Can speak to the reader and refer to reader's circumstances |
| | Uses no contractions | Uses contractions sparingly |
| | Uses no slang or clichés | Avoids slang or clichés unless the reader will understand them |
| | Emphasizes the message rather than who said it or did it | May emphasize the message as well as who said or did it |
| | Is unemotional (uses no emotion-laden words, sarcasm, or exclamation points) | Avoids emotion and sarcasm (uses exclamation points sparingly, if at all) |
| | Uses more passive verbs | Uses more active verbs |
| | Uses no sentence fragments | Uses no sentence fragments |
| | Uses longer sentences and paragraphs | Uses shorter sentences and paragraphs |
| | Uses more abstract words and technical and scientific vocabulary | Uses more specific, concrete words and everyday vocabulary |

informal contractions or slang and, therefore, sounds stronger and more objective.

You can use the formal writing style when you state an opinion but want to avoid stressing that it is merely an opinion. To add strength to your assertions, use the formal, passive writing style in situations such as these:

Formal: "Scheduling the seminar for late October will ensure that it does not conflict with the communications conference."

Informal: "I think the seminar should be scheduled in late October, so it won't interfere with the communications conference."

Formal: "Labor leaders must begin to consider the long-term needs of union members."

Informal: "Everyone knows that labor leaders don't think of anything beyond the short-term needs of their members."

*Certain elements of the formal style can make your writing boring, so use them with care in letters and memos.*

The formal writing style can be useful, but you must be able to determine when it is appropriate. Furthermore, some people feel that the formal, impersonal writing style is dry and boring. You may encounter people who prefer reports written in the informal style, believing it makes them more readable. However, the majority of long reports in the business world are written in the impersonal tone of the formal style. Short reports, on the other hand, tend to blend elements of both the formal and the informal styles. Many short reports use personal you-attitude statements in the beginning and ending paragraphs but employ the formal style in the middle portions. The ability to move back and forth between the formal and informal writing styles is the mark of a skillful writer.

## READABILITY

Enhance the readability of business messages through attention to word choice, sentence and paragraph structure, and format.

In this chapter, you have learned that words should be chosen for their ability to communicate. Word choice, then, is an element of **readability,** or the ease with which meaning can be extracted from a written message. Word choice, alone, however, will not guarantee readability. The other important elements are sentence structure, paragraph structure, and format.

### READABLE SENTENCES

A readable sentence expresses one clear thought. Generally speaking, a document is more readable when its sentences meet the following criteria:

- The subject of each sentence tells what the sentence is about.
- The subject is at or near the beginning of each sentence, and the subject and the verb are close together.
- Most sentences are short, but sentence length varies.
- A variety of sentence types and patterns is used.

**SENTENCE LENGTH.**    Short sentences tend to be more direct, and this directness is what usually makes short sentences more readable. However, if all sentences are short, the writing takes on an annoyingly choppy quality. In addition, some short sentences are less readable than long sentences are, because of the words being used and the concepts being presented.

> Generally, sentences that are short are more readable—unless there are too many short sentences.

There is no ideal sentence length. Try for an average of about 20 words a sentence, but keep in mind that skillful writers often write longer sentences that are clear and concise. Generally, the higher the educational level of the reader, the longer the sentences can be and still remain readable.

Unfortunately, many people believe the longer and more convoluted their sentences are and the more "big" words they use, the more "professional" their writing seems. Such a belief is incorrect.

**SENTENCE TYPES.**    Variety in the length of sentences goes along with variety in the type of sentences. A readable document keeps the reader's interest by combining these three types of sentences:

> Sentences can be categorized on the basis of their combination of independent clauses (which have a subject and a verb and can stand alone as a sentence) and dependent clauses (which have a subject and a verb but cannot stand alone).

- *Simple sentence.* Contains only one independent clause and is clear and direct. (An **independent clause** contains a subject and a verb and can stand alone as one thought.) Examples include:

    "This is an independent clause."

    "I voted."

    "Desktop publishing programs improve the appearance of written work."

    "Aldus PageMaker and Ventura Publisher are two of the most popular software programs." (Compound subject.)

- *Compound sentence.* Contains two or more independent clauses (underlined in the following examples) connected by a conjunction (*and, but, or, nor*) or a conjunctive adverb (*however, therefore*). Because effective sentences contain only one thought, the thoughts in the independent clauses must be closely related. If they are not, the clauses should be separated into two different sentences.

  "This is an independent clause, and this is an independent clause."

  "I voted, but you did not."

  "Desktop publishing programs improve the appearance of written work, and they save money."

  "Aldus PageMaker is a versatile program; however, Ventura Publisher's new edition looks good too."

- *Complex sentence.* Contains at least one independent clause and at least one dependent clause (boldfaced in the following sentences). A **dependent clause** has a subject and a verb but cannot stand alone as a sentence; it must be attached to an independent clause. Complex sentences that contain more than one dependent or independent clause are sometimes referred to as *compound-complex sentences.*

  "***Because it is dependent,*** a dependent clause must remain close to an independent clause."

  "I voted, ***although I did not feel strongly about the issue***."

  "***However much it costs,*** Aldus PageMaker is an excellent investment for a college business student."

  "Ventura Publisher, ***because it has so many features,*** is an excellent investment for people with IBM-compatible computers."

Use a variety of sentence types to improve the readability of your writing. Although simple sentences are easy to read, a good mix of simple, compound, and complex sentences will retain the interest of your readers and give your writing a professional, businesslike quality.

**SENTENCE PATTERNS.**   The sentences you read in kindergarten probably followed the subject and predicate pattern: "Sally runs home," or "Spot chased the cat." However, if all sentences followed this pattern, writing would quickly become boring. More interesting writing includes some sentences in which the order of the elements has been changed. For variety, you can sometimes put the end of a sentence at the beginning:

Without examples to illustrate important points, an author would be at a loss.

The normal pattern would be as follows:

An author would be at a loss without examples to illustrate important points.

**Keep the subject close to the beginning of the sentence.**

When you change the order of a sentence, try to keep the introductory statement (the phrase or clause before the subject) short. The first thing a reader searches for in a sentence is the subject, so readability improves when the opening statement is not too long.

**Keep the subject and the verb close together.**

The next thing a reader searches for in a sentence is the verb, so keep the verb as close to the subject as possible. In the following example, the subject (italicized) and the verb (boldfaced) are separated by too many words:

The *National Council of Insurance Commissioners,* in an attempt to reconcile the regulations placed on automobile insurance companies by the states of California, Nevada, Arizona, New York, New Jersey, and North Dakota, and with the intent of proposing counterlegislation to clarify state-levied mandates, **will meet** on April 23 in Philadelphia.

The following revision puts the subject and verb closer together, but the sentence is still hard to read because it is too long:

The *National Council of Insurance Commissioners* **will meet** on April 23 in Philadelphia in an attempt to reconcile the regulations placed on automobile insurance companies by the states of California, Nevada, Arizona, New York, New Jersey, and North Dakota and with the intent of proposing counterlegislation to clarify state-levied mandates.

Here's a way to solve the readability problem:

The National Council of Insurance Commissioners will meet on April 23 in Philadelphia to do the following:

- Reconcile the regulations placed on automobile insurance companies by the states of California, Nevada, Arizona, New York, New Jersey, and North Dakota.

- Propose counterlegislation to clarify state-levied mandates.

Another potential problem with alternative sentence patterns is wordiness. Avoid using long lead-ins that make the most important parts of the sentence— the subject and verb—seem less important. Delete unnecessary introductory words, as in the following revisions:

Wordy: "I am enclosing a copy of the latest revisions to the Guerrera contract."

Concise: "A copy of the Guerrera contract revisions is enclosed."

Wordy: "I wanted to let you know that the Guerrera contract was signed today."

Concise: "The Guerrera contract was signed today."

Wordy: "Let me begin by announcing that the Guerrera contract was the largest ever signed by this firm."

Concise: "The Guerrera contract was the largest ever signed by this firm."

Notice that the revisions also make the sentences more you oriented and less I oriented.

## READABLE PARAGRAPHS

Readable paragraphs contain only one main idea, expressed in the topic sentence.

Readability depends not just on good sentences, but also on good paragraphs. Sentences concerning the same topic should be grouped together into a paragraph; each paragraph should contain only one main idea. A **topic sentence** at or near the beginning of the paragraph summarizes the main idea and, thus, helps the reader focus on the material. Now read the second sentence of this paragraph again. Notice how, as the topic sentence, it prepares you for a discussion of topic sentences. The following sentences provide further examples of how topic sentences are used to introduce a subject and to explain how it will be developed:

"Company leaders have discussed four new designs for next year's models." (Prepares readers for a discussion of the four designs.)

"Kelby and Prene experienced a radical upswing in the first quarter." (Prepares readers for a discussion of the upswing.)

**Use transitions to tie paragraphs together.**

Another way to enhance readability at the paragraph level is to link paragraphs with **transitions** to form a cohesive message. Transitions show how a new paragraph relates to the previous paragraph. Here are two useful types of transitionary elements:

- Words such as *therefore, however, furthermore, in addition to, Step One, Step Two, finally, consequently, in conclusion, similarly, although,* and *meanwhile.*
- Words repeated from the last line of the previous paragraph. For example:

  . . . is considering implementing new *reform legislation* to allow businesses to invest larger sums in equipment renewal.
  This *legislation* will require the backing of . . .

**Readable paragraphs should be no longer than eight typewritten lines.**

Another way to enhance readability is to keep paragraphs short. Although experts do not agree on the optimal length of a good paragraph, in business writing you should probably try to avoid letting your paragraphs go beyond eight typewritten lines or 125 words. Paragraphs in business letters and memos are usually shorter than in reports; the longest paragraphs should be reserved for technical documents to be read by people with technical backgrounds. Long paragraphs look dense and hard to read. When readers see a document full of long paragraphs, they may avoid reading it altogether. Think about your reaction when you open a textbook that has pages full of long paragraphs.

If you must deal with a complex topic that requires more than eight typewritten lines, break the single long paragraph on that topic into shorter paragraphs, each of which covers a subtopic. This helps the reader by breaking the complex topic into more understandable units.

In business writing, there is no such thing as a paragraph that is too short (unless, of course, it doesn't cover the topic). In fact, one-sentence paragraphs are often used in letters and memos for emphasis, interest, attention and conciseness. One-sentence paragraphs, if they're not used too much, can help lead the reader's eye through a letter, as in Exhibit 5.4. Unusual paragraph constructions command attention because they are unique and the eye tends to read first what is easiest.

To summarize, paragraphs in readable business documents possess the following characteristics:

- Contain only one main idea.
- Usually begin with a topic sentence.
- Are tied together by effective transitions.
- Are no longer than eight typewritten lines.

## READABLE FORMAT

**Format considerations can enhance the readability of a document.**

So far, you have been learning about how your use of words, sentences, and paragraphs can enhance readability. What you may not have considered is the role of **format,** or the way a message is laid out on the page. Readers are more likely to notice and read letters, memos, reports, newsletters, and other kinds of business messages that are arranged attractively and considerately.

**BAARSTEN**
**REALTY SERVICES**

1443 LIZARD RUN SOUTH
ALBUQUERQUE, NM 87102
(505) 617-4432
FAX (505) 617-8205

April 21, 1994

Mr. Franklin Hightower
476 East Lansing, Apt. 223B
Farmington, NM 87401

Dear Mr. Hightower:

And then...?

That's what Joe and Sally Sanders said after they had made the most exciting decision of their lives—to buy a beautiful new house in a perfect neighborhood. Like all first-time buyers, Joe and Sally were anxious to move in and make their house a home. However, they were left to wait...and wait...and wait...and wait. Calls to their realtor went unanswered; they had no idea how long it would be before they could take possession. Unlike Joe and Sally, you will never have to say,

And then...?

When you buy from Baarsten Realty Services, your personal agent will escort you through each step of the sale from the search to the purchase through escrow right up to the front door when you take possession of your dream.

Please call Baarsten today to make an appointment to see one of our premier sales associates. To help you get settled in the home you've always wanted, we'll take $500 off the sales fee if you mention these words when you call—

And then...?

You will receive the friendly, knowledgeable representation you need at such an important time in your life.

Sincerely,

*Gregory Jones*

Gregory Jones
Sales Manager

Readers like plenty of white space on a page, so make sure your documents are not crowded with words. As a general rule, 50 percent of a page should be white space. **White space** includes all four margins as well as the space that appears between letters, words, and lines. Take a look at the wide side margin in this textbook. Doesn't it make each page appear easier to read? Human nature being what it is, what we think is easier usually is.

A readable format should also include everything most readers would expect to see. Not typing a date on a letter might cause the reader to focus on the omission rather than on the message itself. You can imagine the suspicions of some readers if a businessperson failed to sign a letter—"What's she trying to get away with here? What's wrong with this letter that she didn't even want to sign it? Maybe I had better read it better to see what's between the lines!" Another reader might perceive the same writer as careless and sloppy. When all the standard parts of memos, letters, and reports have been included, readers can focus on the content and not on the ulterior motives or carelessness of the writer.

Headings and subheadings are also aids to readability. Look back through this chapter, and try to imagine what it would have been like to read without any of the headings or subheadings. The headings help to guide you through the concepts as you read, and they provide a kind of mental break, time to reflect on what you have read before going on. You can also skim the headings to review for your next exam. Finally, the headings make it easy for you to find specific information as you answer the questions at the end of the chapter, or to refer to the book to solve a communication problem that you encounter at work. Headings and subheadings can do the same thing for readers of reports, letters, and memos.

Another way to help readers absorb and understand your message is to provide lists, illustrations, and tables. For example, step-by-step lists of instructions help to make a complex task easier. Lists also draw attention to important items. In addition, many people are visual learners, so be alert to situations in which you can use illustrations, tables, flow charts, line graphs, and other types of visual aids to highlight the relationships among ideas. Visual aids can also present a great deal of information in a small amount of space.

The relationship between you and your reader will improve when you use a format that makes it easier for the reader to find, read, and absorb what you write. In summary, use these formatting principles to make your documents more readable:

- Select attractive formats that leave approximately 50 percent white space on a page.

- Include all the elements people expect to see.

- Use headings and subheadings to guide the reader.

- Use lists to break large amounts of complex information into easily understood parts.

- Use tables, illustrations, and other visual aids to present large amounts of information in less space.

For more information on visual aids, refer to Chapter 10. Appendix C includes more information on letter and memo formats.

### Using Formulas to Calculate Readability

#### The Flesch Reading Ease Scale

Follow these steps to compute a score for your writing:
1.  Using a sample of approximately 100 words, figure the average number of words in each sentence.
2.  Multiply that number by 1.015.
3.  Compute the average number of syllables in a word.
4.  Multiply that number by .846.
5.  Add the results of steps 2 and 4 together, and subtract the total from 206.835.
6.  The result is your score reported on a scale of 0 (very difficult) to 100 (very easy). The higher the score, the better the readability.
7.  Perform this test on several passages if the document is long to ensure the reliability of the score.

#### The Gunning Fog Index

Follow these steps to compute a grade-level readability score for your writing:
1.  Using a sample of at least 100 words, divide the total number of words by the total number of sentences. (Caution: The independent clauses of a compound sentence are counted as separate sentences.) This yields a number that reflects the average sentence length.
2.  Count the number of words having three or more syllables. Do not count proper names, or combinations of short, easy words such as *bookkeeper, countertop,* or *businessperson.* Do not count capitalized words or verbs that are three syllables as a result of the suffixes *-ed* or *-es* (e.g., *repeated, conceited, excesses*).
3.  Divide this number by 100 to yield a score that reflects the percentage of difficult words in a passage.
4.  Add the average sentence length to the percentage of difficult words in the passage, and divide the total by .4.
5.  The final calculation is the grade level at which a reader should be able to read and comprehend the passage.
6.  If the document is long, run this test on several passages to ensure the reliability of the score.

Source: Based on J. C. Redish, "Readability," in D. Felker (ed.,), *Document Design: A Review of the Relevant Research, 1980.* Reprinted with permission from the Document Design Center. American Institutes for Research, Washington, DC.

## READABILITY TESTS

Some companies and states require that certain types of materials, especially those written for a mass readership, be written at a level that the majority of the population can understand. Usually they have some sort of readability test that they apply to documents. You can do the same thing to ensure that your writing meets the needs of your readers.

Many readability tests have been developed, and some are now available in inexpensive computer programs. Most grammar and style checkers, for example, automatically compute the grade level of your writing, based on the average number of syllables in the words you use and the average length of your sentences.

Even if you do not have a computer program, you can compute the readability scores of your writing by using one of the two most common readability formulas; the steps used to apply the Flesch Reading Ease Scale and the Gunning Fog Index are listed in Exhibit 5.5.

As you write, keep in mind that the average American has an 8th-grade reading level. Many college textbooks are purposely written at a 12th-grade reading level or lower to enhance readability. As a rule, only technical documents for professionals in the same field should be written at a reading level higher than 12th grade.

Most of all, remember that readability formulas are only a guide to effective writing. They do not measure the quality of your writing; they only measure its

*Computerized readability tests can tell you the reading level of your writing, so you can tailor your word choices and sentence structure to match the level of your readers.*

complexity. Also, the formulas do not consider the effects of readability factors that are not language oriented, such as headings, subheadings, and lists, nor do they address the motivation of the reader. However, readability tests can help you avoid using difficult words and convoluted sentence structures that make your writing harder to understand.

If you do a readability test on your writing and find that it is above the reading level you want, take another look at the words you have chosen. Use a thesaurus, if necessary, to find simple, familiar, and specific substitutes for the words that are too unfamiliar or vague. Shorten and simplify your sentences and paragraphs by following the guidelines presented in this chapter. Although format doesn't affect readability formulas, you can use the principles of format selection presented in this chapter to help your reader understand your message.

To write more professionally, avoid using big words and long, complex sentences.

## DISCUSSION QUESTIONS

◤ Avoid words with offensive connotations.

1. Define *connotation* and *denotation*. Provide examples of two words not mentioned in this chapter that take on new meanings when their connotations are considered.

◤ Choose specific words rather than vague words, except when vague words serve a purpose.

◤ Use familiar words in business correspondence.

2. How does the use of specific words and familiar words affect the relationship between the writer and the reader?

◤ Avoid the use of jargon, slang, and colloquialisms.

3. Define *jargon, slang*, and *colloquialism*, and provide two examples of each that are not mentioned in the textbook.

◤ Avoid the use of out-of-date and trite expressions, foreign expressions, redundant expressions, and roundabout expressions.

4. Revise the following redundancies and roundabout expressions to make them concise:
   *a.* important essentials
   *b.* advance planning
   *c.* absolutely necessary
   *d.* brief in duration
   *e.* repeat the same
   *f.* roundtrip and return
   *g.* rules and regulations
   *h.* small in size
   *i.* still remain

◤ Recognize and avoid deliberate distortions and euphemisms.

5. Why are euphemisms less harmful than deliberate distortions? If euphemisms are less harmful, why should they be avoided?

■ Use language that does not discriminate on the basis of gender, disability, age, race, religion, ethnicity, or nationality.

6. Some women do not seem to be offended by terms and phrases such as *manpower, mankind*, and "A way to a man's heart is through his stomach." Would it be acceptable to use these terms or others like them if your listener does not seem to react negatively?

■ Use language that does not discriminate on the basis of gender, disability, age, race, religion, ethnicity, or nationality.

7. How are plural nouns and pronouns used to avoid the overuse and awkwardness of *his or her* and *she or he*? Compose a sentence to demonstrate your understanding.

■ Use positive words as much as possible to avoid negative reactions.

8. "We tend to dislike people who remind us that they have power over us." Do you agree or disagree with this statement? Explain what this means to you. Give two examples of how such power is shown in poorly written sentences.

■ Use active or passive words when each is most appropriate.

9. Why should active verbs be used more often than passive verbs?

■ Use active or passive words when each is most appropriate.

10. Give two examples not mentioned in the chapter of how passive verbs can be used to mislead. Would it ever be ethical to avoid being specific? Why or why not?

■ Choose the writing style most suited to your purpose and your reader.

11. "A passive writing style can make your writing seem more objective and unbiased, even when it is not." Give two examples not provided in the chapter that demonstrate your understanding of this concept.

■ Enhance the readability of business messages through attention to word choice, sentence and paragraph structure, and format.

12. Name four ways to enhance readability.

## Application Exercises

■ Avoid words with offensive connotations.

1. Revise the following paragraph to show your sensitivity to connotative and denotative meanings. Use a thesaurus, if necessary, to find acceptable substitutes for the words with negative connotations.

As one of the largest grantors of earthquake insurance, you have a responsibility to live up to your agreements, not to weasel out of them. That is why your fishy actions since the October quake are nothing short of a ridiculous scam to defraud. There is no good reason for your representatives' long-winded, evasive excuses for failing to acknowledge their intent to pay and refusing to set a date when payment can be expected.

◼ Avoid words with offensive connotations.

2. Come up with terms that have better connotations for those given below:
   *a.* nonconformist
   *b.* oration
   *c.* instability
   *d.* thick-skinned

◼ Choose specific words rather than vague words, except when vague words serve a purpose.

3. Select more specific words to replace the vague words used in the following sentences:
   *a.* The money we offered wasn't enough; they want more.
   *b.* A meeting should be held soon.
   *c.* There was a big drop in operating expenses between 1993 and 1994.
   *d.* The work area must be expanded.

◼ Use familiar words in business correspondence.

4. Revise the following paragraph so it contains words familiar to most readers:

   An ascendance of the profit margin will eventuate from formulation of a conjoined enterprise with a firm in Mexico City. Such an endeavor will effectuate a 30 percent abatement of expenses related to manpower, which will act as a counterweight to an estimated .2 percent ascendance appertaining to materials fees.

◼ Use familiar words in business correspondence.

5. Substitute a more familiar word or phrase for each of the following:
   *a.* analogous
   *b.* stipulate
   *c.* inordinate
   *d.* ineffectual
   *e.* arduous
   *f.* capitulate
   *g.* rejoinder
   *h.* tussled
   *i.* indefatigable
   *j.* amelioration
   *k.* affix a signature

◼ Avoid the use of jargon, slang, and colloquialisms.

6. List at least five slang terms you and your friends use. Define each one, and then compose a paragraph using these five terms that will illustrate for your teacher how the slang is used in everyday conversation.

◼ Avoid the use of out-of-date and trite expressions, foreign expressions, redundant expressions, and roundabout expressions.
◼ Use active or passive words when each is most appropriate.

7. Revise the following sentences:

a.  Postpone the meeting until later.
b.  Send Teri a card from the whole department; she just had a pair of twins.
c.  Are you in a position to send the finished document to me on or before September 9?
d.  To study the effects of culture on nonverbal communication, the team made an investigation of proxemics and kinesics.
e.  To receive reimbursement for travel expenses, you must document your per diem expenditures.
f.  We hereby acknowledge receipt of your recent letter and have come to the conclusion that, in compliance with your request, the group you represent will be allowed to meet in the larger meeting room at no extra charge.
g.  In the event that you are unable to make the full down payment, your $500 deposit will be retained by the seller.
h.  Our foreign counterparts will have to learn "If you can't stand the heat, get out of the kitchen."
i.  We'll have to get up at the crack of dawn if we are going to get ahead of our competition.
j.  It is my personal opinion that we will benefit by solving our mutual problems that are perplexing.

🔲 Recognize and avoid deliberate distortions and euphemisms.

8.  Research the topic of deliberate distortions used by government and business to mislead readers. As you search for deliberate distortions, look for examples of writing that use unfamiliar language and convoluted sentence structure in an attempt to sound more formal or more intelligent. In a two- or three-page report, provide these examples (don't forget to cite your sources). Explain how each example affects communication.

🔲 Recognize and avoid deliberate distortions and euphemisms.

9.  List at least two possible interpretations for each of the following deliberate distortions.
    a.  Management is cautiously optimistic that performance for the year, given the atmosphere of recession, will be acceptable.
    b.  Historical precedence would indicate that the Christmas bonus is vulnerable, but it is our belief that if earnings per share increase or there is no appreciable decrease the bonus will be maintained.
    c.  She has done the job she wanted to do. (to honor an outgoing president)
    d.  First I'd like to thank Sharine, Charlie, Jorgé, Ivan, Patricia, and Rachel who worked with me on this project. They did the jobs of two or three people.

🔲 Use language that does not discriminate on the basis of gender, disability, age, race, religion, ethnicity, or nationality.

10. Revise any terms or phrases in the following sentences that show bias toward age, gender, disability, race, religion, ethnicity, or nationality.
    a.  If you can't make it on Friday, please call my girl, Justine. She'll schedule another appointment.

   *b.*  At 23, he is the youngest participant in the wheelchair race.

   *c.*  Smith? Did you change your name when you came to this country? (in a job interview)

   *d.*  The chairman of the association's board will be elected at the next meeting.

   *e.*  The standard deduction a taxpayer can claim on his return is outlined on the following page.

   *f.*  Bathroom facilities must make provisions for handicapped employees.

   *g.*  Your supervisor would be younger than you are. Would that bother you? (in a job interview)

   *h.*  Patrolmen should be an asset to the police force.

   *i.*  The Democrats want to cut doctors' fees, and the Republicans are going after lawyers' fees. Watch out, Native Americans, the Indian chiefs may be next.

   *j.*  All employees should avoid taking vacations during the Christmas buying season.

◤ Use positive words as much as possible to avoid negative reactions.

11. Revise the following sentences to get rid of the negatives and to improve the "you" attitude. Where appropriate, emphasize what can be done rather than what can't be done.

   *a.*  Thank you for your trouble.

   *b.*  Please do not hesitate to call.

   *c.*  We're very sorry; but, as you know, mistakes are bound to occur.

   *d.*  Be sure not to miss the "How to Survive in Marketing" column in the next issue.

   *e.*  It is against our policy, but because you have been one of our largest accounts, we are willing to grant you another 30 days to pay your bills.

   *f.*  The computer you want cannot be ordered until the new fiscal year.

   *g.*  Decision making is, without a doubt, the most important task of an executive.

   *h.*  It is not possible to increase medical benefits during this round of negotiations.

   *i.*  We don't charge as much for brokerage fees as do other brokers.

   *j.*  If you don't know what you want to do now, don't worry. We can do it for you.

◤ Use active or passive words when each is most appropriate.

12. Identify whether each of the following sentences is active or passive.

   *a.*  You are going to be hired by the accounts receivable department.

   *b.*  Excellence is not achieved by cost cutters.

   *c.*  There are times when negative language is needed to get a point across forcefully.

   *d.*  Negative language sometimes gets a point across forcefully.

   *e.*  Account executives must know the needs of their clients.

   *f.*  Price cutting has been included as a major component of our quality assurance program.

◤ Use active or passive words when each is most appropriate.

13. Revise the passive sentences in exercise 12 so they are active.

◢ Choose the writing style most suited to your purpose and your reader.

14. Identify the writing style—formal or informal—in each of the sentences in exercise 12.

◢ Choose the writing style most suited to your purpose and your reader.

15. For each of the following situations, choose the sentence that best meets the purpose of the writer.
    a. To make the statement seem more objective:
       (1) I believe just-in-time manufacturing will solve the excess inventory problem.
       (2) Just-in-time manufacturing will solve the excess inventory problem.
    b. To make the statement less personal:
       (1) You failed to install the utilities program first.
       (2) The utilities must be installed first.
    c. To set a casual style:
       (1) The first example doesn't show how we can reduce expenses.
       (2) The first example does not show how expenses can be reduced.
    d. To rule out emotion:
       (1) Your explanation does not cover even half of the problem.
       (2) The explanation does not cover the problem in adequate detail.
    e. To concentrate on the message instead of the writer or reader:
       (1) The records were uncovered in time to prove the charges false.
       (2) I found the records in time to prove the charges false.

◢ Enhance the readability of business messages through attention to word choice, sentence and paragraph structure, and format.

16. Determine the reading level of the vignette at the beginning of this chapter. If you have a computer program that will analyze reading levels, do your analysis by computer. If you do not have access to such a computer program, calculate readability using the Gunning Fog Index or the Flesch Reading Ease Scale (explained in Exhibit 5.5). Present the results, with your computer printouts or calculations in a report to your teacher. Is the score or level appropriate for the grade level of this course? If not, what changes do you recommend to increase readability? If you believe the score or level is appropriate, what factors make it appropriate?

# BUSINESS LETTERS AND MEMOS

**CHAPTER 6**

# PLANNING BUSINESS MESSAGES AND SOLVING PROBLEMS WITH CRITICAL THINKING

## OBJECTIVES

When you finish studying this chapter, you will be able to:

- Define critical thinking and explain its importance to business communicators.
- Identify the eight critical thinking skills.
- Explain how critical thinking relates to the problem-solving process.
- Use a four-step process for solving problems.
- Apply the four stages of the message formulation process to your own business messages.
- Apply the five planning steps before composing business messages.
- Demonstrate sensitivity to the legal and ethical responsibilities of businesses and employees.
- Explain the intent of laws that affect business communication.
- Identify the skills needed to write collaboratively.
- Demonstrate the ability to draft business messages.
- Choose the appropriate organizational strategy, given your purpose and the anticipated audience reaction.
- Evaluate business messages and readers' feedback.

WHAT WOULD YOU DO IF...?

**ILLOGICAL.**    A lobbying group, Citizens for Quality Control (CQC), convinced Senator Robert Finch to sponsor a bill requiring American automobile manufacturers to implement stricter safety standards immediately: air bags on both sides in all cars and light trucks, bumpers that can be repaired if hit in a 35-mile-per-hour crash, and windshields that do not shatter or break if struck by passengers' heads during an accident. Senator Finch was especially concerned about automobile safety because his mother was killed in an automobile accident. He had also supported other legislation designed to improve automobile safety standards.

Because of a tight budget and cutbacks in his research staff, Senator Finch readily accepted the CQC lobbyist's data justifying the improved standards. In fact, he presented the following CQC information to the Senate in support of the bill:

- Five years ago, CQC conducted a study of 500 wrecks that involved fatalities. Survivors were asked if they believed that fatalities could have been prevented had the three new standards been in effect. The results were: air bags—89 percent yes, bumpers—92 percent yes, and windshields—93 percent yes.

- CQC conducted a study last year that asked 1,500 chiropractors to predict the percentage of injuries they treat yearly that are related to the three standards. The results were: lack of air bags—25 percent, low-quality bumpers—11 percent, and improper windshields—5.2 percent.

In committee, Senator Finch's bill was attacked for being based on biased and inconclusive data. Lobbyists for the "Big Three" American automakers presented information that contradicted CQC's studies. The committee had to decide whether or not this bill had enough merit to be presented to the entire Senate.

As you read the following chapter, identify the critical thinking errors Senator Finch made. What weaknesses in his thinking make this data questionable? Why is the data of the Big Three also questionable? What kind of data and/or information did the committee members need to make a decision about proceeding with the legislation? How could Senator Finch have planned his message to increase its chances of success?

## CRITICAL THINKING

Business communication typically is associated with writing and reading as well as speaking and listening. What people often forget is that effective business communication also requires a lot of thinking. By learning to think better, you will improve your ability to read and write all kinds of documents, and to comprehend and present oral information. Unfortunately, most of your education has revolved around being told what to think, not how.

All kinds of communication problems, from the most mundane to the most complex, can be attacked using the techniques discussed in this section. Presenting performance data; convincing a co-worker to improve the quality of his or her work; increasing a product's market share; improving the image of a product, a person, or a company; negotiating fair contracts; forming a business; or determining which computers or software to buy—no matter what the problem is or what decisions must be made, higher-order thinking skills will improve your ability to operate efficiently and successfully.

Define critical thinking and explain its importance to business communicators.

Critical thinking enables one to prepare, present, and advocate a point of view and to measure the worth and accuracy of sources, information, arguments, claims, and opinions.

Even though thinking comes naturally to everyone, higher-order thinking, or **critical thinking**, is not automatic. Critical thinking is a process designed to accomplish a set purpose. It includes the following abilities, which are important in the business world:

Analyzing.

Comparing and contrasting.

Explaining.

Evaluating.

Justifying.

Deducing conclusions.

Diagnosing.

Identifying or anticipating problems.

Synthesizing and applying information to solve unfamiliar problems.

The skills used in critical thinking enable business communicators to measure the worth and accuracy of sources, information, arguments, claims, and opinions, and to effectively present their own point of view.

## CRITICAL THINKING SKILLS

Identify the eight critical thinking skills.

**Each of the critical thinking skills is useful in different situations.**

Understanding your thinking processes is the first step in being able to think critically. You need to know what skills are necessary and how to use them. A number of communication theorists have tried to define the specific mental skills involved in critical thinking. B. K. Beyer, for instance, defined the following eight:

Determining the credibility of an observation.

Determining the strength of a conclusion.

Determining the quality of a generalization.

Determining the credibility of a written source.

Distinguishing between relevant and irrelevant information.

Distinguishing between verifiable facts and value judgments.

Detecting bias.

Identifying unstated assumptions.

Exhibit 6.1 presents these eight skills (or operations, in Beyer's terminology) and some of the clues or criteria to be used in exercising them. For example, the committee evaluating Senator Finch's legislation might question the quality of the generalizations drawn from the CQC's first study, because of the nature of the sample. Is a sample made up of 500 survivors of car wrecks enough to give a true picture of all survivors' opinions? The committee's efforts to detect bias might also be at work. As poignant as survivors' opinions may be, are they too emotional and one-sided?

To ensure that you do everything possible to make sound decisions, follow the six steps outlined by Beyer:

Identify your goal and purpose.

Identify the criteria or clues to use.

Search the data piece by piece to find evidence of the criteria or clues.

Identify any pattern within the evidence (how data are connected).

**EXHIBIT 6.1**

**Key Critical Thinking Skills**

**Determining the Credibility of an Observation**

Has only a short time elapsed between the report and observation?
Was the report prepared by the observer him/herself?
Are there minimal inferences?
Does the reporter believe the observation to be accurate?
Is there corroboration by other sources?

**Distinguishing between Relevant and Irrelevant Information**

Has information proved relevant through definition, example, attribute, detail/fact, explanation/reason, evidence for/against, or relationship?
Attribute

**Steps to Employ Critical Thinking Operations:**

1. Identify your goal and purpose.
2. Identify the criteria/clues to use.
3. Search the data piece by piece to find evidence of the criteria or clues.
4. Identify any pattern among the evidence— how they are connected to one another.
5. Match the evidence, clues and pattern found to the ideal/standard.
6. Judge the extent/degree of fit/match between evidence found and the criteria/standards.

**Determining the Strength of a Conclusion**

Are assumptions reasonable?
Does the conclusion explain the evidence?
Is the conclusion consistent with known facts?
Are competing conclusions inconsistent with known facts?
Does the conclusion seem reasonable?

**Determining between Facts and Value Judgments**

Is information precise, certain, objectively demonstrable, testable and free of excessive adjectives?
Is information free of opinion and excessive adjectives?
Does information avoid being subjective and personal?

**Determining the Quality of a Generalization**

Are the data used typical?
Is coverage wide?
Is the nature of the sample consistent with the nature of the larger population?

**Detecting Bias**

Does information avoid a pattern of exaggeration/overgeneralization, "loaded" words, opinions asserted as facts, imbalance (one-sidedness), and loaded images/loaded questions?

**Determining the Credibility of a Written Source**

Does the author have a reputation for accuracy?
Is the author an expert?
Are conflicts of interest absent?
Is the author's reputation at risk?
Has the author used accepted methods?
Does the author agree with other sources?

**Identifying Unstated Assumptions**

Is there a gap between conclusions or assertions and the premises?
Are claims explicitly linked?
Are clues such as *thus, therefore, however,* and *without* used to link claims, conclusions, assertions, and premises?

Source: Adapted from B. K. Beyer, *Developing a Thinking Skills Program,* Copyright © 1988 by Allyn and Bacon. Reprinted by permission.

Compare the evidence to the ideal or standard.

Judge how well the evidence matches the ideal or standard.

You can use these six steps to implement any of the eight critical thinking skills. Imagine that you are reading a report recommending that your company acquire a smaller company. In Beyer's terms, you are evaluating the credibility of a written source. First, you identify your goal as deciding whether to accept the recommendation of the report writer. Second, you choose the criteria to evaluate the writer's use of accepted methods. Third, you search the report for evidence that the writer has relied on such accepted sources as impartial financial analyses, industry forecasts, and the like. In the second and third steps, you determine the credibility of the observation and the strength of the conclusion by asking yourself the kinds of questions shown in the boxes in Exhibit 6.1. After ascertaining the quality of the generalization and the report writer's credibility, you look for evidence of relevancy and bias. At the same time, you assess the data for facts, value judgments, and unstated assumptions. Fourth, you look for a pattern—and in this case you find that some of the evidence comes from the target acquisition itself, which may be biased. The fifth step, comparing the evidence to the ideal or standard, leads to the final step, which is to make a judgment. Because some of the evidence does not match the ideal in this case, you decide that more unbiased evidence is necessary before you can decide to follow the report writer's recommendations.

Critical thinking techniques like these help you filter through the vast amount of information available to today's businesspeople. Your ability to comprehend, interpret, evaluate, and use this information will be a key factor in your success. Leadership comes to those who can find information, expand it, analyze it, and use it for making and evaluating decisions. Critical thinking skills will enable you to anticipate the need for change, analyze developments, and understand the alternatives. It will enable you to arrive at better answers, and it will prepare you to take responsibility for the conclusions you reach and the solutions you implement. Using these skills to evaluate the CQC studies would have helped Senator Finch make sounder decisions.

## CRITICAL THINKING AND PROBLEM SOLVING

Explain how critical thinking relates to the problem-solving process.

**Problem solving and critical thinking are not the same thing.**

Critical thinking is very useful for solving problems, but it is an entirely different process from problem solving. Critical thinking is a number of operations from which you can pick and choose, depending on the situation; problem solving is a series of steps performed in order, no matter what the problem might be. Exhibit 6.2 illustrates the steps of problem solving. Whether your problem is to evaluate a procedure or to select a contractor to build a new superhighway, you will probably follow these steps to solve it:

**Problem solving is a series of steps used to identify a problem and its causes and to generate, evaluate, select, and implement solutions.**

Identify the problem.

Gather information.

Set standards.

Implement and evaluate a solution.

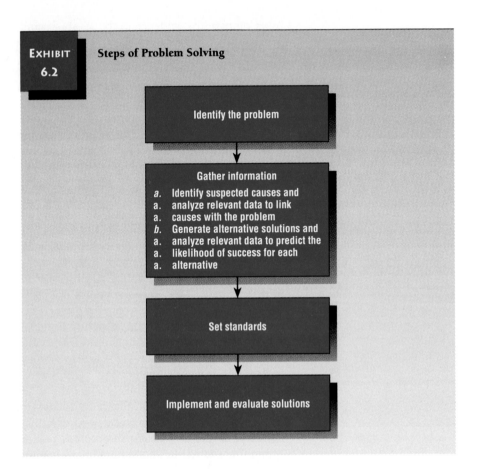

**EXHIBIT 6.2**  **Steps of Problem Solving**

Identify the problem

Gather information
a. Identify suspected causes and
a. analyze relevant data to link
a. causes with the problem
b. Generate alternative solutions and
a. analyze relevant data to predict the
a. likelihood of success for each
a. alternative

Set standards

Implement and evaluate solutions

Use a four-step process for solving problems.

**IDENTIFY THE PROBLEM.**    It is not as easy to determine exactly what a problem is as it might seem at first. Even with knowledge of a field and familiarity with the types of problems that are typical, identifying a problem requires you to sift through multiple possibilities. For example, say that you're a manager in the automobile industry and revenue is down. Because the national economy is in recession, some of the other managers in your industry decide the problem is the economy. After all, when fewer people have jobs and money is harder to borrow, fewer people buy new cars. However, the economy may not be the real problem; perhaps the public thinks the new models lack quality or the designs are unappealing.

Defining the problem in several different ways helps to pinpoint and solve the real problem. For example, if you and the other managers decide the economy is the reason for slow car sales, you might concentrate on lobbying policy-makers to lower interest rates on car loans and increase the number of jobs available so that more people can afford cars. Consequently, you might not do anything to improve quality or design. Do you see how identifying the problem accurately is the first, most basic step in solving it?

The ability to shift perspective, to look at a problem from many different angles, is an element of critical thinking. In the automobile industry example,

Critical thinking requires a willingness and an ability to look at a problem from many different angles.

an astute problem solver would try to view the problem through consumers' eyes. Viewing the new models from this other perspective might help identify the problem in its most elementary form.

Anticipating problems before they occur and perceiving the potential for problems are also valuable skills. After a major problem has occurred, have you ever heard someone say, "I knew that was going to happen!" and then thought, "If you knew it was going to happen, why didn't you warn me?" The ability to see potential problems ahead of time is not easy, nor is it enough. You must be able to warn others about those problems and persuade them to take action before the problems occur. For that you need initiative, and you must be comfortable with uncertainty.

Groups are usually better at anticipating problems and identifying solutions than are individuals. Imagine a discussion in a work group beginning with the statement "Labor unrest is common in our industry. If one of the four unions we deal with were to strike, what would be the result?" All kinds of opinions—realistic and outlandish—might come out in the group discussion, along with all kinds of data. Eventually, however, the work group has a good chance of coming up with a list of reasonable actions the company could take to avoid a strike. Because a group of people usually can draw on greater experience than one person can, groups can usually identify the true problem more accurately.

**GATHER INFORMATION.**   In the second stage of problem solving, you must find or generate the information needed for making decisions. This information takes two forms:

- Suspected causes of the problem and data that link those causes with the problem.
- Alternative solutions to the problem and data that predict the likelihood of success for each alternative.

Analytical research skills (the kind you will learn about in Chapter 12) come in handy as you gather these types of information.

To perform well at this stage of problem solving, you must have a predisposition to seek answers before acting or, to use an old cliché, to look before you leap. You must also be able to determine what information is necessary and know how to go about obtaining it. Because a great deal of information in the business world is obtained face-to-face, your ability to question others effectively and to listen objectively to their answers (see Chapter 3) will improve your chances of getting all the information you need. In addition, the ability to think creatively is of use in generating alternative solutions.

One common technique for generating alternatives is **brainstorming.** Brainstorming is normally performed in small groups. People in the group are free to blurt out anything that comes to mind about the subject. In a spirit of fun, participants are encouraged to say whatever comes to mind without concern for how stupid it may sound. No laughing or commenting on responses is allowed. Ideas are usually written on a board or flipchart as fast as they are uttered. When the group runs out of ideas, the ones already generated are discussed. All alternatives are considered in detail. Through discussion, some are ruled out, but some remain as viable alternatives to solving the problem.

If handled correctly, brainstorming sessions generate many excellent ideas. Creative thinkers are often introverts who seldom speak up in regular meetings,

---

*Sidebar notes (left margin):*

Critical thinking requires the ability to anticipate problems and persuade others to take action to solve the problems ahead of time.

Critical thinking requires a predisposition to seek answers *before* acting.

Critical thinking requires creative thinking.

Creative thinking requires playfulness, patience, persistence, the ability to work with others, tolerance for uncertainty, and the ability to question and to listen.

but the relaxed, unthreatening atmosphere of an expertly handled brainstorming session encourages these people to speak up. The best brainstormers are playful, patient, and persistent. Their ability to work effectively with others and to tolerate uncertainty helps other group members break out of their mindsets and see new possibilities.

**SET STANDARDS.** Many businesspeople make decisions based on "gut feeling," which is actually a form of intuition. Intuition may come in handy when you have to decide between two thoroughly tested alternatives that seem to be equal. However, intuition is not a good standard for making decisions in the early stages of problem solving. All information gathered should be evaluated against rigorous standards of relevance, logic, validity, fairness, clarity, and efficiency. Techniques for testing these standards (to ensure they have been met) should be established before information is gathered.

To evaluate conclusions, you must set standards against which you can assess the relevance, logic, validity, fairness, clarity, efficiency, and evidence of information used for decision making.

The critical thinking skills outlined earlier can be used to evaluate the merits of data to be used for decision making. They can help you determine if the information you have gathered is relevant, identify ambiguous claims, or distinguish between statements of fact and opinion. At this point, widely accepted statistical tests can be applied to quantitative data.

Critical thinking requires a willingness to subject your own ideas and opinions to rigorous evaluation.

This stage of the problem-solving process presupposes a willingness to subject your own ideas to scrutiny. If your ideas do not meet the standards you've set, you must be prepared to modify them. Objectivity and honesty are crucial. Engaging in critical thinking is not just evaluating the work of others; you must evaluate everything you do as well.

**IMPLEMENT AND EVALUATE A SOLUTION.** Critical thinking should also be a major part of the last stage of problem solving. After you have narrowed down the alternatives and taken the steps necessary to solve the problem, you must assess how well the solution is working. If it is not working as your data predicted, you must be willing to start the problem-solving process all over again.

For example, consider again the mistaken assumption that the economy was the problem behind slow car sales. Say that the manufacturer decided the proper solution was to lobby the government to implement policies for bolstering the economy. The final stage of problem solving would be to monitor closely the economy's health as well as the number of cars sold. As soon as company executives see that the new models are still not selling despite an improving economy, they should immediately return to the first stage of problem solving. Critical thinking will show them that their original solution was no solution at all.

## THE MESSAGE FORMULATION PROCESS

Apply the four stages of the message formulation process to your own business messages.

Critical thinking is not just a tool for evaluating others' ideas and solutions to problems; it is equally useful in formulating your own messages. Business messages have a point of view, which must be effectively presented and supported. You will be better prepared to present and support your point of view if you can apply critical thinking skills to your positions, arguments, and conclusions.

The most effective business communicators follow a four-stage process in formulating their letters, memos, and reports:

Plan the message.

Organize the message.

Compose the message.

Evaluate the message.

These stages can be used in creating both written and oral messages. (The process of formulating written messages is the subject of the rest of this chapter; oral communication is covered in Chapters 14 and 15.) Each stage of the process relies on critical thinking skills.

### STAGE ONE: PLAN YOUR MESSAGE

Apply the five planning steps before composing business messages.
Whether your message is to be delivered orally or in writing, you should begin by planning it. Planning involves five steps:

Establish your purpose or purposes.

Choose a medium and a channel.

Consider legal and ethical issues.

Analyze your audience.

Gather the necessary resources.

Use the following sections as a guide when you plan letters, memos, and reports, which are the subjects of the next seven chapters.

**ESTABLISH YOUR PURPOSE OR PURPOSES.**    Before you write a business message, you must consider exactly what you want the message to achieve. Do you want to introduce the reader to a new product? Inform a customer that an error has been corrected? Announce a newly negotiated contract between labor and management? Submit a report to your superior? Persuade a client to increase advertising expenditures?

> A purpose is the goal—the end result—you want your correspondence or report to achieve.

There are many occasions on which a letter or memo will be written to achieve more than one purpose. For example, in a letter responding to a complaint from a citizen, a police chief might want to inform the citizen of how the complaint is being investigated and to restore the citizen's confidence in the police force.

Identifying the purpose before you start writing helps focus your thoughts around the most important points you want to make. Having these points in the forefront of your mind as you write improves your ability to get to the topic directly and discuss it succinctly. The easy-to-understand message that results will elicit more positive reactions from your readers than will a message that rambles without a clear direction.

**CHOOSE A MEDIUM AND CHANNEL.**    A business message can be delivered orally or in writing. To decide which method will work better for achieving your purpose, ask yourself these questions:

> The form the message will take depends on the medium and the channel you want to use.

- *Is a permanent record necessary?* If you need a permanent record for legal reasons or because you may need to refer to the message in the future, the message must be in written form. Contract offers and acceptances, labor and management negotiation proposals, and employee performance appraisals are a few of the messages that should be backed up by written records. Consider, for example, the situation in which banker Hector Villanueva found himself. Federal investigators found a series of monetary transfers that seemed to point to illegal money laundering. Luckily, Hector was able to prove—with dated memos—that he had reported the questionable transfers to his superiors on three occasions.

Minutes of meetings, agreements made during negotiations, the results of problem-solving sessions, and the like should be put in writing as soon as possible to avoid different interpretations of the same event. Because of differences in perception and because we all have a tendency to listen for what we want to hear, it is surprising how many different interpretations there can be of the same event. These written records should be thought of as drafts and should be forwarded to all participants to ensure everyone involved agrees that what is written down is actually what occurred or what was agreed. Participants should be encouraged to respond if changes need to be made. This prevents later misunderstandings that occur when things don't happen as one of the participants expects.

- *Does the material contain complex information or technical data?* As a student, you can certainly appreciate the value of receiving technical information in written form. When complex information is presented in writing, the reader can control the pace at which it is presented and reread difficult passages. Technical or complex information presented orally, however (as in a lecture), is harder to grasp and nearly impossible to review immediately. In addition, raw numbers in lists are hard to absorb. Communication improves when the numbers are converted to graphs and charts.

- *Do you need to control what is included in a message and how it is covered?* Editing your words is much easier when you write than when you speak. Written messages can be critiqued before they are distributed, and words that carry negative connotations can be eliminated. You can heighten the you attitude as well as make any other changes needed to improve the message. On the other hand, very few people have such control over their spoken messages. That is why most corporations and organizations have public relations experts responsible for writing and delivering formal statements to the media in sensitive situations. These formal statements are often read word for word to make sure there is no distortion of the organization's message.

- *Which method is most convenient and least expensive?* If you have to reach a large audience, written messages are usually easier and less expensive to send than oral messages. Within companies—especially companies with locations around the world—sending memos is often preferable to calling large meetings. For example, it might be impossible to get everyone together for a meeting to discuss changes in the hiring procedures. Giving employees a written manual outlining the new procedures would be more convenient and far less expensive. Although voice mail telephone systems now make it easy to send a single message to people within an organization, the technology is not yet available to send the same kinds of electronic messages to large numbers of outsiders. Thus, form letters are often the only viable alternative for reaching large numbers of people.

When you have determined a message should be written, you must then decide on the form of the message. Aside from casual messages, letters and memos are the two most common types of correspondence used in business. Letters are written to people outside the company, such as clients, customers, and suppliers. Memos are sent only to people who work for the same company. The main difference between letters and memos is the format, the way the message is arranged on the page. Appendix C illustrates acceptable letter and memo formats.

Another form of written response, sometimes used because of its speed and convenience, is margin notes. Imagine that a customer has written you, asking where she can buy a product you do not sell. You could simply jot down the name and address of the retailer in the bottom margin of the customer's letter. A signed, handwritten note can be just as effective as a professionally typed piece of correspondence in some cases. The handwritten note might also imply that you wanted to answer the request quickly.

**Margin notes are an effective way of answering someone's questions when response time is a concern and informality will be acceptable to the recipient.**

Demonstrate sensitivity to the legal and ethical responsibilities of businesses and employees.

**CONSIDER LEGAL AND ETHICAL ISSUES.** Most people in business make decisions about what to do based on a deeply felt sense of what is right and what is wrong. However, a few do not. You can rarely pick up a newspaper without reading of bribery, collusion, embezzlement, insider trading, mail and wire fraud, misleading advertising, and cover-ups. When you see stories like these, remember that the media tend to sensationalize the bad examples, whereas the ethical behavior of the majority goes unnoticed.

Being ethical means doing what is right to achieve results that are good. An ethical person, therefore, does the right thing, and, by so doing, achieves good results. Results are good when you have achieved the greatest good for all those involved.

**Ethical behavior entails doing what is right to achieve positive results.**

This requirement is not always easy to meet because ethics is a complex issue. For example, is a corporation more responsible to its stockholders, the public, or its employees? What is right and good for one might not always be right and good for another. Decisions about plant closings, layoffs, forced retirements, mislabeling of products, and misrepresentations of facts are not as clear-cut as stealing, lying, or cheating on an exam.

As you use critical thinking skills to analyze your actions, ask yourself the following questions:

Have I been truthful?

Have I disclosed clearly and completely all that should be communicated?

Have I been fair to all concerned?

Have my actions been beneficial to all concerned?

Have I harmed innocent people in any way?

Have I been loyal?

Have I kept my promises?

Have I given credit to those who deserve it?

Have I shown gratitude to those who deserve it?

Have I accepted responsibility for my actions?

Have I made amends to those who have been harmed by my actions?

Have my actions built goodwill and better interpersonal relationships?

If you can answer "yes" to these questions, you have acted ethically.

In a 1978 speech to Religious Heritage of America in Washington, DC, Donald V. Siebert of JCPenney suggested another way you can evaluate your conduct:

Am I personally proud of this action?

Am I comfortable with this decision?

Would I feel comfortable if it were known by my associates, my friends, my family, and the public in general?

Whichever approach you use, it will help you resist the pressure to compromise your personal ethics in the pursuit of personal and corporate goals.

Most large companies have adopted formal codes of ethics. By publishing these codes of ethics, companies acknowledge reality: Companies do not commit unethical acts; people do. Such codes send the clear message to employees that ethical conduct is as much a goal of the company as profit is.

Exhibit 6.3 is a small portion of the code of ethics of 3M, one of the largest multinational corporations based in the United States. The opening statement carries this message from Allen F. Jacobson, chairman of the board: "It is important for 3M employees to recognize that one constant is our commitment to carry out day-to-day responsibilities in a manner which earns the respect of our customers, our competitors, our suppliers, our shareholders, our fellow employees and the communities in which we do business." All 3M employees are required to verify that they have read and understood the policy. The portion reproduced in Exhibit 6.3 deals with gifts and entertainment. Other topics in the 15-page statement are standards of conduct, use of company facilities and aircraft, political activities and contributions, lobbying, business contacts, and the creation of business relationships.

◢ Explain the intent of laws that affect business communication.

In addition to being ethical, you are expected to abide by the law when conducting business. Large companies normally have departments of lawyers responsible for ensuring that all employees operate legally. (Because of the complexity of the law, this discussion merely introduces the most important legal issues related to business communication. Laws pertaining to employment, credit and collections, and sales are covered in other chapters.)

- *Contracts.* Law schools offer entire courses in contract law. However, as you conduct business you should know that any oral or written communication could be interpreted by the courts as a contract, obligating you and your company to carry out any promises made. Written messages are particularly important, because they serve as legal evidence in court. Your signature on a document means that you approve of and agree with the contents.

- *Defamation.* **Defamation** is any false statement that is made known to others, results in damage, and is made maliciously. The two kinds of defamation are **libel** (written and permanent defamation) and **slander** (oral defamation). You cannot be sued for slander for calling a co-worker lazy and incompetent unless you are overheard by someone else and have no proof. However, permanent records, such as memos or videotapes that damage a person's good name or reputation, act as evidence of libel. As a result, competent communicators are careful to avoid putting in writing anything that cannot be proved objectively. Instead of calling someone lazy, use objective language and verifiable information—such as a written log of the days a co-worker has come in late or left early, or proof of tasks

*Formal statements of an organization's policies pertaining to ethical behavior serve as guidelines for employees who have tough decisions to make.*

*Libel (written and permanent) and slander (oral) are the two forms of defamation of character.*

| EXHIBIT 6.3 | **Sample Code of Ethics** |
|---|---|

The company prohibits making, or causing others to make, illegal payments to advance company interests. 3M recognizes that in the ordinary course of business it may seem appropriate to give or receive some business courtesy, i.e., a gift or entertainment to create or enhance good will for the company. Whether 3M employees should engage in that activity on behalf of the company depends on three basis considerations: the type of business courtesy being extended; the underlying purpose to be served; and the recipient of the courtesy.

The definition of business courtesies may vary. Usually, if someone receives a benefit in the course of business transactions without paying the fair market value, a business courtesy is being extended. Entertainment, recreation, meals, cocktails, hospitality, transportation, discounts, tickets and passes are all examples of typical business courtesies.

In the case of government employees, state and federal regulations may set limits on the amounts and kinds of courtesy that can be extended. (For example, there is a prohibition of gifts, meals or entertainment, or the offer of any of these to Department of Defense employees.) Each employee or agent is responsible for becoming thoroughly familiar with the limits on amounts and kinds of courtesy which are acceptable to the customers he or she serves, and observing these limits.

Employees additionally should be guided by the rule that they should extend or receive no courtesy that could be of such a nature or frequency as to compromise either the reputation or integrity of any supplier or customer, including units of government or its employees, or any 3M employee or the company itself.

In the absence of controlling law or regulations, 3M requires employees to exercise good judgment and moderation when offering or accepting any form of business courtesy, always bearing in mind that their own reputation and the reputation of 3M, as well as that of the recipient, is at stake. Further, 3M desires that employees act in a fashion which would neither embarrass the participants nor give the impression that the recipient of the business courtesy need pay it back.

In sum, if a business courtesy raises an ethical concern in the employee's mind, it probably should not be given or accepted. At the very least, the decision to give or accept the business courtesy should be the subject of discussion with the employee's supervisors.

In the absence of a decision by an appropriate supervisor, or if an employee questions a decision, 3M has a central phone number (612-733-1548) that can be called for assistance. In addition, each employee should feel free to contact the attorney in the Office of General Counsel who is assigned to the employee's business unit ("Division Attorney").

Source: Gifts and Entertainment excerpt from the *Business Conduct Policy*, 3M Corporation. Reprinted with permission of 3M Center, Office of General Counsel, St. Paul, Minnesota.

that have been turned in after deadlines or that were not done at all. To prove that an individual is incompetent, you could show documentation of the person's many mistakes despite your repeated (also documented) attempts to teach him or her how to handle the job correctly.

Fear of being sued for libel or slander is the reason many companies reveal only former employees' length of employment and job title. Even companies that made a practice of only releasing positive information about good employees have been faulted. The courts have ruled that giving no work performance information about poor workers while providing that information for good workers is the equivalent of giving negative recommendations. When companies give negative information, they should be able to document the basis for their conclusions in case they are sued.

- *Fraud and misrepresentation.* **Fraud** is a deliberate misrepresentation of the truth to induce someone to give up something of value. Deliberately

Fraud is a deliberate misrepresentation of the truth to induce someone to give up something of value.

concealing or omitting information you are required to reveal is also fraud. **Misrepresentation** occurs when a false statement is made innocently, with no intent to deceive. Consider the case of a government contractor being paid to develop a new tank for the Pentagon. Typically, this type of work is done on a cost-plus basis (all expenses are paid, plus a specific percentage above expenses). If the contractor deliberately overstates expenses so that the U.S. government will have to pay more than is fair, the contractor has committed fraud. Therefore, the U.S. government could sue the company for the money paid under the terms of the contract and for additional monetary damages. If, however, the contractor could prove that the overstatement was an innocent error, the government could not collect more than the amount it overpaid.

Invasion of privacy is unreasonable intrusion into the private life of an individual.

- *Privacy*. Invasion of privacy is unreasonable intrusion into the private life of an individual. You cannot use sophisticated equipment to spy through the windows at information on someone's desk, and you cannot photocopy the work or property of others without their permission. It is a violation of privacy to tap into a computer network to take information that belongs to an organization or an individual. Privacy is violated by taking or reading information in someone's files or in their company mailboxes unless the person or organization accessing the information has a legal right to it.

Ownership of the information is often the issue in deciding when a person's right to privacy has been violated. For example, companies are allowed to listen in secretly on their employees' telephone sales calls, because companies pay all costs involved and the calls are made within the scope of employees' duties. Other instances of electronic monitoring of employee performance have been upheld by the courts as being legal because employers have argued successfully that supervisors have a right to monitor their subordinates electronically, just as they are allowed to monitor employee performance in person.

You might find yourself tempted to record meetings or telephone conversations when sensitive information is discussed. However, although the courts sometimes give permission to law enforcement agencies to tape the conversations of suspected criminals, you cannot legally record the conversations of others without notifying them they are being recorded.

Many electronic databanks contain detailed information about people's work and personal lives. However, various state and federal laws govern to whom this information can be released. The Fair Credit Reporting Act of 1970 and the Privacy Act of 1974 define the rights of individuals to participate in decisions regarding the disclosure of information collected about themselves. As a result, others, such as mortgagors or credit card companies, cannot determine your salary or how much money you use unless you have signed statements directing the company you work for and credit reporting agencies to release this information.

Although federal and state governments are prevented from releasing information to others about individuals, companies can legally sell some of the information they have collected about their customers. If you have ever ordered something from a mail-order catalog, you probably noticed that you began receiving catalogs from many other sellers almost immediately. Obviously, information about your interests in addition to your name and address are being released to other companies. If you are uncertain of exactly what information about your customers, clients, and employees can be collected and/or sold or given to others, seek the advice of legal counsel. Laws vary from one state to another. For example, some states prohibit gathering telephone numbers electronically. This process identifies and records automatically the telephone number of anyone who telephones a place of business, and some states consider this a violation of privacy and do not allow the process to be used. These states argue that individuals should have the option to decide to whom they provide their telephone numbers.

- *Ownership and copyright.* Letters, memos, and other written materials belong to the person who wrote them. Therefore, even though a letter has been sent to you, it is not yours to do with as you wish. Just as you would not think of using statements from articles or books without the permission of the authors and publishers, you cannot publicize letters or portions of them without the permission of the authors. This law also applies to computer software, compact discs, records, cassette tapes, and other nonprint media. Many companies have been held liable for allowing computer software to be copied by employees.

> **Written material belongs to the writer, not to the buyer or the recipient. It cannot be copied or used without permission.**

The laws affecting business life are numerous. However, you will find that ethical behavior is even more important than a conscious effort to abide by the law. By doing what is right and good, you will almost always find you have automatically met the letter and the spirit of the law. Still, the more legal background you have, the better you will be able to protect your own interests and those of your company against violations of the law. If you have not already done so, consider enrolling in a business law class. It will help you gain appreciation for the legal knowledge necessary to protect yourself in the business world.

**ANALYZE YOUR AUDIENCE.**   In Chapter 4 you learned about the psychological aspects of business communication. Understanding the needs that motivate people to act is a major element of audience analysis. Another important element is understanding how people are likely to react to your message. Before writing any business message, ask yourself the following questions:

> **These questions must be answered before you can decide how a message should be organized.**

Will your reader be interested in the topic and pleased by what you have to say?

Will your reader be interested but react neutrally to what you have to say?

Will your reader be interested in the topic and upset, angry, or disappointed by what you have to say?

Will your reader have little, if any, initial interest in the topic?

The answers to these questions will determine how you organize your message (step two of the message formulation process). They will also help you compose a message that uses effective you attitude and positive wording.

Another consideration when the audience for your message is large is whether you should write individually to each recipient or send a form message. A **form message** is one sent to more than one person with little, if any, attempt made to personalize it. With computers, you can rather easily merge a list of addresses and names with the document itself (although some additional expense is involved) so that each document is personalized with minor bits of information. Exhibit 6.4 compares a standard form letter (on the left) with a personalized form letter (on the right).

> **Form messages are standard letters and memos sent to more than one person containing little, if any, attempt to personalize messages for each recipient.**

**EXHIBIT 6.4**

**Sample Form Messages**

INTER-OFFICE MEMORANDUM

January 16, 1994

Dear Employee:

You and your eligible family members can now take advantage of a new vision care plan that has been added to your health care program. The plan is administered by Vision Care, Inc., a nationally recognized health care provider.

You will be able to receive a complete eye examination yearly; and, with a $10 deductible, any glasses or contact lenses prescribed for you will be covered up to a limit of $150.

Good vision is important. Not only does it improve your outlook on life, it can also save your life. Studies show that many manufacturing accidents result from poor vision and that some health-related problems, such as headaches and backaches, can be cured with corrective lenses.

Please enroll for this critical new program soon. Open enrollment for the current year will end April 28. Enrollment forms are available in the Human Relations Office.

Sincerely,

*Elsie Nightingale*

Elsie Nightingale
Benefits Specialist

**This form letter will be sent to all employees.**

**EXHIBIT 6.4**  Continued

## Vision Care Inc.

1426 EAST BAY STREET
PROVIDENCE, RI 02906
401-881-6000
fax 401-881-6010

_____ (Date)

_____ (Mr./Ms./M. First Name/Last Name)
_____ (Street Address/Apt. No.)
_____ (City, State, ZIP Code)

Dear _____ :   (Mr./Ms./M. Last Name)

Welcome to the Vision Care family! Your enrollment form was received and is being processed rapidly.

As you were probably informed by your company representatives, your policy will take effect on _____ (date). On that date or later, you may complete one of the enclosed forms to receive approval to make an appointment. The form will be sent to you within 10 days of its receipt.

The policy arranged by your company provides for examinations on a _____ (yearly/biyearly) basis with a deductible of _____ ($10/$25) for each person. Restrictions as to approved options exist. Please refer to the enclosed manual.

Please let us process your request for service soon.

Sincerely,

*I. C. Cleare*

I. C. Clearé

Enclosures

This form message contains boilerplate paragraphs. Personal information is merged by computer with the standard paragraphs to create a message unique to each recipient.

Large credit card companies make frequent use of personalized form letters to remind people their accounts are overdue. These letters typically have blanks that computers fill in with the amount due, the due date, the account number, and so on. Such individual information is often merged with what is referred to as **boilerplate**—stock paragraphs that can be merged by computers at the request of the letter "writer." In such cases, letter writing is simply a matter of ordering and combining prewritten paragraphs.

The advantages of form messages are readily apparent. They are an inexpensive way to reach large numbers of people. Because of the speed with which they can be composed and sent, they represent a good method of getting information out quickly. Commonly sent form messages include memos to staff members about upcoming social events, procedural changes, and meetings; public relations announcements; and announcements of new services and products.

The major disadvantage of form messages is the reaction of many recipients. Most form messages have an impersonal tone that offends some readers—or at best, that fails to draw them in. The biggest challenge to companies that market their products by direct mail is to get people to open the envelope and read the message. You probably receive large quantities of such junk mail. How much of it do you actually open? How many of the letters do you actually read?

With careful attention to the you attitude, however, form messages can be effective. As you can see in the examples in Exhibit 6.4, simply using the pronouns *you* and *your* helps make such messages more appealing. The subtle psychological influence of the you attitude draws the reader into the message, even when it is obviously written for many people.

"Reading" your audience is a skill that must be practiced over and over. If you routinely analyze your readers and listeners, you will eventually develop a more effective style. To help you develop this skill, each chapter of this book that deals with written messages and oral presentations contains a section on analyzing your audience.

**GATHER NECESSARY RESOURCES.**    Formulating a business message often requires more than just a pen and paper. If you are already thoroughly familiar with the situation and all that has gone before, you will not have to do much research. However, it might be necessary for you to pull from the files all previous correspondence and other information that pertain to the situation. For example, as a warranty service representative, you might be responsible for answering all letters about a specific product. Before answering a letter from a customer who is trying to collect on a warranty after six months of making telephone calls, sending letters, and completing forms, you would want to catch up on the complete history of the customer's concerns. You want to be able to address all the customer's needs, not just those expressed in the latest correspondence. You might also need other information, such as company policies or boilerplate approved by your company for certain situations.

Anything that should be enclosed with the message when it is mailed should also be gathered before the message is composed. Enclosures might include product brochures, company catalogs, pre-addressed envelopes and postcards, and order forms. Having these enclosures on hand will help you refer to them accurately in your message and remember to include them before you seal the envelope.

Collaborative writing is the
team approach to formulating
business messages.

◼ Identify the skills needed to write collaboratively.

Another sort of resource is the assistance of others. You will write many routine letters, memos, and reports yourself. However, you may sometimes discover that only a team can efficiently complete a writing assignment. **Collaborative writing** is the term used when a document is written by more than one person and when all team members are given credit and held accountable for the finished product.

Collaborative writing makes the most sense under the following conditions:

- The document is too important to the organization to risk letting one person prepare it.

- The complexity of the task requires the participation of people with diverse knowledge, interests, and technical backgrounds.

- The document must represent more than one viewpoint.

- There is not enough time for one person to accomplish the task.

- The document is too long for one person to handle easily.

- Staff members with different views must reach consensus, so everyone involved is committed to achieving success.

- Because of the risks involved, no individual is willing to take personal responsibility for the success or failure of the document.

Collaborative work groups can be organized in different ways. They can be led by one person who assigns the work and dictates the purpose, or they can operate democratically with each person in the group having an equal vote. Groups can be made up of any number of people, but five is often cited as an optimum size—larger groups can be difficult to manage. In general, the larger the group, the more time it will take to reach consensus. However, the larger the group, the broader is its commitment to the finished product. For example, if all eight production supervisors develop and publish a new procedures manual, all of them will be committed to making sure their employees understand and use the new procedures.

At the initial meeting, a collaborative writing group's members should decide on the purpose of the document, analyze its readers, and determine a general plan of organization. They usually divide the writing task as well, assigning group members to write the various parts of the document. Some groups prefer to have one person write the first draft, after which group members evaluate and revise assigned sections. Deadlines are usually set and future meetings planned at the first meeting. To speed up the discussion process, drafts can be distributed to group members before the next meeting. It takes a great deal of time to bring a group to consensus on even the most uncontroversial topics.

Special computer software, called *groupware*, is a big help to collaborative work groups. Anyone in the work group can access a document on a networked computer, edit it, and make suggestions to the writer using standard proofreading symbols—all without changing the original. Notes to the writer can be added in the margins. Major rewrites are signaled in the body of the document, so the original writer can easily refer to the suggestions.

Getting a group to work together effectively can be frustrating. However, collaborative writing groups can work harmoniously and achieve positive results by following these guidelines:

- The leader of the group (if a leader is necessary) should be accepted by all group members. Whether appointed by a high-level executive or elected by group members, the leader must be someone group members respect. A leader cannot lead a group that doesn't agree to follow.

- If all members believe they are part of a team with a purpose important to both the company and themselves, they will work better together. To foster a spirit of teamwork, group members must have time to get to know one another. Respecting one another as individuals will help them respect one another as co-workers.

- All group members should feel free to express their opinions and to question the opinions and work of all group members, including the leader's. Members should agree, however, to use diplomacy and tact in suggesting changes. Leaders must take care not to squelch some ideas in favor of others. All ideas and concerns should be given equal consideration.

- Ways of dealing with conflicting opinions and viewpoints should be worked out when the group is formed. Conflict is a natural part of working in groups; in fact, the differing viewpoints that cause conflict actually improve the final product. Many groups agree to vote when unanimous agreement cannot be reached. Others agree to refer serious disagreements to a higher authority, such as the group's leader or the executive to whom the group reports.

- All members of the group must agree to share the credit or the blame for the final product. They must also agree to put the interests and goals of the group ahead of their personal interests and personal gain. In some work groups, members must sign the final product before it is released to higher levels as an indication that they agree with and approve of the contents. This is so that individual group members cannot try later to undermine the group's efforts by hinting they would have done things differently.

### STAGE TWO: ORGANIZE YOUR MESSAGE

Organizing a message is a two-phase process: freewriting major points and then selecting the best organizational strategy for presenting these points. Normally, only the most experienced business writers are able to compose a mailable document from start to finish without organizing the message first.

◼ Demonstrate the ability to draft business messages.

**FREEWRITE MAJOR POINTS.** **Freewriting** is just what the name implies: Writing without restraint—without trying to observe any rules about content, organization, style, or form. Freewriting means putting your thoughts on paper, as fast as you can think of them, without editing.

*Freewriting is a concentrated effort to write down the purpose and the major points you want to cover as fast as you can think of them.*

To start freewriting a letter or memo, write the purpose of the message at the top of the page. For example, you might write that your purpose is "to inform clients of our new services" or "to convince my boss to approve the purchase of new computer software." Then ask yourself these questions: What do I need to say in this document? What does the reader want or need to know? As you think of the points you want to include in the message, write them down in words and phrases. Do not attempt to use full sentences at this time, and do not try to organize your notes in any kind of order. Do not evaluate each point as you write it down. That will all be done later.

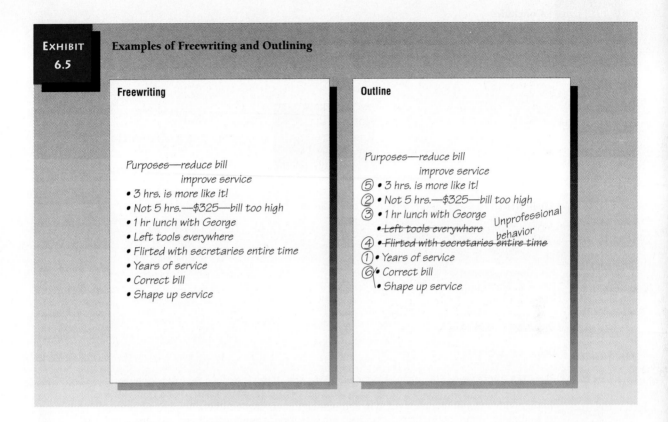

EXHIBIT 6.5

**Examples of Freewriting and Outlining**

**Freewriting**

Purposes—reduce bill
    improve service
• 3 hrs. is more like it!
• Not 5 hrs.—$325—bill too high
• 1 hr lunch with George
• Left tools everywhere
• Flirted with secretaries entire time
• Years of service
• Correct bill
• Shape up service

**Outline**

Purposes—reduce bill
    improve service
⑤ • 3 hrs. is more like it!
② • Not 5 hrs.—$325—bill too high
③ • 1 hr lunch with George    Unprofessional
   • Left tools everywhere    behavior
④ • Flirted with secretaries entire time
① • Years of service
⑥ • Correct bill
   • Shape up service

The first frame of Exhibit 6.5 is an example of freewriting. The second frame shows how the writer can use the notes from freewriting to construct an outline. As you can see, some of the words and phrases the writer first thought of were combined (shown by brackets), some considered unimportant were crossed out, and all those remaining were organized by numbers. The resulting letter is shown in the third frame.

Freewriting works because it frees the writer from the mistaken belief that thoughts have to be "good" before they can be written down. It allows the writer to get the essentials down on paper or on screen. Once all the details are out of the writer's mind, he or she can begin to organize the points into a logical arrangement that takes the reader's needs into consideration.

Choose the appropriate organizational strategy, given your purpose and the anticipated audience reaction.

**CHOOSE AN ORGANIZATIONAL STRATEGY.** The order in which information is presented in a document is as important to setting the tone as are the words used. To determine the best order, you need to analyze how the reader is likely to react to the message. Then you can choose an organizational plan that helps the reader become interested in your message and accept it, while retaining as positive an impression of you and your company as possible.

Before learning about how to choose an appropriate organizational plan, test your knowledge of human nature:

**EXHIBIT 6.5**   Concluded

**AMERICAN**
H • O • M • E
*designs*

April 16, 1994

Ms. Casey Scriven
General Manager
Pro–Com, Inc.
101 Mission Street
Denver, CO 80203

Dear Ms. Scriven:

Pro–Com and American Home Designers have been doing business for many years,
and the work of your computer service technicians has always been of the highest
quality. Knowing how important our computers are to us, you have always responded
immediately to our calls for service, and your technicians have worked diligently to
get our computers back on line quickly.

However, the February 28 visit was not the kind of service your firm normally
provides. Invoice No. 2670–B indicates a charge of $325 for five hours of service.
Although the computer repairs took place over a five-hour period, the actual amount
of time spent by the technician working on the two computers was more like three
hours. After spending approximately two hours working, the technician went to lunch
with one of my employees for an hour. When he returned, he spent about half of the
next two hours working on the computers and half the time visiting and joking around
with the office staff.

Please send a corrected invoice reflecting the charge for the three hours of service
that were actually received. It would also be appreciated if you would see that, in the
future, the technicians you send to us are as professional as those you have sent in
the past.

Sincerely,

*Charles O'Reilly*

Charles O'Reilly
President

126 EAST FILMORE BLVD.
DENVER, CO 80203
303.830.4000
fax 303.830.4100

- Situation 1: You call a client on the telephone to tell her the order she has been expecting is in. What is the first thing you should say to her after identifying yourself? Would you discuss the weather or ask her how her business is going? Would you tell her what she wants to hear—that her order is in? If you are good at dealing with people, you know that the second choice is the one that meets her needs. It immediately gives her the information she needs to know and states it in a positive way.

- Situation 2: You must discuss a negative evaluation with an employee who has only been with the company for six months. How should you begin the meeting? Would you talk about the benefits of working for the company or how hard you must work to evaluate employees? Would you begin by telling her the positive things she has done in the past evaluation period? If you are aware of the complexities of human nature, you will agree that the second option is more appropriate. By stating something positive at the beginning of the meeting, you will put the employee more at ease and prepare her psychologically to receive the bad news that will follow.

- Situation 3: You are writing a sales letter about a new motorcycle your company is marketing. The letter is to go to hundreds of retail motorcycle dealers. How should you begin the letter? Would you start with a detailed listing of the manufacturing specifications for the new motorcycle? Would you thank the dealership for considering the sale of your product? Would you get the reader's attention by beginning with a unique statement designed to take the reader's mind off everyday concerns and focus, instead, on your product? If you understand people, you know that most of us are too busy to read advertising literature unless we see immediately how the product meets our needs. The only way to get most people to read advertising literature is to get their attention and to help them focus on the subject of the message. The you attitude, if used effectively, improves the attention-getting capability of any message. Therefore, the second choice would be the most appropriate beginning for a letter in this situation.

**The anticipated reaction of the reader is the sole determinant of the organizational strategy to be used for a message.**

In all three situations, the first consideration is the probable reaction of the audience. In the first situation, because the information you have to tell is good news, you should begin by telling the reader what she wants to know. In the second scenario, you are attempting to diffuse disappointment by sharing positive information before moving on to the negative information. The third situation is different, because the recipients probably have little interest in reading your message. Therefore, you have to get their attention before they will consider your message.

At first glance, this sort of analysis and problem solving may seem hopelessly complicated. Fortunately, business communication experts have developed some shortcuts for deciding how to organize messages for audiences with particular needs. They have defined three general organizational strategies—direct, indirect, and persuasive—that you can use to sequence the specific ideas in any message. Exhibit 6.6 compares these three strategies. When you use one of these organizational strategies for your business messages, you are actually choosing to organize the message in a way that allows the reader to consider what you have to say without experiencing the negative influences that sometimes affect the reception of a message.

In an earlier section of this chapter, you learned that reader reaction revolves around four questions. The first (will your reader be interested in the topic and pleased by what you have to say) and the second (will your reader's reaction be one of neutral interest in the topic) require use of the direct

**EXHIBIT 6.6**

## Organizational Strategies

| | ▪ Direct | ▪ Indirect | ▪ Persuasive |
|---|---|---|---|
| First paragraph | Get to the point in the first sentence. | If possible, present any favorable news. If there is none, use a relevant, neutral buffer or something on which you and the reader can agree. Do not mention the negative situation. Do not use negative words or phrases. Do not imply *yes* or *no*. | Interest stage: Use a relevant attention-getting theme in the form of a statement or device such as a picture, a sample, or other gimmick that gets the reader's attention and encourages further reading. |
| Middle paragraphs | Include details necessary to fulfill the purpose of the message. Reinforce confidence in the company, its products, its services, etc., in terms of how they benefit the reader. | Make a logical transition between the buffer and the next paragraph. Give reasons for disappointing news in positive, tactful, courteous terms. Prepare the reader for the negative news. Explain the situation, leading naturally and logically to the negative decision, which should be implied diplomatically, if possible, but still be clear. Justify your actions; use the you attitude to tell how the negative news is meant to benefit the reader, if possible. Suggest alternatives or a counterproposal, if appropriate. Reinforce confidence in the company, its products, its services, etc. | Make a logical transition between the opening lines or paragraph to the next paragraph, carrying through the theme established in the opening. When appropriate, use samples, testimonials, trial offers, statistics, and/or guarantees to prove the worth of the product, service, or idea. Desire stage: Use the you attitude to show the reader how your product or idea will benefit him or her personally. Conviction stage: Make the specific request clearly, using reader benefit statements to convince the reader he or she must (1) have the product or service, (2) do what you want him or her to do, or (3) agree with you. |
| Last paragraph | Include a goodwill statement that brings the message to a close. Tie appreciation, if appropriate, to a clear statement of necessary future action. Do not thank in advance. | Include a friendly positive statement that closes the message. Tie appreciation, if appropriate, to a clear statement of necessary future action. Do not thank in advance. Do not refer to the negative situation. | Action stage: Request the action the reader needs to perform next, making it as easy as possible. If appreciation is appropriate, tie it to future action; do not thank in advance. If it does not detract from the serious nature of the message, carry the theme established in the opening through to the end. |

organizational strategy. Because the reader will not be upset by the message and has some interest in the topic, you should get to the point in the first sentence. Do not waste the reader's time by beginning with an essay on how grateful you are that he or she has chosen to do business with your company. There is nothing wrong, of course, with showing gratitude, but it should be done after providing the information in which the reader is most interested. Check Exhibit 6.6 for further details about this organizational strategy.

The following letter uses the direct strategy:

> Your Order No. 28760 will be shipped to you within three days. Thank you for letting Honeywell serve your electronics needs.
>
> By installing Honeywell controllers, you will find the manufacturing of your products to be faster and, even more important, more accurate. Model 10CJV controllers are easy to program and are more reliable than any other controllers on the market.
>
> When you need additional equipment, please let Jason Strange, your account representative, know by calling (612) 555-1221. He will be happy to consult with you personally to discuss your computer numerical control needs.

The major point is made in the first sentence.

The middle of the letter reinforces the reader's belief in the product (through *resale*) because no additional details are needed.

Goodwill is extended via the offer of friendly, eager service.

Many communication situations require a direct strategy. Letters settling disputes (when the dispute is resolved to the reader's satisfaction), announcements of meetings, and even letters of condolence written to someone who has lost a loved one should begin with the most important information first. People do not appreciate your wasting their time; therefore, when you have good or neutral news, tell the reader in the first sentence what he or she needs or wants to know.

However, when you have bad or disappointing news to tell someone, an indirect strategy is more effective. The determining factor in choosing between the direct and indirect strategies is whether the reader will be upset, angry, or disappointed by your message. The indirect strategy, also outlined in Exhibit 6.6, allows the reader to consider your reasons for the negative decision before getting the bad news itself. Take a minute to compare it to the direct outline.

The following letter is organized according to the tenets of the indirect strategy:

> Thank you for supplying such a clear explanation of the program you hope to implement with a Pelle City grant. A recreational baseball league for businesses in the area is an idea that might be of interest to the business community.
>
> The committee spent a considerable amount of time analyzing each of the proposals we received, attempting to discern those that will benefit the greatest number of people within the community. Because of the limited funds available, first priority had to be given to organizations that serve the greatest number of city residents. As a city resident, you have a right to know your tax dollars are being spent on programs that benefit you directly.
>
> Because many of the people who work in Pelle are not city residents, it would be difficult for businesses to limit their baseball teams to only those employees who reside in Pelle. Therefore, the proposal for a business baseball league cannot be funded.
>
> However, the idea has merit and should be reviewed by businesses within the area. You might consider taking your proposal to the leadership of the Kiwanis Club or the Chamber of Commerce. Because these organizations are made up of local businesspeople, they might be able to assist you in getting funding for your proposal.
>
> Good luck to you in securing support for your program.

This buffer is relevant, but it does not say *no*. Goodwill makes the reader feel positive about what she is planning.

The transition between the opening discussion of the program and the committee's making the decision is logical. The situation is explained, and the negative decision is conveyed in terms of how it is intended to benefit the reader.

The negative decision is made clear, but only after the action was justified fully in the second and third paragraphs.

A viable alternative is presented.

The goodwill is appropriate and relevant. The letter closes with no reference to the negative decision.

The benefit of softening the bad news by starting with a buffer paragraph is the subtle psychological influence on the reader. In the sample letter, the writer tried to make the reader feel good about the grant program despite the committee's refusal to help fund the reader's proposal. However, the writer was not misleading; the first paragraph did not imply that a yes answer would follow. The you attitude was used to help the reader understand that a city's dollars should be spent on city residents, just as she, a city resident, would want for herself. The rejection—the bad news—was clear, but it did not have to be brought up until the reader had probably reached the same conclusion herself. By opening and ending with positive words, the writer increases the likelihood the reader will understand and accept the written reasons for rejecting her proposal.

The third type of organizational pattern is used solely for persuasive messages, such as sales letters and collection letters, when the reader has no initial interest in your product or idea. Once again, you must ask what your reader's reaction will be to what you have to say. If your reader has little, if any, initial interest in the topic, use the persuasive strategy outlined in Exhibit 6.6. Compare it with the direct and indirect outlines. Notice how the persuasive outline leads the reader through stages.

The beginning of a persuasive message should be designed to create interest, so the reader will be more likely to read the rest of the message. Notice in Exhibit 6.7, a sales letter sent by the publishers of *PageOne*—a popular desktop publishing magazine, how the interest line and the cartoon at the bottom of the page work together to get the attention of the reader. Notice also how the writer subtly and logically leads the reader from the interest stage to the action stage.

### STAGE THREE: COMPOSE YOUR MESSAGE

If you have carefully planned and organized your message, composing it should be relatively easy. Composing letters and memos is simple when you work from freewritten notes and use one of the three organizational strategies. Look back to Exhibit 6.5. Notice how closely the third frame corresponds to the freewritten notes and to the indirect strategy, which is the appropriate organizational pattern for such a message.

When you compose a message, write it quickly. Do not attempt to make every sentence perfect. While you are learning to write business messages, you will only become frustrated by trying to write the perfect sentence or search for the perfect word. Instead, seek perfection during the evaluation stage. As you become more confident, your ability to compose or dictate nearly perfect copy will improve.

Don't be dismayed if during this stage you experience some form of **writer's block,** that frightening inability to think of what to write. Most writers occasionally go through this. If you are lucky, your writer's block will only last a moment. However, for some people, writer's block is a long-term condition that interferes seriously with their ability to do their jobs. Freewriting is one of the best ways to overcome writer's block.

### STAGE FOUR: EVALUATE YOUR MESSAGE

■ Evaluate business messages and readers' feedback.
The final stage of the message formulation process is to evaluate your message and revise it as needed. Later chapters of this book include evaluation forms—

**EXHIBIT 6.7**

**Persuasive Sales Letter**

*The opening line, combined with the cartoon at the bottom of the page, gets the reader's attention and encourages him or her to keep reading.*

PageOne  P.O. Box 2222, Baltimore, MD 21224

# YOU'RE ABOUT TO BE LEFT ALONE IN THE JUNGLE

Dear Subscriber:

The world of desktop publishing is a jungle—an almost impenetrable thicket of lines, fills, shapes, fonts, and artistic possibilities all requiring your attention.

*The transition between the opening and the third paragraph is logical and relevant. The you attitude is used to build desire for the product by making the reader see how the magazine will be of help.*

For months now you have been relying on PageOne to guide you through this confusing thicket of procedures and techniques. You know that PageOne has the knowledge and instincts of a native tracker—the only magazine dedicated to being your visual guide to the latest in desktop publishing.

However, you won't have PageOne much longer. Your next copy will be the next to the last you will receive on your present subscription. So, if you dread being abandoned to fight your way out alone, be sure to renew your PageOne subscription now. We emphasize now because you won't want to miss a single explanation or illustration. Upcoming issues include ideas for some of the most unique page designs ever seen and step–by–step instructions for mastering even the most complex features of popular software programs.

*The writer continues to create desire for the product.*

*Reader benefit statements are used to convince the reader that he or she must have the product and must order it now.*

Just return the enclosed order form in the envelope provided. Let our trackers lead you safely out of the jungle—before your software programs eat you alive!

*The specific request is made in terms of easy, immediate action. The reader is not thanked in advance.*

Cordially,

*Ralph Streisand*

Ralph Streisand
Editor in Chief

Evaluation forms are provided in the following chapters for each type of correspondence.

designed specifically for the direct, indirect, and persuasive strategies—that you can use as you edit your business messages. Generally speaking, however, you need to tackle the following tasks when evaluating any written message. (Many of these tasks can also be performed to evaluate the effectiveness of oral messages.)

- *Evaluate the opening and the closing.* The opening and closing paragraphs have a big influence on the tone of business messages. Unfortunately, the importance of the opening and closing paragraphs is sometimes overlooked by business communicators, who may resort to boring and often irrelevant clichés. At times, it seems that almost every business letter begins with "Thank you for your letter of . . . " and ends with "Please do not hesitate to call." Opening and closing paragraphs should be as original as possible so that they will be read, so that they express meaning needed to get the message across, and so that the goodwill seems sincere rather than trite. To make sure your beginning and ending paragraphs are effective, follow the advice given in Chapters 4 and 5 on word choice and the you attitude, and follow the organizational patterns recommended in this chapter.

- *Evaluate the message.* To evaluate the message, concentrate on your one-line statement of purpose. Look specifically for the one or two sentences within the message that fulfill that purpose. For example, in Exhibit 6.5 you can see that the two sentences in the last paragraph of the letter clearly and completely fulfill the purpose written at the top of the freewriting frame. The next step is to make sure that nothing in the message contradicts the purpose. Is there anything that might confuse the reader or cause him or her to misunderstand your purpose? Then take another look at word choice. Have you used words that communicate exactly what you want to say? Is your message clear, complete, concise, correct in every detail, and courteous? Next, consider the sincerity of the message. Readers are quick to see through feeble you-attitude statements that are not genuine. Now, analyze whether your message meets the high standards of ethics discussed within this chapter. Would you be happy to have everyone you love or respect know all the details and personal motives surrounding the correspondence? Finally, assess the quality of your arguments, conclusions, generalizations, and assumptions. Do they meet the standards of sound critical thinking?

- *Evaluate the tone.* Look at the words you chose to express your message. Identify specific sentences that show the reader how your goals will also meet his or her needs. To which of the five levels of Maslow's hierarchy of needs (discussed in Chapter 4) did you appeal? Did you use the company's name sparingly or not at all? Did you avoid starting too many sentences and clauses with *I* or *we*? Did you make good use of the pronouns *you* and *your*? Have you substituted positive words for negative ones? Did you demonstrate goodwill? Does the message sound sincere?

- *Evaluate the mechanics.* Correct grammar, sentence and paragraph structure, punctuation, and spelling are important because, if used properly, they allow readers to focus full attention on the message. If they are used improperly, readers' attention is drawn away from the message and to the incorrect usage. Anything that causes readers to focus on something other than the message detracts from the message's effectiveness. Appendix A contains a review of punctuation skills. Computer grammar programs and spell checkers may also help you in assessing the mechanics of the writing you do for this course.

- *Evaluate readability*. Use the Gunning Fog Index or the Flesch Reading Ease Scale (described in Chapter 5) to determine the reading level of your message. Does the reading level suit the needs of your intended audience? If the reading level is too high, consider shortening the sentences and using words with fewer syllables.

- *Evaluate format and appearance*. Like correct mechanics, correct format enables readers to focus on the message instead of on irrelevant factors. If you use one of the formats presented in Appendix C, you will provide all the elements most business readers expect to see in letters and memos. However, if your reader is not from the United States or Canada, consider adopting the format most common in your reader's country. Although businesspeople in most countries are familiar with North American formats, they would probably be honored by your deference to their particular style. General appearance is also important, because it helps set the tone between you and your reader. Unprofessional, sloppy correspondence makes readers feel unimportant. Check the appearance of your document after it has been typed. Is it centered on the page appropriately? Are all corrections made neatly? Is your signature legible?

- *Evaluate reader feedback*. This point applies after the letter or memo has been mailed. Reader feedback can take many forms, depending on the type of correspondence and the subject of the message. For a sales letter, reader response to the message can be evaluated by monitoring orders or increases in sales. For a memo to employees about a new procedure, correct (or incorrect) performance of the procedure provides feedback on your communication effectiveness. For a letter turning down a request for credit, you will know you have done an effective job if the customer or client continues to do business with your company on a cash basis. A collection letter or reminder can be evaluated by tracing accounts that pay up after receiving the message. Be careful not to blame the reader for misunderstanding your message. Examine honestly whether you have some responsibility for miscommunication. If your reader has to request further information or clarification, you did not provide everything he or she wanted and needed to know.

Evaluating each document by these standards will ensure that your correspondence achieves the goals you set and that the relationship between you and your readers will continue and improve.

## DISCUSSION QUESTIONS

🛑 Define critical thinking and explain its importance to business communicators.

1. Define *critical thinking* and discuss its importance in decision making.

🛑 Identify the eight critical thinking skills.

2. What are the eight critical thinking skills? Give an example of how each one can be applied.

◼ Explain how critical thinking relates to the problem-solving process.

3. How does critical thinking relate to problem solving?

◼ Use a four-step process for solving problems.

4. What are the four steps involved in problem solving?

◼ Apply the four stages of the message formulation process to your own business messages.

5. What four stages are involved in formulating business messages?

◼ Apply the five planning steps before composing business messages

6. What are the five steps involved in planning a business message?

◼ Demonstrate sensitivity to the legal and ethical responsibilities of businesses and employees.

7. What does *being ethical* mean?

◼ Demonstrate sensitivity to the legal and ethical responsibilities of businesses and employees.

8. From the list of 12 questions used to analyze the ethics of one's actions (page 167), identify the three that are most difficult for you. Provide examples.

◼ Explain the intent of laws that affect business communication.

9. Legally, what does your signature on a letter, memo, or contract mean?

◼ Explain the intent of laws that affect business communication.

10. To whom does a written message belong—the writer or the recipient? How does this ownership govern what you are able to do with a message you have received?

◼ Identify the skills needed to write collaboratively.

11. What skills and attitudes should a person have to be part of a collaborative writing project?

◼ Demonstrate the ability to draft business messages.

12. How does freewriting aid the message formulation process?

◼ Choose the appropriate organizational strategy, given your purpose and the anticipated audience reaction.

13. How do the opening paragraphs differ in messages organized according to the direct strategy, the indirect strategy, and the persuasive strategy?

◼ Evaluate business messages and readers' feedback.

14. What are the seven major factors by which you should evaluate your business messages? Which is the only factor that is evaluated after the message has been sent?

■ Define critical thinking and explain its importance to business communicators.

1. Refer to the list of eight abilities involved in critical thinking (presented at the beginning of the chapter). Write a two-page paper explaining how each of those abilities relates to the tasks you anticipate performing in your chosen career (or in your college career, if you have not yet chosen a major).

■ Identify the eight critical thinking skills.

2. Choose a federal policy that affects American companies, such as policies on the capital gains tax, free trade, entitlement programs, corporate taxation, or national health care. Then analyze how the policy benefits or harms business and the economy. Apply the eight critical thinking skills to your conclusions. Your professor will let you know whether you should present this information in written form or orally to the class or a small group.

■ Identify the eight critical thinking skills.

3. Attend a speech or a persuasive lecture on your campus. Identify the speaker's major conclusions, and show how he or she supported them. Evaluate the strength of the conclusions. Are they sound? If not, use the eight critical thinking skills to identify what the speaker did wrong. If the conclusions are sound, use the critical thinking skills to identify what the speaker did correctly. Write a two-page paper summarizing your thoughts.

■ Identify the eight critical thinking skills.
■ Use a four-step process for solving problems.
■ Identify the skills needed to write collaboratively.

4. Your instructor will assign you to a collaborative group of six to eight students. As a group, your assignment is to research a current business or economic issue on which there are at least two distinct ways of thinking— for example, free trade versus protectionism, pay for CEOs, the "lazy" American workers versus the "industrious" Japanese worker, compliance with American bribery laws when doing business in other countries, immigration laws and American business, and so forth. Use the advice given in this chapter to organize your group and to assign tasks to group members. Select a topic and get it approved by your professor. In a single memo report to your classmates (submitted by the group), document the following. Your teacher will let you know if you are to present this information orally.

   a. Identify the problem you are researching. Relate how your group determined what the problem is, demonstrating that you looked at the problem from many different perspectives.

   b. Conduct the information-gathering stage of problem solving. One-half of the group members will look at one side of the issue (e.g., free trade), and the other half will look at the other side (e.g., protectionism). According to experts, what are the suspected causes of the problem? What data are used to correlate the causes with the problem?

What alternative solutions have been proposed? What data have been used to predict the success of each alternative?

c. In your group, use the eight critical thinking skills to determine if the standards that have been used by the experts to evaluate alternatives and causes are adequate.

d. In your group, use critical thinking skills to determine if any solutions already implemented are working.

e. In an individual, confidential report to your instructor, evaluate how your group worked together. Did all group members participate equally? Did each group member do what he or she was supposed to do, as assigned by the group? Evaluate your own participation in the group as well. What lessons did you learn from this collaborative experience?

🔹 Explain how critical thinking relates to the problem-solving process.

5. Identify changes or trends that are occurring in your major course of study. Use the eight critical thinking skills and the four problem-solving steps to find answers to these questions: What effects do these trends have on your career preparations? Will you need to change your skills or prepare for changing technology? What can you do to adjust to these changes and trends? Discuss the results in a one- or two-page report to your instructor.

🔹 Apply the four stages of the message formulation process to your own business messages.

🔹 Apply the five planning steps before composing business messages.

🔹 Demonstrate sensitivity to the legal and ethical responsibilities of businesses and employees.

🔹 Demonstrate the ability to draft business messages.

🔹 Choose the appropriate organizational strategy, given your purpose and the anticipated audience reaction.

🔹 Evaluate business messages and readers' feedback.

6. Imagine that you have been asked to write a one-page memo to your co-workers about expanded lunchroom hours and services. Instead of being open only from noon to 1:00 PM, the lunchroom will now be open for two hours—from noon to 2 PM. In addition, the lunchroom will be offering several new food items. Proceed step by step through the message formulation process as you prepare your memo, and turn in to your instructor evidence of your work at each stage:

a. Plan the message. For your instructor, write a line or two about your thinking on each of the seven steps involved in planning.

b. Organize the message. Begin by freewriting, and then edit your notes to show how you will organize the message. Turn this sheet in to your instructor. At the bottom of the page, note which organizational strategy you believe to be most appropriate.

c. Compose your message as instructed in the chapter, and keep the unedited draft to turn in to your instructor. Don't worry about perfection!

d. Evaluate the message. Write a few lines analyzing your draft in terms of the seven elements discussed in the chapter.

■ Apply the five planning steps before composing business messages

7. Choose a letter or memo assignment from Chapter 7, 8, or 9. Perform the following steps in the planning process, and present this information in a typed report to your professor.
   a. Write down an appropriate purpose or purposes.
   b. Determine the appropriate medium and channel.
   c. Indicate which legal and ethical issues are involved.
   d. Analyze the audience and select an appropriate organizational pattern.
   e. Identify the information, materials, and writing team you might need to assemble before you start writing.

■ Demonstrate sensitivity to the legal and ethical responsibilities of businesses and employees.

8. Over the next several days, keep a journal of the ethical issues with which you must deal. Use the list of 12 questions provided in the chapter to help you focus on ethical issues. Describe each situation and tell how you handled it. Be honest; you will not be graded on whether or not you made a decision with which your teacher would agree. If you are currently working, keep the job-related incidents separate from the personal incidents.

■ Demonstrate sensitivity to the legal and ethical responsibilities of businesses and employees.

9. Find an article in a newspaper or magazine about a violation of business ethics. Briefly describe the violation, citing the sources from which you took the information. How might the outcome have differed if the individuals involved had used the 12 questions listed in the chapter or the three questions proposed by the head of JCPenney to guide their behavior? Explain your views in a one-page paper.

■ Demonstrate sensitivity to the legal and ethical responsibilities of businesses and employees.
■ Identify the skills needed to write collaboratively.

10. In a small group organized by your instructor, discuss the following issue: To what extent should businesses be able to monitor the work of their employees? Is it an invasion of privacy to have company-authorized personnel listening in on sales calls made on company telephones during working hours? Checking the contents of employees' electronic mailboxes? Checking up on employees' work by accessing the files stored in their computers? Companies argue that they have a right to monitor the work of their employees and, if that work can be accessed electronically, they should have access to it. Employees, however, argue that it is an invasion of privacy. What does your group think? Is it a legal issue, an ethical issue, or both? Identify the problem and look at it from the perspectives of both the employer and the employee. Your instructor will inform you of the form your group's written report should take.

■ Explain the intent of laws that affect business communication.

11. At the library, look for an article about a legal issue in business communication. On the basis of your reading, what specifically would you recommend

to business writers who want to avoid legal problems? Write up these recommendations in a memo report to your instructor, and include any supporting material necessary to prove how you determined the recommendations.

◼ Demonstrate the ability to draft business messages.

12. For the letter or memo assignment you chose in exercise 7, freewrite the points you believe should be covered.

◼ Choose the appropriate organizational strategy, given your purpose and the anticipated audience reaction.

13. Determine whether a direct, indirect, or persuasive organizational strategy is needed for each of the following situations. Indicate next to your selection what you anticipate the reaction of the reader to be. In some cases, more than one strategy might be appropriate.
   a. A letter to a prominent banker in a nearby community asking her to speak to your college business organization.
   b. A letter to a customer enclosing a check in settlement of a long-standing warranty dispute.
   c. A letter to a new client thanking him for doing business with your firm.
   d. A memo turning down an invitation to lead a workshop at a yearly gathering of co-workers.
   e. A letter to clients who have not been coming in regularly for their weekly appointments at your weight-loss clinic.
   f. A letter to a client asking him or her to pay a bill that has been outstanding for two months.
   g. An acknowledgement of a letter requesting prepared material, which you will mail right away.
   h. A letter of recommendation, at the prospective employer's request, for someone you know well who is highly qualified for the job.
   i. A letter rejecting a customer's demand for an adjustment because an investigation of the situation has determined that the customer is wrong.
   j. A letter to a company asking it to exchange for a bigger size a $45 sweater you ordered that is too small.

◼ Choose the appropriate organizational strategy, given your purpose and the anticipated audience reaction.

14. The organizational strategies recommended for writing essays in literature classes may seem quite different from the three organizational strategies (direct, indirect, and persuasive) recommended for business messages. However, the two types of organizational plans have some similarities. For each of the seven literary-analysis organizational strategies listed below, demonstrate your understanding by composing a business-oriented example. Examples are included here to stimulate your creativity; compose some new examples. Words used to express the same concept are included in parentheses.
   a. *Compare/contrast* (comparing, resemble, have in common, identical, likewise, also, in contrast, instead, differences, however, on the other

hand, nevertheless): "Unlike dictionaries, thesauri propose numerous examples of synonyms and antonyms."

b.  *Problem/solution* (question, dissent, puzzle, assessment, need, issue, solution, outcome, result, solve, satisfy, agreement, therefore, accordingly): "Some say the problem of productivity in the United States can be solved with renewed emphasis on incentives for workers and top-level executives."

c.  *Description* (for example, namely, particularly, illustrates, typically, in addition to): "The bribery issue can best be exemplified by the case of *Weatherly* v. *Gettleman Industries*."

d.  *Sequence* (first, second, before, afterward, soon, currently, later, finally, to start with, following, at the same time, years ago, in conclusion): "From 1987 to 1993 there were four major business failures in the manufacturing industry. In the past year alone, there have already been two major failures."

e.  *Cause/effect* (as a result, since, why, if/then, reason, to explain, therefore, accordingly, led to, in conclusion, consequence, goal): "In the past three quarters, productivity has been rising. We therefore expect that the current quarter will be profitable."

f.  *Concept/example* (for instance, relationship, conceptually, subset, category, connection): "The issue is one of fairness. For example, do you think it is fair for a less-qualified employee to be promoted over another just because of race?"

g.  *Propositions/support* (reason for, in support of, counterargument, suggests, indicate, propose, hypothesize, enumerate, appears, apparently, proof): "The director of admissions maintained his support for race as a factor in student selection by citing dramatic data on the low percentage of graduates among several minority cultures."

Evaluate business messages and readers' feedback.

15. Choose a document you wrote for a previous chapter or in another class and evaluate it using the criteria included in this chapter. Then revise your document to solve its problems. Submit to your instructor the original and your revision.

# CHAPTER 7

# WRITING DIRECT MESSAGES

## OBJECTIVES

When you finish studying this chapter, you should be able to

- Determine when a direct organizational strategy is appropriate.
- Apply the four stages of the message formulation process to direct messages.
- Identify the features of a direct organizational strategy.
- Plan, organize, compose, and evaluate routine requests and announcements.
- Plan, organize, compose, and evaluate routine replies.
- Plan, organize, compose, and evaluate routine claims.
- Plan, organize, compose, and evaluate routine adjustment letters.

## WHAT WOULD YOU DO IF...?

**SAYONARA.**   Elizabeth Sarkanian is the director of finance for PacRim Industries, a medium-sized manufacturer of electronic components headquartered in San Francisco. Her department is responsible for making sure PacRim has sufficient money when it needs it. However, PacRim is already heavily in debt and finds itself needing $2 million more to update its manufacturing equipment. American investors are reluctant to invest in a company as heavily in debt as PacRim, so Elizabeth has written and spoken to a number of foreign investors, many of whom are more accustomed to investing in companies that are in debt.

Luckily, one of PacRim's most important customers, a Japanese firm named Isosaki Enterprises, has responded to Elizabeth's campaign by offering $2 million in exchange for bonds convertible to common stock. PacRim's owners have decided to accept the offer.

Elizabeth instructed her new assistant, a Japanese national named Kiyomi Ito, to draft the letter of acceptance (a formality, because the offer has already been accepted by telephone). However, Elizabeth wants to rewrite Kiyomi's letter. She feels it is boring and indirect, and the acceptance of the offer isn't expressed until the third paragraph. Kiyomi's letter, translated into English, follows:

> I trust that the recent storms Osaka has experienced have left you, your family, and your employees safe. Nature is an element that humbles us all by reminding us of our own vulnerability.

Stormy weather is also a danger for businesses, and our company has experienced many storms in the past. With your help, however, the storms will, at last, subside; and we will once again experience the sunny skies that were meant for us.

Your generous offer of $2 million to clear the clouds from our sky will be used to . . . [details of the transfer of funds].

In deepest gratitude, we look forward to a partnership that will ensure clear skies for Isosaki and PacRim.

As you read this chapter, compare Kiyomi's letter to the principles discussed. Does it follow a direct organizational strategy? Should the letter follow a direct organizational strategy? Should cultural differences be considered? (Chapter 2 might be of help to you here.) Should Elizabeth rewrite Kiyomi's letter to make it more direct? If she does, what changes should she make?

## USING THE DIRECT STRATEGY

■ Determine when a direct organizational strategy is appropriate.

Most letters and memos you will write in your business career will require a direct organizational strategy. Busy, time-conscious people appreciate directness. Think of all of the long telephone messages or letters you have endured. You probably found yourself thinking "Okay, okay, get to the point!" Because it begins with the key idea, the direct strategy forces a writer to get to the point without wasting the reader's or listener's time.

The direct organizational strategy is useful for any message that will not result in a negative reaction from your reader or listener. Memos announcing new company benefits, the places and times of regularly scheduled meetings, and minor changes in policy are examples of situations in which you would be wise to get right to the point in the first sentence. If you are sending requested information to a customer or client, or submitting a refund to a customer, a direct strategy is also appropriate.

■ Apply the four stages of the message formulation process to direct messages.

The stages in the message formulation process that you studied in Chapter 6—planning, organizing, composing, and evaluating—are used in this chapter to guide you through the composition of messages that require a direct approach.

## PLANNING YOUR MESSAGE

Planning any message involves the five steps outlined in Chapter 6:

Establish the purpose.

Choose a medium and a channel.

Consider the legal and ethical issues.

Analyze your audience.

Gather the necessary information.

Each of these steps is explained in the sections that follow.

## ESTABLISH YOUR PURPOSE

"The first step in getting somewhere is determining where you want to go." This old saying applies to many situations in life, including the formulation of business letters and memos. Your first task, therefore, is to decide on your reason for writing and determine what you want to happen as a result of writing.

Direct messages have a variety of general purposes, including the following:

To inform.

To make a routine claim.

To make a routine inquiry or request.

To order a product.

To approve credit.

To thank a client, customer, or employee.

To congratulate a co-worker or client.

To instruct employees how to perform a new procedure.

To submit a report from your collaborative writing group.

To reply to a customer's request for information.

To promote goodwill between the writer and the reader(s).

**A message can have more than one purpose.**

Business letters and memos often have more than one purpose. For instance, you might write a letter to a customer thanking him or her for a recent order and offering congratulations on a promotion to vice president of the company. Or you might write a computer message to a co-worker that includes both the information he or she needs concerning a project on which your group has been working and a request for a copy of the co-worker's final report when it has been completed.

Once you have determined your purpose(s), it is important to have them where you can see them as you are writing the message. The physical act of putting your purpose(s) in writing forces you to clarify concepts, and it also helps you stick to the point when you are composing the message. A clear statement of purpose(s) can shorten the amount of time required to compose any message.

Imagine that you are the director of new student relations for a state university. You must write two form letters to send to prospective students who inquire about your school. One version is for senior high school students who inquire about the school. The other is for younger people who ask for information. What should the purpose(s) of these two letters be? The most obvious purpose is, of course, to send the information each prospective student requests. In this case, it might be a detailed brochure describing the college, the degrees it offers, admissions information, costs, and so forth. A secondary purpose for the high school seniors might be to send an application. A secondary purpose for younger applicants (or for those who have stated they do not plan to apply for the next academic year) might be to let them know they will be placed on a mailing list to receive periodic information about the college and will automatically receive an application during their senior year of high school or the year before they plan to attend. A third and not-so-obvious purpose might be to build goodwill for the college by promoting its fine faculty and/or programs in the hopes that such promotion will persuade good students to apply.

Jotting down your purpose before composing the letters will help focus your attention on the most important elements as you write. It will help ensure your letters are complete and meet the needs of those who read them.

## CHOOSE A MEDIUM AND CHANNEL

Some messages should be presented orally; others are best presented in writing.

The first question is whether a message would be more effectively delivered orally or in writing. Assuming you decide that the message should be written, the next decision is what form the correspondence should take. Should it be in memo form because it is going to a co-worker at your company? Should it be in letter form because it is being mailed outside the company? Next, you must decide whether the message should be sent by computer, conventional mail, or special messenger.

Exhibit 7.1 illustrates another message form that may be appropriate when a speedy response is important: a handwritten note in the margin of the message you received. The extreme informality of jotting a response in the margin must be weighed against the value of a speedy response. Some recipients might view margin notes as unprofessional and react negatively to them. You will have to use your own judgment to determine when to use this type of response.

## CONSIDER LEGAL AND ETHICAL ISSUES

Operating within the law and doing what is right to achieve good results are two principles that stand true no matter what type of message you are writing. You are responsible for having a basic understanding of the ethical issues and laws related to your field. Many companies also have lawyers on staff who make sure all transactions are carried out legally and keep employees informed of laws that affect their business dealings. If your company has not briefed you on the ethical issues and laws related to the industry in which you work, do your own research. The business libraries of most large colleges contain the information you need. Top-level executives are also usually well informed about these matters, so after doing your own research you might ask some of them for clarification or amplification of specific points.

Use dates of previous correspondence, conversations, and meetings only when it works to your advantage.

A common practice among business communicators who are sensitive to contract law is the establishment of dates. For example, most letters requesting a bill adjustment are routine and are settled within a short time to the satisfaction of all concerned. However, when you make a claim against a company or a claim is made against you, protect yourself by keeping a record of all communication. Keep copies of all correspondence and all forms involved in the transaction. Keep detailed notes of any telephone conversations (dates, times, to whom you spoke, and what was said). Being able to report all these details will help if the situation is not settled to your satisfaction within a short time. If you are forced to take the problem to the next level, your case will seem more authoritative if you have documented everything at each step of the transaction.

The best advice in such situations is to be truthful and fair to all concerned. Ask yourself if the message you have composed and the way you are handling the situation make you feel good about yourself. Have you revealed clearly everything the reader wants and needs to know to make informed decisions? Would you be proud to have all the details revealed to everyone you know and respect? Ethical, legal conduct is a major requirement for long-term success in the business world.

**EXHIBIT 7.1**

**Informal Response to a Request**

**AIR NEWARK**

(201) 457-6812
FAX (201) 457-4583

TO:       Marilynn Scalia

FROM:    Herbert Collings, Office of General Counsel

DATE:    December 4, 1994

SUBJECT:  Price-Fixing Investigation

Please send to me immediately the results of your work group's investigation of the fares charged for the past two years by our major competitors, AirYork, Florida Air, and Eastern Airlines. I understand the study was completed last week and is ready for in-house distribution. It will be used to supplement the emergency report I am doing for the CEO in response to the federal price-fixing charge levied against us yesterday.

*Enclosed. Hope it helps!*

Because I assume the information is still confidential, you may be sure it will be seen only by my staff for the report that will be delivered directly to the CEO.

*Try the Maine office— Teri Bernstein. She did a comparison.*

In addition to the data compiled for your study, do you have or know where I can get information related to the fares charged by Noreastern?

Please let me know the dates of any and all correspondence, meetings, and/or telephone calls other than those listed below that you have had with decision makers at any of the airlines named in the suit. If information about future fare plans (theirs or ours) was mentioned at any time with officials or employees of other airlines, please make sure to specify this information.

| | |
|---|---|
| Oct. 15, 1992 | Meeting with AirYork and Florida Air officials at company headquarters. Subject: Possible merger. |
| Oct. 17, 1992 | Telephone call with AirYork and Florida Air officials. Subject: Possible merger. |
| Oct. 22–Dec. 15, 1992 | Correspondence with both AirYork and Florida Air. Subject: Terms of merger. |
| Jan. 5, 1993 | Telephone calls to AirYork and Florida Air. Subject: Cancellation of merger plans. |

5266 Freedom Way
Newark, NJ 07112

EXHIBIT
7.1

Continued

Marilyn Scalia
December 4, 1994
Page 2

Apr. 25, 1993–Jan. 14, 1994  Meetings with Eastern Airlines and
Noreastern Airlines officials. Subject: Possible
sale of 12 routes.

Your prompt response will be appreciated.

*10/4/93  Meeting of Michael Crysome and Danielle Vargas, Noreastern. Subject—Prob. personal but should be investigated.*
*11/7/93  Tele. conv. between D. Vargas & D. Cranston, my asst. Subject—whereabouts of M. Crysome. Status of negotiations on route sales to Noreastern.*

## ANALYZE YOUR AUDIENCE

The more you know about your readers, the easier it will be to write a letter or memo that achieves your goals. As Chapter 4 explains, using the you attitude—both to understand your readers and to show how what you want also benefits them—increases the likelihood that you will achieve what you want.

Imagine that you must write a letter asking a furniture manufacturer, Arcadian, to renegotiate the price of a large shipment of chairs you purchased for resale in your furniture stores. On inspection, you discovered that the chairs are not of the high quality you usually get from Arcadian. Instead of sending them back, you have decided to sell them at a lower price than originally anticipated because your inventory of chairs is too low to wait for another shipment. Because you have done a lot of business with Arcadian over the years, you are fairly sure they will not react negatively to your proposal. Still, in your letter you should stress how Arcadian will benefit from lowering the price. By emphasizing the importance of pride in workmanship (an appeal to esteem and self-actualization needs), the long business relationship (esteem and safety), and the anticipation of a continued relationship (safety), you are likely to receive a response in your favor.

*You* and *your* will always sound better to readers than *I, me, we,* and *our.*

One way to make sure you address your readers' needs is to write down under your purpose statement the specific needs and appeals you can use to show readers what's in it for them. This kind of planning helps you compose messages that avoid overusing *I, me, we,* and *our,* and stress instead *you* and *your.*

The honest, sincere concern for readers that is the basis of the you attitude can help improve the effectiveness of your business correspondence. If you are attuned to the needs of others, the you attitude will come naturally. If you are not, use the techniques proposed in Chapter 4 until they become second nature. Besides knowing your field, no other single attribute determines success in business more than using the you attitude skillfully.

## GATHER THE NECESSARY RESOURCES

After you have analyzed your reader or readers, you must assemble the writing team, information, and materials you need to complete the project. Is this a document that should be written by more than one person? The more important or risky a document is to you or your organization, the more important it is to have a group collaborate on it. At times, collaboration means nothing more than getting the approval of others before mailing the letter or memo you have written. For example, if you were responding favorably to the letter requesting a lower price for the furniture shipment, you might want to make sure that your superiors in the organization agree with your decision to charge less than the original price.

The high cost associated with mass mailings makes collaborative writing more attractive.

Sometimes, however, collaborators should meet formally before the document is written. Form letters sent in large numbers are typically written by groups of people to ensure they represent a variety of views. Because so much money is spent on large mailings, it is sound practice to have the opinions of many experts. Psychologists, marketing experts, technical experts, and financial staff working together can help ensure a successful mailing.

Besides considering who should be involved in writing the message, ask yourself what information you need. Gather from the files any previous correspondence on the topic you might need to refresh your memory. It might also be necessary to familiarize yourself with company policies by reading policies and procedures manuals or, in the absence of written instructions, by speaking to people who have been with the organization longer than you have.

If you plan to distribute enclosures with the letter or memo, it is a good idea to have them in front of you as you compose the message. Their presence not only helps you remember to mention the enclosures, it also forces you to consider whether the enclosures are appropriate. One individual wrote to her bank asking for information about an account that would return her cancelled checks every month. Instead of answering her request, the response from the bank included an enclosure she had already seen that mentioned nothing about the type of account she wanted. Such a response is bad for business.

## ORGANIZING YOUR MESSAGE

Organizing a direct message is the same as organizing any type of message. First, you freewrite the major points; then you choose the appropriate organizational strategy. However, because a direct message is more forthright than an indirect or persuasive message, the organizing stage is often simpler.

### FREEWRITE MAJOR POINTS

After writing your purpose(s) at the top of the page (or computer screen), write the points you want to make as fast as you can think of them and in whatever order they come to mind. At this point, don't concern yourself with what should be said first, and don't attempt to write complete sentences. Avoid evaluating what you freewrite; just write what you think as it comes to you. Freewriting helps beginning writers avoid writer's block.

"No, writer's block is not covered by your
medical insurance, Ms. Ingram."

### CHOOSE AN ORGANIZATIONAL STRATEGY: THE DIRECT STRATEGY

▪ Identify the features of a direct organizational strategy.

The direct strategy should be used only when the reader will probably react pleasantly or neutrally.

This chapter deals with messages that require a direct approach; the next two chapters of this book discuss the indirect strategy and the persuasive strategy. The strategy you will use to organize your messages is determined by your answer to this question: What will my reader(s)' probable reaction be? If you can say that your reader(s) will be happy or unconcerned (not angry or upset)

| EXHIBIT 7.2 | **Direct Organizational Strategy for Good-News and Neutral Messages** |
|---|---|
| First paragraph | Get to the point in the first sentence. |
| Middle paragraphs | Include details necessary to fulfill the purpose of the message. Reinforce confidence in the company, its products, its services, etc., in terms of how they benefit the reader. |
| Last paragraph | Include a goodwill statement that brings the message to a close. Tie appreciation, if appropriate, to a clear statement of future action necessary. Do not thank in advance. |

by what you have to say, you should use a direct strategy. The approach outlined in Exhibit 7.2 is correct for the situations discussed in this chapter.

Americans, Canadians, Germans, Austrians, the French, and, to some extent, the English are major cultures that appreciate directness. People in these cultures are time oriented and resent having it wasted. They expect you to come right to the point as soon as possible when the news will not upset them.

However, a direct approach is offensive in cultures that believe in establishing a social relationship before doing business. Spaniards, Mexicans, most Latin and South Americans, and the Japanese usually approach business indirectly. This indirectness is readily recognizable in their letters. The first paragraph usually has nothing to do with the purpose of the correspondence, dealing instead with the weather or the health of the recipient. Later paragraphs address the purpose, but often even they are less direct than in American messages. For a good example of how these other cultures approach even the best news, refer to the letter written by Kiyomi Ito in the vignette at the beginning of the chapter.

> **A direct strategy may offend some cultural groups.**

Although many businesspeople from these more indirect cultures have grown used to the directness of Americans, many others are offended by it. You will have to use your best judgment when writing to people from other cultures. (More information about this topic is covered in Chapter 2.)

To make sure you understand when a direct outline would be the best way to deal with a situation, consider the following examples. As you read each, determine when a direct outline would be appropriate. The correct answer follows each situation, so cover the answers until you have made a decision. Then verify your answer with the explanation given.

Situation 1: A letter to a customer denying him the discount he requested on purchases over $1,000.

Answer: A direct approach is not appropriate, because the reader will probably be disappointed by the message no matter how well it is written.

Situation 2: A memo to an employee granting her request for a salary increase.

Answer: A direct approach is appropriate, because her reaction should be favorable.

Situation 3: A letter congratulating a client on winning a prestigious community award.

Answer: A direct approach would be best, because the reader should be pleased by the message.

Situation 4: A sympathy letter to an employee whose wife was killed in an auto accident.

Answer: A direct approach would be best. Even though death itself is unpleasant, relatives are pleased when others think of them at a time of loss.

Situation 5: A memo to the Japanese head of the joint venture your company has formed to manufacture Japanese vehicles in the United States.

Answer: You may use either a direct or indirect approach, depending on whether or not the Japanese person to whom you are writing is used to directness. However, there is a possibility a direct approach might not be well received.

Situation 6: A letter to employees announcing the closure of the oil refinery where they work.

Answer: A direct approach would be too harsh because of the anger, anxiety, and sorrow that such an announcement will produce.

Situation 7: A memo restating policies that employees already know but not everyone always follows.

Answer: Use a direct approach. If the memo is properly written to avoid condemning any of the readers, their reaction will be neutral. The message will be viewed simply as a restatement of something they already know.

Situation 8: A letter requesting permission to quote the recipient in a formal company policy statement on ethics your collaborative writing group is composing.

Answer: A direct approach is appropriate because the reader will be pleased by the compliment implied in the message.

Situation 9: A letter to a company asking them to correct a bill you received that is totaled incorrectly.

Answer: A direct approach is appropriate, because the reader should not be upset by the message within the letter. Unfortunately, mistakes are made frequently; as long as your reader does not feel you are unfairly blaming him or her or being too critical, the reaction should be neutral.

Situation 10: A letter to a resident of the city for which you work stating that she is being assessed $600 for sidewalk and street repairs in front of her home.

Answer: Because the reader will probably be upset by this unexpected bill, a direct approach is not appropriate.

Once you have decided on the appropriate organizational strategy, you can assign an order to the topics you wrote down during freewriting. Your arrangement of these major points is every bit as important as what you have to say and how you say it.

## COMPOSING YOUR MESSAGE

After you have planned and organized your direct message, the next step is composing it. This stage is easy when you are working with freewritten notes that have been organized into an outline that follows a direct pattern.

Many kinds of business letters and memos are most effective when the first sentences get right to the point. Four major types of correspondence will be covered in the following sections: routine requests and announcements, routine replies, routine claim letters, and routine adjustment letters. Numerous examples show how to compose direct messages. The comments related to each example are critical to your understanding of direct messages, so read them carefully.

Plan, organize, compose, and evaluate routine requests and announcements.

## ROUTINE REQUESTS AND ANNOUNCEMENTS

When you make an announcement or request something, the message is considered routine if you do not anticipate any resistance from the reader. For example, if you ask a company for information about a new product, the request would be considered routine. However, if you ask for information about a company's research and development activities, your request might not be considered routine. To get this kind of information, you would have to be highly persuasive, using the organizational pattern covered in Chapter 9.

You will find yourself writing a lot of routine requests and announcements as you progress through your business career. Fortunately, they are among the easiest messages to write. Exhibit 7.3 is a good example of a request letter. A description of the subtleties of writing each part of a routine request or announcement follows.

**The first sentence is the most important statement in a direct message.**

When making a routine request, the request should be made in the first sentence of the letter or memorandum. If your purpose is to get the answer to a question, it is appropriate to start with the question. Routine announcements should also begin with the most important part of the announcement in the first sentence of the message. Here are some examples of well-written first paragraphs for routine requests and announcements:

"Please send four copies of your latest catalog to me at the above address, so I may distribute them to the other members of my department who are involved in purchasing furniture for our new offices."

"Does the latest version of WordPerfect operate effectively in the Macintosh System 7.1 environment? I am considering updating my system, but my software program must operate reliably, without frequent crashes."

"The yearly meeting of the Association for Business Communication will be held in Los Angeles on November 13–17."

"Please let me know by March 15 how many of your staff will be attending the Chamber of Commerce luncheon honoring outstanding business leaders in the community."

"Your help in correcting Invoice No. 1437-B would be appreciated. Charges appear for two F-87s, yet only one was ordered and delivered."

The following examples of openings are ineffective, because they do not get to the point:

Ineffective letter applying for a job: "There are so many reasons why the aerospace industry has always appealed to me. The camaraderie, the excitement, and the chance to be at the forefront of technological development are only a few of the reasons I am contacting your company now that my college education has been completed."

**EXHIBIT 7.3**

**Routine Request (Modified Block Format with Mixed Punctuation)**

October 15, 1994

Mr. Michael Solis
Sales Representative
ComUSA
1425 West Sunset Boulevard
Los Angeles, CA 90441

Dear Mr. Solis:

*The first sentence makes the request.* Please send me information about Minolta's Pro Series copiers and comparable Xerox and Canon models.

*The middle paragraph gives additional needed details.* Since your ad in today's *Los Angeles Times* indicates you also sell Canon and Xerox equipment, I would like to know how the larger Minolta copiers, such as the EP 8602 and the EP 8604, stack up to Canon and Xerox machines with comparable qualities. Information about maintenance costs, frequency of maintenance, cost of toner, and how often toner must be added will be important to my decision. Your maintenance records should provide detailed information that goes beyond what the manufacturers publish.

Because your firm has done a superior job of servicing our copiers in the last year, you may be sure I will purchase our new equipment from you if the price is within reason. Therefore, your sending this information before October 31 will be appreciated.

*The last paragraph includes goodwill that will encourage the reader to respond and make sure the price is reasonable. The last sentence ties appreciation to future action and does not thank in advance.*

Sincerely yours,

Franklin Washington

Franklin Washington
President

snl

Ineffective memo informing union members of an important issue: "Once again your union representatives have jumped into the fray for the good of the union. Company representatives met with Charles Vidalia, Joan Degas, Charlie Petersen, Kang Han, and Yumiko Nashimoto and hammered out another tentative agreement for your approval."

Ineffective letter asking for an annual report from a Fortune 500 company: "As I was traveling in Europe, it occurred to me that one can invest to make money in many different ways. Mutual funds, bonds, and tax-sheltered annuities are safe but do not have the growth potential of stocks."

Ineffective letter inquiring about the work performance of a job applicant: "Page-Middleton is a supplier of after-market equipment for water vehicles. We have been in business for 10 years and are looking for someone who can lead our team of designers and engineers into the next decade. That is why we are considering hiring Stacey Franklin, a former employee of yours."

The key to writing an effective first paragraph for a routine request or announcement is to put the most important point in the first sentence. If you need information, state what you need in the first sentence. If you are giving information, state the most important part of that information in the first sentence. In cultures that expect directness, the reader will appreciate your letting him or her know the purpose of the correspondence right from the start.

**MIDDLE PARAGRAPHS.** If your request or announcement requires additional details that do not fit conveniently in the first paragraph, you can put further explanations and information in the middle paragraph(s) of the message. There is no formula for deciding how many paragraphs are necessary. The only guidelines are to use correct paragraph development and to use as many paragraphs as necessary to provide all the information the reader needs.

The following paragraphs are from the middle of the request for four copies of a catalog, the beginning of which appears on page 203. If you only want four catalogs, you do not need a middle paragraph. However, if you need more information, you might write a middle section such as this:

> You gave us a 20 percent discount on our last shipment of furniture, which was a major factor in our decision to order from you. Is this discount still available under your firm's new ownership? Because we intend to place an order of $400,000 or more, it seems that an additional volume discount would also be appropriate.
>
> Pearce Communications is in a growth mode, so we will probably have frequent need for your products. Such a long-term business relationship could be mutually beneficial to both of us.

The middle paragraphs of a routine request or announcement should include all the details necessary to fulfill the purpose of the message (in this case, getting the catalogs and the two discounts). You attitude is used to show the reader how granting the discounts will benefit his or her company. The statement about Pearce Communications is not being used to "sell" the reader on the writer's company; it is only being used to convince the reader that fair pricing would be beneficial to both companies in the long run.

People in business frequently write memos to co-workers giving instructions for handling procedural changes and instituting new procedures and guidelines. You will also often find it necessary to write to customers and clients

Items in a list should be related, balanced in importance, and parallel in construction.

| EXHIBIT 7.4 | **Using Lists and Paragraphs to Write Clear Instructions** |
|---|---|

■ **Using Lists and Paragraphs**

- Use lists when an operation is easy to divide and when items are balanced and require approximately the same amount of space; use paragraphs when steps require long explanations.
- Use transitional words at the beginnings of paragraphs to indicate steps (e.g., *first, second, next, then*).
- Enumerate or bullet lists to make them easy to read and follow.
- Use similar grammatical form in listed items (e.g., all complete sentences, all sentence fragments, all active verbs).

■ **Writing Clear Instructions**

1. When lists appear within text, include a sentence or paragraph to introduce each list, telling why the operation is important.
2. List the materials, information, tools, and equipment needed to perform the operation.
3. Break the operation down into short, easy-to-understand steps, and discuss each step in the order in which it should be performed.
4. Explain each step in specific terms appropriate to the reading level of the reader.
5. Draw the reader in by beginning listed items with active verbs (e.g., *use, draw, insert, attach, check*) that command the reader to perform an action.
6. Indicate, if appropriate, how the reader will know when a step has been performed correctly (e.g., a computer message will appear on the screen).
7. Warn readers ahead of time when a specific step might result in injury or damage if it is not performed correctly.
8. Refer readers, when pertinent, to diagrams or sketches necessary to improve clarity.
9. Within the text and after the list of instructions, sum up the importance of the operation in terms of how the results will benefit the reader.

to tell them how to do something, such as how to complete a form, how to pursue a complaint through an arbitration panel, or how to make specific equipment work with their computer systems. Exhibit 7.4 explains how to give instructions such as these. Notice that each of the listed items in Exhibit 7.4 is related, balanced in importance, and parallel in construction. If you follow these guidelines, your instructions will be easier to follow and will generate fewer questions seeking clarification.

Lists are also useful if you have several questions to ask, so the reader can focus on each one as he or she responds to your correspondence. Numbering the questions helps when they need to be referred to later. You should arrange the questions in some logical order—for example, order of importance, with the most important question at the beginning where it will receive the most attention. Other arrangements that work well include chronological and easy-to-complex order. When you start with easy questions, readers are often drawn gradually into a survey. Once they have started, they are more likely to complete the survey and mail it back to you. Yes/no questions and any other questions that can be answered without research are easy and do not require much time to complete.

The more difficult the questions are, the more important it is that readers have something to gain by answering them. For example, nobody is likely to spend hours researching the answer to a question from a potential buyer unless the buyer seems quite interested in the product. When the reader and the writer work for the same company and the writer has no power to demand information, the reader will have to be convinced to help through appeals to his or her team spirit or whichever of Maslow's needs is most likely to motivate. For example, you might want to use this opening as an introduction to a list of questions:

> As the only network expert on staff, will you please help us with a problem that has slowed down our ability to meet company goals.

**LAST PARAGRAPH.** The last paragraph of a direct request should show appreciation tied to the future—future business or any future action the reader must take. Never thank a reader in advance. Thanking someone before he or she has had the opportunity to choose whether or not to act is presumptuous, and many people resent being taken for granted. The last paragraph in Exhibit 7.3 is a good example of how appreciation can be tied to future action. It expresses gratitude but lets the reader know you are not arrogantly assuming he will automatically jump to meet your request.

Expressions of goodwill are appropriate anywhere in a letter, but they are particularly easy to work into the last paragraph. Although goodwill can be expressed in many ways, it is best used with subtlety. A brief, simple statement of gratitude in the close is an adequate amount of goodwill if the reader's needs have been met in the rest of the letter. Whatever goodwill is used, it should always be sincere and professional. Do not make statements that might seem subservient or patronizing. Any goodwill you use should also be related to the situation discussed in the correspondence.

Here are some examples of closing paragraphs for routine requests and announcements:

> Effective memo announcing a holiday party for company employees: "Please call Ext. 2989 to let me know whether or not you will be attending. Happy holidays!"
>
> Critique: This last paragraph is appropriate because the memo discusses plans for a holiday party.
>
> Ineffective letter requesting information about a new product: "Merry Christmas!"
>
> Critique: As a last paragraph, this closing is not appropriate because the letter does not discuss Christmas. Goodwill should be related to the purpose of the message. In addition, the writer runs the risk of seeming culturally insensitive because the reader might not celebrate Christmas.
>
> Ineffective memo to your boss asking for a pay raise: "Thank you so much for reading this memo and for considering my request."
>
> Critique: The menial tone might leave the reader with the impression that you are weak and docile (not the sort of qualities for which people get pay raises).
>
> Effective letter congratulating a co-worker on his promotion: "Good luck to you in your new position! Let me know what I can do to help."
>
> Critique: If sincere, this expression of goodwill is appropriate in the last paragraph.

A polite request sounds like a question, but it is not. Use a period at the end of a polite request.

## ROUTINE REPLIES

Plan, organize, compose, and evaluate routine replies.

When you write routine replies, you should use a direct approach because routine replies are not likely to elicit a negative reaction from your reader. Because you are not delivering bad news, you can come right to the point. Elizabeth Sarkanian, the director of finance for PacRim Industries (see the vignette at the beginning of the chapter) thought her reply to the Japanese investors could take this simple, straightforward approach. She could simply accept the offer in the first paragraph, discuss the necessary details in the middle, and end with a cordial look toward the future relationship of the two companies. The direct strategy would, in fact, have been perfectly acceptable for readers in this country. However, for Japanese readers, whose culture is less direct, Elizabeth would perhaps be better off using the indirect letter written by her assistant.

Exhibit 7.5 is an example of a well-written routine reply. Read it carefully and note how it follows the direct approach. Writing routine replies is easy if you use the direct strategy as a guide. Coupled with good word choice and an effective you attitude, the direct strategy is usually more favorably received by readers because it gets to the point without wasting their time.

**Respond quickly to requests to promote goodwill.**

One of the most important factors in writing effective replies is promptness. A delayed response sends a negative message to the reader; a prompt response earns goodwill for yourself and for your company. Respond quickly to any request made of you, so the reader feels you are concerned about his or her needs.

**FIRST PARAGRAPH.** When you write a routine reply, you are not delivering bad news. Therefore, you should get to the point in the first sentence. Do not waste the reader's time by discussing anything other than what he or she wants or needs to know.

Compare the following examples of first paragraphs of routine replies. They are responses to earlier examples of routine requests and announcements.

Effective: "As you requested, enclosed are four copies of our latest catalog. You will see that the catalog contains the latest ergonomic designs in office furniture."

Ineffective: "We were happy to hear from you once again. Fulfilling your need for the latest ergonomic designs in office furniture is what we do best."

Effective: "Yes, the latest version of WordPerfect operates effectively in the Macintosh System 7.1 environment."

Ineffective: "The information you requested about WordPerfect and System 7.1 is summarized in subsequent paragraphs of this letter."

Effective: "As you requested in your announcement, I plan to attend the November 13–17 meeting of the Association for Business Communication in Los Angeles."

Ineffective: "The November 13–17 meeting of the Association for Business Communication sounds interesting. I wouldn't miss it for the world."

Effective: "Five of our employees will be attending the Chamber of Commerce luncheon honoring outstanding business leaders in the community. Thank you for inviting us."

**EXHIBIT 7.5**

**Routine Reply (Memo)**

## BARNNES, HORN & ALBRIGHT, INC.

ATTORNEYS AT LAW

To: Frank Jerome

From: Merle Okambe

Copies To: A. Roche, A. Loston, D. Cano

Date: February 3, 1996

Subject: Gender Equity Report

*The subject line is an essential part of the message; therefore, it should get right to the point.* The enclosed report provides the requested information on gender equity. You will see from reading the preliminary results of the study now underway that we have made strides in the last four years toward providing equal pay and equal opportunity at all levels of employment. On the other hand, the results reveal that we still have a way to go before we have a workplace free of gender discrimination.

*The first sentence gets right to the point, and the requested results are summarized.* In particular, you will be interested in the charts on page 4 that show we have almost an equal number of men and women working in Category 2—clerical, secretarial, computer programming, and data entry. Four years ago this job category was 72 percent female. The study also revealed that, after adjustments for length of employment, women in Category 2 are earning 92 percent of what men in the same category are earning. It is clear equal pay is still not a reality in Category 2, significant progress has been made since the last major study. At that time, it was revealed Category 2 females were earning only 76 percent of what Category 2 males were earning.

*The next three paragraphs summarize the details the reader requested.* The most disheartening results can be seen in a comparison of Category 2 employees with Category 3 employees—painters, carpenters, welders, and electronics technicians. Because Category 3 is on the same level as Category 2, salary for both categories is supposed to be comparable (a goal established by

Frank Jerome         2         February 3, 1996

management three years ago). However, little progress has been made. At the time of the last affirmative action study, Category 3 employees were earning 34 percent more than Category 2 employees. The latest results show that, despite a high number of retirements in Category 3, they are still earning 31.9 percent more than Category 2 employees.

Data collection is still taking place for mid-management and upper-level management categories. Let me know if you want this information when the results have been interpreted and are ready for dissemination.

This information should help you monitor how well your interviewers are meeting our hiring goals and initial salary establishment goals. As soon as all categories have been completed, final recommendations will be made. Please let me know if you need further information before then.

Enclosure

*The you attitude is used to show the reader how the requested results will help him and his department. It (and the previous paragraphs) provides further information in which the reader might be interested. The last sentence is a sincere offer of further assistance.*

Ineffective: "Thank you for inviting us to the Chamber of Commerce luncheon. Five of us will attend to honor outstanding business leaders in the community."

Effective: "Enclosed is a corrected invoice. Thank you for bringing the errors in the last invoice to our attention."

Ineffective: "When you contacted us regarding a possible error in Invoice No. 1437-B, we immediately began to research the matter. All your recent purchase orders were matched against the shipping orders; and we found, as you stated, only one F-87 was ordered and delivered. Therefore, a corrected invoice has been enclosed."

All of the ineffective examples have one error in common: They don't get to the point immediately. When you want to communicate good news or neutral news that won't anger or disappoint the reader, tell it without wasting the reader's time. Any expressions of gratitude and further information can be included later. In fact, readers will be more receptive to the extra information after reading the good news.

**MIDDLE PARAGRAPHS.** As with routine requests and announcements, the middle paragraphs of routine replies include all the details needed to fulfill the purpose of the message. As you write a reply letter or memo, refer frequently to the message you are answering to make sure your response is complete. If the request asked for answers to specific questions, respond to those questions in the same order they were asked. The middle paragraphs of the memo in Exhibit 7.5 illustrate how those of a routine reply should be constructed.

> Goodwill must be sincere or it will not be believable.

**LAST PARAGRAPH.** As with all business correspondence, the last paragraph of a routine reply should include some expression of goodwill. Sometimes it is nothing more than a sincere offer of further assistance. The key word here, however, is *sincere*. Do not offer further assistance if you do not want the reader to take you up on your offer.

The following examples of last paragraphs would be appropriate for routine replies:

"The enclosed brochure explains other services we offer that might be of interest to you. Please be sure to let us help you whenever we can."

"I look forward to seeing you May 19."

"Your business is appreciated, and we pledge to do our utmost to see that you are always satisfied with LizEx products."

"Thank you for giving us the pleasure of serving you. We look forward to hearing from you again."

"Please call if you need further information."

"Thank you for your support of AirDynamics."

> Statements such as this are appropriate only if the reader has indeed expressed support for your product or company, either by praising or purchasing your products.

"Now that you have the operating instructions, you should find your Drillmate easy to operate and essential to your home repair needs. Please call our technical support representatives at (602) 555-4900, Ext. 9603, whenever you need advice about the use of any of your quality Blackwell tools."

## ROUTINE CLAIM LETTERS

◤ Plan, organize, compose, and evaluate routine claims.

**Claim letters** are written by the buyer to the seller or manufacturer of a service or product. Claim letters seek some type of corrective action to resolve a conflict situation.

Has everything you ever ordered through a catalog been the quality, color, or fabric you expected? Has every software program or piece of equipment you have ever purchased worked exactly as it was supposed to? Has every mechanic or car dealer treated you fairly and courteously? Have all the parts been included with every product you have ever purchased? Have you always been satisfied with the services you received from a government agency or a professional, such as an accountant or a doctor?

When you were disappointed with the product or service you received, what did you do? Too many people do little more than complain to their friends. However, well-written claim letters are usually effective in resolving problems like these. Most companies are eager to keep customers satisfied and willingly replace or repair substandard products. When quality of service is the problem, companies are usually quick to apologize and sometimes offer discounts and free products or services to compensate customers for their inconvenience. On one occasion, a person wrote about rude service at a gas station. In addition to the apology she requested, she also received a free tank of gasoline and was treated like royalty on each subsequent visit. Another person once received a free box of candy bars when he asked for his money back for a candy bar that contained a nutshell.

A claim letter anticipates and specifies the action needed to resolve a problem.

It is important for you to understand that a claim letter is not a complaint letter. A complaint letter merely complains; it does not expect action on the part of the seller or manufacturer. Claim letters presume that some action will be taken, and specify what is needed to resolve the issue.

Exhibits 7.6 and 7.7 are examples of effective routine claim letters. As you read them, notice the emphasis placed on the action desired—replacement of the product as well as a messenger to pick up the defective desk (Exhibit 7.6) and a refund check (Exhibit 7.7).

Be sure you decide the action you desire before you begin writing. If the action you want is reasonable and you believe the recipient will respond favorably without much persuasion, a direct approach is best. If you take care not to dwell on the negative side of the problem, a direct approach will usually get positive results. If, however, you believe it will be difficult to convince the company to take the action you desire, an indirect approach (Chapter 8) or a persuasive approach (Chapter 9) would be more appropriate.

**FIRST PARAGRAPH.** Begin directly by stating the problem in the first sentence and, if possible, the desired action. However, the action you want the company to take to correct the problem may be explained elsewhere in the first paragraph if it does not fit smoothly and logically into the first sentence. In a subject line at the top of the letter or in the first paragraph, include order numbers, policy numbers, account numbers, and any other information the reader might need in order to find your file. Making the problem easy to solve is a good you-attitude tactic.

The following examples are effective openings for routine claim letters:

EXHIBIT
7.6

**Routine Claim (Simplified Style)**

CHANCE VOUGHT
ENGINEERING          3261 Boyington Boulevard          Santa Fe, NM 87501          (505) 448-8692

March 27, 1994

Customer Service Representative
Hon & Hon, Incorporated
15144 North Kensington Boulevard
Santa Fe, New Mexico 87440

*The optional subject line tells exactly what the letter is about.*

REPLACEMENT OF ITEM RECEIVED WITH ORDER NO. 136-BX

*This paragraph explains the problem that needs to be solved.*

Please arrange to have someone pick up and replace the desk (No. 14888-ls) received with the above order. Two of the five drawers stick and are difficult to open and close because the runners are bent. It also appears that one of the drawers is too large for the intended opening.

*With a lighthearted tone, the writer justifies the proposed solution so it seems reasonable and fair.*

Since my old desk was given away when the new one arrived, it is important you send a replacement at the same time the defective desk is picked up. I realize that the usual procedure would be to send back the defective merchandise and wait for a replacement. However, working without a desk while the problem is solved would be more than just a little difficult.

*This goodwill helps the reader feel good about the writer's company and should make the reader want to keep the writer happy.*

You will be glad to know that all the other items received with the order were of your usual high quality.

Please call me at Ext. 9641 as soon as you receive this letter to let me know when I may expect a replacement.

*This paragraph courteously stresses the action the reader needs to take. "As soon as" is used to stress the need for immediate action.*

James D. Wang

JAMES D. WANG
ENGINEERING SPECIALIST

snl

1019 Eucalyptus Street, Apt. B
Hesperia, CA 91010
April 2, 1994

Because personal business letters are from individuals who do not have personal letterheads, an address at the top of the letter above the date is essential. The writer's name is typed at the bottom of the letter.

Mr. Bruce Goswin
Warranty Representative
Yamaha Motor Company
66555 Katella Avenue
Cypress, CA 90603

Dear Mr. Goswin:

Please see that I am reimbursed $172.80 for the cracked WaveRunner seat for which I was incorrectly required to pay. The attached receipt shows that one of your dealers charged me for replacement of the seat, which I found out later should have been covered under the warranty.

On January 9, I took the WaveRunner seat into Marine Specialties in Sun Valley because it was cracked and ready to break. At that time, I was told by the manager, Steve Keller, the seat was not a warranty item even though I called to his attention that the pins that align the seat on the new 1994 WaveRunner models were not the same on the 1993 model. Therefore, I paid $172.80 for a replacement.

When I took the WaveRunner to my regular dealer, Ted Evans, for maintenance, he told me that the damage should have been covered by the warranty. As a result, I wrote the attached letter to Marine Specialties on March 1 but have received no response despite repeated telephone calls (March 11, 12, 13) that were not returned by the owner or the manager. The names of the individuals I left messages with and for are also attached.

Your help in resolving this matter promptly would be greatly appreciated. Ted Evans has the cracked seat if you need to see it.

Sincerely

Stacey Leonard

Stacey Leonard
(818) 555-4327

Attachments: Receipt
Letter
Telephone record

As a warranty representative, the reader deals with this kind of problem regularly. Therefore, his reaction should be neutral.

The writer summarizes the situation without dwelling on the emotional aspects of the unfair treatment.

The reader is informed of what he needs to do to resolve the problem, and the writer mentions forthcoming appreciation for such an action.

A telephone number can be provided after the writer's name if it has not been mentioned in the message itself.

The attachments make it easy for the reader to see what has been done so he can make a quick decision.

Memo to a fellow department head concerning a trade between departments that did not work out as planned: "As we feared, the seventeen 486 computers inherited from your department do not work with my department's network. Therefore, as we agreed, I would appreciate your having the computers removed and seeing that the $37,000 we transferred to get them is returned to this department's budget."

Letter seeking an apology for poor service and reprimanding those who were in charge: "Please speak to those in charge about the unusually poor service we received this week at your Wilmington hotel. Because the staff has always been exceptional in the past, we once again scheduled our annual meeting at your facility despite the higher convention rates."

**MIDDLE PARAGRAPHS.**    Now that you are familiar with the direct organizational pattern, you know the middle paragraphs should contain all the details the reader needs in order to deal with the problem. Make good use of the you attitude throughout the letter. During the planning stage, you should have asked yourself this question: What will make the reader want to correct the problem and agree that my proposed solution is appropriate? Keep the answer in mind as you compose the message.

Your claim letter will get a better reception if you keep two things in mind:

- Companies want customers to be satisfied with their products and services. Most firms know that repeat business and word-of-mouth advertising costs very little, and they are willing to go to great lengths to meet any reasonable claims.

*State your claim calmly and unemotionally to avoid creating a negative reaction.*

- Companies need to know that you are willing to continue doing business if they solve the problem to your satisfaction. Don't dwell on the inconvenience you have experienced; state it once unemotionally and then focus on solving the problem. If your reader thinks you have given up on the company or the product, there is no reason to solve your problem.

The following statements do not provide much incentive for the readers to try to make the writer happy:

Ineffective letter attempting to resolve a problem with an executive's company car: "You can rest assured we will buy no more vehicles from your dealership."

Ineffective letter requesting replacement of a malfunctioning photocopier: "We've been able to use our copier on only 35 days of the last three months. As a result, three of us have had to go down six floors every time a copy had to be made on the days the copier was malfunctioning. I stopped counting when I made my 250th trip! Perhaps your competitor could make my life easier!"

*Make it easier for your reader to solve the problem by including all documentation that establishes the validity of your claim.*

Make it easier for the reader to help you by including copies of all documentation needed to support your claim. The letter in Exhibit 7.7, for example, includes numerous attachments. Any receipts, invoices, order forms, and so forth you provide will not have to be gathered by the person reading your letter, and so perhaps your request will get immediate attention. Be specific about dates and names, and discuss everything in chronological order. Include copies of previous correspondence and, when applicable, provide a summary of all telephone calls made in attempts to resolve the problem.

**LAST PARAGRAPH.**  Read the final paragraphs of Exhibits 7.6 and 7.7. They both politely mention what the reader needs to do to resolve the issue. As with other direct letters, the final paragraph should also contain goodwill, unless there is an adequate amount of goodwill in the rest of the letter. However, your gratitude should be expressed in terms of the action the reader will take in the future (i.e., *will be appreciated*), because taking people for granted by thanking them in advance is a sure way to get a negative response.

In some cases it might be necessary for you to specify a date by which the matter should be handled. After all, your own idea of what *soon* means might be very different from your reader's interpretation of the word. The examples below show two ways to specify and justify a date:

"Because we have a heavy production schedule for April, it is critical the FB349 be replaced by March 27. Your personal attention in expediting the replacement before that time would be greatly appreciated."

"Your company has always bent over backwards to provide superior service. Once again, I hope you are able to achieve your usual high standards by rushing the replacement part to us by September 15, the latest date that will allow us to meet our publishing deadline. Please call to let me know whether you will be able to ship the part by September 15."

Although it is important that you assume a reasonable solution will be carried out, it is also important that this assumption does not come across as arrogance on your part. A statement such as the following would probably cause a negative reaction. In fact, there is a good chance your request might be placed at the bottom of a very tall stack of papers!

Ineffective: "You will correct this error immediately, I am sure."

However, a request stated with too much humility might also create a negative reaction. Most Americans, Canadians, and people from other direct cultures do not react well to begging or signs of weakness. As a result, avoid final paragraphs such as the following:

Ineffective: "Please forgive me for the trouble this causes you. I only wish it could be handled in some other way."

Ineffective: "Don't let this unfortunate occurrence bother you. These things happen. However, if you would try your best to take care of the problem soon, we would be forever grateful."

## ROUTINE ADJUSTMENT LETTERS

Plan, organize, compose, and evaluate routine adjustment letters.

**Adjustment letters** are written in response to claim letters. Routine adjustment letters are those that grant what the customer desires. Because they deliver good news, these letters should follow a direct organizational pattern. Adjustments that do not grant what customers want require an indirect organizational strategy.

Companies that receive many routine claims usually develop form letters that can easily be individualized for particular situations. These form letters are usually not as direct as individually written adjustment letters. Exhibit 7.8 is an example of such a form letter. Notice that it starts by displaying good you attitude. It also lets the reader know the organization is glad the claim was

Form adjustment letters are, by necessity, less specific than adjustment letters written for specific individuals.

METROPOLITAN POLICE DEPARTMENT
CHIEF
DARYL GUTS
TOM BRADLUM
MAYOR

**123 LAWLESS AVENUE**
**HARDINSBURG, KY 40143**
**(606) 717-6448**

October 11, 1995

*This form letter could be used for all routine complaints about police personnel. It does not admit the officer was at fault, and it treats the reader with respect. A well-written letter such as this will go a long way toward restoring the reader's confidence in the police department.*

Mrs. Tanya Rubenstein
119 Garfield Street
Hardinsburg, KY 40143

Dear Mrs. Rubinstein:

The letter in which you expressed dissatisfaction, and rightfully so, with the behavior of one of our officers was referred to me by Mayor Tom Bradlum. The matter has been referred to Rampart Field Services Division for review and investigation.

One of our officers should have already discussed this matter with you. If this is not the case, please call the Rampart Division at (606) 555-4070. Personnel complaint investigations are always given high priority because of the importance of maintaining confidence in our police force. You will be informed of the disposition at the conclusion of the investigation.

*The goodwill seems sincere and makes the reader feel like a public-spirited citizen instead of a complainer.*

It is the department's goal to provide the best possible police service. Only with input from concerned citizens such as yourself may the accomplishment of this goal become a reality. Thank you for bringing this matter to our attention.

Very truly yours,

*Daryl F. Guts*

Daryl F. Guts
Chief of Police

mgl

brought to the attention of those in charge, thereby putting the reader at ease. Companies can set the same sort of tone by mentioning that feedback from their customers helps them develop better products and services.

**FIRST PARAGRAPH.**    Read the first paragraph of Exhibit 7.9. Consistent with the requirements of a direct approach, the first sentence states what the reader wants to hear: The problem is being corrected.

As you read the rest of Exhibit 7.9, you will see that the claim is not granted grudgingly, nor is there anything to imply the customer might be lying about the damaged windshields. Most companies know that customers do not write to make a claim unless they feel strongly about their case. Therefore, when you write adjustment letters, do not use words implying that the customer's request is silly or unworthy of your consideration. An arrogant tone may increase the customer's dissatisfaction with your product or your company.

The following poor examples would probably dismay customers rather than reassure them:

> Ineffective: "Despite the condition of the item you returned, my department supervisor instructed me to send you the enclosed check."

> Ineffective: "Newquick has been one of our most reliable products. We have never had any complaints before about its quality. Therefore, we were quite surprised at your allegations that Newquick did not work as instructed. However, we will take your word for it; enclosed is a coupon for a free can of Newquick and $10 in coupons for some of our other fine baking products."

> Ineffective: "Your refund is enclosed. We see no reason to quibble over a $100 order."

**MIDDLE PARAGRAPHS.**    As you know, the middle paragraphs of a direct message should include any details the reader wants or needs to know. The tone of these paragraphs is important, because the goal is to reestablish consumer confidence.

In a routine adjustment letter, the middle paragraphs often contain a brief explanation of how the error occurred (see Exhibit 7.9). The first rule of such an explanation is to avoid blaming the reader. In addition, take care not to make excuses or blame one of your employees. Avoid sounding flippant—do not use phrases such as "Mistakes are bound to occur" or "These things happen." You don't have to admit there have been a number of complaints about a product, service, or individual. You don't have to discuss the inefficiency of your accounting department or the fact that you think a few disgruntled employees are sabotaging shipping. In all likelihood, your customer will be satisfied just knowing that the error has been corrected.

If you or your company actually did something wrong, you may apologize. However, do not be overly apologetic, and never apologize more than once. You may have seen letters that apologize in the first paragraph and then conclude with "Again, we are sorry" at the end. Dwelling on what you have done wrong or the damage and inconvenience your error has caused may prompt the thought "Well, you ought to be sorry!" Don't risk turning good news into an opportunity for negative thoughts.

*In a routine adjustment message, tell the reader the good news in the first sentence.*

*Don't feel compelled to tell how a mistake was made.*

*Apologize only when you've done something wrong.*

**EXHIBIT 7.9**   Routine Adjustment (Block Style with Open Punctuation)

**FLOYD GLASS WHOLESALERS**

625 Watersgone Ave.
Minneapolis, MN 55402
(612) 805-6347
FAX (612) 805-7058

October 13, 1995

Mr. Esrat Hegabe
Purchasing Agent
Santa Monica Glassworks
1900 Pico Place
Sun River, MT 59483

Dear Mr. Hegabe

Re: Order No. 83789

*Begin with the good news.*

Two new windshields were shipped to you today by Air Express. You should receive them before this letter reaches you.

*If you explain how the error was made, do not make the explanation sound like an excuse. In an effort to restore confidence in the company and its products, this letter justifies the error in terms of how haste was meant to benefit the reader.*

At the time your order was received, our supply of windshields was depleted due to exceptionally high demand. Knowing you needed your order immediately, we rushed the five windshields as soon as they were received from the manufacturer. In our haste, two of the cartons were evidently not opened for inspection.

Thank you for allowing us to correct the situation. The defective windshields will be picked up at the same time the new ones are delivered. You may be sure I will do everything I can to ensure that your next order is filled promptly and properly.

*The goodwill is based on the assumption that the relationship between the two companies is still intact and that future business is anticipated.*

Sincerely

Kelly Clearman

Kelly Clearman
President

mgl

In this type of letter, it may also be tempting to make unrealistic promises about the future: "Trust me, this will never happen again" sounds good. However, even if you own the company, can you honestly say you have complete control over every billing or shipping clerk? Every salesperson? Your suppliers? Your partners? Rarely make promises, because people take them seriously and expect you to stand up to them—even when doing so is not under your control.

Resale is an important feature of adjustment letters.

One of the most important components of the adjustment letter is **resale,** the regeneration of confidence in the organization, its products, and its services. Resale is usually best suited for the middle paragraphs of a letter, but it can also be included in opening or closing paragraphs. A routine adjustment letter is a perfect opportunity for resale, because it is a letter the customer wants to read and it contains good news. Many companies include a complete paragraph promoting new products or services in which the reader might be interested. In Exhibit 7.9, the resale is more subtle. Statements such as "exceptionally high demand" reaffirm that the product is worth waiting for. Furthermore, the image of workers rushing around to meet the reader's need for haste depicts a positive picture of a company bending over backwards for its customers. In Exhibit 7.8, resale occurs when the writer speaks of the public's confidence in the police force and the department's goal of providing the best police service possible.

**LAST PARAGRAPH.** If there is anything the reader needs to do to complete the transaction, such as calling to reschedule a delivery date or sending an item back to you, clarify this need for action at the end of the message. However, under no circumstances should you again mention the negative situation. As you write the last paragraph, assume everything is satisfactory between you and the reader. After all, you have honored the reader's request.

No matter how many goodwill statements you have used throughout an adjustment letter, try to include some type of goodwill in the last paragraph as well. The message should end on a note of courtesy and warmth.

## EVALUATING YOUR MESSAGE

Once you have planned, organized, and composed your message, you should evaluate its effectiveness. Exhibit 7.10 is a checklist you can use, either individually or collaboratively, to assess the effectiveness of all your direct messages before they are sent.

The only major factor not included in the evaluation checklist is the last point on which any message should be evaluated: reader feedback. This type of evaluation comes in many forms. In the case of instructions, you can tell your message is understood if people perform the instructions easily and without excessive questioning. If a customer continues to do business with you after you have resolved a complaint or claim, you know your handling of the problem was acceptable. If someone agrees to comply with a request you have made and the tone of the reply is courteous and sincere, your message is probably effective.

On the other hand, if you do not receive a response or if a response indicates the other party did not understand your questions or instructions, reevaluate your message to determine the changes that should be made. Such rewriting is particularly important for form messages and for instructions that

**EXHIBIT**

**7.10**

## Checklist for Direct Messages

Answer the following yes/no questions. (A "no" answer indicates room for improvement.) A few of the points do not apply to all types of messages. If a point does not apply, put n/a (not applicable) in the blank.

### ■ Opening and Closing

___ Did you begin with the most important news (in the reader's opinion) in the first sentence?

___ Are pertinent order numbers, dates, etc., mentioned?

___ Is effective you attitude used in the opening paragraph?

___ Are negative references to the situation avoided in the opening and closing paragraphs?

___ Is goodwill in the closing relevant to the situation?

___ Does the closing paragraph avoid trite, overused words and phrases?

___ Does the closing paragraph inform the reader politely of what he or she should do next (if appropriate)?

___ Does the closing avoid thanking the reader in advance?

___ In the closing, is gratitude tied to any action the reader should perform?

### ■ Message

___ Have you disclosed clearly and completely everything that should be communicated?

___ Does the message achieve the purpose(s) established during freewriting?

___ If pertinent, have details of previous contact or correspondence been summarized?

___ Will the quality of your arguments, conclusions, generalizations, and assumptions stand up to scrutiny?

___ Did you avoid negative words?

___ Did you use resale when appropriate to reestablish confidence in your products, services, or company?

___ Did you mention anything that will be enclosed with the correspondence?

___ Did you tell the reader clearly what you have done and what you will do?

___ For replies and adjustments, have all requests or questions been addressed?

___ For adjustment messages, if you or your company did something wrong, did you apologize briefly without dwelling on the negative impact of your mistake?

___ For claim and adjustment letters, did you avoid blaming anyone (your firm, your employees, the reader)?

___ For adjustment messages, did you avoid unrealistic promises about the future?

___ If you can't do everything the reader wants, do you explain why the decision was made in terms of how it actually benefits the reader?

### ■ Tone

___ Did you avoid overuse of *I, me, my, our, we,* and the company name?

___ Did you emphasize *you* and *your* and the reader's needs?

___ Is goodwill sincere and appropriate to the situation?

___ Has the reader been treated with courtesy and respect?

### ■ Mechanics

___ Are the name and title of the reader spelled and used correctly?

___ Have all words been spelled correctly?

___ Is correct sentence structure used for all sentences?

___ Is correct paragraph structure used for all paragraphs?

___ Are there transitions between each paragraph?

___ Is punctuation correct?

### ■ Readability

___ Is the reading level appropriate for the intended reader(s)?

___ Are lists used when necessary to improve the clarity of complex information or questions?

### ■ Format and Appearance

___ Is the format one of those recommended in the textbook? (See Appendix C.)

___ If appropriate, has reader reaction to a form message been considered?

___ Are side margins equal?

___ Are corrections undetectable?

___ Has the letter or memorandum been folded correctly?

___ Is your signature readable?

### ■ Other

___ Is the entire message truthful?

___ Have you been fair to all concerned?

___ Would you be proud if everyone you know were aware of all the details of this transaction?

___ Is your communication within the bounds of the law?

___ Have you collaborated with appropriate individuals?

___ Did you reply promptly?

___ Have you avoided deliberate distortions, slang, discriminatory language, clichés, redundancies, roundabout expressions, and confusing foreign expressions?

___ Did you analyze the reader and his or her needs thoroughly?

are used repeatedly. In situations like the one faced by Elizabeth Sarkanian, who was communicating about very important matters with people from a different culture, you might also follow up with a phone call or face-to-face meeting to make sure you have successfully conveyed both your meaning and your wish to continue the relationship.

## DISCUSSION QUESTIONS

■ Determine when a direct organizational strategy is appropriate.

1. What does the reader's probable reaction to a message have to do with the selection of a direct organizational strategy?

■ Determine when a direct organizational strategy is appropriate.

2. What impact does culture have on the selection of a direct strategy?

■ Apply the four stages of the message formulation process to direct messages.

3. How are the four steps of the message formulation process used for direct messages?

■ Identify the features of a direct organizational strategy.

4. What are the features of a direct organizational strategy?

■ Plan, organize, compose, and evaluate routine requests and announcements.

5. What four points recommended for writing clear instructions seem to be most important to you? Why?

■ Plan, organize, compose, and evaluate routine replies.

6. Define *resale,* and give two examples of when resale would be appropriate in a direct message.

■ Plan, organize, compose, and evaluate routine claims.

7. Give two examples of products or services about which you would like to complain or about which you would like to write a claim letter. Give reasons.

■ Plan, organize, compose, and evaluate routine adjustment letters.

8. Respond to this statement using the reasoning presented in this chapter. "If you tell the reader the good news in the first sentence of an adjustment letter, it is unlikely he or she will read the rest of the letter; therefore, it is better to put resale before the good news."

## APPLICATION EXERCISES

■ Determine when a direct organizational strategy is appropriate.

1. Analyze the following situations to determine whether a direct strategy would be appropriate and what the reader's probable reaction would be to

the message. In some cases, there might be more than one possible reaction. If so, is a direct message still the best choice?

a. A letter asking a reference for information about a job applicant.

b. A memo to your boss asking for a raise in pay.

c. A letter acknowledging an order from a customer who hasn't purchased anything from your firm in three years.

d. A memo asking a co-worker for confidential information.

e. A memo congratulating a co-worker on his appointment to a lower-level management position.

f. An adjustment letter that denies a customer's claim.

g. An adjustment letter suggesting a way to handle a claim in a manner other than what the customer wanted.

h. An adjustment letter with an apology to someone who objected to sexist connotations in an advertisement for your product.

i. A letter to a local newspaper objecting to inaccurate reporting in an article about the owner of your firm.

j. A memo to your boss objecting to her new policy requiring employees to get her permission whenever they leave the office area for any reason.

🔳 Apply the four stages of the message formulation process to direct messages.
🔳 Identify the features of a direct organizational strategy.
🔳 Plan, organize, compose, and evaluate routine requests and announcements.

2. Evaluate the following memos. Then rewrite them so they adhere to the guidelines presented in this chapter.

a. Memo to all first-year employees from the benefits manager.

Before long you will reach the end of your first year with SMC, so I thought it would be a good idea for us to get together on an informal basis. Lunch will be served, so you will need to arrange with your supervisor for someone else to cover your desk if you do not normally go to lunch at that time.

Please join me on Tuesday, November 4, at 11 AM in the Porter Room on the second floor to discuss the benefits to which you are entitled once you have worked for SMC for one full year. This meeting is mandatory.

b. Memo to eight supervisors from the general manager of a hotel:

The National Association of Industrial Psychologists is holding its ninth annual meeting at our hotel next week, November 14–18. They are planning many fascinating sessions on topics of interest to anyone with supervisory responsibilities. Four of these (Dealing with the Difficult Employee, Making Jumping through Hoops Seem Like Fun, Designing an Effective Incentive Program, and Disciplining and Terminating within the Law) seem particularly pertinent to the work we do here at the Hyatt.

These topics looked so interesting to me that I thought you supervisors might also like to attend. Therefore, I arranged for you to go by offering a discount on hotel services to the NAIP. A complete schedule of the sessions, including dates and times, will be available on the first day of the conference. Please let me know which sessions you plan to attend.

Thanks for your team effort!

🔳 Identify the features of a direct organizational strategy.

3. Evaluate whether the following openings are appropriate for direct messages. State what is wrong with those that are not appropriate.

    *a.* "Thank you for your order for 1,500 enamel pins. Grayson Novelties is always happy to welcome a new customer."

    *b.* "Your order was received today. It will be shipped to you within two days. Thank you for doing business with Grayson Novelties."

    *c.* "Please send a replacement cartridge for the HP DeskWriter I purchased from you yesterday (Invoice No. 2359). The one that came with the printer is apparently old because the print quality is faint, as you can see in this letter."

    *d.* "PacRim has been one of our most important clients for many years, and it has been a pleasure doing business with you. That is why we are willing to make a donation to your scholarship fund drive for your local community college."

    *e.* "Thank you for suggesting Lucy Jimenez as a speaker for our Women in Business Exposition. She was informative, energetic, and humorous. The audience liked her and her message as well."

■ Identify the features of a direct organizational strategy.

4. Evaluate whether the following closings are appropriate for direct messages. State what is wrong with those that are not appropriate.

    *a.* To acknowledge a new customer's order: "If you have any questions, please feel free to call."

    *b.* To ask for correction of an error in the computation of your sales commission: "Your taking care of this so the money will appear in my next paycheck would be greatly appreciated."

    *c.* To send a co-worker complex information he or she requested: "If the information is not clear to you, let me know. I'll be happy to explain it further."

    *d.* To announce a meeting for new employees: "I look forward to seeing you Tuesday in the Nguyen Lounge."

    *e.* To request a replacement for a defective printer ink cartridge: "Thank you for taking care of this replacement today. We urgently need the cartridge."

For the remaining exercises, you are to compose a letter or memo as instructed. Assume any reasonable details to make the messages realistic. Unless a job title is specified for you, make up a title that is appropriate to the situation. As you do the exercises, follow these steps:

1. Plan your message:
   *a.* Establish your purpose.
   *b.* Choose a medium and channel.
   *c.* Consider legal and ethical issues.
   *d.* Analyze your audience.
   *e.* Gather necessary resources.

2. Organize your message:
   *a.* Freewrite major points.
   *b.* Choose an organizational strategy.

3. Compose your message.

4. Evaluate your message:
   *a.* Use Exhibit 7.10 for self-evaluation.
   *b.* Evaluate feedback from your instructor.

Your instructor will tell you whether to turn in your freewritten notes or any other evidence that you have performed each step of the message formulation process. You will also be told whether the message must be written individually or collaboratively.

### Routine Requests and Announcements

◥ Apply the four stages of the message formulation process to direct messages.
◥ Plan, organize, compose, and evaluate routine requests and announcements.

5. *Thank you letter to clients.* You are the accounts manager for a large furniture manufacturer, Ozarkanian. Your company needs $575,000 in orders each month to maintain its profitability. However, during the last six months, orders have dropped off considerably. You have assigned a team to research the problem, but in the meantime, you have decided to send a form letter to all your active accounts and to any other accounts that haven't ordered within the last year. A business communication course you are taking at your local college has stressed the you attitude, and you have begun to doubt that your company has done anything to make its customers feel special.

   Write a letter thanking customers for their business. Let them know this is the sort of letter that isn't sent often enough. Make it seem as though the only purpose of the letter is to let them know they are appreciated. However, as a smart businessperson, you can't let a perfect opportunity for resale go by. Include resale about some of your latest designs and products or about your company's reputation for quality and service.

   Each letter will be individually addressed by computer; however, you should address your letter to the first business on the list (Mr. Jason Ulibarri, Chief Purchasing Agent, Appalachian Furniture, Inc., P.O. Box 355, Horatio, AR 71842).

◥ Apply the four stages of the message formulation process to direct messages.
◥ Plan, organize, compose, and evaluate routine requests and announcements.

6. *Request for justification of a biweekly report.* Every two weeks your department is required to report to payroll clerks the period's positive attendance (the exact number of hours every person has worked each day in the time period). Because all your employees are on salary (no one is paid by the hour) and all are full time, you do not see any reason for reporting positive attendance. Vacations, sick leave, maternity/paternity leave, and similar absences are already reported to the payroll department on another form. In your opinion, the payroll clerks should be able to compute how many hours people work by subtracting the vacation and leave days from each person's established work hours. You understand the reason for reporting positive attendance for part-time workers who do not work a set number of hours and are paid by the hour, but you see no need to do it for full-time salaried workers.

   You want to propose the following alternative:

   - Positive attendance be reported only for part-time employees who are paid by the hour and do not work a set number of hours per week.

- A column be added to the vacation and leave form to report unauthorized absences or leaves that should be deducted from the pay of full- and part-time employees who work a set number of hours per week.

You think your proposal would actually save time for the payroll clerks. They would have to deal with only the vacation and leave form for each employee rather than fill out two separate forms. Because the computers already keep track of the scheduled work hours for full- and part-time employees as well as their pay rates, all the clerks would have to do is enter into the computer the number of hours for the various classifications of vacations, leaves, and absences (paid and unpaid). The computer could be programmed easily to subtract from pay only for unauthorized leaves or absences.

However, being a reasonable person, you recognize that there might be a legitimate need to verify positive attendance for every employee of the company. Therefore, write a memo to Linda Sinclair, head of the payroll unit of your accounting department. Ask her to explain why reporting positive attendance for full-time employees is necessary. Submit your ideas to her as a time-saving measure. Send a copy of your memo to vice president Franklin Kee.

🔻 Apply the four stages of the message formulation process to direct messages.
🔻 Plan, organize, compose, and evaluate routine requests and announcements.

7. *Memo announcing a negotiating agreement.* You are the chief negotiator for your local union, and you have been involved in months of negotiations over several issues with the management of ConRed. On one major issue, parking, you recently reached agreement. The company president, Jason Feinberg, and the union president, Patrick Nielsen, will send a joint announcement about the agreement to all employees because the agreement pertains to everyone, not just union members. Your job is to draft the joint memo from both presidents on plain paper and to submit it to them for their approval (someone in the graphics department is designing a suitable letterhead that combines the union's logo and the company's logo).

To date, parking has been free for all employees, and it has been plentiful. However, the Air Quality Management District (AQMD), a state agency with the authority to fine businesses who do not comply with major efforts to decrease pollution of the environment, has mandated that companies with more than 25 employees must make every effort to increase ride sharing and other forms of mass transportation. The agency's goal is to keep people off the freeways from 6–10 AM, the peak pollution period. ConRed must soon send AQMD its plan to decrease the number of employee vehicles in the company parking lot by 25 percent. However, because parking is part of the labor–management contract, the company could not make changes unilaterally. To avoid possible fines of $25,000 a day, the company had to come to terms with the union.

The agreement includes changes in workdays and times that will begin on February 1, approximately three months from today. All management and office employees who choose to do so will be allowed to work 10-hour days instead of the current 8-hour days. These employees may then take either Monday, Wednesday, or Friday off (to be determined by each employee and his or her supervisor). In the offices, employees who wish to work 10-hour days may choose to work from 7 AM to 6 PM or from 9 AM to 8 PM (includes the usual one-hour lunch break); however, each person's schedule will be established by the employee and his or her immediate supervisor.

In the manufacturing plant and maintenance categories, all employees will be required to work 10-hour days instead of the current 7 AM to 3:30 PM and 3 PM to 1:30 PM schedules, unless they can justify not doing so (for example, because of responsibilities for the care of a child or an aging parent that cannot be fulfilled under the new schedules). Otherwise, manufacturing and maintenance employees must apply for one of the following work schedules: 6 AM to 4:30 PM or 4 PM to 2:30 AM (with a half-hour lunch). They may choose any day of the workweek (Monday through Friday) as their day off. The numbers of employees working each shift will have to be balanced, of course, but the company has agreed to make every attempt to accommodate employee preferences. Preference will be given to employees with seniority, and others will be placed on a waiting list. In other words, if too many day-shift employees want to take Friday off, that day off will be given to day-shift employees with the most seniority. Employees who do not get their first choice of shift or day off will be placed on a waiting list.

Each month, employees who share rides to work with at least two other employees or who take a bus, walk, or ride a bicycle to work will receive a bonus of $15 and will be entered in a company lottery for a $2,000 prize. More information about this plan will be distributed by the new parking services director, LeAnne Leonard.

In your memo, tell employees that the forms to be used in selecting work times and days off will be distributed by their immediate supervisors within one week. Employees may consult their union representatives, their immediate supervisors, or the parking services director if they still have questions about the plan after receiving the forms.

◆ Apply the four stages of the message formulation process to direct messages.
◆ Plan, organize, compose, and evaluate routine requests and announcements.

8. *Letter to a successful job applicant.* You are the human resources director for Fanuc Controls, and you just completed two weeks of interviews to hire a new sales manager for your western division. As soon as you, the president, and the retiring sales manager made the difficult decision about whom to hire, the president telephoned the successful applicant, Leigh Constantine, to announce the decision. To formalize the president's telephone message, you will send a letter to Ms. Constantine welcoming her to the company. Her annual salary will be $75,000 plus commission, as discussed during the interviews (you are not sure if she and the president discussed this during their telephone conversation). Let her know the company has also agreed to her request that she be furnished a car with a maintenance and mileage allowance of $2,000 a year (she wanted an allowance of $3,500, but the current sales manager felt that was too much).

Ask Ms. Constantine to let you know within two weeks of the date of your letter whether she will be able to begin work on June 1 or on July 1, so that the sales manager can finalize his retirement date. (Ms. Constantine wasn't sure how soon she would be able to finish up her current responsibilities.) Ms. Constantine's address is 2376 Oak Forest Circle, Minneapolis, MN 55432.

🔲 Apply the four stages of the message formulation process to direct messages.
🔲 Plan, organize, compose, and evaluate routine requests and announcements.

9. *Inquiry about a product.* You are the training director for Executive Temps, a temporary employment agency that specializes in executive assistants. In addition to administering a staff of five trainers, you also train new temporary employees in the use of computer software.

After a full year of searching for good books and correlated software to teach the latest version of PageMaker (a desktop publishing program), you finally found a package that is thorough and well written. *PageMaker: A Tutorial Program for the Professional* is written by Janine Yasui and John Floyd and is published by Parachute Publishing International. It has a large software library of previously created graphics and text that can be imported into the PageMaker documents the trainees are required to create. This package also gives them experience creating a number of documents with the kinds of graphics and word processing programs they will be required to use on the job.

Because you have employees training on as many as 12 different programs at once, it is important that their books and programs be easy to follow. When software doesn't work as the book says it should, trainees become extremely frustrated. The trainers, who must take time away from other trainees to track down the problem, also become frustrated.

One problem with the new software that you and your trainers have not been able to solve is that many of the word processing documents stored in the training software sometimes do not transfer into PageMaker. When you attempt to, the message "This document cannot be placed" appears on the monitor. You have not been able to determine why the documents sometimes place and sometimes do not. To solve the problem, you have had to save the document, exit PageMaker, save the document to a word processing program, quit the word processing program, and then import the document to PageMaker from the newly created word processing document. Needless to say, this time-consuming "solution" is not an acceptable alternative. You want a program that works as it is supposed to.

Write a letter to Phil Lund, software support services representative for Parachute Publishing (6438 City East Parkway, Miami, FL 52001) and ask him what you can do to make the program work correctly. Perhaps the publisher has already corrected the problem. Assuming they have, ask them to send an updated version of their software. You believe any update that solves a serious deficiency should be sent free of charge.

🔲 Apply the four stages of the message formulation process to direct messages.
🔲 Plan, organize, compose, and evaluate routine requests and announcements.

10. *Inquiry about a product or service.* Write to the manufacturer or seller of a product or service about which you have a number of questions. Addresses for most companies can be found in the reference section of your college or local library. To improve the clarity of your questions, consider using a list.

11. *Instructions to trainees.* You are still waiting for a reply to the request you sent Parachute Publishing (for exercise 9). In the meantime, you have decided to write a memo to your trainees telling them how to place the documents that occasionally do not import into their PageMaker documents. These instructions will work only for word processing documents; graphics are handled another way. However, there have been no problems with the placement of graphics files.

The purposes of these instructions is to tell trainees what they need to do to place the files on their own. First, they should try to place the file one more time. If this method does not work, they should exit PageMaker, making sure to save the document and remember the name they give the file. Next, they should open the word processing software on the hard disk and from it choose the "Open" command. Then, they should use the dialog box to open the document file that PageMaker could not place. Once the file is open, they can use the "Save as" command to save the file to their own floppy disk. After quitting the word processing software, they should open the PageMaker document they were working on and move the file from their floppy disk.

Let trainees know that you are trying to get the problem worked out with the software's publisher, but that following your instructions is actually a more realistic way of working with documents. They will probably be creating their own documents from start to finish on the job, so they are actually learning how to create and save a document in one program and import that document into another program.

Address the memo to the first trainee on your list, Alan Barnaby. Send copies of the memo to your five trainers.

### Routine Replies

◆ Apply the four stages of the message formulation process to direct messages.
◆ Plan, organize, compose, and evaluate routine replies.

12. *Letter of recommendation for a professor.* One of your favorite business professors, Louis Galoob, is being considered for tenure at the end of this school term. You saw an announcement on a bulletin board in the hallway asking for student comments that will help the committee make a decision.

Send your letter to the Tenure Review Committee, and use the department and address of the school you are attending. You have taken two courses with Professor Galoob. Name the two courses, and tell all the reasons you believe this teacher deserves to be tenured. The committee will probably be interested in such things as the professor's teaching ability, the standards he sets and maintains, how he relates to students and others outside the classroom, his ties to area businesses, his research, and any contact he might have with the community. Address any of these topics about which you have information. You may also include other information you believe the committee might use to reach its decision.

◆ Apply the four stages of the message formulation process to direct messages.
◆ Plan, organize, compose, and evaluate routine requests and announcements.

13. As training director of your firm, you are constantly being asked to clarify operating instructions and procedures. You have often wondered why manufacturers and publishers often seem incapable of writing clear

instructions. Recently, you have been asked by department heads to clarify the following topics. Write a form memo that includes step-by-step, clear instructions for performing one of the following procedures or for operating one of the following pieces of equipment.

   *a.* Operating a fax machine (identify the model).

   *b.* Performing a procedure using a software program (e.g., merging an address list with a form letter, setting up a table, etc.).

   *c.* Using a telephone modem.

   *d.* Creating and changing a message on a voice mail system.

   *e.* Inserting and printing envelopes on a specific computer–printer setup.

   *f.* Ordering and receiving supplies.

   *g.* Keeping track of expenses and filling out an expense report.

   *h.* Other (get approval from your professor).

> Apply the four stages of the message formulation process to direct messages.
> Plan, organize, compose, and evaluate routine replies.

14. *Form response to requests for a company's annual report.* Potential investors often write to your company for copies of its annual report, an expensive 15-page four-color document including, among other things, BorderBund's yearly balance sheet and its statement of income and expense. The diverse interests of the company (including the import of exotic fish, birds, and animals into the United States; the export and sale of Appalachian arts and crafts in the United States, Europe, and Africa; and the distribution of foreign films to theaters in the United States) are detailed in the annual report. Write a form letter to accompany each annual report you send out.

> Apply the four stages of the message formulation process to direct messages.
> Plan, organize, compose, and evaluate routine replies.

15. *Letter granting a customer's request for a discount.* You are the owner of 3M&G Builders' Supply, a small company in a small town. One of your best customers, Greg Sanchez of Sanchez Construction, wrote the following across the bottom of his last invoice: "How about a discount for an old customer? Thompson Lumber's prices are often lower than yours."

   For the last 15 years, Greg has been buying from you the majority of his lumber, plumbing, roofing, and electrical supplies for the homes and businesses he builds in your area (approximately 20 each year). However, by looking at the records, you can tell that Greg occasionally has purchased some of his supplies elsewhere. Obviously, you do not want him taking the rest of his business to Thompson Lumber.

   Thompson Lumber is a member of a large chain. They pay less for their supplies because of large-scale buying. Therefore, they can afford to charge less for their building materials. However, their prices are often so close to yours (and sometimes even more) that you believe they are actually overcharging customers.

   You know the most important advantage 3M&G has to offer its customers is commitment to the community. You have cut your prices (and your profit margin) to the bone because of a slump in the local economy. You are an active member of many community organizations. Generations of your family have grown up in this town, you took over the business from your father, and you know 3M&G will always be a critical part of the community.

Trying to meet Greg's request, you have spent hours calculating ways to give him a discount. You have determined that you cannot grant a discount on small orders. However, if he orders all the lumber, plumbing, electrical, and roofing supplies for each of his projects at one time, you will be able to give him a 5 percent discount. In addition, you will increase his credit limit from $75,000 to $150,000 and will continue the usual 2 percent discount for cash payment within 30 days of the invoice. You will also deliver the materials to each building site free of charge as soon as the materials are received from your supplier. (Actually, the real reason for free delivery is that you cannot afford to dedicate any of your own storage space to materials for any of your customers.)

Write a positive letter to Greg telling him the good news. His address at Sanchez Construction is P.O. Box 782, Casa Grande, AZ 85222. Greg and his wife Marlene own Sanchez Construction.

■ Apply the four stages of the message formulation process to direct messages.
■ Plan, organize, compose, and evaluate routine replies.

16. *Reply to a student's request for information about a program.* You are a counselor in the business department of your college. Your job is to evaluate students who want to enter the MBA program and to decide whether to accept them. Then, as part of a committee, you work with students who have been accepted as interns of various programs in the business department.

You received the letter in Exhibit 7.11 from an upset applicant. You have not been able to determine why she was never notified of her acceptance into the program; however, you have made sure she will be receiving official notification from the admissions people. In the meantime, you are writing to answer her questions. Tell her all you have done to find out what happened to her acceptance, and how the admissions department will be following up. In the meantime, let her know the good news.

Tell Ms. Pebbles that she has been approved for admission into the MBA program as soon as she has completed four units of ACCT 420 Financial Accounting. She may take a full schedule of graduate-level business classes for one semester before she is officially admitted into the program. As soon as she finishes ACCT 420, she will be eligible for a Pierce Grove internship. Although it is not advised, Pierce Grove interns may work if they are able to find a job that allows for a heavy class and internship schedule. The eight units Ms. Pebbles is speaking about will count as elective units; however, none of them will substitute for any of the MBA requirements. A full schedule of graduate seminars and courses is offered in the summer session, and students enrolled in the summer average six units. Only one four-unit course is offered in the winter intersession (the one scheduled this year is BUS 576 Ethical and Legal Management Issues). Students often take independent study courses; however, they are completely subject to the discretion of the professors, who must agree to work with a student. Another suggestion would be to take one of the lower-level MBA courses at the local state university. Tell her to get the state university's catalog and then to get in touch with you so you can find a suitable substitute.

8912 Buffalo Bill Drive
Hermosa, SD 57744
March 12, 1995

School of Business and Economics
Idaho State University
1500 State University Drive
Boise, ID 83707

Application for Graduate Admission

I submitted my application for admission to your MBA program in December; however, I have received no notification from you as to the status of that application. Because the deadline for admissions is only weeks away, I need to know if you received the application, and if so, whether I have been accepted into the program.

Because a counselor in admissions assures me she received and evaluated my transcript before sending it to your office, I am assuming you have the information I need.

1. Does my degree in industrial psychology qualify me for immediate entry into the MBA program?

2. Will the eight units of graduate psychology and business courses I took as part of my undergraduate program substitute for any of the MBA requirements?

3. Will my educational background in industrial psychology disqualify me from acceptance into the Pierce Grove internship program?

4. May Pierce Grove interns work at other employment during the internship?

5. Do you offer a full program of graduate courses during the winter and summer intersessions? Approximately how many units do MBA students take during these times?

**EXHIBIT**

**7.11**

Continued

6. The company for which I currently work has agreed to give me a one-year leave of absence to work on the degree. However, I anticipate I will still have one four-unit course to complete after that time. Would it be possible for me to take an independent study course to complete those last four units? If not, do you have any other suggestions?

Please let me know the answers to these questions soon. I need to be able to plan my life, and so far, I have been left hanging out on a limb.

Sincerely yours,

Anita Pebbles

In your letter, do your best to show Ms. Pebbles that your college cares about students and that what happened to her is not the way students are treated normally. Make her feel that you and the college care about her.

◣ Apply the four stages of the message formulation process to direct messages.
◣ Plan, organize, compose, and evaluate routine replies.

17. *Letter confirming details of a job.* You have arranged to build a deck and install a hot tub for a family in your community. The clients, Mr. and Mrs. Buckley, gave you a check for $1,500 to seal the bargain and asked that you let them know as soon as possible when you can begin. At the time, you were not sure when your crews could get started, because good redwood is becoming hard to find. You also had to order another pump, because the client wants a larger unit than you keep in stock. You just received word today from your supplier that the pump is being shipped to you today and should arrive by the end of the week. Yesterday you purchased enough redwood to build the deck, and you have the hot tub in stock. Another client canceled an order so you can install the deck and hot tub sooner than you had originally anticipated.

    You tried to call the Buckleys to give them the good news but have been unable to reach them. Therefore, you must write a letter to the Buckleys (768 North Brown Street, Underwood, ID 51576). Let them know you have scheduled a work crew to begin the deck two weeks from today (check your calendar), and ask them if that date is acceptable. You anticipate the deck and hot tub will take three weeks to install, but you cannot guarantee a firm completion date. Reassure the Buckleys that you will use No. 1 grade treated redwood and that the two-horsepower pump will be worth the extra expense. The entire cost of the project as contracted is $15,600. At your last meeting, the Buckleys made a minor change in the size of the deck, so you had to redraw the plans; enclose two copies of the new plans with your letter. Let the Buckleys know that they will be responsible for obtaining a building permit from the city and that you need a copy of the permit before you can begin the job.

    Finally, tell the Buckleys to make sure their back gate is left unlocked during the project. Because they have a dog, suggest they make other arrangements for the animal to avoid his escaping during the construction. The heavy equipment that will be moving in and out of the gate will make it impossible to supervise the gate closely.

### Routine Claim Letters

◣ Apply the four stages of the message formulation process to direct messages.
◣ Plan, organize, compose, and evaluate routine claims.

18. *Memo correcting a department budget.* You are an assistant financial analyst for an investment firm. Among the many things you have to do is to make sure that the accounting department has billed your department for the correct expenses and that your department is staying within its approved budget. Today you noticed that the monthly expense allocation sheet shows a $13,000 deduction for telephone and mileage expenses. However, the voucher form you submitted to accounting showed expenses of only $7,632.

Write a memo to Penny Filborne in accounting, asking her to correct the error. Send another copy of the voucher form showing the correct total. Ask her to let you know once the error has been corrected.

◖ Apply the four stages of the message formulation process to direct messages.
◖ Plan, organize, compose, and evaluate routine claims.

19. *Letter seeking recourse for poor hotel service.* You were in charge of the Fifth International Conference of Sister Cities held last week in Atlantic City, New Jersey, at the Madison Hotel. The conference was attended by 1,500 representatives of 356 cities in the United States and their sister cities in countries around the world. Coordinating such an effort was, needless to say, a tremendous undertaking. Arranging the conference took a year. Already you have begun to plan next year's conference, which is scheduled to take place at the Madison Hotel in Los Angeles.

Overall, this last conference went well. However, the hotel's service was not what it should have been. These are your main complaints:

- You were told the airport shuttle would run every 30 minutes; however, on the last day of the conference, many participants complained of having to wait over an hour. In addition, the delegations from Hong Kong, Taiwan, and China missed their flights because the shuttle dropped them off at the wrong terminal.

- The sound system and the audio-visual equipment for the opening speaker did not work properly. Although the hotel staff was able to substitute equipment after a delay of 25 minutes, the microphone worked only half the time. As a result, many frustrated participants left the room during the middle of the speech.

- The meal for the banquet was not what had been ordered, and it was poorly prepared and served. You had ordered and paid for filet mignon, and the staff served "rubber" chicken. The program for the banquet went nearly an hour over the schedule because too few servers were employed for the size of the crowd.

You believe that your organization deserves a partial refund or some sort of financial reimbursement, because the hotel did not live up to its promises. Write a letter to the president of Madison Hotels Inc., Malcolm Vandeveer (11349 East 57th Street, New York, NY 11286), and ask him for a price break on next year's conference. You know the Madison in Atlantic City was undergoing a labor dispute during your conference there; however, you do not believe your delegates should have been subjected to such poor service. You have always been pleased with Madison hotels in the past, and you would like to continue dealing with them in the future. However, you have your own reputation to protect, and you want to be able to reassure the others on the conference planning committee that such problems will not occur again.

◖ Apply the four stages of the message formulation process to direct messages.
◖ Plan, organize, compose, and evaluate routine claims.

20. *Letter correcting an invoice.* You are the account manager for a company that makes jackets for records, compact discs, and cassette tapes. Deciding on

the artwork to be used for a new album involves choosing from hundreds of photos, so you spend a lot of money developing film. Recently, you sent 20 rolls of film to be developed at a lab you have used for years. Usually, the charge to develop a roll of film to your size specifications and on the type of paper you require is $70. Therefore, the charge should have been approximately $1,400. However, the invoice you received (No. 14702) listed a charge of $1,725. The invoice listed 14" x 17" prints instead of the 11" x 14" prints you received. Write to Chu Dai Hui, commercial account representative, asking her to correct the invoice so you can authorize payment of the bill. She works for Right Way Commercial Photography Services, 118 Sherwood Drive, Rockville, NC 20852.

- Apply the four stages of the message formulation process to direct messages.
- Plan, organize, compose, and evaluate routine claims.

21. *Letter correcting an inaccurate newspaper report.* You are the owner of a new bookstore, Book 'Em, that specializes in mystery fiction. Two days ago you had a book-signing party for a well-known writer of mystery novels, Edith Burns. During the party, which you videotaped, a local newspaper reporter interviewed Ms. Burns. You were pleased to see the reporter, because an article mentioning your store should bring in a lot of business.

    You were not pleased, however, to read the account of the interview in this morning's newspaper. Ms. Burns was misquoted. In response to the question, "Where do you get the ideas for your plots?" the reporter cited Ms. Burns as saying, "The stupidity of the general public provides all the intriguing ideas I need." You reviewed the videotape because you were sure Ms. Burns would never aim such a gross insult at the people who buy her books. What she really said was, "Studied scrutiny of the general public provides all the intriguing ideas I need."

    Write a letter to the editor of your local newspaper (research the name and address) and ask him or her to print a correction in the next issue. Send a copy of the videotape to verify your assertion. Ask the editor to return the tape to you.

## Routine Adjustment Letters

- Apply the four stages of the message formulation process to direct messages.
- Plan, organize, compose, and evaluate routine adjustment letters.

22. *Memo correcting a department budget.* Reread exercise 18. You are now Penny Filborne, associate accountant. Write to assistant financial analyst Gregory Sandahl to let him know you have corrected the error in his departmental budget. You don't know for sure how the error occurred. You believe that a new accounting clerk may have debited the $13,000 total expenses for the public relations (PR) department from both PR's and Gregory's accounts. Send a corrected monthly expense allocation sheet to Mr. Sandahl.

- Apply the four stages of the message formulation process to direct messages.
- Plan, organize, compose, and evaluate routine adjustment letters.

23. *Letter granting recourse for poor hotel service.* Reread exercise 19. You are now Malcolm Vandeveer, president of the Madison hotel chain. Write a letter to Charlotte Mazapah, conference chairperson for the International

Conference of Sister Cities (ICSC). Apologize for the quality of service her group received at your Atlantic City hotel. Give her the price break she wants on next year's conference. Tell her you have already called the manager of the Los Angeles Madison Hotel, Carl Hanser, and the conference representative, Molly MacDuff, to discuss the matter. Together, the three of you decided ICSC will receive a 6 percent discount on the usual prices for next year's conference. Tell Ms. Mazapah that Ms. MacDuff has been given the authority to employ extra shuttles for the conference if necessary. Ms. MacDuff has also decided to assign the hotel's most experienced audio–visual specialist to oversee every aspect of the group's electronic needs. Discuss the superior quality of the food at the Los Angeles Madison; it was given a superior rating by both *Gourmet Magazine* and Elmer Dills, a major food critic.

You have also spoken to the manager of the Atlantic City Madison, who is upset about the quality of the service ICSC received. The Atlantic City manager should be contacting Ms. Mazapah and will be sending ICSC a check for $353.17, the difference between the cost of the filet mignon meal for which they paid and the chicken dinner they were served at their last conference.

Ms. Mazapah's address at ICSC is 1800 Rockland, Wilmington, DE 19850-1837. Include in your letter plenty of resale to regain her confidence in Madison hotels. Try to show her Madison works hard to satisfy the needs of its customers.

◤ Apply the four stages of the message formulation process to direct messages.
◤ Plan, organize, compose, and evaluate routine adjustment letters.

24. *Letter correcting an invoice.* Reread exercise 20. You are Chu Dai Hui, commercial account representative for Right Way Commercial Photography Services. You received a letter from Clinton Agonini, a customer for more than seven years, asking you to correct an error on your invoice No. 14702. You double-checked the invoice and discovered that the $1,725 he was charged was, indeed, incorrect. You mistakenly charged him the price for a grade of paper that is superior to the paper his company prefers. Send Mr. Agonini an invoice that includes the correct charge of $1,423.79. Clinton Agonini is the accounts manager for Pugel Commercial Photographers, 7823 E. Chase Street, Baltimore, MD 21213-7823.

◤ Apply the four stages of the message formulation process to direct messages.
◤ Plan, organize, compose, and evaluate routine adjustment letters.

25. *Letter correcting an inaccurate newspaper report.* Reread exercise 21. As the editor of your local newspaper, write a letter to Ms. Gina Asti, the owner of Book 'Em (8427 East Becker Road, in your community). Apologize for the fact that a reporter working for your newspaper misquoted Edith Burns, the author Ms. Asti mentioned in her letter. Tell her a correction will appear in tomorrow's newspaper. Do your best to reassure her of the quality of your newspaper and your reporters. The letter will be enclosed with the videotape you are returning to her. Thank her for making it so easy to verify the correction.

# WRITING INDIRECT MESSAGES

## OBJECTIVES

When you finish studying this chapter, you should be able to:

- Determine when an indirect organizational strategy is appropriate.
- Apply the four steps of the message formulation process to indirect messages.
- Identify the features of an indirect organizational strategy.
- Plan, organize, compose, and evaluate indirect replies.
- Plan, organize, compose, and evaluate indirect claims.
- Plan, organize, compose, and evaluate indirect adjustments.
- Plan, organize, compose, and evaluate indirect announcements.
- Plan, organize, compose, and evaluate indirect collection letters.

### WHAT WOULD YOU DO IF...?

**RIGHT BETWEEN THE EYES.** Brady Aeronautics Corp. (BAC) has bad news to tell its employees. Nearly one-half of the Brady workforce must be laid off because of a dramatic decline in government defense spending. More than two-thirds of BAC's income over the past 13 years has come from Department of Defense contracts.

Employees have known for a long time that the company has been losing money and that layoffs were being discussed with union negotiators; however, they thought layoffs would not be necessary until July, six months from now. At a meeting of the board last night, the decision was finally made to lay off 2,482 people at the Aurora facility. The board hopes this drastic decrease in personnel costs will enable the company to keep its expenses in line with its income.

Brady's chief operating officer, Helen Cohen, directed the public relations staff to draft a press release about the layoffs. However, she has decided to write a form memo herself to be given to all company employees before the public is informed. She also wants every employee to know his or her own status before reading about the layoffs in local newspapers or hearing about them on television. Ms. Cohen believes it would be more humane for all employees to hear the bad news from company leaders.

Exhibit 8.1 on page 239 is Ms. Cohen's first draft of the form memo. Read the memo; then read the rest of this chapter. Compare the memo to the principles taught within the chapter. Does the memo meet all the requirements of effective indirect messages? Does it follow an indirect organizational strategy? Are the words and phrases clear and positive? Have the readers' needs been considered? Is the you attitude used effectively? How would you feel if you were one of the laid-off employees, or if you were one of those who retained your job? Does the goodwill seem sincere? What changes, if any, should be made to soften the blow of this horrible news without sacrificing clarity?

## Using the Indirect Strategy

▸ Determine when an indirect organizational strategy is appropriate.

*A major purpose of any business message is to continue good relations between the writer and the reader.*

You will find as you read this chapter that Helen Cohen made many mistakes in her memo. Although her purpose of informing employees of the layoffs was fulfilled, her memo probably did more harm than good. Bad news that is skillfully delivered makes the meaning clear but creates a minimum of offense to the reader, which is an underlying purpose of any business message. However, because many readers consider bad news to be a form of personal rejection, they automatically react to the writer and the message with anger or hurt. Therefore, formulating a negative message that still preserves good relations takes extra care. Good relations are far easier to maintain when you are delivering good news or neutral news. However, if you follow the principles within this chapter, you will find you can deliver disappointing information to people in a way that makes it easier for them to accept and understand.

"Oh, I just loooooove writing business letters!
How else are you going to tell someone the bad news?"

Few people enjoy composing correspondence that delivers bad news. Yet, there will be many times in your career you will have to do it. Among the kinds of messages that require the indirect organizational strategy presented in this chapter are replies, claims, adjustments, and announcements that will disappoint readers, as well as collection letters.

Take a moment to study the indirect organizational strategy outlined in Exhibit 8.2. A major difference between this strategy and the direct strategy you

EXHIBIT
8.1

Ineffective Indirect Memo

TO:        All Brady Employees

FROM:      Helen Cohen, Chief Operating Officer

DATE:      January 15, 1995

SUBJECT:   Permanent Dehiring of 2,482 Members of the Brady Family

*Avoid making the same mistakes Helen did if you want to "win friends and influence people."*

If a family can be defined as a cohesive group of people related by common purposes and goals, then Brady has been blessed with one of the closest families anyone could expect. Together, we have weathered the many ups and downs of government funding, and we have a proud record of innovative products to show for the years of striving together for common goals.

The board of directors has decided that, effective April 1, a permanent layoff of 2,482 employees must take place to return Brady to a position of strength in the industry. These layoffs will affect only employees at the Aurora facility, which is not in a position to retool to the level needed to meet the requirements of our current contracts and those anticipated for the future. A reduced cadre of employees, however, will keep that facility operating at a minimum level in anticipation of Brady's being awarded the new contract to develop Opus 5.

Most of the cuts were made at Level 3 and below, although a number of upper-level positions were transferred to other facilities. Employees affected by the layoffs met with their supervisors this morning.

Every attempt has been made to ease the transition of affected employees. The Human Resources Department has opened a new Transfer Office to aid each individual in finding another job. They have begun a diligent telephone and letter-writing campaign to publicize to other companies that many skilled people are now available. The Transfer Office is available to help in the preparation of resumes and letters and will be conducting job-hunting seminars.

In addition, a generous severance package has been arranged for the members of our family who are leaving. Union representatives will be announcing the details of the severance package as well as provisions for early retirement.

Think of this unfortunate event not as losing family members but as having some of our family move away. Families pull together in times of loss. Our smaller family will be much stronger as a result of this move and will be able to better achieve its goals.

| EXHIBIT 8.2 | **Indirect Organizational Strategy for Negative News Messages** |
|---|---|
| First paragraph | If possible, present any favorable news. If there is none, use a relevant, neutral buffer or something on which you and the reader can agree. Do not mention the negative situation. Do not use negative words or phrases. Do not imply *yes* or *no*. |
| Middle paragraphs | Make a logical transition between the buffer and the next paragraph. Give reasons for disappointing news in positive, tactful, courteous terms. Prepare the reader for the negative news. Explain the situation, leading naturally and logically to the negative decision, which should be implied diplomatically, if possible, but still be clear. Justify your actions; use the you attitude to tell how the negative news is meant to benefit the reader, if possible. Suggest alternatives or a counterproposal if appropriate. Reinforce confidence in the company, its products, its services, etc. |
| Last paragraph | Include a friendly, positive statement that closes the message. Tie appreciation, if appropriate, to a clear statement of future action necessary. Do not thank in advance. Do not refer to the negative situation. |

studied in Chapter 7 is the first paragraph. Most people prefer to have bad news presented to them gradually rather than being confronted with it in the first sentence. Those of you who are people oriented have probably used the indirect approach many times to avoid seeming blunt and rude when delivering bad news. You will immediately recognize the value of the following approach to a discussion with a subordinate:

> The sincere compliment serves as a buffer to the negative news that will follow. It makes Joe happy to continue the conversation.

Hey Joe, that was a great report you did. I really liked the way you tied the conclusions to the company's goals. I think your report will help us make better decisions.

> An explanation of why the study should have been done a certain way precedes the negative news.

However, Vincent and Joan are concerned that you didn't consult with them before submitting the final report. Didn't we agree that the report was to be a collaborative effort of all the department heads? Even if they weren't actively involved in doing the study and the writing, I wanted to be sure the final report represented the perspectives of all the major players.

Please, next time, be sure you consult all the people who are involved. I want them to be committed to the changes that'll come out of the study. If we don't have their cooperation, we might not be able to get the same kind of teamwork we need to accomplish things.

> The goodwill closing lets Joe know everything is okay despite the problem that was discussed.

Well, I have a meeting. Joe, keep up the good work. You have a real future here.

The indirect approach that many people take in conversation is just as useful for written messages.

Apply the four steps of the message formulation process to indirect messages.

By now, you are familiar with the four steps in the message formulation process. Following these steps (planning, organizing, composing, and evaluating) will help you maintain positive relations with your readers even when you cannot say "yes" to them.

## PLANNING YOUR MESSAGE

The more experience you get at writing business letters and memos, the less time it will take to plan your messages. Much of the planning stage will eventually become automatic, much as you are now able to climb a set of stairs without conscious thought. In the meantime, until the planning stage has become habit, follow the five planning steps presented in the following discussion.

## ESTABLISH YOUR PURPOSE

As you consider your specific purpose in writing a message that delivers bad news, keep in mind the underlying purpose: maintaining or creating the best possible relations between the writer (or the company) and the reader. Some of the common purposes for indirect messages are

> To refuse an unreasonable request.
>
> To get a customer to pay an overdue bill.
>
> To tell job applicants the position has been filled by someone else.
>
> To refuse an employee's request for a raise or promotion.
>
> To announce that an order cannot be delivered on time.
>
> To announce that a project will have considerable cost overruns.
>
> To proclaim the unfeasibility of an idea about which the reader is enthusiastic.
>
> To let a customer know you no longer can provide free services.
>
> To deny a request for special services or special treatment.
>
> To deny a customer's request for a discount.
>
> To decline a speaking invitation.
>
> To tell employees some of their benefits have been canceled.

To help focus your thoughts, write down a purpose statement.

Whatever purposes you decide on, write them down at the top of your paper or on the first line of your computer screen. Keeping the purposes within your field of vision will help you make sure your messages achieve the results for which they have been written. It is too easy to lose sight of the major points when you are also trying to maintain good relations. Although you should make every effort to avoid angering the reader, you must not sacrifice the clarity of the message to achieve this goal.

## CHOOSE A MEDIUM AND CHANNEL

In some cases, it might be better to deliver bad news orally. By speaking to the other person, by telephone or in person, you can address all the individual's concerns as they come up. Writing does not always provide such an opportunity and could be perceived as a cold and cowardly way to avoid a difficult situation. For example, can you imagine being told in a letter you have been fired? Wouldn't it seem more compassionate for your supervisor to deal with you face to face? Granted, you probably would not leave the encounter happy, but at least you would have the satisfaction of knowing you were treated with dignity. Your supervisor would also have a chance to explain how termination might be in your own best interests, despite your disappointment.

On the other hand, in a difficult situation a writer has complete control over what is said and how it is said. For this reason, some people prefer to write negative news instead of delivering it in person. In addition, handling bad news personally may not always be feasible. For example, Helen Cohen could not have spoken individually with all the employees whose jobs were being cut; a meeting for so many employees would also have been difficult to arrange. Similarly, companies that deal with hundreds or thousands of accounts receivable often cannot afford to telephone each client every time an account is overdue. Even small companies that operate with small staffs often find it easier and more efficient to send written messages in the early stages of bill collection. In most cases, a simple overdue notice assuming payment is forthcoming is all that is needed to make clients pay. For accounts that are long overdue, these companies often switch to personal contact.

## CONSIDER LEGAL AND ETHICAL ISSUES

Ethical and legal issues are a particular concern when writing indirect messages. First, the subject matter is by definition sensitive. Furthermore, readers are in a state of heightened emotion, which may predispose them to take offense.

*Ethical messages are fair to all concerned.*

As with all other messages, ask yourself whether you would be proud if everyone you know and respect were to discover all the circumstances and your motives involved in the communication situation. In addition, consider if you have introduced any deliberate distortions (described in Chapter 5) in an effort to soften the message. *Indirect* refers only to the arrangement of the major points in a message, not the clarity of those points. Words such as *dehiring, downsizing,* and *negative employee retention* are deliberate distortions that obscure the true meaning—people are being fired.

In addition to the legal issues mentioned in Chapter 6, special legal concerns apply to three areas that frequently require indirect messages: claims, credit and collections, and employment.

**CLAIMS.**   As a business communicator, you should be aware that a letter refusing to honor a claim—no matter how reasonable—always runs the risk of unleashing considerable hostility. Dissatisfied customers cannot always be satisfied. In some cases, if dissatisfied customers believe they have been treated unfairly and a lot is at stake, they may charge the company with fraud. Fraud, as Chapter 6 explains, is a deliberate misrepresentation of facts in order to deceive or to conceal. If a sale is found to have resulted from fraud, the company can be held liable for the actual amount of the loss as well as additional penalties.

Well-managed companies forestall fraud charges by making every effort to communicate clearly and truthfully with customers. The courts infer that writers who use technical terms unlikely to be understood by the average consumer have intended to conceal or obscure information. Thus, careful companies try to write consumer contracts in everyday language. In fact, some states have plain language laws requiring contracts, policies, and the like to be written in language that can be understood by the average reader.

In addition, careful companies make sure their salespeople understand the importance of being honest and open about a company's products. They do not want anyone to come back claiming that they did not understand the limitations of the product they were sold. For similar reasons, retail outlets make sure their return and exchange policies are clearly stated and can be plainly seen by customers.

**CREDIT AND COLLECTIONS.**   Laws related to credit and collections are among the most important areas of concern for people writing indirect messages. Before you compose letters or notices pertaining to people's credit, you should become well versed in these laws. The following laws are only those established at the federal level; some state laws are even more strict.

- *Truth in Lending Act of 1968.* Credit policies must be stated in writing, using language the consumer is likely to understand. Most companies have developed, with legal advice, printed policies that are the only messages pertaining to credit that employees may distribute to customers and clients.

- *Federal Wage Garnishment Law of 1968.* With a legal judgment, an employer can be required to withhold a portion of an employee's pay for payment of a debt. However, the employee cannot lose his or her job because wages have been garnished.

- *Fair Credit Reporting Act of 1970.* This far-reaching law regulates credit granting and reporting agencies and collection agencies, and it protects the confidentiality, accuracy, and relevancy of information about credit applicants. Creditors cannot check a loan applicant's credit history unless the applicant signs a statement giving them permission. A company that turns down a loan applicant because of something negative in his or her credit report must inform the applicant of the name and address of the credit reporting agency. The applicant then has the right to contact the agency to receive a free copy of the credit report. (For a fee, anyone may also receive his or her own credit report at any time.) If the report is erroneous, the applicant can write to the credit reporting agency and explain the problem. The agency must then notify anyone who inquires into the applicant's credit that he or she is protesting that particular part of the file. In the meantime, the applicant must also write to the company that filed the erroneous information to get it corrected. Explanations of the basis on which an applicant has been denied credit are usually carefully worded by company lawyers to ensure compliance with the law.

- *Equal Credit Opportunity Act of 1974.* This law forbids discrimination because of marital status or gender. Later legislation extended protection to individuals discriminated against because of their age, race, religion, national origin and color. However, these laws do not stipulate that credit must be extended to everyone; they only stipulate that credit decisions must be based only on past credit history and ability to repay and must be applied equally to all applicants.

- *Fair Debt Collections Practices Act of 1978.* This law, which prohibits excessive use of force and harassment in the collection of debts, significantly changed debt-collection practices. The law requires bill collectors to telephone or visit a debtor only between the hours of 8 AM and 9 PM. In addition, bill collectors must identify themselves, even in written messages. They may not disguise their envelopes, letters, or statements to make them look like something they are not—for example, official court notices or correspondence from government agencies. Bill collectors have the right to contact the debtor to request payment. However, once an individual has written to the agency instructing it to stop contacting him or her, the agency can make no further oral contacts. Usually, bill collectors then give up on the account and consider harsher means of collection, such as a lawsuit. To avoid such drastic measures, many companies are willing to discuss with debtors other ways of resolving the problem, such as a revised payment schedule or reasonable reduction in the amount due.

Bankruptcy laws, which protect individuals who owe money and those to whom money is owed, are also important, but they vary from state to state. The type of bankruptcy determines who will be paid first and who will run the company while it is being reorganized. In some cases, a company's current management will continue to oversee the company while it is going through bankruptcy. In other cases, a court might appoint others to oversee the company, the sale of assets, and payment of debts to creditors. Bankruptcy laws pertaining to individuals allow them to keep their homes, a minimum level of assets needed to sustain their lives, and, sometimes, a car in which they can get to and from work.

**EMPLOYMENT.**   The Civil Rights Act of 1964 (with 1972 and 1978 amendments) prohibits employment discrimination based on race, age, religion, gender, or national origin. However, special interest groups wrote into these laws preferential hiring for Native Americans and veterans. In addition, religious and educational institutions may discriminate in favor of persons of a particular gender or religion. Communist Party members are not protected by the Civil Rights Act, and, for positions of importance to national security, companies may discriminate in favor of American citizens. For example, the FBI, the CIA, congress, and defense contractors seldom hire anyone but American citizens.

Companies and organizations that receive government funds are required to advertise job openings publicly, as "equal employment opportunities." The goal is to ensure that diverse applicants have equal chances to compete for the job.

## ANALYZE YOUR AUDIENCE

The main reason to use the indirect approach in a written message is the probable reaction of your audience, the reader. When you believe your reader will probably be angry, disappointed, or otherwise upset by your message, an indirect strategy can be used to soften the negative news.

Remember, however, that all negative news does not cause a negative reaction. Some negative situations are routine. For example, warranty representatives at many companies deal daily with claims, so the negative news in a claim letter would not make them angry, disappointed, or otherwise upset. Instead, their reaction would be neutral, and so an indirect strategy would not be needed.

Remember that your reader is not like you and probably will not share your viewpoint. Anticipate all possible objections, and prepare counterarguments.

To be able to predict with some degree of accuracy the likely response of your readers, you must have the ability to understand another's perspective or point of view. First, you must acknowledge that your reader is not exactly like you. Second, you must recognize that in a negative news situation, your reader probably will not share your viewpoint. Third, you must be able to anticipate the possible objections your readers will have toward your message. Finally, you must be able to provide counterarguments.

Maslow's five levels of needs: physiological, safety, belonging, esteem, and self-actualization.

Maslow's hierarchy of needs can be used to determine how to explain the bad news in a way that meets readers' needs. Here are some of the reasons you might use to justify bad news:

- *Refusing a request for a discount.* Granting such a discount to everyone would force a rise in prices (safety needs).

- *Refusing a request to change an employee's vacation date.* If too many employees are gone at the same time, the remaining employees would be forced to work overtime to get the work done (belonging needs).

- *Refusing a credit order because the company is over its credit limit.* Credit limits are established for all customers according to a formula intended to ensure that customers do not overextend themselves and are able to conduct their business without undue financial stress (safety needs, belonging needs).

- *Refusing an employee's request to condense a 40-hour week into three days.* Working 13 or more hours a day could be bad for one's health (safety), would not allow adequate contact with upper-level decision makers (self-actualization, esteem, belonging), and would prevent one from communicating effectively with colleagues (belonging).

The point of using such reasons is to let the reader know you understand and have addressed his or her needs.

### GATHER NECESSARY RESOURCES

To save yourself time and to ensure the effectiveness of your message, gather all necessary information and materials before you begin to compose the correspondence. If you have access to your company's computer database, review the customer's account, any previous correspondence, and records of telephone calls. In companies that are not so computerized, this same information should be available in files. By reviewing what has already happened, you can be sure to answer all the reader's concerns and questions.

At this point, you should also decide whether you will write the letter or memo yourself or with a collaborative writing group. Because indirect messages require special sensitivity to readers' feelings and concerns, you may want the perspective of more than one person. Collaborators can be particularly helpful in coming up with all the possible objections a reader might have to your position, and can help you design positive counterarguments to those objections. Groups are also good at determining ways to show the reader how your position benefits him or her as well.

## ORGANIZING YOUR MESSAGE

The major difference between direct and indirect messages is how they are organized. As you read the information that follows, focus on the psychological reasons for using an indirect organizational pattern.

### FREEWRITE MAJOR POINTS

As you will recall, freewriting helps focus your attention on the topic, the fastest way of putting all the major and minor ideas down on paper or on computer, and frees you of the concerns that often cause writer's block.

Before you freewrite, write your purpose or purposes at the top of the page. Then, off the top of your head, write down phrases that represent everything you want to say in the message. Don't concern yourself with whether your notes are appropriate; just write or type anything and everything related to the message that comes to mind.

## CHOOSE AN ORGANIZATIONAL STRATEGY: THE INDIRECT STRATEGY

Identify the features of an indirect organizational strategy.

Once you have freewritten the major points, consider the probable reaction of your reader to the message and choose the organizational strategy that meets the reader's needs. The topic of this chapter is indirect correspondence—letters and memos that contain news likely to make the reader feel disappointment or anger. Exhibit 8.2 outlines the features of an indirect strategy: **buffer** (a relevant but neutral opening), reasons for the bad news, the bad news itself, and the close.

As you learned in Chapter 2 and Chapter 7, many cultures do not normally use a direct approach. Most businesspeople in England, Japan, Mexico, and much of Latin and South America prefer to use the indirect approach at all times, believing it is important to establish a social climate before doing business. The first paragraphs of business letters in these cultures typically do not deal with business at all. Instead, they begin with sociable, friendly statements.

Test your ability to determine whether an indirect strategy is the proper approach by considering the following examples. (Cover up the answer to each situation until you've made your determination.)

In many other countries, the indirect strategy is used for almost all correspondence.

Situation 1: A letter to a customer denying him a requested discount of 5 percent on orders over $1,000.

Answer: Yes, an indirect outline is appropriate. The customer would not have written to request the discount if he or she did not think it was fair. Therefore, he or she will probably be angry or disappointed with your response.

Situation 2: A letter of sympathy to a client whose child was killed in an automobile accident.

Answer: A direct approach would be better. The client should react positively to a sincere expression of sympathy during a difficult time.

Situation 3: An unsolicited form letter selling a new product.

Answer: An indirect strategy would not be correct. Because the reader has little initial interest in the topic, a persuasive strategy would be better.

Situation 4: A memo to a subordinate denying her request for a raise.

Answer: An indirect strategy would help ease the reader into the negative news.

Situation 5: A letter announcing to a client that his request for the replacement of a defective machine tool has been granted.

Answer: An indirect strategy should not be used. Tell the client the good news in the first sentence.

Situation 6: A memo acknowledging a request for a report you will send as soon as it is printed and bound.

Answer: A direct strategy would be the best choice. The reader will be happy to learn that the information he or she needs is on its way.

Situation 7: A letter to a delinquent account urging the client to give an explanation for the three-month delay in paying her bill.

Answer: An indirect strategy should be used. Although the reader knows the account is overdue, many people avoid anything that is unpleasant because it is upsetting to them.

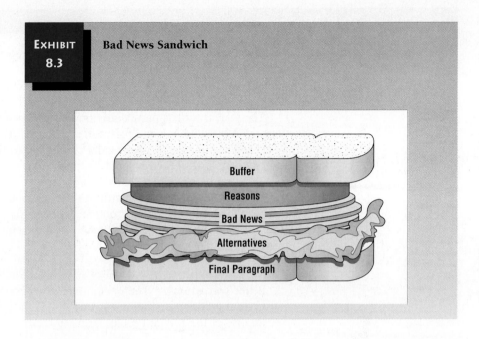

**EXHIBIT 8.3**   **Bad News Sandwich**

Buffer

Reasons

Bad News

Alternatives

Final Paragraph

Situation 8: A memo to the chief executive officer of your company (about whom you know very little) asking her to speak to the national conference of the Future Business Leaders of America, a high school organization.

Answer: An indirect strategy would not be appropriate, because there is no reason to believe the request would upset her in any way. If you knew she would be pleased or would react neutrally, a direct strategy would be appropriate. In some cases, the persuasive strategy might also be appropriate.

Situation 9: A letter granting a customer's request for a discount on purchases, but denying his request for free delivery of orders over $1,000.

Answer: An indirect strategy is appropriate, because you can begin with the good news in the first sentence before going on to the reasons for the refusal and the refusal itself in the middle paragraphs.

Situation 10: A letter to a customer who does not qualify for credit.

Answer: An indirect strategy would be best, because it would help to soften the blow of the negative news.

Once you have determined that an indirect strategy should be used, assign an order to the words and phrases you wrote down during the freewriting step. The indirect strategy is similar to the sandwich illustrated in Exhibit 8.3. The soft bread serves as a buffer around the tougher meat (the bad news). The lettuce and tomatoes (the reasons and the alternatives) help explain why the bad news is necessary.

To summarize, an indirect strategy is appropriate whenever your reader is interested in what you have to say but will probably be upset, disappointed, or angry about your message.

## Composing Your Message

Once you have planned and organized your message, composing it becomes much easier. The proper strategy, coupled with a you attitude and positive phrasing, will enable you to make your point without bruising your reader's ego.

The you attitude is particularly important when you explain the reasons for your refusal and when you present the bad news. It is important to explain why a decision was made, so your reader can be led to the same logical conclusion you reached. Even if the reader is disappointed about the outcome, your goal is to prove that he or she has been treated fairly.

One way to apply the you attitude is to use *you* and *your* whenever possible (except when you are telling someone that he or she did something wrong). Here are some examples of how to incorporate the you attitude into negative messages:

> Poor you attitude: "You failed to read the operational instructions."
>
> Better you attitude: "The operational instructions enclosed include a step-by-step guide to operation of your XB237. You will see that page 7 details the use of the forward rocker arm."

> Poor you attitude: "You did not do what I told you to do."
>
> Better you attitude: "The procedure we decided on at the beginning of the project apparently was not followed."

> Poor you attitude: "Your workgroup was responsible for the loss of over $1,200 in receipts over the last two months."
>
> Better you attitude: "Over $1,200 in receipts for the housewares department has been unaccounted for over the past two months."

**Avoid playing the part of the executioner.**

Be particularly careful to avoid *I, me, my, we,* and the company name. Instead of "I must reject your offer," substitute "the offer cannot be accepted." Instead of "I am unable to," say "it is not possible to." People are uncomfortable when they feel someone is standing in judgment of them like an executioner waiting to swing the axe. Remove the human element from the bad news, and it becomes easier to accept.

The you attitude also focuses on the benefits to the reader rather than the needs of the writer or his or her company. Find a way to convince your readers you have considered their interests, without preaching or lecturing to them. For example, if you were trying to explain why it is necessary to cut back everyone's work schedule one day a month, you might emphasize that this simple measure is the fairest solution and will prevent layoffs, foster teamwork through sharing the economic burden, and keep a full staff ready to remobilize when the situation improves without overburdening any employees. If you were, instead, to spend a paragraph or two preaching about how important it is to share burdens and pull together as a team through both good and bad times, many readers would resent your holier-than-thou attitude. Effective use of the you attitude requires straightforward recognition of the reader's interests.

**"Company policy" is a phrase that inflames.**

It is especially important in negative situations to avoid hiding behind company policy. More than once you have probably encountered a statement such as the following: "We're sorry, but company policy does not permit . . . "

The words *company policy* have been used far too often to avoid having to explain why things are the way they are. For some reason, letter writers and anonymous voices on the telephone expect us to accept the decision without question when we hear these words. However, these words are as negative as any other if the reasons for the refusal are not justified in terms of how they might benefit the reader.

Well-written reasons for refusals or bad news should be positively worded as well as you oriented. Admittedly, when you discuss a negative situation, you will find it challenging to avoid the negative. Remember, however, that words such as *dissatisfied, damaged, fault,* and *blame* elicit a negative reaction from your reader.

Even an apology can cause a negative reaction. If you or your company has actually done something wrong, it does not hurt to apologize briefly and positively in the middle of the letter (never at the beginning or the end). However, if you have not done anything wrong, do not apologize. Simply disagreeing with a reader or not granting his or her request does not require an apology. Notice the negative tone established by excessive apologies in the following message:

> Ineffective: "We are very sorry we cannot grant your request for free copies of the Top 40 hits of the year. We wish that we were able to do so. Unfortunately, even the music industry has been hit by hard economic times. We hope this decision does not cause you undue hardship. Perhaps without too much more effort, you will find a company that can contribute to your worthwhile cause. In the meantime, we hope you understand our position and you will continue to promote our artists and their work in your production."

After you have stated the reasons, it is time for a brief but clear statement of the bad news. If possible, imbed the bad news in the middle of a paragraph. Never let the bad news stand alone in a one-sentence paragraph. However, do not hide the bad news. Your reader must understand the information but, at the same time, recognize that it is final and not negotiable.

The rest of this section covers five typical kinds of negative documents: indirect replies, indirect claims, indirect adjustments, indirect announcements, and indirect collection letters. As you read about each type of message, pay close attention to the exhibits and to the margin notes that accompany them.

*Margin note: Don't be overly apologetic or apologize when you haven't done anything wrong.*

## INDIRECT REPLIES

Plan, organize, compose, and evaluate indirect replies.

Unfortunately, people in business sometimes have to say "no" to customers or coworkers. For example, someone might ask you for confidential information or for free products or services you cannot provide. How will you handle a request from a charitable organization that asks you to donate time you do not have? Will you be able to write an effective reply to an important stockholder who has proposed a ridiculous plan that could lose the company millions of dollars? These are only a few of the many types of indirect replies you might be called on to write in your business career.

The three major parts of the indirect organizational pattern are explained later. Before you continue, however, read the letters in Exhibits 8.4 and 8.5 to see good examples of indirect replies.

**EXHIBIT 8.4**

**Indirect Reply (Block Style with Open Punctuation)**

June 17, 1995

**Farm Fresh**
INDUSTRIES

1000 Anderson Avenue
Raleigh, NC 27610
919-704-8400
fax 919-704-8401

*The buffer refers to the situation but does not imply that the request will be granted or denied. It states the condition that must be met (economic feasibility) before requests can be granted.*

Ms. Alexandria Davis
Reardon Farms, Inc.
2308 Coe Avenue
Albuquerque, NM 87106-2300

Dear Ms. Davis:

Your request for an extension of the 60-day requirement for payment of your account has been carefully considered. We always try to comply with the requests of our customers whenever it is economically feasible to do so.

*Resale takes the form of a reminder of the other good things the writer has done for Reardon Farms.*

This commitment to meeting your needs went into the recent doubling of the credit limit on your account; and from the increase in your orders since then, it is apparent your customers must also appreciate the superior quality of Farm Fresh products.

*This paragraph clearly implies the negative news and explains how not granting the extension benefits the customer.*

Because we value the successful relationship our companies have established, we wish it were possible to also extend the time required for payment. However, such an increase would negatively impact the cash flow needed to keep our prices low and our inventory high.

*More resale reminds the reader what she gets from a business relationship with Farm Fresh. The business-as-usual tone will help her see the benefits of a continued relationship with Farm Fresh.*

As an alternative, you may wish to take advantage of the current low prices on Dorita Valley strawberries and Culberson peaches. Nature and the economy were good to farmers this year, and you may harvest the benefits by paying only 40 cents a bushel for the peaches and $2 a flat for the strawberries. Our usual quantity discount applies even to these lower-than-ever prices for such quality products.

*Additional reader-benefit statements lead to a statement of the specific action required of the reader.*

Please let us know the quantity of strawberries and peaches to reserve for you. We'll rush them to you right away so your customers can savor the fresh-picked juicy flavor of Dorita Valley strawberries and Culberson peaches.

Sincerely,

*Kathleen Brooker*

Kathleen Brooker
Sales Supervisor

snl

# COLORADO
## *outfitters*

August 19, 1995

Mr. Charles Waters
Waters Productions
16909 E. Patterson, Suite 246
Levittown, PA 19058

Reference No. 459923-JL

Dear Mr. Waters

*The opening is relevant. It does not give away the bad news, yet it does not imply credit will be granted.*

Thank you for the opportunity to consider your request for credit. Colorado Outfitters is always happy to sell quality camping and sporting gear on credit terms to local businesses that have established good credit records.

*Resale about Colorado Outfitters' products and services paves the way for the reasons and the bad news in the next paragraph.*

Day after day, quality-minded customers like you turn to Colorado Outfitters to meet their need for a wide variety of rugged products at affordable prices. You can depend on our representatives to provide the personal attention you require to ensure all your needs are considered and met—with no regard for whether your orders are small or large, or whether you pay cash or charge the order.

*Reasons for the refusal are given in terms of how they benefit the reader. The writer does not imply that the reader would not pay or that his business would pay slowly. The explanation helps the reader see that he is being treated in the same way as all other new businesses.*

So that we can continue to offer you the same attentive service, it is important we have a minimum number of accounts receivable. An active, steady cash flow enables us to place large orders with our suppliers, which in turn allows us to offer lower prices and a varied inventory to you. Therefore, accounts are opened only for businesses that have established steady records of prompt payment. According to your TRW report, your business has not been in operation long enough to establish a long-term record. As a result, a business account cannot be opened until you have operated successfully for two years.

**656 Hillsbire Rd.**
**Du Bois, PA 15801**
**814-371-6600**
***fax* 814-371-6611**

**EXHIBIT 8.5**    Continued

Charles Waters
August 19, 1995
Page 2

*An alternative is presented with reader-benefit statements.*

However, you may reapply for credit now under the provisions of a personal business account. Such an account would have the same provisions as the business account, but it would require you to guarantee personally the financial obligations incurred by your business. In this way, your business is able to establish a credit history; and, within time, it would qualify for a standard business account.

*Goodwill is included in the offer of prompt, enthusiastic service. The action required of the reader is courteously stressed. There are no clichés or apologies.*

Please complete the enclosed credit application form for a personal business account. As soon as your application is received, it will be rushed through the approval procedure. In the meantime, your cash orders will be enthusiastically filled by our expert staff.

Sincerely

*Michael Carley*

Michael Carley
Credit Sales Manager

Enclosure: PL273

*The law requires that the reader be informed of his rights to obtain a copy of his credit report.*

You have the right to view the specific information in your credit report. You may request your report by writing TRW, 14370 Sunset Boulevard, Los Angeles, CA 90422, or by telephoning them at (213) 555-5555 between the hours of 9 AM and 5:30 PM within 60 days of this letter. Refer to the reference number above when you contact the credit agency.

Tone is the relationship between the reader and the writer.

**FIRST PARAGRAPH.**   The opening paragraph of an indirect reply—the buffer—should contain no negative words or phrases because its function is to set a positive, professional tone that will permeate the rest of the document. Therefore, the first paragraph can refer to the negative situation only vaguely. However, the buffer should not sound too positive, or else our reader will think you are going to grant his or her request—later on, when the reader discovers the bad news, his or her anger will be intensified because of the misleading first paragraph.

The buffer must also be relevant to the situation. Readers in cultures that admire directness hate to have their time wasted too obviously. Do not discuss the weather, the economy, or the reader's health unless they have direct bearing on the purpose of the correspondence. A good opening paragraph is relevant and leads naturally and logically to the paragraphs that follow.

You might occasionally have both good news and bad news to tell. Take, for example, the situation in which Ron Jones found himself. Ron had to write a memo informing a company's absentee owners of the progress made in the past month on a construction project. Knowing the owners would be upset that delays in delivery of materials had put the project one week behind schedule, Ron chose to tell them the good news in the first paragraph—that he was able to negotiate a 10 percent decrease in the price of lumber and roofing materials. He also informed them that labor issues that posed problems in the past had been worked out to the mutual satisfaction of the company and labor leaders. Reading this good news put the readers in the right frame of mind to read the bad news about the delay, which was postponed until the middle of the letter.

The following are examples of poor opening paragraphs:

Ineffective letter denying a request for giveaway donations for an annual awards banquet: "We can certainly see how using Parker pens as giveaways at your annual awards banquet would be just the right touch for an organization such as yours."

Critique: This misleading opening sounds as though the writer is going to grant the request; therefore, the reader's disappointment will increase when the bad news is finally made clear.

Ineffective memo refusing to release confidential information: "It is company policy to hold projections about future earnings and expenses confidential until the board feels they can be released to dependable sources."

Critique: Did the writer just insult the reader by implying that he or she is undependable? This opening is negative and insulting, and it hides behind company policy.

Ineffective letter denying a student's request to extend the deadline for a financial aid application: "We are sorry we cannot comply with your request."

Critique: The bad news should not be in the first paragraph in an indirect situation. The bearer of bad news is too visible.

Ineffective letter refusing to accept an individual's personal check. "This is a letter regarding our recent receipt of your personal check in the amount of $1,000 as payment for the reservation of dates at the Civic Auditorium. We regret to inform you that, after speaking with the director of finance and the city administrator, we cannot accept a personal check as a deposit for payment for any events scheduled to be held at the Civic Auditorium.

Critique: The bad news should not be in the first paragraph. The paragraph is too wordy, contains unnecessarily obvious statements ("This is a letter," "in the amount of"), and uses negative executioner-oriented phrases ("We regret to inform you," "we cannot accept").

Ineffective letter turning down an offer to buy 15 percent of the shares of a corporation: "I hope this letter finds you in good health and that your golf game is, as usual, up to par."

Critique: This buffer is completely irrelevant to the situation. Goodwill is appropriate in any letter, but it should not be the sole topic of the first paragraph. A personal exchange such as this could take place only after the purposes of the letter are fulfilled, perhaps in the last paragraph.

Ineffective memo denying an employee's request for transfer: "This memo is to inform you that there is no room for you in the production department."

Critique: The condescending sarcasm of the out-of-date phrase ("This memo is to inform you") sets the tone for the insult that follows. Would you like to work for this individual?

Take a minute now to read the good opening paragraphs in the sample letters and memos in this chapter. They should give you an idea of the principles that make the opening paragraphs of indirect correspondence effective.

**MIDDLE PARAGRAPHS.**   Read once again the middle paragraphs of Exhibits 8.4 and 8.5. Middle paragraphs are critical components of an indirect strategy, because they must clearly express the unfavorable news and the reasons for it while also displaying skillful use of the you attitude to maintain a favorable relationship.

As you read Exhibit 8.5, pay close attention to the skillful way the writer shows the reader that the denial of credit is fair and that the policy actually benefits the reader and similar businesses. Can you identify the specific sentences that give reader-benefit reasons for the refusal? Can you determine which elements of the letter are required by law? By necessity, a letter such as this is often a form letter, used for all small businesses that have not been in operation long enough to establish a solid credit history. However, even form letters should be written to appeal on a personal level to anyone who reads them. By speaking to the reader as an individual, the letter in Exhibit 8.5 appears composed for the reader alone.

Businesses are sometimes denied credit for reasons other than the one mentioned in Exhibit 8.5. Often a business is considered risky because it has an unusually high debt-to-equity ratio or too much inventory. Without lecturing, you might suggest that such a business reduce its inventory or buy its outstanding bonds to improve the debt-to-equity ratio before reapplying for credit. You could also stress the benefits, such as discounts, of paying cash for small orders.

In some cases, such as when individuals are denied credit because of extremely sensitive factors in their records (e.g., prison sentences, drug convictions, or a long history of short-term jobs), you might want to avoid being specific about the reasons for denying credit. Avoid giving reasons if you think you might be sued by an individual upset by something that seems unfair but is

Avoid giving reasons for the bad news only when the reader might take legal action against you. When unsure, consult an attorney.

actually legal. Even if you and your company are operating within the law, lawsuits are expensive.

**LAST PARAGRAPH.**   The last paragraph of an indirect reply should contain no negative words or references to the bad news. There is no need for an apology at the end because, if you or your company were at fault, you would have apologized in the middle of the message. The last paragraph should have a positive, friendly tone that assumes everything is okay between the reader and the writer. If there is something the reader needs to do, such as return a postcard or call the company, courteously request that he or she do it. If it is appropriate, you can tie appreciation to this action by using a statement such as the following:

> "Your completing the information in the highlighted blanks will be appreciated. Getting it back to us soon will ensure that we can consider your request for credit right away."

All of the examples of effective indirect messages within this chapter contain well-constructed final paragraphs. Take a moment now to read them, and then see if you can determine what is wrong with the following closing paragraphs:

> Ineffective: "We hope that you understand and accept our position in this matter and that you will continue doing business with Garfield Industries."
>
> Critique: "We hope" shows doubt and introduces a negative into the situation that might anger the reader once again.
>
> Ineffective: "Thank you for your understanding."
>
> Critique: Presumptuous statements such as this might rekindle the reader's anger. Never thank in advance.
>
> Ineffective: "We are so sorry, Mrs. Patrini, that we are unable to fill your order. Perhaps we will have better luck on your next order."
>
> Critique: Never apologize in the last paragraph; never finish with a negative. "Perhaps" makes it sound as though the next order is likely to have problems as well.
>
> Ineffective: "Please let us know if we can be of further assistance to you in the future."
>
> Critique: This seems a bit insincere in a message that denies the reader what he or she wanted.
>
> Ineffective: "You have my personal assurance that nothing like this will ever happen again."
>
> Critique: Never guarantee anything over which you do not have complete control. Don't refer to the negative situation in the last paragraph.

## INDIRECT CLAIMS

◣ Plan, organize, compose, and evaluate indirect claims.

Claim letters are written by the buyer to the seller or manufacturer of a product or service that has failed to satisfy. The claim letters covered in Chapter 7 were direct claims, those that will probably not upset the reader in any way. This chapter covers claims that might upset the reader; therefore, they must be written using an indirect strategy. The indirect arrangement is also sometimes effective if your direct letter did not result in any kind of action. In one respect, direct and indirect claim letters are the same: Both should identify the remedy you expect from the recipient of the message.

**FIRST PARAGRAPH.** The buffer of an indirect claim should mention something on which you and the reader can both agree—for example, your long business association or the reputation of the company to whom you are writing:

> "For the past five years, we have known that we could depend on Hollisters to get our orders to us on time. Because of your dependability, we have not even considered another supplier in a long time."

> "American Furniture has a reputation for quality products. That is why we furnished three offices with your Art-Deco line."

> "Your sales receipt says 'The Customer is King.' This attitude has always brought us to Redway for our paper products."

> Opening for an annual meeting: "Employees must be encouraged to be more entrepreneurial in their thinking, to become more innovative, and to experiment without undue fear of failure. This is the way to develop innovative new products that will put Kroehler back in the forefront of the industry."

Openings such as these are effective because they get the attention of the reader and draw on the reader's pride in his or her product or company. To maintain this sense of pride, the reader might work harder to satisfy the writer. As long as such statements are sincere and relate to the purpose of the letter or memo, they help to ease the reader into the middle paragraphs where the negative information is discussed.

**MIDDLE PARAGRAPHS.** The middle paragraphs of an indirect claim present the reasons for the claim and state specifically what needs to be done to remedy the situation to the reader's satisfaction. As with any other indirect message, the middle paragraphs should contain plenty of reader-benefit statements.

The transition between the buffer and the middle paragraphs is particularly important. Without effective transitions, the sentiments expressed in the first paragraph can seem insincere and irrelevant. The following example shows how a smooth transition can be made from the first paragraph to a justification of the claim and a clear statement of the claim itself:

The buffer is relevant, goodwill oriented, and you oriented.

The transition between buffer and second paragraph is effective. You-oriented statements let the reader know you haven't given up on his or her company.

> For the past five years, we have known that we could depend on Hollisters to get our orders to us on time. Because of your dependability, we have not even considered another suppler in a long time.
>
> That is why we were so puzzled by the unusual delay of Order No. 34449 and the lack of response to our June 18 letter. As I explained in that letter, because the order was delivered 15 days later than the scheduled date, we had to suspend construction for two weeks, which required the rescheduling of five subcontractors. In addition, interest on the construction loan will have to be paid for an extra two weeks.

Justification for the claim continues.

It is highly unusual that someone from your office did not notify us of the delay in time for other arrangements to be made; your representatives are normally right on top of things. That is why we were not initially concerned when the order was late and why we did not immediately reorder the items from another supplier.

The claim is clearly stated.

As mentioned in the previous letter, a fair settlement of this issue would be a 10 percent discount on our next order of Andersen windows, an order we would agree to keep at approximately the same size as the previous order.

**LAST PARAGRAPH.**   The last paragraph of an indirect claim letter or memo follows the same pattern as other indirect messages. The following would be a good last paragraph for the claim letter to Hollisters:

The close includes a positive look to the future, appreciation tied to future action, and a push for immediacy. Reader benefit is emphasized.

> Your personal attention in seeing that this discount is approved soon will be appreciated. In the past, you have always met our needs, and we should soon be ready to place another large order with you.

A good closing paragraph for an indirect claim ends the message in a friendly, positive manner and is specific about what the reader should do. It expresses appreciation only for action in the future ("will be appreciated").

For some readers, asking them to do something for you "soon" or "as soon as possible" is the same as saying "I'm in no hurry; do it whenever you have some spare time." If the timing is important to you, set a deadline for action and explain why it is important. For example, you might say "Your taking care of this matter by January 22 will be appreciated because our conference is scheduled to begin the following week."

## INDIRECT ADJUSTMENTS

Plan, organize, compose, and evaluate indirect adjustments.

An adjustment is a response to a customer's or client's claim letter. There are many reasons why a company might deny the claim of a customer or client, thereby necessitating an indirect organizational strategy. Even though people are basically honest, they are not always reasonable. For example, retail salespeople say it is not uncommon for customers to return items such as bedspreads that have been used for two years, demanding a full refund or replacement on the grounds that a good bedspread should last longer.

Individuals are not the only ones to whom you will have to say "no." Companies also make unreasonable requests. One small aerospace development firm wrote a claim letter to the U.S. Department of Defense, demanding early payment of a contract they had signed. Their justification was that the government should have known the company wouldn't be able to produce what it said it would produce within the time it said it could be done. The Department of Defense denied the claim because the major reason the company was awarded the contract in the first place was that it had accepted a payment schedule tied to stages of product development.

Exhibit 8.6 is an example of an indirect adjustment letter. As you read it, notice how the use of an indirect approach and good you attitude help the reader accept the denial of her request, a full refund of the price of her ticket. The writer of this letter did an excellent job of resolving a difficult situation. Maintaining the goodwill of each dissatisfied customer is important because that one customer can easily spread dissatisfaction to at least 10 other people.

**EXHIBIT 8.6**

**Indirect Adjustment (Block Style with Mixed Punctuation)**

**MESA AIRLINES**

756 Washington Blvd.
Lincoln City, IN 47552

(812) 453-2300
FAX (812) 453-4600

September 2, 1995

Ms. Mickie Poletski
501 Jefferson Street
Morgan Center, VT 05854

*The relevant buffer agrees with the reader's claim. Resale stresses that the airline goes out of its way to meet the needs of passengers.*

Dear Ms. Poletski:

You are right. Airline food should be appetizing, tasty, and nutritious. That is why Mesa works closely with nutritionists and chefs to create meals that meet these high standards. In addition, we try to offer delicious food that appeals to the varied preferences of our diverse clientele.

*The reason for not having the reader's preferred meal is explained in a way that should lead her to the same logical conclusion.*

Although our research has shown that most people prefer high-protein meals consisting of chicken, ham, or beef, we also offer vegetarian meals for passengers who request them. Although it is customary for people on special diets to call ahead to arrange special meals, we always stock a few extra vegetarian meals on each flight.

Unfortunately, on your flight all the vegetarian meals had already been distributed before the flight attendant took your order. Therefore, it was not possible to serve you a vegetarian meal. Had you reserved a meal beforehand, you would, of course, have received your order.

*A reader-benefit statement is used to justify the bad news. The bad news is subordinated by placing it at the end of the paragraph.*

As hard as we try to meet everyone's dietary preferences and needs, it simply is not possible to predict with 100 percent accuracy what will be required for each flight. If we were to refund the full cost of tickets because meal preferences could not be met, we would not be able to offer you the same superior service at such low prices.

*An alternative is suggested. (Alternatives are not always available, however.)*

However, enclosed is a coupon for an upgrade to a first-class meal for your next Mesa flight. You will find the food served to first-class passengers to be the epitome of elegance and fine dining.

**EXHIBIT 8.6**    Continued

Ms. Mickie Poletski
September 2, 1995
Page 2

*The friendly, positive closing looks to a future business relationship and suggests what the reader needs to do next.*

Just let your Mesa ticket agent know ahead of time to reserve an appetizing, tasty, and nutritious first-class vegetarian meal for you on your next Mesa flight. Your order will be waiting for you.

Sincerely,

*T. J. Rosenberg*

T. J. Rosenberg, Vice President
Customer Satisfaction and Service

Enc: First Class Food Upgrade

**FIRST PARAGRAPH.**   The first paragraph of an indirect adjustment should try to establish some type of common ground with the reader. Search for something within the individual's claim letter you can support. You could also express appreciation, give a sincere compliment, tell the good news (if there is any), show understanding, or present a fact or principle so general that you are positive the reader will agree.

Read the following examples of poor opening paragraphs, and see if you can identify what is wrong with each one:

Ineffective: "Thank you for your complaint of January 23."

Critique: The gratitude sounds insincere. *Complaint* is a negative word when combined with *your*. As far as most of us are concerned, we don't complain—we have justified concerns.

Ineffective: "You claim that you did not wear the swimsuit you returned. However, it smells of chlorine, a smell usually associated only with suits that have been worn in swimming pools."

Critique: This sarcastic paragraph will do nothing to create a positive relationship with the reader. An indirect message should never give away the negative news in the first paragraph.

Ineffective: "The operational instructions that came with your wide-screen TV state specifically that the set should be connected only to external speakers that are UL approved."

Critique: This buffer is not neutral. A buffer is not supposed to give reasons for the refusal.

An effective opening paragraph sets the tone for the rest of the message. It puts the reader in a receptive mood for the rest of the letter—the reasons for the refusal and the refusal itself.

**MIDDLE PARAGRAPHS.**   In the middle paragraphs of an indirect adjustment, present the reasons for the refusal. The best reasons are those that stress the benefits to the reader or to someone other than the writer.

Notice how the letter in Exhibit 8.6 states the reasons in positive language, showing that the airline works harder than necessary to meet the needs of all its passengers. It makes what happened to the reader seem to be an understandable, unusual occurrence that could easily have been prevented by the reader herself. Ms. Poletski is led through a logical, clear argument that any reasonable person would accept as fair. Thus, she is fully prepared for the negative news before it is presented in the next to the last paragraph. Immediately presenting an alternative should make Ms. Poletski feel that the airline has, at least, offered her some compensation. Resale is included throughout the letter in an attempt to make the reader see that the airline is worthy of her confidence and her continued patronage.

Negative news should always be presented in impersonal language. In other words, avoid using terms such as "your claim," substituting instead, "the claim." Avoid lecturing or seeming to condescend. Take care not to make your reader feel he or she is the child and you are the stern parent delivering advice and denying privileges. The tone of the argument will determine whether or not you are able to maintain a favorable relationship with the reader once you have refused a claim.

**LAST PARAGRAPH.**   The final paragraph of an unfavorable adjustment should not mention the refusal or include an apology. It should also be original, avoiding insincere, meaningless clichés such as "If you have further questions" or "Please feel free to call." These kinds of statements make the negative decision seem less final and might result in another letter or telephone call from a reader attempting to negotiate further. If possible, however, the paragraph should include resale to foster confidence in the company, its products, or its services.

If appropriate, offer best wishes to the reader in the last paragraph, but avoid any that are insincere or irrelevant. For example, it would be ridiculous to say "Keep up the good work" in a memo denying an employee's request for a raise on the basis of poor performance. Such a statement would do more harm than good to the relationship between the reader and the writer.

In addition, avoid words like *hope* and *trust* that indicate you doubt the reader's willingness to accept your decision as reasonable and fair. A positive statement concerning a continuing business association between you and the reader will return the relationship to a "business as usual" mindset. Exhibit 8.6 contains a prime example of a future business statement appropriate for an indirect adjustment.

## INDIRECT ANNOUNCEMENTS

Plan, organize, compose, and evaluate indirect announcements.

Indirect announcements range from memos sent to thousands of people announcing the closing of a major plant (like Helen Cohen's memo to Brady employees) to personal letters of resignation. Memos or letters detailing procedures about which employees will be unhappy, delays in filling orders, new policies that limit retailers' ability to discount your product, or increases in charges on all bank accounts are only a few examples of the many kinds of indirect announcements you might have to write.

**FIRST PARAGRAPH.**   By now, the pattern for the first paragraph of all indirect messages should be familiar to you. A buffer opening is used to put the reader in the right frame of mind to receive the bad news.

The sample letter shown in Exhibit 8.7 illustrates one way you might begin a memo telling employees that they will receive no vacations this year because the company has been acquired by new owners. However, instead of presenting what little good news there is (payment for vacation days not taken) later in the memo, you could have presented it in the first paragraph. Alternatives may be presented in the beginning when they will be considered acceptable and reasonable to the reader. However, placement of alternatives after the negative news can lift the reader's spirits.

Read and critique the following opening paragraphs for indirect announcements:

> Letter recalling an automobile: "If you still own the car, please call your Oldsmobile dealer immediately for an appointment to repair your 1995 Streak. A recall for this vehicle has been issued because of the unusually high number of cars that shift into reverse without warning."

> Critique: It gets the message across; however, it is so blunt there is a danger it will panic the reader.

**EXHIBIT 8.7**    Indirect Announcement (Memo)

TO:        Sunoco-Southwest Employees

FROM:      Mason Vesarian, Southwest Division V.P.

DATE:      March 13, 1995

SUBJECT:   Bellingham Transition

*The buffer is a reminder of the positive changes coming about at a time of uncertainty.*

As you already know, the acquisition of Sunoco by Bellingham Oil and Gas has brought about many positive changes. The infusion of funds into Sunoco has meant we have been able to take real action toward meeting many of the goals and objectives set by both employees and management. One of the most immediate benefits is the hiring of 11 new employees to help with your heavy workload.

*The reasons for having everyone on duty during the transition provide justification for the bad news. A sincere apology is reserved for the last sentence.*

To help relieve the workload, these new employees must be trained as soon as possible and the two new Bellingham managers must be made thoroughly familiar with all aspects of Sunoco operations. They must see how your job fits into the overall picture, which can be done only if you are present. No one else can articulate as well as you what you do and how the organization can back you up. Attempting to give the new people such information when as many as one-sixth of our employees are on vacation would not be effective. Therefore, all vacation days not taken by April 30 must be canceled. We are sensitive to the disappointment this may cause and are sorry for the necessity of implementing this measure.

*The alternative is a bit of good news.*

To compensate you in some small way, Bellingham has agreed to pay you for your vacation days at your regular rate of pay plus one-half. The vacation checks will be distributed on May 7. In the meantime, you may ascertain what this measure will mean for you personally by visiting with either of the representatives in human resources.

Moving under the umbrella of Bellingham will magnify the strengths of Sunoco-Southwest and its superior staff. Your help in making the transition go as smoothly and as quickly as possible will be invaluable.

mgl

*Goodwill and resale, to remind readers of the good things happening as the result of this acquisition, provide an optimistic close.*

Letter recalling automobile tires that should not be used in extreme heat: "Your Waterhugger tires are the result of a marriage of science and technology. Years of research went into designing a tire that will keep you safe when you drive on wet and icy roads."

Critique: The buffer reassures the reader that the company tried hard to develop a superior product. When the bad news (the tires are unsafe on extremely hot roads) is delivered, readers might be comforted by the emphasis on safety and the fact that the company has volunteered to correct its mistake.

A big problem with Helen Cohen's memo is that it begins with a buffer that could be misleading. Would you expect to hear about massive layoffs if you had just read that "we have weathered the many ups and downs of government funding"? In addition, Ms. Cohen's subject line trumpets the bad news at the very beginning, rendering the buffer pointless.

**MIDDLE PARAGRAPHS.** The middle paragraphs of indirect announcements contain the same progression of logic used in other indirect messages.

1. Justification of the bad news in terms of how it benefits readers.
2. The bad news stated in positive, tactful, courteous terms.

Helen Cohen's memo to Brady employees violates this progression. In the second paragraph in Exhibit 8.1, she immediately announces the bad news and then justifies it. Furthermore, she does not justify the bad news in terms of how it benefits readers. She might have said, for example, that returning Brady to a position of strength in the industry would secure the jobs of the remaining employees and perhaps allow Brady to rehire some of the laid-off employees when the new contract is signed.

For better examples of the middle paragraphs of indirect announcements, look at Exhibit 8.7 and the following, which continues the message about Waterhugger tires:

A select group of top scientists worked closely with our specialists to develop an innovative process that helps maintain the bond between tire and road despite the presence of dangerous rain or ice. You will be glad to know that, once our products are on the market, this same attention to your safety does not stop. Our researchers continue to work to ensure the safety of you and your loved ones.

Continued research on the Waterhugger tire has revealed that, despite its superior handling in wet and icy conditions, it does not perform well at temperatures exceeding 100 degrees. The tread tends to separate from the tire, and blowouts are a factor at temperatures exceeding 110 degrees.

Your safety is important to us. If your Waterhugger tires are driven in areas where road temperatures rise above 100 degrees, please make an appointment to see your dealer within 30 days. **Show the enclosed certificate and your Waterhugger warranty to your dealer, who will replace your Waterhuggers with the new Roadhugger II, a tire designed for high- and low-temperature performance.**

If your vehicle is not driven in high-temperature areas, you may be sure your Waterhuggers will continue to give you the safest ride available today.

Boldface is used in this letter to make sure the most important part of the message is read. With an indirect strategy, there is always a danger that the reader will assume the communication is merely an unsolicited sales letter.

Because the safety of readers is concerned and there is a danger of lawsuits, the company must do everything it can to ensure that its recall letter is actually read. Boldface will pique the reader's interest, making him or her more likely to read the entire message.

**Last Paragraph.**   The last paragraph of a message announcing negative news should be friendly and positive. If the reader needs to do something that has not been covered previously, the final paragraph is an appropriate place to mention it.

Read the final paragraph of the Waterhugger tire letter:

> This voluntary recall is only part of our ongoing commitment to service and quality. You may be sure Hugger tires will keep you out of harm's way.

This final paragraph is followed by the usual complimentary close and the writer's signature lines. The following underlined statement would then appear at the bottom of the letter as an extra inducement to read the letter. Good use of the you attitude helps the reader understand why he or she should read the letter.

> No matter how many miles your Waterhugger tires have been driven, you will receive your new Roadhugger IIs free of charge!

Take a moment to read once again all the parts of the Waterhugger letter. Note how closely it corresponds to the indirect strategy presented at the beginning of this chapter. By following this indirect arrangement, the company's reputation for a quality product is more likely to survive the recall (a situation that has proved devastating to more than one company).

### Indirect Collection Letters

Plan, organize, compose, and evaluate indirect collection letters.

Messages intended to collect money from overdue accounts take many different forms, ranging from photocopied invoices to letters announcing an account has been turned over to a collection agency. Although companies differ a great deal in the number of written messages they send customers whose accounts are overdue, most go through the following stages:

1.  *Informal reminder:* A new invoice showing a past due amount or a photocopy of the original invoice with an attention-getting device emphasizing the past-due amount (e.g., a stamp or sticker).

2.  *Formal reminder:* A friendly, indirect letter or informal note (which may include detailed payment information) attached to another invoice.

3.  *Discussion:* A friendly, concerned letter urging the reader to tell you why he or she has not paid the invoice. An indirect strategy is most appropriate, although a persuasive strategy can also be effective. A copy of the invoice should be included unless the payment and account information are provided in the letter.

4.  *Persuasion:* A persuasive letter urging final payment before stronger measures are taken. (Chapter 9 discusses this stage in greater detail.)

5.  *Action:* A direct letter announcing the account has been turned over to an attorney or collection agency.

Some firms do not send each of these types of messages; others send several messages in each of the first three or four stages. The amount of time allowed for each stage also varies a great deal from one company to the next.

The first, middle, and last paragraphs of collection letters are like those in other direct and indirect messages. Collection letters that use good you attitude, follow the appropriate strategy and appeal to honor, fair play, and protection of one's credit rating are likely to be successful.

## EVALUATING YOUR MESSAGE

Once you have planned, organized, and composed your indirect message, you should evaluate its effectiveness. You can use the checklist in Exhibit 8.8 to assess all types of indirect messages before they are mailed. If you have composed a message as part of a collaborative team, each member of the team should complete the checklist before the results are compared.

In a business situation, it would also be necessary to evaluate feedback from your readers. Angry telephone calls and written responses would indicate that your written message was not successful in furthering good relationships. On the other hand, it is not safe to assume you have accomplished your purposes just because you do not receive angry responses. Follow through to determine if the reader has taken the action you recommend or if the client or customer continues to do business with you. In the case of memos, assess the initial reactions of your co-workers, superiors, or subordinates after they have received an indirect message. When it is obvious your reader understands the negative message, yet he or she continues your business relationship, you may assume your message was successful.

## DISCUSSION QUESTIONS

Determine when an indirect organizational strategy is appropriate.

1. How does a reader's likely reaction determine when an indirect strategy should be used?

Determine when an indirect organizational strategy is appropriate.

2. What impact does culture have on the selection of an indirect strategy?

Apply the four steps of the message formulation process to indirect messages.

3. Name the four steps in the message formulation process used for business messages. Which one is the most difficult for you? Could a collaborative writing group improve this difficult step for you? If so, how?

Identify the features of an indirect organizational strategy.

4. What are the features of an indirect organizational strategy?

Plan, organize, compose, and evaluate indirect replies.
Plan, organize, compose, and evaluate indirect announcements.

5. Identify four situations, other than those discussed in this chapter, for which indirect replies and announcements would be appropriate.

**EXHIBIT**

**8.8**

## Checklist for Indirect Messages

Answer the following yes/no questions. (A "no" answer indicates room for improvement.) Some of the points do not apply to all types of messages. If a point does not apply, put n/a (not applicable) in the blank.

■ **Opening and Closing**

___ Is the buffer opening relevant to the situation?

___ Did you avoid implying that positive news follows?

___ Does the first paragraph lead naturally and logically to the next paragraph?

___ Did you present any good news in the first paragraph or later on in the letter?

___ Are pertinent order numbers, dates, etc., mentioned?

___ Is effective you attitude used in the opening paragraph?

___ Are negative references to the situation avoided in the opening and closing paragraphs?

___ Is goodwill in the closing relevant to the situation?

___ Does the closing paragraph avoid trite, overused words and phrases?

___ Does the closing paragraph inform the reader politely of what he or she should do next (if appropriate)?

___ Does the closing avoid thanking the reader in advance?

___ In the closing, is gratitude tied to any action the reader should perform?

■ **Message**

___ Were reasons given in positive terms?

___ Did you stress how the policy or decision benefits the reader?

___ Is the bad news clear, but diplomatic?

___ For replies and adjustments, have all requests or questions been addressed?

___ Have you disclosed clearly and completely everything that should be communicated?

___ Does the message achieve the purpose(s) established during the freewriting?

___ If pertinent, have details of previous contact or correspondence been summarized?

___ Will the quality of your arguments, conclusions, generalizations, and assumptions stand up to scrutiny?

___ Did you avoid negative words?

___ Did you use resale when appropriate to reestablish confidence in your products, services, or company?

___ Did you mention anything that will be enclosed with the correspondence?

___ Did you tell the reader clearly what you have done and what you will do?

___ For adjustment messages, if you or your company did something wrong, did you apologize briefly without dwelling on the negative impact of your mistake?

___ For claim and adjustment letters, did you avoid blaming anyone (your firm, your employees, the reader)?

___ For adjustment messages, did you avoid unrealistic promises about the future?

■ **Tone**

___ Is goodwill sincere and appropriate to the situation?

___ Has the reader been treated with courtesy and respect?

___ Did you avoid overuse of *I, me, my, our, we,* and the company name?

___ Did you emphasize *you* and *your* and the reader's needs?

■ **Mechanics**

___ Are the name and title of the reader spelled and used correctly?

___ Have all words been spelled correctly?

___ Is correct sentence structure used for all sentences?

___ Is correct paragraph structure used for all paragraphs?

___ Are there transitions between each paragraph?

___ Is punctuation correct?

■ **Readability**

___ Is the reading level appropriate for intended reader(s)?

___ Are lists used when necessary to improve the clarity of complex information or questions?

■ **Format and Appearance**

___ Is the format one of those recommended in the textbook? (See Appendix C.)

___ If appropriate, has reader reaction to a form message been considered?

___ Are side margins equal?

___ Are corrections undetectable?

___ Has the letter or memorandum been folded correctly?

___ Is your signature readable?

■ **Other**

___ Is the entire message truthful?

___ Have you been fair to all concerned?

___ Would you be proud if everyone you know were aware of all the details of this transaction?

___ Is your communication within the bounds of the law?

___ Have you collaborated with appropriate individuals?

___ Did you reply promptly?

___ Have deliberate distortions, slang, discriminatory language, clichés, redundancies, roundabout expressions, and confusing foreign expressions been avoided?

___ Did you analyze the reader and his or her needs thoroughly?

🔳 Plan, organize, compose, and evaluate indirect claims.

    6. Identify two situations not discussed in this chapter that would require you to write indirect claim letters. Explain why an indirect organizational plan would be better for these situations. How would you begin each of these letters?

🔳 Plan, organize, compose, and evaluate indirect adjustments.

    7. Name two situations in this chapter for which a company would have to write indirect adjustments. How would you begin each of these letters?

🔳 Plan, organize, compose, and evaluate indirect collection letters.

    8. Name the five stages of collection letters. What considerations might go into a company's decision about how many messages to send to someone whose payments are overdue?

## APPLICATION EXERCISES

🔳 Determine when an indirect organizational strategy is appropriate.

    1. Analyze the following situations to determine whether an indirect strategy would be appropriate and what the reader's probable reaction would be to the message. In some cases, there might be more than one possible reaction. If so, is an indirect message still the best choice?

       *a.* A letter announcing to a customer that his request for an extension of time in which to pay his bill has been denied.

       *b.* A memo announcing to employees that a mandatory meeting will be held before working hours next week.

       *c.* A memo to human resources personnel detailing the implications of a new law concerning hiring disabled employees.

       *d.* A letter announcing a discount cannot be given to a client only on the basis of your long business relationship.

       *e.* A short memo report to a client announcing the results of a survey of his or her employees, which reveal that productivity is down because their morale is low.

       *f.* A letter to established customers announcing a new product.

       *g.* An adjustment letter that grants a customer's claim.

       *h.* A memo to another manager asking her to instruct her subordinates to follow procedures they have been violating.

       *i.* A letter accepting an invitation to join an organization but refusing to speak at their annual conference.

       *j.* A memo to your boss asking for permission to take an extra week off without pay.

🔳 Apply the four steps of the message formulation process to indirect messages.
🔳 Identify the features of an indirect organizational strategy.

    2. Evaluate the following memo. Then rewrite it so it adheres to the guidelines presented in this chapter.

I regret that it has become necessary to send this strong message. Because efforts to force reconciliation of these issues among yourselves have met with no success, I must issue the following directives:

- Because of his experience, Elton will be in charge of inventory control. Once the products to be stocked have been determined, Elton will use established formulas to determine how much of each product to order to meet sales targets. As shortages of merchandise are noted, Elton will take care of the reordering. Elton may not meet with buyers who are confused by the different messages they are receiving from the two of you.

- Besides myself, Donald is the only person authorized to represent the company with local and corporate buyers. In conjunction with buyers, Donald will determine quarterly the product lines and specific products to be made available for purchase in our stores. If Donald (or anyone else for that matter) notices shortages of specific products, he may recommend in writing that Elton purchase additional inventory. However, Elton will have the final say on whether more merchandise is ordered.

To make a long story short: Donald, you will decide what to order; and Elton, you will decide how much to order. This division of responsibilities should allow you to work together without embroiling buyers, your staff, and upper-level management in unnecessary territorial squabbles. I do not expect to hear any more complaints from anyone on this matter.

🔩 Identify the features of an indirect organizational strategy.

3. Evaluate whether the following openings are appropriate for indirect messages. State what is wrong with those that are not appropriate.
    a. "Thank you for your order no. 23477. Grayson Novelties is always happy to welcome a new customer."
    b. "Thank you for writing to Peachpit Press. The book about which you ask is in the process of publication but is not available at this time."
    c. "Satisfying the needs of Allen Productions has been one of our most important goals for many years. The mutual business relationship we have established is important to us."
    d. "Your account is now 60 days overdue. Please send a check for the amount specified below within 10 days to avoid prosecution."
    e. "Unfortunately, shipment of your order for eight Rosewood doors must be delayed six months. However, to compensate you for the inconvenience, Haskell Hardware is cutting the price by 5 percent."

🔩 Identify the features of an indirect organizational strategy.

4. Evaluate whether the following closings are appropriate for indirect messages. State what is wrong with those that are not appropriate.
    a. "It is our hope this delay will not cause you undue inconvenience. Our goal is to satisfy, not to dissatisfy."
    b. "Your order will be rushed to you as soon as it is in stock unless you instruct us to do otherwise by completing the form below. Your satisfaction is important to us, so let us know how we can best meet your needs."
    c. "Please let me know this week that it is okay for me to take an extra week's vacation without pay so I can meet the deadline for the cruise reservations."

    *d.* "Please let me know if there is anything else I can do to help your cause. Perhaps I could send brochures or product samples for your seminar."

    *e.* "I look forward to seeing you at the meeting Tuesday."

For the remaining exercises, you are to compose a letter or memo as instructed. Assume any reasonable details to make the messages realistic. Unless a job title is specified for you, make up a title that is appropriate to the situation. As you do the exercises, follow these steps:

1. Plan your message:
   *a.* Establish your purpose.
   *b.* Choose a medium and channel.
   *c.* Consider legal and ethical issues.
   *d.* Analyze your audience.
   *e.* Gather necessary resources.

2. Organize your message:
   *a.* Freewrite major points.
   *b.* Choose an organizational strategy.

3. Compose your message.

4. Evaluate your message:
   *a.* Use Exhibit 8.8 for self-evaluation.
   *b.* Evaluate feedback from your instructor.

Your instructor will tell you whether to turn in your freewritten notes or any other evidence that you have performed each step of the message formulation process. You will also be told whether the message must be written individually or collaboratively.

## Indirect Replies

- Apply the four steps of the message formulation process to indirect messages.
- Plan, organize, compose, and evaluate indirect replies.

5. *Form letter to unsuccessful job applicants.* You were just hired as the office manager of a small manufacturing facility. Your job is to run the entire office with the help of a part-time accountant and a clerical assistant. All these tasks used to be done by the owner; however, he hired you so he could spend more time developing the manufacturing side of the business.

    One of the most important changes you have made is updating the hiring procedures to comply with legal guidelines. The owner, a brilliant metal worker and machinist, had little knowledge of legal hiring procedures. Whenever he needed a new employee, he merely advertised in the local newspaper for a week or two, interviewed everyone who came in the door, and hired the first person who seemed to fit the job.

    Now you must write a form letter to be sent to all unsuccessful applicants who interview for positions. You will be informing each reader that someone else has been hired for the job for which he or she applied. This form letter will be used for all types of positions. You will use a mail-merge computer program to personalize each letter with an individual's name and address and the title of the job for which he or she applied. Use good you attitude to make the reasons for denial seem reasonable and logical and to help the reader feel that you are speaking to him or her as an individual. Because you will be conducting all interviews in the future, the letter should be written in your name. Address your letter to Mrs. Alluwana Tears, 101 Ala Moana Blvd., Waikiki, HI 96815. She interviewed for an opening as a computer numerical control programmer.

🐾 Apply the four steps of the message formulation process to indirect messages.
🐾 Plan, organize, compose, and evaluate indirect replies.

6. *Form letter announcing a job is being readvertised.* Reread exercise 5. As the office manager, you must now write a form letter announcing to those who have sent in resumes or filled out applications that the job is being readvertised; no interviews will be conducted at this time.

   There are many reasons a job might be readvertised. For example, perhaps none of the applicants meet the qualifications the company is looking for, or perhaps the pool of applicants does not reflect the ethnic and gender makeup of the community. (Many government contractors and public organizations are required to do everything in their power to ensure applicant pools reflect roughly the ethnic and gender makeup of the general population of an area.)

   Encourage the reader of this letter to reapply for the job, and use care to make sure you do not give the impression that he or she was not qualified. Address the letter to the same person described in exercise 5.

🐾 Apply the four steps of the message formulation process to indirect messages.
🐾 Plan, organize, compose, and evaluate indirect replies.

7. *Memo refusing an employee's request.* One of the employees you supervise, Nancy Au, sent you a memo asking for a 10 percent raise in pay. In her memo she stated that she has been with the company for one year without an increase in her starting salary; her rent just went up; and, because she just signed up for the medical insurance available through the company, her take-home pay has actually gone down.

   You are surprised Nancy would request a raise, because she knows you are not happy with her performance. One month ago, you went over Nancy's yearly performance appraisal with her and made it clear she needs improvement in three areas: attendance, attitude, and productivity. Nancy has taken the maximum amount of sick days, one day at a time, usually on a Friday or a Monday. She is frequently rude to clients; as the receptionist, Nancy is the first person most people encounter when they come into the office. She also seems to resent being told what to do, does not ask questions when she does not understand how to do things, and makes the same mistakes repeatedly. You feel she is capable of doing much better, however, and believe her poor performance is the result of a bad attitude. You discussed all of these things with her during the performance appraisal interview, which resulted in a rating of "Needs further improvement" for Nancy. As required by company policy, Nancy signed the form to indicate she had met with you to go over it. At that time, you and Nancy established written goals for her, which have not yet been met.

   Raises and promotions are granted to employees only when their supervisors recommend them. Your policy has always been to consider raises or promotions only for those who meet or exceed their yearly goals. Write Nancy a memo turning down her request for a raise. Use good you attitude to tie reconsideration of a raise to her next performance appraisal. Do not promise her a raise, because you never know what the future economic condition of the company might be. For selfish reasons, you want Nancy's performance to improve (training a new receptionist is a time-consuming task you do not relish). Compose a memo that will keep Nancy as an employee while making her want to improve.

### Indirect Claims

- Apply the four steps of the message formulation process to indirect messages.
- Plan, organize, compose, and evaluate indirect claims.

8. *Memo to management about a union concern.* You are the chief negotiator for a small union of health care professionals (you also work full time for the hospital as a nursing supervisor). As chief negotiator, you lead a seven-member negotiating council that represents 567 nurses and nursing assistants. Four months ago, you reached agreement on a two-year contract. That contract requires your members to pay $80 a year for parking in the facility's parking lots; however, it guarantees a specific number of spaces for all staff, excluding doctors and four top-level administrators who have assigned parking spaces. Getting this guarantee was a big success for you, because parking space is hard to find; and, even though the number of hospital employees has grown in recent years, the number of staff parking spaces has diminished. The specific number of spaces in effect at the time the contract was signed were 207 in Lot A, 84 in Lot B, 210 in Lot C, and 225 in Lot D.

At the request of Marilee Bird and Daniel Schumer, two nurses, you investigated and discovered that four staff spaces in Lot B have been assigned to two new doctors and two new administrators, and that eight staff spaces (four each in Lots C and D) are now wider than before and designated for handicapped use only. You, of course, have no objections to parking spaces for handicapped people; however, converting the spaces did decrease the number available for the union members you represent as well as other employees. All parking spaces for handicapped people, regardless of whether they are in employee lots or not, can be used by handicapped members of the public. In addition, security officers seem to have decreased the ticketing and towing of vehicles that park illegally in employee spaces.

Write a memo that will convince hospital administrators to honor the contract by returning the spaces they took. Remember that you work with these people on a daily basis, so you will have to use good you attitude to point out why it is in everyone's best interest to live up to the agreement. Don't assume the removal of spaces was an intentional violation of the contract. Send copies of the memo to the nine hospital board members and to Dr. Dorothy Gelvin, chief administrator. Address the memo to the hospital's main negotiator, Alan Largesse. (By the way, even though your memo will be typed on the union's letterhead and not the hospital's, you decided to use a memo format instead of a letter format because you want to emphasize that you are all employees of the hospital with the same interest at heart—superior health care.)

⬛ Apply the four steps of the message formulation process to indirect messages.
⬛ Plan, organize, compose, and evaluate indirect claims.

9. *Letter refusing to pay a bill.* Write a letter to Margarita Romero, one of the owners of CompuService, the small local company from which you purchased the 11 computers and printers in your office. Tell her that you will not be paying the bill (No. 1473-ZX) for $567.49 that you recently received for the repair of a computer that should still be under warranty for another two months. On the bill you received was the following statement: "Warranty nullified due to unauthorized access to internal housing."

   You checked with Jim Hughes, the person who uses the computer in question, and he said one of CompuService's technicians told him by telephone how to make the computer start up when it would not do what it was supposed to. Jim said the technician, whose name he does not remember, remained on the telephone while instructing Jim to open the case housing the central processing unit and to tap a pencil on top of the hard drive while turning the computer off and on. According to Jim, this technique worked, and he was able to put off the servicing of the computer for nearly three months. Jim said he never would have tried this method had he realized that it would void the warranty; he thought he was saving the company money on a service call.

   You do not believe the charge is justified under these circumstances. Send the letter to Ms. Romero at 1301 East Mission Street, Rombauer, MO 63962.

⬛ Apply the four steps of the message formulation process to indirect messages.
⬛ Plan, organize, compose, and evaluate indirect claims.

10. *Follow-up letter to an automobile dealer.* Your three-year-old pickup truck has been experiencing a number of electrical problems. It keeps blowing fuses; as a result, you never know when you will be able to use the lights, turn signals, air conditioning, or radio. Four weeks ago (August 2) you had the truck repaired; however, within one week, the problem had returned. Because the receipt you received states that all repairs are guaranteed for six months, you took the truck back in on August 10. At that time, the mechanics said they couldn't find anything wrong with it. However, two weeks later (August 23) the fuses are still blowing, and the repair shop wants to charge you at least another $150 with no guarantee that the problem will be fixed.

   On two occasions (August 10 and August 23) you spoke to Grady Spinner, the service manager, who was rude, implying that you must be doing something to blow the fuses, such as pulling a trailer that is improperly wired. You explained to him that the boat you used to pull was sold two years ago. However, it was obvious he did not believe you.

   Because you paid $355.14 for the repair on your personal Visa charge account, you have notified Visa of the problem. Although the parties are making progress toward settling the matter, Visa will not pay the auto repair shop, and you will not be charged interest on the disputed amount. One of Visa's requirements, however, is that you attempt to settle the matter personally with the repair shop.

   Write a personal business letter to Frank Cortez, owner of Cortez Auto Services, 1600 East Valley Boulevard, Minneapolis, MN 55414. Tell him the bill will not be paid by Visa until the repairs are done to your satisfaction. Mention the rude treatment you received from the service manager. Remember your primary purpose: getting the pickup fixed once and for all under the terms of the original repair order. Send a copy of the original repair order so that Mr. Cortez does not have to look it up. Tell him you can take the truck in for repairs on any Saturday, but it must be returned on the same day because you have no other transportation (unless they are willing to lend you a vehicle if they need more time to track down the problem).

## Indirect Adjustments

Apply the four steps of the message formulation process to indirect messages.
Plan, organize, compose, and evaluate indirect adjustments.

11. *Letter denying part of a customer's claim.* Reread exercise 9. You are now Margarita Romero, one of the owners of CompuService, a small shop that sells and services computers. The warranty for the computers you sell explicitly states that all repairs and alterations must be done by certified technicians during the nine-month warranty period. This fact appears in large, boldface type at the bottom of the warranty, on the wrapping for each computer component, and on the purchase order delivered with each computer.

    After reading the letter from Rachel Ward, accounting manager of Missouri Power Users, you investigated her claim that an employee was instructed by one of your technicians to attempt a personal repair of a malfunctioning machine. After speaking with five technicians, you discovered that Enrique Mendoza, a new technician, did tell Mr. Hughes how to access the hard disk manually. However, while replacing the hard disk that was malfunctioning, your technician also found that someone had apparently tampered with the circuits. One of the reasons this type of computer is so cheap is that the circuits are permanently soldered in place. They cannot be removed and replaced as circuits can be in some other computers. Removing the circuits causes permanent damage, requiring replacement of all the main circuitry.

    Write a letter to Ms. Ward, explaining to her that the $567.49 charge is for the new circuitry and that, while your technician was wrong to tell Mr. Hughes how to make his own temporary repairs on the hard disk, no one who is not certified by the computer manufacturer should have attempted to work with any other part of the computer. As a compromise, tell Ms. Ward that once the bill has been paid, you will extend the warranty for another nine months on the entire computer, not just on the circuitry, because of the misunderstanding and because of the excellent business relationship your two companies have established over the past five years.

Apply the four steps of the message formulation process to indirect messages.
Plan, organize, compose, and evaluate indirect adjustments.

12. *Letter responding to a citizen who wants to buy American.* Gerald Smith, a citizen in your community, wrote to the mayor and the city council complaining that city officials are irresponsible because they have been, in recent years, purchasing some Honda motorcycles for the police force. His

major arguments revolve around his belief that the economy would be much improved and everyone would have jobs if Americans and, in particular, government agencies always bought American products. He cites the fact that a General Motors assembly plant in your community closed down two years ago, leaving many people unemployed.

As assistant to the mayor, you have been instructed to prepare a response to Mr. Smith's letter for the mayor's signature. As you consider what to write, a number of thoughts run through your mind. You agree with his statements about the importance of keeping jobs in this country by buying American products. You know that the city purchases large numbers of computers, typewriters, and other equipment from firms that do not have their main offices in the United States. However, the city is required to get bids on large purchases, such as fleet purchases of automobiles and motorcycles. The bidding process requires the city to specify exactly what it needs and to accept the lowest bid for products that meet those specifications. In recent years, Honda has been the lowest bidder for motorcycles, and they have been the only bidder able to prove it can meet the specifications for reliability and lower repair costs. In addition, Harley-Davidson, the American motorcycle manufacturer Mr. Smith promotes in his letter, uses many parts that come from other countries in its motorcycles. Therefore, there are no completely American-made motorcycles. You also consider police personnel's safety of primary importance, and you are under the impression that most police officers consider the Honda to be a safer motorcycle.

You know that some cities require preference be given to American products and firms when purchasing items or contracting for services. However, such a proposal has never come before your city council for consideration. You decide to mention this as an alternative to Mr. Smith and to include a list of city council members' addresses and telephone numbers. To get a proposal such as this on the agenda for a meeting, Mr. Smith will have to get the sponsorship of one of the council members.

Send the letter to Mr. Smith at his business address: Sunset Corp., P.O. Box 1444, New Canton, IL 62356. He lists himself as chief executive officer of that corporation.

◣ Apply the four steps of the message formulation process to indirect messages.
◣ Plan, organize, compose, and evaluate indirect adjustments.

13. *Memo denying an employee's request for full reimbursement of expenses.* You are the finance manager for *Southwest Cycling,* a magazine for bicycle enthusiasts. You recently sent a photographer, Wesley Brickett, who had worked for you for eight months, to Washington, DC to cover a major bicycle race. While there, he was supposed to photograph the race and sell advertising for future issues of the magazine. Your company purchased his airline tickets and arranged for a rental car. Wesley was given a company credit card to pay for hotel accommodations during his one-week stay, but, following company policy, he was to pay for his own meals and would be reimbursed for the cost on his return. You and Wesley's supervisor told him before he left to keep expenses to a minimum.

You were surprised when Wesley returned and gave you credit card receipts totaling $3,675. Apparently, Wesley was not content with the usual inexpensive accommodations used by your employees, so he checked himself into rooms averaging $225 a night. He upgraded the economy car that had been reserved for him to the most expensive car the agency rented. In addition, Wesley requested reimbursement for meal receipts totaling $2,100 ($300 a day!). Unfortunately, Wesley brought back only $575 worth of advertising.

You and Wesley's supervisor met with the publisher of the magazine and the company's lawyer to discuss what to do about Wesley's request. Instead of firing him at this time, you decided to warn him that such behavior would not be tolerated in the future. In addition, you were instructed to write him a memo accompanying a check for $1,050, half the amount he requested for his meals. His supervisor, Lisa Spulanti, has already met with Wesley, so he knows how unhappy the company is with his performance. In all likelihood, he will never be allowed to travel alone again.

Write your memo, explaining why the check is for less than Wesley is expecting. Use the you attitude skillfully to see if you can inspire Wesley to mend his ways.

## Indirect Announcements

◼ Apply the four steps of the message formulation process to indirect messages.
◼ Plan, organize, compose, and evaluate indirect announcements.

14. *Form memo announcing 30 days off without pay.*  You are the personal assistant to Robert de Carelli, president of Pasta Magoo, a company that supplies pasta to restaurants in the southeastern part of the United States. Business has not been good for over a year now; more and more of the restaurants you supplied have gone out of business, because people seem to be eating out less often. In addition, your company has lost a large percentage of its marketing share to a new company that supplies a lower-quality product at a cheaper price than Pasta Magoo. Four months ago, you had to lay off one-third of your workforce (most of it in manufacturing and maintenance).

Now you find yourself with another unpleasant task. Mr. de Carelli has instructed you to compose a memo in his name to be given to all employees of the company. The memo should announce that all salaried employees, except you, Mr. de Carelli, and five salespeople, will be required to take 30 days off without pay during the next year, with a minimum of one or two days each month. Employees who wish to take more than the minimum in any one month may do so. All salaried employees must select the dates they will be taking off and must submit the dates to their supervisors by the end of this month. All employees paid by the hour will be cut back by approximately eight percent. Supervisors will be meeting with hourly employees individually to go over new work schedules.

This cost-saving measure will ensure that no more layoffs are necessary, at least for the time being. Most employees are aware of the downturn in business; however, this information is bound to be a shock to them, because it amounts to a large cut in total pay.

Mr. de Carelli has contacted two consultants associated with a local university who will conduct a study to determine how the company's products can be better marketed. The consultants will compare the sales and marketing strategies of other successful companies and suggest ways to improve Pasta Magoo's share of the market. While the study is being conducted, the five-member salesforce has been instructed to redouble its efforts to create new sales and recapture lost accounts. Assure your employees that as soon as business improves, everyone will return to full production status. Use the you attitude effectively to improve morale by showing your employees how this temporary slowdown will benefit them in the long run.

Write the memo to the first employee on your list, Martha Abraham. Once Mr. de Carelli has approved the memo, computer equipment will be used to print an individual memo addressed to each employee of the company.

◗ Apply the four steps of the message formulation process to indirect messages.
◗ Plan, organize, compose, and evaluate indirect announcements.

15. *Form letter increasing rent.*  You are the finance manager for a firm that just purchased several apartment buildings in Los Angeles. Los Angeles is a rent-control city, which means owners of rental units may not raise the price of rent more than 7 percent a year. Because the new owners are anxious to recoup some of their investment as soon as possible, you have been instructed to increase rents the maximum allowed by law. Your computer search has produced a file of 172 renters who have not had their rent raised within the last year.

Write a form letter to accompany a formal Notice to Change Terms of Tenancy agreement. The notice is actually a contract that the renter must sign and return to you within one month of the date of the letter, indicating that the renter intends to remain at the new rate. If you do not receive this form by that date, you will assume that the reader is vacating the apartment, and you will begin advertising it. Tell your reader the rent is being increased by the 7 percent allowed yearly by the city's rent-control ordinance. Specify the new amount of rent that will be charged each month commencing with the first day of the month (two months from the date of the letter). Your computer equipment will insert automatically the amount of the rent corresponding to each renter's name.

Of course, you hope your renters will remain with you instead of finding other housing because of the expense involved in getting an apartment ready for new renters. However, you are confident you will be able to rent any units that are vacated, because a comparative study shows the rents charged for apartments in your buildings are reasonable and are, in many cases, lower than those in surrounding buildings. In fact, the buildings owned by your company are superior in many ways to other apartments. Increased security has been added in recent months and maintenance costs have always been high because of the owners' commitment to their tenants, a commitment the new owner, CodeCo Enterprises, intends to continue.

Address the first form letter to Ms. Stephanie J. Shaevel, 1822 Purdue Avenue, Apt. 5, Los Angeles, CA 90025. The rent on her apartment will be $991. Don't forget to enclose the Notice to Change Terms of Tenancy form. Send the letters by certified mail so you will have proof that the renters actually received the correspondence.

▪ Apply the four steps of the message formulation process to indirect messages.
▪ Plan, organize, compose, and evaluate indirect announcements.

16. *Form letter announcing a price increase.* You are national sales manager of The Page Guitar Company. You must write a letter to your authorized dealers announcing a 10 percent increase in the price of your two most popular lines, the C. F. Page line and the Shenandoah line. This price increase is necessary because the prices charged you by your supplier have risen, and there is an ongoing shortage of high-quality wood. Without increasing prices, Page would be forced to lower its rigid quality standards. Because you have not changed the prices of your guitars in nearly two years, this increase does not seem unreasonable to you, but you are not sure what the reaction of your dealers will be.

    Tell your readers the price increase will take effect two months from the date of the letter, but the old prices will be honored for all orders received prior to that date if the instruments are in stock. Address the first letter to McCabe's Guitar Shop, 3101 Pike Boulevard, Cleveland, MN 56017.

## Indirect Collection Letters

▪ Apply the four steps of the message formulation process to indirect messages.
▪ Plan, organize, compose, and evaluate indirect collection letters.

17. *Formal reminder letter.* You are the accounts manager for *Southwest Cycling*, the bicycling magazine discussed in exercise 13. You are not happy with the poor results of your staff's collection efforts, which consist mostly of telephone calls and copies of overdue invoices sent to those who advertise in your magazine. Therefore, you are going to attempt to improve the success of the company's bill collection efforts by preparing form letters.

    Your first task is to design a stage 2 letter, a friendly letter that will be attached to a copy of the invoice. This letter will be sent eight weeks after an original invoice is mailed. By that time, recipients will have received the following: the original invoice, an invoice marked "Overdue" three weeks later, and a telephone call six weeks after the original invoice.

    Write a reminder letter that uses good motivational technique to convince readers to pay for the advertisements they placed in your magazine. Use effective resale because your ultimate hope is that each reader will not only pay the bill but will also continue to advertise in *Southwest Cycling*. Send the first letter to Marsha Adema, who owns E-Ticket Bicycles, a small bicycle shop in your community, at 427 Main Street.

▪ Apply the four steps of the message formulation process to indirect messages.
▪ Plan, organize, compose, and evaluate indirect collection letters.

18. *Discussion letter.* Reread exercise 17. You are still the accounts manager for *Southwest Cycling*. Your task now is to write a discussion stage letter for accounts that are 10 weeks overdue. Use good you attitude to get the reader to either send the money owed or tell you why she has not paid and when she will do so. Assume you are writing it to Marsha Adema, the individual mentioned in exercise 17.

# CHAPTER 9

# WRITING PERSUASIVE MESSAGES

## OBJECTIVES

When you finish studying this chapter, you should be able to:

- Determine when a persuasive organizational strategy is appropriate.
- Apply the four steps in the message formulation process to persuasive messages.
- Identify the features of a persuasive organizational strategy.
- Plan, organize, compose, and evaluate sales correspondence.
- Plan, organize, compose, and evaluate persuasive collection messages.
- Plan, organize, compose, and evaluate persuasive requests.

### WHAT WOULD YOU DO IF...?

**MONEY PLEASE!**    Caesar Caruso received a letter from Cotswold Enterprises attempting to collect on a bill that was 120 days overdue. The letter asked Caesar to pay the $672.44 due or explain why it had not been paid and state when it would be. Caesar had not paid the bill because his laser giftware business had not been doing well—he was spending 12 to 14 hours a day making sales calls, overseeing production, and doing the work of two employees he was forced to lay off. Although Caesar knew he owed the money, he could not pay it now. He hoped to pay all the company's bills as soon as business got better; however, he had no idea when that would be.

Caesar reacted angrily to the letter and responded by calling Cotswold Enterprises, a supplier with whom he had done business for several years. What Caesar needed was an extension of time to pay the bill. This is his side of the conversation with an accounting clerk:

> I can't believe you don't have anything better to do than harass a small operation like mine. Six hundred dollars is nothing to you; you must have hundreds of accounts 10 times the size of mine. Why don't you leave me alone? I'm an honest man; I always pay my bills. If you want to slap an interest charge on me, go right ahead! If you want to turn my account over to a collection agency, go ahead! I can easily find another supplier, so you won't be hearing from me again!

Venting his anger made Caesar feel better at first; however, as he calmed down, he began to wonder if he could have handled the situation in a better way, without showing his anger.

What do you think will be the consequences of Caesar's angry telephone call? Do you think Cotswold Enterprises will agree to let him pay the bill "as soon as possible?" As you read the following chapter, consider how Caesar's situation could have been handled better. Would you recommend a letter or a telephone call? What would be an appropriate organizational strategy for the message?

## USING THE PERSUASIVE STRATEGY

■ Determine when a persuasive organizational strategy is appropriate.

When a reader has little or no initial interest in the topic about which you are writing or speaking, you need an approach different from either the direct strategy or the indirect strategy—namely, the persuasive organizational strategy. Sales letters for magazines, fund-raising letters from charitable organizations to potential donors, and memos from union leaders encouraging members to vote in favor of a negotiated contract are examples of the kinds of situations that require the strategy discussed in this chapter. The persuasive strategy would also have been appropriate in Caesar Caruso's situation, because Cotswold Enterprises was probably uninterested in negotiating alternative terms. Caesar needed to convince them that working out a special payment plan would benefit them.

Before you read further, study the persuasive organizational strategy outlined in Exhibit 9.1, which is based on techniques used by effective salespeople. Anyone who has made a living by selling knows that a sale is seldom made to a buyer who is not interested in a product. If interest does not already exist, a good salesperson first gets the attention of customers and points out how a product will meet their needs. Once customers are interested in a product, the salesperson tries to encourage their desire to have the product and solidify that desire into conviction that the product will meet their needs. Finally, the salesperson suggests a specific action—buying the product. The persuasive pattern works well in many situations: selling products, services, and ideas, whether the sale is being made face-to-face, by telephone, or by mail.

■ Apply the four steps of the message formulation process to persuasive messages.

The act of writing persuasive correspondence proceeds through the same four stages used in formulating any other kind of business correspondence: planning, organizing, composing, and evaluating.

## PLANNING YOUR MESSAGE

Planning is just as important (or more so) when you write persuasive letters and memos as when you write direct or indirect messages. Inducing people to change their minds or to take some action that they had not even considered is very difficult. You must have a clear idea of what you want to accomplish and how your goals and the readers' interests might coincide. Planning is especially critical for expensive sales and fund-raising letters sent in mass mailings.

| | |
|---|---|
| **EXHIBIT 9.1** | **Persuasive Organizational Strategy** |

| | |
|---|---|
| First paragraph (or opening line at top of page) | Interest stage—Use a relevant attention-getting theme in the form of a statement or device, such as a picture, a sample, or a gimmick, that gets the reader's attention and encourages further reading. |
| Middle paragraphs | Make a logical transition between the opening lines or paragraph to the next paragraph, carrying through the theme established in the opening. When appropriate, use samples, testimonials, trial offers, statistics, and/or guarantees to prove the worth of the product, service, or idea. |
| | Desire stage—Use the you attitude to show the reader how your product or idea will benefit him or her personally. |
| | Conviction stage—Make the specific request clearly, using reader-benefit statements to convince the reader that he or she must (1) have the product or service, (2) do as you wish, or (3) agree with you. |
| Last paragraph | Action stage—Request the action the reader needs to perform next, making it as easy as possible. If appreciation is appropriate, tie it to future action; do not thank in advance. If it does not detract from the serious nature of the message, carry the theme established in the opening through to the end. |

## ESTABLISH YOUR PURPOSE

The purpose of most persuasive correspondence is easy to determine. For example, the purpose of a sales letter is, of course, to sell the product, service, or idea the letter is promoting. The purpose of a fund-raising letter is to prompt sympathetic readers to send a donation to the charitable organization. Other purposes for persuasive messages include the following:

- To persuade a customer to continue ordering from your company, despite an increase in prices.

- To persuade your subordinates to attend a job-related seminar on their own time or at their own expense.

- To convince the employees of your firm that a new management reorganization plan will positively affect operations.

- To convince retailers of the fairness of a new marketing policy that restricts their right to advertise your line of quality health care products.

- To persuade your employees to schedule, on their own time, a physical examination paid for by the company's medical benefit plan.

- To persuade a listener or reader to participate in a study you are conducting.

One of Caesar Caruso's problems in the vignette at the beginning of the chapter is that he did not carefully define his purpose before calling Cotswold Enterprises. He ended up venting his anger instead of arranging a manageable payment plan. In business communication, venting anger is not an acceptable purpose. Caesar could have avoided embarrassment by first writing down his angry thoughts to get them out of his system and then tearing up the paper. After that he could have logically planned a more effective message.

Persuasive messages often have more than one purpose. For example, a letter announcing a new marketing policy might be designed to both give the reader the information needed to understand the new policy and convince the reader the policy will enhance the product's image for consumers, resulting in additional sales. As you write, centering your thoughts on the central purpose(s) will help you design an effective message.

## Choose a Medium and Channel

As you consider the most appropriate medium and channel for your message, put yourself in your reader's position. Will the reader's reaction be affected by the form of the message? Some people are hard to reach or are irritated by unsolicited phone calls seeking to persuade them to do or buy something; a letter or memo would work better for them. In Caesar Caruso's case, a letter might have given him greater control over his emotions.

Should an oral message be delivered in person or by telephone to improve its effectiveness? Face-to-face communication offers more nonverbal feedback about the reaction your message is provoking, but a phone call is quicker and easier when the other person is not close by. If you must reach large numbers of people, can you afford individual messages to each person, or will a form letter or memo be more feasible?

The same techniques used to sell by mail can be used to telemarket products and services.

A channel unique to persuasive messages is **telemarketing.** Using the telephone to sell products and services, solicit donations, and collect overdue accounts has become a multimillion-dollar industry. Companies use large databases to get the names of thousands or millions of people to call. The same techniques recommended for written persuasive messages in this chapter can be used to sell by telephone or in person. You will also notice these strategies' similarities to those used by television, radio, and print advertisers.

## Consider Legal and Ethical Issues

The power to persuade (a power that can be learned) helps present information about products, services, and ideas to people who might have a need for them. Unfortunately, some people misuse this power by manipulating others into agreeing to do things that are not in their best interests. To be ethical, persuasive messages must be truthful, sincere, and fair to all concerned.

Many ethical and legal pitfalls await those who formulate sales messages. A major problem is the temptation to write sales letters that contain deceptive claims about the product. Deceptive claims include the following:

- *Irrelevant claims.* These claims are truthful but have nothing to do with the product being discussed. The hope is that people will connect the product with the claim. For example, what difference does it make that a celebrity drinks a certain soft drink or wears a certain brand of underwear? A person's choice of soft drink or underwear has nothing to do with his or her fame, and being a celebrity does not automatically make someone an expert on products such as these.

- *Advantage claims.* When you state the advantages of candidates, ideas, or products, make sure that they are genuine. For example, consider the following claim for a vitamin product. "Vita-Ro won't cause unsightly skin blemishes." This claim makes it seem as though other vitamins cause blemishes (which they do not). Even though the statement is technically truthful, the implication that other products cause blemishes is unethical. As another example, consider politicians who claim to be more in touch with the public than their rivals are because their childhoods were marked by poverty. What does being poor have to do with understanding people's needs? It is conceivable that someone who felt deprived as a child might become obsessed with material things and power as an adult. Such an upbringing might also make some people insecure as adults, less able to deal confidently with important people.

- *Voodoo claims.* Some sales messages refer, without scientific validation, to a mysterious ingredient or device that produces magic results—for example, facial creams containing fruit acids that make lines disappear in days and mentholated creams that provide "peace of mind" by mysteriously relieving headaches. If these products contained magic ingredients, would those ingredients be revealed? Intelligent people immediately dismiss voodoo claims as advertising hype and lose respect for the company and the writer using them.

- *Confusing claims.* Some claims seem to have merit but, upon examination, are contradictory. For example, claiming that manufactured cubic zirconias are "rare" might make them attractive; however, what does the word *rare* mean? The word certainly has nothing to do with any product that can be produced in quantity, like cubic zirconias. The temptation to use confusing claims is strong among those who believe that people hear what they want to hear. However, intelligent and educated people are likely to reject ideas backed by confusing claims.

**In sales correspondence, use plain language, avoid fine print, and explain technical terms.**

Consumers have the responsibility to critically analyze deceptive advertising for themselves. However, as previous chapters explained, consumers are protected by law from deceptive sales contracts. (Any communication is a contract if an offer or commitment has been made and something of value has been exchanged.) Sales offers must not conceal vital information, and technical terms must be fully explained. Anyone selling products and services by mail is advised to have an attorney check the language for possible illegalities, which vary from state to state.

You must, of course, avoid fraud—deliberately making a false statement to induce another party to give up something of value, or deliberately concealing information that must be revealed. However, only factual statements can be fraudulent. For example, consider this statement: "The Hitachi is the only television on the market that has an inset screen that allows you to have up to four channels on the screen at once." It is fraudulent because it is not true. However, this next statement is an opinion and value judgment and is, therefore, not fraudulent. "The Hitachi multiscreen system is the easiest to use and has the clearest reception of any television on the market."

Consumers are protected by law from deceptive sales practices. Fine print—the tiny, often hidden details sometimes seen at the ends of sales offers—may be interpreted by the courts as an attempt to conceal vital information a buyer needs to know. Technical terms must be fully explained, and many states require the use of plain language (words that may be understood by the average reader). Obfuscation—intentional misuse of language to confuse or to conceal—should never be employed when composing effective persuasive messages.

**Use of information about debtors or credit applicants is protected by law.**

The laws relating to credit and collections (briefly described in Chapter 8) apply to persuasive messages as well as indirect messages. Make sure you understand these laws before you write any letters relating to consumers' credit or debts.

People who owe money are also protected by The Fair Credit Billing Act of 1974. This act was written to protect consumers from unfair or inaccurate credit card practices. It requires creditors to respond to written complaints about bills within 30 days and to investigate and resolve complaints within 90 days. No interest may be charged on the amount in question until 10 days after the creditor has solved and answered the debtor's inquiry. Other stipulations of The Fair Credit Billing Act deal with timelines for closing an account, reporting information to credit-rating organizations, and collection procedures that can take place while a bill is being disputed.

When composing persuasive messages, the ethical/legal dimension should be foremost in your thoughts. Make sure every detail is accurate and fair. Include everything readers want and need to know in such a way that the meaning is clear.

## ANALYZE YOUR AUDIENCE

The persuasive strategy outlined in Exhibit 9.1 works because it requires writers to consider the needs of their readers. Persuasive writers know that their chances of achieving their goals increase significantly when they are specific about how a product, service, or idea meets the potential buyer's needs. Everything you learned about the you attitude in Chapter 4 will be useful to you in designing persuasive messages.

Learning to use Maslow's hierarchy of needs is an important first step in analyzing your audience, whether you are selling automobiles, convincing people to stop smoking, or informing stockholders of the benefits of closing a plant. However, even if you are already automatically considering the needs of your readers, to write persuasive messages you must be particularly sensitive to how your readers will benefit from what you are proposing. For example, consider the various reasons people select certain types of cars:

- *Safety needs.* Large, solidly built cars that might serve as barriers in an accident, cars with powerful engines that allow one to get out of dangerous situations quickly, cars with anti-lock brakes that will not skid when applied suddenly and forcefully, basic transportation that is more reliable than public transportation (might allow one to keep a job rather than having to depend on unreliable public transportation).

- *Belonging needs.* Cars like those one's peer group or colleagues are driving.

- *Esteem needs.* Powerful sports cars and luxury cars that most people cannot afford, unusual cars others will admire because of their uniqueness.

- *Self-actualization needs.* Cars that, because of their uniqueness, provide a challenge to the owner (e.g., cars that are unusually fun to drive or cars that require mastery of a complex pattern of gear shifting), cars that symbolize to you alone that you have "made it" (e.g., if your successful mother drove a Cadillac, you might aspire to a Cadillac as an indicator to yourself that you have finally achieved the same level of business success), economy cars that conserve gas and are, therefore, better for the environment, alternative fuel vehicles that make the United States less dependent on foreign oil.

In most cases, it would not be practical or effective to send persuasive letters to, for example, everyone who wants to buy a car or to every address in a

Narrow your list of recipients down to those most likely to buy your product, service, or idea, and investigate their needs thoroughly.

city. Thus, mail advertisers try to narrow the list of recipients to those whose needs are most likely to be met by buying the product. Advertisers can either buy or compile lists of people who have indicated, through prior purchases, that they are predisposed to certain products. Persuasive messages sent to those people are more likely to produce sales than messages sent to people who have never purchased related products. Associations, such as the Association for Business Communication, often compile and sell directories of their members' names and addresses. Such lists are useful in determining who, for example, should receive sales information about new business communication textbooks. Chambers of commerce are a common place to learn about businesses within cities, and city directories available in most libraries can be useful to find information about people who live within a given city. Lists can also be purchased from other companies that communicate with customers by mail, or from companies that specialize in compiling mailing lists.

The more you know about your readers, the more successful your persuasive writing will be. Therefore, a large part of the budget for many companies is spent trying to determine what potential buyers need and want. Secondary sources also provide useful information about potential buyers. Exhibit 9.2 reveals some of the information available from one of these sources, SRI International. SRI has categorized people into eight groups based on lifestyles, attitudes and values, and demographic characteristics such as gender, age, and education. This information helps those who advertise in the newspaper to develop effective advertising.

Demographic data about the employees of your company might also be available. Companies usually keep records of the percentage of employees who fall into various racial groups, the number of females and males, and the average salaries in each job classification. Check with your human resources department to determine what type of information is available, and use this information to analyze the readers of your in-house persuasive messages. For example, if you must write a memo persuading employees to donate their time tutoring students of a nearby elementary school, it would be useful to know how many employees live in the area served by the school. If a lot of staff members live in the area, your sales appeal might emphasize how they can help the children in their own neighborhoods (belonging needs). If most of your employees live outside the elementary school area, you might decide to emphasize esteem and self-actualization needs in addition to pointing out clearly how a company and its employees are an essential part of the surrounding community (belonging needs).

Learn as much as you can about your intended readers. If you can discover the needs that make them act, you will be more successful at convincing them to do what you want them to do. Selling products and services will be easier, and you will also improve your ability to motivate co-workers, superiors, and subordinates.

## GATHER NECESSARY RESOURCES

You are already aware of the importance of gathering ahead of time all the information and materials necessary to write a letter or memo. This time-saving recommendation is equally important when you write any kind of persuasive message.

**EXHIBIT 9.2**    **Demographic Information**

## ACHIEVERS

—**21.0%** of all
U.S. adults
—**22.7%** of adults
in the Greater
Los Angeles
Area
—**23.6%** of Sunday
Los Angeles Times
adult readership

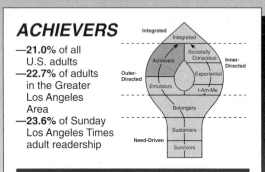

—The leaders in business, the professions
and government
—Competent, self reliant and efficient
—Materialistic, hard working, oriented to fame
and success, comfort loving
—Have created the economic system in
response to the American dream
—The defender of the economic status quo
—Traditional consumers, also willing to
experiment with new technologically based
products
—The leaders in establishing norms and
fashions
—Support top-of-the-line markets, including
luxury and gift items, the "new and
improved"

### DEMOGRAPHICS (U.S. Adults)

| | |
|---|---|
| Female | 42.3% |
| Median Age (Years) | 42.3 |
| Median Household Income | $43,584 |
| Graduated College | 25.1% |
| Professional, Manager | 32.1% |
| Married | 81.2% |
| Caucasian | 94.1% |

## BELONGERS

—**38.0%** of all
U.S. adults
—**27.4%** of adults
in the Greater
Los Angeles
Area
—**17.5%** of Sunday
Los Angeles Times
adult readership

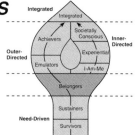

—The large, solid and comfortable middle
class
—Main stabilizers of society and preservers of
the moral status quo
—Conservative, conventional, nostalgic, senti-
mental, puritanical, conforming
—Key drive is to fit in; adhere to the rules
—Family, church, home and tradition are
important
—Prefer traditional over "new and improved"
products

### DEMOGRAPHICS (U.S. Adults)

| | |
|---|---|
| Female | 58.1% |
| Median Age (Years) | 56.7 |
| Median Household Income | $17,762 |
| Graduated College | 3.2% |
| Professional, Manager | 1.0% |
| Married | 70.9% |
| Caucasian | 89.2% |

Source: Excerpts are from VALS (Values and Lifestyles). SRI International, Menlo Park, CA. Illustrated are two of the eight types of people who fit into four major lifestyles. This pamphlet is intended to help advertisers develop their marketing strategies and to define their customers. Reprinted by permission.

**Collaborative writing teams
should consist of experts
knowledgeable of the potential
customers, the product or
service, and the competition.**

Collaborative writing teams are an essential resource in developing effective sales messages. Economically, it makes sense to use a group to analyze potential readers and compose sales messages that appeal to the needs of different kinds of people. The more diverse your collaborative writing team is, the more likely your letters and memos will appeal to a diverse readership. An ideal collaborative writing team consists of people who have expert knowledge of the product, the customer, and the competition.

## ORGANIZING YOUR MESSAGE

You have already studied the arrangement of direct and indirect messages. Therefore, you will recognize immediately the major differences between the strategies for those messages and the persuasive strategy outlined in Exhibit 9.1. The reader's interest in the topic of your message and the reader's probable reaction to your message are the primary factors in determining how your message should be organized.

### FREEWRITE MAJOR POINTS

At this stage, do not concern yourself with designing an eye-catching or attention-getting campaign. Just write down as fast as you can all the things that need to be said in your persuasive message. No matter how illogical or silly some of your initial points (or those of your partners in a collaborative writing group) may be, do not pass judgment on anything during the freewriting stage. Resist any attempt to place the items in a particular order, just put down your thoughts as fast as they come to mind.

As with direct and indirect messages, it helps to have the purpose of the message at the top of the page before you begin freewriting. With the purpose in front of you, you will find it easier to stick to the topic.

### CHOOSE AN ORGANIZATIONAL STRATEGY: THE PERSUASIVE STRATEGY

Identify the features of a persuasive organizational strategy.

Think about the number of persuasive sales letters that cross your path in a week's time. How many of them do you actually read? If you are like most of the recipients of the more than 65 billion pieces of direct mail sent annually in the United States, you probably throw away most sales letters without opening them. What is it about those you don't throw away that gets you to open the envelope and read what is inside? Chances are that those letters do a good job of attracting your attention and piquing your interest. They make you want the product (desire) and convince you that you must have it (conviction). Finally, they tell you exactly what to do to get the product (action). Persuasive collection messages and persuasive requests follow the same sequence.

Read the sample letter presented in Exhibit 9.3. Notice how the words and the organizational strategy work together to lead the reader through the interest, desire, conviction, and action stages.

You should use a persuasive strategy only when you can answer "Yes" to this question: Is the reader likely to have little or no initial interest in your message? This is the question that Caesar Caruso should have asked himself before he called Cotswold Enterprises. The accounting clerk he talked to was not initially interested in arranging an alternative payment plan, much less interested in knowing how Caesar felt. The clerk was only interested in hearing that the payment was on its way.

Consider whether a persuasive strategy should be used in each of the following situations. Cover up the answers until you have made your decision.

Situation 1: You must write a letter convincing a prominent liberal politician to speak free of charge to your conservative business group.

> Use a persuasive organizational strategy only when a reader is likely to have little, if any, initial interest in your product, service, or idea.

*T H E*
*A m e r i c a n*
**H O M E**
*B u i l d e r*

862 Meridian St
Indianapolis, IN
FH: 317.281.1427
FAX:317.286.0855

*Interest is piqued by the attention-getting cartoon theme that is used throughout the letter.*

*If you want the answer, ask Beall.*

January 12, 1995

Dear Mr. Beall:

With a subscription to *The American Home Builder*, you will have the answers to the hundreds of questions that come up when you are building anything—whether you are planning a new home, remodeling a room, or building a new desk.

*The answers theme is used in the transition to the next stage.*

*The Latest and the Best* is a monthly feature highlighting the newest and most innovative products for use in your home. Products planned for upcoming months include everything from built-in electronic home entertainment centers to kitchen sinks.

*Desire is generated through you-oriented statements that show the reader how the magazine will benefit him.*

Knowing about new products isn't enough, however, so we also tell you how to install them. To provide everything you need to know to get the job done, the upcoming April issue includes information about the most burglar-proof security system available today as well as in-depth diagrams and step-by-step installation instructions. It also includes information to enable you to easily modify these instructions to install any security system no matter the cost.

*Conviction relies on reader-benefit statements linked to a specific request to purchase.*

You don't need a security system? Perhaps a new Japanese soaking tub or a Swedish sauna would be more to your liking. Sending in the attached order form today will ensure that you receive the March issue, containing full-color instructions for selecting and installing these wonderful additions to your life style. You may be surprised how little space they require and how easy they are for one person to install with very few tools.

Whether you are updating your writing, remodeling a closet, or starting from scratch on a new home, you will find step-by-step guidelines, informative tidbits, detailed diagrams, and expert advice in *The American Home Builder*.

**EXHIBIT 9.3**

**Continued**

Mr. Beall         2         January 12, 1995

Read the enclosed copy of a recent article to see how useful AHB will be to you. By subscribing today, you can find the answers to all your building needs. Send in the enclosed order form to make sure you receive the next issue.

Sincerely,

*Frank G. Hammer*

Frank G. Hammer
Editor in Chief

*The action the reader should perform to get the product is specified and made easy. A sample of the product is provided. The answers theme ends the message.*

If you want the answer, ask Beall.
862 Meridian St
Indianapolis, IN
FH: 317.281.1427
FAX:317.286.0855

*The cartoon on the envelope should encourage the reader to open the envelope.*

**Yes, I want to have the answers.** Sign me up for:

*Puchase of the product is made as easy and as financially painless as possible. The theme is continued to the end.*

_____ 2 years ($82.50—*a $12 savings*)

_____ 1 year ($47.40)

Payment instructions:

_____ Bill me in 3 monthly installments.

_____ Check for full amount enclosed.

_____ Bill my charge card:    MasterCard No. _____

                           Visa No. _____

                   Expiration Date _____

                          Signature _____

Answer: A persuasive strategy would increase the likelihood that this individual would agree to speak to a group that is unsympathetic to him or her on many issues.

Situation 2: You must write a letter to your dental patients informing them you are moving your office to a location 10 miles away from its current site.

Answer: A persuasive strategy would not be appropriate, because most patients would be interested in a message from their dentist. You may want to use elements of persuasion to convince your readers that your services are worth driving 10 miles for, but you do not need the kind of dramatic opening statement used in persuasive messages.

Situation 3: You are composing an application letter for a job that was advertised in a professional publication.

Answer: A persuasive strategy is not needed; an attention-getting opening statement would not be appropriate. Because the job was advertised, the reader will be interested in reading letters from job applicants.

Situation 4: You must write a memo urging employees to donate money to the United Way, a charitable organization.

Answer: A persuasive strategy might get their attention long enough for you to persuade them to give up some of their hard-earned money to help others less fortunate than themselves.

Once you have determined that a persuasive strategy is appropriate, follow the pattern presented in Exhibit 9.1 as you organize your freewritten notes into a coherent message.

## COMPOSING YOUR MESSAGE

*Persuasive messages can appeal to emotions or to reason.*

Effective persuasive messages are organized to propel the reader through four stages: interest, desire, conviction, and action. In addition, effective persuasive messages have a theme. The theme can either appeal to the emotions, as in a sad story about an orphan intended to solicit donations to a charity, or to reason, as in a campaign to convince assembly-line workers to better their chances of job success by improving their reading skills. Notice in Exhibit 9.3 how the four stages are centered around a rational theme—answers—that runs throughout the message.

*Devise a theme or central appeal for your message.*

Devising a theme, the central appeal, is a key task in developing a direct mail sales campaign. Much time and money are usually expended to make sure the appeal is innovative and will be interesting to potential customers. Even if you have not been trained in advertising and marketing, you can use your imagination and sense of fun to develop persuasive themes. Collaborative writing groups are particularly helpful at this stage, because groups are usually able to generate more ideas. Once these ideas are put forth, they may be discussed and evaluated for their appeal to the intended readers.

The following statements might help you find good themes:

- "The needs my product, service, or idea will satisfy are . . . "
- "The most dramatic statement I can make about the product or idea is . . . "

- "The most challenging question I can ask readers to get them thinking about each feature or benefit is . . . "
- "The best visual illustration of each of these features and benefits is . . . "
- "The most interesting story that will glamorize each of these features and benefits is . . . "

Some complex sales campaigns use all of these statements to prompt new ideas, although most sales messages focus on one or two. Completing these statements for your product or idea will help you compose interesting messages that are more likely to achieve results.

Here are some examples of persuasive themes, expressed in the openings of letters:

For a new computer, a message accompanied by an official-looking seal of quality. "One company just redefined how computer quality is measured. It goes further than the lab, further than the warranty period."

For a resort, a message that appears to be a personal party invitation (centered several lines below the statement was a line with the reader's name):"If your name appears below, you are cordially invited to play on the golf course selected for this year's Master's competition."

For a security system, a message followed by a photograph of a burglar breaking into a house: "Someone may be collecting in your area soon. Do you have any unwanted stereos, VCRs, computers, or expensive jewelry?"

For a boat show: "The most affordable time to take possession of your new sailboat or motor yacht is Friday, October 25, or Saturday, October 26 . . . and the most opportune place to make your deal is at the Harbor Boat Show."

For a new soft drink, a message accompanied by a photograph of a very large, sweaty football celebrity quenching his thirst after a hard workout. "When you have a thirst this big . . . "

For a hospital, a message accompanying a dramatic, heartrending statement of a parent (pictured with the child) whose child's life was saved by the hospital's superior physicians and facilities: "When you need them, they'll be there for you, too."

The following sections explain some of the special requirements of the types of persuasive messages most often used in the business world: sales correspondence, persuasive collection letters, and persuasive requests. The examples show how theory can be translated into effective persuasive messages.

## SALES CORRESPONDENCE

Plan, organize, compose, and evaluate sales correspondence.

Of all business messages, sales messages require the greatest creative skills. If you have an imagination, understand human nature, and possess a sense of fun and drama, you will enjoy writing letters and promotional literature that sell products and services. Even if you have never had an opportunity to test these abilities before, you may discover, like many students, that you have what it takes to write innovative, persuasive sales messages.

Refer to Chapter 10 for more ideas about visual aids that might be used to add interest to sales messages.

You can learn a great deal by studying the direct mail messages you receive. Which envelopes do you open? Which letters do you read? If you don't read three- and four-page sales letters, don't compose lengthy letters of your own. Ask the same questions of others. Can you find anyone who actually reads letters that are longer than one or two pages? If you are like most people, you probably resent it when you have to hunt for the price of a direct mail product. Does it make you feel as though the seller is hiding the price because there is something negative about it? Are you as tired as most people of the same old phrases, such as "Free gift," "Don't miss out," and "Limited-time offer"? Common sense would tell you, then, to keep sales messages short, concise, and original and to make the price and terms of payment straightforward and clear. If you follow this advice, your sales correspondence will be more successful than the hundreds of letters you throw away every year.

Use good you attitude to interest your reader.

**FIRST PARAGRAPH: INTEREST.**   Once you have devised a theme, use it to grab the reader's attention at the beginning of the message. If you fail to get the reader's interest, your letter will probably be ignored.

For sales messages, the theme is often printed on the envelope to entice readers into opening the envelope (see Exhibit 9.3). Piquing interest with the envelope increases the likelihood that readers will open it and read the message inside. Avoid phrases such as the following, however; people have seen them so often that they no longer motivate:

> "Dated material—open immediately."
>
> "Urgent message."
>
> "Mailogram."
>
> "Official document enclosed."
>
> "Western Union Transmittal! Open Immediately!"

Be sure to choose a central appeal that is relevant to the product, idea, or service discussed in your message. Irrelevant appeals can get a reader's attention for a short time, but as soon as the reader discovers that the appeal is not directly related to the topic of the message, he or she will feel cheated and toss the message in the trash can. Avoid irrelevant attention getters like the following:

> "**SEX!**
> Now that we have your attention, you might be interested in knowing about the savings you can receive this week at Wilson Tires."

> "Congratulations! You won the enclosed pen as the result of a drawing we conducted of all our past customers.
> Because the cost of postage is so high, we want to take advantage of this opportunity to also invite you to come in once again to see our new showroom models."

> **News Flash!**—What president of a Fortune 1000 company has been charged with insider trading?
> Fortunately, not Megan Fishbeck, president of Harper Enterprises, your investment counseling experts."

Continue the central appeal from the beginning of the document to the end.

Once you have decided on a relevant theme and developed an attention getter that will generate interest in your product or idea, compose a message that uses the theme from beginning to end. A central theme leads readers through the message, almost like a story that readers feel compelled to finish.

Smoothly link the opening appeal to the rest of the message.

**MIDDLE PARAGRAPHS: DESIRE AND CONVICTION.**   Making a smooth transition from the opening appeal to the middle paragraphs is one of the most important parts of a sales message. To draw your readers into your persuasive campaign and maintain their level of interest, you must lead them through the letter with skillful use of words and logic. Read the first sentence following the opening statement of each of the letters presented in this chapter. These demonstrate how you can tie the opening appeal into the rest of the message.

After reading the positive examples in each of the exhibits, read the following examples of poor transitions:

For a new computer, a message accompanied by an official-looking seal of quality: "One company just redefined how computer quality is measured. It goes further than the lab, further than the warranty period."

Poor transition: "If your company is like most companies, you have probably purchased many different kinds of computers, and you have probably had to endure thousands of complaints from users who are dissatisfied with their machines."

Analysis: The appeal to quality that goes beyond the lab and the warranty period are not included in any way in the transition; therefore, the reader is likely to lose the interest generated by the opening theme.

Better transition: "The Koreus II went six months against the IPC and the MacDougall and outperformed them in a real-world test. Twenty-five users were asked to . . . "

For a resort, a message that appears to be a personal party invitation (centered several lines below the statement was a line with the reader's name): "If your name appears below, you are cordially invited to play on the golf course selected for this year's Master's competition."

Poor transition: "When the pressures of life get to you, when you need time for yourself—only Rocky Beach will satisfy."

Analysis: The transition does not carry through the invitation theme used in the opening.

Better transition: "This is your personal invitation to take advantage of all Rocky Beach has to offer. See for yourself how . . . "

For a security system, a message followed by a photograph of a burglar breaking into a house: "Someone may be collecting in your area soon. Do you have any unwanted stereos, VCRs, computers, or expensive jewelry?"

Poor transition: "AlarmTek is the symbol of security found in front of more than 50,000 homes in New Jersey."

Analysis: This paragraph is not a transition because it introduces an idea that has nothing to do with the opening appeal.

Better transition: "Install an AlarmTek Security System now, and keep your family's valuables from going to an unworthy cause."

The desire and conviction stages show readers how the product or service will benefit them personally.

Once you have composed an effective transition, build desire for the product or service. You can do this by pointing out to readers how they will benefit if they purchase your products or hire your company to perform services for them. Everything you have learned about the you attitude can be put to good use. Your audience analysis will also be helpful.

Goal of the desire stage: "I want this product."

In addition to an explanation of benefits, many people expect to see proof of your product's quality. You can offer proofs like these to substantiate your claims:

Sample (the product itself, sample of work done for other customers).

Statistics (test results, user satisfaction surveys).

Testimonial (statement from a celebrity or a user of the product).

Guarantee (replacement or repair for a specific period).

Trial offer (full refund within a certain period or subscription cancellation).

Limited-time offer (extra discount for a certain time).

These forms of proof appeal to the reader's reason.

Goal of the conviction stage: "I *must* have this product."

There is no visible dividing line between the desire and conviction stages of a sales letter. Your goal is to provide enough reader-benefit statements to eventually convince the reader that he or she must have what you are selling.

**LAST PARAGRAPH: ACTION.**   Once your message has generated conviction, you can make your specific request. Statements such as the following gently push the reader into purchasing the product or service:

"By ordering your copy of Edit 5.0 today, you will . . . "

"Just say 'Yes,' and your first copy of *Business Monthly* will be shipped directly to you."

"Telephone 1-800-555-348 today to find out how you can have access to the finest legal minds, available for just pennies a day."

Prompt your reader to act immediately, and make it easy for him or her to get your product or service.

Even if you asked the reader to order in previous paragraphs, it is important to make one final request in the last paragraph. You want to persuade the reader to order the product or service before he or she does anything else. Many people buy on impulse and will forget about the product if they don't order it immediately.

Make it as easy as possible for your reader to order your product or service. If possible, don't make the reader send money right away; people always think twice when they have to write out a check. Many people prefer to pay by credit card, but it is also good to accept checks and to offer the option of being billed in monthly installments. Return-reply envelopes with prepaid postage do not require the reader to hunt for postage stamps, and 800-numbers allow readers to telephone an order in without having to pay for the long distance call. Successful direct mail advertisers use wording like the following in the final paragraph:

"Send no money now. You will be billed in three easy installments of $19.95."

"To receive your Wonder Widget, just place a checkmark in the appropriate box on the reply envelope enclosed."

"Please send or call in your order now while you're still thinking about it."

"Please write the Super Sales dates on your calendar now."

*Don't end with presumptuous or negative statements.*

As you learned when you studied direct and indirect messages, you should not thank a potential customer in advance. No one likes to be taken for granted, and it is particularly unwise when that person is in the process of deciding whether or not to buy your product. Ineffective statements such as the following should never be used in direct mail sales messages:

"Thank you for your order."

"Thank you again for sending in your enrollment form and for making the decision to try Charter Membership in the Library. I promise it's one you will not regret."

"Your spending your valuable time to read this message is appreciated."

It is equally important that you do now show doubt when making the request. Avoid using negative words that threaten readers or remind them that some products do not live up to their expectations. The following kinds of ineffective statements should be avoided:

"If you would like to order . . . "

"You won't regret ordering a . . . "

"I hope you see how useful a Wonder Widget would be."

Use the theme to wrap up the letter in the final paragraph. In this chapter's exhibits, you will see that the central appeal leads the reader through the entire letter. Here is an appropriate theme-oriented ending to the letter about the security system:

"Don't let someone else decide when you'd be better off without your stereos, VCRs, computers, and jewelry. Send in the enclosed card today to arrange for a security check of your home by an expert personal security consultant."

If you use your creative skills and the advice presented within this section, you can produce sales messages that get results. Take care not to duplicate the mistakes so many direct mail marketers make.

## PERSUASIVE COLLECTION MESSAGES

Plan, organize, compose, and evaluate persuasive collection messages.
Chapter 8 described the five stages of the collection series: (1) informal reminder, (2) formal reminder, (3) discussion, (4) persuasion, and (5) action. A persuasive strategy can be used to write effective third- and fourth-stage collection messages. Stage 3, the discussion stage, consists of one or more friendly, concerned messages urging the reader to tell you why he or she has not paid the invoice. Stage 4, the persuasive stage typically includes only one letter. It consists of a final appeal to the reader to pay before the account is turned over to a collection agency or an attorney.

Before you read the rest of this section, take a moment to read Exhibits 9.4 and 9.5. The margin notes included with these figures indicate how persuasive strategy, positive tone, and effective you attitude combine to present logical, motivating collection letters.

AUBREY

Office Machine Inc.

*The unusual format of the letter is an attention getter (interest stage).*

June 30, 1995

Dr. Marion H. Krekorian
Krekorian Medical Services
167 North Broadway, Suite 212
Laguna Beach, FL 32413

Dear Dr. Krekorian:

### Every story has two sides

**Here's Our Side of the Story:**                    **Now Please Tell Us Your Side:**

As the enclosed statement indicates, your Account No. 2423 is now long overdue.

*Be specific about all the contacts that have been made before continuing the story theme.*

Over four months have passed since the last monthly payment for copier maintenance was received. You also received reminders and telephone calls in February, March, April, and May. However, we have heard nothing. No payment. No explanation.

Is something wrong? If so, please tell us your side of the story in the space at the right. If there is something we can do to serve you better, or to make payment on this

3131 W. Ocean Dr.

Palm Bay, FL 56740

PH: 305.345.6756

FAX: 305.345.7665

**EXHIBIT 9.4**

**Continued**

*The continuous-page heading is often omitted in form letters.*

account easier, let me know. I am also available if you would prefer to handle this personally. Just call; I'm available to meet with you by telephone or in person.

Otherwise, just attach your check and return it with your statement in the enclosed envelope.

*Incorporate the request with the benefit to the reader of performing the action.*

Your payment will allow us once again to honor our part of the enclosed service agreement, which you and I signed last year. It will also ensure that your Canyon 230 receives the complex maintenance it requires to meet your high-volume copying needs.

*Prompt action by setting a date. Continue using the theme.*

Please let us hear from you by July 10. Your side of the story matters to us.

Sincerely,

Bill Shuman

Bill Shuman
Sales Manager

*Make action easy by providing the information the reader needs (the statement) and a return envelope.*

Enclosures (2)

P.S. If you've already mailed your payment, thank you very much. You will be contacted soon to determine the monthly maintenance schedule that best suits you.

*Add a thank you in case he recently mailed a payment.*

AUBREY

Office Machine Inc.

May 18, 1995

*The cartoon is used as an attention getter (interest stage).*

We've looked everywhere for your check.
Could it still be in your checkbook?

Dr. Marion H. Krekorian
Krekorian Medical Services
167 North Broadway, Suite 212
Laguna Beach, FL 32413

Dear Dr. Krekorian

*The theme is continued in the first paragraph.*   No, no check today. Every day we search and search and search for your check, confident that it will arrive.

So far, our records show that no checks have been received on Account 24-490S since November. Nevertheless, since you agreed to pay $52.70 plus parts and toner for monthly maintenance of your copier, we are sure the overdue payments have probably just been an oversight. That is why we wanted to contact you one more time to give you a chance to clear up this matter before other means must be taken to collect.

*The theme works as a transition to a reminder of what the reader agreed to do and how he has benefited from the product and the service (desire stage). The next step (collection action) is mentioned tactfully to ensure that the reader keeps reading.*

As you probably remember, when our agreement was signed, the maintenance amount was based on the 1,500 copies each month you estimated. Even though your Canyon 230 has been registering nearly 2,500 copies each month, the monthly maintenance fee has not been raised. In fact, we are proud of your copier and are happy to service it. Even though the Canyon 230 is best known in the industry for high-quality production of a limited number of copies, for you it has performed like a much more expensive, high-powered copier.

To better assist you, our technicians have always responded to your calls for additional assistance within 24 hours. On one occasion, Nelson Scudder was there less than one hour after your secretary made the

*A drive for conviction is accompanied by the request.*

3131 W. Ocean Dr.
Palm Bay, FL 56740
PH: 305.345.6756
FAX: 305.345.7665

EXHIBIT
9.5

Continued

Dr. Marion H. Krekorian
Page 2
May 18, 1995

call! This is the kind of service you will continue to receive once you
have brought your account up to date.

Dr. Krekorian, please remove a check from your checkbook, make it
out for $368.90 (seven months' maintenance), and send it today. Your
payment must be received by July 10 to prevent stronger collection
efforts. This is not a step we want to take with a valued customer; but
without your payment, there is no other option available to us.

Sincerely yours

*Ivan O. Won*

Ivan O. Won, Clerk
Accounts Receivable

*Striving for conviction, the letter states
more specifically the action the reader must
perform as well as the consequences of not
acting. The checkbook theme is continued.*

P.S. If your check crosses this letter in the mail, thank you.

*An expression of
appreciation is
included in case
the check was
sent recently.*

Have you ever considered why people don't pay their bills? The reasons why are many and varied:

- They forget to pay the bill or overlook it.
- They do not now and will probably never have the money.
- They do not have the money but intend to pay as soon as possible.
- They cannot pay the full amount but could pay a little at a time; however, they do not know how to approach you to suggest such an arrangement or are not aware such an alternative might be available.
- They feel the price, service, or the product purchased was unsatisfactory and are protesting by withholding payment.
- There is a misunderstanding surrounding the details of the sale.
- Your invoice did not reach them or is erroneous.
- From the moment they bought the product or service, they intended to commit fraud by not paying for it.

Most customers do not intend to defraud. If most people did have this intention, businesses would have to demand cash on delivery. Fortunately, most people are honest and intend to pay for what they buy or contract.

The prime asset in writing collection letters is a positive outlook, because your goal is to prompt payment of the debt while maintaining a favorable relationship among you, your company, and the reader.

> To establish a positive tone in your persuasive collection letters, it is necessary for you to believe that most people are basically honest and want to be fair.

**FIRST PARAGRAPH: INTEREST.** You can use the same techniques in persuasive collection letters that you use in all persuasive communication to gain the attention of the reader. However, there is a major difference between collection letters and sales letters. Because you have already done business with the reader and have probably sent several bills before writing discussion stage or persuasive stage letters, the reader is familiar with your name and the negative subject you wish to discuss. Therefore, some recipients might not even open the envelope.

There are many ways you can use collection letter envelopes to gain attention. Some companies believe addressing an envelope by hand without a return address increases the likelihood the reader will open the envelope, thinking what is inside might be a personal instead of business letter. If you use this idea, continue the handwriting theme on the inside or explain it is a friendly attempt to reach the client (see Exhibit 9.6). If you do not, the handwritten letter is likely to elicit a negative reaction from a disappointed reader.

You may also choose to include a printed message or cartoon on the envelope to get the attention of the reader. If you use such a device, however, continue the theme in the letter. For example, if your envelope has a sketch of a finger with a string tied around it, the drawing might be repeated at the top of the letter with a statement such as, "Sooner or later we all forget something." The cartoon in Exhibit 9.5 could also be used on the envelope. However, instead of completing the full caption, these words alone might appear on the envelope: "We've looked everywhere . . . " If readers become curious about the cartoon and what it is about, they might open the envelope.

Here are some examples of attention-getting envelope statements:

| EXHIBIT 9.6 | **Opening for a Handwritten Collection Letter** |
|---|---|

*We know a handwritten business letter is somewhat unusual. However, it is one way to show you how sincere we are in wanting to maintain the friendly business relationship we have both benefited from.*

"Discount coupon enclosed."

Caution: Use this only if the first thing you announce in the letter is a discount coupon good on the customer's next order once the customer's account becomes current.

"This Is Your Life!"

Caution: Use this only if the first thing you mention in the letter is the old television show "This Is Your Life!" and tie it into a discussion of what is happening in the reader's life that has caused him or her to get behind on payments.

"Your personal invitation is enclosed!"

Caution: Use this when the attention getter in the letter is a personal invitation for the reader and the writer to sit down together to discuss the circumstances surrounding the debt and, possibly, an easier way for the debtor to pay it off.

Remember that the attention getter you use on the envelope establishes a theme that must be used throughout the letter.

Of course, the envelope of a collection letter does not have to contain an attention-getting device. Using envelopes to gain attention depends on the situation and a firm's image of itself. For example, it is hard to imagine a prestigious law firm that would be comfortable using this sort of sales-oriented tactic to get clients to open an envelope. If the account is owed by anyone other than a very small company or an individual, you can probably depend on your correspondence being opened and read (if your letter is well written) without a special envelope. However, if your client or customer is an individual not representing a company, envelope devices can be effective.

As you determine a theme for your collection message, consider its purpose. In the discussion stage, your purpose is to continue a business relationship and prompt either full payment of the overdue amount or, if that is not possible, a discussion with the debtor concerning reasons for the delay. In the end, both parties might agree on an alternative plan to pay off the debt (e.g., smaller payments made over a longer period of time). In the persuasive stage, your purpose is to obtain full payment of the overdue amount because all previous attempts at discussion have failed. Of course, an equally desirable purpose would be both parties committing to continue their business relationship despite the late payment.

Can you determine which of the following would be appropriate opening statements for collection letters? Cover the answers as you consider the effectiveness of each statement.

> Opening 1: "Overdue Account No. 2748-B."
>
> Answer: This is not an effective opening because it is negative. The reader knows the bill is overdue because of previous correspondence, and he or she is not likely to read further.
>
> Opening 2: "Final payment urged."
>
> Answer: Like the first example, this statement is too negative.
>
> Opening 3: "Your business is important to us."
>
> Answer: If what follows is well written, this opening might disarm a reader who is expecting the usual negative collection letter. It might help the reader see that you want to continue doing business.
>
> Opening 4 (accompanied by a drawing of a runner in track shoes and shorts, running a race, with sweat beading into the air around him or her): "Life can be a race sometimes, can't it? . . . a rat race . . . a race to succeed . . . a race to the finish line . . . a race to keep up with the competition . . . "
>
> Answer: As long as this theme is followed through to a final appeal to call "time out" long enough to pay the bill, this could be an effective attention-getting opening.

Using a persuasive strategy to create interest at the beginning of a third- or fourth-stage collection letter is a good way to convince a reader that your message merits further reading. Without an interesting opening, it is not likely that debtors will want to read about what they already know and would prefer to avoid—they owe you money. Because all other correspondence about the

**Goals of a discussion stage letter: immediate payment or discussion of the reasons for the delay with a specific commitment to pay, accompanied by continuance of a good business relationship.**

**Goals of a persuasive stage letter: immediate payment in full and continuance of a good business relationship.**

debt to this point has been direct or indirect, the uniqueness of the persuasive strategy increases your chances of getting the reader to read what follows.

**MIDDLE PARAGRAPHS: DESIRE AND CONVICTION.** In the middle paragraphs of persuasive collection letters, attempt first to create a desire in your reader to pay the money owed. After creating that desire, convince your reader to either pay the bill or contact you to discuss the matter.

Before you can engender desire and conviction, however, you must provide a transition from the interesting opening lines into the rest of your message. Abrupt changes in thought can cause the reader to lose interest and discontinue reading your letter. Imagine how disjointed the letter in Exhibit 9.5 would seem if the attention-getter was followed immediately by "Please let us know why your bill has not been paid."

Just as you can create desire for products and services in sales messages, you can create desire to pay a debt with skillful use of the you attitude. Tell your reader how he or she will benefit from paying for the goods or services received. It is sometimes effective to remind a reader of the benefits he or she has already received from the product or how well the product is thought of in the industry. Stressing the reliability of the company succeeds, in some circumstances, in convincing debtors to maintain their association with the company by honoring their debts. If you understand the reader's motivations, you can also use Maslow's hierarchy of needs to develop an effective appeal:

- Physiological needs—the need for creditworthiness necessary to have money for food and drink.
- Safety needs—the need to qualify for credit to provide for other needs.
- Belonging needs—the need to be accepted by others as fair; the need to provide for loved ones.
- Esteem needs—the fear of the reader's losing the admiration of those important to him or her.
- Self-actualization needs—the personal satisfaction of living up to one's obligations.

*Avoid lecturing to or threatening the reader.*

Appealing to needs is more likely to convince your reader to take action than making threats will. Threats run the risk of turning the reader angry. For example, the lecturing tone of this remark is sure to anger a reader: "People with honor take pride in saying 'I always pay my bills.' " Although the following threat might result in the bill being paid, the reader is not likely to want to continue to do business with a company that sends this sort of message: "No payment on your account, a bad credit rating. It's that simple. Pay your bill if you want to maintain your positive credit standing."

In a discussion stage letter, you can ask the reader to telephone you, or contact you by mail or in person, to discuss the bill. Be specific about which of these options is acceptable to you. In most instances, you will eventually be able to obtain the money owed if you can get the debtor to acknowledge that he or she does owe you money and then to specify when the debt will be paid in full or the amount and the dates of payments.

Some credit-granting companies have strict policies to guide their employees in renegotiating payment terms; others allow a great deal of latitude. Some companies can afford to renegotiate liberal repayment terms; others must demand immediate payment of the full amount plus interest. If you are not sure of your company's policies, check with your supervisor to determine how much authority you have to renegotiate loan provisions.

**Last Paragraph: Action.**   The last paragraph of a persuasive collection letter should urge immediate action. Whether the letter is in the discussion stage or the persuasive stage, request payment of the full amount in the last paragraph. In a discussion stage letter, you must also tell the reader whether to write to you or telephone. Referring to the opening theme (if it doesn't seem too light hearted) can help give the message a friendlier tone.

The following examples would be good closing paragraphs for persuasive collection letters:

> "Please send in your check for the full amount today to ensure that you receive the latest spring catalog, a unique opportunity to view the latest designer fashions in the comfort of your own store. It's the closest thing you can get to a fashion show without strolling down the runway yourself!" (assuming the opening theme dealt with fashion shows).

> "Please send a check for $2,114.87 today to bring your account up to date. However, if that is not possible, please send one-half ($1,057.44) the amount owed today and return this letter with a note on the bottom indicating when you will be sending the remainder. Please specify a date between now and February 28 when we may expect to mark your account paid in full."

> "Please, Mr. Winfrey, rush full payment of your account today; or tell us in the space below what we can do to make it easier for you to pay this account. We want to work with you to ensure a long, mutually satisfying business relationship. Your reply by January 13 would be appreciated."

Because there is a possibility the bill might have been paid by the time your letter reaches the recipient, many companies add postscripts like those at the bottom of Exhibits 9.4 and 9.5. A note like the following is appreciated by those who have recently paid a bill: "If you have sent your check since the date of this letter, thank you. Your business and continued goodwill are important to us." Without such a statement, a reader who has already made the payment might react angrily to receiving another letter.

## Persuasive Requests

▶ Plan, organize, compose, and evaluate persuasive requests.

**A written request should follow the persuasive pattern when you believe the reader has little initial interest in granting your request.**

Persuasive requests include all the other types of memos and letters intended to persuade others to agree with you or to do what you want them to do. For example, a memo to your boss requesting the opportunity to attend a conference during a busy time or a memo requesting additional staff would both require a persuasive approach. Another example is a letter requesting acceptance into a top-notch graduate business program or a letter requesting a scholarship. Caesar Caruso's response to Cotswold Enterprises' collection message could also have been a persuasive request. Using the persuasive strategy in situations like these might increase both the reader's interest in your request and your chances of getting what you want.

Many business messages include persuasion, but persuasive requests have one distinguishing feature—an attention-getting opening. For example, a persuasive organizational strategy might not be appropriate for some job application letters such as for an executive or professional position. A cartoon or a dramatic statement such as the following would seem unprofessional: "Have you looked everywhere for a good project engineer? Well, look no more. I'm the person for the job."

Before writing a persuasive request, follow all the usual steps in planning and organizing your message. Once you have written the purpose(s) at the top of the page and have freewritten the major points as they occur to you, you are ready to use the persuasive strategy discussed in this chapter to compose the message. Take a moment to read the example in Exhibit 9.7, paying close attention to the comments in the margins. Notice how the principles of good you attitude work together with the persuasive strategy to create interest, desire, conviction, and action.

**FIRST PARAGRAPH: INTEREST.**  As with all other types of persuasive messages, begin your persuasive request with a relevant statement or device to get the attention of the reader. To understand the effect of an attention getter, put yourself in the place of an employee receiving the memo in Exhibit 9.7. If you are like most people, you are probably used to dry, uninteresting memos that impart nothing but information. The unusual beginning of the Rose Carver memo increases the chance that you might take time from your busy day to read it.

Evaluate the following openings for persuasive requests. While you read each example, cover up the answer. After you have determined your answer for each one, see how closely your answer matches.

Purpose 1: To convince a reluctant boss to invest in new computers because of the loss of productivity caused by out-of-date equipment.

Opening: "No, dear, I can't make it home for the children's holiday program. Our computers went off line again today, and we're already two days behind. Unfortunately, telephone calls such as this are becoming commonplace around here at closing time. Over the last two months, the computers have gone off line seven times, resulting in order delays, inventory errors, and customer loss."

Answer: As long as the writer concentrates on the benefits of the change to the company and does not dwell on the problems the computers have caused him or her personally, this could be an effective way of getting your boss's attention.

Purpose 2: To persuade those who hold season tickets to a light opera series to donate funds to help the theater company cover the full cost of performances.

Opening: "A life with music is a life filled with magic. Joyous musical performances, actors and musicians at their best—that's what's in store for you as a season ticket holder of the Granville Civic Light Opera. This year you will become part of the magic as you enjoy *Barnum, Phantom of the Opera, Carousel,* and *Hello Dolly*."

Answer: This opening might get the attention of some readers who are pleased with the organization; however, because it doesn't get to the point

**EXHIBIT 9.7**

**Persuasive Request (Memo)**

**Washington Hardware Corp.**
611 Ridge Rd • Thorton, WA 62213 • 206.312.5552

TO:

FROM:     Darrell Clemmensen, President

DATE:     August 23, 1995

SUBJECT:  *Why don't they do something?*

The subject line and the story work together to create interest.

Eight-year-old Rose Carver stares blankly out her window with tears in her eyes, crying for her sister Stefani. Stefani, her beautiful, bubbly little tag-along, was killed last Wednesday in another random shooting. Another family grieves, and the rest of us wonder why *they* don't do something to stop these senseless acts of violence.

Does it seem to you, as it does to me, that heart-tugging stories such as this are occuring almost daily? When we hear something often enough, it becomes easier and easier as time goes by to ignore its impact on our own lives. **After all, these things only happen to other people, don't they?**

The you attitude is used to show how the story relates to readers and to create a desire to help.

Every so often something happens, however, that shatters this perception and makes us realize the part we are meant to play in these stories. For those of us at Washington Hardware, that revelation comes in the form of the sad story of Rose and Stefani.

Rose and Stefani are the granddaughters of Philip Carver, a maintenance supervisor who has worked for 32 years for Washington. As Philip walked home from work last week, he was one of the first to arrive on the crime scene. Little Stefani was killed as she played in her front yard on Wilson Street, only two blocks from the front entrance to our main office.

It is time for *them* to do something. The *they* we often speak of is not a nebulous overburdened and underfunded government agency; it is you, and it is me. We are the concerned citizens who must act to curb the violence encroaching on our lives.

**EXHIBIT 9.7**    Continued

(Name of recipient)
Page 2
August 23, 1995

That is why Washington Hardware is joining together with the Hillside YMCA to sponsor a program of activities aimed at getting young people off the streets. It is modeled after a successful program in St. Louis and will play on the eagerness of teens to compete and to pursue their personal areas of interest. It will include sports activities of all kinds (basketball free-throw competitions, tournaments, tennis matches, soccer games, card games, etc.) as well as programs designed to teach job-related skills in an innovative way. Arts and crafts classes and shows, child care classes, and keyboarding and software sessions are only a few of the activities our $600,000 donation will help to fund.

"Help" is the critical word here. Six hundred thousand dollars donated in memory of Stefani Carver will provide only half the money needed to offer enough interesting and useful activities to keep kids off the street and away from the pervasive reach of gangs.

*This is where you come in...*

*The reader is motivated to want to help through an explanation of how participating will benefit him or her and is shown what he or she can do to help.*

Your help is needed. Money, of course, is always useful; however, even more critical than money are your time and your expertise. May I include your name and office telephone number in a bulletin of volunteers available to help these kids? Before you put this memo down, don't say this:

> *I can't do anything; they wouldn't want me.*

**Yes, we do need you.** Think for a moment. Have you ever shot a basketball? Do you have a tennis racket? Do you play a musical instrument of any kind? Did you ever learn to sew? Do you know how to type a memo or set up a spreadsheet formula? Can you use a hammer and a saw? Can you sketch cartoons or paint a house? Do you play pool, jog, or do aerobics to keep in shape? Do you cook? Can you give advice about interviewing to teenagers? Do you have children of your own?

These are only a few of the skills these kids are interested in learning. The YMCA activity organizers will use the booklet of volunteers to call you when you are needed. You alone will determine if, when, and how

EXHIBIT
9.7

Concluded

(Name of recipient)
Page 3
August 23, 1995

many hours you dedicate to the program. However, between now and December 31, <u>for every hour you dedicate to the Hillside YMCA as a volunteer, you will earn one hour of additional vacation time.</u> Volunteers and contributors will also be featured in our monthly newsletter, *The Inside Outer.*

As you have probably figured out, we have an ulterior motive in being so generous in rewarding employee participation. We believe that, once you take an active part in this worthwhile program, you will become hooked on the deep feeling of satisfaction that comes from working with these wonderful young people. Imagine how much happier Rose's life would be if she could share it with little Stefani. Your active participation in just one activity might make such a difference for another child.

Please let me list your name along with mine in the volunteer's bulletin. Just complete the enclosed questionnaire today telling us how you will be able to participate in the program. **Together, we can do something!**

Enclosure

*The action the reader must perform is specified. The theme established at the beginning finishes the message.*

sooner, there is a danger some ticket holders might assume this is just another sales letter urging the general public to buy season tickets. (If the reader already has tickets, why read further?)

Effective opening statements and paragraphs should create interest in your idea. To create interest, the part of your message must contain good you attitude. Maslow's hierarchy of needs can be used to determine the appeals most likely to make your readers react favorably to your request.

**MIDDLE PARAGRAPHS: DESIRE AND CONVICTION.**   As you move from the opening of the message to the middle paragraphs, double-check to see that the transition is relevant. Read again the third and fourth paragraphs of the memo in Exhibit 9.7. The fourth paragraph is the beginning of the stage intended to make the reader want to do something about gang violence. The transition comes in the form of repeating the names of the girls discussed in the story. The reader is then shown how the story of these girls affects the reader's own life.

If the third paragraph of Exhibit 9.7 read as follows, the attention getter and the rest of the message would not be effectively linked:

> Washington Hardware is joining together with the Hillside YMCA to sponsor
> a program of activities aimed at getting young people off the streets. It is
> modeled . . .

This paragraph is ineffective, because it does not immediately show readers how the information that follows relates to the story in which they have become engrossed.

Building desire and conviction is the same for persuasive requests as for sales messages and collection letters. The better your ability to determine what motivates a person to act, the better you will be at getting people to do what you want them to do.

**LAST PARAGRAPH: ACTION.**   In the final paragraph, repeat courteously what it is you want the reader to do next, and make that request easy to comply with. If you want the reader to fill out a questionnaire, make it short and simple, with boxes to check off or spaces for very short responses. If you need authorization for a new computer, include a completed purchase order that requires only the reader's signature.

You may show appreciation tied to the action you want the reader to perform, but remember not to thank the reader in advance. Statements such as these work well in the final paragraph of persuasive requests:

> "Your completing this questionnaire today would be appreciated."

> "Because the results must be reported soon, your filling out and returning this questionnaire in the enclosed envelope by February 11 would be greatly appreciated."

> "Your signature on the attached purchase order will be more than appreciated by all of us in the production services department."

Finally, return to the theme you established at the beginning of your persuasive request. Notice how the last paragraph of Exhibit 9.7 correlates with the subject line of the memo. Simple devices such as this help the reader assimilate the information and the request. They almost force the reader to mentally review the interest, desire, conviction, and action stages of the message.

Goal of the action stage: to persuade the reader to do whatever it is you want him or her to do next (this should be relatively easy for the reader to do).

## EVALUATING YOUR MESSAGE

Once you have planned, organized, and composed your persuasive message, evaluate it in two stages: before mailing and after mailing. If your message was written collaboratively, it should be evaluated by all members of the writing team.

The first evaluation should take place before you mail the message. Use the evaluation checklist in Exhibit 9.8 to assess the opening and closing, the message itself, tone, mechanics, readability, and format and appearance. Pay special consideration to the ethical and legal content of your persuasive message. With the high stakes involved, there is great temptation to act unethically. Is your message truthful, and does it contain everything the reader wants and needs to know to make an informed decision? Is the message and the way the points are expressed open and clear, with no attempt to hide meaning behind doublespeak? Have you been fair to everyone involved in the situation?

The second evaluation of a persuasive message should occur after it is mailed. A major test of a message's persuasiveness is reader response. Did the reader order your product? How would you know if an increase in business was due to advertising, letters, or nebulous factors such as word of mouth or unique packaging? Most companies recognize how hard it is to assess which of its advertising components are working. Some try to overcome the problem by using different post office box numbers to identify the source of a customer's information. For example, a reply card in a magazine advertisement might list P.O. Box 234, and a sales letter for the same product might specify P.O. Box 235. Creative ideas such as this can help you measure the effectiveness of your various sales messages.

The success of other types of persuasive messages is more easily measured. Did your boss approve the purchase of the computer you requested? Did the reader pay off the overdue account? With collection letters, however, it is also helpful to keep statistics on any form letter that is used repeatedly. Over time, you will be able to tell which letters bring results. Because continuation of a business relationship and goodwill are also goals of persuasive collection messages, a company should keep track of the number of continuing customers and clients.

## DISCUSSION QUESTIONS

■ Determine when a persuasive organizational strategy is appropriate.

1. How does the reader's likely reaction determine when a persuasive strategy should be used instead of a direct or indirect strategy?

■ Apply the four steps in the message formulation process to persuasive messages.

■ Plan, organize, compose, and evaluate sales correspondence.

2. Identify a product or service you might be able to sell, and identify appropriate purpose statements for a sales letter for it.

**EXHIBIT 9.8**

**Checklist for Persuasive Messages**

Answer the following yes/no questions. (A "no" answer indicates room for improvement.) Some of the points do not apply to all types of messages. If a point does not apply, put n/a (not applicable) in the blank.

## ■ Opening and Closing

___ Is the attention-getting statement, question, visual illustration, or story relevant to the situation?
___ Is it likely to get the attention of the reader?
___ Does the attention getter encourage the reader to keep reading?
___ Does the attention getter and/or the first paragraph lead naturally and logically to the next paragraph?
___ Are pertinent order numbers, account numbers, amounts, dates, etc., mentioned?
___ Is effective you attitude used in the opening paragraph?
___ Are negative references to the situation avoided in the opening and closing paragraphs?
___ Is goodwill in the closing relevant to the situation?
___ Does the closing paragraph avoid trite, overused words and phrases?
___ Does the closing paragraph inform the reader politely of what he or she should do next?
___ Does the closing avoid thanking the reader in advance?
___ In the closing, is gratitude tied to any action the reader should perform?
___ Is the action the reader should perform next specified in the final paragraph?
___ Is the action the reader must perform made as easy as possible?
___ Was the theme used in the closing paragraph?

## ■ Message

___ Were reasons given in positive terms?
___ Did you stress how your product or what you want the reader to do or think benefits him or her?
___ For collection messages, is the message clear but diplomatic?
___ Have you disclosed clearly and completely everything that should be communicated?
___ Does the message achieve the purpose(s) established during freewriting?
___ If pertinent, have details of previous contact or correspondence been summarized?
___ Will the quality of your arguments, conclusions, generalizations, and assumptions stand up to scrutiny?
___ Did you avoid negative words?
___ Did you use resale when appropriate to establish confidence in your products, services, or company?
___ Did you mention anything that will be enclosed with the correspondence?
___ If pertinent, did you tell the reader clearly what you have done and what you will do?
___ Were statistics, testimonials, guarantees, trial offers, and/or limited time offers used to create desire, conviction, and action?
___ For collection letters, did you avoid blaming anyone?

___ For discussion stage collection letters, did you communicate clearly both options (i.e., payment and/or discussion of the problem)?

## ■ Tone

___ Is goodwill sincere and appropriate to the situation?
___ Has the reader been treated with courtesy and respect?
___ Did you avoid overuse of *I, me, my, our, we,* and the company name?
___ Did you emphasize *you* and *your* and the reader's needs?

## ■ Mechanics

___ Are the name and title of the reader spelled and used correctly?
___ Have all words been spelled correctly?
___ Is correct sentence structure used for all sentences?
___ Is correct paragraph structure used for all paragraphs?
___ Are there transitions between each paragraph?
___ Is punctuation correct?

## ■ Readability

___ Is the reading level appropriate for intended reader(s)?
___ Are lists used when necessary to improve the clarity of complex information or questions?

## ■ Format and Appearance

___ Is the format one of those recommended in the textbook?
___ If appropriate, has reader reaction to a form message been considered?
___ Are side margins equal?
___ Are corrections undetectable?
___ Has the letter or memorandum been folded correctly?
___ Is your signature readable?

## ■ Other

___ Is the entire message truthful?
___ Have you been fair to all concerned?
___ Would you be proud if everyone you know were aware of all the details of this transaction?
___ Is your communication within the bounds of the law?
___ Have you collaborated with appropriate individuals?
___ Did you reply promptly?
___ Have deliberate distortions, slang, discriminatory language, clichés, redundancies, roundabout expressions, and confusing foreign expressions been avoided?
___ Did you analyze the reader and his or her needs thoroughly?
___ If pertinent, are duplicate statements and other supporting material enclosed, and are they mentioned in the letter?

■ Apply the four steps in the message formulation process to persuasive messages.
■ Plan, organize, compose, and evaluate sales correspondence.

3. Identify an idea you would like to persuade someone else to agree with. Then specify purpose statements for a letter promoting your idea.

■ Apply the four steps in the message formulation process to persuasive messages.
■ Plan, organize, compose, and evaluate persuasive requests.

4. Identify a request you might like to make that would require a persuasive strategy. Then specify purpose statements for a letter or memo making the request.

■ Apply the four steps in the message formulation process to persuasive messages.
■ Plan, organize, compose, and evaluate persuasive requests.

5. Read the following paragraphs of a persuasive request. Evaluate the message using the checklist in Exhibit 9.8. Identify at least four points this message violates.

The just-in-time policy you instituted last year has reduced productivity in my department. Without an inventory of raw materials readily at hand, my people are often forced to shut down the line while we wait for a delivery truck. By the time the materials finally arrive, it is very difficult to motivate my employees to get back to work.

Please consider making changes that will allow us to have at least a minimum amount of raw materials in the warehouse to get us through these down periods when deliveries are late.

■ Identify the features of a persuasive organizational strategy.

6. In your own words, describe the difference between the desire and conviction stages of a persuasive message.

■ Identify the features of a persuasive organizational strategy.
■ Plan, organize, compose, and evaluate persuasive collection messages.

7. From the following openings for persuasive collection messages, choose the one that is best:
   a. "Your account, No. 2437-B12, is overdue. Please send $412.88 today to bring your account up to date."
   b. (Accompanied by a sketch of a computer) "Hello, I am the computer. As yet, no one but me knows Acct. No. 2437-B12 is overdue. However, if I do not receive a payment from you by February 14, the humans are bound to discover soon that it is overdue."

■ Identify the features of a persuasive organizational strategy.
■ Plan, organize, compose, and evaluate persuasive collection messages.

8. Choose the best closing for the messages in question 7:
   a. "Without an immediate payment, your account will be turned over to a collection agency."

  *b.* "Please send in your check today or by February 14 at the latest. I'm only a computer, and I won't be able to hold off the humans much longer."

▸Identify the features of a persuasive organizational strategy.
▸Plan, organize, compose, and evaluate persuasive requests.

9. Evaluate the following requests made to a business communication teacher. Which one has the best you attitude?
   *a.* "Please send a copy of the study you presented at the Association for Business Communication conference in Phoenix."
   *b.* "Please use the enclosed stamped envelope to send a copy of the bibliography on male and female communication styles discussed in your informative article in *The Forum*. With this bibliography, two eager graduate students will be able to continue your important groundbreaking research."

▸Identify the features of a persuasive organizational strategy.
▸Plan, organize, compose, and evaluate persuasive requests.

10. Evaluate the following justification for a request made by a paralegal who wants permission to work four 10-hour days instead of five 8-hour days. Which one has the best you attitude?
    *a.* "Longer hours would enable me to spend longer periods of time researching and preparing cases for you. Currently, valuable time is lost each morning rereading and reviewing what was done the day before and what still needs to be done."
    *b.* "Working four 10-hour days makes sense. I would be working the same amount of time and would be helping to decrease congestion on the freeway."

▸Plan, organize, compose, and evaluate sales correspondence.
▸Plan, organize, compose, and evaluate persuasive collection messages.
▸Plan, organize, compose, and evaluate persuasive requests.

11. How could you make use of statistics, testimonials, guarantees, trial offers, and limited-time offers in sales messages? In persuasive collection letters? In persuasive requests?

## APPLICATION EXERCISES

▸Determine when a persuasive organizational strategy is appropriate.

1. Analyze the following situations to determine when a persuasive strategy would be appropriate. Next to each "yes/no" answer, predict what the reader's initial reaction to the subject of the message would be. In some cases, there might be more than one possible initial reaction. If so, how would this change your decision about the type of strategy that would be most appropriate?
   *a.* A form letter selling memberships in a new health club.
   *b.* A letter to a customer who is 10 days overdue in paying his bill.

c. A memo to seven co-workers inviting them to join a professional organization of which you are an officer.

d. A memo from a vice president to division managers announcing a change of time in the weekly meeting.

e. A letter report from a consultant to the individual who contracted for her services. The letter announces a delay in the completion date of the study conducted by the consultant.

f. A letter to a customer who is 60 days overdue in paying her bill. An indirect letter and two telephone calls resulted in the debtor committing to make a partial payment seven days ago; however, no payment has yet been received.

g. A second request to convince your boss to send you to a two-day seminar to learn the software program you have been attempting unsuccessfully to use for the past three months. You feel you have been unable to learn anything more than the basics of the program because of the constant pressure of work to be completed and all the interruptions that are a part of your job. Because no one else in your organization knows the program, you have had to spend hours on the telephone consulting the free hotline specialist.

🔖 Apply the four steps in the message formulation process to persuasive messages.

2. In this chapter, you were advised to complete the following statements to develop themes for sales messages:

- "The most dramatic statement I can make about the product or idea is . . . "
- "The most challenging question I can ask my reader to set him or her thinking about each feature or benefit is . . . "
- "The best visual illustration of each of these features and benefits is . . . "
- "The most interesting story that will glamorize each of these features and benefits is . . . "

   a. Select a product or service now on the market and write a letter to your professor describing it. Complete the preceding statements for the product or service. For each statement, include a paragraph or two evaluating its chances for success in a sales letter.

   b. Pretend you work for the company that sells the product or service you chose (give yourself an appropriate title). To your boss, write a memo specifying the theme that might be used for advertising by mail. Recommend and justify the one attention getter you believe would bring about the highest number of sales.

🔖 Apply the four steps in the message formulation process to persuasive messages.
🔖 Identify the features of a persuasive organizational strategy.
🔖 Plan, organize, compose, and evaluate sales correspondence.
🔖 Plan, organize, compose, and evaluate persuasive collection messages.
🔖 Plan, organize, compose, and evaluate persuasive requests.

3. Select a sales letter, collection letter, or persuasive request you have received recently or that your company uses. Use Exhibit 9.8 to evaluate that message.

    *a.* Write a one-page memo to your professor discussing the message's good points and the major changes you would make if you were to rewrite it. Be specific in your evaluation, highlighting passages that exemplify the points you are making. Attach the evaluation form and letter to the memo you turn in to your professor.

    *b.* Write a memo report with recommendations for changing the letter to the person who, as part of a collaborative writing team, composed it. The team has sent the message to you and five other people, asking for your assessment of the message before it is actually mailed. Make positive recommendations for changing the message to increase its chances of succeeding.

    *c.* Rewrite the message so it incorporates the changes you recommend.

🔲 Apply the four steps of the message formulation process to persuasive messages.

🔲 Identify the features of a persuasive organizational strategy.

🔲 Plan, organize, compose, and evaluate sales correspondence.

4. Think of a new product idea or identify a product now on the market that could be used in a new way or that could be improved significantly. Imagine yourself as the sales manager for the company that makes the product. You are responsible for composing and sending form letters to sell the product by mail. Your task is to write a memo report to your supervisor about the approach you intend to take in the sales letter. These are the topics you should cover in your memo:

    *a.* For the product you choose, how would you complete the statements listed in exercise 2? Use the principles you have learned in this chapter to justify each of the statements; one or two paragraphs for each statements should be sufficient.

    *b.* What type of people are most likely to purchase this product? How will you find the names and addresses of those who should receive a sales letter?

    *c.* What kinds of samples, statistics, testimonials, guarantees, trial offers, and limited-time offers might be used to sell your product? Discuss the advantages and disadvantages of each of these items.

    *d.* How will you evaluate the success of the letter after it has been mailed?

🔲 Apply the four steps in the message formulation process to persuasive messages.

🔲 Plan, organize, compose, and evaluate sales correspondence.

5. Select a sales letter you have received in the mail. Apply the evaluation criteria in Exhibit 9.8 to the letter and write a short memo about your findings. Then rewrite the letter with the purpose(s) at the top of it. Turn in the original letter, the evaluation memo, and the revised letter.

🔲 Identify the features of a persuasive organizational strategy.

6. Evaluate whether the following openings are appropriate for persuasive messages. State what is wrong with those that are not appropriate.

    *a.* "Please send your $27.89 payment on Account No. 76690 today to prevent further legal action."

       *b.* "At this time of year, you should be able to gaze out your front window at the camellias that are just starting to bloom.

          "After carefully studying your wishes and local conditions, our professional staff of landscapers planned and planted your garden with the greatest care to ensure you would be able to enjoy color all year long."

       *c.* "**The very day you came to work at Eckman Industries, you began to make a difference.** You see, whether you realize it or not, your very presence affects the lives of the people who work here and the customers so important to our business."

▌Identify the features of a persuasive organizational strategy.

   7. Evaluate whether the following closings are appropriate for persuasive messages. State what is wrong with those that are not appropriate.

       *a.* From the letter begun in exercise 6c: "There are several ways you can make a difference by contributing to United Way. Please take the time to read the enclosed information and to complete the form, indicating whether you prefer to make your contribution by check or by automatic payroll deduction."

       *b.* From a letter accompanying a survey conducted by a marketing research firm: "Feel free to call me at (319) 589-2806 if you have any questions regarding this survey. I appreciate your time and professional cooperation and look forward to receiving your response."

       *c.* From a discussion stage collection letter: "Please send us today a check and your explanation, Ms. Grecinian. Your reasons and your suggestions for settlement will be carefully considered."

For the remaining exercises, you are to compose a letter or memo as instructed. Assume any reasonable details to make the messages realistic. Unless a job title is specified for you, make up one that is appropriate to the situation. As you do the exercises, follow these steps:

   1. Plan your message:
       *a.* Establish your purpose.
       *b.* Choose a medium and channel.
       *c.* Consider legal and ethical issues.
       *d.* Analyze your audience.
       *e.* Gather necessary resources.

   2. Organize your message:
       *a.* Freewrite major points.
       *b.* Choose an organizational strategy.

   3. Compose your message.

   4. Evaluate your message:
       *a.* Use Exhibit 9.8 for self-evaluation.
       *b.* Evaluate feedback from your instructor.

Your instructor will tell you whether to turn in your freewritten notes or any other evidence that you have performed each step of the message formulation process. You will also be told whether the message must be written individually or collaboratively.

### Sales Correspondence

- Apply the four steps in the message formulation process to persuasive messages.
- Plan, organize, compose, and evaluate sales correspondence.

8. *Sales letter for an innovative product.* For the product you chose in exercise 4, write a sales letter that incorporates your decisions and the principles described in this chapter. Address the letter to the first person on your mailing list.

- Apply the four steps in the message formulation process to persuasive messages.
- Plan, organize, compose, and evaluate sales correspondence.

9. *Sales letter promoting your services.* Choose a service for which you have been paid or for which you believe you could be paid. Identify the most likely customers of that service, and then write a sales letter that incorporates the principles described in the chapter and in Exhibit 9.8. Address the letter to someone who might actually be interested in purchasing these services.

- Apply the four steps in the message formulation process to persuasive messages.
- Plan, organize, compose, and evaluate sales correspondence.

10. *Sales letter promoting an idea.* You are the local director for a cause you believe in (your choice). Your goal is to find sympathetic people in the area who will volunteer or make a donation. Compose a letter that will achieve your goals.

### Persuasive Collection Messages

- Apply the four steps in the message formulation process to persuasive messages.
- Plan, organize, compose, and evaluate persuasive collection messages.

11. *Collection letter for the persuasion stage.* You are the new collections coordinator for a small company that has not been having much luck collecting its overdue accounts. The following letter has been used as a model for the persuasion stage. Referring to the criteria listed in Exhibit 9.8, rewrite the letter so it will be a more effective model.

Re: Collection Notice on Acct. No. 30089555462

Dear Ms. Ratzke:

**THIRD NOTICE!!!**

This is the third notice you have received demanding payment on the above account. Your account, which stands at $657.22, is now 60 days overdue.

My last notice to you asked you to send partial payment and an explanation; however, you still have not responded.

What will get you to respond? Do I have to send this account to a collection agency to get the money? Your failure to respond leads me to believe this is probably the only course of action I can follow. After all, we have to pay our bills too. Times are tough for everyone, yet we do not expect our creditors to carry us while we get our act together!

Please, Ms. Ratzke, only you can make the third notice the last notice. We want to continue doing business with you, but unless you soon write a check in full payment of this account, that will be impossible.

🔲 Apply the four steps in the message formulation process to persuasive messages.
🔲 Plan, organize, compose, and evaluate persuasive collection messages.

12. *Form letter using persuasion for the discussion stage of collections.* You are the accounts manager for *Southwest Cycling*, a bicycle magazine. As part of your effort to improve collections of overdue advertising accounts, you are formulating a series of collection letters.

Your task now is to compose a persuasive letter that will be used in the discussion stage. It will be sent to any advertiser with a bill that has gone unpaid for four months. Such accounts should already have received the original invoice, an invoice marked "Overdue" 3 weeks later, a telephone call 6 weeks after the original invoice, a reminder letter sent 8 weeks after the original invoice, and a discussion stage letter (using an indirect strategy) sent 10 weeks after the original invoice.

Make sure your persuasive discussion stage letter uses an attention-getting opening. The letter will be individualized, with names, addresses, account numbers, and balances to be inserted automatically. For now, however, address the letter to Mrs. Doris Christopher, Owner, Energy Cycles, 1510 East Westridge, Chattanooga TN 37402 (Account No. 77DC08, $142.35 balance, plus $15 in finance charges and penalties).

🔲 Apply the four steps in the message formulation process to persuasive messages.
🔲 Plan, organize, compose, and evaluate persuasive collection messages.

13. *Form letter for the persuasive stage of collections.* As the accounts manager for *Southwest Cycling* magazine (see exercise 12), you now need to write a persuasive stage collection letter to be sent to any account that is six months old. This letter should, of course, attempt to collect full payment of the account. However, you should inform the reader that this is to be the last letter before the account is sent to an agency for collection. Send the letter to the same person specified in exercise 12 (the balance is now $157.35, plus a $3.15 finance charge).

🔲 Apply the four steps in the message formulation process to persuasive messages.
🔲 Plan, organize, compose, and evaluate persuasive collection messages.

14. *Discussion stage form letter persuading credit card customers to pay.* Write a discussion stage letter to be used by a major credit card company. This letter will be sent to all account holders who have not made monthly payments on their accounts for the past three months. Assume you have already sent copies of the invoices with finance charges added each billing period. In addition, your representatives received promises by telephone from each debtor to make a regular monthly payment within one week of the call. However, no payments were received. Therefore, this letter, to be

sent two days after the promised receipt date, should be written to accomplish three things: to get the payment that is currently overdue, to propose a plan for paying off the account at one-half the normal monthly payments (the usual finance charges will continue), and to receive from the reader a written note agreeing to accept these terms of payment.

Address the first letter to Mr. Carl Aragon, 2025 Milan Avenue, Hockingport, OH 46739 (Account No. 465752162-0028; balance on account is $11,263.45; amount of payments overdue is $675.78; normal monthly payment is 2 percent of the highest daily balance).

◄ Apply the four steps in the message formulation process to persuasive messages.

◄ Plan, organize, compose, and evaluate persuasive collection messages.

15. *Persuasive form letters to credit card customers.* Refer to exercise 14. Your job now is to write a series of three persuasive collection letters to be used by the same major credit card company. The first letter will be sent to all account holders who have not made a payment on their account within the past four months. The second letter will be sent after five months with no payment. The third letter, sent after six months, is the last one that will be sent before the account is officially closed (after seven months with no payment). Once an account is closed, full payment of the entire account is due immediately. The only recourse the debtor has at this stage is to pay all the overdue monthly payments.

Again, address the letters to Mr. Carl Aragon, 2025 Milan Avenue, Hockingport, OH 46739. The monthly payment should be 2 percent of the account each month. If a payment is not made, the account balance must be increased by an additional 1.2 percent each month.

### Persuasive Requests

◄ Apply the four steps in the message formulation process to persuasive messages.

◄ Plan, organize, compose, and evaluate persuasive requests.

16. *Persuasive request for a new payment plan.* Refer to the vignette at the beginning of the chapter. Compose a letter that will achieve Caesar Caruso's goals. Address it to Jill Barrett, Accounts Supervisor at Cotswold Enterprises.

◄ Apply the four steps in the message formulation process to persuasive messages.

◄ Plan, organize, compose, and evaluate persuasive requests.

17. *Persuasive memo requesting educational benefits.* You have been employed at Albright Bulk Products for four years and have worked your way up from an accounting clerk position to your current job as Accountant II, the highest level you will be able to achieve without a bachelor's degree. You are only one year away from completing your degree but cannot afford to pay the tuition and fees, and you do not qualify for financial aid.

Albright, a small family-owned company with 75 employees, has no formal policy for reimbursing its employees for education that directly benefits their jobs. However, you found out recently that the president reimbursed Franklin Strawberry, a senior manager, for the last four semesters of his degree in management. Franklin suggested you write to the owner, Francine Spada, requesting reimbursement for the cost of tuition, fees, and books for the 30 units you still have remaining in your degree. As Franklin suggested, you want to submit the receipts for payment at the end of every semester (or quarter if that is the system you are on) along with a copy of your grades (verifying a grade of at least a B in each class).

Write a persuasive memo to Mrs. Spada, convincing her that what she and the company will get for the money will be worth far more than what she will have to pay. If you have not had advanced accounting courses, you might need to visit with an accounting major or read the descriptions of advanced accounting courses in your collect catalog. Doing so will enable you to be specific about the kinds of topics covered in upper-division accounting classes.

▮ Apply the four steps in the message formulation process to persuasive messages.
▮ Plan, organize, compose, and evaluate persuasive requests.

18. *Persuasive memo seeking support.* If you currently work, identify a request you want to make of someone with whom you work, a request that will require use of your persuasive skills. Would you like to have new equipment or software, a new procedure, more employees, an assistant, time off, a ride-sharing program, or something else that requires an attention getter to create interest? Write a memo to the individual who has the power to grant your request. Use good you attitude to show the individual how he or she will benefit from granting your request.

If you do not currently work, use a circumstance from your last job. If you have never worked at all, talk with a classmate who works to get an idea of the kinds of requests about which you might write.

▮ Apply the four steps in the message formulation process to persuasive messages.
▮ Plan, organize, compose, and evaluate persuasive requests.

19. *Persuasive letter requesting reduced lease payments.* Write a persuasive letter to the landlord who holds the two-year lease on the building your corporation uses. You are currently leasing 35,000 square feet of space at a cost of $7,000 a month. The manufacturing facility, encompassing 20,000 square feet, produces parts for airplanes used in the defense industry. In this facility, you at one time had a management, support, and manufacturing staff of 37 people.

When you signed the lease, business was good. However, in the last year changes in the defense industry have cut the demand for your products in half. As a result, you have had to let all but 20 of your employees go and can no longer afford to pay the monthly lease. You have exhausted all sources of funds and cannot borrow more money from anyone.

You have spoken to the landlord, Bernard Johnson, by telephone about solutions to your problem. Unfortunately, he will not let you out of your lease so you can find a smaller facility more appropriate to your reduced cash flow. You considered declaring bankruptcy, but because you guaranteed the lease with your personal assets, bankruptcy would result in your losing your home.

However, you have found someone who is willing to pay you $2,700 a month for two of the offices and about one-third of the manufacturing plant. This arrangement would enable you to keep operating and paying the lease. Hesselbarth Inc. would use the space to operate a specialty advertising business that sells its products (pens, T-shirts, frisbees, notepads, etc., that are imprinted with a company's name). They sell mostly by catalog, telephone contact, and personal visits, although a certain amount of light customer traffic is still to be expected. The owner, Jim Hesselbarth, would have two employees—a salesperson and a clerical assistant. The Hesselbarth share of the manufacturing area would be used to store inventory.

Your current lease does not allow you to sublet any part of the facility. Mr. Johnson believes the parking area is too small to support more than one business, and he thinks that more than one business sign on the building would make it look unattractive.

Using a persuasive strategy, write a letter to Mr. Johnson requesting his permission to sublet the facilities to Hesselbarth Inc. Provide an estimate of the number of cars that would be using the parking lot compared with the number that used to park when you had 35 employees and considerably more business. Hesselbarth has agreed to keep his sign small and to match the lettering and style used by your own company. In fact, he has agreed to get Mr. Johnson's approval of any sign before it is ordered and installed. Point out to Mr. Johnson benefits to him of keeping your company as his tenant.

◗ Apply the four steps in the message formulation process to persuasive messages.

◗ Plan, organize, compose, and evaluate persuasive requests.

20. *Persuasive form letter seeking participation in a survey.* You are the research director for a marketing research firm that is studying the spending patterns of various ethnic groups. You have selected a sample of 5,000 people across the United States whom you want to complete a two-page survey. The survey measures, among other things, the purchases over $100 each reader has made within the last three months, along with income range, ethnicity, age, and marital status. You will be asking about those purchases over $100 they plan to make within the next three months, the next six months, and the next year; and you are interested in knowing their reasons for choosing specific products and brands. You will also attempt to determine what product qualities are most important to them when they purchase items. You want people to complete the survey and return it to you within two weeks.

    The questionnaire is laid out in easy-to-read and easy-to-respond fashion; it requires only checkmarks except for the last question, which asks readers to indicate purchases over $100 that are not included in the survey (as you know, no matter how comprehensive your list of products is, there is always something unique you didn't think of and about which the reader wants to respond).

    The sample was compiled from lists purchased from companies that hold the warranties on appliances. Registration of these warranties proved that these people currently buy such products as personal computers, espresso machines, refrigerators, freezers, microwave ovens, vacuum cleaners, air conditioners, dehumidifiers, stereos, car radios, compact disk players, and so on.

To save time and money, an individualized letter will not be sent to each person on your list. Therefore, you should use a generic salutation or a letter style that does not require a salutation. You will enclose a pre-addressed, stamped envelope with each letter to improve the chances of getting a response. Write an effective persuasive letter to accompany the questionnaire.

PART **THREE**

# BUSINESS REPORTS

# CHAPTER 10

# PRODUCING VISUAL AIDS

## OBJECTIVES

When you finish studying this chapter, you should be able to:

- Decide when to use a visual aid.
- Present numerical data effectively and ethically.
- Incorporate visual aids into written presentations.
- Incorporate visual aids into oral presentations.
- Apply the general principles of constructing graphics of all types.
- Select the best type of visual aid for displaying different kinds of information.
- Evaluate graphics for effective construction and usage.

## WHAT WOULD YOU DO IF...?

**NUMBER GAMES.** Because Alan Troxell recently received a degree in marketing, he has been reassigned from a retail outlet to the marketing department of his firm's home office. ElectroMart has 55 electronics stores in the United States and 5 in Mexico. The two other marketing specialists, Nancy Washington and Mac Jurgenson, just completed the first draft of a report on their survey of customer buying behavior in all the stores. This is the first such report for the three-year-old company. Alan's supervisor has asked him to read the report and suggest any changes he feels are needed.

The data for this study came from brief questionnaires completed by customers at the cash register or at home on a mail-in postcard, depending on the policy of the particular store. ElectroMart wants to know what products sell best in each store, what kind of customer is buying various products, and why the customer is buying them. This information will be used to determine what products each store should carry to appeal to the type of customer who shops at that particular store. The conclusions will also be used to make key decisions about new product research and development.

The questionnaire asks for specific product information (type of product, model, price, etc.) and customer information (age, income level, intended use of the product, reason for purchasing that particular brand and model, and source of information about the store). Statistics were compiled for each store and each country.

As he read the report, Alan noticed that Nancy and Mac included no graphs or charts to illustrate the data. In addition, he was disturbed by some of the conclusions they reached and by their explanations. For example, the survey results indicated that 42 percent of Anchorage customers in the $45,000 to $54,000 income range and 38 percent in the $35,000 to $44,000 income range purchase stereo equipment (versus 10 to 27 percent for all other stores). Nancy and Mac have concluded that people in Anchorage at these income levels must like music more than people in other store areas. They also concluded that people in Mexico are not as concerned about their personal comfort because only 1.2 percent of the sales in Mexican stores are for air conditioners (American stores vary from 5 percent to 25 percent). Alan believes there might be other reasons for these results, and he is not willing to sign the report without further study.

What should Alan recommend be done to produce a better report? What are other possible explanations for the results? What kinds of visual aids should be included in the report to illustrate the information? How can Alan justify his recommendations to his supervisor? What should he say to Mac and Nancy? As you read the following chapter, consider how numerical data and visual aids must be used if they are to effectively support a business message.

## USING VISUAL AIDS EFFECTIVELY

**Visual aids can be used to present data and concepts.**

A **visual aid** is any graphic representation of data or a concept, whether it is used in letters, memos, reports, or oral presentations. Tables, lists, graphs, charts, photographs, maps, drawings, and so on are all visual aids. Because visual aids are part of the communication process, the process of planning, preparing, using, and evaluating visual aids is similar to the process for formulating written messages.

In Chapter 9 you learned that visual aids can help get the attention of a reader who must be persuaded. Visual aids can also make your message more interesting and easier to understand, particularly when the concept you are writing or speaking about contains numbers. In addition, as Exhibit 10.1 shows, visual aids can help you present complex ideas and data with fewer words.

### DECIDING WHEN TO USE VISUAL AIDS

▪ Decide when to use a visual aid.

Visual aids should be used only to supplement and support the words in your message, never to replace the words. Furthermore, no matter how well done, visual aids should never be used exclusively to impress a reader or an audience. They must be a critical part of the message.

When should you use visual aids?

**Graphics may be used to create interest, to supplement, to emphasize, and to explain.**

- When you want to organize facts and figures into a readable, easy-to-follow format.

- When you need to clarify technical information and make it easy for even nontechnical people to understand.

- When you are communicating with people who learn best visually or who are able to grasp immediately the significance of numerical data.

- When you want to improve retention and recall of important information (people remember better when they can visualize as well as read or hear a message).

**EXHIBIT 10.1** **Visual Aid versus Text**

This graph says it all...

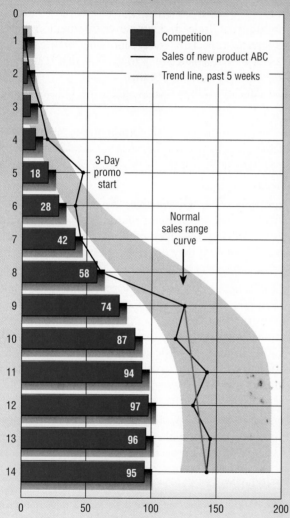

**Product ABC**
**Sales and Competitive Position**

- Competition
- Sales of new product ABC
- Trend line, past 5 weeks

3-Day promo start

Normal sales range curve

**Putting the same information into words looks like this...**

Sales began week 1 with 1 unit sold. During week 2, 4 units were sold. Week 3, 18 units sold. Week 4, 20 units sold. Week 5, 48 units sold. Week 6, 42 units sold. Week 7, 46 units sold. Week 8, 60 units sold. Week 9, 125 units sold. Week 10, 120 units sold. Week 11, 146 units sold. Week 12, 132 units sold. Week 13, 149 units sold. And Week 14, 148 units sold. By the end of week 4, an upward trend was indicated. In order to boost sales performance, a three-day promotion was run, beginning at week 5. This promotion resulted in actually lower sales figures, as they declined from 48 at week 5 to 42 at week 6, and rising slightly to 46 at the end of week 7. Following this period, another upward trend began with volumes up to about 125 in the next two weeks. However, from that point on sales became erratic. A study of sales performance during the last five weeks of the period indicates an approximate 27 unit-per-month increase to date. However, the erratic behavior of product sales (week 9: 125 units sold; week 10: 120 units sold; week 11: 146 units sold; week 12: 132; week 13: 141; and week 14: 148), coupled with the fact that volumes never hit the 150 unit sales point would indicate a leveling off of demand. Compared to expected normal sales ranges, a standard pattern was followed without any exceptionally good indications. On the contrary, during weeks 7 and 8, it was about minus 5 to minus 10 against the worst-case of 53 and 76 respectively. With the exception of the promotional period—during which greater sales were achieved, sales that exceeded the normal sales range— sales were consistently toward the lower-end side. Even though sales did not exceed normal sales upper limits, they were favorable from a competitive-position perspective. After the initial phase where sales were 1, 4, and 18 for the first three weeks, against 3, 6, and 11 for the competition, we were above the competitive levels consistently. It should also be noted that as our sales began to flatten, so did the competition. In week 5, our sales were at 48 units, while the competitive product was at 18 units. In week 6, we were at 42 while the competitor was at 28. In week 7, we were at 46, they were at 42. In week 8, we were at 60, while they were at 58. During week 9, we were at 125, they were at 74. In week 10, we sold 120 units, they sold 87. Week 11, we sold 146, they sold 94. Week 12, we experienced a decline in sales to approximately 132 units. Our competitor, on the other hand, was at 97 units. In week 13, we were at 149, and they were at 96. In the 14th week, the final week of tracking sales, our sales were 148, while our competitor's were at 95.

- When you want to make your message more credible and persuasive.
- When you want a concise way to summarize data explained in more detail in the text.
- When you want to simplify complex concepts and procedures.

- When the reader or the audience expects visual aids.

- When you want to stimulate interest and focus attention on your message.

As you can see, visual aids have many legitimate uses. All kinds of business messages can incorporate visual aids that are relevant and effective.

## PRESENTING NUMERICAL DATA

Present numerical data effectively and ethically.

In the vignette at the beginning of the chapter, Alan Troxell's colleagues have drafted a marketing report that presents a great deal of complex, interrelated numerical data. That is not unusual. Indeed, quantitative information makes up the bulk of most business reports, especially given computers' ability to compile and report great masses of data. The challenge is to present that data in a way that accurately conveys its meaning and significance.

*Seek to make numerical data interesting and readable, while preserving their accuracy and meaning.*

As you use numerical data in your messages, keep the following suggestions in mind:

- *Make sure your figures are accurate.* Verify all computations, including those from other sources.

- *Explain all computations.* When statistical tests are used, explain clearly how the figures were derived.

- *Round off large numbers whenever possible.* An exact number like $6,467,905.67 is difficult to absorb. Consider rounding off—to $6.5 million in this case—instead of specifying the full amount. In many cases, people do not need to know exact amounts. If they do, exact amounts can be used in a table while the generalized amounts are used in the text discussion.

- *Express large numbers in simple terms.* Because large numbers are hard for the average person to relate to (after all, most people deal in bank accounts that go down to zero every month), express them in terms that have more to do with everyday life. For example, you might say, "Your share of the national debt is $6,000" instead of, "The national debt is $1.5 trillion." Stating that one out of every three new small businesses will fail within the first two years has greater impact than saying that approximately 230,000 new small businesses will fail within the next two years.

- *Group related numbers in visual aids.* Avoid putting too many numbers in sentences. When entire paragraphs are filled with numbers, readers become confused and frustrated. A better approach is a visual aid, such as a table, graph, or chart, that shows how the numbers relate and provides a snapshot of trends (like Exhibit 10.1).

- *Explain the significance of the numbers presented in visual aids.* All readers might not be able to see the importance of specific figures or trends indicated in your tables, charts, or graphs. Point out in the text the high and low figures, exceptions, ranges, averages, and so on—anything that is critical to interpreting the data used in reaching conclusions.

*Statistics and graphics must be interpreted and portrayed ethically.*

It is one thing to construct graphics poorly or to use numbers ineffectively; it is another thing to deliberately misuse them so the data will be misinterpreted. Although graphic and numerical data can be misused in many ways, you will avoid the most common problems if you follow this advice:

The mean, the median, and the mode are all averages.

- *Avoid confusing mean, median, and mode.* These three types of figures are all averages, but they are calculated differently. Suppose that you are working with seven numbers (14, 15, 17, 19, 21, 28, 28). The average could be

  | | |
  |---|---|
  | Mean | 20.3 (the total of all seven figures, divided by 7) |
  | Median | 19 (the number that appears in the middle when the numbers are arranged from low to high) |
  | Mode | 28 (the number that appears most often) |

  Usually, the term *average* refers to the mean. However, unethical communicators may count on your making that assumption. For example, a salesperson could tell you that he or she sold an average of 20.3, 19, or 28 units each day last week, and, technically speaking, any of those figures would be correct. Clarity and accuracy demand that you specify which average you are using.

Avoid misleading your readers or audience by omitting essential data.

- *Include even the inconvenient data.* It is unethical to leave out information that might lead to another interpretation of the results. The bar chart on the left side of Exhibit 10.2 backs up an unethical communicator's statement that "Sales have increased steadily since I took over." However, that statement could be challenged if the missing year is included, as the chart on the right shows. Clearly, sales have increased over the years, but leaving out the year in which sales declined significantly is misleading.

Make sure the proportions of graphic elements give an accurate impression of relative size.

- *Keep sizes proportionate.* The size of the bars, lines, or icons used in a graph should indicate the true size relationship between items. Exhibit 10.3 illustrates the kind of misinterpretation that can occur when proportion is ignored. The icon used to show 1997 sales for Suspicion Systems is fatter than the icon used in the graph showing sales of its major competitor, which might lead you to believe that projected sales are greater for Suspicion Systems. However, the height of each bag is the true indicator of projected sales, and thus the actual statistics are roughly equal for the two companies.

Begin scales at zero, and use consistent numbering to avoid distortion.

- *Begin at zero and number consistently.* Usually, the numerical scales used in charts and graphs should begin with zero. Scales that do not begin at zero have the effect of cutting off the bottom of a line or a bar, which may distort the picture. If you decide for some reason to drop off zero and lower numbers on the scale, make sure you clearly explain to the reader that you have done so. Scale breaks, as illustrated in Exhibit 10.4 (page 331), are a related problem. Even when the reader knows that the scale jumps from $200,000 to $500,000, the size of the money bags may give the wrong impression. Without the scale break, the bag symbolizing 1995 profits would appear much smaller than the bags symbolizing 1996 and 1997 profits.

If you want to produce reliable information that can be used to make sound decisions, you will avoid these four mistakes when presenting numerical data in graphic form.

## INCORPORATING VISUAL AIDS INTO WRITTEN MESSAGES

Incorporate visual aids into written presentations.
Because all visual aids are supposed to supplement, emphasize, or clarify the topic, the text should explicitly refer to each visual aid. The only times you might not refer in the text to a visual are when it is included for interest value

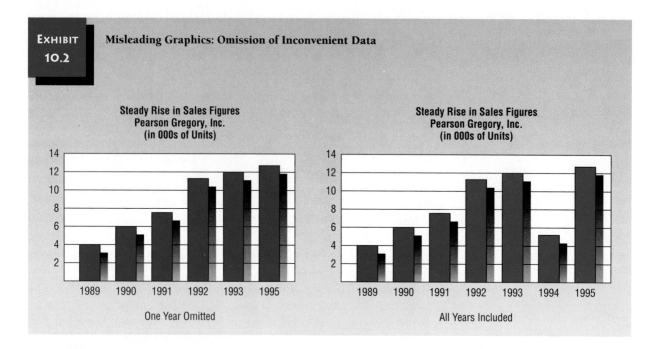

**EXHIBIT 10.2**   **Misleading Graphics: Omission of Inconvenient Data**

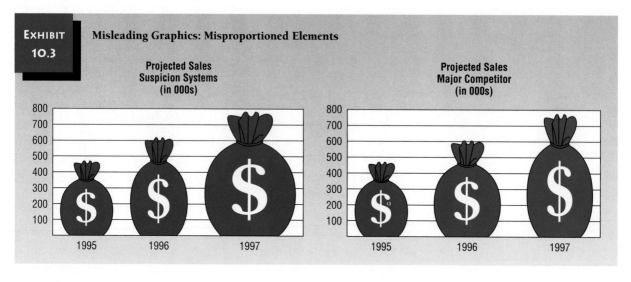

**EXHIBIT 10.3**   **Misleading Graphics: Misproportioned Elements**

only (cartoons and photographs often fall into this category) and when its point is obvious. Then, if the reader ignores it, the overall message is not harmed in any way.

> Mention two or three things you want your readers to see in the visual.

After you have told your reader to look at the visual, tell in your own words what you want the reader to see. Do not state every detail of the graphic, because describing every detail defeats a major advantage of using visual aids. You should discuss only those elements that need to be called to the reader's attention. Point out significant relationships, trends, cycles, averages, ranges, or exceptions in your analysis. In other words, you are simply helping your reader by interpreting the graphic and explaining its significance. The text in Exhibit

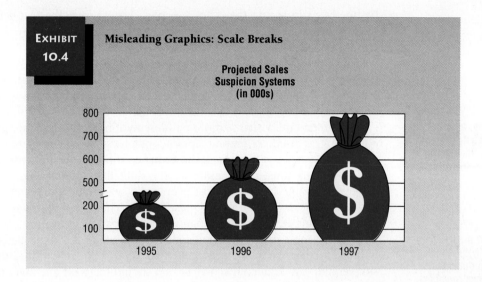

**EXHIBIT 10.4**

**Misleading Graphics: Scale Breaks**

**Projected Sales
Suspicion Systems
(in 000s)**

10.1 is an example of how *not* to explain a graphic. When every detail is explained, the reader loses sight of the real generalizations to be made from the visuals.

Number visuals, and refer to them by their numbers.

An in-text display is a visual, such as a table or list, that appears within the text and is an essential part of the discussion.

Each visual aid you include in a document should be numbered for easier reference, except when you are only using one or two visuals or when the visual element is an **in-text display,** such as a bulleted list. There are many ways of numbering visuals in a large document. In this textbook, for example, all graphics are numbered consecutively. However, you may also number graphics by type. For example, if you had a report containing two tables, four charts, and two photographs, you might number them Table 1, Table 2; Chart 1, Chart 2, Chart 3, Chart 4; and Photograph 1, Photograph 2. You might also number tables separately from figures, which would be everything that is not a table. Then the tables in the example would still be numbered Table 1 and Table 2, but the four charts and two photographs would become Figure 1, Figure 2, Figure 3, Figure 4, Figure 5, and Figure 6. Another method is to call them all exhibits and number them consecutively (the numbering system used in this textbook).

Present a visual as soon as possible after mentioning it to your reader, preferably on the same page.

The visual aids themselves should be placed as close as possible to where they are first referred and discussed. The ideal location is immediately following the point where you tell your reader to look at the visual. A more convenient alternative is to place the exhibit immediately after the paragraph in which it is discussed. If you are using a desktop publishing program or a word processing program that allows you flexibility in placing graphics and text on the same page, you may even be able to place the visual aid right beside the text where you discuss it. If necessary, a graphic may be placed on the following page, although you run the risk of frustrating readers who want to read your explanation and look at the visual aid at the same time.

If a visual is so large that it must be folded and is not critical to readers' understanding, it may be placed at the end of the chapter or in an appendix at the end of a report. For example, a table of 50 variables of which only two or three are pertinent to the discussion might be handled this way. The variables that apply to the discussion are, of course, revealed in the text. However, the entire table may be included at the end of the report for readers who might also be interested in seeing the other variables. Just be sure the text refers to this table within the discussion of the relevant variables.

◼ Incorporate visual aids into oral presentations.

Any of the visual aids discussed in this chapter can be used to present information during an oral presentation. However, instead of putting a chart or a diagram on a piece of paper, as part of a document, you probably will display it separately using some other medium, such as a flipchart or transparency.

> In presentations, as in documents, visuals are not just pretty pictures; they are an essential part of the message.

Very often, the visual part of oral presentations is rather slick. Sophisticated equipment is used to present colorful graphics, some of them prepared at considerable expense to impress the audience and grab their attention. It is true that presenters must compensate for the difficulties of absorbing information through listening. However, most people will see through any attempt to cover up a weak message with a slick presentation. The media with which you present visuals are less important than their information value.

> Visuals used in presentations should generally be simpler than visuals used in documents, because audience members cannot study the visuals at their own pace.

For the most part, visual aids for oral presentations look just like those for written documents. The major difference is that presentation aids must be simpler and less detailed. Each visual aid should focus on one main idea. It will be shown briefly during the presentation, and the audience cannot go back and refer to it again as the reader of a written message can. For example, a list projected onto a screen should have no more than about half a dozen items; those items should be written in short phrases, not sentences, so they can be scanned and understood quickly. The speaker's words can fill in the missing details. Similarly, a graph projected onto the screen should chart two or three lines at most and include only enough data points to illustrate the speaker's main point. It is more important for the audience to have visual reinforcement of the speaker's points about the data than to know the details.

> Introduce visual aids to the audience before showing them, telling the audience what to look for.

Before showing a visual aid, prepare the audience for what they are about to see. Tell them how the message fits into the presentation as well as how they can use the information. In essence, your preview is like the reference you would use in a written document to direct the reader's attention to a visual aid and explain its importance. (Chapter 15 gives more information about using visual aids in oral presentations.)

## PREPARING VISUAL AIDS

◼ Apply the general principles of constructing graphics of all types.

Whether they are bound into a report, folded into an envelope with a letter or memo, or shown during an oral presentation, your visuals should be prepared skillfully and presented professionally. Doing so takes nothing more than time—time to select the most appropriate type of graphic, time to prepare each graphic so it highlights the appropriate information and keeps interest high, and time to determine the most effective way to present each visual to your audience or reader.

Here are some general rules for preparing visual aids that serve the needs of your readers or audience:

- *Avoid using a tiny background grid.* Too many lines in a background grid make the page appear cluttered. If necessary, however, you may add a few lines to assist readers in determining figures.

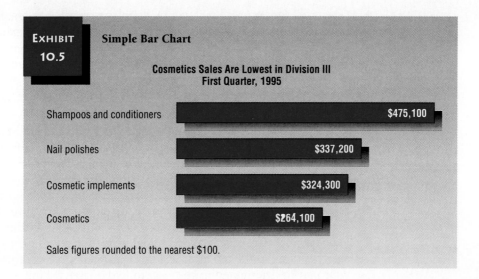

**EXHIBIT 10.5**

**Simple Bar Chart**

**Cosmetics Sales Are Lowest in Division III**
**First Quarter, 1995**

Shampoos and conditioners — $475,100

Nail polishes — $337,200

Cosmetic implements — $324,300

Cosmetics — $264,100

Sales figures rounded to the nearest $100.

- *Label everything clearly, using phrases or words instead of whole sentences.* Using a simple typeface and upper- and lower-case type, name both axes, and identify each component of the graph so the reader knows what he or she is reading. Give the chart an appropriate, specific title, and number it if you are using several figures or exhibits in a document. Use a key at the bottom or on the side of your chart to indicate the meanings of any color or fill patterns. Identify whether numbers are rounded off in thousands, in millions, and so forth.

- *Use color and fill patterns that are not distracting.* Color is an excellent attention getter, and expertly crafted colored charts are generally well received by readers and audiences. However, colors should complement one another without clashing. For example, a dark blue column would look much better than pink when placed next to a red column. Use an artist's color wheel if you need help selecting colors. Fill pattern such as bricks, herringbones, and stripes running left, right, or sideways can entertain the person preparing the chart, but they can confuse readers when too many or similar patterns are used. Use complex fill patterns sparingly, if at all.

- *Use borders and rules around graphics that occupy less than a full page.* Borders improve the appearance of tables, charts, and so forth, and help to set them off from the text. Choose borders that enhance the visuals but are not overpowering. Avoid excessive use of underlining within a table—too much can make the table appear cluttered and difficult to read.

- *Convey only one message on each visual.* Attempting to convey more than one message in a chart can be confusing. Look briefly at Exhibit 10.5. This chart portrays a division's weakest product in comparison to its other products. Imagine how confusing the chart would become if you tried to combine all three of this organization's divisions with their 15 different product categories on one chart. Consolidating the three divisions into one chart might save space; however, this benefit is without merit if the message is lost.

- *Make the X axis (the left) and the Y axis (the bottom) meet at zero.* Except when negative numbers are clearly labeled, readers believe you are hiding something from them if you begin with anything other than zero.

- *Give credit for borrowed material.* A doublespace below a graphic, cite the source of any secondary information you are using. The exhibits in this chapter that are not original show a detailed way of documenting sources. Refer to style manuals for other citation styles recommended by other authorities. If the material you are writing is for publication, avoid violating copyright laws by getting written permission from the source to use its data or reproduce its figure.

- *Reduce or fold figures or exhibits that are too large for the page.* Many architectural drawings and blueprints are too large to include within a normal 8½″ × 11″ report. As long as the figure is readable, it may be reduced on a photocopy machine to fit a standard page. However, if reduction would hinder readability, you may fold the page and bind it with the rest of the report (although the cost of doing so might be prohibitive if you must reproduce a large number of copies). Of course, large exhibits must be folded so that a reader can easily unfold, read, and refold the pages as he or she goes through the report. It will probably take some experimentation on your part to determine the best way to fold a large exhibit.

◼ Select the best type of visual aid for displaying different kinds of information. The following subsections will give you more tips for producing specific types of graphics: in-text displays and lists; tables; flowcharts and organization charts; bar charts; pie charts; line charts; pictographs; fishbone diagrams; computer clip art, photographs, drawings, and diagrams; and statistical and geographic maps. They will also help you choose the best type of visual aid for displaying different kinds of information.

## IN-TEXT DISPLAYS AND LISTS

Bulleted or numbered lists are useful in any kind of business message—one of the most common types of list in business messages is a step-by-step explanation of how to perform a particular act. Depending on the subject, in-text displays such as formulas and equations may also be useful. Setting off information in such a way makes it more interesting and draws attention to it.

In-text displays and lists are dependent on the text and not separated from it, as are other kinds of graphics.

In-text displays and lists are easy to type. They may include only words, only numbers, or a combination of the two. Unlike other visual aids, however, lists and other kinds of in-text displays do not contain separate titles because they are completely integrated into the text. They are not intended to stand alone; they should be read as they are introduced.

Here's an in-text list that tells you how to prepare an in-text list:

This list is an example of an in-text list that gives instructions. Notice the use of active verbs at the beginning of each item.

- *Introduce an in-text list in the paragraph preceding it.* Introductory phrases, such as *the following* and *the list below,* should be used in the sentence or paragraph before a list to tell a reader when to read the list and how it fits into the topic of discussion. When a sentence that immediately precedes a list contains such introductory words, that sentence should end in a colon. However, if the closest sentence before a list does not contain such introductory words, a period is used at the end of the sentence appearing immediately before the list. In addition, do not use a colon if the list follows a verb or a preposition. In this case, the items in a list function as complements or objects to the verb. (An example of this type of list is included as numbered items in the last entry of this bulleted list.)

- *Group items in lists only if they are related.* Because lists are used only to group items together for the purpose of improving readability and comprehension, each item in the list must be related. Imagine a list of department tasks that might be included in a short report (e.g., "Increase order turnaround time by 7 percent by May 25," "Reconfigure Team A by March 2," "Replace inventory control software by March 15," etc.). You can see how illogical it would be to include an explanation of the history of the company in the middle of such a list.

- *Begin each item in the list with an active verb when the list gives instructions.* Take a moment to look at the first words of each item in this list (e.g., *introduce, group, begin, use, format,* etc.). Active verbs such as these help you, the reader, understand exactly what you need to do to construct effective lists.

- *Use the same type of construction and grammatical form for each item in the list.* If any item in a list contains only a single word, no other item should contain more than one word. If a complete sentence is used for one item in the list, a complete sentence should be used for all items. Imagine how ineffective the list you are reading would be if, after using active verbs in the first three list items, this one began as follows: *"It is important that the same type of construction and grammatical form be used for each item in the list."* Changing the syntax or grammar changes the emphasis of the entire list. In this case, the item would become a statement of fact rather than an action you should perform.

- *Format the list effectively to make it easy to read and follow.* You may use the same margins as the rest of your document, or you may indent the list on the left (approximately one-half inch is suggested). Most experts suggest indenting successive lines of a list so the first line containing the number, the bullet, or other distinguishing element stands out. This list and the bulleted list in the previous subheading are examples of this type of format. Format can increase a reader's ability to follow step by step what you have to say.

- *Punctuate, capitalize, and construct items in a vertical list in accordance with accepted conventions.* If the items in a list are complete sentences, punctuate the ends just as you would any sentence. However, if the items are phrases or single words, most experts recommend not using ending punctuation after each item. Whether a list contains complete sentences or not, it is considered correct to capitalize the first letter of the first word in each item.

- *Punctuate, capitalize, and construct items in a horizontal list in accordance with accepted conventions.* Horizontal lists are those that are part of a paragraph; they are not set off from the rest of a paragraph. In addition, they are an integral part of a sentence. With a horizontal list (such as the one included in this sentence), you should (1) follow the rules given in Appendix A for the use of commas and semicolons in a simple series, (2) type the items in the list without capitalizing the first letter of the first word in each series item, and (3) include the word *and* before the last item in the series.

## TABLES

A table is an arrangement of numbers or words in rows and columns.

A table is a systematic arrangement of data and/or other information in rows and columns. Tables are best for organizing large amounts of data concisely. They are among the easiest of all visuals to construct, and they are the most used of all graphics. However, they can also be the least interesting to look at.

EXHIBIT 10.6

**Table Reporting Research Data**

**Disclosure of Nonfinancial Information in Annual Reports**

| Industry | Number of Companies | Percentage of Items Disclosed by Each Industry | Percentage of Disclosed Items by Category in Each Industry | | | | |
|---|---|---|---|---|---|---|---|
| | | | I | II | III | IV | V |
| | | D = 32 | D = 14 | D = 4 | D = 3 | D = 7 | D = 4 |
| Petroleum | 6 | 31 | 11 | 58 | 67 | 57 | 0 |
| Aerospace | 2 | 39 | 14 | 100 | 100 | 50 | 0 |
| Entertainment | 8 | 23 | 7 | 31 | 63 | 46 | 0 |
| Transportation and public utilities | 2 | 34 | 32 | 38 | 50 | 50 | 0 |
| Services | 6 | 27 | 8 | 46 | 78 | 43 | 8 |
| Insurance | 4 | 27 | 13 | 6 | 92 | 54 | 0 |
| Construction | 2 | 31 | 14 | 50 | 50 | 57 | 13 |
| Health care | 6 | 21 | 7 | 4 | 72 | 50 | 4 |
| Banking, S&L, & real estate | 21 | 27 | 9 | 29 | 70 | 57 | 0 |
| Computer products | 8 | 20 | 5 | 78 | 63 | 46 | 0 |
| Manufacturing | 13 | 29 | 7 | 60 | 74 | 51 | 0 |
| Retail & wholesale | 9 | 17 | 5 | 22 | 37 | 40 | 3 |
| Total | 87 | 25.5 | 8.5 | 40.2 | 67.0 | 50.3 | 1.5 |

**Key:**

| | | | |
|---|---|---|---|
| Disclosure items | = D | Investment programs | = III |
| Human resources | = I | Organizational structure | = IV |
| Production | = II | Environmental measures | = V |

Source: The annual reports of 87 corporations located in the Los Angeles area. Reprinted by permission of Adnan Abdeen, "Social Responsibility Disclosure in Annual Reports," *Business Forum,* Winter 1991, California State University, Los Angeles, p. 24. Reprinted by permission.

One typical use of tables is to present numerical research results. For example, Exhibit 10.6 reports data from a study of the nonfinancial information included in companies' annual reports. By reading the key, the column headings, and the data in the exhibit, you can determine that six health care firms disclosed 21 percent of the 32 types of nonfinancial information listed in the study. Of those, 7 percent were variables dealing with human resources; 4 percent, production; 72 percent, investment programs; 50 percent, organizational structure; and 4 percent, environmental measures. This sort of detailed table would be very useful in presenting the statistical information outlined in the vignette at the beginning of the chapter.

Exhibit 10.7, on the other hand, is a table that includes only text rather than statistical data. It consists of two columns that demonstrate, step by step, how a meeting can be organized. Many readers would find it easier to get such information from a table than from a paragraph in the text.

Exhibit 10.8 (page 338) shows the standard format of a complex table. Use the exhibit and the following suggestions to construct tables that achieve the purpose you intend:

• Number the figure when a written message contains more than one graphic.

• Use a title that identifies the topic of the table immediately and fully.

**EXHIBIT 10.7**

**How to Plan a Better Meeting**

■ **Steps**  ■ **Guidelines**

| | |
|---|---|
| 1. Plan | Plan the meeting, being clear about<br>• Why the meeting is needed<br>• What outcomes the group wants<br>• Who should attend<br>• What arrangements need to be made<br>• What agenda items need to be made<br>• How items will be addressed (what processes will be used—brainstorming, diagnosing a problem, developing solutions, selecting a solution, reaching consensus, etc.)<br>• How much time will be needed to achieve the desired outcomes |
| 2. Inform | Inform meeting participants of<br>• The purpose of the meeting<br>• The desired outcomes<br>• The agenda items (the *what*)<br>• The processes to be used (the *how* of addressing agenda items)<br>• The date, time, and location<br>• Any premeeting assignments |
| 3. Target | Target a plan for developing productive discussion by<br>• Stating and clarifying the purpose of the meeting<br>• Getting agreement on the desired outcomes<br>• Allowing for modification of the agenda (including adding or deleting items, changing the order, or adjusting the times allocated)<br>• Getting agreement on the processes to be used when addressing agenda items |
| 4. Contain | Contain the discussion to the agreed-on agenda by<br>• Designating a facilitator and a recorder<br>• Adhering to the agenda unless the group explicitly agrees to alter it<br>• Confronting behavior that diverts the group from attaining its desired outcomes<br>• Encouraging each group member to address all his or her information to the issue at hand<br>• Reaching agreement on action steps, responsibilities, and target dates |
| 5. Hasten | Hasten the completion of agreed-on action steps by<br>• Summarizing the meeting<br>• Recording the decisions that were made<br>• Recording the names of persons responsible for implementing action steps and target dates<br>• Agreeing on a date for the next meeting<br>• Evaluating every meeting and agreeing on ways to "pitch" a better meeting<br>• Putting unfinished business on the agenda for the next meeting<br>• Following up and encouraging task completion<br>• Monitoring and evaluating the results achieved by the group |

Source: U.S. Department of Labor, Bureau of Labor–Management Relations and Cooperative Programs, Module 2 "Effective Meetings," *Skillbuilding for Labor–Management Groups*, 1991, pp. 1–2. Reprinted by permission.

● Use borders and spacing above and below headings to increase readability.

● Identify each row (a horizontal line of a table) and each column (a vertical element of a table) as well as groupings of columns or rows in complex tables.

● If totals or subtotals are necessary, they should be separated slightly from the rest of the data; this will make them readily identifiable. Double lines and/or boldfacing are often used with totals.

● Significant numbers may be boldfaced for emphasis.

EXHIBIT
10.8

**Standard Table Format**

### Table Number
### Table Title (may go on same line as Table Number)
### Secondary Title (if necessary)

| Row Head | Decked Heading (spans several columns) | | |
|---|---|---|---|
| | Column Title | Column Title | Column Title |
| Row name | xxxx | xxxx | xxxx |
| Row name | xxxx | xxxx | xxxx |
| Row name | xxxx | xxxx | xxxx |
| Row name | xxxx | xxxx | xxxx |
| Row name | xxxx | xxxx | xxxx |
| Total | xxxx | xxxx | xxxx |

**Position tables on one page and, if possible, within the normal margins of your document.**

- Position the table on one page and within the same margins as the rest of the written document. If a table is too wide for a normal page, it may be turned sideways on a separate page. When it is bound, the table's title should appear on the left (closest to the binding).

- Sources of secondary data must be identified at the bottom of the table.

- Use asterisks, cross hatches, and so on to add footnotes for elements that should be explained further. Repeat the symbols with the noted information at the bottom of the table.

- Simplify figures for reading ease. However, identify the units being discussed. For example, a column heading or a key at the bottom should state that numbers are expressed in millions, thousands, or hundreds, not in single digits.

## FLOWCHARTS AND ORGANIZATION CHARTS

**Use flowcharts to diagram processes and organization charts to diagram hierarchies.**

Businesses use flowcharts to illustrate processes and organization charts to illustrate lines of authority within a branch, department, or company. Illustrating such information clarifies the relationships among the components.

Exhibit 10.9 is a flowchart of the job-search process. To perform a job search, one only has to do what is specified in each box, following the arrows from one step to the next. Notice the different shapes used in the flowchart and the meaning of those shapes. These are standard shapes developed by the computer industry for data-processing flowcharts. The more complex the process you are illustrating, the more important it is to use standard shapes.

Instead of depicting a process, organization charts depict the structure of some entity at some point in time. An organization chart reflects the lines of authority, levels of responsibility, and working relationships in a company. Exhibit 10.10 (page 340) shows the organizational hierarchy of one department of the textbook's publisher. At the bottom of the chart are those segments, positions, or people with the least power. Those at the top have the greatest decision-making power.

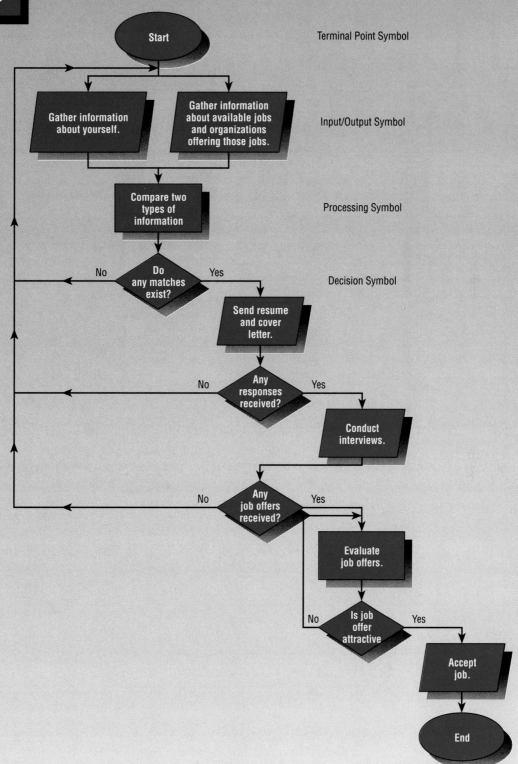

**EXHIBIT 10.9**

**Flowchart of the Job-Search Process**

Start

Terminal Point Symbol

Gather information about yourself.

Gather information about available jobs and organizations offering those jobs.

Input/Output Symbol

Compare two types of information

Processing Symbol

No — Do any matches exist? — Yes

Decision Symbol

Send resume and cover letter.

No — Any responses received? — Yes

Conduct interviews.

No — Any job offers received? — Yes

Evaluate job offers.

No — Is job offer attractive — Yes

Accept job.

End

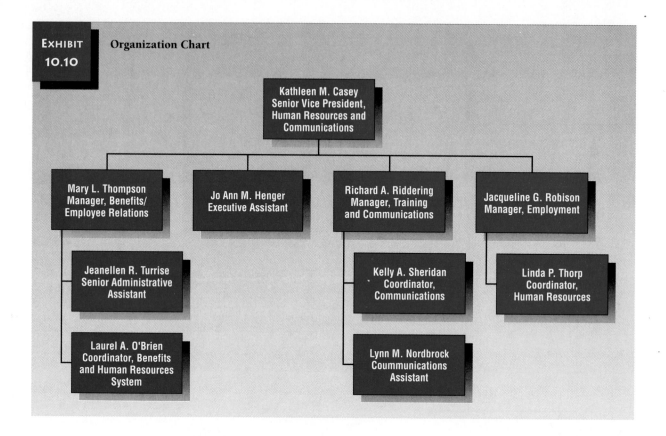

**EXHIBIT 10.10**   **Organization Chart**

The information in organization charts is useful for new employees and people outside the firm as they attempt to make sense of the interrelationship of one part of a firm to other parts. Drawing up such a chart also gives an organization the chance to streamline its operations. Such charts highlight any duplication of efforts and help to ensure that the lines of authority within a firm make sense. For example, one of the basic precepts of good management is that an employee should have only one immediate supervisor. A detailed organization chart that lists positions rather than divisions or departments clearly reveals who works for whom.

## BAR CHARTS

Use bar charts to compare several variables at one time or one variable at several points in time.

Bar charts are most useful for comparing several variables at one time or one variable at several points in time. Bar charts are used often in business because they are easy to both create and understand. They would be an excellent choice for presenting some of the information described in the vignette at the beginning of the chapter. Desktop publishing software can be used to prepare effective bar charts. With a spreadsheet program (the most sophisticated type of computer programs for creating charts) you merely key the data into the computer, and the program designs a chart for you.

The simple bar chart illustrated earlier, in Exhibit 10.5, makes it readily apparent that shampoos and conditioners enjoy much greater sales than cosmetics do. Notice that it uses horizontal bars. Another bar chart that makes the same point is shown in Exhibit 10.11. However, this type of bar

**EXHIBIT 10.11**

**Column Bar Chart**

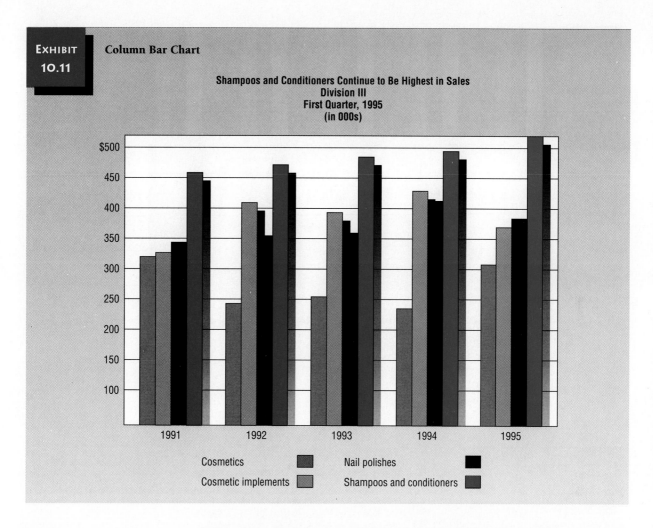

**Shampoos and Conditioners Continue to Be Highest in Sales**
**Division III**
**First Quarter, 1995**
**(in 000s)**

chart, often called a *column chart*, includes more information about the company's products and shows the four product categories over a period of five years. A column bar chart of this type is good for comparing several variables over time.

Exhibit 10.12 is a divided column bar chart. In this case, the entire column represents total gross revenue from sales; however, each segment of the column shows the amount of sales in each of the company's three product categories. One disadvantage of this kind of chart, however, is that exact figures for each product category are difficult to determine. Therefore, some people prefer to type exact or rounded dollar figures directly in each segment of each bar. It will be up to you to consider the degree of specificity necessary to satisfy the people who see your graphics.

When you need to show negative numbers, the column bar chart portrayed in Exhibit 10.13 is useful. To see how easy such a chart is to read, look at the exhibit and answer the following exercises:

In what four months did the mutual fund dip below the average growth figure for 1993?

Answer: February, March, August, and September.

EXHIBIT
10.12

**Divided Column Bar Chart**

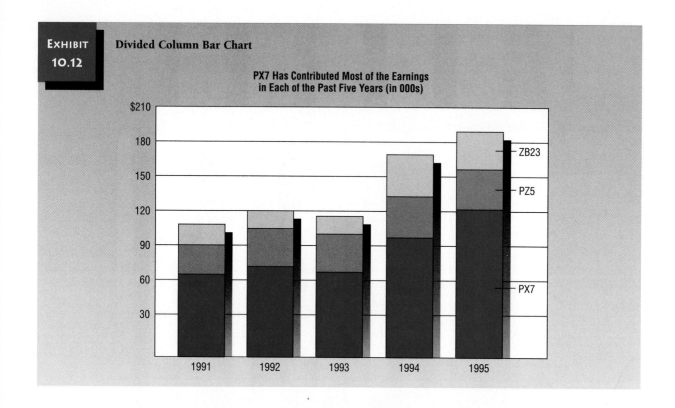

**PX7 Has Contributed Most of the Earnings
in Each of the Past Five Years (in 000s)**

EXHIBIT
10.13

**Column Bar Chart Showing Positive and Negative Numbers**

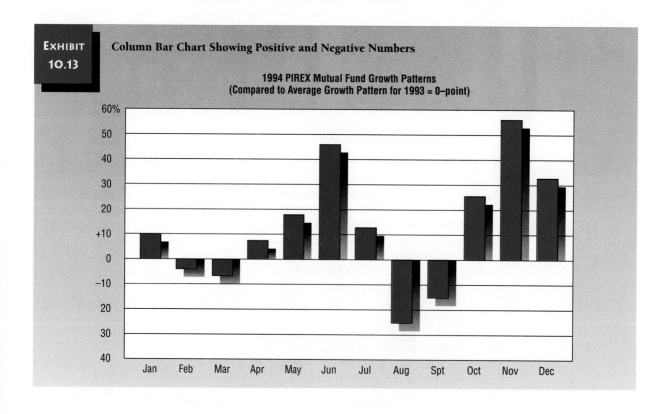

**1994 PIREX Mutual Fund Growth Patterns
(Compared to Average Growth Pattern for 1993 = 0–point)**

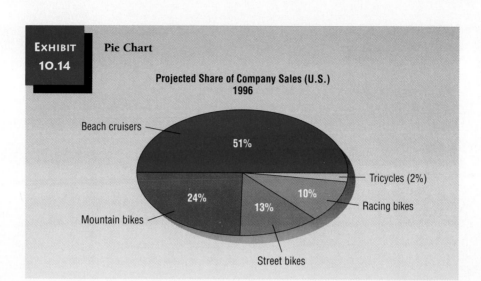

**EXHIBIT 10.14**   **Pie Chart**

**Projected Share of Company Sales (U.S.)**
**1996**

Beach cruisers

51%

Tricycles (2%)

10%

13%

24%

Racing bikes

Mountain bikes

Street bikes

Locate the lowest growth month for the mutual fund. In one sentence, state what that figure means.

Answer: In August 1994, the PIREX Mutual Fund dipped approximately 26 percent below the average growth of 1993.

## PIE CHARTS

*Pie charts are used to show the parts of a whole.*

Use pie charts to show the parts of a whole. These charts get their name from the fact that each segment looks like a piece of pie. The total of all the segments should equal 100 percent. Exhibit 10.14 shows a pie chart that was prepared using a computer spreadsheet program.

Pie charts work particularly well when you want to show percentages or shares and when you have no more than five components. It is customary to lump together segments that are very small and to label their total as "other" or "miscellaneous."

Some people will tell you that the largest share should begin at the 12 o'clock position (imagine the chart to be the face of a clock). However, several computer software programs do not follow this rule when they automatically create pie charts. Therefore, most people have come to accept pie charts in any form that is easy to read and clearly labeled.

Exhibit 10.15, an "exploded" pie chart, combines a pie chart and a bar chart. The bars provide details about the missing piece of the pie. This pie chart's similarity to a Pac-Man game character can also bring an element of fun to the message the graphic contains, although one has to wonder if such light-heartedness is appropriate in this case.

## LINE CHARTS

Line charts, also referred to as *graphs,* are useful to show changes over time. Numerical data that identify trends or cycles are particularly adaptable to line charts. Sales figures, price changes, changes in racial or gender categories in

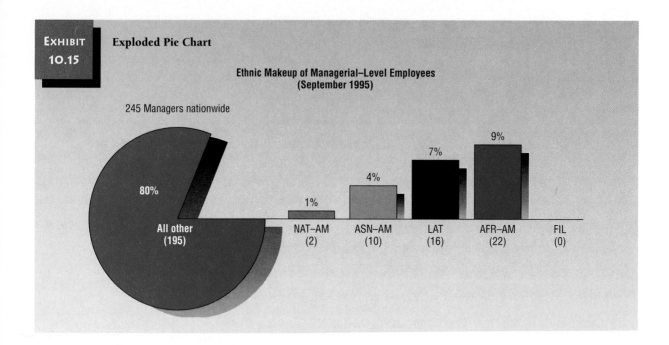

**EXHIBIT 10.15**

**Exploded Pie Chart**

**Ethnic Makeup of Managerial–Level Employees**
**(September 1995)**

245 Managers nationwide

80%

All other
(195)

1%

NAT–AM
(2)

4%

ASN–AM
(10)

7%

LAT
(16)

9%

AFR–AM
(22)

FIL
(0)

Line charts (graphs), which are used to show changes over time, make it easy to see trends and cycles.

management positions, and quarterly production figures are examples of the types of information typically shown in line charts. Anything that fluctuates, grows, or diminishes over time can be illustrated in a graph. You can pick up any major business publication to view a variety of types of graphs to show how current economic indicators compare to those of the past.

When you construct a line chart, use a continuous line that moves from left to right, with the earliest figures reported at the left of the chart and the latest figures at the right. Illustrate actual figures as a solid line and projected figures as a dotted line. Clearly label time values (e.g., the year or the month), which are normally shown across the bottom of the chart (the horizontal axis). Scale values such as money, percentages, number of hours, barrels of oil, and so on are normally shown on the vertical axis (the left side). Graphs sometimes include a grid—hatched lines that allow the reader to trace data points to specific numbers on the axes. However, too many lines in a background grid make the graph appear cluttered. It is best to use only a few lines to assist readers in determining values.

Exhibit 10.16 is a simple line chart. Dashed lines are commonly used in line charts to indicate projected figures. Imagine Exhibit 10.16 as a bar chart, with the market share for each year as a bar. Which do you think would be most effective—the line chart or your imagined bar chart? If you responded "The line chart would be most effective," you are right. A line chart provides the reader with more information and makes the trend toward a greater market share easier to see immediately. Exhibit 10.17 is a more complex line chart containing more than one set of data points.

Another type of line chart is commonly called a *surface chart* (also called an *area chart*). In this type of visual, the top line represents the total of all the items, and the areas between the lines represent the component parts of the total. In Exhibit 10.18 (page 346), some of the figures from the divided column

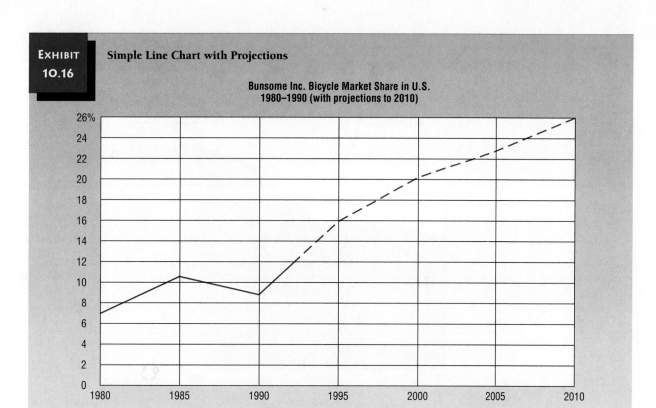

**EXHIBIT 10.16**

**Simple Line Chart with Projections**

Bunsome Inc. Bicycle Market Share in U.S.
1980–1990 (with projections to 2010)

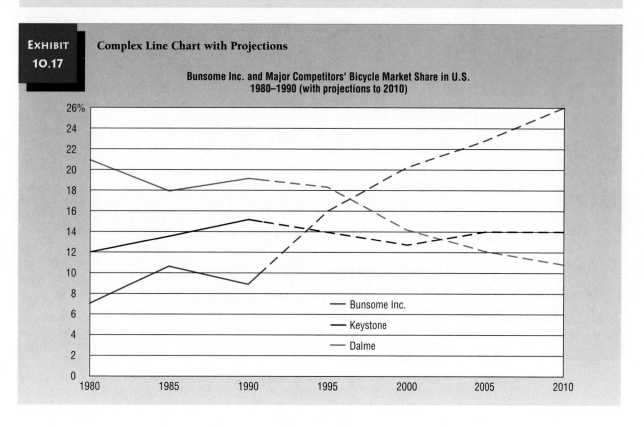

**EXHIBIT 10.17**

**Complex Line Chart with Projections**

Bunsome Inc. and Major Competitors' Bicycle Market Share in U.S.
1980–1990 (with projections to 2010)

— Bunsome Inc.
— Keystone
— Dalme

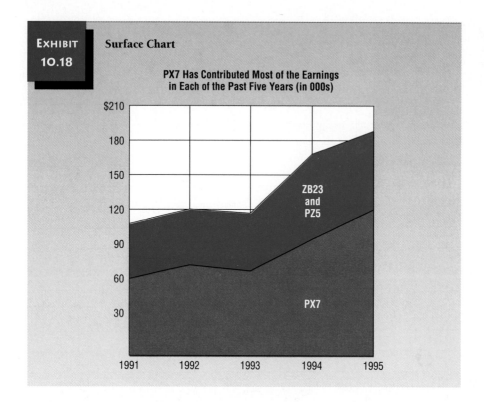

**EXHIBIT 10.18**

**Surface Chart**

**PX7 Has Contributed Most of the Earnings
in Each of the Past Five Years (in 000s)**

ZB23
and
PZ5

PX7

bar chart (Exhibit 10.12) have been converted to a graph. Take a moment to compare the two. The impact of the one product on the company's earnings is easier to see on the surface chart.

### PICTOGRAPHS

*Pictographs use icons to create interest, and they sometimes convey information more quickly than words and numbers alone.*

A pictograph is a bar chart that uses a row or column of icons in place of the bars. Each icon is the same size, and each represents a standard unit of measure.

The benefit of using a pictograph instead of a bar chart is the interest value such icons give a chart. The bandaid drawings in Exhibit 10.19 are appropriate for illustrating the number of workers' compensation claims. When you're using a pictograph, you can be creative; for example, icons of telephones could be used to illustrate an increase in the number of residential telephones in Russia. Population figures are sometimes portrayed with stick figures of people.

### FISHBONE DIAGRAMS

*Use fishbone diagrams to portray graphically the steps necessary in planning and implementing major projects.*

A fishbone diagram is particularly useful for planning new processes or procedures directed toward a given outcome. Cause and effect analysis can also be illustrated with fishbone diagrams. The slanted lines, each of which is used to link a particular subitem to the process, form the chevron pattern typical of a fish's bones.

The fishbone diagram in Exhibit 10.20 (page 348) shows the technology, budget, processes, and people a company has dedicated to updating its telephone system. The diagram could be easily tailored to match any problem or effect being studied. For example, for a manufacturing firm that has a large

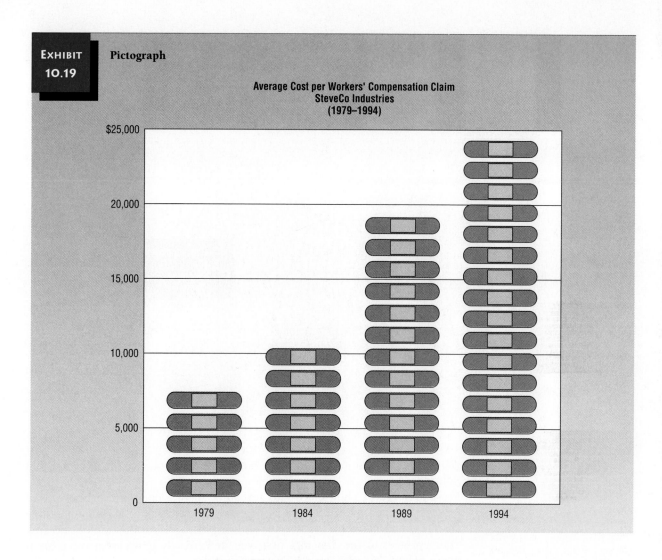

**EXHIBIT 10.19**

**Pictograph**

**Average Cost per Workers' Compensation Claim
SteveCo Industries
(1979–1994)**

order to fill, the fishbone diagram might substitute these headings: machines, materials, processes, and people.

## CLIP ART, PHOTOGRAPHS, DRAWINGS, AND DIAGRAMS

Depict objects with clip art, photos, drawings, and diagrams.

A grab bag of visual aids is available to improve writers' and speakers' ability to communicate. What clip art, photographs, drawings, and diagrams all have in common are their interest value and their ability to depict objects. Imagine how difficult it would be to visualize the extent of the damage caused by an automobile accident if it were only described to you. However, if you were to see a photograph of the car with its roof caved in, you would instantly understand the accident's seriousness.

Clip art consists of drawings that can be cut from a collection of images and pasted into your own message. The types of pictures available range in style from cartoons to sketches and detailed illustrations to photographs. You can obtain them from printed catalogs or computer software. Computer clip art is easily transferred into word processing and desktop publishing programs. Many

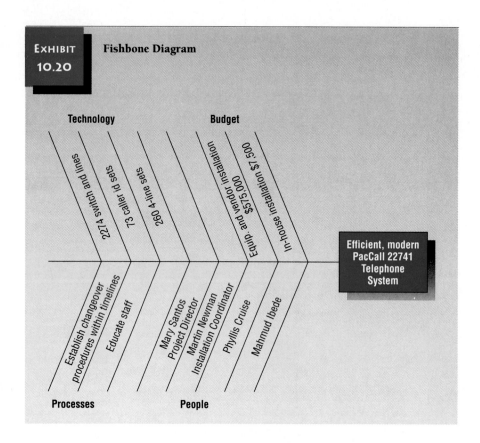

**EXHIBIT 10.20** **Fishbone Diagram**

Technology

Budget

2274 switch and lines

73 caller id sets

260 4-line sets

Equip. and vendor installation $575,000

$7,500

In-house installation

**Efficient, modern PacCall 22741 Telephone System**

Establish changeover procedures within timelines

Educate staff

Mary Santos Project Director

Martin Newman Installation Coordinator

Phyllis Cruise

Mahmud Ibede

**Processes**

**People**

programs allow you to electronically cut, resize, and enhance the images to suit your needs.

Exhibit 10.21 shows how clip art can be incorporated into other kinds of visual aids. The Irish coffee cups pictured on the graph make it more interesting than it would be with only the line showing rising sales. In addition, because your eye goes to the drawings first, you immediately grasp what the chart is about before you read the title or numerical data.

Computers also make it easier to use photographs in written documents. Photos with little fine detail and good contrast between dark and light tones can be scanned by a computer and turned into electronic data, enhanced with desktop publishing or other graphics software, and integrated into word processing programs. In this way they do not have to be pasted manually into the text of a report or brochure. Scanned photographs can also be electronically manipulated to produce dramatic original art. Exhibit 10.22 (page 350) shows how photos can be enhanced to look like drawings with the use of page layout programs.

### STATISTICAL AND GEOGRAPHIC MAPS

Maps can be used to present statistical or geographic information.

A good way to communicate statistical and other kinds of information about geographic areas is to use maps. For example, the report discussed in the vignette at the beginning of the chapter could have incorporated a map showing the location of the company's stores in relation to temperature zones.

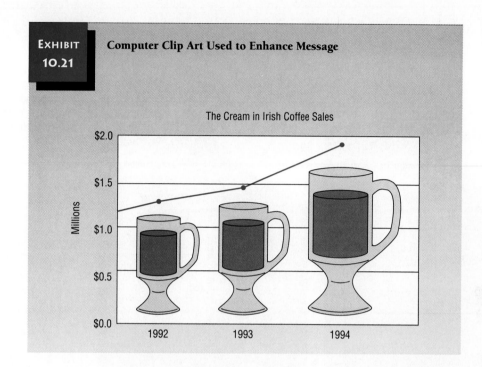

**Exhibit 10.21**

**Computer Clip Art Used to Enhance Message**

The Cream in Irish Coffee Sales

The map of the world shown in Exhibit 10.23 (page 351) reveals visually where the members of an international organization live. This portrayal makes it easy to see how much of the world is represented by the organization's membership, a message that is more easily conveyed graphically than it would be by listing the countries in columns.

Statistical differences can be shown on maps with numbers, colors, shading, or patterns. If something other than exact numbers is used, an explanation must be added to the map to explain the meaning of each distinguishing device. See Exhibit 10.24 (page 352) for an example of a map that uses color shading to indicate specific information.

You may also combine bar charts or pie charts with geographic maps. Notice how easy Exhibit 10.25 (page 353) is to read. You can see immediately that the regions being discussed are Arizona, Texas, and New Mexico. As a reader, if you are only interested in an approximation you will probably not look beyond the size of the bars. If you desire more specificity, however, you will read the figures and the key at the bottom. Sometimes this information is printed on the bars themselves.

## EVALUATING VISUAL AIDS

Visual aids can be evaluated by asking others for feedback or by comparing them to criteria for effective graphics.

🔖 Evaluate graphics for effective construction and usage.

Once you have planned and prepared your visual aids, their effectiveness should be evaluated. Show your graphics to colleagues whose opinions you respect. Have them critique your finished product, but ask them specific questions, such as the following:

**EXHIBIT 10.22**   **Computer Enhancement of Photographs**

**Original**

**Result**

Enhanced with
PageMaker's Image
Control feature

**Original**

**Result**

Enhanced with
QuarkXPress's
Picture Contrast
Specifications

Source: Reprinted by permission of ThePage 65, 1993, p.16.

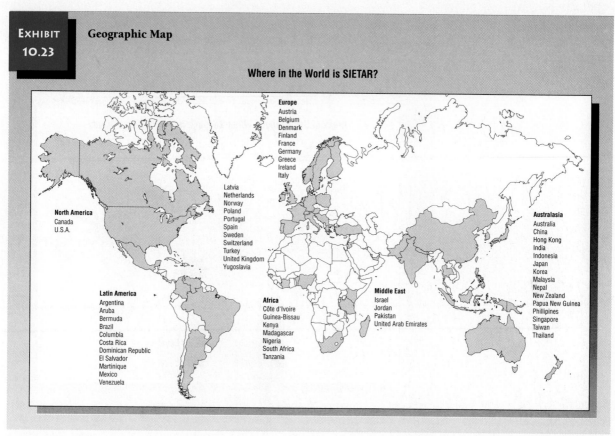

**EXHIBIT 10.23**

**Geographic Map**

**Where in the World is SIETAR?**

**Europe**
Austria
Belgium
Denmark
Finland
France
Germany
Greece
Ireland
Italy
Latvia
Netherlands
Norway
Poland
Portugal
Spain
Sweden
Switzerland
Turkey
United Kingdom
Yugoslavia

**North America**
Canada
U.S.A.

**Australasia**
Australia
China
Hong Kong
India
Indonesia
Japan
Korea
Malaysia
Nepal
New Zealand
Papua New Guinea
Phillipines
Singapore
Taiwan
Thailand

**Latin America**
Argentina
Aruba
Bermuda
Brazil
Columbia
Costa Rica
Dominican Republic
El Salvador
Martinique
Mexico
Venezuela

**Africa**
Côte d'Ivoire
Guinea-Bissau
Kenya
Madagascar
Nigeria
South Africa
Tanzania

**Middle East**
Israel
Jordan
Pakistan
United Arab Emirates

*Source: SIETAR Communiqué* XXI, no. 3 (April/May 1991), p.9. SIETAR International is an interdisciplinary membership organization serving professionals in intercultural fields. SIETAR has 1,800 members in 60 countries worldwide. For information on membership benefits and services, contact SIETAR International Secretariat, 808 17th Street NW, Suite 200, Washington, DC 20006, USA, (202) 466-7883.

- "Is the title clear, and does it really summarize what is contained within the visuals?"

- "As you go through it, is there any place that confuses you?"

- "Would another type of chart make the message clearer?"

- "What are the two most important conclusions you reach from this graphic?"

- "What can I do to get the message across better?"

These and other open-ended questions will elicit more honest and thoughtful answers than "Is this okay?"

Another evaluative technique that works well for many people is to read once again the section of this chapter dealing with the type of graphic you prepared. Do this with the graphic and the report or speech in front of you. Make a point to turn each suggestion in the book into a question, and take the time to answer it. For example, when you read in the book that a graphic should be introduced in the text before it appears on the page, turn that statement into questions such as these and answer them:

- "Did I refer the reader to the graphic, by number, at the time the reader needs to view it?"

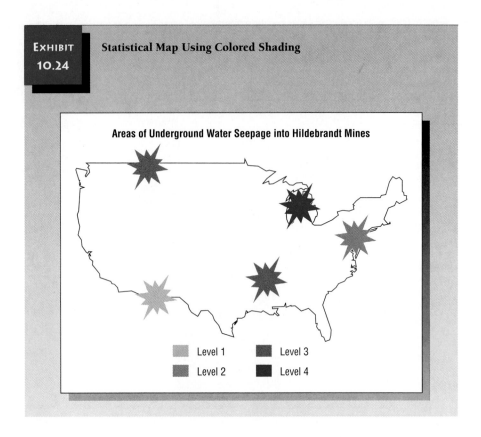

**Exhibit 10.24**  **Statistical Map Using Colored Shading**

Areas of Underground Water Seepage into Hildebrandt Mines

Level 1    Level 3
Level 2    Level 4

- "Does the graphic appear at the bottom of the page or as soon as possible after its text cite?"

If possible, the evaluation should also extend to feedback from your intended readers or listeners. This is usually easier in oral presentations, because you can detect confusion by observing body language, and, if there is an opportunity, the audience will ask questions about anything that is unclear. In many oral presentations, you will have a chance to immediately correct any confusion caused by poorly prepared visuals.

Feedback on graphics used in reports and other written documents usually comes in the form of questions from readers—if you are present at the time. However, if you are not there to immediately clear things up, you may never know what readers really thought of your work. Obviously, it is much better to plan carefully and to evaluate all graphics thoroughly *before* they go to their intended readers or audience.

## DISCUSSION QUESTIONS

 Decide when to use a visual aid.

1. List five advantages of visual aids.

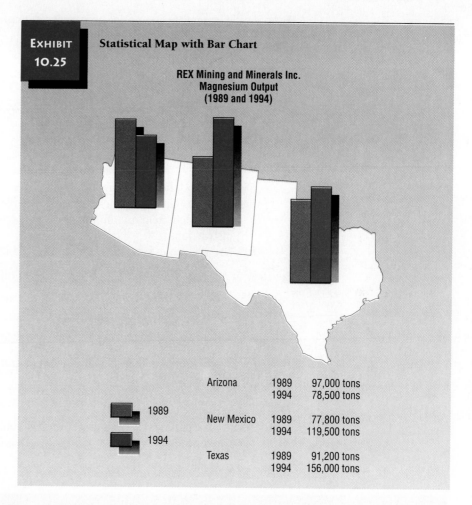

**EXHIBIT 10.25**

**Statistical Map with Bar Chart**

REX Mining and Minerals Inc.
Magnesium Output
(1989 and 1994)

| | 1989 | |
| | 1994 | |

| Arizona | 1989 | 97,000 tons |
| | 1994 | 78,500 tons |
| New Mexico | 1989 | 77,800 tons |
| | 1994 | 119,500 tons |
| Texas | 1989 | 91,200 tons |
| | 1994 | 156,000 tons |

🔳Present numerical data effectively and ethically.

2. This chapter presents 12 suggestions for presenting numerical data. What is the overall purpose of following these suggestions?

🔳Present numerical data effectively and ethically.

3. For the following set of figures, specify the mean, the median, and the mode: 17, 74, 73, 74, 12, 44, 19, 82. Round your answers to the nearest whole number.

🔳Incorporate visual aids into written presentations.

4. Explain two different numbering options available for a report that contains several tables and several graphs.

🔳Incorporate visual aids into written presentations.

5. Give two examples of how you might refer to visuals in the text of a report.

🔳Incorporate visual aids into oral presentations.

6. What is the main difference between visual aids prepared for written messages and visual aids prepared for oral presentations? What is the reason for the difference?

🔖 Apply the general principles of constructing graphics of all types.

  7. What are the five general principles listed in this chapter for constructing visual aids of all types?

🔖 Select the best type of visual aid for displaying different kinds of information.

  8. What type of information is best portrayed by each of the following: tables, flowcharts, bar charts, pie charts, line charts, pictographs, and fishbone diagrams?

🔖 Select the best type of visual aid for displaying different kinds of information.

  9. Discuss what the following principles of using in-text displays and lists mean to you. Give examples of each principle.
     *a.* Begin each item in the list with an active verb when the list gives instructions.
     *b.* Use the same form for each item in the list.

🔖 Select the best type of visual aid for displaying different kinds of information.

  10. Give examples of the problems that might arise from using colors or patterns in a bar chart.

🔖 Select the best type of visual aid for displaying different kinds of information.

  11. What are some of the specific ways computers can be used to prepare visual aids?

🔖 Evaluate graphics for effective construction and usage.

  12. Name two methods recommended in this book for evaluating the effectiveness of your visual aids.

## APPLICATION EXERCISES

🔖 Decide when to use a visual aid.
🔖 Incorporate visual aids into written presentations.

  1. In which of the following situations would you use a visual aid? If you recommend using one or more visuals, what advantage will be gained by doing so? If you do not recommend using visuals, why not? Write your results in a memo to your instructor, giving your answers in an in-text list.
     *a.* You are composing a report on body language in which you plan to include about 20 tables and charts to illustrate the findings from films and from surveys you and a team of researchers have conducted. You have found a statistic saying that 72 percent of the interpretation of spoken words is derived from a speaker's body language. You are wondering whether or not to use a pie chart.
     *b.* You are preparing a persuasive letter to be sent to all company employees. The purpose of this letter is to persuade people to contribute to a major charitable organization, one that makes grants to at least 17 different local organizations. You know that a common criticism of charities is that they keep so much of the donated money for running

the organization; however, this charity keeps only 11 percent (the mean of other major charities is 32 percent). You are wondering how to express this information, and are also wondering if it might be beneficial to include a table showing the amounts given to each local organization last year as well as a chart showing how the amount donated to this charity has declined in the last three years.

c. You have compiled the following data from warranty registrations of people who have purchased your company's products: type of product; model number; whether the product was purchased for self or a gift; age, address, and telephone number of purchaser; family income level; name and location of store where the purchase was made; and how the purchaser first heard of the product. You are wondering whether all this information should be summarized in visuals, or whether only significant bits of information (that affecting marketing and research and development decisions) should be reported.

⬛ Present numerical data effectively and ethically.
⬛ Incorporate visual aids into written presentations.

2. For each of the following exhibits (shown within this chapter) write an introductory paragraph as if you worked for an organization that might be using the data to make decisions. Then write at least two sentences explaining two or three points of significance illustrated by each graphic.
   a. Exhibit 10.12.
   b. Exhibit 10.13.
   c. Exhibit 10.15.
   d. Exhibit 10.17.

⬛ Present numerical data effectively and ethically.
⬛ Incorporate visual aids into written presentations.
⬛ Apply the general principles of constructing graphics of all types.
⬛ Evaluate graphics for effective construction and usage.

3. Select two of the latest issues of two of the following publications: *The Wall Street Journal, Business Week, Fortune, U.S. News and World Report,* and *Time.* As you look through the publications, record the number of times each of the following visuals is used: in-text displays and lists, tables, bar charts, line charts, pictographs, fishbone diagrams, pie charts, flowcharts, organizational charts, diagrams, and statistical and geographic maps. Prepare an appropriate graphic for displaying the results of your survey, and include it in a report to your teacher.

   As you discuss the results of your survey in the report, address the following (as well as any other information you believe your professor will need to appreciate the results of your study):

   • Types of graphics most often used.
   • Types of graphics least often used.
   • Appropriateness of titles, with examples of good and poor titles.
   • Reliance on dependent visuals (in-text displays) versus independent visuals.

   Include at the end of your report photocopies (with appropriate source notes) of a good example of each of the 12 visual categories mentioned above (or fewer if your publications did not contain examples of all the categories). Decide how to best present these visuals to minimize space and to save paper without sacrificing readability.

Include photocopies of at least two visuals that were confusing or misleading. Provide suggestions for improving them.

■ Present numerical data effectively and ethically.
■ Incorporate visual aids into written presentations.
■ Evaluate graphics for effective construction and usage.

4. In a memo report to your professor, give an example of each of the following: omission of inconvenient data, misproportioned elements, and scale breaks. Be sure to give proper credit for all words and visuals borrowed from other sources. Number each graphic, cite it at the point in your memo at which your professor should turn to the graphic, and explain clearly where the error in layout or interpretation occurs.

■ Incorporate visual aids into written presentations.
■ Select the best type of visual aid for displaying different kinds of information.

5. For each of the items below, what kind of graphic should be used to best display the information? Justify your answer in a letter to your professor, and use an in-text list. Your professor will tell you if you are to provide an example of the graphic for each case (you may assume any reasonable details necessary to prepare each graphic).
   a. Results of a survey showing that chief executive officers believe the business problems of the late 1990s will be profitability (37 percent), inflation (20 percent), regulation (13 percent), technological changes (10 percent), foreign competition (12 percent), and other (8 percent).
   b. Annual sales for Eyewitness Production, Inc., over the past eight years.
   c. A breakdown showing that your company spends $15,320 a month on security services compared to the following amounts for three other similar businesses: C&E Cycling ($12,999), San Dimas Wheels ($11,459), and Bodholdt Lane ($11,321).
   d. The process to program a machine to make tiny parts for airbag mechanisms. The process involves a yes/no decision after the third step. At this point, the operator must branch out to a new set of instructions depending on which answer is given.
   e. Change in the number of new home sales for each of the past five years in your community.
   f. A multimillion dollar painting purchased by one of your clients and insured by the firm for which you work.
   g. The locations of the 15 stores your company owns in New York and Florida.
   h. Results showing that people making between $45,000 and $55,000 a year have invested more in bonds for each of the past three years than those making over $100,000 a year.
   i. A comparison of the mortgage interest rates for home loans of $300,000 and larger offered by 15 institutions, as of today.
   j. The change in interest mortgage rates for home loans of $300,000 and larger offered by one bank in your local community over the past 10 years.

■ Incorporate visual aids into oral presentations.
■ Apply the general principles of constructing graphics of all types.
■ Select the best type of visual aid for displaying different kinds of information.

6. For two of the examples in exercise 5 (if your teacher does not specify which ones you are to do, you may choose any two examples in the list), prepare the graphics for an oral presentation and justify your selection in an oral presentation to your classmates. Your instructor will let you know if you will be expected to turn in an outline of your presentation.

# CHAPTER 11

# WRITING SHORT REPORTS

## OBJECTIVES

When you finish studying this chapter, you should be able to:

- Identify the uses of the short report.
- Apply the four steps of the message formulation process to short reports.
- Choose the correct short report format for the situation, distinguishing among the standard letter, memo, and manuscript formats.
- Plan reports of suitable length.
- Select the appropriate organizational strategy, distinguishing between direct and indirect outlines.
- Make the content of short reports more accessible with appropriate headings, subheadings, and visual aids.
- Use informal and formal writing styles to best advantage.
- Plan, organize, and compose progress reports, feasibility studies, justification reports, problem-solving reports, and business and government proposals.
- Plan, organize, and compose business plans.
- Evaluate short business reports and business plans.

## WHAT WOULD YOU DO IF...?

**THE RIGHT MACHINE FOR THE JOB.** Ralph Spanswick, the staff development specialist in the human resources department of a large company, is drafting a memo report at his computer. He is recommending the purchase of computers, updated software, films, and other equipment to be used for training employees. Specifically, he is recommending 15 computers be purchased at a price of $778 each from MicroTech, a small company owned by Ralph and two partners. In the report, Ralph plans to justify the purchase of MicroTech computers by showing the higher price bids he received from five other companies.

Ralph is wondering if he should disclose his association with MicroTech. He is confident that the computers are exactly the ones needed for training purposes and that $778 is the best price available anywhere. He is afraid, however, that others might veto the purchase if they feel a conflict of interest exists. If he must order computers at the next lowest price ($895), he would be able to order only 13 computers instead of 15. The department would then be able to train fewer employees than it has in the past in a typical computer training session.

Should Ralph reveal to his boss that he owns MicroTech? What are the ethical implications of this purchase? What might be the possible effects of this sale on Ralph himself if he does not disclose the information? What effect might this sale have on the company if Ralph does not speak up and the information comes to light later? As you read the following chapter, consider what information a report of this type should contain. If you were going to disclose Ralph's association with MicroTech, where in the report would you include it?

## USING SHORT REPORTS

■ Identify the uses of the short report.

Short reports are used extensively in business. Short reports such as those discussed in this chapter are generally prepared by subordinates and sent to managers and executives. These individuals, in turn, base their decisions on the data and conclusions in the short reports.

Short reports vary widely in purpose and appearance. They may be anything from columns of sales figures generated weekly by a computer to grant proposals written to obtain government funding for company projects. This chapter covers the kinds of short reports used most often in the business world—progress reports that bring management up to date on a project, feasibility reports that establish the viability of various options, justification reports such as that written by Ralph in the chapter-opening vignette, unsolicited problem-solving reports that identify problems and recommend solutions, and proposals that solicit support for various ideas. You will also be studying how to write effective business plans. Should you need start-up or expansion money for your business, a good business plan will increase your chances of success when you meet with bankers.

■ Apply the four steps of the message formulation process to short reports.

As you write any short report, you will follow the same message formulation process you use to prepare letters and memos. To refresh your memory, planning the report is the first stage in the process; it involves establishing a purpose, choosing a medium and channel, considering legal and ethical issues, analyzing the audience, and gathering the necessary resources. The second stage is organizing, which includes freewriting and selecting an organizational strategy. Composing the short report, the third stage, requires you to include the elements that people expect to see in the various types of short reports. The final stage in the process is evaluating the report before it is distributed, as well as considering feedback from the report's readers.

## PLANNING A SHORT REPORT

Planning means developing a strategy by which a short report can achieve the purpose for which it was intended.

It is difficult to conceive of a short report that can be written without planning. Even reports consisting of computer-generated numerical data are the result of planning. Someone had to decide what information is needed, what form it should be reported in, and how and when the information should be collected.

Planning can be thought of as the strategy by which a short report achieves the purpose(s) for which it is intended. Devising an effective strategy will be easier if you follow the suggestions presented in the following sections.

## ESTABLISH YOUR PURPOSE

Decide whether the information or data should only be reported or whether it should also be analyzed.

Before you write a report, first establish what you want it to accomplish and why you are preparing it. Overall, short reports have one of two general purposes:

- Informational: Do you intend to report only information you have compiled?

- Analytical: Do you need to analyze information you have compiled, reach conclusions, and then provide recommendations to management about how problems can be solved?

Of course, both informational and analytical reports include information.

You should also establish a specific purpose before you begin writing. Specific purposes for short reports include the following:

- *Progress reports.* To inform others of a task group's progress toward completing a project; to outline problems encountered on a project and the future steps necessary to reach a specific goal; to periodically report sales figures, production totals, and quotas; and to provide a detailed, factual record of what transpired during a meeting.

- *Feasibility studies.* To assess the feasibility of purchases, mergers, and acquisitions, new products, services, and procedures.

- *Justification reports.* To justify the purchase of equipment, the hiring or firing of personnel, and the investment of money.

- *Problem-solving reports.* To analyze a current problem and recommend solutions to a superior.

- *Proposals.* To propose new products, services, or plans to a client; to seek monetary grants advertised by government agencies in exchange for manufacturing a product, research and development, or performing a service; and to seek approval to do research on a specific topic.

- *Business plans.* To influence readers into investing funds in the company for which the plan is developed.

- *Periodic reports.* To report sales figures, production totals, and quotas.

If the report you are writing was assigned to you by someone else, be sure the two of you agree on the purpose. You may even want to document the purpose by getting it in writing, perhaps through a progress report. A few days into the study (or a few weeks, depending on the time available) send a short report that restates the purpose as you understand it while bringing your supervisor up to date on what you are doing. Your supervisor will then have a chance to correct your impression of the purpose, if necessary.

## CHOOSE A MEDIUM AND CHANNEL

Before you organize or compose your report, you need to consider how it will be presented. If your report is routine, something that is prepared on a regular basis, you generally will be expected to adopt the format and length that has been used in the past. A search of the company files or computer database will reveal the information you need to comply with expectations. However, if this is a special situation, an issue not studied previously, or one unlike other situations in the past, you may be required to make decisions of your own about format and length.

Four basic formats are used for short reports:

■ Choose the correct short report format for the situation, distinguishing among the standard letter, memo, and manuscript formats.

**Reports written on a regular basis generally require a standardized format to allow information from one period to another to be compared easily.**

- *Standard form.* Preprinted forms or computer-generated forms are often used for reports produced on a routine basis. Often the information is produced by a computer in the form of numerical data and requires no analysis. Those who use this information to assess progress and to make decisions expect the data to be in the same place from month to month or week to week. Therefore, standardization is important.

- *Memo report.* If your report is to be sent to someone within your company, you may use the standard memo format, which is the most common format for short, informal reports. (Appendix C explains the standard elements of this format.) In addition, memo reports may contain headings and subheadings in the same way they are used in formal reports.

- *Letter report.* Short reports that are compiled for individuals outside your company may be formatted as letters if they are not too long. It is recommended you use the letter report format only for reports no longer than five pages; however, preferences vary from one organization to another. All the normal parts of a letter should be included in a letter report (see Appendix C). You may also use subject lines, headings, and subheadings in any letter report.

**Manuscript format is covered in detail in Chapters 12 and 13.**

- *Manuscript.* The manuscript format is considered more formal than any of the the other formats. Manuscript format is generally used for reports longer than 10 pages; however, this format may also be appropriate for some shorter reports. Take a moment to look at the formal report illustrated in Chapter 12 to see how it differs from the short reports illustrated in this chapter. When the manuscript format is used for short reports, many standard parts may be omitted. For example, in a six-page report, it is probably unnecessary to include a summary, a table of contents, or a list of tables and figures.

## CONSIDER LEGAL AND ETHICAL ISSUES

**Ethical reports are those that are honest, objective, accurate, and complete.**

Legal and ethical issues concerning the composition of short reports center around the need for honesty, objectivity, and accuracy. What you say must be truthful, and the information and findings you report must be real, not manufactured to prove a point for which real evidence could not be found. Executives make key decisions based on the reports their subordinates compile. If this information is faulty, the company's survival may be at stake.

Objectivity requires you to report all sides of any issue, not just information relevant to solutions you would prefer. This is not always as easy as it sounds, however, because each of us views the world differently. Because your ability to describe what you see will always be tied to your values and beliefs (two qualities that are seldom objective), you must guard against letting your biases influence your ability to report and interpret data impartially. Make sure to tell your reader everything he or she wants and needs to know to assess the accuracy and feasibility of your information, conclusions, and recommendations. The vignette at the beginning of this chapter is a good example of this issue. Ralph Spanswick should tell his boss about his involvement with MicroTech, as well as MicroTech's superior bid, so he can make an informed decision.

Because it is essential that reports be accurate, your information and research must be correct. Verify the data on which your conclusions and recommendations are based. Doublecheck statistical tests for accuracy and appropriateness.

Here are some guidelines that will help you meet acceptable ethical and legal standards as you prepare short reports:

- *Avoid bias.* Avoid exaggeration, overgeneralizations, and "loaded" words. Don't assert opinions as facts. Facts are precise, certain, demonstrable, and testable; opinions are not. This biased statement from a report assessing the feasibility of merging with another company was prepared by an executive who feared losing his job in the merger: "Terrorist tactics cannot be tolerated in our organization." Use of the word *terrorist* was highly biased; it implied that the strategy of the acquiring firm was dishonorable when actually it was not.

- *Avoid generalities; express facts, data, and events specifically.* Replace a general statement such as "The data justifies a large increase in consumer rates" with a specific statement like "A 20 percent decline in usage and a 12 percent rise in costs justify an increase of $.23 per unit in consumer rates." Specific language will help to ensure that the message is accurately understood.

- *Give credit for borrowed material.* Acknowledge the source of anything taken from someone else's work. If your report is solely for internal company use, it is not necessary for you to obtain written permission to use the work of another to support your study. However, you must still give the author credit for borrowed material. If your report is to be published outside the company, avoid copyright infringement by obtaining written permission from the publisher or author for any material you use that was created by someone else. Federal copyright law protects a wide range of creative works, including the words, ideas, data, or graphics of another person or organization. (Chapter 13 tells how to document the sources of information and data included in a report.)

- *Provide plenty of valid evidence for conclusions.* The preponderance or weight of evidence must prove your conclusions. Use the principles detailed in Chapter 6 to strengthen the credibility of your observations, conclusions, and generalizations. Explain the expertise of your sources, and distinguish between statements of verifiable facts and opinions. If you cite someone else's work, identify his or her possible unstated assumptions.

- *Base the recommendations on the conclusions.* Bias-free recommendations are derived solely from the conclusions reached in the report.

## ANALYZE YOUR AUDIENCE

Your reader's familiarity with the topic of the report and his or her likely reaction to the information and recommendations dictate the report's length and the arrangement of information. Therefore, take a few minutes to analyze your reader(s) before you begin composing any short report. To whom will the report be distributed? How receptive are your readers to the topic? What expectations will they have of the format and the degree of formality?

If the reader is expecting the report and is familiar with the topic, the introductory material may be limited.

Business reports are either **solicited**—authorized by another person—or **unsolicited**—prepared on the writer's own initiative. If your report was solicited, and your reader is, therefore, expecting it, you may not need to include as much introductory material. If management wants you to investigate a problem in sales, for example, you will not need to spend much time updating the scope of the problem. After all, your recommendation to solve the problem is what management is really interested in.

Unsolicited reports, however, generally require more introductory material, either to explain the full extent of a problem or to provide enough background on a topic so readers understand and appreciate the need to study it. Consider, for example, an unsolicited report from a receptionist justifying the purchase of $500,000 in new telephone equipment and recommending training in telephone etiquette and procedures for all employees, including management. It is possible management does not even know there is a problem. Therefore, the receptionist will have to convince the readers first that the company's current telephone equipment is causing it to lose business or to lose productivity. Readers will not be psychologically ready to read the rest of the report until they have been convinced that a problem exists.

The reader's expectations and probable reaction to your conclusions and recommendations will determine the arrangement of information within the report.

You must also consider the likely reaction of your readers to either the information or the recommendations within the report. If the recommendations may cause an angry reaction, you should put them at the end of the report, not at the beginning. This gives the reader time to read, absorb, and think about the problem before the recommendations are presented. If the evidence you provide in the report is rational, unbiased, and sufficient in quantity and quality, readers are more likely to reach the same conclusions on their own before you get to the logical recommendation. For example, after a six-month study of ways to cut costs in a firm, a consultant wanted to recommend, among other things, eliminating the job of the human resources representative who served as the company's liaison on the project. Putting the recommendations at the end of the report ensured that everyone, including the human resources representative, read the rationale before the harsh news was presented.

## GATHER NECESSARY RESOURCES

If the report you will be writing requires research, gather all the information you will need before you begin. Most short reports for use within the company are based on data available in company files. (However, if you need to perform library research or go outside the company for information, you may want to read Chapter 13 for advice.)

Will you need visual aids of any kind in the report? If so, will you prepare them yourself, or does your company have a graphics department better able to prepare professional-looking visuals? How much time and money are available to spend on graphics and to wait for them to be produced? Greater effort and expense are sometimes expended for reports sent to people outside the organization, depending on the importance of the intended readers to the firm.

If writing the report is to be a group effort, decisions must be made about procedures, timelines, and responsibility. The entire group should undertake the planning stage. A number of other decisions must also be made: Who will be responsible for each element of the research? By what date must the research be completed? How will the writing be handled, and when must each draft be completed?

Collaborative writing of a short report, common in today's business world, is easier with new software that gives all group members, even those at remote locations, easy and effective access to the document.

You might want to take advantage of computer software that allows everyone in a group to access and comment on a document as it is being written. All users must be on the same computer network or possess modems that allow access to the system over the phone lines. Collaborative group members may then call up draft copies of a document and make comments or suggest revisions, identifying the notes as their own with special code numbers. These suggested changes do not become a permanent part of the report unless the primary writer chooses to make them so.

Without such software, you will have to decide on procedures that will allow each collaborator to research, write, revise, and endorse the draft copies as well as the final report. Collaborative efforts often take more time than individual efforts; however, combining the thinking power of many people often produces a better report.

## ORGANIZING A SHORT REPORT

The length of your report depends on the topic, the purpose, and the reader.

How short reports are organized depends on many things, including your topic and purpose, the familiarity of the reader with your topic, and her or his probable reaction to the contents. The length of your report depends on these things as well.

■ Plan reports of suitable length.

Generally speaking, the newer or more unusual the idea or the more significant the problem is, the longer the report. In a problem-solving report, for instance, you may need extra space to explain possible solutions and analyze various alternatives' chances of success. Furthermore, informational reports are generally shorter than analytical reports, because analysis requires that information not only be reported but interpreted as well. In addition, analytical reports often include separate sections or headings for conclusions and recommendations.

The readers and their technical backgrounds and educational levels also affect the length of any report. Achieving clarity when reporting on complex, highly technical topics often requires more space. In addition, when readers are not familiar with your topic, you may need to spend more time filling them in on the background. Statistical tests may have to be explained in detail if your readers are not used to reading and absorbing such information.

The organization stage of writing a short report is much the same as the organization stage of writing a letter or a memo. You begin by freewriting to determine the major points, and then you choose an appropriate organizational strategy.

### FREEWRITE MAJOR POINTS

Freewriting helps many people get their initial thoughts down on paper as quickly as possible. These ideas can then be organized into a coherent whole. The process of freewriting is explained in detail in Chapter 6; however, these are the major steps:

- Write the purpose(s) of your short report at the top of the page so you will always have it (or them) in mind.

- Using words and phrases, not complete sentences, write down as fast as you can and in whatever order they come to mind everything you can think of that should be said in this study.

## CHOOSE AN ORGANIZATIONAL STRATEGY

Select the appropriate organizational strategy, distinguishing between direct and indirect outlines.

Once you have determined the points you need to cover in your short report, you can figure out the best pattern for arranging those points. Your goal is to choose an organizational strategy that will meet the reader's needs and expectations. In a short report, you also have the option of using headings and visual aids to help the reader navigate the document and find the required information.

**DIRECT AND INDIRECT ARRANGEMENTS.**   Just like letters and memos, reports of all kinds can be arranged in the direct (deductive) or indirect (inductive) order. The choice of arrangement depends on what you want to emphasize. For example, if you were compiling a problem-solving report for your supervisor, who you are sure will be receptive to the conclusions and recommendations, you might choose to get to the point and put the conclusions and recommendations at the beginning. This would save her the trouble of reading through several pages before she finally comes to what interests her most.

On the other hand, you might believe that your supervisor will disagree with or be suspicious of what you have found. In this case, it would be preferable to use the indirect order, putting the conclusions and recommendations at the end of the report. By putting them at the end, you give your supervisor a chance to come up with the same ideas on her own as she reads all the data on which the conclusions and recommendations were based. In the end, she may be more receptive to taking the steps necessary to put your suggestions into action. Ralph Spanswick, from the vignette at the beginning of the chapter, should have chosen the indirect arrangement. His supervisor is likely to be suspicious of Ralph's motives in recommending a purchase from MicroTech. However, Ralph had a good rationale for his recommendation, and he could ensure that rationale would be considered by placing it before the recommendation.

Short reports may contain a variety of features that are not found in letters and memos. Some reports, for example, might benefit from a lengthy introduction or a summary. Reports written for the purpose of providing information only, without analysis, have no need for recommendations; however, recommendations are one of the most important parts of an analytical report.

Take a moment to compare the elements of the direct and indirect arrangements outlined in Exhibit 11.1. As you can see, the main difference is the placement of the conclusions and recommendations—either at the beginning (in the direct arrangement) or at the end (in the indirect arrangement). Decisions about which arrangement to use should be based on your reader's information needs, probable reaction to your report, and expectations.

| | |
|---|---|
| **EXHIBIT 11.1** | **Direct and Indirect Arrangements for Short Reports** |

| ■ **Direct Arrangement** | ■ **Indirect Arrangement** |
|---|---|
| Conclusions and recommendations (may be stated or implied) | Introductory material, such as background, purpose, research methods, and other explanatory information |
| Introductory material, such as background, purpose, research methods, other explanatory information | Findings |
| Findings | Conclusions and recommendations (may be stated or implied) |

🔖 Make the content of short reports more accessible with appropriate headings, subheadings, and visual aids.

**HEADINGS AND VISUAL AIDS.**   Consistent use of clear, appropriate headings helps guide the reader through your report. In addition, skillful placement and use of graphics will add interest to your short reports and help you convey your message in fewer words. When your use these elements in your short reports, you will find your writing is consistently well received.

Short reports may also contain headings, subheadings, and visual aids. Look at the examples of short reports in this chapter to see how these elements are typically used. Chapter 12 illustrates the format of longer reports; you may use that chapter as a guide to formatting short reports in manuscript form. The headings for major divisions of your report may be centered or placed at the left margin as long as they are consistent. Depending on how and where you type the major headings, you may position subdivisions by indenting or placing them on the left margin. You also may choose to capitalize all the letters of main headings, although words completely capitalized are harder to read. Indentations for paragraphs may also vary, depending on whether or not you are using flush left (unindented) letter or memorandum styles (although you should always indent paragraphs when typing reports in manuscript format).

The number of spaces before and after headings and subheadings varies in practice. Some companies prefer to put a triple space (two blank lines) after a major heading and before first-level subheadings, but many merely place a double space (one blank line) before and after headings and subheadings, regardless of whether a report is single or double spaced.

Visual aids are used in short reports in exactly the same way they are used in longer reports. Chapter 10 went into detail about the types of visual aids available to you. However, these are the major rules for using visual aids:

- Introduce each visual aid in the text at the point the reader needs to refer to it.

- Center a visual aid within the established margins as soon as possible after you refer to it, preferably at the end of the paragraph in which it is introduced.

- Number each visual aid if there are more than three or four in a short report.

Your goal in using visual aids is to help the reader. Keep this in mind when deciding what to represent visually and how to present it.

---

**Exhibit 11.2**　　**Formal and Informal Writing Styles**

| ▪ **Formal Writing Style** | ▪ **Informal Writing Style** |
|---|---|
| Adds power to technical writing by emphasizing facts and analysis. To achieve this power: | Adds personable tone by emphasizing the reader and his or her needs. To achieve this tone: |
| • Do not use first- or second-person personal pronouns (e.g., *I, me, you,* and *your*). | • Emphasize second-person personal pronouns (*i.e., you,* and *your*). |
| • Avoid using third-person pronouns (e.g., *we, our, us, their, they,* and *them*). | • Deemphasize we-oriented third-person pronouns (e.g., *our* and *we*). |
| • Avoid referring to yourself as "the writer." | • Deemphasize all references to the writer (e.g., *I, my,* company name). |
| • Do not use slang or clichés. | • Avoid slang and clichés unless the reader will understand them. |
| • Do not use contractions (e.g., *can't, wouldn't,* or *it's*). | • Avoid using contractions. |
| • Emphasize passive verbs (e.g., "These responsibilities can be related to . . ."). | • Emphasize active verbs (e.g., "Relate these responsibilities to . . ."). |
| • Do not use emotional language (i.e., excessive adjectives and adverbs) or exclamation points. | • Avoid emotional language and exclamation points. |

---

## COMPOSING A SHORT REPORT

▪ Use informal and formal writing styles to best advantage.

Once you begin to compose your short report, you will have already determined whether the report should be presented directly or indirectly. Before you actually start writing, you should also decide on an appropriate writing style— informal, formal, or a combination of the two.

The writing style most often used in letters, memos, and conversations is the informal style; that is what the previous chapters emphasized. (The you attitude is characterized by its informal style.) Although the informal writing style is sometimes employed in short reports, it is most often confined to the opening and closing paragraphs of letter and memo reports.

Exhibit 11.2 is an overview of the formal and informal writing styles. Formal writing style is sometimes referred to as *scientific writing style* because it has always been used by scientists and other scholars to report the results of experiments and research. Although some people say the formal style is dry and uninteresting, it has advantages.

*The formal writing style adds strength by emphasizing the content rather than the writer or the reader.*

The main benefit of the formal writing style is the strength it can add to your ideas by emphasizing what is being said rather than who is saying or reading it. Consider this sentence written in an informal style:

"I determined 17 variables that affect our production capability."

Because the pronoun *I* is at the beginning of the sentence and is the subject of the verb, the writer is the one receiving all the emphasis. Compare it to the emphasis in this formal sentence:

"Seventeen variables that impact production capability were determined."

Now the sentence emphasizes the 17 variables; who determined them is not important.

Formal writing style has other advantages as well. Consider the following informal statement:

"I think the only viable solution is to hire more people."

This is the speaker's opinion, but by including the words *I think*, the writer is almost begging someone to disagree. Now consider how much stronger this formal revision is:

"The only viable solution is to hire more people."

Of course, no matter how this idea is stated, it is still only an opinion. However, the formal statement is so emphatic that it may forestall argument.

Most business writing, even that with an informal tone, is more restrained than casual writing. For example, it is best not to use exclamation points in business letters, memos, or especially reports. Except in the case of sales letters, exclamation points detract from the professional tone of your message. Similarly, many adjectives and adverbs add an emotional tone to writing that should be avoided in reports. For example, say the following sentence to yourself with feeling:

"This is a great improvement over the original draft!"

The adjective *great* (with its enthusiastic connotation) and the exclamation point add excitement, but they remind the reader of the writer and his or her emotion. Note the more professional tone of these formal revisions:

"This is an improvement over the original draft."

"This is a significant improvement of the original."

Both the revisions make the statement sound more factual. Even though another adjective (*significant*) has been substituted for *great* in the second formal example, the difference in the connotations of the adjectives is easy to see.

Slang and clichés lend a touch of informality to any message. However, they increase the risk of miscommunicating because the reader might not understand their meaning. Furthermore, using slang and clichés is considered unprofessional. Consider the following expressions:

- Slang: rad, disin', cool, thumb's up, killer, kick back.
- Clichés: cat who swallowed the cream, E-ticket, Midas touch, out of the blue.

You wouldn't use words such as these when speaking to your company's top management, would you? Slang and clichés may be used sparingly, if at all, in business letters and memos when you are positive that the reader will understand what is being said and will not be surprised by the unprofessional nature of the words. However, neither should be used in reports.

Contractions such as *wouldn't*, *can't*, and *they're* are also inappropriate in formal writing. They are seldom used in even informal business writing. Instead, write *would not*, *cannot*, and *they are*.

One reason some people prefer to write reports with an informal writing style is an aversion to the passive nature of the sentences in the formal style. A major strength of active verbs, the ability to draw the reader personally into the action, is lost in formal writing style. (To refresh your memory, passive verbs are "being" verbs that do not perform an action, like *is*, *are*, *was*, *were*, and *am*.) To illustrate this principle, read the following passive, formal sentence:

> "The construction quality of both buildings was analyzed and is about the same."

Proponents of the informal writing style argue that an informal sentence like the following is far more readable:

> "We analyzed the construction quality of both buildings, and we consider it to be about the same."

**The formal writing style is the more common style used for writing reports in the business world.**

Although the informal writing style is sometimes used in short reports, formal writing style is far more common in the business world. A reasonable compromise for those who dislike passive sentences would be to avoid excessive use of being verbs, as in this formal revision:

> "Analysis shows the construction quality of both buildings to be approximately equal."

In summary, formal writing style is the preferred style for reports, whether they are short or long. When you write letters and memos, you will use a predominantly informal style of writing. However, the advantages of formal writing style—its seeming objectivity and impersonality—may also be exploited anytime you express an opinion.

Plan, organize, and compose progress reports, feasibility studies, justification reports, problem-solving reports, and business and government proposals.

## PROGRESS REPORTS

**Progress reports inform management of the progress made during a specific period toward completing a task or project.**

As is implied by the name, a **progress report** (sometimes called a *status report* or *periodic report*) is a review of progress made toward reaching a goal. Progress reports are typically used for projects that will take a month or longer to complete. They are written periodically to assure management or a funding agency that you are proceeding as planned and will be finished on schedule. The time period between progress reports varies—weekly, biweekly, monthly, and so on.

Progress reports, being internal documents, are usually written in memo format. The writing style may be either formal or informal; check your company files if you are uncertain which writing style will be expected by your intended reader(s). The format and the arrangement of information should follow the pattern of previous reports to facilitate comparisons from one period to the next.

Because progress reports are usually written to people already familiar with the project, very little explanatory material is needed at the beginning; the subject line often serves as the only introductory element. However, if the report will be read by anyone unfamiliar with the project, you should mention the study's purpose.

Whether written for business, government, or education, effective progress reports focus on what you have done and what remains to be done. They usually contain the following elements:

1.  *Progress toward meeting the project's goals on the original time schedule.* Briefly describe activities relating to your normal responsibilities, and provide the facts and figures always included in this specific type of progress report

(e.g., sales or production data, profit and loss statistics, completion status of each component of a large construction project, or meetings with potential clients). State specifically whether the project is still on schedule; if it is not, indicate how far behind the project is. Identify any problems encountered, their impact on the time schedule, and proposed solutions with timelines, if possible. If problems are beyond your control, request higher-level assistance.

2. *New activities undertaken during the period.* Briefly describe any new activities that are not part of your ongoing responsibilities but move the project closer to completion (e.g., an unplanned public relations activity undertaken because the opportunity presented itself, unplanned hiring of key personnel to replace some lost during the period, or initiation of the next phase of a project). If these activities will change the time schedule, clarify their impact.

3. *Activities to be undertaken in the next period.* Describe briefly what you will concentrate on or begin during the next reporting period.

This arrangement places in the first section a discussion of any problems encountered. However, some companies prefer to put problems in a separate section, either after the initial section or at the end of the progress report. Reporting problems separately emphasizes them and helps ensure that readers pay closer attention to them. Refer to existing reports of the same type or use your judgment when deciding whether to place problems in a separate section or to include them elsewhere in the report. The important thing is that you be honest about problems; do not try to hide them. If you report problems in a timely fashion, both you and upper-level management will be able to take corrective action.

Take a minute to read Exhibit 11.3, a progress report written by an individual in charge of building a new home for a client. Because progress reports for this project are written on a regular basis, there is no need for a long introduction. Notice how the problems and time schedule changes are reported.

After reading Exhibit 11.3, take a look at Exhibit 11.4, which is a typical student progress report written to inform a professor of progress on a research project. Progress reports such as these are used by many business communication teachers in the same way progress reports are used in the business world. They serve as an indicator for the supervisor, in this case the professor, that everything is going well. If there is obviously a problem such as slow progress or the omission of crucial steps in the research process, the professor can step in to correct the situation before it is too late.

## FEASIBILITY STUDIES

**Feasibility studies analyze actions to determine if they are advisable, viable, or attainable.**

**Feasibility studies** are used to analyze the impact of proposed actions on a firm's goals. For example, they may be written to answer question such as these:

"Will profit goals be realized if we go ahead with the Lakeside Project?"

"Who is likely to win if we sue Sanyito for copyright violation?"

"Do the advantages of a merger outweigh the disadvantages?"

"Will a computer or software purchase meet the needs of our company?"

3616 Main Street

Riverside, CA 92501

PH: 714.777.9018

FAX: 714.777.9019

February 18, 1994

TO:        Linda Beamer

FROM:     Rocky Young

SUBJECT:  *Progress on Grafton Property Construction*

The Grafton cabin in Lake Arrowhead is now approximately 72 percent complete, approximately 12 days behind schedule due to a significant delay expected because of a recent change order (enclosed).

<u>Period Activities and Timelines</u>

*Problems are identified within the discussion of activities.*

The period began with the project three days behind schedule due to delays in delivery of cedar shakes and roofing materials ordered to replace those stolen from the construction site.

Two of these days were made up during the past two weeks by pushing ahead at an increased pace on the inside of the home. However, the homeowner has delayed the completion of the ceiling that, at this point, was supposed to be 70 percent complete. Mrs. Martoni's decorator feels the No. 280 beams are too large and has requested No. 250 beams be substituted. An initial check of supply in the area and in Los Angeles revealed that there are only 12 No. 250 beams in stock (Builders' Suppliers), whereas the project requires 110. Perhaps you or Debbie can use your influence to speed up the delivery of these beams because much of the interior work must be delayed until they are installed.

*The last sentence of the paragraph is written in an informal style.*

The current completion figures for the project are

|  |  |
|---|---|
| Outside walls | 82% (behind schedule) |
| Roof | 70% (behind schedule) |
| Ceiling | 35% (behind schedule) |
| Interior walls | 25% (behind schedule) |
| In-wall electrical | 87% (on schedule) |
| Flooring | 40% (on schedule) |

**EXHIBIT 11.3** Continued

Linda Beamer
February 18, 1994
Page 2

*A second-page heading like this is appropriate for a multipage memo or letter report. Today, however, many people simply number each page of a multipage report, regardless of the format.*

| | |
|---|---|
| Internal plumbing | 100% (completed) |
| Well | 100% (completed) |

Security Activities and Impact on Timeline and Costs

Because of the theft of items stored on the construction site, increased security has been employed at an additional cost of $150 per month, plus $585 for the fence, gate, and labor. All materials and equipment are now secured nightly behind a sturdy chain link fence with a chained, locked gate. A guard dog supplied by Dober Security remains within the fence nightly. It is estimated that taking the time to secure equipment and materials will add an extra two days to the project.

Upcoming activities

*The next to last sentence of this paragraph speaks directly to the reader and is, therefore, informal. The following paragraphs also contain elements of the informal writing style.*

Completion of the flooring will continue on schedule. Drywalling and electrical work will continue in the three rooms not requiring the new beams. Plumbing will be completed in the kitchen and both bathrooms. Cabinetry in the kitchen must be delayed until after the beams are installed; therefore, arrangements must be made to store the cabinets away from the site until they are needed. Please have Debbie arrange for this storage or delay delivery until the cabinets are needed. The installation of the kitchen cabinets is tentatively scheduled for March 23.

These delays will probably require the temporary laying off of about 40 percent of the Category 3 labor and 20 percent of Category 2. Ideally, this layoff should occur today; however, I will delay making the announcement until Friday in the hope that you will have more luck finding the beams than I had.

Please let me know when the new beams will be delivered and what arrangements have been made for storage and later delivery of the kitchen cabinets. As soon as a delivery date is set for the beams, a new time schedule can be drawn up and the homeowner can be informed of the monetary impact of her change order.

Enclosure: Change order

1529 K Street, Apt. 23
San Diego, CA 92180
February 15, 1996

Dr. Benson Minh
Professor of Organizational Communication
School of Business and Economics
San Diego State University
San Diego, CA 92182-0034

Dear Dr. Minh:

**Progress Report on Research Project**

Since you authorized my analytical research study on January 11, I have done the following activities. As you will remember, the purpose of this project is to determine the effect of communication style on perceptions of managerial competence.

1. I gathered secondary research on the topic in three area libraries. I have had trouble finding information specific to communication styles of executives. Most sources deal with communication styles in general.

2. I developed survey instruments to measure both submissive and dominant communicators. I field-tested surveys by observing three conversations between six executives (two female and four male) in two companies. I revised the survey in accordance with the results of field test.

3. I scheduled 25 blind observations with executives of 10 companies and completed six.

4. I completed writing the introduction.

During the next month, the following steps will be undertaken to complete the project. Timelines for the completion of each step are included.

1. Use company database to do a wider search to find studies dealing with supervisory/subordinate relationships—completion date March 12

**EXHIBIT 11.4**   Continued

Dr. Benson Minh                    2                February 18, 1996

2.  Write a review of current literature—completion date March 19

3.  Complete blind observations—March 24

4.  Compile and analyze results of blind observations—March 31

5.  Complete first draft of study—April 5

6.  Complete second draft—April 9

7.  Meet with professor—April 10, 2:30 p.m.

8.  Complete and bind final draft—April 17

If you have questions about my progress on this study or suggestions you feel will improve the final results, please let me know.

Sincerely,

*Holly Calhoun*

Holly Calhoun
8-9:30 a.m. OSBE 301 Class

"What is the likelihood a product can be produced by a specific time? Within a specified cost? With current personnel?"

"Is privatization of a city's services a feasible alternative to city-run services?"

Feasibility studies analyze two or more alternatives and determine which is the best. The alternatives may involve doing something or not doing it. For example, should a city contract with private companies to provide its landscaping and lighting services or not (in other words, should or shouldn't it privatize those services)? Sometimes the decision to do something has already been made, and then the feasibility study analyzes the options available for doing it: Should a city select a company submitting the lowest bid on a project, or should it select another company providing better quality? Information relevant to these decisions is gathered and analyzed, and this analysis results in a recommendation.

Feasibility studies may be arranged in direct or indirect order, and they may be written using either the formal or informal writing style or a combination of the two. Long feasibility studies may contain all the parts of a long formal report (see Chapters 12 and 13). Short feasibility reports, those of no more than 10 pages, usually include the following elements:

1. *Short background, purpose statement, and description of research methods.* This section provides reasons for the study and clarifies the problem in no more than four or five paragraphs. It describes how the problem was studied and by whom.

2. *Conclusions.* Generalizations or implications arising from the study are presented in list or paragraph form.

3. *Recommendation(s).* The action(s) urged as a consequence of the conclusions may also be presented in list or paragraph form.

4. *Criteria.* The standards for deciding which recommendation to follow are described and justified in as few paragraphs as necessary.

5. *Comparison of alternatives.* The alternatives are evaluated in light of the criteria, and the conclusions are described and justified. If the analysis takes more than two pages, this section should be divided into subsections. Tables and other visual aids often improve readability. If other sources have been consulted, they should be documented.

This sequence of elements is a direct arrangement. Do you recall why? If you answered, "Because the conclusions and recommendation(s) are presented before the findings," you are right. Feasibility studies may also be arranged indirectly, with conclusions and recommendations typed at the end of the report.

Spend a few minutes reading the feasibility report illustrated in Exhibit 11.5. It is written in direct order, because the city council for which it was compiled is anxious to know its conclusions. The study could have been expanded to include tables and charts showing the specific data from which the conclusions were derived. Doing so would have been more important if the committee preparing the report had come up with conclusions that the city council might have questioned. However, because the conclusions are favorable and the full study is accessible, there is no need to include all the information in this report.

### The City of South Pasadena

*367 Mission Street*

*South Pasadena, CA 91030*

**TO:**     City Council Members

**FROM:**     Fereshda Sesarian, City Manager

**COPIES TO:**     Privatization Committee Members: B. Sanchez, N. Theiss, L. Simpson, J. Prickett, L. Luigi

**DATE:**     July 17, 1995

**SUBJECT:**     **Privatization of Landscaping and Lighting Services**

The Privatization Committee, commissioned on September 5, 1994, has completed its study. The primary features of the study are included in this report; a more detailed analysis with charts and tables is available in the City Clerk's Office for you and members of the general public who would like more information. This information will be presented in detail at the August 2nd City Council meeting.

*The purpose is stated clearly at the beginning.*

As you will recall, the purpose of this study was determining if privatizing the city's landscaping and lighting functions would save the city money without sacrificing service, safety, or environmental esthetics. This study was necessary because of the projected loss, over the next three years of $3.2 million from the state.

*Methods of researching the problem are mentioned in the brief introduction.*

The committee thoroughly investigated the experiences of 35 cities, 5 in the surrounding area, who have privatized these services over the past five years. Committee members visited four of the cities whose services have been in the hands of private landscaping or lighting companies for four or more years. Committee members were able to see for themselves whether safety and environmental esthetics were being maintained. It also gave the committee an opportunity to informally survey citizens to determine their reactions to the effects of privatization.

EXHIBIT
11.5

Continued

Privatization of Landscaping and Lighting Services
Page 2
July 17, 1995

**Conclusions**

The study of the experiences of other cities led to these conclusions:

Direct
arrangement
places the
conclusions
and the
recommendation
right after the
introduction
and before the
discussion of
the findings.

1. A compelling majority of cities who have privatized their landscaping and lighting services within the past five years report satisfaction with the service of the contractors, as well as satisfaction with the safety and environmental esthetics.

2. Savings to the cities who have privatized their landscaping services has averaged $.45 per square foot of landscaped ground per year.

3. Savings to the cities who have privatized their lighting services has averaged $7 for each light pole, regardless of type, in each year.

4. At these rates, the City of South Pasadena could save approximately $925,000 over the next three years by privatizing its landscaping and lighting services.

**Recommendation**

This data within this study and its conclusions led to the following recommendation:

*The recommendation is emphasized by typing it in bold type.*

**The City of South Pasadena should privatize its landscaping and lighting services.**

**Current and Projected Expenses**

When the salary and benefits of the grounds supervisor and four groundskeepers are added to the cost of supplies, bushes, trees, flowers, and so on, the city spent $1.60 a square foot for landscaping last year. That figure will be approximately $1.68 this year because of an increase in the cost of medical benefits and a 2 percent salary increase.

**Exhibit 11.5**   Continued

Privatization of Landscaping and Lighting Services
Page 3
July 17, 1995

To maintain the City's lighting, two full-time individuals are employed.
Their salaries, benefits, and the budget given their department resulted
in a figure of $27 necessary to maintain each light pole within the city
limits in 1994. The cost of medical benefits, a 2 percent salary
increase, and the planned replacement of 23 poles should increase this
cost to $34 this year.

**Survey Results**

At the last convention of city managers, 35 cities in the state who have
privatized either their landscaping or lighting services were identified.
The city managers of each of these cities were contacted and asked to
complete a survey. Twenty-two of those surveys were returned
completed. Follow-up telephone calls resulted in completion of the
remaining surveys, realizing a 100 percent return rate.

Four of the cities surveyed had lighting and landscaping budgets
approximately the same as that of South Pasadena and were judged
comparable in overall size and population. Therefore, these cities were
selected for visitation by two committee members. Except in one
instance, committee members found these cities' services and facilities
to be satisfactory; and in most cases, the committee was surprised to
discover that many citizens were unaware a change had occurred. Most
citizens felt that privatization had resulted in no decrease in services
or esthetics, and most believed the quality of landscaping had
improved.

In one instance, although the city manager of Mokesto indicated city
officials were satisfied with the level of services, safety, and esthetics,
committee members were not satisfied. Many streetlights lacked
working bulbs, and what little landscaping existed was in need of
weeding and pruning. However, citizens themselves believed there had
been no change in the level of service since a private company took
over the city's responsibilities. Therefore, committee members
concluded that, although the situation would not be satisfactory in
South Pasadena, no decrease in services, safety, or esthetics had taken
place as a result of Mokesto's privatizing its landscaping and lighting
services.

**EXHIBIT 11.5**  Concluded

Privatization of Landscaping and Lighting Services
Page 4
July 17, 1995

Eighty-two percent of the city managers surveyed registered their
complete satisfaction with privatization and its resultant savings over
a period of three or more years. For those cities where privatization
has been in force for two or fewer years, the figure rose to 86 percent.
In only one case did privatization result in higher costs, and this could
be attributed to the unusual expenditures necessary after a flood.

As you can see from this brief summary of the results of the study, as
well as the complete study to be presented at the next City Council
meeting, privatization promises to be a feasible alternative to
city-operated services. Not only will it save a considerable amount of
money, it should also ensure the continuation of safety, quality service,
and esthetic surroundings typical of our fair city.

If you have any questions about this study, please telephone me at my
home number, (818) 441-4352, or at my office (310) 450-5455. I will
be more than happy to discuss the results of the study with you.

Because feasibility studies are written to answer simple questions, the primary focus of the report is the conclusion(s) reached. However, feasibility studies are analytical; information is reported only because it must be analyzed in order to make decisions. The reader must be reassured that the conclusions have been arrived at honestly and objectively; thus, the research itself must be clearly presented and interpreted.

## JUSTIFICATION REPORTS

Justification reports seek approval for projects, ideas, or expenditures by persuading management of the benefits to the company.

A **justification report** is a proposal to management seeking its approval for a project, an idea, or an expenditure. The emphasis is on the proposal and the reason for it. This is the type of report that Ralph Spanswick was writing to persuade his supervisor to recommend the purchase of employee-training materials. Many justification reports are unsolicited. An employees sees a need, proposes a course of action, and uses persuasive skills to convince management to take that action.

The ideas behind a justification report may be presented orally, although it is sometimes advantageous to put the proposal in writing. When you write, you have the advantage of time—time to plan carefully and to choose just the right words to persuade. In addition, a written report may overcome some supervisors' tendency to react negatively to any proposal without really thinking it through. Reading the report gives such a supervisor time to think about your proposal before reacting.

Justification reports should be written in direct order and should focus the reader's attention on what needs to be done. Therefore, you may want to organize everything around your recommendation(s). For example, if you wanted to persuade your company to research the Asian-American market as a way of increasing sales, you might organize it as follows:

1. Direct subject line: "Focusing Market Research on Asian-Americans."
2. Concise reasons for the recommended action: "Currently we know nothing about this market. Surveys show we're not selling many products to it."
3. Direct proposal: "Dedicate 15 percent of next year's market research budget to this population."
4. Gains to be derived from this act: "Potential benefits include increased market share via targeted advertising and development of products, entry into a market virtually untapped by other American companies, and the possibility of increased exports to Pacific Rim nations."
5. Wrapup: "If management decides to pursue this course, I will be happy to assist with or be in charge of the research."

Another arrangement that works well for justification reports is this:

1. Introduction, including explanation of need for recommended action.
2. Short, clear statement of action recommended.
3. Justification of that action in terms of how it will benefit the reader.
4. Further explanation of what the recommended action will entail (if necessary).
5. Offer to assist with the recommended action.

## PROBLEM-SOLVING REPORTS

Problem-solving reports analyze a problem and alternative solutions to determine which one best meets the needs of the company.

The major difference between a justification report and a problem-solving report is objectivity. Whereas justification reports use persuasive skills to convince management that a desired course of action is sound, **problem-solving reports** analyze data and recommend only those actions supported by the evidence. In a problem-solving report, the evidence discovered during the study is what drives the decision.

For example, Paul Moyer, a consultant, was directed to find out what to do about the declining sales of FunPro National's snack food division. Management was thinking about either selling the division or changing its focus. Paul's consulting firm first investigated the current situation to determine the full extent of the problem. Next, they investigated trends in the market by surveying a large number of snack food buyers across the country. The third step was to study government data on the topic. The report Paul wrote at the end of his investigation is included in Exhibit 11.6. Notice that Paul's recommendation is at the end of the report. Paul could easily have put the recommendation at the beginning, but he wanted to be certain FunPro's executives understood the amount of research the study encompassed. However, the recommendation is printed in boldface type, which draws attention to it. Notice also the use of headings to guide readers.

## BUSINESS AND GOVERNMENT PROPOSALS

Some proposals seek new business from a client; others respond to government agencies that have published RFPs (requests for proposal) for specific work that needs to be done or an order that needs to be filled.

**Proposals** are reports that explain how you intend to meet your readers' needs. For instance, you might write a proposal to a potential client explaining how your company can improve his or her telephone system. Proposals to government agencies are also common.

Various federal state, county, and city agencies issue announcements inviting companies, organizations, or individuals to submit proposals for providing goods or services. These announcements may be called RFPs (requests for proposal), RFQs (requests for qualifications), or bid requests. For example, proposals might be solicited for developing a new product, performing research vital to national security, hiring and training unemployed workers, opening a factory in a blighted urban area, moving a company to a new city or state, or supplying uniforms to a fire department. After the deadline passes, the government agency thoroughly evaluates all the proposals it has received. If your proposal is selected over all the others, your company will be given a contract.

If you are responding to a proposal at the invitation of a government agency, follow the pattern requested in the RFP. Use its headings and subheadings, its numbering system, and its terminology, and present these items in the same order as in the RFP. To illustrate, if a request for proposal uses a heading such as "Background of Proposed Project Director," then you should use that same heading as you discuss this topic.

Address very specifically all categories and criteria in exactly the same order in which they are listed in the RFP. Most proposals are evaluated by several different people, who use a point system corresponding to the RFP specifications. Exactly following the recommended format makes it easier for each evaluator to assess how well your project meets the RFP's terms. In some cases, you might be required to limit your proposal to a specific number of pages. If so, make sure you do not exceed that number, or it is likely the evaluator will not

# BANDOLIER CONSULTING GROUP

Specialists in Management Operations

*1019 Gibson Blvd. Albuquerque, NM 87117*

August 4, 1996

Ms. Jodi Florez
Vice President of Operations
FunPro National
Snack Food Division
23771 Lomas Boulevard
Albuquerque, NM 87108

Dear Ms. Florez:

*The purpose is identified in the first paragraph.*

The study you and Paul Clendenning requested on April 25 has been completed and is included within this letter. As you will recall, the purpose of the study was analyzing the declining sales of the Snack Food Division to determine the best course of action for the firm.

*The alternatives to be studied are identified in the last sentence of this paragraph.*

In our initial meeting, FunPro's executives expressed the consensus that a change in public preferences is the cause of the decline. The executives felt that increasing interest in healthier foods and overall physical fitness has caused the public to eschew snack foods other than fruits and vegetables and to concentrate their purchases on food served at main meals only. Since the snack foods made by this division are primarily potato chips, peanuts, and crackers, unacceptable to a health-conscious public, it was believed that the Snack Food Division should be either sold or its focus changed to other types of food.

*The research methods are described to lend credibility to the findings.*

To study this issue, one team of Bandolier consultants concentrated on a search of sales and accounting records to ascertain the full extent of the current decline and to compare it to the performance figures of the past. At the same time, other teams surveyed marketing trends in snack foods. This consisted of an on-site study of snack purchases made by 1,000 people in 100 grocery stores in the states of California, Kansas, Alabama, and Pennsylvania. A third component of the study included a search of USDA studies to determine the overall amounts spent by the American public on traditional snack foods and on fruits and vegetables.

*The reader is specifically directed to the visual aid, which is positioned within the report's margins immediately following the paragraph in which it is first mentioned.*

### Division and Company Performance

Figure 1 reveals that the Snack Food Division's sales have declined almost steadily since 1989, paralleling the drop in overall company gross

*Telephone 505•821•4444*          *FAX   505•821•4380*

EXHIBIT
11.6

Continued

profits during that time. The same linkage was revealed by records of the two previous five-year periods—that overall company profits rose as snack food sales rose. It can be said, throughout FunPro's 17-year history, that overall success has been tied to the progress of the Snack Food Division.

**Figure 1**

**Correlation of Division Sales and Company Performance**

Company gross profits (in millions)

## Survey and Marketing Results

Teams of two Bandolier researchers did on-site studies of 100 buyers in each of 100 grocery stores in four states: 35 in California, 20 in Kansas, 20 in Alabama, and 25 in Pennsylvania. Over a three-day period, these individuals recorded the snack food purchases of individuals purchasing food at randomly selected times and at rotating checkout stands. Their findings resulted in these conclusions:

• Plain potato chips, peanuts, and crackers of the types made by FunPro account for 8 percent of the total snacks purchased.

• Tortilla chips and low-fat, low-salt chips account for 20 percent of the total snacks purchased and 82 percent of total chip sales.

• Freeze-dried peanuts and cashews account for 7.5 percent of snack food sales and 78.5 percent of the snack nut sales.

• Low-fat, low-salt crackers account for 11 percent of snack food sales and 84 percent of the total cracker sales.

*Conclusions related to management's alternatives are set off in a list so they are easier to find.*

2

**EXHIBIT 11.6**

Continued

• Fresh fruits and vegetables account for 20 percent of total snack food sales, a figure that has risen only 2 percent since 1983.

• Candy, cookies, cakes, and other foods account for 33.5 percent of total snack food sales.

• Snack foods account for 14 percent of the total food dollar spent in grocery stores, a figure that has risen 3.5 percent since 1983.

See Figure 2 for a breakdown of snack food sales.

**Figure 2**

**Total Snack Food Sales**

| |
|---|
| 7.5%<br>Freeze-dried peanuts and cashews |
| 8%<br>Plain potato chips, peanuts, and crackers |
| 11%<br>Low-fat, low-salt crackers |
| 20%<br>Tortilla chips and low-fat, low-salt chips |
| 22%<br>Fresh fruits and vegetables |
| 31%<br>Candy, cookies, cakes, and other |

**EXHIBIT 11.6**     Concluded

The above figures lead to this recommendation:

**Because the tastes of the American public have changed, the Snack Food Division should focus its production on healthier versions of its current products.**

According to USDA data, the sale of fruits and vegetables has only increased two percent over the past 10 years, and the sale of snack foods has risen 3.5 percent in that same period. It does not appear that the public has completely abandoned prepared snack foods in favor of fruits and vegetables. In fact, the general public is spending a significantly larger portion of its disposable income on snack foods in general. All of the growth in snack food sales revolves around healthier versions of the traditional foods—crackers, nuts, and chips.

The increasing importance of snack foods to the American public makes the Snack Food Division of increasing importance to FunPro. As a result, minor retooling of equipment, revamping of production lines, and reformulating existing products should return the Snack Food Division to its former position of strength.

It was a pleasure doing this study for you. To ensure you have all the data you need to make a sound decision on this critical issue, Bandolier concentrated its resources in the field (the only way to get valid results in any marketing survey). You may be sure that we will dedicate this same level of resources the next time you need to pinpoint the specifics of your marketing, sales, or production characteristics. I look forward to presenting this report to the board next week. In the meantime, please let me know if there is anything that needs clarification.

Sincerely yours,

Paul Moyer
Vice President

snl

read the rest of your proposal and may even deduct points for your failure to follow instructions.

Whether you are writing a proposal for a government agency or a private company, use good you attitude to show how the reader, his or her organization, or the public will benefit from accepting your proposal. Tell exactly what your company will do in return for the money. For example, if a county maintenance shop has advertised for equipment that cuts screw threads at a specific tolerance level, state that your particular machine will do exactly that. In fact, because bidding for government contracts is so competitive, you might explain what your company can offer beyond the minimum level stated in an RFP. In writing a proposal for a training grant, for instance, you might offer to hire and train 23 people for the same amount the agency is willing to pay for training 20 people.

A long history of successfully completing other projects should be mentioned in a proposal. However, if your company is new, you might stress the benefits of going with a firm that has new, innovative ideas and is still young enough to be able to get things done quickly without the red tape of larger or older, more bureaucratic companies.

If an RFP asks you to supply a budget, be specific and truthful about what you plan to do with the money. Government grants are usually subject to audit, and the penalties for fraud can be severe. In both business and government proposals, you should describe honestly what you are going to do. Moreover, you must avoid getting caught up in the competition. Make realistic commitments, because you and your company will be expected to deliver whatever promises you make.

## BUSINESS PLANS

Plan, organize, and compose business plans.

> Business plans give lenders the information they need to decide whether to lend money to a new business or to an existing business for expansion.

A **business plan** is a detailed report describing the nature of a business, the target market, what the company offers that its competitors do not, the budget required to turn a profit, and the resources and qualifications of the owner(s). Business plans are generally required of new businesses seeking funding, as well as of existing businesses needing outside funding to expand their operations. Most bankers and potential investors want to examine a business plan to evaluate the idea's potential for success and the likelihood that the investment or loan will be repaid.

> Most business plans are ineffective because they do not include everything lenders require or because they are not specific enough.

Most business plans fail in providing such reassurance, however, because they are incomplete and not specific. Their writers don't understand the kinds of information and the level of detail required. Although business plans are usually no longer than 12 pages (10 pages are the ideal), they include a great deal of information, such as:

1. *Executive summary with product or service description.* Begin with a two- or three-page overview of the proposed venture. Concisely describe the key elements of the project and its major goals and objectives. What makes the product or service better, more unique, or more desirable than competitors' products or services? Supply patent information (if applicable).

2. *Company background* (for existing businesses only). Provide previous balance sheets, income and expense statements, cash flow statements, and so forth. Describe the industry (showing that it is flourishing or likely to do so soon) and the company's position within it.

3. *Management.* Supply brief resumes of the entire management team and the consultants (if any) who will provide skills that management lacks. Explain each person's responsibilities. Describe his or her expertise and experience in critical areas such as planning, product development and pricing, distribution, promotion and marketing, management, production and operations management, accounting, and finance. Explain each key person's level of commitment (financial and time) to the business. Letters of reference and personal financial statements may be included in an appendix.

4. *Financial plan.* Provide a realistic, conservative five-year projection of income and expenses. If you are seeking funding to manufacture a product, tie projections to the stages of the product's life cycle (introduction, growth, maturity, and decline). Explain briefly how the figures were derived (generally, with assumptions based on known trends). Mention all sources of funding, personnel requirements, and accounting procedures. Identify the factors that might affect projections. Sketch best-case and worst-case scenarios.

5. *Capital requirements.* State exactly how much money is needed for the project and how the funds will be used. Describe the financial commitment of the owner(s). If possible, offer a personal guarantee of the loan.

6. *Marketing plan.* Provide sales forecasts for a five-year period. Set a price for the product or service (based on research), and compare its weaknesses and strengths with those of its competition. Describe planned marketing research, promotional activities, and advertising campaigns. Analyze the target market and market size. Summarize all the marketing research that has already been conducted (copies of sources and/or a bibliography may be included in an appendix).

7. *Manufacturing plan* (if appropriate). Describe the production capacity of the plant, plant size, inventory on hand, inventory control method, personnel required, machinery and computers required, quality control efforts, and so on.

8. *Location.* Verify that the location is accessible and desirable to the target market. Analyze traffic patterns and parking availability. Provide a demographic analysis of area consumers. Describe competitors' locations.

Doublecheck business plans for accuracy and consistency.

Once you have written your business plan, have an accountant or financial analyst verify the accuracy of your figures and financial analyses. Ask him or her to make sure that totals are correct and consistent throughout the plan. For example, the marketing costs specified in the marketing plan section should agree with the projections for marketing listed in the financial plan; the machinery called for in the manufacturing plan should be listed in the financial plan. If the numbers do not add up, your business plan is likely to be turned down. Careless errors such as these imply that the owner will be careless in other aspects of the business.

By preparing a business plan before you meet with a banker or venture capitalist, you increase your chances of success. To further increase your chances, take an accountant with you. Bankers will want to speak to you to make sure that you are both passionate and realistic about the new venture; however, they don't expect you to have the financial or accounting background necessary to answer all their questions in these areas.

## EVALUATING A SHORT REPORT

◆ Evaluate short business reports and business plans.

After you have finished planning, organizing, and composing a short business report, take the time to evaluate it before you distribute it. What is the likelihood the report will achieve its major purpose and maintain a favorable relationship with the reader(s)? Use the checklist in Exhibit 11.7 to assess your short report. If the report was written by a collaborative writing team, have each member of the team complete a checklist, and then discuss the results as a group.

Once you are satisfied that the report meets the checklist's criteria, you may distribute it. Then the final step of your evaluation may take place. What was the result of your report? Did you get what you wanted? Was your supervisor, client, or prospective client satisfied with the information you submitted? Did your reader have to seek clarification about anything?

If they are asked, evaluators of government proposals will sometimes discuss the strengths and weaknesses of a proposal. Listen carefully to what they say, and avoid the tendency to defend your proposal against any and all criticism. A good relationship at this stage might result in a successful proposal in the future.

As a businessperson, you will write many different kinds of short reports. By following the suggestions and guidelines within this chapter, your reports will be more likely to please your clients, your colleagues, and your superiors. The more effective your short reports are, the more you demonstrate that you have what it takes to be successful in the business world.

## DISCUSSION QUESTIONS

◆ Identify the uses of the short report.

1. Describe the purpose of each of the six main types of short reports, and give an example of a situation that would necessitate each.

◆ Apply the four steps of the message formulation process to short reports.

2. Identify the four steps in the message formulation process for writing short reports. For each step, compose one sentence that explains it.

◆ Apply the four steps of the message formulation process to short reports.

3. Name two advantages and two disadvantages of writing a short report collaboratively.

◆ Choose the correct short report format for the situation, distinguishing among the standard letter, memo, and manuscript formats.

4. Describe the differences between a report written in manuscript format and one written in letter format.

EXHIBIT
11.7

**Checklist for Short Reports**

Answer the following yes/no questions for the sections that apply to the type of short report you have written. If a point in a general section does not apply, put n/a (not applicable) in the blank.

■ **Progress Reports**

___ Did you consider the reader's expectations in deciding how much information is needed in the introduction?

___ Are problems you encountered included, and are they honest?

___ Did you include all these elements: progress toward meeting goals, new activities this period, activities for next period, and problems encountered?

___ Have you disclosed clearly and completely everything that should be communicated?

___ Does the message achieve the purpose(s) established during freewriting?

___ Will the quality of your arguments, conclusions, generalizations, and assumptions stand up to scrutiny?

■ **Feasibility Studies**

___ Did you consider the needs of your reader in deciding how much information is needed in the introduction?

___ Did you consider the expectations and reaction of your reader when deciding between a direct and indirect outline?

___ Did you include all these elements: short background, purpose statement, research methods, conclusions, recommendations, criteria, and comparison of alternatives?

___ Will the quality of your arguments, conclusions, generalizations, and assumptions stand up to scrutiny?

___ Have you disclosed clearly and completely everything that should be communicated?

___ Does the message achieve the purpose(s) established during freewriting?

■ **Justification Reports**

___ Did you consider the needs of your reader when deciding how much information was needed in the introduction?

___ Did you consider the expectations and reaction of your reader when deciding between a direct and indirect outline?

___ Did you include all these elements: direct subject line, concise reasons for the recommended action, direct proposal, reader-centered gains to be derived from the action, and offer to assist?

___ Will the quality of your arguments, conclusions, generalizations, and assumptions stand up to scrutiny?

___ Have you disclosed clearly and completely everything that should be communicated?

___ Does the message achieve the purpose(s) established during freewriting?

■ **Business and Government Proposals**

___ Did you follow exactly the RFP's order of items?

___ Did you use the same headings and wording?

___ Did you address all criteria and categories requested in terms of how they will benefit the funding organization or firm?

___ Are your proposed budget and all other figures reasonable, correct, and consistent?

___ Are your commitments reasonable and sincere?

■ **Problem-Solving Reports**

___ Did you consider the needs of your reader in deciding how much information was needed in the introduction?

___ Did you consider the expectations and reaction of your reader when deciding between a direct and indirect outline?

___ Did you include all these elements: short background, purpose statement, research methods, conclusions, recommendations, criteria, and comparison of alternatives?

___ Will the quality of your arguments, conclusions, generalizations, and assumptions stand up to scrutiny?

___ Did you include all relevant research on the topic?

___ Have you disclosed clearly and completely everything that should be communicated?

___ Does the message achieve the purpose(s) established during freewriting?

■ **Business Plans**

___ Are all elements included (executive summary with product or service description, company background, management, financial plan, capital required, marketing plan, manufacturing plan, location analysis)?

___ Have you disclosed clearly and completely everything that should be communicated?

___ Are the content and figures accurate and consistent?

___ Will the quality of your arguments stand up to scrutiny?

■ **Mechanics**

___ Have you decided to use the formal writing style, the informal writing style, or a combination of the two?

___ If formal writing style is used, have you avoided using all first- and second-person personal

**EXHIBIT 11.7**

**continued**

pronouns? Avoided slang and contractions? Avoided *our* and *we?* Avoided referring directly to the reader? Avoided excessive use of adjectives and adverbs? Avoided emotional words and punctuation?

\_\_\_\_ If informal writing style is used, does it emphasize the benefit to the reader, using *you* and *your?*

\_\_\_\_ Are the name and title of the reader spelled and used correctly?

\_\_\_\_ Have all words been spelled correctly?

\_\_\_\_ Is correct sentence structure used for all sentences?

\_\_\_\_ Is correct paragraph structure used for all paragraphs?

\_\_\_\_ Are there transitions between each paragraph?

\_\_\_\_ Is punctuation correct?

■ **Readability**

\_\_\_\_ Is the reading level appropriate for intended reader(s)?

\_\_\_\_ Are lists used when necessary to improve the clarity of complex information or questions?

\_\_\_\_ Are visual aids used to aid in the flow of information?

\_\_\_\_ Are visual aids introduced in the text and inserted as soon as possible after their introduction?

■ **Format and Appearance**

\_\_\_\_ If standardization is important, did you use a standardized format?

\_\_\_\_ For internal reports, did you use memorandum format or manuscript format?

\_\_\_\_ For external reports, did you use letter format or manuscript format?

\_\_\_\_ Have subsequent pages been properly labeled?

\_\_\_\_ Are side margins equal?

■ **Other**

\_\_\_\_ Is the entire message truthful?

\_\_\_\_ Have you been fair to all concerned?

\_\_\_\_ Would you be proud if everyone you know was aware of all the details of this transaction?

\_\_\_\_ Is your communication within the bounds of the law?

\_\_\_\_ Have you avoided deliberate distortions, slang, discriminatory language, clichés, redundancies, roundabout expressions, and confusing foreign expressions?

■ Choose the correct short report format for the situation, distinguishing among the standard letter, memo, and manuscript formats.

5. What are the options for labeling the second and third pages of a three-page memo report? (See the chapter exhibits.)

■ Plan reports of suitable length.

6. What influences the length of a report?

■ Select the appropriate organizational strategy, distinguishing between direct and indirect outlines.

7. Identify two things about the reader that you should consider before deciding whether to present the conclusions and recommendations at the beginning or the end of a short report.

■ Make the content of short reports more accessible with appropriate headings, subheadings, and visual aids.

8. What is the value of using headings and visual aids in a short report?

■ Make the content of short reports more accessible with appropriate headings, subheadings, and visual aids.

9. Identify two formatting alternatives for using the heading "Problems Encountered" in a letter report.

■ Use informal and formal writing styles to best advantage.

10. Identify two advantages and two disadvantages of formal writing style.

🔖 Use informal and formal writing styles to best advantage.

11. Read the following excerpt from a report written in informal writing style. Underline the words and other elements that would have to be changed to convert the sentences to formal writing style.

I said that I don't think we should study the feasibility of merging with Clinton Industries! You know as well as I do that their spectacular profits make them an unlikely target for a takeover.

🔖 Plan, organize, and compose progress reports, feasibility studies, justification reports, problem-solving reports, and business and government proposals.

12. What is the difference in the way recommendations are presented in a justification report and in a problem-solving report?

🔖 Plan, organize, and compose business plans.

13. What does this statement mean to you?

Doublecheck the accuracy and consistency of the information within the business plan.

What would you advise the business plan's author to do in light of this statement?

🔖 Evaluate short business reports and business plans.

14. What is the ultimate test of a short report's effectiveness?

## APPLICATION EXERCISES

🔖 Identify the uses of the short report.
🔖 Plan, organize, and compose progress reports, feasibility studies, justification reports, problem-solving reports, and business and government proposals.
🔖 Evaluate short business reports and business plans.

1. Get a copy of a short report (10 or fewer pages) from a business. (You will need to get permission from the company and the report's writer.) Critique that report using the checklist in Exhibit 11.7 as a guide. In some instances, because you did not write the report, you might not be able to answer a question. For example, one of the questions in the checklist is "Have you decided to use the formal writing style, the informal writing style, or a combination of the two?" You can't really answer that question "yes" or "no"; however, you can look at the report to determine what the writer apparently decided to do, and you can assess whether or not the writer's approach was effective. If your professor instructs you to do so, rewrite the short report to make it more effective. Turn in a copy of the original report stapled to the back of your revision.

🔖 Choose the correct short report format for the situation, distinguishing among the standard letter, memo, and manuscript formats.
🔖 Plan reports of suitable length.
🔖 Evaluate short business reports and business plans.

2. As directed by your professor, use the checklist in Exhibit 11.7 to evaluate a report written by one of your classmates. What changes would you recommend to the report's writer? If you can't answer a question, look at the

report to determine what the writer apparently decided to do, and assess whether or not the writer's approach was effective. Are the format and length appropriate for the topic, the purpose, and the reader? After your evaluation, write a memo report to the student (with a copy to your professor) specifying changes you recommend and justifying your viewpoint. Do not rewrite the student's report; just critique it. Be honest—insincere praise does no one any good. Use good you attitude to inform the student of the benefit to be gained from making your recommended changes.

🔻 Select the appropriate organizational strategy, distinguishing between direct and indirect outlines.

🔻 Plan, organize, and compose progress reports, feasibility studies, justification, reports, problem-solving reports, and business and government proposals.

🔻 Evaluate short business reports and business plans.

3. Read the notes below for a memo report justifying the complete ban of smoking in all company restaurants. The writer arranged the items into two patterns: direct and indirect. Which pattern best considers the needs of the reader, a boss who smokes? Justify your answer, and then write the short report using the organizational pattern you selected.

---

**EXHIBIT 11.8**

**Application**

| ▮ **Direct outline** | ▮ **Indirect outline** |
|---|---|
| Subject line—complete ban on smoking in company restaurants | Subject line—Restaurant smoking policies |
| Introduction/identification of problem (loss of customers to no-smoking restaurants) | Introduction/identification of problem (loss of customers to no-smoking restaurants) |
| Recommendation—ban | Data presentation/justification of ban (benefits to company—regain customers lost, image of healthiness and caring, increase in sales, decrease in workers compensation claims; benefits to society) |
| Data presentation/justification of ban (benefits to society—death rates from lung cancer, emphysema, and second-hand smoke) | Recommendation—ban |
| Offer to oversee institution of new policy | Offer to oversee institution of new policy |

---

🔻 Use informal and formal writing styles to best advantage.

4. Rewrite each of the following informal sentences to make them comply with the principles of formal writing style:

   a. "We sent two teams to research your sales problem, and they found just what we expected. It's hard to believe, but your sales representatives have decreased their overall contacts by 33 percent."

   b. "Over a three-month period, our sales dropped an unbelievable 24 percent!"

   c. "Do not forget to include the recommendations in your report."

   d. "To ensure you have everything you need to make a decision, Diaz & Associates surveyed, oh, I'd say, somewhere between 500 and 700 buyers of personal computers."

e. "I assumed there is a marked similarity between the problems of a new bicycle shop and those of a camera shop."

f. "Personally, I believe the second alternative is best. Its use of the fantastic new polymers will decrease our product failures a lot!"

g. "Briefly describe activities relating to your normal responsibilities, as well as facts and figures that you always include in your progress reports."

🔖 Use informal and formal writing styles to best advantage.

5. Make each of the following formal sentences impersonal and informal:

a. "Progress reports are written periodically to assure management that progress is being made on an activity."

b. "Sales figures should show an 11 percent increase with the inception of the recommended marketing campaign."

c. "A one-month concentrated program of media promotional activities will increase public awareness of the company's efforts to reduce harmful emissions."

d. "Color tints can be combined with the spot overlay feature of the software program to improve the cumulative effect of the tinted colors as they print on top of one another."

e. "The insurance policy allowing monthly payments at a 14.5 percent interest rate is recommended."

f. "Keyboards should be 25 to 27 inches from the floor for users to avoid carpal tunnel syndrome, a wrist injury associated with repetitive motion."

🔖 Plan, organize, and compose progress reports, feasibility studies, justification reports, problem-solving reports, and business and government proposals.

🔖 Evaluate short business reports and business plans.

6. Compare the annual reports of two Fortune 1000 firms that are in the same industry. Critique the two reports on the following factors:

a. The overall appearance.

b. The sincerity, completeness, and accuracy of the information.

c. The specificity of the wording.

d. The treatment of negative information.

e. The writing style.

f. The use of headings and subheadings.

g. The use of visual aids.

h. Its ability to appeal to the needs of its readers (stockholders).

Write a memo report to your instructor evaluating these factors and detailing any improvements you would make. Attach the annual reports or copies of them to your memo.

🔖 Evaluate short business reports and business plans.

7. Make four photocopies of Exhibit 11.7. Fill one out for each of the reports in Exhibits 11.3, 11.4, and 11.5. In some instances, because you did not write these reports, you might not be able to answer a question. For example, one of the questions is "Have you decided to use the formal writing style, the informal writing style, or a combination of the two?" You can't really answer that question "yes" or "no"; however, you can look at the report to determine

what the writer decided to do. After completing the checklists, write a memo to your instructor about the revisions you suggest for each of the reports.

For the remaining exercises, you are to compose a short report as instructed. Assume any reasonable details to make the messages realistic. Unless a job title is specified for you, make up a title appropriate to the situation. As you do the exercises, follow these steps:

1. Plan your message:
    *a.* Establish your purpose.
    *b.* Choose a medium and channel.
    *c.* Consider legal and ethical issues.
    *d.* Analyze your audience.
    *e.* Gather necessary resources.

2. Organize your message:
    *a.* Freewrite major points.
    *b.* Choose an organizational strategy.

3. Compose your message.

4. Evaluate your message:
    *a.* Use Exhibit 11.7 for self-evaluation.
    *b.* Evaluate feedback from your instructor.

Your instructor will tell you whether to turn in your freewritten notes or any other evidence that you have performed each step of the message formulation process. You will also be told whether the message must be written individually or collaboratively.

### Progress Reports

▪ Apply the four steps of the message formulation process to short reports.
▪ Choose the correct short report format for the situation, distinguishing among the standard letter, memo, and manuscript formats.
▪ Plan reports of suitable length.
▪ Select the appropriate organizational strategy, distinguishing between direct and indirect outlines.
▪ Make the content of short reports more accessible with appropriate headings, subheadings, and visual aids.
▪ Use informal and formal writing styles to best advantage.
▪ Plan, organize, and compose progress reports, feasibility studies, justification reports, problem-solving reports, and business and government proposals.
▪ Evaluate short business reports and business plans.

8. *Progress report on a site for a new plant.* You have just returned from a business trip to Mexico and Canada, during which you investigated where to locate a new plant for MALRACO, the company for which you act as operations manager. MALRACO assembles computers for brand-name manufacturers. Your company's business has grown tremendously within the five years it has been operating, and your two North American plants (one in Mexico and one in Texas) are no longer able to handle the volume of work. Increasing personnel costs, government regulations, and taxes in the United States have led you to conclude that a new facility must be opened in either Mexico or Canada. The labor and tax advantages in either country currently make them more desirable locations than the United States.

You have visited three areas and talked with local politicians and city representatives to determine the concessions, if any, each is willing to make to attract this facility. The plant will hire about 2,000 local citizens.

Your first visit—with Carlos Gutierrez of Guaymas, Mexico—was held on Tuesday, two weeks ago (supply a date). You discovered that city officials are willing to donate land in an acceptable location, although the plant's full construction costs will have to be paid by MALRACO (approximately $5.5 million). They have promised, however, to shorten the city's approval process from six months to three months; however, there is no guarantee, nor are you confident they can achieve this goal. The city will also provide the land, water, and electricity for the homes and apartment units necessary to house employees. The company will have to build and maintain the homes and apartments (building costs $20 million; annual maintenance $600,000). You toured the proposed plant and housing sites and found the view of the ocean breathtaking. There is an adequate number of citizens to staff your plant in the city and in the surrounding area; however, the level of education is very low. Most people do not speak English and would have to be trained for even the low-skilled assembly jobs. No proof was available that employees for higher-skilled jobs and middle-level management positions are available in the area.

Your second visit, with Diego Rivas-Piatas four days later in Juarez, Mexico, revealed that they are also willing to donate the land for the plant and housing facilities as long as the company pays the cost of constructing the buildings. However, the available workforce in Juarez is slightly better educated than that in Guaymas and, because of Juarez's proximity to the United States, is able to speak English with limited proficiency. There are also many highly educated Mexicans as well as Spanish-speaking Americans looking for work in the area; and, because a free trade zone has been in operation there for many years, many Mexicans have worked for American companies. Housing units would be less expensive because fewer would have to be built. There is available housing in Juarez already; however, many Mexicans have come to expect to move into company housing when they are hired by American companies. Therefore, it appears the company will still be expected to provide housing if it wants to hire the best people available. Labor costs are higher in Juarez, however, than in Guaymas. The average beginning wage per hour for an assembly line worker is $10.25, including a minimum level of medical benefits and housing. (In Guaymas it is $8.65). The comparable figure for workers in the U.S. plant is $15.25, including all medical benefits, workers' compensation, life insurance, and so forth. Housing is not provided in the United States. The Juarez site is in a large industrial park at the edge of the city and on the Juarez/El Paso border, near an upper socioeconomic American housing area. Operations could probably begin six to eight months after the Mexican government approves the project.

The Calgary, Canada, site is 15 miles from town in a new industrial park where there will be no charge for a 25-year lease. Housing would not have to be provided for Canadian workers, who are well educated and English-speaking. A suitable building is already available and may be refitted for an approximate cost of $2.5 million. According to Francoise de'Alatore, the Calgary representative with whom you met, the average wage of a beginning-level worker in Canada is $16.85 (including all benefits, as well as the high taxes necessary to support a state-run medical program available to all). Start-up could probably begin six months after approval.

The cost of transportation for finished products and materials varies a great deal from one facility to the next, and these costs are still being investigated. You are having trouble getting the transportation breakdown per computer from your existing plant in Mexico, and you question the figures from the plant in Texas. They gave you a figure of $78.30 per computer, yet last year their transportation costs were $65 per computer. Because their profits were down this year, and the number of computers assembled was about the same as in previous years, you wonder if this is a correct figure. You must decide how to verify the figure because, without it, you will not be able to compare all the possible locations for the new facilities. The cost of transportation would be higher at the Canadian plant because it is not in a seaport. Juarez is on a major railroad hub; however, the computer parts would have to be shipped into the area from the nearest seaport. Guaymas is on the ocean and only 20 miles from a port.

You still have two more sites (one in Vancouver, Canada, and one in Ontario, Canada) to check, and will schedule those visits today. You hope to go sometime within the next two weeks if local representatives can meet with you.

Write a progress report in memo format. Inform your boss, Charlene Tappen, of your activities. Include everything Charlene wants and needs to know to make sure the project is continuing as she intended. Use a table or other visual aid to organize the information, and devise appropriate headings.

- Apply the four steps of the message formulation process to short reports.
- Choose the correct short report format for the situation, distinguishing among the standard letter, memo, and manuscript formats.
- Plan reports of suitable length.
- Select the appropriate organizational strategy, distinguishing between direct and indirect outlines.
- Make the content of short reports more accessible with appropriate headings, subheadings, and visual aids.
- Use informal and formal writing styles to best advantage.
- Plan, organize, and compose progress reports, feasibility studies, justification reports, problem-solving reports, and business and government proposals.
- Evaluate short business reports and business plans.

9. *Progress report on your research report.* Using letter format, write a report to your professor discussing your progress on a formal research report that has been assigned. Use appropriate headings to show work or tasks that are already finished, work in progress, and work yet to be initiated. Include timelines showing when each task will be completed. Discuss any problems you have had and solved, as well as any that have not yet been solved.

If the research report is a group project, discuss the entire group's progress as well as your own. Be specific about what you have done to contribute to the success of the project. Discuss any problems the group is having, and be honest. If there are members of your group who are not participating as they should, discuss how you and others have attempted to resolve the problem, and the results of those attempts.

If you are having problems or need further clarification on the report, request a conference with your instructor.

## Feasibility Studies

- Apply the four steps of the message formulation process to short reports.
- Choose the correct short report format for the situation, distinguishing among the standard letter, memo, and manuscript formats.
- Plan reports of suitable length.
- Select the appropriate organizational strategy, distinguishing between direct and indirect outlines.
- Make the content of short reports more accessible with appropriate headings, subheadings, and visual aids.
- Use informal and formal writing styles to best advantage.
- Plan, organize, and compose progress reports, feasibility studies, justification reports, problem-solving reports, and business and government proposals.
- Evaluate short business reports and business plans.

10. *Feasibility study of a new retail outlet.* Write a feasibility study to determine if Norsetrumbs Dept. Store, the company for which you work, should sell its fashions and accessories via Television Shopping Network (TSN). Home shopping services such as this are being used for more than just jewelry these days; it has become a $2 billion-plus industry and is growing about 20 percent a year. Staks Fourth Avenue and two major designers have gone on the network and consider their forays successful.

     TSN has plans to offer a sort of video mall, where television shoppers will browse through channels as they do through individual stores, ask for information and advice, order, and pay—all without leaving home. TSN now reaches 60 million viewers around the country, and this audience is expected to grow 5 or 6 million a year as new shopping services are offered. There are also plans to broadcast in Japan, Canada, Mexico, and Great Britain.

     Norsestrumbs' executives have two concerns—will your sophisticated upper-middle- and upper-class customers actually order fashions by television, and will overall sales increase without cutting into current store sales? Sales growth in each of the past two years was less than 2 percent (the usual is 4 percent), so management needs to increase sales but is worried about gambling so much on what might be a risky venture.

     You did some research to compare shoppers and determined the following: The average television shopper is between 25 and 34 years old (36 percent), and 32 percent of Norsestrumbs' shoppers are that age. Only 10 percent of TV shoppers are over 65, whereas 15 percent of your shoppers are over 65. The average household income for TV shoppers is $34,500; your customers' average household incomes are $36,900. However, 12 percent of your shoppers earn over $70,000 a year, whereas only 9.5 percent of TV shoppers earn over that amount. You also found that 24 percent of TV shoppers are open to new styles and trends, 27 percent prefer traditional things, and 32 percent choose value or comfort over fashion. Forty-eight percent of TV shoppers are males, and 29 percent of TV shoppers have attended college. Of Norsestrumbs' shoppers, 31 percent have attended college, and 39 percent of them choose value or comfort over fashion. Fifteen percent of Norsestrumbs' shoppers are open to new styles and trends, and 33 percent of them prefer traditional things. Your survey shows that 43 percent of your shoppers are male.

     You found in your research that the companies that have successfully sold via television did not attempt to sell all their products and, in fact, did not even feature the same products sold in the stores. To encourage telephone orders and avoid cannibalizing their own retail store sales, they featured fashions that could not be obtained in the stores and were available for only a limited time, in limited numbers, and at bargain prices.

The two biggest expenses of retailers are rent, sales personnel, and advertising. Home shopping could help you slash all three. When you sell on TV, the selling and advertising are done all at once, and you could target your market better than you are able to do in your usual newspaper advertisements.

Maxeys, the largest retailer in the United States, is introducing its own 24-hour shopping service at the end of this year. L. L. Peas, J. C. Dime, and Blunter Image are renting air time on TSN and seem to be successful. J.C. Dime, which attempted television sales years ago and failed, plans to give it another try with a different product mix. They will not feature the same products as they sell in the store.

Write a feasibility study on this issue for Barry Malone, CEO of Norsestrumbs. Organize the above information and use it to justify your recommendation.

- Apply the four steps of the message formulation process to short reports.
- Choose the correct short report format for the situation, distinguishing among the standard letter, memo, and manuscript formats.
- Plan reports of suitable length.
- Select the appropriate organizational strategy, distinguishing between direct and indirect outlines.
- Make the content of short reports more accessible with appropriate headings, subheadings, and visual aids.
- Use informal and formal writing styles to best advantage.
- Plan, organize, and compose progress reports, feasibility studies, justification reports, problem-solving reports, and business and government proposals.
- Evaluate short business reports and business plans.

11. *Feasibility study on a site for a new plant.* Read exercise 8. Assume you have finished all the visits and must now write a feasibility study recommending one of the sites. Analyze the five sites (make up appropriate information for the Vancouver and Ontario sites) and recommend one to management. Use a memo report style and appropriate headings to improve readability. Use a visual aid to illustrate the information needed for comparing the five sites.

- Apply the four steps of the message formulation process to short reports.
- Choose the correct short report format for the situation, distinguishing among the standard letter, memo, and manuscript formats.
- Plan reports of suitable length.
- Select the appropriate organizational strategy, distinguishing between direct and indirect outlines.
- Make the content of short reports more accessible with appropriate headings, subheadings, and visual aids.
- Use informal and formal writing styles to best advantage.
- Plan, organize, and compose progress reports, feasibility studies, justification reports, problem-solving reports, and business and government proposals.
- Evaluate short business reports and business plans.

12. *Feasibility study on a subject of your choice.* Write a feasibility study for one of the following situations. In each case, specify a limited number of criteria and alternatives. Make up the data necessary to determine feasibility, or do research to find the data you need.

    a. Should the city you live in privatize some of its services (e.g., trash services, fire or police department, accounting, landscaping, lighting, or street maintenance)?

    b. Should the company you work for establish on-site child care and elder care centers for its employees?

    c. Should your company cut costs by eliminating its training program?

    d. Should your city allow a marina to be developed on unused swampland?

    e. Should your city allow a proposed expansion of a local amusement park?

    f. Should your company expand its facilities?

    g. Should a charitable organization build a needed office building if it means increasing the amount of money going to the charity's administration from 12 percent to 19 percent?

    h. Should a large department store offer various kinds of contest incentives to its sales staff?

### Justification Reports

◆ Apply the four steps of the message formulation process to short reports.

◆ Choose the correct short report format for the situation, distinguishing among the standard letter, memo, and manuscript formats.

◆ Plan reports of suitable length.

◆ Select the appropriate organizational strategy, distinguishing between direct and indirect outlines.

◆ Make the content of short reports more accessible with appropriate headings, subheadings, and visual aids.

◆ Use informal and formal writing styles to best advantage.

◆ Plan, organize, and compose progress reports, feasibility studies, justification reports, problem-solving reports, and business and government proposals.

◆ Evaluate short business reports and business plans.

13. *Justification report on a topic of your choice.* Write a justification report for one of the following topics:

    a. Purchasing a piece of equipment for your department (e.g., new computer, printer, photocopier, telephone modem, or facsimile machine).

    b. Purchasing a software program for your department.

    c. Purchasing a new computer network or altering the current one.

    d. Switching to a new operating system for all company computers.

    e. Advocating a policy or a change of policy aimed at increasing gender and ethnic diversity in your company's management ranks.

    f. Influencing your company to look at the international arena as a market for its products.

    g. Leasing company cars instead of purchasing them (or vice versa).

    h. Buying the equipment to do desktop publishing in-house rather than sending it out to a printer.

    i. Switching to a different method of accounting.

  *j.* Instituting a new procedure for your department.

  *k.* Instituting a new procedure for your college (e.g., registration, parking, program change, course offerings, addition or deletion of general education or major courses, or placement services).

  *l.* Recommending a political party whose national platform will improve the economy.

  *m.* Recommending a mutual fund to an investor.

  *n.* Instituting a new U.S. trade policy.

- Apply the four steps of the message formulation process to short reports.
- Choose the correct short report format for the situation, distinguishing among the standard letter, memo, and manuscript formats.
- Plan reports of suitable length.
- Select the appropriate organizational strategy, distinguishing between direct and indirect outlines.
- Make the content of short reports more accessible with appropriate headings, subheadings, and visual aids.
- Use informal and formal writing styles to best advantage.
- Plan, organize, and compose progress reports, feasibility studies, justification reports, problem-solving reports, and business and government proposals.
- Evaluate short business reports and business plans.

14. *Justification report for the chapter-opening vignette.* Write the report described in the vignette at the beginning of this chapter. Assume you are Ralph Spanswick and that you have decided to reveal your ownership of MicroTech in the report. However, convince your supervisor that MicroTech computers will benefit the company and should be purchased regardless of your personal interest in the matter.

- Apply the four steps of the message formulation process to short reports.
- Choose the correct short report format for the situation, distinguishing among the standard letter, memo, and manuscript formats.
- Plan reports of suitable length.
- Select the appropriate organizational strategy, distinguishing between direct and indirect outlines.
- Make the content of short reports more accessible with appropriate headings, subheadings, and visual aids.
- Use informal and formal writing styles to best advantage.
- Plan, organize, and compose progress reports, feasibility studies, justification reports, problem-solving reports, and business and government proposals.
- Evaluate short business reports and business plans.

15. *Justification report for a real estate agency.* You work as an agent for Lalama Action Realtors. You have been asked by your company's management to write a justification report suggesting ways to increase real estate sales. You have two ideas:

  • Abolish exclusive listings by registering all homes with a multiple listing service (a database to which real estate agencies subscribe). This service advertises all the homes for sale by every agency subscribing to the service. If Lalama subscribed to a multiple listing service, its agents' listings could be sold by any real estate agent in any agency. The chances of selling homes increase, but Lalama's listing agents would only get half the usual commission (the other half goes to the agent who found the buyer). However, you feel the loss of commissions will be more than offset by an increase in the number of sales.

- Personalize the firm's weekly advertising by featuring the three top agents in addition to the homes for sale (traditionally the focus of newspaper ads). You believe that once people in the community feel they know these three agents, they will think of these agents first when they need to buy or sell a home. This idea would also increase the firm's overall performance, because agents would compete with one another for the privilege of being featured.

Write a memo report to the owner of your real estate firm, Alan Robins, justifying your two ideas. Use your persuasive skills to show him how the firm will benefit from instituting these suggestions. Before you begin writing, consider these questions: Is a formal writing style, an informal writing style, or a combination of the two most appropriate? Would headings help to guide the reader in this case? Are there any visual aids that might improve Alan's receptiveness to your ideas?

## Problem-Solving Reports

- Apply the four steps of the message formulation process to short reports.
- Choose the correct short report format for the situation, distinguishing among the standard letter, memo, and manuscript formats.
- Plan reports of suitable length.
- Select the appropriate organizational strategy, distinguishing between direct and indirect outlines.
- Make the content of short reports more accessible with appropriate headings, subheadings, and visual aids.
- Use informal and formal writing styles to best advantage.
- Plan, organize, and compose progress reports, feasibility studies, justification reports, problem-solving reports, and business and government proposals.
- Evaluate short business reports and business plans.

16. *Problem-solving study on a lawsuit.* You work for Vettco, a small company that restores Corvettes and mounts new bodies on Corvette frames, creating sports cars with a completely new look. To accommodate these new bodies, you had to make changes in the frames, and one of those changes has resulted in four lawsuits. The lawsuits are for varying amounts; however, they total $4.4 million, an amount that will put your company out of business.

According to the plaintiffs and their expert witnesses, your design caused the gas tanks to be improperly secured. They say the tanks pull away from the gaslines and, in two instances, have caused fires that resulted in serious injuries to two people. Your company's owners, Francesca and Nick Girodino, have spent over $80,000 on tests to determine if the design could be at fault. In each case, three different tests, conducted by an independent automobile expert, showed that the tanks are secure and could not have caused the accidents described in the lawsuits.

This fight has been going on in the courts for more than a year now, and it has already cost your company over $350,000. The three attorneys representing the four plaintiffs have approached the owners' attorney about an out-of-court settlement. The plaintiffs have indicated that they will accept the following:

- For the two cases involving no injuries: The cost of the cars themselves, the repairs, and the legal expenses ($250,000 total).

- For the two cases involving bodily injury: $2.5 million total.

One advantage of this settlement would be that Vettco could state formally that it is not guilty of the charges. Another is that the plaintiffs would agree to drop all charges and remain silent about the case.

Francesca and Nick have asked you to do a problem-solving study to determine whether they should pay the out-of-court settlement or take their chances and hope the juries will exonerate them. It is estimated that it will take three more years for all the suits to go through the trial and appeal process, and it is estimated that the total cost to you for legal services, expert testimony, and additional tests will run about $2 million. Francesca and Nick are most concerned about keeping the expenses to a minimum in the hope that the company can survive these bad times; however, Vettco's reputation is also important to them. Write a memo report and, depending on the conclusions you reach, recommend a course of action to Vettco's owners. Use appropriate headings to increase readability.

- Apply the four steps of the message formulation process to short reports.
- Choose the correct short report format for the situation, distinguishing among the standard letter, memo, and manuscript formats.
- Plan reports of suitable length.
- Select the appropriate organizational strategy, distinguishing between direct and indirect outlines.
- Make the content of short reports more accessible with appropriate headings, subheadings, and visual aids.
- Use informal and formal writing styles to best advantage.
- Plan, organize, and compose progress reports, feasibility studies, justification reports, problem-solving reports, and business and government proposals.
- Evaluate short business reports and business plans.

17. *Problem-solving report on security measures.* You were hired last week as head of security for Simply Perfect, a large interior design firm. Already you find yourself faced with your biggest challenge yet. Yesterday, every computer on your network stopped working and flashed this message: "Have a nice day!" Because all layouts, ordering, scheduling, corresponding, inventory, and accounting are handled by computer, no work could be done. After four hours the message disappeared, and you discovered that the files of 12 of your biggest clients had been wiped out. Fortunately, most of the work can be reconstructed; however, it will take at least two months to get things in order again.

In addition, it has become apparent that some of the company's new ideas and designs are being stolen and sold to competitors. In at least two cases, other firms have underbid Simply Perfect on jobs that would have brought more than $800,000 into the firm. These competing bids were only $200 to $500 lower than your own bids, and their designs were remarkably similar to what your designers had worked on for months.

Such white-collar theft of designs is common in the design industry; however, the sabotage of company computers by planting a computer virus designed to wipe out files is new. You have been instructed to study the problem and come up with ways to improve security. You have identified two antivirus programs and will evaluate them. You have also been directed to evaluate several alternatives for safeguarding Simply Perfect's information, data, and designs:

- 12-hour guards at the four building entrances and exits to check briefcases, purses, and so forth.

- Computer access numbers coded by four levels of security (ranging from A for those able to view all company information to D for those allowed computer access only to input clerical and data information).

- Controlled printing of designs and bid sheets.

- Purchase of paper shredders and screen savers.

- Education of company employees about security issues.

- Limiting access to the building after and before hours to only employees with level A security clearance.

- A ban on taking home any work and computers.

Write a report evaluating the computer virus problems and the alternative security measures and recommending those you believe are appropriate for Simply Perfect. As you analyze each alternative, reach conclusions about its appropriateness and justify your conclusions. Follow an indirect report arrangement, and use headings to arrange the analysis for better readability.

- Apply the four steps of the message formulation process to short reports.
- Choose the correct short report format for the situation, distinguishing among the standard letter, memo, and manuscript formats.
- Plan reports of suitable length.
- Select the appropriate organizational strategy, distinguishing between direct and indirect outlines.
- Make the content of short reports more accessible with appropriate headings, subheadings, and visual aids.
- Use informal and formal writing styles to best advantage.
- Plan, organize, and compose progress reports, feasibility studies, justification reports, problem-solving reports, and business and government proposals.
- Evaluate short business reports and business plans.

18. *Problem-solving report on a subject of your choice.* Write a problem-solving report on one of the following issues. Reach conclusions, and make recommendations for action based on those conclusions.

  *a.* Investigate a grocery store's 20 percent increase in workers' compensation claims due to carpal tunnel syndrome, back pain, headaches, and eye strain.

  *b.* Investigate the recent 25 percent increase in the number of customer complaints at an auto dealer's service and auto body repair facilities.

  *c.* Investigate an 11 percent decrease in the number of orders processed per day by a company's shipping department.

d. Investigate why a city's fire and police departments are not making progress toward the city's goal of having their labor force reflect the city's gender and ethnic makeup (45 percent females, 24 percent Hispanics, 14 percent Afro-Americans, and 3 percent Asian-Americans).

e. Investigate a startling increase in the number of accidents involving company vehicles over the last two years.

f. Investigate the reasons why a company's costs have doubled over the past five years when inflation has only increased 4 percent.

g. Investigate three candidates for a management job (to have fun with this one, imagine that you are selecting someone to be your own boss).

h. Investigate the three-year work history of an individual you are recommending be fired.

i. Investigate why a company's downtown store's sales have slipped to 40 percent below those of their suburban stores.

### Business Plans

▪ Apply the four steps of the message formulation process to short reports.

▪ Plan, organize, and compose business plans.

▪ Evaluate short business reports and business plans.

19. *Business plan for your great idea.* If you have an idea for a new product, service, or business, use that as the basis for a business plan. If not, be creative; is there a product you have always wished someone would make (e.g., a new design for a glass ketchup bottle from which the ketchup actually flows easily)? A service you think other people need and can't get now?

Once you come up with your idea, write as much of the plan as you can. Obviously, if you do not have an accounting or finance background, that section of your plan will not be as complete or well thought out as that of someone who has such a background. However, you should be able to estimate the kinds of expenses you will have, the price for your product, the approximate income anticipated, an approximate amount of profit, and so forth.

# CHAPTER 12

# PLANNING AND ORGANIZING FORMAL REPORTS

## OBJECTIVES

When you finish studying this chapter, you should be able to:

- Describe how organizations use formal reports.
- Differentiate between formal and informal reports.
- Define and limit the problem to be studied, and devise a purpose statement that defines it.
- Address readers' needs by choosing a direct or indirect arrangement and an appropriate writing style.
- Develop logical, parallel outlines for informational and analytical issues.
- Prepare a formal proposal.
- Assemble all the necessary parts of a formal report.
- Use manuscript format correctly.

## WHAT WOULD YOU DO IF...?

**JUST THIS ONCE!**    Patricia Mantabe, a college senior, is taking a business communication course and two other classes so she can graduate at the end of this semester. Patricia has two children, ages 3 and 5, whom she is raising on her own. She is also working full time as an accounting clerk.

Patricia has been so busy with her job and her family that she underestimated the amount of work involved in her classes this quarter and did not plan her time well. In her business communication class, a report is due in two weeks, but Patricia hasn't even been to the library since her report proposal was approved. Patricia is desperate; she needs this course to graduate but knows she can't do a good job on the report in so short a time. Because she must receive a grade of C or better in the class, Patricia is afraid she will not be able to graduate in time to get the promotion she is anticipating when the staff accountant retires next month.

Her friend, Franklin, told Patricia that she is foolish to worry about the report when she can simply buy one from a report-writing service. For about

$100, which Patricia could borrow from her credit union, she could buy an informational report on her topic, change it a little to make it analytical, and turn it in for a better grade than what she could probably do on her own. When Patricia told Franklin that buying a report composed by someone else was like cheating, he responded, "Everyone is doing it; teachers expect too much anyway, and it isn't really fair that we have to work so hard for just one class."

Patricia has mixed feelings. She feels she has to graduate this semester; however, she is just too busy to do things the way they ought to be done. After all, she has to work, and her children take so much of her time. However, she is afraid of getting caught, failing the course, and possibly being suspended for plagiarism. On the other hand, Patricia knows other people who have submitted purchased reports in the past, and they didn't get caught. What harm could it do?

What do you think Patricia should do? What are the implications of purchasing a report from a report service? Is it fair for anyone, regardless of their outside responsibilities, to bend the rules a little to get through school? As you read this chapter, think about Patricia's dilemma; determine how you would handle it if you were her.

## USING FORMAL REPORTS

Reports are prepared to gather and present the information necessary to make decisions.

🔖 Describe how organizations use formal reports.

When a mass of complex information must be carefully considered, a formal report is indispensable. In the business world, executives base most of their important decisions on the data contained in reports. For example, executives usually study the probable impact of new products, services, and procedures on company goals before making any changes. Once such changes are introduced, executives rely on reports to track the changes' effects. In addition, people throughout the organization need to know how to implement the changes and whether the changes are producing positive results; formal reports are their handbooks throughout the process.

Business reports are generally written by people considered to be the most knowledgeable on a specific topic or by those who are most affected by a particular problem. Management is usually interested in these individuals' opinions. Therefore, it is entirely appropriate for someone who has been asked to write a formal report to analyze the information, compare it to the company's needs, and produce conclusions and perhaps recommendations for action. At that point, company executives determine whether they will act on the recommendations, study the topic further, or take some other course of action.

Despite the usefulness of formal reports, the need for them varies with the size of the organization. Generally speaking, the larger and more complex an organization is, the more it needs formal reports to keep decision makers informed. Fewer formal reports are prepared in small businesses, because there is less need for formal documentation of concerns and propositions. Where owners and employees work side by side, discussing and solving problems together, everyone who needs to know about a situation is involved from the beginning. However, even small businesses prepare formal reports and proposals to apply for government grants, to bid on contracts for providing services or goods to the government, and to propose new business ventures.

People who can write good reports are often noticed by upper-level decision makers. Many successful businesspeople attribute their promotions to the recognition earned by their writing skills. The better the information you gather and the more logical and insightful your conclusions and recommendations, the more your work will be appreciated for its contribution to the organization's goals.

The stages in the process of formulating formal reports are the same as the stages in the process of formulating letters, memos, and short reports:

Writing long formal reports requires you to plan, organize, compose, and evaluate—the same steps necessary for writing business letters and memos.

- *Planning:*
  Establishing the purpose.
  Choosing a medium and channel.
  Considering legal and ethical issues.
  Analyzing the audience.
  Gathering the necessary resources.

- *Organizing:*
  Freewriting major points.
  Choosing an organizational strategy.

- *Composing.*

- *Evaluating.*

As you read the rest of this chapter, keep these stages in mind. Although this chapter is not organized to cover them in sequence, they serve as an effective guide to the report-writing process.

## DEFINING THE NATURE OF A REPORT

Early in the planning stage, you must define the nature of the report you are about to write. Formal reports are not all alike:

- They may report information only, without analysis, or they may analyze information, reaching conclusions and making recommendations.

- They vary widely in content, format, length, purpose, and scope.

- They may be prepared for internal use, generally moving up the chain of command, or they may be prepared for external distribution (e.g., for clients, the media, government agencies, or stockholders).

- They may be written for one reader, a small group of readers, or a large group of readers.

- They may be written by an individual, or they may be the collaborative effort of many people.

- They may vary in writing style (although formal writing style is preferred).

- They may include all the parts of a formal report, everything from the prefatory elements to a final appendix, or they may include only some of the standard components of a formal report.

These are all factors that must be considered as you compose formal reports that reveal clearly, objectively, and honestly everything a reader wants and needs to know about a topic.

## INFORMAL AND FORMAL REPORTS

Differentiate between formal and informal reports.

A report is considered formal when it

Uses formal writing style (see Chapter 11).

Adheres to formal format expectations.

Contains specific preliminary and supplementary parts (e.g., title page, summary, introduction, bibliography, and appendixes).

The writing style of informal reports may be formal, informal, or a combination. However, formal reports almost always are written in formal style. In addition, formal reports are always typed in manuscript format, whereas informal reports may be typed in letter, memo, or manuscript format. Later in this chapter, you can learn the details of manuscript format, along with the supplementary elements typical of formal reports. However, not all formal reports contain all of these elements. In some cases, for example, there is no need for a list of tables and figures, nor for an appendix. Whatever elements you decide to include, however, never format a formal report as a memo or a letter.

Informal reports, typically short reports, are described in Chapter 11. If you have not yet studied that chapter, look it over briefly after you finish reading this one. You will then have a complete picture of the differences between formal and informal reports.

## INFORMATIONAL AND ANALYTICAL REPORTS

Informational reports present information only; analytical reports analyze information and reach conclusions.

Formal reports are used frequently in the academic world, so you may already have written one. Most often, however, college reports tend to be informational, not analytical. In the case of Patricia Mantabe, the subject of the chapter-opening vignette, her professor was probably requiring an analytical report to give students experience they will find useful in the business world. There, formal reports are usually analytical in nature, although occasionally a formal report will present only preliminary information that will be analyzed later by someone else.

The topic of a report has nothing to do with whether it is informational or analytical. In your business career, for example, you might be asked to write a formal report on topics such as the following:

Costs of two different computer networks.

Color psychology or office ergonomics.

Cultural differences in negotiation styles.

Yearly sales figures for the past five years.

Department budgets for the past 10 years.

If your purpose in writing any of these reports was solely informational, you would only present the facts. However, if your purpose was also to analyze the information you gathered, reach conclusions, and make recommendations, the report would be analytical. For instance, you might compare the two computer networks, analyze which one best meets your company's needs, and recommend its purchase. Your analysis of people's reactions to various colors could be used to select colors for new products, commercials, or office furniture. You might analyze an individual's sales for the past five years to determine if she should be retained or laid off. Your analysis of department budgets might justify a request for additional funding to improve productivity. In any of these situations, you would be writing an analytical formal report.

Compiling and documenting information on a periodic basis is often the topic of short reports and the purpose of college reports. However, long, formal reports in the business world are seldom solely informational in nature. Because business reports are generally written by people considered to be the most knowledgeable on a specific topic or by those who are most affected by a particular problem, management is usually interested in these individuals' opinions. Analyzing the data and information in a report and comparing it to the needs of a company leads to conclusions and recommendations for action. At that point, upper-level management determines whether it will act according to the recommendations, whether the topic should be studied further, or whether another course of action is more feasible.

Even though those at the top of an organization will ultimately make the final decision, it is helpful for them to know how those at lower levels view a particular problem. People who write clear, objective reports are often noticed by upper-level decision makers. As a result, many people attribute their promotions to recognition of their writing skills. The better the information you gather and the more logical and insightful your conclusions and recommendations, the more your work will be appreciated for the positive effect it has on the organization's goals.

## DETERMINING THE PROBLEM, PURPOSE, AND SCOPE

▶ Define and limit the problem to be studied, and devise a purpose statement that defines it.

Your first impulse, when given a topic to report on, may be to go to the library or search through company files to gather information. However, you should first define the problem you are studying, your purpose in conducting the research, and the scope of (or limitations on) the problem. The way you define a problem shapes the way you study it, and limiting the scope of your study prevents you from wasting time collecting and analyzing information you don't need.

Consider the case of Leon Singleton, who has been asked to investigate the problem of absenteeism at a large factory. That's a rather vague request. Should he determine the causes of the absenteeism and recommend ways to encourage better attendance? Should he determine the characteristics common to workers with excessive absences and recommend not hiring people who have these characteristics? Should he investigate the effects of absenteeism on product quality and productivity, recommending ways to lessen the negative effects? Of course, Leon's decision about what to report should be cleared with his supervisors to make sure they agree on his definition of the problem and the purpose of the study. Doing so will save Leon time and keep him from turning in a report that fails to meet his supervisor's expectations.

## DEFINING THE PROBLEM

Use a journalistic approach to define the problem you plan to investigate: Who? What? When? Where? Why? How?

The first step is to define the problem, which may be more difficult than it seems. In Leon Singleton's case, for instance, it was not enough to say that the problem was absenteeism, because it had a number of dimensions. One way to make sure you address the multiple dimensions of a problem is to answer the following questions:

*Who?* Who is involved in the situation?

*What?* What must be determined?

*When?* When did the problem begin? When does it occur?

*Where?* Where is the problem centered?

*Why?* Why does the problem exist? Why is it important to study this issue?

*How?* How did the problem begin? How did it get to this point?

These are the same questions journalists use to write news stories to make sure they address all the questions people normally have about a topic. Your answers to these questions will eventually be incorporated into your report's introduction.

## STATING THE PURPOSE

With the answers to these preliminary questions in mind, your next step is to develop a specific statement of purpose, often referred to as a study's *objectives* or *goals*. Sometimes the purpose statement is included as a part of the problem's explanation in the introductory section of a formal report. However, putting the statement of purpose in a separate section emphasizes its importance.

The purpose statement guides the entire research project. In addition, in informational reports the title and the outline echo the purpose statement; in analytical reports the conclusions and recommendations must address the issues raised in the purpose statement. Once you and the person authorizing the report agree on a purpose statement, you may begin the research knowing exactly what is expected of you.

Use a question, an infinitive phrase, or a declarative statement to establish the purpose of your formal report.

Purpose statements may be written in one of three forms:

- *A question.* "This study answers the question, Should Ortiz Manufacturing purchase Boauch Inc.?"

- *An infinitive phrase.* "The purpose of this study is to determine if Ortiz Manufacturing should purchase Boauch Inc."

- *A declarative statement.* "The viability of Ortiz Manufacturing's purchasing Boauch Inc. will be determined."

Analytical reports used to determine which alternative is the most appropriate to solve a particular problem are based on comparison. Thus, one of the following phrases, or something similar, should be part of your purpose statement: *the most feasible, the most profitable, the best, the most appropriate.* For example, an analytical purpose statement written in question form might read as follows:

This study answers the following question: Of the three alternatives, which best meets the needs of Ortiz Manufacturing?

Many research reports have more than one purpose. The following example for an analytical report states the primary and secondary purposes and is written using infinitive phrases:

> The primary purpose of this study is to determine if there is evidence in the literature of an increase in productivity among businesses that have instituted in-house child care centers. If evidence of an increase in productivity is found, a secondary purpose of this study will be to determine the characteristics of good in-house child care centers.

This purpose statement indicates that the report writer will use only secondary sources, researching the issue in libraries.

The following example, also for an analytical report with two purpose statements, indicates that the writer will do a different kind of research. The report will be used by the executives of a securities firm who are trying to decide if formal education should be required of people hired to counsel clients and sell investments. This purpose statement uses a declarative for the primary purpose and an infinitive for the secondary purpose.

> In this study, the relationship between salary and commissions of investment account managers and formal financial and accounting coursework will be determined. If a correlation is found, a secondary purpose will be to determine the accounting and finance courses executives believe have been most helpful to them in evaluating investments.

Look closely at the above purpose statements again. Can you see how they dictate what the title and overall outline of each report must look like? The child care center purpose statement dictates a report that concludes whether or not providing child care facilities has increased productivity in other companies. If that evidence is found, the report must reach conclusions about the characteristics of successful in-house child care centers. The logical recommendation in the report would be whether or not the company should institute an in-house child care center. What types of conclusions and recommendations do you envision as a result of the purpose statement dealing with investment account managers?

## LIMITING THE SCOPE OF THE REPORT

Specifying the scope of your formal report means deciding what it will cover.

Once you have identified a problem and written a purpose statement, you must determine the **scope** of the report, or its boundaries. In deciding what the report will include, you will also have to decide what *not* to include. The six questions you answered in defining the problem—who, what, when, where, why, and how—will help with this task. Imagine yourself involved in a study to determine why the number of work-related accidents has increased in your company's factories. You might decide to study only the data for the past two years, even though a slight increase has been occurring each year for the past five years. You might decide to survey a random sample of 300 of the more than 1,600 injured employees. You might decide to study only one segment of the problem (e.g., your automobile assembly plant, rather than all your plants). If many possible causes and solutions have been identified, you might narrow the study to three or four of the most obvious.

In the section of the report covering scope, you should also mention what your report does not address that some people might expect to find. Some people refer to excluded factors as *delimitations*. Whether you use the term or not, it is important to tell readers why these factors have been excluded. For example, for the report on work-related accidents, you will have to justify going back only two years if the readers expect you to discuss the record over the past five years. If readers might question why you did not discuss all possible causes and solutions, you will have to explain your reasons for omitting some of them.

Be honest about any limitations that might detract in any way from the report or its findings and conclusions.

Along with the scope of your study (what you will include), you should also determine its limitations. *Limitations* are limiting factors that detract from the study in some way. One limitation in a business report might be lack of information due to fire, theft, or sabotage. If a survey of employees was to be included in your study of work-related accidents and you find that a large number of injured employees has left the company, you should explain this limitation. If you have not had enough time to study a phenomenon thoroughly, that should be mentioned as a limiting factor. For example, analyzing the effectiveness of new procedures that have only been in place a week or two might yield significantly different results from analyzing those procedures after they have become routine six months later.

A complete explanation of your report's scope and a sincere acknowledgement of your study's limitations help to protect you against criticism. A good description of the scope and limitations also assists readers, because it enables them to decide if the report meets their needs before they read it. You may include a separate section on scope and limitations in the introduction, or describe the scope in the section of the report dealing with research methods. Take a moment to read the Scope and Limitations section of the sample report at the end of this chapter (Exhibit 12.8) to see if it ties in with the explanation of the problem and the statement of purpose.

## MEETING READERS' NEEDS

Address readers' needs by choosing a direct or indirect arrangement and an appropriate writing style.

Readers' needs must be considered before you compose a formal report. You must assess how much they need to know about a topic based on their experience and knowledge, their probable reactions to the conclusions and recommendations, and their expectations. Answers to these questions will determine the report's arrangement and writing style. As you will learn later in this chapter, your readers' needs will also determine the elements your report includes and the way it is formatted.

### DIRECT AND INDIRECT ARRANGEMENTS

A direct report presents the summary, conclusions, and recommendations at the beginning; an indirect report places them at the end.

Formal reports—like short reports, memos, and letters—may be arranged in indirect (inductive) or direct (deductive) order. The arrangement you select will determine where in a report you will place the conclusions and recommendations—at the end (indirect) or at the beginning (direct).

Some businesspeople and many teachers prefer the indirect arrangement in a formal report because it allows them to follow the writer's logic and to read first the research on which the conclusions are based. The indirect arrangement is also desirable when there is a chance that readers might object to or disagree with your conclusions and/or recommendations. If your logic is sound and based on objective research, requiring readers to analyze the findings before reading the summary, conclusions, and recommendations softens the blow somewhat. It also gives readers a chance to deduce the same results before you have to state them. To summarize, use the indirect order when:

- The reader expects an indirect report.
- The reader might react negatively to your summary, conclusions, and/or recommendations.

As useful as indirect arrangement may be, most people in business and many teachers prefer reports to be arranged directly. Reading the summary, conclusions, and recommendations first gives readers immediate answers to the questions that spawned the research; in fact, readers who are pressed for time may not read the rest of your report. Direct arrangement is particularly suitable when you have been chosen to write a report because of your expertise on the subject. In that case, the reader is less likely to react negatively to a challenging conclusion or recommendation, even when it is placed at a report's beginning. However, you should not be too cavalier about the rest of the report. Many readers will read the entire report thoroughly, especially those who are directly involved and those who disagree with your results. To summarize, use a direct arrangement when:

- Your reader expects a direct report.
- Your reader is time conscious.
- You are an acknowledged expert on the topic.
- Your reader will react positively or neutrally to your summary, conclusions, and recommendations.

## FORMAL AND INFORMAL WRITING STYLES

Most formal reports use a formal, impersonal writing style, although there is a trend toward using more informal writing.

Your readers' expectations also determine the writing style you will use in your formal reports. The following paragraph is written in formal writing style:

> Experiments and surveys have inherent constraints. For example, an inherent constraint of experimental studies is the Hawthorne effect. In the field study, it was found that the Hawthorne effect contributed to the positive results. However, subsequent revision of the procedures removed this element from the study.

Now read a paragraph on the same topic written informally:

> We know that experiments and surveys have tremendous inherent constraints. As you are probably aware, one inherent constraint of experimental studies is the Hawthorne effect. In my field study, I found that the Hawthorne effect actually contributed to the positive results! Afterwards, however, I removed this element from the study by revising the procedures.

The second paragraph, written in informal style, contains an emotional element (the exclamation point); first-, second-, and third-person personal pronouns (*we, you, I, my*); and unnecessary qualifiers (*tremendous, actually*). These elements are fine if informal language is acceptable; however, they should not be used if formal writing style is expected. Although formal writing style is the style most used in business, the informal writing style is gaining in popularity.

As Chapter 11 explains in great detail, formal writing style adds power to your writing by emphasizing the facts and the analysis rather than who wrote or is reading it. Focusing on the findings forces a writer to be more objective, and it makes writing seem less biased and more fair. The formal writing style was first used by scientists to report the results of their experiments. It was and still is the most widely accepted writing style for professional journals, doctoral dissertations, master's theses, and other technical and scientific reports. However, in recent years many people have argued that the formal writing style is less interesting and less readable than the informal style. They criticize it for excessive use of passive verbs and a lack of first- and second-person personal pronouns. These people argue that technical writing should be more personal, thereby more interesting, and that this can be achieved without using biased language.

The way to add a personal tone, if you determine it to be acceptable, is to use the informal writing style, which is the preferred style for letters and memos. Informal writing style emphasizes the reader and his or her needs; and, although it de-emphasizes the writer, first-person pronouns are not avoided completely as they are with formal writing style. Informal writing is more like everyday conversation; therefore, it sometimes makes technical writing seem more interesting and understandable (if readers are receptive to informality).

You will have to use your own judgment in determining which writing style is most appropriate in any given situation. If you know that your reader prefers informality, use it with discretion; what is referred to in business as *informal* writing style is still a great deal more formal than conversational language. The ability to switch easily from one writing style to another will be useful to you as you compose all kinds of business messages, not just reports. Many skillful writers have learned the benefits of blending the two styles together.

## OUTLINING FORMAL REPORTS

■ Develop logical, parallel outlines for informational and analytical issues.

As soon as you have determined the problem, purpose, and scope of your project and have analyzed your readers' needs, you can prepare a tentative outline. The purpose statement should be your guide. Consider this purpose statement once again:

> The primary purpose of this study is to determine if there is evidence in the literature of an increase in productivity among businesses that have instituted in-house child care centers. If evidence of an increase in productivity is found, a secondary purpose of this study will be to determine the characteristics of good in-house child care centers.

A logical outline for a report with this purpose would have two sections, one reviewing the literature to answer the productivity question and one analyzing the characteristics of good child care centers. Research must be conducted to develop the outline further. However, the purpose statement dictates the preliminary outline, which tells the writer exactly what to look for as he or she

| EXHIBIT 12.1 | Outline Styles |
|---|---|

| ■ Topic Outline | ■ Summary Outline |
|---|---|
| I. Profit potential<br>  A. Santa Monica<br>  B. Marina del Rey<br>  C. Long Beach<br>II. Target market demographics<br>  A. Santa Monica<br>  B. Marina del Rey<br>  C. Long Beach<br>III. Competition<br>  A. Santa Monica<br>  B. Marina del Rey<br>  C. Long Beach | I. The potential profitability of the Long Beach site exceeds Santa Monica and Marina del Rey by 8 to 12 percent.<br>  A. Profit projections for Santa Monica are estimated to be 7 percent above costs.<br>  B. Profit projections for Marina del Rey are estimated to be 5 percent above costs.<br>  C. Profit projections for Long Beach are estimated to be 13 to 19 percent above costs.<br>II. The demographics of the Long Beach site most closely match the ideal target market.<br>  A. The high socioeconomic level of the surrounding community and the diversity of cultures in the area do not closely resemble the products' intended market.<br>  B. The high socioeconomic level of Marina del Rey and its predominately white American and heavy European population does not match the products' intended market.<br>  C. The predominately middle-class Hispanic demographic makeup of the Long Beach site and Los Angeles's largely Hispanic population (easily accessible by rail) most closely resemble the products' intended market.<br>III. There are no competitors in the Marina del Rey area; however, the competition in Long Beach would not negatively impact profits.<br>  A. The Santa Monica area contains two major competitors that report low profits.<br>  B. Marina del Rey contains no major or local competitors.<br>  C. The competition in the immediate area of the Long Beach site consists of more outlets; however, they are not likely to have much impact on profits. |

searches for answers. After a little exploratory research, the writer can then develop a full outline for the study. Although this outline may change as the study progresses, roughing out the major sections and breaking each into smaller subsections will guide the research and writing and prevent the writer from straying too far from the topic.

## OUTLINE STYLES AND FORMATS

*Use a topic outline with short phrases or a summary outline with short sentences to identify segments of a report.*

There are many kinds of outlines, the two most common being the topic outline and the summary outline (see Exhibit 12.1). A topic outline is one that uses short phrases, not complete sentences, to identify segments of a topic. A summary outline uses a sentence for each level to summarize the major conclusion reached in that section.

In the report, your outline will be converted to headings and subheadings, which are typically words and short phrases. Therefore, it may be better to use a topic outline to guide your research. If you use a summary outline, you will have to convert it to a topic outline when the report is typed.

Long headings distract readers; therefore, choose words that are short but descriptive. When using a summary outline, keep the sentences short. Do not

**EXHIBIT 12.2**

**Outline Formats**

| ■ **Alphanumeric Outline** | ■ **Decimal Outline** |
|---|---|
| I. Chapter title | 1. Chapter title |
|   A. Subheading |   1.1 Subheading |
|     1. Sideheading |     1.1.1 Sideheading |
|     2. Sideheading |     1.1.2 Sideheading |
|     3. Sideheading |     1.1.3 Sideheading |
|   B. Subheading |   1.2 Subheading |
|     1. Sideheading |     1.2.1 Sideheading |
|     2. Sideheading |     1.2.2 Sideheading |
| II. Chapter title | 2. Chapter title |
|   A. Subheading |   2.1 Subheading |
|     1. Sideheading |     2.1.1 Sideheading |
|     2. Sideheading |     2.1.2 Sideheading |
|     3. Sideheading |     2.1.3 Sideheading |
|   B. Subheading |   2.2 Subheading |
|     1. Sideheading |     2.2.1 Sideheading |
|     2. Sideheading |     2.2.2 Sideheading |
|   C. Subheading |   2.3 Subheading |
|     1. Sideheading |     2.3.1 Sideheading |
|     2. Sideheading |     2.3.2 Sideheading |

attempt to grab the reader's attention by using cute or attention-getting words and phrases. Clear, professional words are preferable to the curiosity-building words that advertisers employ to get the attention of people uninterested in a topic.

In addition to choosing an outline style, you will have to choose an outline format. Exhibit 12.2 illustrates the two most-used formats. Either is perfectly acceptable, although the organization for which you work might prefer one over the other. The decimal format, for example, is popular in the armed services and many other government agencies. It is also often used for government grants and bids.

As you look at the outlines shown in Exhibit 12.2, notice that at no time is there an A without a B or a 1 without a 2. Any time you divide something by giving part of it a subtitle, you must also name the other part. This concept is easy to understand if you picture a big apple in the middle of your kitchen table. The title of this object is "Apple." Now take an imaginary knife and slice the apple in half. Give one of the halves the subtitle "Bad half." Do you see how naming one half mandates that you give the other half a name too? Let's name it "Good half." The new outline we have created with this imaginary apple is logical and balanced. Of course, if you wanted to, you could keep cutting the pieces smaller and smaller, but each time you would have to name the pieces. A report is the same way. Each time you divide a chapter (or any subsection), you must have at least two subsections, and each subsection must be named.

## OUTLINING PRINCIPLES

Some reports, such as funding proposals, follow a prescribed outline, so you will not need to figure out how to organize the information. However, for most other formal reports you have much latitude in deciding how to organize the information. Your goal is to prove to readers that your conclusions and/or recommendations are rational consequences of the analysis within the report. An outline that helps you reach this goal will structure your argument logically and be phrased consistently.

**LOGICAL PRESENTATION.**   Even before you have finished the research for your report, you must decide how to show the logic behind your conclusions (for analytical reports) and how to present the information clearly (for both analytical and informational reports). Pretend that you are considering where to locate a new store and have narrowed your search to three alternatives: Santa Monica, Marina del Rey, and Long Beach. Furthermore, you have decided on three criteria for choosing a location: the profit potential, the target market demographics, and the competition. One way to organize the report would be to subdivide your analysis by the three alternatives:

> **Presentation of Alternatives: Option One**
> Santa Monica
> > Profit potential
> > Target market demographics
> > Competition
>
> Marina del Rey
> > Profit potential
> > Target market demographics
> > Competition
>
> Long Beach
> > Profit potential
> > Target market demographics
> > Competition

Another option is to organize your analysis by the three criteria:

> **Analysis of Criteria: Option Two**
> Profit potential
> > Santa Monica
> > Marina del Rey
> > Long Beach
>
> Target market demographics
> > Santa Monica
> > Marina del Rey
> > Long Beach
>
> Competition
> > Santa Monica
> > Marina del Rey
> > Long Beach

Both organizational plans present the same information, but the criteria-based option has a major advantage: It emphasizes the decision-making process and allows you to match each of the locations to the factors used to make a final decision. You can compare one city to another by saying such things as the following:

Although the proposed site in Marina del Rey is larger, a lack of public transportation makes it less accessible to potential customers. The Long Beach site, on the other hand, with its easy access to rapid transit facilities, attracts an average of 4,000 potential customers a day from outside city boundaries.

If you decided to organize your report on the basis of alternatives, you would have no place to write this sort of argument. Your only choice would be to present the information about each site, without comparison. You could reach conclusions about each site, but you would have to argue about why one is better or worse than another in a section separate from the presentation of information about the three sites.

Sometimes neither of these two organizational plans is appropriate. For instance, if the purpose of an analytical report is to determine why a problem has occurred, you may want to suggest the probable causes—that is, you may want to formulate hypotheses—and then present the information needed to prove or disprove each hypothesis. The hypothesis-based outline that follows shows the logic of studying an issue in such a way. In the actual report, you would use phrases instead of complete sentences in the headings to make them more succinct and easier to follow.

### Evaluation of Hypotheses
Purpose: Why are sales down in Division III?

I.  Hypothesis: The number of sales personnel has dropped.
    A.  How many sales personnel are there compared to previous sales periods?
    B.  Why has the number dropped?
    C.  What has been the impact on sales of the drop in number of sales personnel?

II.  Hypothesis: The product's price has increased beyond the means of our target market.
    A.  How has the product's price changed?
    B.  Has the price kept pace or moved beyond the means of the target market?
    C.  How has price affected sales?

III.  Hypothesis: The product's quality has declined.
    A.  What is the product's quality compared to that of previous sales periods?
    B.  What has caused a change in quality?
    C.  Has a drop in quality affected sales?

**Informational reports may be organized to present the information step by step, chronologically, geographically or spatially, in order of importance, in terms of advantages or disadvantages, or by type or category.**

Informational reports may use a variety of other arrangements that are not suitable for analytical reports. Reports that present information can be arranged in the following patterns:

- *Step by step.* Use a sequential arrangement to show how a process works or the steps necessary to achieve a particular goal. A report on how to form a corporation could be logically arranged as a step-by-step sequence.

- *Chronological.* Events occurring over a period of time may be presented by date. For example, if a large plant is being completely retooled over a period of one year, you might arrange the report according to what must be done in each month of that year.

- *Geographical or spatial.* When location is the basis of a study, the report may be divided according to location. For example, the names of a company's various sales districts might be used as headings. When the plans for a new ocean liner are being discussed, it might be most logical to discuss one deck at a time.

- *Importance.* Some information might be best presented in order of importance. In some cases, it might be better to begin with the least important factors; in other cases, you might decide to put the most important alternative first. One logical arrangement for data about a company's products would be to list first the product that represents the largest percentage of company profits.

- *Advantages and disadvantages.* When there are distinct advantages and disadvantages or arguments for and against something, but no need to analyze that outweighs the other, you may organize information according to the pros and cons. An important decision is whether to present advantages or disadvantages first. The last argument carries the most psychological weight, so save the best for last.

- *Type or category.* When it is necessary to study the distinct facets of a topic, you may arrange the information according to those facets. For example, a study of computer software might be divided according to the type of program (spreadsheet, database, word processing), program name and version, or general functions of such programs (sorting, drawing, linking).

Scope, importance, and size are three considerations in balancing the segments of a formal report.

In addition to arranging your sections logically, you must also consider the logical scope of the sections. Although each chapter of a report need not have the same number of pages, it would seem odd for one chapter to contain only two pages if other chapters contain eight, nine, or more. In addition, the topic of each chapter must relate to the report's purpose, and each chapter must be equally important to the report's purpose. For example, it would be illogical for the first three chapters of a report on the effectiveness of the company's organizational hierarchy to cover the company's history if the final chapter covers the advantages and disadvantages of the company's organizational chart. The link between the report's purpose and the company's history is far weaker than the link between the purpose and the analysis of the organizational chart. If anything, it would be more logical to have one chapter on history and three on the organizational chart.

Take a minute to look at this book's table of contents. As you look at the headings and subheadings, you can see that they are approximately equal in their influence on the topic—they are balanced in scope.

At each level of an outline, the headings or subheadings should contain the same parts of speech and be constructed the same way.

**GRAMMATICAL AND STRUCTURAL PARALLELISM.** The headings and subheadings in an outline must not only be logical in their organization and balanced in scope, they must also be parallel in grammar and structure. That is, the wording at each level of the outline must be the same part of speech. If you use a phrase, the other headings at that level within that section must consist of the same type of phrase. If a chapter title uses an adjective–noun pattern, the other chapter titles must also use that pattern.

In the following outline, can you identify which headings are not parallel to the others?

**Human Resources Functions**

   I. Hiring
      A. Advertise openings
      B. Reviewing files
      C. Conduct interviews

  II. The process of conducting training
      A. Assessing the needs of employees
      B. The consultant and session design
      C. Evaluating the session and the consultant

 III. Evaluating employee performance
      A. Providing information about expectations
      B. Setting mutual goals
      C. Evaluating performance

 IV. Terminating employees
      A. Documentation
      B. Termination meeting

Look first at the four headings, designated by roman numeral. Are they the same parts of speech? Do they use the same structural pattern? If you said "no," you are correct. The heading in item I is a noun, item II contains a prepositional phrase, and items III and IV are gerund phrases. They are parallel in scope, because each identifies an important part of what a human resources department does; however, they are not grammatically or structurally parallel. Following is one of the several ways you could make these four headings grammatically parallel:

   I. Hiring employees
  II. Conducting training
 III. Evaluating employee performance
 IV. Terminating employees

Now review the subheadings under item I. Do they each begin with the same part of speech? As you can see, they do not. You could choose to stay with the gerund pattern established by the major headings, or you could use the verb–noun pattern used in A and C. Either would be correct. Following is how the section would look if all the subheadings followed the verb–noun pattern:

  A. Advertise openings
  B. Review files
  C. Conduct interviews

Now look at the subheadings under item II. It is easy to see that they are not parallel either. You could reword them as gerunds to make them grammatically and structurally parallel:

  A. Assessing employee needs
  B. Hiring consultants and designing sessions
  C. Evaluating the session and the consultant

Finally, evaluate the subheadings under item III. If they look fine to you, you are correct. These subheadings are all grammatically and structurally parallel.

Parallelism is important in an outline—and in titles and headings—for one main reason: It helps readers follow your train of thought and understand the relationship between concepts.

# PREPARING FORMAL PROPOSALS

■ Prepare a formal proposal.

A formal proposal can be defined as a report written to get a specific reader or readers to consider something. As Chapter 11 explained, proposals may be solicited (requested by the reader) or unsolicited (prepared for the reader without a specific invitation to do so). The following sections discuss the circumstances surrounding proposal writing, so you will have a better idea of the readers' needs.

## BUSINESS AND GOVERNMENT PROPOSALS

*A proposal for business or government is a formal report in which an offer is made to undertake specific tasks or to provide particular products or services in return for something.*

Many organizations seek outsiders to do specific research or provide particular products or services. A request for proposal (RFP) may be issued by the organization, offering all qualified providers an equal opportunity to prove they can do the job. Consider Comet Enterprises, a company that owns several large office buildings. The offices in these buildings are rented to other businesses, but Comet is still responsible for maintenance and upkeep. Comet hires outside contractors to clean the offices. Its first step in selecting companies to provide these services is to issue an RFP, which explains the specific services required, the level of service expected, bonding requirements to guard against employee theft and fraud, deadlines for submitting the proposal, and so on. Once all proposals are received, Comet executives evaluate them and select the contractor they believe will best meet their needs.

Sometimes proposals follow an initial meeting between the parties involved. Mergers between two businesses usually begin in such a way. Similarly, a consultant typically meets with a company representative and then prepares a detailed written proposal. The services a company provides a city are also often discussed beforehand. For example, the city's leaders might get together with a taxi company to discuss whether it can meet the city's needs for the next five years. After the meeting, the taxi company would submit a proposal containing detailed information about the number of cars, drivers, routes, prices, services to be performed, the quality of service, and so forth.

In the purchase of goods or services, the law usually requires government agencies to contract with the organization that submits the lowest bid, assuming that organization's product meets the agency's specifications. However, research proposals do not require the same standard of evaluation. Research contracts are generally awarded to those who submit the most creative or unique ideas or who provide proof of successful past results. Although research proposals are typically evaluated by a committee, the decision remains subjective; therefore, it is critical that you convince evaluators of your ability to do what you propose within their timelines and budget and according to their standards.

Follow these guidelines when writing a solicited proposal in response to an RFP (see Chapter 11 for more detail):

- Address specifically each category and each criterion requested in the RFP or in the initial meeting, ignoring or omitting nothing.

- Arrange your proposal in the same order as listed in the RFP, using its headings, numbering system, and terminology.

- Adhere to special requirements, such as number of pages, letters of reference, accounting statements, and so forth.

- Include a project summary, a project description, personnel qualifications, and budget.

- Be realistic about the price and your capabilities. If your proposal is accepted, you are legally obligated to perform all the services and products you promised at the price quoted.

- Explain what you and/or your company will do that goes beyond the minimum expectations.

- Instill confidence in your company.

- Describe your service or product in terms of how it will benefit the soliciting organization; use good you attitude.

- Meet all proposal deadlines.

Good you attitude is especially important in unsolicited proposals. For example, in an unsolicited proposal about a new inventory system, you should concentrate on explaining the system thoroughly and showing how your idea will benefit readers.

Some unsolicited proposals fall into a category that can more accurately be called *expected.* For example, it is not unusual for large companies to have as many as seven or eight different agencies handling their advertising. These companies often let it be known that they are considering changing advertising agencies or that they are thinking of a new type of advertising for a new product. The implication is that they are open to proposals for new ideas. By making a simple telephone call to the right person, you might be able to determine if a proposal for new business would be welcomed. You will not have an RFP to let you know exactly what information these organizations require to make a decision, but good proposal-writing skills and some persuasive techniques (see Chapter 9) should help you sell your ideas.

## ACADEMIC RESEARCH PROPOSALS

If you are in college to get a degree, you may write several proposals for formal research. Research proposals are usually considered to be short reports; however, they are covered in this chapter because most professors require proposals before approving students' formal research studies. In the vignette at the beginning of the chapter, Patricia Mantabe had successfully completed this sort of proposal. Exhibit 12.3 shows an academic research proposal in manuscript format. (Academic proposals may also be written in memo or letter formats.)

As you prepare an academic research proposal, consider the information a professor needs to understand exactly what you plan to do. First, because the title of a research study is critical to a reader's understanding of the content, specify a preliminary report title. Then, explain the problem and its significance. Next, include a clear statement of your purpose, followed by an explanation

**EXHIBIT 12.3**

Academic Research Proposal (Manuscript)

## PLAN FOR RESEARCH PROJECT

By Patricia Mantabe

### Tentative Title

The Influence of Interruptions on Male and Female Supervisors

### Problem and background

Research discussed in class shows that communication skills are one of the key determinants of success in management. It was reported that the ability to use verbal and nonverbal language to influence people is critical for anyone who wants to get ahead in business. Yet the textbook reports that men and women communicate differently, using different words, syntax, and body language to get their messages across. One of the most reported differences has focused on interruptions—that women allow men to interrupt them. The effect of these interruptions is male control of the flow of conversation and control of the topics discussed.

Research reported in major publications shows that women are not present in significant numbers in upper-level management nor do they make the same salaries as men at any level in any profession.

Many reasons have been raised for these differences. However, if effective communication skills are as important as reported, a reasonable question is: "Could the communication skills of women cause them to be viewed by those in power as weak and submissive thereby less capable of handling managerial positions?" An issue this broad must be broken down into components for study. Therefore, a second question is: "Do women in business allow men to interrupt them?"

### Purpose Statement

The purpose of this study is to determine if women in supervisory positions allow others to interrupt them more than supervisory males allow others to interrupt them. This information will be used to advise women of the effectiveness of their communication style related to interruptive behavior.

### Scope and Limitations

This study will include a review of secondary research related to the interruptive behavior of men and women. It will also include observations of 10 hours of female-male business dyads. While an attempt will be made to

EXHIBIT
12.3

Continued

2

match the types of encounters and the positions of the individuals studied, it is assumed that some variation will exist that cannot be controlled. Every attempt will be made to select individuals in businesses of the same size and type.

One limitation of this study is its sample size. Observations, by nature, take a great deal of time; and since the study must be completed within 10 weeks, the number of communication encounters must be limited.

**Research Methods**

Secondary sources will be searched to determine what is currently known about interruptions in social and business settings. Arrangements will be made with two large organizations willing to allow an observer to observe and record a total of 10 hours of male-female interactions—5 hours with five female supervisors and five hours with 5 male supervisors. Every attempt will be made to match the positions, ages, and experience of these individuals. The individuals involved will not be informed of the real purpose of the study because of the influence such knowledge would have on their interactions. However, they will be assured of confidentiality.

This information will be used to develop a survey form, which will be completed from the recording after each observation. A field test of one male and one female will be conducted to ensure the efficacy of the survey form. Chi-square analysis will be used to determine the significance of the interruptions identified in the observations.

**Preliminary Outline**

    I. Interruptive behavior in the literature
      A. Interruptions in social settings
          1. Among women
          2. Among men
      B. Reasons for allowing interruptions
          1. Roles in society
          2. Lack of awareness
      C. Effects of interruptive behavior
          1. Loss of control of conversation
          2. Loss of speaking time
          3. Perceptions of submissiveness and weakness
   II. Interruptions in business
      A. Types of interruptions
      B. Immediate results of interruptions
      C. Perceptions of interrupters and interruptees

EXHIBIT
12.3

Concluded

**Work Plan and Timelines**

| | |
|---|---|
| Get approval of purpose and outline | September 9 |
| Arrange test sites | September 9-15 |
| First National | |
| Ardco | |
| First Interstate | |
| Mutual Life | |
| Complete database search | September 15 |
| Complete study of periodicals and books | September 19 |
| Compose first draft of literature review | September 23 |
| Draft survey | September 19-23 |
| Field test survey | September 25-30 |
| Finalize survey | November 5 |
| Complete observations | November 7-16 |
| Complete survey forms from recordings | November 17 |
| Run multivariate analysis | November 25 |
| Run chi-square analysis | November 27 |
| Compose first draft of findings | December 1 |
| Edit all chapters | December 9 |
| Complete final draft of report | December 14 |
| Photocopy and bind report | December 15 |
| Submit formal report | December 17 |

of the scope and any limitations you face as you study the topic. Your professor will also want to know how you plan to study the issue; therefore, include at least one paragraph detailing your sources and methods of collecting data. The more complex the research, the longer this section will be.

A preliminary outline should also be included in your academic research proposal. Of course, this outline may change several times before your study is finished; but for now, include at least the first two levels of your outline (chapter titles and first-level headings).

The last part of your academic research proposal should be a personal work plan, showing the specific tasks you will perform in studying the issue and the schedule you have established for completing each task. Be as specific as possible as you break your tasks down. For example, "Finish the research by December 1" is too general. Breaking the research goal into more detailed tasks, as in Exhibit 12.3, is a better way to make sure you accomplish the overall goal. Be realistic as you establish deadlines, and update your timelines daily as you perform the study. The best research studies usually come from people who have not only prepared detailed work plans but have followed them and updated them regularly. There is no substitute for good time management in completing academic research.

## ASSEMBLING FORMAL REPORT ELEMENTS

The elements used in a formal report and the order in which those elements are arranged vary from one report to another.

■ Assemble all the necessary parts of a formal report.

Exhibit 12.4 illustrates the parts of formal reports and their arrangement in both direct and indirect organizational schemes (notice the placement of the summary, conclusions, and recommendations). Few formal reports contain all these elements. If you are uncertain which elements to include in your reports, look through your company's files to determine the type of reports your coworkers are used to reading. Many of the following elements are pictured in the sample report in Exhibit 12.8 at the end of this chapter.

### PREFATORY PARTS

A formal report's findings are most commonly prefaced by a title page and a table of contents. An abstract, letters of transmittal and authorization, and a list of illustrations may also be included. In the direct arrangement, the summary, conclusions, and recommendations are also prefatory parts.

**TITLE PAGE.** The title page does exactly what its name implies—it presents the title of the report. It should also contain the date and the author's name and affiliation. In the case of an academic report, the affiliation would be the name of the institution where the research was conducted. For a formal report prepared for a business's internal use only, the name of the business would probably be unnecessary; however, the writer might decide to put a job title after his or her name. A consultant might give the name of his or her own company immediately after his or her name and list the organization for which the research was performed in another area of the title page. When more than one person writes a report, all the names should be included, although it is also

**EXHIBIT 12.4**

**Direct and Indirect Arrangements of Formal Reports**

| ■ Direct Arrangement | ■ Indirect Arrangement |
|---|---|
| Prefatory parts | Prefatory parts |
|   Title page |   Title page |
|   *Abstract/synopsis/executive summary |   *Abstract/synopsis/executive summary |
|   *Letter of transmittal |   *Letter of transmittal |
|   *Letter of authorization |   *Letter of authorization |
|   Table of contents |   Table of contents |
|   *List of illustrations |   *List of illustrations |
|   Summary | |
|   Conclusions | |
|   Recommendations | |
| Body | Body |
|   Introduction |   Introduction |
|     Background/problem |     Background/problem |
|     Purpose statement |     Purpose statement |
|     Scope and *delimitations |     Scope and *delimitations |
|     *Limitations |     *Limitations |
|     Research methods |     Research methods |
|     *Definitions |     *Definitions |
|   Findings |   Findings |
|     Results and discussion |     Results and discussion |
|       (broken into chapters) |       (broken into chapters) |
| |   Summary |
| |   Conclusions |
| |   Recommendations |
| Addenda | Addenda |
|   Bibliography |   Bibliography |
|   *Appendix |   *Appendix |
|   *Glossary |   *Glossary |
|   *Index |   *Index |

*Optional—used only when necessary or expected by the reader(s).

acceptable to list a department or task force name rather than the individual names of everyone involved in the study.

Use your creative skills to design appealing title pages. On a typical title page, all the elements are centered vertically and horizontally, with an equal number of lines between each section. However, if you know how to use desktop publishing software, you can create unique title pages to appeal to readers.

The title of your report should be concise, yet descriptive and comprehensive. Its wording should indicate the content of the report. Formal report titles should not be cute or interesting; they should express exactly what is contained in the study.

**ABSTRACT.** An **abstract**, sometimes referred to as a *synopsis* or *executive summary,* is a brief, comprehensive summary of the formal report. An abstract is usually limited to between 75 and 150 words—it is a great deal shorter than the section of the report referred to as the *summary.* Abstracts are often omitted from business reports, but they are almost always required by editors before publication of a research study.

An abstract should describe the following:

The purpose of the study (in one sentence, if possible).

The sources used as well as the subjects studied and their characteristics.

The research methods, data-gathering procedures, and statistical tests used.

The findings, conclusions, and recommendations.

If you are expected to compose an abstract for your formal report, keep in mind that the abstract is read first; and, in the case of articles, it may be the only thing people read. Many people skim the abstract to decide if they want to read the rest of the article. Good abstracts should be accurate, able to stand on their own without further reading, concise and specific, and readable.

**LETTER OF TRANSMITTAL.**   A letter of transmittal is a letter or memo from you to the person who authorized you to write the report. The letter may be bound with the report, or it may be clipped to the top. Letters of transmittal are not always required in business reports.

A letter of transmittal gives a consultant or a company employee a chance to put in a few extra personal words. For example, the letter of transmittal for one consulting report had three purposes: to submit the report, to inform the person who commissioned the report that the findings were questionable because the study's subjects—the company employees—were distrustful of the researchers because of tension within the firm, and to offer to guide the company in instituting the recommendations (an opportunity for another consulting contract). The letter was not bound with the report, because the consultant knew the company would not want its internal problems to be made public.

If you are expected to include a letter of transmittal, follow the same guidelines you would follow in composing any direct message. Get to the point in the first sentence. Then discuss the report briefly, along with any information the reader needs to know. The last paragraph should, of course, contain goodwill and, if appropriate, request action on the part of the reader. For example, if you are hoping to be the person selected to head the project studied in a report, your last paragraph should include an offer to undertake the job. Alternatively, an offer to answer questions about the report is an appropriate ending to such a letter.

**LETTER OF AUTHORIZATION.**   Letters or memos of authorization are among the least-used report elements discussed in this section. However, they are sometimes necessary. These letters, written to the person or group commissioned to do the report, serve as evidence of what the writer was told to investigate and, sometimes, how he or she was instructed to investigate the problem.

If you must write a letter or memo of authorization, follow a direct strategy. State the purpose of the letter first (the request or instructions to perform the study). Then give all details necessary, such as the date the study should be completed, the specific problem to be studied, the report's purpose as you see it, and the scope of the problem. For example, in the details portion of a memo, you might instruct one of your employees as follows:

Specifically, the board asks that you determine the correlation between employee absenteeism and employees' demographic characteristics. Analyze the following categories of employees: women with children; men with children; women and men, ages 18–30; women and men, ages 31–40; women and men, ages 41–55; and women and men over 55. Even though earlier data is available, please confine your study to absences within the past five years.

As we discussed earlier, the report with conclusions should be ready for presentation at the July 14 meeting of the board. George says he will need at least a week to edit and publish the report, so your final draft should be completed by July 7.

In some cases, the letter of authorization may be replaced by a contract between the two parties or a one-page document authorizing the study. Whatever form it takes, the letter of authorization should include details about the study, who is to perform it, and the signature of the individual authorizing the study.

A table of contents should contain all the section and chapter titles and first-level headings used in the report.

**TABLE OF CONTENTS.** A table of contents is a detailed listing of all the sections in a report with their page numbers. Because only sections that follow the table of contents are listed, anything that comes before the contents page will not appear. The table of contents should include the chapter headings and first-level subheadings in each chapter. The headings and subheadings in the table of contents must match the words used within the report.

Tables of contents are generally arranged in two columns, with the titles and headings on the left and the beginning page number of each aligned on the right margin. Although you may list the page number of all subheadings no matter how minor they are, it is not necessary to do so. However, the longer your report, the more important it becomes to include page numbers for subheadings as well as for chapter headings.

Although most business reports do not usually include roman numerals and other outline designators, you may do so if your reader will not object. However, if you use numbers and letters in a table of contents, you should also use the same numbers and letters for the headings within the report itself.

Take a minute to look at the table of contents contained within Exhibit 12.8, the sample report at the end of the chapter. Notice how the leaders (dotted lines) guide the eye from the left column to the page numbers on the right.

**LISTS OF ILLUSTRATIONS AND TABLES.** If your report contains a lot of tables, figures, and other visual aids, a list of illustrations with their page numbers should follow the table of contents. A single list of illustrations that includes all graphs, tables, and figures is generally acceptable; however, if you have many figures and many tables, you should probably cite them in separate lists.

Each title in the list of illustrations must appear exactly as it does within the report. As with all titles, the initial letter of all words other than articles, prepositions, and conjunctions should be capitalized.

A good summary answers the questions implied in the report's purpose statement.

**SUMMARY.** The summary is one of the most important parts of a formal report, especially one using a direct arrangement. A good summary should make it unnecessary to read the rest of a report unless a reader is interested in the supporting data that led to the conclusions.

If the organization for which you work expects you to include a summary in your formal analytical reports, begin with your overall recommendation in the first sentence. Unless it is obvious from the recommendation, state the purpose of the study or the hypotheses tested. Paraphrase the major conclusions of your report in the order in which they were presented in the body, but avoid repeating the same words used in conclusions and recommendations sections. The reasons for reaching the conclusions and one or two pieces of supporting statistical evidence may also be included in a summary, as long as they can be stated succinctly.

The length of a summary varies with the length and complexity of the report. It may range from a few paragraphs to no more than two pages. The most important rule is that a summary should be long enough to tell the most important facts the intended reader wants to know. It should answer clearly and succinctly whatever was posed in the purpose statement. Complex scientific studies intended for readers unfamiliar with a topic would require longer summaries, because readers must be educated at the same time results are presented. However, if your readers are fully aware of the problem being investigated and the purpose of the study, you might be able to answer the major questions and present the main reasons behind the conclusions in only a few paragraphs.

Read the summary presented in Exhibit 12.8 at the end of the chapter for an idea of what a summary should include. Then read the rest of the report to get a feel for how the summary evolved from the conclusions reached within the test itself.

**CONCLUSIONS.**   Conclusions are the answers to the hypotheses, questions, or statements you specified in the purpose statement. They are the most read part of analytical reports, but they may not be necessary in informative reports that do not require analysis.

> Conclusions, an essential part of analytical reports, may be written in list form or in paragraph form, but should contain no new information.

To understand the close tie between a report's purpose statement and the resulting conclusions, consider the example below. If you were assigned to determine if there is a correlation between employees' absences and their ages, genders, and children, your conclusions might be something like the following:

Based on the findings within this study, the following conclusions are drawn:

1.  Women between the ages of 18 and 30 with children were found to have a significantly higher number of absences than all other women.

2.  Men between the ages of 18 and 30 with children were also found to have a significantly higher number of absences than all other men; however, when compared to women of the same age with children, the number of male absences was significantly lower.

3.  No other correlation was found between age, gender, and children and the number of employee absences.

These conclusions are in list form preceded by an introductory paragraph. Conclusions are sometimes presented in paragraph form, especially when there is only one. In that case, this section would be titled "Conclusion" instead of "Conclusions." When there is more than one conclusion, however, lists carry an advantage: Each item is a single sentence, in which the writer clearly and concisely answers each research question. Lists force the writer to get to the point.

No new information may be presented in the conclusions section. Each conclusion should also be discussed within the report body, where the statistics and other pertinent facts are reported and analyzed. The conclusions section restates the report's major conclusions (*only* those that tie directly to the purpose statement) in a concise manner.

**Recommendations tell a report's readers what steps should be taken as a result of the conclusions reached in the study.**

**RECOMMENDATIONS.**    Recommendations are the action items that result directly from a report's conclusions. They tell the person or organization commissioning the report what should be done to solve the problem. Imagine that you are writing a report on the feasibility of merging with another company. In your recommendations section, you must tell the readers whether they should or should not merge with the other company. A marketing survey report might recommend a company discontinue its plans to spend $2 million promoting a new product that the survey found the public didn't like. As you can see, the recommendations are of prime importance in an analytical report. They are the ultimate reason for investigating any problem—to determine exactly how to solve it.

The recommendations are supported by the conclusions, which are, in turn, backed up by data within a report. Thus, recommendations are based on logic and reason, not opinions.

If there is more than one recommendation to be made, they are best presented as a list. Because recommendations appear on the same page as the conclusions or on the page immediately following, there is little, if any, need to justify them. Just use wording that gives advice, directing the organization or individual to act. Active verbs and the word *should* are key components of recommendations. Notice how they are used in the following recommendations:

The conclusions contained within this study support the following recommendations:

1.  Murdock Enterprises should investigate the feasibility of instituting an on-site child care center to alleviate attendance problems of its employees with children.

2.  Murdock Enterprises should investigate other ways to meet the needs of working parents without sacrificing productivity and quality.

The purpose of this study was to determine the correlation between several demographic variables and absenteeism. Such a correlation was found and reported in the conclusions. However, the purpose of the study was not to determine solutions to the problems of absenteeism. Therefore, the recommendations above are appropriate. The writer cannot tell the organization to start a child care center, because the conclusions do not support such a recommendation. However, the first recommendation is logically based on the assumption that, because children were the only common denominator found among frequently absent employees, children might logically be a direct cause of their parents' absences. Although this point is still arguable without further substantiation, an investigation into the feasibility of instituting a childcare center could include a search of the literature or a survey of other businesses to determine if childcare centers improve attendance. The second recommendation leaves management open to propose and study other ways of solving the problem.

## THE REPORT BODY

The report body contains the introductory material and the findings. The introduction normally consists of a description of the background or problem, a purpose statement, and a description of the study's scope, research methods, and results. Optional sections are the delimitations of the study (combined with the scope), the limitations, and definitions. The findings (results and discussion) are divided into as many chapters as are needed to answer the questions proposed by the purpose. In indirect reports, the summary, conclusions, and recommendations are also placed in the body. Check Exhibit 12.4 for a list of these elements in the proper sequence.

**BACKGROUND AND PROBLEM.**    The background section of a study describes a pertinent situation or the history of a problem. In business, the background (or the *statement of the problem,* as it is sometimes called) establishes the fact that there is a problem worthy of study, a dilemma that has affected the organization in some way or that will do so in the future if nothing is done. For example, in the absenteeism report, the writer might describe a dramatic increase in absenteeism over the past five years. To prove the problem is worth studying, the writer might cite studies that tie high levels of absenteeism to decreased productivity and poor quality. An appropriate title for this section would be "Problem and Background."

> The background or problem should contain enough detail to convince your readers that the topic being studied is worthy of their time.

In academic research reports, the background section is also an appropriate place to identify the report's intended readers. Different topics may be handled in different ways depending on who is reading them. A report investigating the problems of installing multimillion-dollar scrubbers on power plant smokestacks would be written differently if it were prepared to educate the general public than if it were intended for lawmakers or plant engineers needing to solve complex installation issues. Somewhere in the background section, or immediately following the purpose statement, a statement such as the following should be included:

> This analysis will result in recommendations to state lawmakers as to the necessity of their intervening in the decision making of one of the state's most critical industries.

**PURPOSE STATEMENT.**    After proving there is a problem that should be studied or a question that should be answered, a report writer should clearly state the purpose of the report. The purpose statement may be part of the problem and background section; however, many people feel the importance of the purpose statement warrants a separate subheading.

As you learned previously in this chapter, a clear purpose statement is critically important in a formal report. It establishes the overall elements of the outline, and it guides the writer as she or he researches the topic. Finally, the purpose statement tells the writer exactly what needs to be addressed in the conclusions and the recommendations.

> Tell your readers exactly what your report is going to cover and what it is not going to cover that they might be expecting.

**SCOPE AND DELIMITATIONS.**    As you will recall from an earlier section of the chapter, the *scope* section of a report details what the report is going to cover. The *delimitations* section refers to excluded variables, characteristics, factors, subheadings, topics, or issues that some readers might expect to find in a report on this particular topic.

Although delimitations are often omitted from formal business reports, there is an advantage to mentioning them. At the same time you tell your readers what is being left out, you can justify the exclusion. This advantage was Joe Otto's motivation for stating delimitations in a report he composed. Joe's purpose was to select a location for a new hotel. Management instructed him to compare four locations, which he did. However, they and he knew that stockholders would want to know why a site in Eastern Europe was not considered. This particular site had been announced at the last annual meeting. Rather than ignore the site and hope no one would notice its omission, Joe told his readers that the location had been ruled out because of unrest in that part of the world. Properly worded delimitations help to forestall challenges to the quality of the research.

**LIMITATIONS.** The limitations of a formal research study are those factors that detract from the study in some way. As stated before, limitations are often detailed in the section where the scope of the study is discussed. It is also common to discuss limitations as a part of the research methods section when the limitations prevent the research from being as scientific as possible. For example, lack of money might prevent a company from surveying as many people as necessary to achieve valid results. An informational report on gender differences with advice for businesswomen provides another example. The limitations section should explain that most published studies have been done on women in general and much of data come from surveys of college students. That information may not be generalizable to businesswomen.

Some people prefer not to mention limitations, hoping instead that readers will not notice the fallacies of their research or reasoning. However, readers are not stupid. It is better to be honest about the limitations of the research to avoid the appearance of deception. For example, the writer of the report on gender differences should mention the possible limitation, but justify it with a statement such as the following:

> Because the findings are true of women in general, they may be assumed to be true of women in business as well.

Even though the point is still arguable, the writer has avoided the appearance of trying to deceive readers.

**In the research methods section, describe your subjects; the apparatus, materials, and/or data you used; and the procedure by which you studied the problem.**

**RESEARCH METHODS.** The methods section of a formal report describes how a study was conducted. It should concisely tell the reader *what* you did and *how* you did it. The description allows the reader to evaluate the appropriateness of your methods and the reliability and the validity of your results. *Reliability* refers to the extent to which an experiment, survey, or measuring procedure yields the same result when repeated. *Validity* is the extent to which the conclusions of a study are based on sound reasoning, objective truth, and a preponderance of evidence.

First, identify the subjects of the study. If your subjects were people, who were they? Include demographic information about those subjects. How many subjects did you study? How were they selected? For example, in a report on new hotel locations, you might list the locations you studied and mention the basis on which they were compared, the kinds of data gathered, and the procedures for gathering the information.

Next, you can describe any apparatus or special materials used and the types of data gathered. A study of the safety of a company's car models would probably include many different tests with highly sophisticated machinery. One of these tests would probably be a test of the front bumper at measured speeds. Machines that regulate the speed of each automobile and evaluate the amount of damage incurred would be described or illustrated, as would the computerized dummies used to estimate how much damage human beings would experience in such a crash.

The third component of the research methods section should include a summary of each step in the execution of the research. Instructions given to the subjects or the people conducting the surveys, how any groups studied were formed, and so forth, should be summarized. If you are using the information gathered from your subjects to generalize to the public as a whole, convince the reader that the sampling technique you used was random and is, therefore, generalizable. Counterbalancing techniques, control features, and standard testing procedures should be discussed. In addition, it might be necessary to justify any inferential statistics (e.g., $t$-test, $F$-tests, chi-square) used. In many cases, statistical justification may be only a referral to other respected studies in which the same test was used. It is beyond the scope of this book to explain statistical presentation. However, other sources should be consulted for further information about accepted statistical practice.

**A definitions section may be included if the report uses a lot of new, complex technical terms that readers may not remember as they read the report.**

**DEFINITIONS.**    When a report includes a lot of technical terms that your readers will not understand, you may dedicate a section to definitions. It is usually best to define a difficult word at the time it is introduced. However, you may put technical definitions in a separate section if readers might have to refer to them frequently.

Definitions and abbreviations may be combined to conserve space, or they may be presented in two different sections. Definitions and abbreviations may also be placed in a glossary at the end of a report. If you do this, however, be sure to tell your readers in the introduction that a glossary is included and refer readers to the glossary whenever a new term is used. The following sentence shows how such a referral would be made:

> The third step in the process is the engagement of the whirling wire (see the Glossary).

**The results and their discussion may be presented in one section, two separate sections, or together in chapters appropriate to the topic.**

**RESULTS AND DISCUSSION.**    In an indirect arrangement, the findings section of the report consists of the results and discussion, summary, conclusions, and recommendations. In a direct arrangement, however, the summary, conclusions, and recommendations are prefatory parts, and so the findings section consists solely of the results and discussion.

Depending on the type of study, the results and their discussion may be presented together ("Results and Discussion") or in two different sections ("Results," "Discussion"). An alternative is to divide the findings into topic-related chapters, each containing both results and discussion. Scientific studies and many academic reports generally use one of the first two options. However, many business studies use the third, especially when the discussion is relatively brief and straightforward.

If results are presented by themselves, you should first briefly state the main results or findings and then report the data in sufficient detail to justify the conclusions. Be objective when you report results, making sure to give even those results that run counter to your beliefs, your preferences, or your hypotheses. Similarly, when you are using secondary research to determine the answer to a problem, avoid biasing your conclusions by presenting only those sources that agree with you. For example, if you personally prefer a certain word processing program but your task is to select a program that best meets the needs of a particular company, make sure you include the comments of reviewers who favor other programs as well. You are expected to put forth a balanced presentation of both or all sides of an issue. Readers do not respect work that is obviously biased, and you will be judged by the quality and professionalism of the reports you submit.

Use tables and figures to present data clearly and economically. However, do not use tables or figures for information that can be given in two or three sentences. Tell your reader what to look for in each visual, providing sufficient explanation to make the significance of the visual readily apparent.

If data were manipulated by statistical tests, include all the information necessary to judge their reliability and validity. If your reader has knowledge of statistics, you will not have to explain or justify these tests. Otherwise, it might be necessary to go into more detail.

Wherever you put the discussion, evaluate and interpret the implications of the results as they relate to your purpose statement. Open with a clear statement of the conclusions as they relate to your purpose, without repeating points already made. Examine, interpret, and qualify the results as you draw inferences from them. Cite the source of all quotes, paraphrases, and references to other sources (Chapter 13 shows how to cite sources). If some of your results are negative, don't try to explain them away; just state them and move on. If there are shortcomings in your research, such as subjects' reluctance to speak truthfully, they should be mentioned, but it is not necessary to dwell on them.

In the discussion, concentrate on answering these two questions:

- How has the study helped to resolve the problem identified in the purpose statement?

- What conclusions related to the purpose statement can be drawn from the information gathered for the study?

### ADDENDA

A formal report may end with a bibliography, an appendix, a glossary, and/or an index, depending on the reader's expectations.

At the end of a formal report, addenda are sometimes used. The most common is a bibliography listing all the sources referred to in the study. However, some studies may require an appendix, a glossary, or an index.

**BIBLIOGRAPHY.** A bibliography is an alphabetical listing of all secondary sources cited in a formal report. Some writers also list additional sources, such as interviews they conducted with experts on the topic. In addition, researchers sometimes list seminars or classes from which references were drawn to support their research. Some people also include recommended reading on the topic under discussion.

Bibliographies will be discussed in detail in Chapter 13 along with citations of works listed in bibliographies. However, you may want to take a minute to familiarize yourself with the bibliography shown in the sample report in Exhibit 12.8.

**APPENDIX.** The need for complete documentation often dictates the inclusion of an appendix or appendixes at the end of a formal report. An appendix might consist of folded visual aids that were too large to go within the chapter of a report, questionnaires, raw computer data, or statistical calculations for complex statistical tests not readily intelligible to readers. Appendixes are not for "nice to know" information; they are for information and materials that apply directly to the topic and the purpose statement. Each item in an appendix must be referred to within the body of the report.

**GLOSSARY.** Although glossaries are not present in most business reports, they are an important part of lengthy scientific treatises that contain words unfamiliar to readers. New terms created by the author and seldom-used or new acronyms are often arranged in alphabetical order in a glossary. Including a glossary in a formal report does not release you from the necessity of defining each term when it is used within the report, however; a new term should be defined the first time it is used, and an acronym should appear in parentheses after the words for which it stands:

> The United States Department of Agriculture (USDA) has not approved a grading system for fish. However, the USDA has issued a preliminary report on the subject.

Once an acronym has been introduced, it does not have to be explained again, unless a number of pages of text intervene between its uses. In those cases you may want to remind the reader of what the acronym means.

*An index is an alphabetical listing of important topics in a study, with the page numbers on which important information about those topics can be found.*

**INDEX.** Most business reports do not need an index—an alphabetical listing of important topics in a study and the page numbers on which important information about those topics can be found. However, indexes can be helpful, particularly when a reader will be frequently referring to a report for information.

Reports of 30 pages or so can usually get by without an index. However, an index is useful in some scientific research reports encompassing several volumes. Many defense industry contracts, for example, require a confidential auditing report (a comprehensive accounting of the entire project from its inception to its completion) at the end of a project. These detailed reports describe each step of the product's development in minute detail and highly technical language. When readers need to look up specific details, they should be able to turn to an index to find the location of that information.

## FORMATTING THE FORMAL REPORT

■ Use manuscript format correctly.

Consistently using a single style throughout a formal report for headings, margins, page numbers, footnotes, spacing, indention, visual aids, references, and the like ensures that readers will be able to concentrate on the content. That is why many schools require all students to lay out their formal reports, theses, and dissertations in the same way. Some businesses do the same thing; however, there is usually more flexibility in the way a business report may be set up.

**Major Style Manuals**

Achtert, W. S., and Gibaldi, J. *The MLA Style Manual.* New York: Modern Language Association, 1985. One of the most popular references for what is referred to as *MLA style,* it is used frequently for academic writing.

American Psychological Association. *Publication Manual of the American Psychological Association.* 3rd ed. Washington, DC: American Psychological Association, 1983. Referred to as *APA style,* this style uses the efficient author–date system of citations.

Campbell, W. G., et al. *Form and Style.* 6th ed. Boston: Houghton Mifflin Company, 1982. Used often in colleges, this guide shows both the MLA and Chicago styles of citation and documentation.

*The Chicago Manual of Style.* 14th ed. Chicago: University of Chicago Press, 1993. Referred to as the *Chicago style,* this style is used frequently in publishing and the academic world.

Turabian, K. L. *A Manual for Writers of Term Papers, Theses, and Dissertations.* 4th ed. Chicago: The University of Chicago Press, 1973. This manual covers the Chicago style but is smaller than *The Chicago Manual of Style.*

*U.S. Government Printing Office Style Manual.* Revised ed. Washington, DC: U.S. Government Printing Office, 1984. Referred to as the *GPO Manual,* this guide is particularly useful for documentation of government publications.

If you are unsure how to format a business report, look through your company's files. How do the other reports in those files look? What parts do they contain? Which arrangement is used most often—direct or indirect? After you have finished this chapter and the next and have done a formal report of your own, you will have the knowledge to critique the format of the reports you see in your company's files. Do they look readable, or do the pages appear cluttered and hard to read? Is each component of the report labeled clearly and easy to find?

Some large companies put a great deal of effort into designing a readable format and prepare their own "house" style manuals containing guidelines for all company reports. In the absence of a customized style manual, you can refer to one of the major published manuals. Exhibit 12.5 lists the most commonly used guides to formatting. They all provide advice on capitalization, use of numbers, page layout, reference styles, and so on, although each has its own particular recommendations. Anyone who writes reports should become familiar with one or two such manuals.

The sections that follow cover commonly accepted ways of formatting formal business reports. These guidelines will help you present your research and information in such a way that readers can focus on the content. As you read, refer to the sample report in Exhibit 12.8 and pay close attention to the notes in the margins. They will serve as an excellent guide to formatting (as well as to the other topics covered in this chapter).

## HEADINGS AND SUBHEADINGS

Headings and subheadings help the reader by telegraphing the content of the report and showing the relationship of one part to another. For example, if a heading reads "Word Processing Programs" and the subheadings under it are "Microsoft Word©," "WordPerfect©," and "WordStar©," the reader can more easily find the information and knows from the format that these are word processing programs.

As a student, you already know the benefit of good headings and subheadings. When answering questions or studying for an exam, how many times have you skimmed a chapter looking for a particular section? When you do this, you probably look at the headings and subheadings to find the section you want. Good readers also know to read first all the headings and subheadings in a technical paper to get a general overview of the entire topic before reading the paper line by line. Doing so lets a reader know where a writer is headed with a topic and keeps the reader focused on the major points as he or she reads.

Exhibit 12.6 shows two commonly used ways to use headings and subheadings in formal reports. Whether you use one of the styles illustrated or devise a plan of your own, the major principle is consistency. Each level of heading must be typed in the same way. For example, if you center the first chapter title and use 14-point boldface type, all other chapter titles must be centered and boldfaced in 14-point type. Inconsistency confuses readers and negates the benefits of using headings and subheadings.

## MARGINS

Use report margins that match the style manual you are following and take into account how the report will be bound.

Rules about the size of the margins in a formal report vary, depending on the style manual you follow and the way you bind the report. However, the bottom margin is always set at one inch. Exhibit 12.7 shows the commonly accepted margin widths for leftbound, unbound, and topbound formal reports.

Many formal reports are stapled in the upper-left corner or paper-clipped together instead of being bound. In that case, the titles of all prefatory and supplementary pages (e.g., bibliography, table of contents) and the first page of text should begin 1-1/2 inches from the top of the page (some reference manuals specify 2 inches). The text on all other pages of the report should begin 1 inch from the top. If you choose to begin each chapter of a report on a new page, the title should be typed 1-1/2 inches down. However, if each chapter does not begin a new page, you may simply leave one blank line (when double spacing) or two blank lines (when single spacing) between the chapter title and the end of the previous chapter.

When reports are to be bound at the left or the top, the margins have to be increased to make room for the part of the page taken up by the binding. If your report is to be leftbound, use a 1-1/2-inch left margin but leave the right margin at 1 inch. If the binding will be at the top, increase the top margin of each page by 1/2 inch, making pages with titles start at 2 inches and all other pages start at 1-1/2 inches. Centering titles on leftbound pages is easy if you are using a computer that automatically centers between the margins. However, if you are using a typewriter, you will have to remember to move the center point to the right 1/4 inch so the title will appear at the visual center of the page after it is bound.

**EXHIBIT 12.6**   Headings and Subheadings in Formal Reports

■ **Example No. 1**
(Five Levels)

**CENTERED UPPERCASE CHAPTER TITLE**

**Centered Uppercase and Lowercase Heading**

**Centered, Underlined, Uppercase and Lowercase Subheading**

**Flush Left, Underlined, Uppercase and Lowercase Side Heading**

    **Indented, underlined, lowercase paragraph subheading with a period.**

For Example:

---

**PHASE ONE: INTERVIEWS**

**External Validation**

**Method**

    Text begins here and continues . . . . . . . . . . . . . . . . . . . . . . . . . . . . . . . . .

**Subjects**

    Text begins here and continues . . . . . . . . . . . . . . . . . . . . . . . . . . . . . . . . .

    **Solicited.** Text begins here and continues . . . . . . . . . . . . . . . . . . . . . . . . .

    **Unsolicited.** . . . . . . . . . . . . . . . . . . . . . . . . . . . . . . . . . . . . . . . . . . . . .

**Apparatus**

    . . . . . . . . . . . . . . . . . . . . . . . . . . . . . . . . . . . . . . . . . . . . .

---

■ **Example No. 2**
(Four Levels)

**CAPITALIZED CHAPTER TITLE**

**Centered Heading**

**Flush Left, Uppercase and Lowercase Side Heading**

    **Indented, uppercase and lowercase paragraph heading with a period.**

For Example:

---

**PHASE ONE: INTERVIEWS**

**External Validation**

    Text begins here and continues . . . . . . . . . . . . . . . . . . . . . . . . . . . . . . . . .

**Method**

    Text begins here and continues . . . . . . . . . . . . . . . . . . . . . . . . . . . . . . . . .

    **Subjects.** Text begins here and continues . . . . . . . . . . . . . . . . . . . . . . . . .

    **Apparatus.** . . . . . . . . . . . . . . . . . . . . . . . . . . . . . . . . . . . . . . . . . . . . .

---

**EXHIBIT
12.7**    **Report Margins**

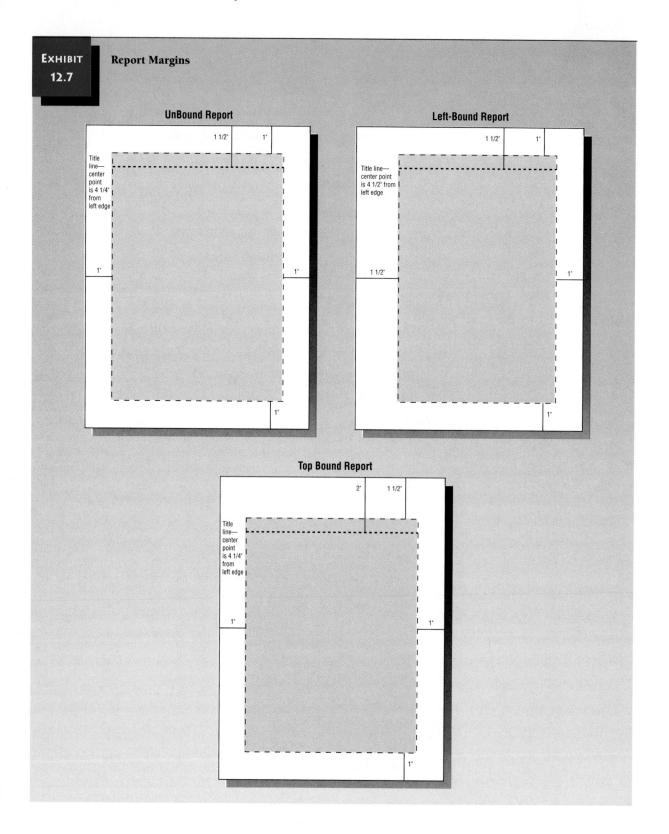

Most word processing programs give you the option of **justifying** the right margin so that every line of text ends exactly on the right margin. The pages of this book are justified. Many computer programs are able to justify text by adding a tiny amount of space between words and between letters, and condensing or expanding imperceptibly the amount of space each letter uses. However, not all software programs and printers do a good job of justifying. Do not justify the right margin of a formal report if the extra spaces between words are noticeable. The appearance advantage is lost when extra spaces between words hinder readability.

## PAGE NUMBERS, HEADERS, AND FOOTERS

Page numbers may be combined with a footer at the bottom of a page or with a header at the top of a page.

Page numbers are often combined with a **header,** an identifying element that appears at the top of report pages. Headers may contain all or part of a report or chapter title. (A **footer** is like a header, except that it appears at the bottom of the page.) The ease with which headers can be created using word processing programs has made them popular for many business reports. The following example is a running head you could use for the report in Exhibit 12.8 which is titled "The Relationship between Interruptions and Gender in Superior–Subordinate Interaction at Chamberlain Mathiba"; the running head includes only part of the report's title and the page number:

Gender-Related Interruptions
12

Depending on the style manual you are following, page numbers may be placed by themselves in the upper-right corner of the page (at the 1-inch margin, or 1/2 inch from the top of the page), may be part of a header at the top right corner of the page (1/2 to 1 inch down), or may be centered at the bottom of the page (1/2 inch from the bottom).

Some style manuals require a running head and page number on every single page of a report. However, to prevent page numbers from interfering with titles, pages that begin with titles are usually not numbered when a top-of-the-page numbering system is used for a report. Most modern word processing programs may be set to automatically omit page numbers on pages that begin new sections, such as those containing centered titles. However, when page numbers appear at the bottom, many people include numbers on all pages, including the first page of a chapter or of some other major section.

Some style manuals require the use of arabic numerals for all the pages in a report; others specify a mix of roman and arabic numerals, with some pages being counted but not numbered. The sample report in Exhibit 12.8 uses the second type of numbering system; after reading this paragraph, take a minute to observe the use of roman numerals and arabic numerals in the sample report. Typically, the page count begins with the title page, although a page number does not appear on the page. If a bottom-of-the-page numbering system is used, the rest of the prefatory pages would be numbered at the bottom with small roman numerals (e.g., ii, iii, iv). The introduction is typically the first page of a formal report that uses arabic numbers, and the page number should be typed at the bottom of the page. From that point on, use arabic numerals for all pages.

## SUPPLEMENTAL NOTES, FOOTNOTES, AND ENDNOTES

**Supplemental notes** are asides that amplify or explain the discussion in the text. They may be placed at the bottom of the page, or they may be included in a separate section at the end of either a chapter or the report. However, when the explanation is placed at the bottom of the page where it is referenced, it is easy to find and readers are more likely to take the time to read it.

Bibliographic details about a cited source may be placed at the bottom of a page (footnotes) or at the end of a section, chapter, or report (endnotes).

Footnotes contain complete bibliographical details about the source paraphrased or quoted in the text. They appear at the bottom (the foot) of the page on which they are cited. Most style manuals say to single space the footnotes even when the rest of the report is double spaced. Correctly formatted footnotes end exactly 1 inch from the bottom of a page. Because footnotes vary in length and because the number of footnotes varies from one page to another, positioning them correctly is tricky. However, many word processing programs contain advanced features that place footnotes automatically.

Because footnotes are hard to position correctly, many people prefer to put the reference details at the end of each chapter or at the end of the report. In this case, they are referred to as *endnotes* or *reference notes*. If you are using endnotes, place them on a separate page. Format the title exactly as you did the chapter titles within your report. Chapter 13 discusses the arrangement of items within footnotes and endnotes.

## SPACING AND INDENTIONS

Line spacing and spacing above and below headings should be consistent throughout a report.

Formal reports used to always be double-spaced (one blank line between every two lines of type) so they would be easier to read. However, in business today, single spacing is as common as double spacing—a result of environmental concerns and efforts to conserve paper. With effective use of graphics, margins, headings and subheadings, and other visual elements, readability need not suffer with single spacing. Look at the sample report in Exhibit 12.8 to see how the spacing of lines and report elements contributes to readability.

Most style manuals used in the academic world still specify double spacing for the text of a report, with footnotes and the bibliography being single spaced. Double-spaced text provides more room to make notations to students. For the same reason, collaborative writers often double space their initial drafts even though they may single space the final report. The extra spaces encourage everyone involved to make suggestions that will aid in the development of the final product.

Recommendations for spacing on the title page vary. Most style manuals require equal top, bottom, and side margins, as well as an equal number of lines between the blocks of type. If you are not restricted by a style manual, strive for interest and originality. Just make sure that the title is emphasized more than the other elements on the page.

Recommendations for spacing above and below titles and other headings also vary among style manuals. Whether a report is single or double spaced, one of these two conventions is usually recommended:

- Triple space above a chapter title (when it does not appear at the top of a new page) and above first-level subheadings; double-space below.

- Double-space above and below titles and first-level subheadings; double-space above second- and third-level subheadings except for those that are indented five spaces from the left margin.

Whether the report is single or double spaced, the first line of every paragraph and every footnote should be indented 1/2 inch, although sometimes the first line below a title or heading is not indented. All other lines should begin at the left margin, with obvious exceptions such as title lines of tables, tables that do not need the full line width, indented subheadings, and so forth. Chapter 13 covers the rules for indenting long quotations.

## VISUAL AIDS

Use graphics to present information concisely and to create interest.

Most formal reports contain visual aids. Graphs, charts, illustrations, tables, and so forth are used frequently as a concise and interesting way of presenting technical information. Most businesspeople speak a numerical language, and they expect to see information presented visually. (Chapter 10 discussed the use of graphic aids in detail.) If you have not already done so, read that chapter before you begin to work on your next report. To summarize, keep in mind the following:

- Each visual aid must be referred to within the text at the point at which the reader should look at the graphic.

- Unless they are larger than the page, visual aids should be placed as soon as possible after they are introduced, preferably at the end of the paragraph.

- If there are more than two visual aids in a document, they should be numbered.

- Although each visual aid should be clear enough to stand on its own without explanation, significant results revealed by the graphic must be discussed within the text.

- Each visual aid should have a clear, descriptive title, and all elements of the graphic should be labeled clearly.

- Visual aids should be constructed to adhere to commonly accepted guidelines.

The visual aids in Exhibit 12.8 demonstrate how consistent formatting adds to the readability and credibility of a formal report.

**EXHIBIT 12.8**   Formal Report (Excerpts)

**Chandler & Associates**
Communication
and Management
Consultants

January 13, 1996

Dr. Linda Beamer
Affirmative Action Representative
Human Resources Department
Chamberlain Mathiba
1677 Thatcher Road
Boston, Massachusetts 02136

Dear Dr. Beamer:

Attached is the study of interruptive behavior you commissioned on September 3, 1995.

As you can see, the results do not bear out your initial perception that subordinates at Chamberlain Mathiba practice interruptive behavior, thereby revealing a lack of respect for their female superiors. In addition, no significant difference was found in the number of interruptions exhibited by upper-level executives toward male or female middle-level managers. However, the findings did reveal that female middle-level managers allow their superiors to take control of discussions at a far higher rate than do males at that level.

We enjoyed working with you on this project, Linda. If you decide to present this report formally to the board, please let me know. I have a few ideas for a 15-20 minute multimedia presentation that will make the topic interesting and thought-provoking.

The next component of this three-part study should begin within the next month, possibly February 13. If that date is fine with you, please let me know. At that time, we can finalize the study plan.

**EXHIBIT 12.8**    Continued

Dr. Linda Beamer                 2                 January 13, 1996

In the meantime, you may be glad to know that we are putting together a series of interactive workshops on issues related to communication differences. Should you decide to pursue this issue aggressively, my staff and I will be happy to work with your employees. These workshops are fun. They are designed to teach effective communication techniques without placing the blame for miscommunication on either gender.

Sincerely,

*If appropriate, close with an offer of additional assistance. While goodwill should be included throughout the letter, it is particularly pertinent in the closing paragraphs.*

Joseph Otto
President

Attachment

**EXHIBIT 12.8** Continued

If you know how to do so, use desktop publishing software to create an interesting title page. If not, center each block of type in the middle of the page horizontally.

Make the title stand out; it should be the most prominent feature on the page. If you are not able to boldface the title, capitalize it.

# The Relationship between Interruptions and Gender in Superior–Subordinate Interaction at Chamberlain Mathiba

Include the author's name and the date of the report. In some cases, it may be necessary to identify who commissioned the report.

Prepared for Chamberlain Mathiba
by Joseph Otto, Chandler & Associates
162-A Kearney Square
Lowell, Massachussetts 01852

January 1996

The top and bottom margins should be equal, and the amount of space between sections of the title page should be balanced.

**EXHIBIT 12.8**    Continued

*Include all chapter headings and first-level subheadings in the table of contents. Page numbers should be included for all major headings, but they may be omitted for suheadings.*

## CONTENTS

**EXHIBIT
12.8**

Continued

*A summary may begin with the
conclusions and recommendations
(direct order), or it may present the
conclusions and recommendations at
the end (indirect order). This summary
is organized using an indirect pattern.*

**SUMMARY**

The purpose of the study was to determine if middle-level
female managers are interrupted more often than their male
counterparts by their subordinates, colleauges, and superiors. In
addition, the study ascertained the number of successful
interruptions directed at male and female middle-level managers
by their subordinates, colleagues, and superiors.

*Write the summary
in your own words;
do not use
quotations and
paraphrased
information.*

To study the issue, a team of observers audiotaped five
Chamberlain Mathiba middle-level executives, three females and
two males who gave their permission to be taped and who were
assured of confidentiality. Results of these observations were
tallied, and tests were conducted to determine the significance of
the results.

*Make sure your
summary actually
summarizes each of
the sections of your
report. Do not
confuse it with an
introduction. If a
topic is important
enough to be a
section of the
report, it should
be part of the
summary as well.*

It was found that Chamberlain Mathiba women who are
employed in middle-level managerial positions are interrupted
more often than their male counterparts. These attempts to
violate accepted turn-taking conventions to seize control of
dialogue were practiced by colleagues and subordinates as well
as by the female managers' superiors.

However, it was determined that the middle-level females
studied were as successful as their male counterparts in
resisting the interruptive attempts at domination of their
colleagues and subordinates. By successfully resisting these
interruptive attempts, females and males are able to maintain
power, thereby lessening perceptions of weakness and lack of
assertiveness. Nevertheless, such equality was not found in
dyads of these women and their superiors. Females were less
successful than males in retaining the floor when interrupted by
their superiors.

To fully investigate other issues related to communication
style differences and their impact on managerial gender
diversity, the currently planned studies of verbal differences
are recommended. Workshops on interruptions and other

**EXHIBIT 12.8**    **Continued**

communications styles are recommended at the conclusion of this three-part study.

## CONCLUSIONS

*The conclusions may be in list or paragraph form. Keep the purpose in mind as you address each of the questions or hypostheses presented in your purpose statement.*

Comparison of the interruptive behavior directed toward male and female middle-level managers leads to these conclusions:

1. Female middle-level managers are interrupted more frequently by their colleagues, subordinates, and superiors.

*Use your own words to phrase conclusions; do not paraphrase or quote sources.*

2. Most interruptive attempts by colleagues and subordinates were unsuccessful when directed at male and female middle-level managers.

3. Male middle-level managers were significantly more successful in retaining control of the floor when interrupted by their superiors.

## RECOMMENDATIONS

The conclusions of this study lead to these recommendations:

1. Chamberlain Mathiba should continue to study communication style differences as a possible contributor to the gender disparity among its upper-level managerial staff.

2. Chamerlain Mathiba upper- and middle-level employees should participate in workshops designed to foster an appreciation of the differences in communication styles and to develop an awareness of the impact of their own interruptive behavior.

iv

**EXHIBIT 12.8**

Continued

## INTRODUCTION

Chamberlain Mathiba prides itself on the diversity of its employees. It has long been the belief of its board of directors that people of all genders should have an equal opportunity to succeed in the company. This credo is spelled out in detail in Chamberlain's Affirmative Action Policy Manual, a manual distributed yearly to all employees and made a part of every position announcement. However, there is reason to believe the convictions of the company have fallen short of expectations.

### Background

*The background should set the stage for the problem. Why is it so important? Just what is the problem the reader should know or care about?*

On September 3, 1995, the Board of Directors of Chamberlain Mathiba met in closed session to consider charges of discrimination leveled against the company by three of its middle-level female managers. Their charge was that they had been repeatedly passed over for promotions and that there was a climate of discrimination against women that was preventing women from achieving top management positions. After taking testimony from all involved, the board found no proof of the basis behind the charges; however, they did determine that although women are being promoted in sufficient ranks to first-level management positions (34 percent), only 15 percent of middle-level management and 2 percent of top-level management are female. Since 48 percent of lower level employees are female, it is apparent that something is preventing women from rising within the company.

At the direction of the board, Chandler & Associates, a firm specializing in communication and management consulting and training, was called in by Dr. Linda Beamer to investigate the issue. Chandler & Associates conducted an attitude survey of all employees. This survey, presented to the Board in July 1995, revealed a significant number of employees believe that most women are too weak to handle the challenges presented by management positions and that most women are unassertive communicators.

**EXHIBIT 12.8**   **Continued**

Disturbed by these findings, the board decided to investigate the issue of communication style to determine how it manifests itself in management-subordinate relationships. Chandler & Associates was commissioned to study the issue, and a series of three studies was planned.

Chandler presented the three major differences in male and female communication styles as defined in communication literature. It was decided to divide this study into three components. This study is the first of those three segments.

## Purpose Statement

*An infinitive purpose statement is used to indicate clearly what the researchers are trying to determine. This study has a two-part purpose.*

This, the first of three studies, deals with one of the key techniques people use to control conversations and topics—interruptions. Because control of conversations results in a perception of power, interruptive behavior may be one cause of what some describe as the bias against female managers at Chamberlain. The purpose of this study is to determine if middle-level female managers are interrupted more often than their male counterparts by their subordinates, colleagues, and superiors. It will also ascertain if there is a significant difference in the number of successful interruptions between male and female middle-level managers.

## Scope and Limitations

*Tell what the report covers (its scope), and be honest with readers about any limitations that might detract from the viability of the study's results.*

This study included on-site visual observation of the daily business dialogue of three female and two male managers at Chamberlain, and it dealt only with interruptive behavior. Study of each individual was limited to five hours of dialogue on five different days over a period of three months.

A major limitation of the study was its intrusive nature. Subjects, who agreed to be studied, were aware of the presence of consultants. Although they were not told that interruptions were being studied or even that their communication styles were being examined, it may be surmised that what was observed may have been different had subjects not been aware of the presence of a stranger.

2

**EXHIBIT 12.8**  Continued

In addition to on-site observations, a review of literature dealing with interruptive behavior was conducted and is included in this report. This information is provided to give Chamberlain decision makers the background necessary to appreciate the importance of interruptive behavior as an influence on perceptions of competence.

## Research Methods

*Describe the study's subjects, and show that their inclusion as subjects is objective and represents the population as a whole. Give detailed information about how the issue was studied and how the data and information gathered were analyzed.*

The subjects of this study were three middle-level women and two middle-level men. The subjects were randomly selected from a list of middle-level managers who have been in their current positions for two or three years and who have received only satisfactory performance reviews. The female subjects represented two different races as did the male subjects. Their ages were balanced as well with the mean age of each group falling between 35 and 40.

Each of these individuals was approached first by the head of human resources and a Chandler researcher to determine if he or she would consent to being observed and audiotaped by a researcher. The nature of the study was not revealed; the subjects were told that nothing in the findings would identify the study's participants. They were assured that the tapes would be confidential, would be heard only by Chandler & Associates, and would be destroyed at the conclusion of the study.

In each instance, participants were given only one day's notice that the researcher would be visiting them the following day. Study of each individual included the researcher's shadowing him/her, recording all in-person conversations with a tape recorder hidden on the researcher. The subjects' conversational partners were told that the researchers were university business students participating in a classroom assignment.

In each case, researchers pulled together at least one hour of dialogue for each subject (a half hour of dialogue with each subject's superiors and a half hour with each subject's subordinates and colleagues). In each case, the first 30 minutes of dialogue were isolated and additional dialogue on the tape was ignored.

EXHIBIT
12.8

**Continued**

Once the appropriate communication dyads were isolated on the tapes, they were analyzed by researchers. Score sheets were used to tally the total number of interruptions as well as the number of successful and unsuccessful attempts.

A chi-square technique recommended by Bruning and Kintz (1977) was used to determine the degree of relationship between interruptive behavior and gender. This technique is often used for determining whether the frequencies observed differ greatly from a logically expected frequency.

### REVIEW OF RELEVANT LITERATURE

As early as 1922, research was being conducted on the notion that the different sexes communicate differently. One such notion that has been noted in organizational and in interpersonal communication research is the use of interruptive behavior. Studies by Kanter (1977) and Allen and Grey (1974) show that males use more interruptive and topic-changing behaviors than do females. Zimmerman and West (1975) found that males tended to dominate non-intimate conversations through the use of simultaneous speech (Thorne, 1973).

Though Rogers and Jones (1973) and Tannen (1990) have questioned whether an interruption can really be called a *contest of wills,* most of the existing literature on the subjects suggests that men use frequent interruptions to assert their dominance over women and to gain control of conversation. *Dominance* is defined here as any communication device or strategy which lessens the communication role of another (Markel, Long, Saine, 1973). Meltzer, Morris, and Hayes (1971) argued that the act of interrupting another can be viewed as attempted dominance. Glass (1993) also treated interruptions as a domineering act.

Lakoff (1975) has suggested that men and women differ in their styles of speech in ways that result from sex stereotypes and reinforcement of these stereotypes. Lakoff asserts that, "sex differences in speech styles are said to contribute to maintaining images of men as assertive, self-confident, and definite, and images of women as vague and lacking in confidence."

*Any statistical tests you may have used should be justified. Explain statistical tests only when you believe your reader will not understand the computations.*

*If necessary, provide a review of literature to show readers what is already known about a topic. This section is usually included in academic reports, but it is not always found in business reports.*

*The author–date method is used here to cite the sources of information. Footnotes and endnotes are also common in both business and formal academic reports. More information on the various ways to cite sources is included in Chapter 13.*

**EXHIBIT 12.8**  **Continued**

and Lawler, 1980), provides legitimacy for accepted modes of communication between superiors and subordinates.

As women continue to enter the ranks of professionals, the question of how male-female stereotypes are reinforced through patterns of interruptive behavior becomes increasingly important, especially in situations where the recipient of the behavior is in a more powerful position, such as a typical superior-subordinate relationship. Will the interruptive behaviors of males continue when the female is in a position of authority? How does this differ from their behavior toward a male superior? Do females relate differently to their fema[...] superiors? Will the resul[...] for those females who a[...] behavioral characteristic[...] attitudes hold true in lig[...] superior-subordinate rela[...] stress, "Since the crucia[...] others to accept any wor[...] consider to be an exclusi[...] factor even more critical[...]

Accepted modes of co[...] are often seen as consen[...] or procedural rules that[...] the flow of messages (Go[...] regulate the taking of tu[...] the dominant communica[...] superior or authority wh[...]

Sacks et al. (1974) se[...] speak that is allocated to[...] this right as being value[...] be considered a violation[...] complete a turn or to rea[...] conversation where the t[...]

However, Tannen (19[...] are not attempts to domi[...] one's culture. She sees s[...] speakers, those for whor[...]

Bradley's (1980) use of the "expected states theory" in postulating how men use various tactics to gain and assert dominance and control in problem-solving situations provides additional support for the idea of control and dominance via interruptive behavior. She argues that work or task groups often focus on the value of a group member's status in the outside or real world—that is, in their societal context or role. The work group then infers that a person's ability to contribute to the group is based directly on his or her external status, even if there is no logical relationship between a task and that person's role. In effect, Bradley compares a person's sex or gender to the concept of "external status" and how a "disvalued" state forces the person to overcompensate to prove that his or her contributions are worthwhile and valid. Bradley's argument is that women have always been considered second class and passive and will always be judged on this societal context.

Rosen and Jerdee's (1973) research demonstrates that "Men and women share common perceptions and expectations regarding what constitutes appropriate behavior for males and females in supervisory positions and their attitudes are often influenced by sex-role stereotypes." Societal acceptance of the docility of women has allowed interruptive behaviors to become fully implanted in conversational interactions. This concept of accepted societal interaction rules carries over into the business and professional world as well. Lillian Glass (1993) reported that a Gallup poll she commissioned showed that 90 percent of the people questioned perceived interruptions to be the most annoying talking habit.

Pilotta (1983) discusses the communication difficulties that women encounter in business which women themselves say are unique to them. If these communication difficulties cause women to lose power in supervisory relationships, let alone in interpersonal relationships, this might explain the belief held by many that women are too weak to be effective managers and leaders.

Aspects of power and dominance permeate interpersonal and business relationships. The distribution of power, primarily hierarchical in nature (Pfeffer, 1983; Bacharach

**EXHIBIT 12.8**    Continued

acceptable. She posits that high-involvement speakers, consisting of both men and women, do not view interruptions as violations of turn-taking behavior or as attempts to dominate.

Men are hierarchical communicators who view a speaker as the dominant person, the one in control (Tannen, 1990). Therefore, they attempt to achieve this power by being speakers themselves rather than listeners. Since women are not hierarchical speakers but are consensus builders, they are more inclined to allow men to interrupt.

### ANALYSIS OF INTERRUPTIVE BEHAVIOR

*This section reports and discusses the findings. In longer studies, the findings might be discussed in several chapters with numerous subheadings.*

For the purposes of this study, interruptions are characterized as "cases of simultaneous talk in which the turn of the speaker with the prior claim on the floor is cut short of its projectable point of completion" (McLaughlin, 1984). They also include interruptions that occur when the interrupter starts to talk while the original speaker is still talking, but the original speaker retains the floor. Interruptions emitted for the purposes of clarification or insult were not considered in this research. Each interruption was determined to be "successful" or "unsuccessful." All attempts to gain control of the topic or to change the topic, whether successful or unsuccessful, were considered.

From the audiotapes for each of the managers studied, coders isolated 30 minutes of dialogue with superiors and 30 minutes of dialogue with subordinates and colleagues. Tallies were made of the total number of interruptions for each individual, and subtotals for successful and unsuccessful interruptions were discerned. These figures are presented and analyzed in the following subsections.

#### Subordinates and Colleagues

To determine if subordinates and colleagues interrupt female middle-level managers at a greater level than male middle-level managers, Table 1 was constructed.

**EXHIBIT 12.8**

Continued

*Introduce visual aids in the text, telling your reader when to look at them. Number each visual aid and use a clear, descriptive title. Explain and label all elements of the visual aid.*

Table 1
Interruptive Behavior of Subordinates and Colleagues

| | Successful Interruptions | Unsuccessful Interruptions | Total |
|---|---|---|---|
| Three middle-level female managers | 25 | 50 | 75 |
| Two middle-level male managers | 7 | 22 | 29 |
| Total | 32 | 72 | 104 |

*Present the information or data, and point out their significance.*

Tabulation of the data results in $x^2 = 7.59$ with one degree of freedom, significant at the .05 level. It is concluded, therefore, that there is a significant relationship between the number of interruptions aimed at female middle-level managers and those aimed at males at the same level. Seventy-two interruptive attempts is significantly greater than the two-thirds of the total that would be expected if the two populations were treated equally.

The number of successful interruptions, however, was not significant. The chi-square figure was not significant at .9153 with one degree of freedom. Therefore, it may be concluded that, although female middle-level managers are interrupted more often than their male counterparts, most of these interruptions are not successful.

### Superiors

Coders analyzed a total of two and one-half hours of dyadic interaction between the five managers studied and their superiors. Once again, they tallied the number of successful and unsuccessful interruptions. These figures are reported in Table 2.

EXHIBIT
12.8

**Continued**

Table 2
Interruptive Behavior of Superiors

|  | Successful Interruptions | Unsuccessful Interruptions | Total |
|---|---|---|---|
| Three middle-level female managers | 72 | 30 | 102 |
| Two middle-level male managers | 31 | 26 | 57 |
| Total | 103 | 56 | 159 |

At 1.12, chi square proved to be insignificant at the .05 level with one degree of freedom. With female managers making up 60 percent of the population studied, 102 interruptions out of a total of 159 results in 64 percent of the interruptive attempts being aimed at that population.

However, 72 of those 102 interruptions were successful, and this number proves significant when compared to the fact that only 31 of 57 interruptions were successful in male managerial interactions. Comparison of these figures results in a correlation of 4.133, significant at the .05 level with one degree of freedom. Therefore, it is concluded that, while female middle-level managers at Chamberlain are not interrupted at a significantly higher rate by their superiors than are male middle-level managers, the women relinquish the floor at a much greater rate than do their male counterparts.

### IMPLICATIONS OF RESULTS

*Reach conclusions that address the issues raised in the purpose statement.*

The implications of these results are not clear by themselves. When combined with the next two components of this study, investigation of the effects of gender-related verbal differences, researchers might be able to determine if such distinctions play a part in explaining why women do not hold a larger number of upper-level management positions.

9

**EXHIBIT 12.8**    Continued

However, it does appear that because they are forced to deal with a higher number of interruptions from their subordinates and colleagues, Chamberlain's middle-level managerial females are successful at asserting their control of dialogue. They do not readily turn over control of conversations with their colleagues and subordinates. Therefore, previous surveys showing that Chamberlain female middle-level managers are considered to be weak communicators are not supported by this study of interruptive behavior.

Still, the three female managers studied did not assert themselves at the same rate as the two male managers when the source of interruptions was a superior. Although women were not interrupted by their superiors at a higher rate than males, they were 17 percent more likely to yield control of converation to these individuals. It is possible that this may be a component in decisions to promote more assertive speakers to upper-level managerial positions.

## BIBLIOGRAPHY

*The bibliography should list only those sources cited in the study unless you are instructed to use a reference manual that allows the inclusion of all sources consulted.*

Allen, D.E. and R. F. Grey (1974). *Conversational analysis: the sociology of talk.* Mouton: The Hague.

Bradley, P. (1980, June). Sex, competence, and opinion deviation: an expectation states approach. *Communication Monographs, 47,*101-110.

Bruning, J. and B. Kintz (1977). *Computational handbook of statistics* (2d ed.). Glenview, Illinois: Scott, Foresman and Co.

Glass, L. (1993). *He says, she says—closing the communication gap between the sexes.* New York: Perigee Books—Putnam.

Glass, L. (1987). *Talk to win—six steps to a successful vocal image.* New York: Perigee Books—Putnam.

Goffman, E. (1955). On face-work: an analysis of ritual elements in social interaction. *Psychiatry, 8,* 213–31.

**Exhibit 12.8**    Continued

Henning, M. and A. Jardim (1977). *The managerial woman.* Garden City, New York: Anchor Press.

Kanter, R. (1977). *Men and women of the corporation.* New York, Basic Books.

Lakoff, R. T. (1975). *Language and woman's place.* New York: Harper & Row.

Markel, N., J. Long, and T. Saine (1973). Sex effects in conversational interaction: another look at male dominance. *Human Communication Research*, 2, 356–64.

Marsh, P. (1988). *Eye to eye—how people interact.* Topsfield, Massachusetts: Salem House Publishers.

McLaughlin, P. (1984). *Conversation: how talk is organized.* Beverly Hills, California: Sage.

Meltzer, L., W. Morris, and D. Hayes (1971). Interruption outcomes and vocal amplitude: explorations in social psychophysics. *Journal of Personality and Social Psychology*, 18, 392-402.

Nie, N. H. et al. (1975) *Statistical Package for the Social Sciences* (2d ed.). New York: McGraw-Hill Book Company.

Pearce, W.B. and F.B. Conklin (1979). A model of hierarchical meanings in coherent conversations and a study of indirect responses. *Communication Monographs*, 46, 75-89.

Pfeffer, J. (1981). *Power in organizations.* Marshfield, Massachussetts: Pitman Publishing Inc.

Pilotta, J. (1981). Trust in power in the organization: an overview. *Women in organizations: barriers and breakthroughs.* Illinois: Wakeland Press, 1-10.

Rogers, W.T. and S.E. Jones (1973). Effects of dominance tendencies on floor holding and interruption behavior in dyadic interaction, 113–21. Facts of publication missing.

**EXHIBIT 12.8**    Continued

Rosen, B. and T.H. Jerdee (1973). The influence of sex-role stereotypes on evaluation of male and female supervisory behavior. *Journal of Applied Psychology,* 57, 44-48.

Sacks, H., E. Schegloff, and G. Jefferson (1974). A simplest systematic for the organization of turn-taking for conversation. *Language,* 50, 696-735.

Tannen, D. (1990). *You just don't understand.* New York: William Morrow.

Zimmerman, D. H. and C. West (1975). Sex roles, interruptions and silences in conversation. *Language and sex: difference and dominance.* Edited by Barrie Thorne and Nancy Henley. Rowley, Massachussetts: Newbury House Publishers, Inc.

12

# DISCUSSION QUESTIONS

🔲 Describe how organizations use formal reports.

1. Give an example of a business decision that might be made based on the information and analysis contained in each of the following types of formal report: business proposal, government proposal, feasibility study, and justification report.

🔲 Describe how organizations use formal reports.

2. Discuss the advantages and disadvantages of collaboratively writing formal reports. How does the collaborative process work in the composition of formal reports?

🔲 Differentiate between formal and informal reports.

3. What is the difference between a formal and an informal report?

🔲 Differentiate between formal and informal reports.

4. What is the difference between an informational and an analytical report?

🔲 Define and limit the problem to be studied, and devise a purpose statement that defines it.

5. What six questions must be answered to determine the true nature and full extent of a problem in need of study?

🔲 Define and limit the problem to be studied, and devise a purpose statement that defines it.

6. Give an original example of a purpose statement written as a question, one written as an infinitive phrase, and one written as a declarative statement.

🔲 Address readers' needs by choosing a direct or indirect arrangement and an appropriate writing style.

7. What is the difference between a report written to follow a direct arrangement and one written to follow an indirect arrangement?

🔲 Address readers' needs by choosing a direct or indirect arrangement and an appropriate writing style.

8. Under what circumstances would you use an indirect report arrangement? A direct report arrangement?

🔲 Address readers' needs by choosing a direct or indirect arrangement and an appropriate writing style.

9. Identify the sentences below that are written in formal writing style. Underline the words in each informal sentence that you would have to change if you were going to make the sentence formal.
   a. "Conclusions resulting from this analysis reveal the need for further study."
   b. "It can't be concluded that further study is necessary."
   c. "My committee recommends further study of the issue because, as you know, the findings were very inconclusive."

d. "It is recommended that Pearson-George purchase the Philadelphia facility."

■ Develop logical, parallel outlines for informational and analytical issues.

10. For each of the following organizational patterns, give an example of an issue that might be logically studied using the pattern: step by step, chronological, geographical or spatial, importance, advantages and disadvantages, and type or category.

■ Develop logical, parallel outlines for informational and analytical issues.

11. For each of the examples you gave in question 10, where in the report would you analyze fully how the various courses of action compare?

■ Prepare a formal proposal.

12. Give an original example of an unsolicited proposal one business might make to another and an original example of a solicited proposal that one organization might request.

■ Assemble all the necessary parts of a formal report.

13. What should be included in a formal analytical report's summary?

■ Use manuscript format correctly.

14. Report format varies somewhat, depending on the style manual used. Either choose a style manual or use the format recommendations made in this chapter to answer the following questions. If you choose a particular style manual, cite your source.
   a. In inches, what are the measurements of all four margins of the first page of a chapter? Subsequent pages of a chapter?
   b. Does each chapter have to begin on a new page?
   c. Select one way of positioning headings and subheadings in formal reports. Then describe how and where each level of heading is typed. From this list, specify which headings should be centered, typed flush left, capitalized, or underlined. How many blank lines should you leave above and below each level of heading?
   d. State the two ways in which left-bound and unbound reports differ.
   e. State the way in which unbound reports and top-bound reports differ.
   f. Which parts of a formal report use Arabic numerals? Which use small Roman numerals?

## APPLICATION EXERCISES

■ Describe how organizations use formal reports.
■ Address readers' needs by choosing a direct or indirect arrangement and an appropriate writing style.
■ Use manuscript format correctly.

1. With permission from the company, get a copy of a typical problem-oriented company report and analyze the following issues: How is the

company likely to have used this report? Is the report arranged in direct or indirect order? Is the writing style formal or informal? How does the format of the report compare to the format specifications given within this chapter? What improvements would you recommend for improving the appearance of the report? Include a copy of the report with your analysis.

◤ Differentiate between formal and informal reports.
◤ Define and limit the problem to be studied, and devise a purpose statement that defines it.

2. Determine whether each of the following purpose statements is analytical or informational. Redo the purpose statements that are poorly written, justifying your changes.
   a. "The purpose of this study is to develop an effective marketing plan for Tasty Toasties cereal."
   b. "This study will determine if sex discrimination exists at the managerial level in American businesses and will analyze sex discrimination in business."
   c. "This study answers the question of whether Ali Industries should mount a hostile takeover of RJB Tabasco."
   d. "This study answers the question of whether there is evidence of productivity improvement and/or improvement in labor–management relations among companies that have achieved parity in the hiring of minority middle-level managers."
   e. "Have the drug abuse programs instituted in 1990 by EAL Mink had a significant impact on absenteeism? A secondary purpose will be to determine whether alcohol abuse coverage is feasible."
   f. "The purpose of this study is to determine the yields of 15 mutual funds for the past five years."
   g. "The purpose of this study is to inform the reader of the health problems related to exposure to computer monitors, give the experts' opinions, and let the reader decide for him- or herself what to do about the problem."

◤ Define and limit the problem to be studied, and devise a purpose statement that defines it.
◤ Develop logical, parallel outlines for informational and analytical issues.

3. Create a purpose statement and an outline for two of the topics suggested in exercise 11.

◤ Define and limit the problem to be studied, and devise a purpose statement that defines it.
◤ Develop logical, parallel outlines for informational and analytical issues.

4. Read each of the purpose statements below. Then determine if the accompanying outline addresses all of the purpose statement's elements. If the topic is analytical, does the outline contain a logical way to argue one course of action over another under the same subheading? Can conclusions be reached within the analysis? Are the headings and subheadings grammatically and structurally parallel?

    *a.*   Analytical purpose: "The purpose of this study is to compare the latest-model Macintosh and IBM computers to select the one that best meets the needs of the Graphic Design Department of Keenan Rogers."

        Outline:  I.  Macintosh (latest model)

                A.  Desktop publishing and graphics software interface

                B.  Compatibilty with service bureaus

                C.  Hardware requirements and cost

           II.  IBM (latest model)

                A.  Desktop publishing and graphics software interface

                B.  Compatibility with service bureaus

                C.  Hardware requirements and cost

    *b.*   Informational purpose: "This study answers the question of how office work stations are analyzed for ergonomic soundness."

        Outline:  I.  Role of Ergonomics in the Office

                A.  Costs

                B.  Benefits of Ergonomic Sensitivity

           II.  Work Station Analysis

                A.  Height of Work Surface

                B.  Video Display Terminals

                    1.  Eyestrain

                    2.  Female Reproductive Concerns

                    3.  Cumulative Trauma Injuries

                C.  Chair Design must be considered

    *c.*   Informational purpose: "The purpose of this study is to determine the effects of the proposed health care reforms on Endeavor Enterprises and its employees."

        Outline:  I.  Employees

                A.  Full-time Nonmanagerial Employees

                    1.  Eligibility

                    2.  Coverage

                    3.  Costs

                B.  Part-time Employees

                    1.  Eligibility

                    2.  Coverage

                    3.  Costs

                C.  Management

                    1.  Eligibility

                    2.  Coverage

                    3.  Costs

           II.  Direct Expenses

◼ Define and limit the problem to be studied, and devise a purpose statement that defines it.

◼ Assemble all the necessary parts of a formal report.

  5.  Write a two- or three-paragraph problem statement for the following situation, giving the background necessary for stockholders (even those unfamiliar with the inner workings of the company) to understand the extent of the problem and why it needs to be studied. Assume any details necessary to make the problem statement more realistic.

Who? Atlan Industries' Southwestern Division—four manufacturing plants

What? The feasibility of consolidating the four electronics assembly plants under one roof in Mexicali, Mexico, in a facility approximately the size of two of the plants, that could turn out (after initial training of Mexican workers) 63 percent of what is produced by the four American plants, at a cost of 20 percent less per electronic component.

When? Division started losing money in 1988 ($2.2 million). Losses in 1989 ($1.3 million), 1990 ($1.6 million), 1991 ($1.9 million), 1992 ($1.7 million), and 1993 ($1.8 million).

Where? Southwestern Division plants in Albuquerque, Dallas, Phoenix, and Tucson.

Why? Recent attempts to sell the division failed; attempt to merge with PacCo failed when they withdrew their tender offer earlier this week.

How? Origins of problem coincided with a two-thirds increase in Japanese electronics imports to U.S. and a 9 percent salary settlement after a three-week strike. Attempts to bring costs under control in 1989 by shutting down the Laredo, Texas, plant resulted in short-term relief only. All other attempts to attract additional funds, increase market share, cut expenses, and so forth have failed.

◼ Define and limit the problem to be studied, and devise a purpose statement that defines it.

6. Critique the following problem statement. Does it contain everything necessary to convince its readers that the problem is worthy of study? Does it give the reader everything he or she needs to know to understand the background? What is missing?

The wine-making industry in California has existed since the 1800s. California wine is considered by many to be equal and, in many cases, superior to much more expensive French wines. Since the introduction of the first known commercial grape vineyard near San Francisco, the California wine industry has survived many economic crises, most notably the period in the 1920s and 1930s when Prohibition ruled.

 The current crisis, however, is likely to change the face of wine making in California forever. Increasing costs associated with water, labor, and taxes as well as a more health-conscious public have caused the forced sale of many wineries. Sixty-two percent of the small- and medium-sized wineries that have gone out of business in the past five years have been purchased by huge foreign conglomerates.

◼ Develop logical, parallel outlines for informational and analytical issues.

7. Develop a logical outline that will allow you to study one of the topics presented in the following purpose statements:
 a. "This study will determine the changes necessary to make the student cafeteria (or bookstore) more profitable and appealing to students."
 b. "The viability of using various energy conservation techniques at (name of business or name of college) will be determined."

    *c.* "The purpose of this study will be to determine the feasibility of increasing productivity with fewer employees at DOTS Inc."

    *d.* "This study will determine the best form of advertising for Cheepos (a new discount electronics store)."

    *e.* "This study will answer the question of what is the most feasible way of ensuring that full-time associate degree students are able to graduate within two years and full-time bachelor's students within four years."

■ Develop logical, parallel outlines for informational and analytical issues.

8. For each of the following organizational patterns, give an example of an issue that might studied using that pattern, and provide a preliminary outline for the issue:

    *a.* Step by step.

    *b.* Chronological.

    *c.* Geographic or spatial.

    *d.* Importance.

    *e.* Advantages and disadvantages.

    *f.* Type or category.

■ Prepare a formal proposal.

9. Prepare an unsolicited proposal that addresses one of the issues listed in exercise *7a*, *7b*, or *7e* above. Include everything that people with the authority to grant your recommendations will need to know. Your professor will let you know whether you will be expected to perform secondary and primary research before preparing this proposal or whether it will be necessary for you to make up reasonable details.

■ Prepare a formal proposal.
■ Assemble all the necessary parts of a formal report.

10. Write a proposal responding to the following request for proposal (RFP), assuming that you are Russell Colburn, president of Earth Reflections, a company specializing in environmental consulting and services. The RFP is from Kaiser Permanente, a large health maintenance organization (HMO) that operates three clinics in your area. Kaiser wants a consulting firm with a background in environmentalism to study their usage of paper, office supplies, aluminum, plastics, and so forth, and recommend ways to save money. Kaiser also wants the same firm to pick up and dispose of the recyclables in bins to be provided as part of the proposal. The RFP asks for a firm that can supply, at competitive prices, office products that are of recycled materials (at least 50 percent post-consumer material).

    Disposal of hazardous material and dangerous medical waste is already handled by another company, so you won't have to consider this in your proposal. The vice president of your organization, Carley VanCott, is a registered nurse who worked for years in large hospitals. Therefore, you believe your firm can do an excellent job of determining how Kaiser can save money and be environmentally sensitive at the same time. If awarded the contract, your firm will provide the following:

    • *Study of needs.* On-site evaluation of needs; search of records to determine purchasing and disposal patterns and costs for past two years;

secondary search of literature concerning corporate and medical environmental programs.

As an added benefit and at Kaiser's direction, Earth Reflections will study the energy and water usage as well as the green waste of the clinics and make recommendations for improvement. (Green waste is the waste generated by gardening.) Cleaning supplies will also be included in this study. This extra study will also include analysis of paint; wall, window, and floor coverings; and furniture.

Timeline—three months, culminating in a multimedia presentation to the board of directors. Cost of needs study—$23,000.

- *Services.* Waste disposal estimates are $96,000 a year for each clinic (approximately 10,000 cubic yards a year), $19,500 less than Kaiser is currently paying for trash pickup and disposal. You figure that, on this part of the operation, your company can make about $48,000 (approximately $40 per ton for paper products and $45 per ton for commingled products) a year over and above trash pickup expenses by selling the trash to recycling brokers. Services would include once-daily pickup of large bins (Kaiser employees would empty the smaller bins) and cleaning of all bins as needed. Earth Reflections also agrees to make additional runs as needed. Disposable printer cartridges will be picked up as needed once daily. Earth Reflections will also provide pickup for commingled products (plastic and glass bottles, cans, clamps, pencils, etc.).

- *Products.* Various types of sorting bins are available: $32 (a waste basket with a side sorter to replace each waste basket—estimated 75 per clinic), $110 (estimated 12 per clinic in appropriate locations), and $1,550 (estimated 3 large dumpsters per clinic to be located in current trash pickup area), depending on requirements identified in the study of needs.

Earth Reflections also offers a full range of recycled paper in all weights and qualities—photocopy paper, computer paper, letterhead stationery, card stock, newsprint, envelopes, invoices, forms, scratch pads, note pads, cash register tapes, report covers, and so forth. Any paper Kaiser needs, even bond stock, your company can provide at competitive prices in a wide variety of color and weights. Other recycled and recyclable products your company can provide at competitive prices include: computer printer cartridges; file folders, file dividers, and plastic tabs; index cards; markers; highlighters; pens; pencils; paper clips; paper clamps; notebooks; recyclable Styrofoam cups and plates; calendars; boxes; scissors; rulers; drawer dividers; desktop letter trays; waste baskets; mobile carts; carpet underlayment; fabric-wrapped panels; sound board; tackboard; coffee pot filters; and industrial packaging.

Write a proposal responding to Kaiser's RFP. Include the information necessary to persuade the Kaiser board to select your company. Before you write the proposal, do the research necessary to show how your product's prices compare to those of your competitors. In addition, include an introduction and a transmittal letter that discuss the kinds of savings of natural resources that can be achieved through individual corporate efforts to conserve.

■ Prepare a formal proposal.
■ Assemble all the necessary parts of a formal report.
■ Use manuscript format correctly.

11. Write an academic proposal for one of the following report topics. In Chapter 13 you will be asked to write the complete report. Your professor will let you know how long your report should be, whether it should be informational or analytical, whether it is to be an individual effort or a collaborative effort, how much research you are expected to do, and when the complete report (and any portions of the report) are due. Many of these suggested topics are very general and will, therefore, have to be narrowed down.

Employer drug testing in transportation jobs.

Analysis of applicants' lying behavior in interviews.

Improvement of listening skills in the office.

Selection of a new location for a new store (branch office, plant).

Selection of insurance for a fleet of company vehicles.

The glass ceiling encountered by female executives.

The progress made by women (and/or other minorities) in business and management since equal employment laws went into effect.

Evaluation of a restaurant (or any business) operation.

Feasibility of starting a student business organization at your college.

Feasibility of starting a student-run bookstore (or day care center) on your campus.

Preventing carpal tunnel syndrome (and/or other job-related) health problems.

Making meetings successful.

Electronic presentation skills.

Feasibility of increasing donations to and funding of a nonprofit organization.

Collaborative writing in business.

The controversy over collaborative writing in business writing classes.

Comparison and selection of software or equipment for a particular corporation.

Economic projections for a country, region of the world, or company.

The patent process for a new product (come up with an idea of your own).

A sales proposal for a new product or service (better form letters, newsletters, annual reports).

A marketing plan for a product or service.

Analysis of corporate annual reports.

Analysis of businesses' collection letters and policies.

Compliance with the Americans with Disabilities Act.

Selection of a mutual fund for Ann D. Vidual.

The negotiating styles of businesspeople from other countries.

The feasibility of a particular company's expanding into another product or service area.

Sampling techniques in business.

Questionnaire construction.

Analysis of presentation and desktop publishing software as a component of report and speech success.

The psychology of color, with implications for business professionals.

Sales potential of a particular product.

The feasibility of a corporate fitness plan for a particular company.

The viability of a particular kind of store or service for a specific area or city.

Corporate energy conservation.

Corporate environmental policies.

The feasibility of several franchises for (an individual—supply a name).

Giving operational instructions.

Economic reform in Russia (or other regions).

The impact of NAFTA (or European Economic Community) on particular industries.

Latest developments in business technology.

Reduction of costs at a particular company.

The effects of the decline in manufacturing jobs in the United States.

Creating jobs in a particular company (or region) through government intervention.

Analysis of advertisements in major magazines related to African-Americans (women, Hispanics, gays and lesbians, Asian-Americans, etc.).

The effects of health care reform (immigration policies, tax changes) on U.S. businesses.

Attitudes toward diversity in management ranks.

The effects of bank (or particular company) mergers on U.S. citizens.

The effects of airline deregulation on U.S. citizens (or on the airlines themselves).

The effects of executive salary inflation on corporation stability.

The effects of professional athletes' inflated salaries on team profitability.

The economic effects of foreign purchase of U.S. banks (movie studios, wineries, etc.).

The viability of common economic indicators as a predictor of a country's economic soundness.

The short- and long-term effects of a country's export and import policies (industrial, taxation, domestic subsidies, tariffs, industry protection, etc.).

International monetary policies and how they affect U.S. businesses.

Conducting communication audits of businesses.

How to start a corporation in a particular city.

The effects of incorporating in Delaware instead of in one's home state.

Analysis of motivational techniques at a particular company.

Selection of a form of business ownership for a particular group of individuals.

The effects of corporate in-house day care on recruitment, retention, and productivity of employees.

The controversy over the effects of electromagnetic fields.

Alternative forms of employee compensation.

The effects of organized lobbying efforts on foreign and domestic businesses as well as on U.S. taxpayers.

Comparison of supermarket prices for a list of commonly used products.

Comparison of corporate salaries for specific jobs.

Employment outlook and salary expectations for graduates with specific degrees.

Effects of a company's reorganization on intrapreneurship.

Alternatives to layoffs.

Federal, state, local, and private financing alternatives for small business (startup and expansion).

The viability of investing in particular companies' stocks.

The role of small companies in the economy.

The effects of worker empowerment.

Analysis of buyers (domestic and global) for a particular product or service.

The trend toward customization of products for individual consumers.

The electronic linking of businesses and consumers.

A long-term analysis of Democratic and Republican business policies on the U.S. economy.

Analysis of the effects of the Federal Reserve's efforts to control the U.S. economy.

The role of U.S. businesses in linking the world electronically.

Improvement of labor–management negotiations.

Labor unions in Mexico.

Volunteer activities of U.S. executives.

Corporate donations.

Ways in which business can work with colleges and public schools to reform and improve education.

Time management (stress management, depression) for executives (and other levels).

The personality of the entrepreneur.

Using Internet to solve business problems.

Common characteristics of Fortune 1000 executives.

Selling to the European Community (Mexico and Canada, Asian Community, or various ethnic groups in the United States).

Use of personality testing for hiring.

The latest information technology battle (or developments).

# RESEARCHING AND DOCUMENTING FORMAL REPORTS

## OBJECTIVES

When you finish studying this chapter, you should be able to:

- Understand the role of research in the report-writing process.
- Identify and use the three main types of sources for secondary research.
- Design and conduct a survey or interview, when appropriate, as a method of primary research.
- Determine when permission is needed to use material from another source.
- Use various styles of reference citations to document sources of information in formal reports.
- Compile bibliographies that include all the information necessary for the reader to find the source.

## WHAT WOULD YOU DO IF...?

**GANG POWER.** Jacarta Ibu manages a group of graphic artists, journalists, and word processing specialists who share a networked system of 45 micro-computers. The operating system in place for the past 11 months has never operated properly, and because of the way it interfaces with the network, some of the most important features of the group's software programs operate only occasionally or do not work at all. Frequent failures of the entire system have caused loss of information, loss of time, and loss of productivity.

Jacarta read an article in a computer magazine citing frequent problems with this operating system. However, Jacarta's supervisor, Forrest Greenberg, believes the problem is the staff's inability to operate the software, not the operating system itself. Mr. Greenberg says that he paid a top consultant $11,000 to research and set up the current system, and the consultant said that the network would compensate for any problems that are "supposedly" present in the operating system. Instead of spending approximately $5,000 for the operating system update the article says will solve the problems,

Mr. Greenberg sarcastically suggested additional training for the department's key employees, including Jacarta.

Jacarta believes the real problem lies in Mr. Greenberg's reluctance to admit to his own boss that he made a mistake. Jacarta is convinced that, no matter how much training his staff receives, the current operating system will continue to cause problems. Therefore, he has decided to research the topic thoroughly on his own and to present a full study of the issue in report form. Copies of this report will be presented to both Mr. Greenberg and the vice president, Mr. Greenberg's immediate superior. Jacarta figures that, although one article didn't convince Mr. Greenberg, an entire collection of them might.

Jacarta went to two bookstores, looking for pertinent books and magazine articles. However, he has been unable to find anything about the problem. He is stymied about what to do next.

What would you recommend to Jacarta? Where should he go to find additional information on the topic? What specific sources would you advise him to search? As you read the following chapter, write down anything that you believe would be useful to Jacarta in his search. Help him amass a large number of comments from experts on the topic that might persuade Mr. Greenberg and the vice president to give Jacarta's staff the tools they need to do their jobs.

## RESEARCH AND THE FORMAL REPORT

Understand the role of research in the report-writing process.
The formal reports so important to decision making in business are not just writing projects; they are also, to a great extent, research projects. When you write a letter, memo, or short report, the information you need is often close at hand—a letter or memo to which you must respond, sales and marketing literature, a calendar or activity log, or recent files. The purpose of a formal report, however, is to provide decision makers with information not readily available. Therefore, to write a report, you must dig deeper to find the facts that will let you draw sound conclusions and make solid recommendations. The value of your report depends on the quality of your investigation. Similarly, the health of the company—and your own reputation—depend on your ability to conduct thorough research as efficiently as possible.

There are two main types of research: primary and secondary. **Secondary research** is the search for information that someone else has gathered—that is, secondhand information. Magazines, journals, and books are secondary sources. A company report that you pulled from the files may also be a secondary source if you use the writer's analysis as backup for your findings. **Primary research,** on the other hand, is your own, firsthand search for information about a specific topic. Your original surveys and interviews with experts are primary research. Primary research also includes your analysis of data from a company report that has been gathered for another purpose. Both secondary and primary sources are useful when you need to research an important problem. Exhibit 13.1 lists the types of sources available for primary research and secondary research.

| EXHIBIT 13.1 | **Primary and Secondary Information Sources** |
|---|---|

**Primary and Secondary Information Sources**

■ **Primary (based on first-hand material not gathered, analyzed, and published by others)**

Surveys
Interviews
Personal observations and expertise
Experimentation
Isolated data contained within company documents

■ **Secondary (based on the writings and published research of others)**

Books
Magazines and journals
Newspapers
Data in company files gathered and interpreted by someone else
Indexes and abstracts
Encyclopedias
Dictionaries
Manuals and handbooks
Almanacs and yearbooks
Pamphlets, bulletins, and brochures
Films and videos
Television and radio programs
Business and corporate directories
Government documents
On-line subscriber services and computer databases

## SOURCES OF SECONDARY RESEARCH

You gather secondary research to determine everything others have learned about the topic you are studying.

Identify and use the three main types of sources for secondary research.

Most people begin a research project with secondary research. Why go to the extra effort of conducting a survey, for example, if someone else has already gathered the data you are looking for? In addition, the report's readers will often be expecting you to provide an overview of what others have already found. For example, formal academic reports typically require a review of the literature, a summary of the major facts about a topic that have already been proved by research or are widely believed to be true. Analytical reports in business also often include a review of the existing literature on a topic, so readers have all the information they need to fully appreciate and understand the report writer's analysis.

When you think about doing secondary research, you are likely to think first of books, journals, and magazines. However, as Exhibit 13.1 shows, these are not the only kinds of secondary sources. Company files are another readily available source of secondary data. You might, for example, gather information from sales reports over the past 15 years to determine if there is a correlation between the sales of certain products and major economic trends. The sales figures are secondary data you can use in your analysis.

When secondary sources are to be an essential part of your report, you should begin your search for such information as soon as you have a definite purpose statement. A research librarian can assist you in finding secondary sources on your topic. Usually, you will use three types of resources to find the information you need: on-line computer services and databases, card catalogs and indexes, and company and industry directories. As you read about them in the following sections, think about which might be useful to Jacarta Ibu as he researches the problem identified in the vignette at the beginning of the chapter.

## ON-LINE SERVICES AND COMPUTERIZED DATABASES

Electronic databases provide easy access to hundreds of sources on any topic. Depending on which electronic database you are using, it is possible to get copies of entire articles, abstracts of articles, or lists of books and articles pertinent to your topic.

As computers have become more popular, more and more resources have been catalogued electronically. Today many libraries have fully computerized indexes of their own collections. In addition, electronic databases and on-line services allow computer users to search the files of other computers around the world.

The simplest electronic system is a library database containing information about each item in the collection (A **database** is a storehouse of organized facts.) In addition to providing the same information about books and periodicals (magazines, journals, and newspapers) that was once recorded on cards, library databases now tell you whether the publication is on the shelf. If it is not, the database will specify when the publication is due to be returned. These "electronic card catalogs" can also tell you where a reference is located, even if it is in another library somewhere else on campus; some of them will allow you to place a temporary hold on a book, giving you time to find it and check it out.

Searching electronically through a library's collection is simple. At the terminal, you are usually asked to indicate whether you want to search by subject, author (or organization), title, call number, or key word (taken from a title, author, or subject). To determine appropriate subject headings for your topic, you can consult a copy of the *Library of Congress Subject Headings*, which would normally be located near the computer terminals.

Most libraries now store hundreds of thousands of text pages on a single electronic disc the size of a record. These discs are known as CD-ROMs.

Many libraries also possess **CD-ROM** (compact disc—read only memory) devices. A CD-ROM can store masses of data, as many as 200,000 text pages on a single disc. *CD-ROMs in Print* is a catalog that lists the CD-ROMs available.

Libraries, schools, companies, and individuals may also link up, via telephone line and computer, with electronic databases compiled by others. In the last few years, at least 2,000 electronic databases have become available, covering almost every subject. These databases can provide you with a list of books, magazines, newspaper articles, and other resources on your research topic. Because these services are **on-line,** you can "talk" directly to the computer and receive an immediate response. You tell the computer what terms it should look for, and then it conducts the search for you. For example, you might tell the computer that you want a list of all the works a particular author has published in the past five years. If you choose to do so, you may then print the list. Some databases also show on-screen abstracts or complete copies of articles, dissertations, theses, and the like. Some full-text articles are free, although often you will be charged to get a copy (you can simply key in your credit card number). Fees for entire articles vary; however, to give you an idea of the cost, one major database provides a copy of a journal article for $10.

Internet is an electronic service that provides access to many library and government collections.

One major electronic resource is **Internet,** a network of computer networks that serves as a clearinghouse for databases around the world. When you link up with Internet, you get access to the databases of some of the largest university libraries in the United States, the Library of Congress, and many government agencies. You also get access to electronic mail services, weather information around the world, games, and electronic bulletin boards and user forums. With these capabilities, you can not only search the databases for the names of books and periodicals on a particular topic, but also participate in an electronic dialogue with others interested in the topic and move copies of relevant files from a distant computer to your own.

Many commercial database collections are now available as well. Some you might find useful are The Dow Jones News Retrieval Service, ABI/Inform, Predicasts Terminal Systems, Knowledge Index, and Accountants' Index. DIALOG Information Services is a huge inventory of more than 1.75 million records, including bibliographic indexes, abstracts, and entire articles. Bibliographic Retrieval Systems is similar to DIALOG, but is smaller. LEXIS/NEXIS and ERIC (Education Resources Information Center) give you access to many other databases. Government publications can be accessed through databases such as MARCIVE or CARL UnCover. Many of the materials in these databases are also available in printed form, but almost daily it seems that another printed database goes electronic.

Using an on-line service usually requires you to first open an account and get a password. You can get access through Internet, information services such as CompuServe, Prodigy, and America On-Line, and, while you are a student, through your school's library. Some libraries charge for the service; many do not. You may have to sit down with a librarian to narrow the scope of your research and then do your own search, or a librarian may do the search for you. However you obtain access, you will find a wealth of information available electronically.

## CARD CATALOGS AND INDEXES

The advantages of electronic information searches are many; however, in many libraries you will still have to search manually through card catalogs and indexes. Even some libraries possessing computer databases have kept their card catalogs for those who prefer not to use computers.

Card catalogs contain information about books. Searching a card catalog requires you to specify a subject, title, or author. If you are having a hard time finding sources on a topic, read the descriptors at the bottom of the cards—they will often give you clues as to other subject headings you may search for more information. In addition, look through a copy of *Library of Congress Subject Headings* for more ideas.

You might also find relevant book titles by checking *Books in Print*, an index showing all the books currently in print, by author, title, and subject. The *Cumulative Book Index* and *Paperbound Books in Print* may be helpful as well.

Printed indexes to periodicals are numerous (many of them may also be viewed electronically). Searching by author or subject, you can find articles or papers that have been published on your topic. Some of the indexes also provide abstracts, or short summaries, of articles and dissertations.

The indexes listed below might be of use to you as you search for information on business-oriented topics. They can help you research specific products, companies, regions, countries, and industries. If you have not used these indexes before, you will be glad to know that directions for their use are usually included at the beginning of each volume.

*Accounting and Tax Index.*

*American Statistics Index: A Comprehensive Guide and Index to the Statistical Publications of the United States Government.*

*Applied Science and Technology Index.*

*Business Education Index.*

*Business Periodicals Index.*

*Communication Abstracts.*

*Dissertation Abstracts International.*

*Economic Abstracts.*

*The Education Index.*

*Employment Relations Abstracts.*

*Funk & Scott Index of Corporations and Industries.*

*Funk & Scott Index International.*

*Funk & Scott Index Europe.*

*Insurance Related Abstracts.*

*Human Resources Abstracts.*

*Journal of Economic Literature.*

*Los Angeles Times Index.*

*Market Research Abstracts.*

*Monthly Catalog of United States Government Publications.*

*New York Times Index.*

*Personnel Management Abstracts.*

*Psychological Abstracts.*

*Public Affairs Information Service Bulletin.*

*Sage Public Administration Abstracts.*

*Social Sciences Index.*

*Sociological Abstracts.*

*Statistical Theory and Method Abstracts.*

*Wall Street Journal Index.*

*Wall Street Transcript.*

*Work Related Abstracts.*

## Business and Industry Directories

Businesspeople frequently refer directly to specialized printed and electronic directories for facts about particular companies and industries. Some of the most used sources of data about companies and industries include the following:

*American Statistics Index* (electronic version: *Statistical Masterfile*).

Dun and Bradstreet publications (*Million Dollar Directory, Middle Market Directory, Principal International Businesses*).

*European Marketing Data and Statistics.*

*Forbes* (January issue).

Guide to Doing Business in [Name of Country] (a Price Waterhouse publication).

Moody's Manuals (*Bank and Financial Manual, Industrial Manual, Municipal and Government Manual, OTC Industrial Manual, Public Utilities Manual, Transportation Manual*).

Standard & Poor's reports (*New York Stock Exchange, American Stock Exchange, OTC*).

Standard and Poor's industry surveys.

*Standard and Poor's Trade and Securities: Statistics.*

Predicasts *F & S Index.*

*Value Line Investment Survey.*

*U.S. Industrial Outlook* (a U.S. Department of Commerce publication).

*Almanac of Business and Industrial Ratios* (by Leo Troy).

*Annual Statement Studies* (by Robert Morris Associates).

*Key Business Ratios* (a Dun and Bradstreet publication).

*Encyclopedia of Business Information Sources.*

*Business Information Sources* (by Lorna Danielle).

## METHODS OF PRIMARY RESEARCH

Primary research consists of conclusions you reached on your own based on data you accumulated through research you designed and conducted.

Primary research is gathering data yourself. Surveys, interviews, observations, experiments, and your own expertise are sources of primary data. Gathering information from company files is also primary research when you assemble and analyze the data.

### SURVEYS, INTERVIEWS, AND PERSONAL OBSERVATION

Design and conduct a survey or interview, when appropriate, as a method of primary research.

A lot of useful information may be obtained by either asking questions or observing people act or interact. For example, Jacarta Ibu, in the chapter-opening vignette, may have been able to support his analysis of the operating system's weaknesses by sending other businesses a questionnaire asking about the operating systems they use, or by interviewing a few selected individuals who manage groups like his. To counter his boss's claim that Jacarta's staff is misusing the operating system, Jacarta could carefully observe them at work and document their actions when problems arise.

The three techniques Jacarta could use—surveys, interviews, and observations—are closely related. **Surveys** require the researcher to ask a number of people a standard list of questions to find out about their experiences or opinions. If the population being studied is quite large, a sample will be selected (preferably randomly, so the results can be generalized) to complete the questionnaire. The responses are then analyzed statistically to produce generalizations about the surveyed population. **Interviews** also rely on questioning, but the focus is a single individual and the questions may be more open-ended and unique for each person interviewed. **Observations** involve a coder, who counts specific instances of the behavior or activity under observation. In a study of lying behavior, for example, coders might note the number of times people telling lies touch their cheeks, necks, or ears; avoid eye contact; fidget; and so on. They would also observe the body language of a similar number of people who are telling the truth to determine if liars, and only liars, typically exhibit lying behavior.

We may use these methods of investigation casually in our daily life. However, using them scientifically to generate reliable, valid data is harder than you might think. You don't just jot down a few questions or sit down with someone and carry on a conversation. The consistency of the questions is what makes generalizations possible. Therefore, even interviews and observations begin with a plan.

Observations are less common in business research than are surveys and interviews. Therefore, this chapter focuses on surveys and interviews. Neither is always the better choice, however; each has advantages and disadvantages (see Exhibit 13.2). Most of the disadvantages inherent in surveys are the result of poor respondent selection and poor questionnaire design. Most of the disadvantages of interviews relate to the fact that they are expensive, time consuming, and often less generalizable than surveys. The following sections will help you choose the right method for a given situation and overcome its disadvantages.

**DESIGNING SURVEY AND INTERVIEW QUESTIONS.**   To prepare good questions for either an interview or a questionnaire, you must be thoroughly familiar with your topic. In-depth review of the literature is the only way to determine which questions about your topic remain unanswered or the major points of disagreement in the field. You can then frame specific questions that seek to either answer the unanswered questions or clarify the points of disagreement.

Surveys and interviews normally seek answers to two types of questions—those that gather demographic information and those that gather information pertaining to the research questions. Demographic questions help to define the people who are answering the questions; they elicit such information as age, general income level, position, number of years in current position, and so on. Research questions provide the data to be analyzed.

Demographic questions are often asked at the beginning because, if correctly worded, they are easy to answer. Once the respondents have started filling out the survey, they are more likely to finish answering the research questions as well. You can also encourage complete responses by making sure you ask only those demographic questions needed for your study. Say, for example, that a salsa manufacturer is conducting an in-store marketing survey of consumers' taste preferences. If the company wants to analyze those preferences on the basis of age and ethnic background, it would not ask questions about marital status, income, or number of children.

Research questions—those designed to get the information necessary for analysis—also require careful preparation. Here are some guidelines:

- Position easy-to-answer questions at or near the beginning of the survey.
- Carefully word questions so they don't influence respondents to provide the answers they believe are desirable. The following examples are so-called leading questions, because they lead respondents to answer in a certain way:

  "Do you usually purchase the best-quality electronic products?"

  "Do you always drink moderately?"

Wouldn't you be inclined to answer "yes" to both these questions? Most people would not want to admit that they buy the lesser-quality products

---

*Interviews allow you to clarify confusing or difficult questions; however, it is difficult to interview a sample large enough to make generalizations from the data.*

*Surveys should be composed only after you have researched everything that has already been written about a topic.*

*Surveys consist of questions about the respondents themselves (demographic questions) and the topic being studied (research questions).*

**EXHIBIT 13.2**

## Advantages and Disadvantages of Surveys and Interviews

| ■ Method of Gathering Data | ■ Advantages | ■ Disadvantages |
|---|---|---|
| Survey | •Allows many individuals to be contacted at the same time.<br>•When sent through the mail, is less expensive to administer than an interview.<br>•Allows subjects to respond at their own convenience.<br>•Permits participation by people in remote or distant areas.<br>•Ensures that each respondent receives the same questions.<br>•Gives respondents anonymity, freeing them to answer honestly, without embarrassment.<br>•If properly constructed, allows easy tabulation of responses.<br>•Eliminates need to select and train interviewers.<br>•Avoids interviewer biases.<br>•Because there is a written record of questions, it can be administered later to test long-range implications. | •May not be returned in adequate numbers.<br>•May require follow-up letters and telephone calls to increase response rate.<br>•Does not provide information about causes of poor response rate.<br>•Does not provide feedback on what really motivated respondents to complete and return survey.<br>•Does not permit participation of those who cannot read or write.<br>•May prevent respondents from saying what they really feel.<br>•Does not provide a way to determine whether respondents interpreted questions and statements as intended.<br>•May be completed by someone besides the intended respondent.<br>•Depends on the availability of enough names, addresses, or telephone numbers to construct a suitable sample.<br>•Is not generalizable if those who respond are not representative of the population.<br>•Allows some respondents to avoid completing entire survey. |
| Interview | •Allows respondents to take as much time as they need to express themselves completely.<br>•Allows respondents to seek clarification of questions, if necessary.<br>•Permits observations of respondents' nonverbal behavior.<br>•Allows participation of those who cannot read or write.<br>•More easily elicits personal information, attitudes, beliefs, feeling, and perceptions.<br>•Achieves high rate of participation.<br>•Allows follow-up questioning and probing for leads. | •Is time consuming and difficult to schedule.<br>•May be prohibitively expensive because of interviewer salary and training.<br>•Can only be conducted in limited numbers when time is an issue.<br>•May yield questionable results, because people are often reluctant to tell the truth directly to another individual, especially when it causes embarrassment or puts the interviewee in a bad light.<br>•Produces biased responses if interviewer gives inappropriate introduction, shows approval or disapproval of answers, or makes carelessly worded statements when asked for clarification.<br>•May be coded incorrectly when interviewer has to make subjective judgments about responses.<br>•Does not allow use of large samples, thereby increasing chance that results are not truly representative or generalizable. |

or they drink too much. These revisions would elicit more honest responses:

"Do you own a VCR? If so, what brand do you own?"

"How often do you drink more than two alcoholic beverages at a sitting?"

Here's another example of a leading question:

"Which of the following sources do you use to research major purchases—consumer magazines, word of mouth, telephone calls or letters to manufacturers, interviews with sales staff?"

The way this question is worded, respondents may believe that they should do research before buying anything. They may choose an untruthful answer just to avoid the embarrassment of confessing that they don't do any research before purchasing. These questions would elicit a more honest answer:

"If you were going to do research before making a major purchase, which of these sources would you be most likely to consult?" (List of responses).

"Which have you consulted within the past year?"

- Each question should address only one topic. The question "Are you satisfied with the number of flights and the service on those flights?" is too complicated. Are people who answer "no" saying they are dissatisfied with both the number of flights and the service, or are they only responding to one part of the question? Two distinct questions is a better alternative:

  "Are you satisfied with the number of flights?"

  "Are you satisfied with the service on flights?"

- Avoid ambiguous words:

  "Do you believe in a closed campus?" (Will your respondents know what a closed campus is?)

  "What type of transportation do you prefer?" (What does *type* mean? Will your respondents answer "train," "car," "bus," or "plane," or perhaps "quiet," "luxurious," "sporty," "inexpensive"?)

  "Do you often eat out?" (How often is *often*? A better question is "How many times a week do you eat out?")

- Address sensitive areas (e.g., age, income, religion, race, gender, values, personal habits, personal likes, dislikes, and sexually related activities) discreetly.

  Indiscreet: "As a school dropout, what are your plans for the immediate future?"

  Discreet: "Within the next two to three months, which of the following are you planning to do? Enroll in a general education diploma (GED) program, enroll in the home school program, enroll in a private trade or technical program, work, other (please specify)?"

  Indiscreet: "Do you bathe daily?"

  Discreet: "In the past seven days, how many baths or showers have you taken?"

Discreet: "How often do you think people should bathe? Twice daily, daily, two to three times weekly, weekly, other (please specify)?"

- Avoid words that provoke biased or emotional responses as well as those that carry undesirable connotations. Words such as *wrong, right, happiness, terrorist, democracy, socialism, capitalism,* and so on cause people to react emotionally instead of objectively.

    Loaded words: "Is it wrong to market sugared cereals during children's television programs?"

    Objective words: "In your opinion, which of the following products are acceptable for advertising during children's television programs: sugared cereals, low-sugar cereals, war toys, dolls, trucks . . . ?"

- Arrange the questions in logical order, with each set of items addressing a single topic. For example, don't ask for level of income after asking respondents if they have ever lost a close friend or relative through violence.

- Produce a questionnaire that looks and is easy to answer. At least 50 percent of the page should be white space. The questions should require short answers and, if possible, should be answerable with check marks or other easy-to-use devices. Respondents should not have to search their memories or do computations to answer the questions. Include an addressed, stamped envelope for easy return.

**CONDUCTING THE SURVEY OR INTERVIEW.** A key to a useful survey or interview is to carefully select respondents. Are you surveying or interviewing enough people to get an accurate picture? Are they truly representative of the whole population under study? Will you be able to generalize what you learn about the respondents to the rest of the population you are studying? Were your respondents randomly chosen? If not, can you defend your choices against criticism that they were chosen intentionally to gain specific results? For example, if you are researching the effects of motivational techniques on productivity by studying the 25 employees of a small manufacturing company, you might run into criticism if you try to make generalizations about the effectiveness of motivational techniques for all businesses.

> **Choose your subjects carefully, so they are representative of the larger population you are studying.**

Another key is preparation, particularly for an interview. Make sure you are thoroughly familiar with the topic you are discussing. Can you imagine a bank loan officer's dismay if a student interviewer asked, "Could you please tell me everything you know about lending money to small businesses?" Just where would the loan officer begin? Any busy businessperson would be frustrated by such a question, and any researcher should be embarrassed to admit to such ignorance.

> **Give the survey in a pilot test before administering it to the larger group of subjects.**

Before conducting your survey or interview, test your questions first on a few people who are representative of the other respondents. Afterward, discuss the questions with each person so you can eliminate or rephrase any that are unclear, offensive, or unanswerable.

If your survey is to be conducted by mail, include a good cover letter and a stamped, addressed return envelope. The letter should explain the importance of the study, motivate the reader to respond promptly, and provide a reasonable deadline for action. Use good you attitude to let the reader know what he or she will get out of responding to your survey. It might be nothing more than the satisfaction of participating in something of importance (e.g., being included in a study that might bring about changes to a state's business policies). One questionnaire that received an usually large response had two pennies taped to the cover letter. Using a persuasive sales pattern, the letter began with the statement "Give us your two cents' worth!" Two cents does not even begin to pay a respondent for his or her time, but the humor and uniqueness of the approach probably motivated many people to complete the survey.

If questionnaires are to be administered face-to-face by more than one person, train all questioners to ensure that their methods are the same. In addition, make sure everyone understands that people who conduct surveys can have a great deal of influence on the responses unless they answer respondents' questions in a noncommittal fashion.

In instances where observers are tallying results, train coders thoroughly to ensure that their evaluations are consistent. A pilot test is one way of testing coders' consistency. However, statistical tests can also be used to adjust numerically for the differences among coders that cannot be controlled. Another way to increase reliability is to tape or video record the activities being observed, with the permission of participants. Then you can see how each coder is doing and recognize where additional training may be needed.

## EXPERIMENTS

In business, people are seldom the subjects of experiments; however, experimentation is common in product research and development.

**Experiments,** which measure the change that occurs when something is manipulated, are used more often in science than in business. For example, scientists may test the effects of a new drug on a disease. The main application of business experiments is for product development. Makeup, skin care products, products containing dyes and perfumes, food, safety products, and so on may be tested on people or by computer simulation. Tests such as these are carried out under strict guidelines, particularly for products that need government approval before they can be marketed.

Experiments are far less common on the behavioral side of business. One big reason is the ethical implications of interfering in people's lives without their knowledge. Because people often behave differently when they know they are part of an experiment, most experiments are designed to hide the true purpose. In addition, people are complex, and it is very difficult to control their lives enough to guarantee that only the manipulation under study is responsible for the results. For example, employees at one factory were given 5 percent less pay than employees at the company's other factory. Researchers were testing the hypothesis that productivity would not decrease with a pay cut if, at the same time, medical benefits were increased and each employee was given the choice of working a 40-hour week over either four days or the usual five days. Instead, researchers found that productivity dropped drastically because employees resented the pay cuts. Any research involving people must be carefully planned and conducted to avoid negative reactions that have nothing to do with the manipulation being studied.

## DOCUMENTATION OF REFERENCES

You must acknowledge the originators of any words, visuals, and ideas you borrow.

After you have done the research for a formal report, you will presumably have good data from other sources that you can use to back up your analysis. The originators of these data must be given credit—to acknowledge their contribution to your work and to give your report greater credibility. Documenting your sources shows your readers which ideas, words, and graphics were created or devised by someone else.

## COPYRIGHT AND FAIR USE

Determine when permission is needed to use material from another source. Acknowledging the contribution of others is not just a matter of ethics; it is a matter of law. Copyright laws protect the intellectual property of writers and artists, giving only them the right to profit or benefit from their work. Most countries have established copyright laws, so, to avoid being sued, your company should investigate the laws of all countries in which you do business.

Intellectual property is much more than just the printed material in books and periodicals. Copyright laws in most countries cover the following:

Books and articles.

Graphical and artistic works.

Audiovisual materials.

Computer programs and data files.

Tables.

Mailing lists.

Movie and television scripts and interviews.

Speeches.

Letters, memos, and reports.

Voice mail.

Electronic messages.

Song lyrics and poetry.

In short, anything written or expressed by someone else is intellectual property. Copyright laws do not generally cover the following:

Symbols and designs that have become familiar to most people.

Names of people.

Titles of books songs, people, and so on.

Short phrases and slogans.

Ideas, discoveries, concepts, and devices (aside from their written descriptions or illustrations).

When you use copyrighted material, you are expected to get written permission from the author and/or the publisher. These are the situations requiring written permission:

- When you quote 250 or more words from a published source.

- When you quote a poem, song, play, television program, film, or other creative work.

- When you reproduce tables, graphs, charts, and so on from commercially produced material.

- When you distribute multiple copies of published material for noneducational purposes.

- When your use of material might deprive the work's author and/or its publisher of the opportunity to sell or distribute the work from which the material was taken.

You may be expected to pay a fee for using copyrighted material, especially if you are going to use it in a publication you will sell for profit. For instance, all of the material in this textbook that was taken from other works required permission. The fees for using some of the artwork ranged from $100 to $150.

Under some circumstances, it is all right for you to use the work of other people without their written permission. Copyright laws include **fair use** provisions, which generally allow you to use limited amounts of a work for research, criticism or comment, or teaching purposes. For example, in academic research papers you may quote from other sources without getting permission as long as you properly credit each work and don't use too much of any one source. You don't have to get written permission to quote from books published before 1907 or from news articles more than three months old. The material published by U.S. government agencies may also be used without written permission.

Even when you are not required to obtain written permission, you must give credit to the source. If you don't, you are guilty of **plagiarism,** a serious offense in most academic institutions and a source of public embarrassment and loss of credibility in the business world.

## REFERENCE CITATIONS

Use various styles of reference citations to document sources of information in formal reports.

A **reference citation** is the vehicle by which you give credit to secondary sources. Whenever you quote or paraphrase someone else in your report, you must provide a reference citation. **Paraphrasing** is rewording a quote or expressing someone else's words and ideas in your own words. Quotations, on the other hand, are the other person's exact words. Quotations either have quotation marks around them or, when they are 35 words or more, are typed as **extracts**—set off from the surrounding text, with an extra half-inch margin on both sides.

Use the exact words of others (direct quotations) only when they are so memorable that there is no better way to express the thought.

In most cases, you should paraphrase. However, sometimes an author says something so uniquely or so forcefully that you cannot do it justice in a paraphrase. It is hard to imagine anyone improving on this famous statement attributed to Abraham Lincoln: "Whatever men do, they do in response to motives. Discover the motives that cause them to act and you can make them do your bidding." Paraphrased, that same statement might read something like this: "People are motivated to act. To get them to act as you want, you must first discover what motivates them."

Both sentences mean the same thing, but Lincoln's words are definitely more memorable. In addition, using the exact words of such an esteemed figure might add considerable weight to your argument, even when the wisdom of the statement is obvious. Quotations from authoritative sources are useful backup when you take a controversial position or lack expertise. Quotations are also the most accurate way of expressing someone else's opinion.

The rules for citing other sources vary from one style manual to the next. (Refer to Chapter 12 for a list of the style manuals used most often for writing business reports.) However, most recommend one of four basic styles of reference citation: superscript system, author–date system, author–page system, or key-number system. If the company for which you work prefers a specific system, you will of course use that system for your formal reports. If it does not seem to have a preference, however, select the system that suits you best. All are easy to understand and use.

Whichever system you select, be consistent. The style and placement of the citations must be uniform, so that readers can easily find the information they need.

**SUPERSCRIPT SYSTEM.** **Superscripts** are symbols or numbers placed slightly above the line of type. Superscripts signal the reader to look elsewhere for complete details about the source of the statement. Superscripts usually appear immediately following quotations and at the ends of paraphrased sentences or paragraphs. However, to avoid confusion, superscripts may be placed right after the reference statement.

Some writers use the superscript system with **footnotes,** complete reference citations corresponding to the superscripts that are typed at the bottom of the page. The advantage of using footnotes is that a reader can see at a glance the complete details about a statement's source. Most major word processing programs are able to number and position footnotes automatically. However, you must still be familiar with the correct order for presenting the information in a footnote.

A similar system uses endnotes instead of footnotes. As the name implies, the **endnotes** corresponding to the superscripts are typed at the end of each chapter or the report. Endnotes are easier to type than footnotes, but they are not as handy for the reader. A reader who wonders where a particular note or paraphrase comes from would have to thumb through the report to find the endnotes.

Exhibit 13.3 shows how superscripts and footnotes are typed, following the rules recommended in the style manual published by the University of Chicago. Endnotes look like footnotes, except they are not typed at the bottom of the page.

Notice that the fourth footnote in Exhibit 13.3 has the words *op. cit.,* meaning "the work cited." This Latin abbreviation is used when references to the same source follow each other closely but are not consecutive. Reading the example, the reader would know that it refers to the previous work by the same author. Other Latin abbreviations that may be used in the superscript system are *ibid.* and *loc. cit. Ibid.* means "in the same place" and is used for the second reference when two consecutive references to the same source appear together on a page. *Loc. cit.* is an abbreviation meaning "for the place cited." *Loc. cit.,* like *op. cit.,* is used when another entry comes between references to the same source, except that *loc. cit.* is used to indicate that the citation is on the same page as the related citation.

**AUTHOR–DATE SYSTEM.** The **author–date system** puts basic information about a source—the author's last name and the date of publication—into the text with the quote or paraphrase:

*Footnotes at page bottoms make it easy for the reader to see complete details about a quoted or paraphrased source and are easy to use with modern word processing programs.*

*Op. cit. means "the work cited."*
*Ibid. means "in the same place."*
*Loc. cit. means "for the place."*

EXHIBIT
13.3

**Superscripts and Footnotes**

### ■ Superscripted Quotation

"In push strategy, the producer uses advertising, personal selling, sales promotion, and all other promotional tools to convince wholesalers and retailers to stock and sell merchandise. If it works, consumers will then walk into the store, see the product, and buy it. The idea is to push the product down the distribution system to the stores."[1]

### ■ Superscripted Paraphrase for the Same Passage

A push marketing strategy focuses promotion and advertising on convincing wholesalers and retailers to stock a product, knowing that it will then be seen and purchased by consumers.[1]

### ■ Superscripted Paragraph with Paraphrases and Quotations

Araujo has written that managers should bring a positive bias to the supervisory relationship. He defines a positive bias as "the source of eternal optimism that employees will aspire to excellence if it is expected of them."[2] On the other hand, Dunne argues that, regardless of expectations, penalties for not meeting expectations must be stressed. Penalties, not positive bias, are the source of motivation.[3] Araujo concurs that penalties, when not obvious, should be made known from the outset; however, they should be de-emphasized. When penalties are stressed, they become demotivators, as Araujo found in his study of 152 New Jersey factory workers.[4]

### ■ Matching Footnotes at Bottom of Page:

[1]William G. Nickels, James M. McHugh, and Susan M. McHugh, *Understanding Business,* 2d ed. (Homewood, IL: Irwin, 1990), p. 290.
[2]Ismael Araujo, "Positive and Negative Bias in Supervisory Relationship," *Personnel Journal* 44 (February 1993): 122.
[3]Freida Dunne, "Debunking Positive Bias Theory," *Human Relations* 28 (May 1994): 32.
[4]Araujo, op. cit., 122–23.
Note: "Op. cit." could also be "loc. cit." when the two related footnotes appear on the same page.)

Araujo (1993) has written that managers should bring a positive bias to the supervisory relationship. He defines a positive bias as "the source of eternal optimism that employees will aspire to excellence if it is expected of them" (p. 123). Others have argued that penalties, not positive bias, are the source of motivation (Dunne, 1994, p. 33). Araujo concurs that penalties, when not obvious, should be made known from the outset; however, they should be de-emphasized. When penalties are stressed, they become demotivators, as Araujo found in his study of 152 New Jersey factory workers.

The full reference appears at the end of the chapter or report in a bibliography. As you can see, the author–date system often incorporates the name of the author into the text, with the year of publication (and the page number for quoted material) in parentheses immediately following the name. When the name of the author is not used in the sentence itself, the parentheses should contain the author's last name, the year, and the page number of the direct quotation.

Within a single set of parentheses, you may cite more than one work. You simply list the two citations in alphabetical order and separate them with a semicolon:

. . . a much-studied phenomenon (Daley, 1991; Krasowitz, 1989).

When you refer to more than one work by the same author within the same parentheses, this is the way it should appear:

Past research (Ramos 1989, 1991) . . .

When a source was written by three to five people, the citation should contain all their names the first time it appears. After that, you may use only the surname of the first author and *et al.* For example:

First citation: Williams, Yaki, Washington, and Huntley (1991) found . . .

Subsequent citation: The study by Williams et al. (1991) revealed . . .

Sources written by six or more authors should always use only the first author's name and *et al.,* even for the first citation.

Some works are not published under an individual author's name; instead, the "author" is the group or organization that publishes or distributed the work. If you were citing a booklet put out by the Bureau of Land Management, you would need to give your reader enough information to find the complete reference in the bibliography at the end of your report. Your citations would look like this:

First citation: In early 1993, the Bureau of Land Management (BLM) stated that no evidence of the Hanta virus has been found among the tribes in Northern Arizona (U.S. Department of the Interior, 1994, p. 11).

Subsequent citation: A follow-up study of Hanta victims conducted by the BLM revealed that 92 percent of them had visited or lived on the Navajo and Hopi reservations at the time they were stricken (U.S. Department of the Interior, 1994).

When a publication has no author at all, you must provide enough information so the reader can find the complete details in the bibliography. For example, a newspaper or magazine article with no named author but titled "What's So Hot about the Outsiders?" would be alphabetized in the bibliography under "W." The text citation for that article would look like this:

Chief Executive Officers who are hired from the outside tend to know best " . . . how to size up a situation quickly, create the right vision, and then swiftly and effectively implement it" ("What's So Hot," 1994, pp. 113–14).

There is no need to type the full title of the article, because the partial title is enough to enable the reader to find the source in the bibliography.

The author–date system has a major advantage that makes many writers prefer it. Because the author and the date of the reference appear in the text itself, the reader does not have to look away to find the most important information about the source. In addition, changes are easier because there are no superscripts to renumber when sections of text are deleted or added. The most-used style manual advocating the use of the author–date system is published by the American Psychological Association. As a result, the author–date system of citation is frequently referred to as *APA style.*

**AUTHOR–PAGE SYSTEM.**    Another major type of citation is the **author–page system.** It is much like the author–date system, except that no date is included within the parentheses. The author–page system is promoted by the Modern

APA-style documentation places the author and the date within the sentence where a quotation or a paraphrase is used.

The MLA style of documentation is much like APA style; however, it includes the author and the page, not the year, within the sentence containing a quote or paraphrase.

Language Association (usually referred to as the MLA). The citations for this form of reference appear within parentheses, usually at the end of the sentence:

> The study of depression among top executives shows that medicine must be given right away; there is almost no evidence of psychotherapy alone being successful in eliminating severe depression (Gardner 144).

The parenthetical citation would not be placed at the end of the sentence, however, if you were presenting opposing views within the same sentence:

> Although Fortunici argues that American high-tech jobs will increase with the passage of "NAFTA, the greatest opportunity for American business in the last 100 years" (26), not everyone agrees with her.

A citation for a work with two or three authors is handled the same way as a work with one author (e.g., Crittenden and Poole 147). However, when a work has more than three authors, you may either list all the names or use the first name followed by *et al.* When referring to a government document or a work with corporate author, you should try to work the name of the author into the text:

> A 1991 report by the New Mexico Department of Transportation predicts a gradual increase in shipping traffic (6).

> "The executive branch was absolved of charges that it was involved in a cover-up of unequaled proportions" (CIA 13).

This is the style recommended for an indirect source (one source quoted or cited by another source):

> John Ramirez, executive director of the Small Business Administration, maintains that even small manufacturers should spend at least 11 percent of net profit on research and development (qtd. in Boyd 54).

As you may have noticed, the parenthetical citations in the author–page system are placed before the punctuation at the end of the sentence. The citation would appear after the sentence- or paragraph-ending punctuation only after a long, set-off quotation. The indentation of the extract on both sides makes it easy for readers to see where the quotation starts and stops, so they are not confused by parentheses appearing outside the end-of-sentence punctuation.

In the CBE style documentation, a number is assigned to the source cited within the paraphrased or quoted sentence. For more information about the source, readers must refer to the bibliography at the end of the report.

**KEY-NUMBER SYSTEM.**   In the key-number system, which is described in the style manual published by the Council of Biology Editors (CBE), each source is numbered in the order in which it is first presented in the report. The number assigned to a source is then used throughout the text for subsequent references. If readers want to know about the source of a statement, they can turn to the bibliography and find the source by number.

In the following examples of key-numbered citations, notice the placement of the citation. The numbers are usually in parentheses within the sentence or placed at the end of the sentence (if that is the only logical place).

> Two standard references (1, 2) use this term . . .

> These forms of bankruptcy have been extensively researched (3).

> According to one report (3, p. 242), "research into some forms of bankruptcy is almost nonexistent."

> Allyn (1) did not discuss reorganization.

A reader would know that the first citation refers to the sources in the bibliography numbered 1 and 2. Because these two sources are cited first in the paper, they appear first in the bibliography. The last name of the author is not used to determine the order of bibliographical entries. Page numbers are included in the parentheses only for quotations (see the third example).

## BIBLIOGRAPHIES

Compile bibliographies that include all the information necessary for the reader to find the source.

A **bibliography** is a complete list of sources that appears at the end of the report, before the appendix. Some people refer to bibliographies as "works cited" or "references." There are three main forms of bibliographies:

- An alphabetical listing (by author's last name) or numerical listing (in order of citation within the text) of sources cited.

- An alphabetical listing of all sources cited and consulted.

- An alphabetical listing of all sources cited and consulted, as well as those recommended for further reading.

The last two forms, which contain more sources than those referred to in the report, are seldom used in business reports; however, they are sometimes seen in academic reports. The first type of bibliography is the one used most often in business. However, you might find that a bibliography is unnecessary when you have already listed all the entries in endnotes or footnotes. The longer and more formal a report is, however, the more you will be expected to have a separate bibliography.

Listing only the sources actually cited in a report is recommended for three of the citation systems discussed in this chapter: the author–date system, author–page system, and key-number system. The type of information contained within each entry is essentially the same for all three, but there are slight differences in the way the information is arranged and presented. Sample bibliography entries for all three styles are illustrated in Exhibit 13.4.

## VISUAL AID SOURCE NOTES

The sources of all the visual aids you borrow from another work to use in your reports must also be cited. (See Chapter 10 for information about constructing and using visual aids.) In reports that use footnotes or endnotes, the source notes for visual aids are usually complete bibliographic references, usually placed just below the graphic. The source of the visual aid is then listed in the bibliography at the end of the report, mixed in with the other sources cited in the text itself.

If you are using the author–date system, the key-number system, or the author–page number system for documenting your sources, you may also use that form of citation for visual aids. With the author–date system, for instance, you would type "Source:" followed by the author's last name and the publication date right under the visual aid.

Either way is acceptable in most business environments. However, academic settings often require a particular style. If you are compiling reports for college, be sure to ask your teachers which method they expect.

**Exhibit**

**13.4**

**Sample Bibliography Entries**

| ■ Type of Source | ■ APA Style | ■ Chicago Style | ■ MLA Style | ■ CBE Style |
|---|---|---|---|---|
| Book with one author | Able, J. R. (1994). *Objective human resource management.* Philadelphia: Atheneum. | Able, J. R. *Objective Human Resource Management.* Philadelphia: Atheneum, 1994. | Able, J. R. *Objective Human Resource Management.* Philadelphia: Atheneum, 1994. | 1. Able, J. R. (1994). Objective human resource management. Philadelphia: Atheneum. |
| Book with two authors | Adam, M. G., & Taburi, J. J. (1993). *A complete and utter transformation* (2d. ed.). New York: Columbia University Press. | Adam, Mary G., and Jason J. Taburi. *A Complete and Utter Transformation,* 2d ed. New York: Columbia University Press, 1993. | Adam, Mary G., and Jason J. Taburi. *A Complete and Utter Transformation,* 2d. ed. New York: Columbia University Press, 1993. | 2. Fischer, M. G.; Taburi, J. J. A complete and utter transformation, 2d. ed. New York: Columbia University Press; 1993. |
| Book with editor | Conner, A. (Ed.). (1992). *Production principles.* Cincinnati: Gresham Vanity Press. | Conner, Abigail, ed. *Production Principles.* Cincinnati: Gresham Vanity Press, 1992. | Conner, Abigail, ed. *Production Principles.* Cincinnati: Gresham Vanity Press, 1992. | 3. Conner, A., editor, Production principles. Cincinnati: Gresham Vanity Press; 1992. |
| Journal article | Dinnoti, J. (1993). A study of the production factors present in post-generative firms. *Personnel Management, 30,* 155–72. | Dinnoti, Jason. "A Study of the Production Factors Present in Post-Generative Firms." *Personnel Management* 30 (1993): 155–72. | Dinnoti, Jason. "A Study of the Production Factors Present in Post-Generative Firms." *Personnel Management,* 30 (1993), 155–72. | 4. Dinnoti, J. A study of the production factors present in post-generative firms. Personnel Management 30: 155–72; 1993. |
| No author | *The essential element.* (1994). Augusta, GA: The Society of Manufacturing Engineers. | *The Essential Element.* Augusta, GA: The Society of Manufacturing Engineers, 1994. | *The Essential Element.* Augusta, GA: The Society of Manufacturing Engineers, 1994. | 5. The essential element. Augusta, GA: The society of manufacturing engineers; 1994. |
| Interview | Gregorio, S. (March 15, 1993). Interview. Director of Manufacturing, International Business Machines. | Gregorio, Susan. Personal interview. 15 March 1993. | Gregorio, Susan. Personal interview. 15 March 1993. | 6. Gregorio, S. Director of Manufacturing, International Business Machines; March 15, 1993. |
| Season or month necessary for identification | Harding, S., & Nwezeh, W. (1994, February 7). Electronic training and development techniques. | Harding, S., and W. Nwezeh. "Electronic Training and Development Techniques." *Telecommunications* | Harding, S., and W. Nwezeh. "Electronic Training and Development Techniques." *Telecommunications* | 7. Harding, S.; Nwezeh, W. Electronic training and development techniques. Telecommunications Finance; February |

**EXHIBIT 13.4**

**Continued**

| ■ Type of Source | ■ APA Style | ■ Chicago Style | ■ MLA Style | ■ CBE Style |
|---|---|---|---|---|
| | *Telecommunications Finance, 8,* 31–34. | *Finance* 8 (February 7, 1994): 31–34. | *Finance,* 8 (February 7, 1994), 31–34. | 7, 1994: 31–34. |
| Group or corporation as author | Rand Corporation. (1994). *Government investment in people: Training and development of human resources.* Malibu, CA. | Rand Corporation. *Government Investment in People: Training and Development of Human Resources.* Malibu, CA: author, 1994. | Rand Corporation. *Government Investment in People: Training and Development of Human Resources.* Malibu, CA: author, 1994. | 8. Rand Corporation. Government investment in people: training and development of human resources. Malibu, CA; 1994. |
| Newspaper article, no author, discontinuous pages | Study finds German training methods have a place in U.S. firms. (1993, December 15). *The Wall Street Journal,* pp. 1, 25. | "Study Finds German Training Methods Have a Place in U.S. Firms." *The Wall Street Journal,* Western ed., 15 Dec. 1993, Sec. 1, pp. 1, 25, col. 1, 4. | "Study Finds German Training Methods Have a Place in U.S. Firms." *The Wall Street Journal,* Western ed., 15 Dec. 1993, Sec. 1, pp. 1, 25, col. 1, 4. | 9. Study finds German training methods have a place in U.S. firms. (1993, December 15). The Wall Street Journal, pp. 1, 25. |
| Government publication | U.S. Department of Education. Task Force on Manufacturing Performance. (1990, February). *A longitudinal study of training in the manufacturing industry,* Washington, DC: U.S. Government Printing Office. | U.S. Department of Education. Task Force on Manufacturing Performance. *A Longitudinal Study of Training in the Manufacturing Industry,* (Washington, DC: U.S. Government Printing Office, February 1990). | U.S. Department of Education. Task Force on Manufacturing Performance. *A Longitudinal Study of Training in the Manufacturing Industry,* (Washington, DC: U.S. Government Printing Office, February 1990). | 10. U.S. Department of Education. Task Force on Manufacturing Performance. A longitudinal study of training in the manufacturing industry. Washington, DC: Government Printing Office; February 1990. |
| Source found through electronic database | Zimbarro, W. (1987). *How valid are small business training methods?* Los Angeles: University of Southern California, Center for Business Organization and Development. (ERIC Document Reproduction Service No. ED 122 497). | Zimbarro, Wallace. *How Valid Are Small Business Training Methods?* Los Angeles, CA: University of Southern California, Center for Business Organization and Development. ERIC Document Reproduction Service, ED 122 497, 1987. | Zimbarro, Wallace. *How Valid Are Small Business Training Methods?* Los Angeles, CA: University of Southern California, Center for Business Organization and Development. ERIC ED 122 497. | 11. Zimbarro, W. (1987). How valid are small business training methods? Los Angeles: University of Southern California, Center for Business Organization and Development. (ERIC Document Reproduction Service No. ED 122 497). |
| **Formatting and content principles** | •Entries appear in alphabetical order according to last name of author(s). | •Entries appear in alphabetical order according to last name of author(s). | •Entries appear in alphabetical order according to last name of author(s). | •Entries appear in order of their citation in text. |

**EXHIBIT**

**13.4**

**Continued**

| ▪ Type of Source | ▪ APA Style | ▪ Chicago Style | ▪ MLA Style | ▪ CBE Style |
|---|---|---|---|---|
| **Formatting and Content Principals (cont'd)** | When no author exists, entry is alphabetized under first important word of title (articles such as *the*, *a*, and *an* are not used in alphabetizing entries).<br><br>•Each entry begins on new line, and first line begins at left margin. Subsequent lines of each entry are indented ¼ inch from left margin.<br>•Authors' names are separated by commas (more than two authors) or by & (only two authors) and are followed by periods. All authors' names must be included. | When no author exists, entry is alphabetized under first important word of title (articles such as *the*, *a*, and *an* are not used in alphabetizing entries).<br><br>•Each entry begins on new line, and first line begins at left margin. Subsequent lines of each entry are intended ½ inch from left margin.<br>•All authors' names are inverted (last name first). Names of two authors are separated by *and*. When there are three authors, all but the last two names should be separated by commas. When there are more than three authors, use only the name of the first author, followed by a comma and *et. al.* (meaning "and others"). | When no author exists, entry is alphabetized under first important word of title (articles such as *the*, *a*, and *an* are not used in alphabetizing entries).<br><br>•Each entry begins on new line, and first line begins at left margin. Subsequent lines of each entry are indented ½ inch from left margin.<br>•First author's name is inverted (last name first); all other authors' names are written first name first, last name last. Names of two authors are separated by *and*. When there are three authors, all but the last two names should be separated by commas. When there are more than three authors, use only the name of the first author, followed by a comma and *et. al.* (meaning "and others"). | •Each entry begins on new line and is numbered. Subsequent lines of each entry begin directly under first word of first line.<br><br>•Authors' names are separated by semicolons and are followed by periods. |
| | •Authors' first and middle names are represented by initials.<br>•Only in journal and newspaper titles (*not* article titles) are any but first word of title capitalized; for books and article titles, all words after first are lower case (except following a colon). | •Authors' middle names are represented by initials.<br>•All important words in titles (excluding articles, prepositions, and conjunctions, unless they are first or last word) begin with capital letters. | •Authors' middle names are represented by initials.<br>•All important words in titles (excluding articles, prepositions, and conjunctions, unless they are first or last word) begin with capital letters. | •Authors' first and middle names are represented by initials.<br>•Only in journal titles are any but first word of a title capitalized; for books and article titles, all words after first are lower case. |

| EXHIBIT 13.4 | Continued | | | |
|---|---|---|---|---|
| **■ Type of Source** | **■ APA Style** | **■ Chicago Style** | **■ MLA Style** | **■ CBE Style** |
| **Formatting and Content Principles (cont'd)** | | •Titles of articles are enclosed in quotation marks. | •Titles of articles are enclosed in quotation marks. | •No punctuation follows journal's title and volume number. Page numbers and volume numbers are separated by colons. |
| | •Bibliography may be single- or double-spaced to match text or report unless supervisor has specified otherwise. | •Names of months are spelled out. •Bibliography is single-spaced and has same margins as rest of report. | •Names of months are abbreviated. •Bibliography is single-spaced and has same margins as rest of report. | •Bibliography may be single- or double-spaced. |

## EXPLANATORY NOTES

Explanatory notes are the asides that provide additional information beyond what readers need to understand the text of your report. Typically, a supplemental note is signaled with an asterisk at the end of a sentence. A reader who sees the asterisk can then look immediately to the bottom of the page for further information. Here's an example of an explanatory note:

> *Departmental climate surveys were first introduced at Westingburg in January 1988, at which time it was determined that the development of the survey instruments themselves must begin with a coalition of management and labor. A result of the first surveys was the formation of climate teams of three to five employee representatives and an equal number of managers, including at least two outside managers.

This note includes a little of the history of climate surveys at a particular company. Readers who are familiar with the history don't need to read the note. Moreover, those who are not familiar with the history can understand the rest of the text without reading the note.

Explanatory notes should never take the place of information needed to understand a topic. As their name implies, they are intended to explain and supplement text, not to replace it.

## DISCUSSION QUESTIONS

◤ Understand the role of research in the report-writing process.
◤ Identify and use the three main types of sources for secondary research.
◤ Design and conduct a survey or interview, when appropriate, as a method of primary research.

1. For each of the following topics, specify the type of research you would do to investigate the topic. Describe the information you would seek from each source.

    *a.* A study of the market potential of a new dish detergent.

    *b.* A study of the improvements necessary to increase the profitability and effectiveness of your campus bookstore.

    *c.* Comparison of the effectiveness of annual reports.

    *d.* Study of how to fund a new business venture.

    *e.* Study of the effects of in-house child care centers on productivity.

■ Determine when permission is needed to use material from another source.

  2. How could you legally avoid getting permission to use material from another source in a formal report?

■ Use various styles of reference citations to document sources of information in formal reports.

  3. Name the primary differences between the author–date system of citing reference sources and the author–page system.

■ Use various styles of reference citations to document sources of information in formal reports.

  4. What is wrong with the following citations, assuming you are using the specified citation system?

    *a.* Paraphrased author–date system: "In the course of events, Imagine Productions . . . used its influence to cause the bankruptcy of its smaller competitors." (Reiner, 1993, p. 2-b)

    *b.* Quoted author–page system: The private screening of *Vivian's Planet* was set for two weeks before Thanksgiving, but it was "shelved by its producers," says film historian George Shelstein (172) "to deliberately deprive its lead of the profits she would derive from the early release."

    *c.* Superscript system: Modern technology may not be able to improve the productivity of all areas of the service industry, but many can benefit from it, according to Wards (p. 33).[1] "However," says Sphinx (p. 1)[2] "the fixed productivity of a single laser-enfused, computer-controlled musical performance is a good example of the quality improvement that results in increased profitability."

■ Compile bibliographies that include all the information necessary for the reader to find the source.

  5. What are the main pieces of information included in each bibliography entry, regardless of the bibliographic form a report uses?

## APPLICATION EXERCISES

■ Understand the role of research in the report-writing process.
■ Identify and use the three main types of sources for secondary research.
■ Design and conduct a survey or interview, when appropriate, as a method of primary research.

  1. Write a business plan for a business you would like to start (or for the expansion of a firm that is currently operating). Do the research necessary to provide all the information a financial backer would need to know to

make a decision about financing the proposal. Check with your professor to find out the parts of your business plan that must be based on research and how much may be estimated or fabricated.

■ Understand the role of research in the report-writing process.
■ Use various styles of reference citations to document sources of information in formal reports.
■ Compile bibliographies that include all the information necessary for the reader to find the source.

2. Refer to exercise 11 in Chapter 12, for which you were to write an academic proposal. Now it is time to write a formal report on the topic you chose. Before you begin, determine the following:
   a. Is the report to be informational or analytical?
   b. Is the report to be directly or indirectly arranged?
   c. Is it to be an individual effort, or is a collaborative effort of several students permissible?
   d. Is your report to be a justification report or an objective analysis of all sides of an issue?
   e. What format and binding expectations does your professor have?
   f. What type of documentation is expected?
   g. How much library research will you be expected to do?
   h. What are your professor's expectations concerning secondary and primary research?
   i. What are the due dates of the complete report and any of its portions?
   j. How many copies of the report must be turned in?
   k. Are you expected to keep your notes and rough drafts?
   l. What report parts will your instructor expect?
   m. Does your instructor prefer formal or informal writing style in formal reports?
   n. Will you have to turn in a progress report? If so, when?

■ Identify and use the three main types of sources for secondary research.

3. To what on-line databases does your college library subscribe? Your local library or company library? What are the steps one must go through to get on-line and to find specific research sources? What forms of output are available to the user (paper copies of entire articles; paper abstracts of articles, studies, and books; on-screen-only views of abstracts, on-screen-only views of bibliographical information, and so on). Write a short memorandum report to your instructor answering these questions.

■ Identify and use the three main types of sources for secondary research.

4. What is the easiest way for you to get access to the Internet collection of databases? (Your college or local library or your company's information services department should have this information.) What do you have to do to use Internet? Will there be a charge? Write a short memorandum report to your professor answering these questions.

■ Identify and use the three main types of sources for secondary research.

5. Prepare a list of periodicals that apply to your major field of study.

◼ Identify and use the three main types of sources for secondary research.

6. Do an on-line database search for information on two different business topics. In a memo report to your instructor, prepare a detailed list, showing step by step what you did to preform the search. Submit copies of the computer printouts.

◼ Identify and use the three main types of sources for secondary research.
◼ Design and conduct a survey or interview, when appropriate, as a method of primary research.

7. Research the use of closed, open, direct, indirect, ranking, checked response, and fill-in-the-blank questions in surveys and questionnaires. Devise a questionnaire using good examples of these types of questions. Devise another questionnaire using poor examples of these types of questions. (The questions should apply to your major field of study.)

◼ Identify and use the three main types of sources for secondary research.
◼ Design and conduct a survey or interview, when appropriate, as a method of primary research.

8. Research the following sampling techniques: random cluster samples, strategic random samples, systematic random samples, and simple random samples. Give examples of how these samples are selected, how they are used, and the types of business problems for which they would be used.

◼ Identify and use the three main types of sources for secondary research.
◼ Compile bibliographies that include all the information necessary for the reader to find the source.

9. For one of the topics in application exercise 11 in Chapter 12 (besides the one you chose for your formal report project), prepare a bibliography of research sources.

◼ Design and conduct a survey or interview, when appropriate, as a method of primary research.

10. Using a survey prepared by another researcher (master's theses, doctoral dissertations, and consumer mail surveys are good sources), analyze the questionnaire. What improvements do you recommend? Do the questions address thoroughly and clearly the purpose for which they were intended? Present your analysis and your recommendations in a letter report to your professor. Include a copy of the questionnaire.

◼ Determine when permission is needed to use material from another source.
◼ Use various styles of reference citations to document sources of information in formal reports.
◼ Compile bibliographies that include all the information necessary for the reader to find the source.

11. Research the subject of fair use of copyrighted materials from the perspective of a businessperson writing formal reports. Write a short informational report in memo format explaining to the reader, your boss, how report writers in your department can make sure they do not run afoul of the copyright laws. Use a consistent style to document your sources, and construct a complete bibliography of your sources.

- Determine when permission is needed to use material from another source.
- Use various styles of reference citations to document sources of information in formal reports.
- Compile bibliographies that include all the information necessary for the reader to find the source.

12. Research the subject of fair use of copyrighted materials from an academic perspective. Pay particular attention to the issue of copying materials for use in class. Write a short informational report in letter format for your instructor. Use a consistent style to document your sources, and construct a complete bibliography of your sources.

PART FOUR

# ORAL PRESENTATIONS

# CHAPTER 14

# PLANNING BUSINESS PRESENTATIONS

## OBJECTIVES

When you finish studying this chapter, you should be able to:

- Identify instances in which knowing oral presentation skills is useful to businesspeople.
- Compare the steps for planning oral messages to those for planning written messages, and use these steps in preparing effective oral presentations.
- Identify the general and specific purposes of formal presentations.
- Select an appropriate organizational strategy for a presentation after analyzing your topic and purpose and predicting the audience's probable reaction to the message.
- List the seven ways to introduce oral presentations, and choose the appropriate one for any given presentation.
- Develop major and supporting points within the body of an oral presentation.
- Develop appropriate conclusions for a presentation.
- Prepare for the question-and-answer period after an oral presentation.
- Prepare notes that will help you deliver an oral presentation.

### WHAT WOULD YOU DO IF...?

**BETTER LATE THAN NEVER?** Robert DeSantangelo is the head of human relations for a major aeronautics firm. Over the past couple of months, several supervisors have asked him for advice about how to handle tardy employees. For example, one of the receptionists has a habit of being 15 to 30 minutes late at least three days each week. This means the other receptionists have to do her job as well as their own. As a result, callers and visitors often do not receive the kind of courteous treatment the company expects its receptionists to provide.

The tardy employees have given all kinds of reasons for being late: child care problems, car breakdowns, and personal troubles. To a certain extent, Robert is sympathetic and wants to accommodate employees' needs. However, when employees are tardy, their co-workers usually have to make up for their absence, which affects morale throughout the company. In addition, the company's productivity and reputation often suffer because of the absence of key workers.

The supervisors who have consulted with Robert on this issue have tried a number of tactics. Some have tried giving the tardy employees' favorite assignments to more reliable workers. Some have tried teasing tardy employees about being late, hoping they will get the point. Some have lost their tempers and threatened disciplinary action, even termination. However, these approaches have produced, at best, only temporary improvement among some of the habitually tardy employees. What the supervisors really need to do is to discover the individual reasons for each employee's tardiness, make sure each employee understands the effect of tardiness, and help each employee work out a plan for resolving the problem.

Because tardiness has become so widespread, Robert has decided to conduct a brief seminar for supervisors about getting employees to be more reliable. At first he thought he might just write a memo on the topic. However, a presentation will allow him not only to share his expertise but also to answer the supervisors' questions about applying the principles to specific cases. The give and take should be instructive for everyone.

As you read the following chapter, think about the kind of presentation Robert should prepare. What should he tell the supervisors, and how can he present the information so they will understand, accept, and act on it?

## RECOGNIZING BUSINESS PRESENTATION OPPORTUNITIES

■ Identify instances in which knowing oral presentation skills is useful to businesspeople.

**Oral communication skills are becoming more important in the business world.**

The opportunities to orally present your point of view or those of the company for which you work are numerous. As occupations become more people oriented and less paper and number oriented, the need for people with good oral communication skills is increasing. Most of the communication you do on the job is oral, and most of it is informal. Explaining company procedures and policies to a client or customer, giving instructions to a new employee, offering your opinion in a department meeting, and asking for a pay raise are only a few of the cases in which oral communication skills are useful.

Occasionally, however, you will be asked to make a more formal oral presentation. As you become more knowledgeable in your job, you may be expected to make presentations about work-related issues to co-workers (as Robert De Santangelo did in the chapter-opening vignette), company executives, or stockholders. In addition, businesspeople are often asked to speak to community, educational, and professional organizations. Knowing the value of good public relations, many companies encourage their employees to participate in such opportunities. Whether you are justifying the purchase of a new computer system, presenting a plan to introduce a new product or service, leading public tours through the company's facilities, publicly announcing a recently negotiated contract, or explaining your job to students at a local school, you will find that mastering the skills discussed in this chapter will help further your goals and your company's goals.

Speaking informally comes naturally to most of us, so we seldom spend much time thinking about active steps we should take to improve our effectiveness. However, when asked to give a speech, we usually spend time planning and preparing for it. These same steps help ensure effective communication whether you are working to improve your informal or formal presentation skills. The more time you spend planning and organizing what you are going to say and how you are going to say it, the better your oral messages will be received by listeners. This and the following chapter concentrate on the preparation and presentation of formal business presentations. However, the information will be useful to you in improving the quality of your informal day-to-day oral communication activities as well.

**Anyone can learn how to make an effective presentation.**

As you study these two chapters, remember that making presentations is a learned art; people are not born effective public speakers. Good oral communicators learn by observing others who speak well and by evaluating and improving their own performance each time they make a presentation.

## PLANNING A PRESENTATION

Compare the steps for planning oral messages to those for planning written messages, and use these steps in preparing effective oral presentations.

Planning presentations is much like planning written messages: You must establish your purpose, choose a medium and a channel, consider legal and ethical issues, analyze your audience, and gather the necessary resources.

### ESTABLISH YOUR PURPOSE(S)

Identify the general and specific purposes of formal presentations.

Your purpose depends to a considerable degree on your topic. Most of your business presentations will be about a predetermined topic—either a need you've identified or a subject someone else wants you to address because of your expertise. On rare occasions, such as a conference or awards banquet, you will have to come up with your own idea for a topic. In those cases, ask yourself the following:

What are you qualified to talk about?

Do you clearly have something to say?

How much research must you do?

How does your topic meet the audience's needs?

In-depth assessment of these considerations will help you select a topic that interests and involves the audience.

**Presentations are generally made to inform or to persuade.**

Presentations, like written messages, have general purposes and specific purposes. The general purposes are mainly to inform and to persuade. For example:

- *To inform.* Reports on competitors; reports on manufacturing, vendor, or other problems; periodic sales reports; progress reports regarding ongoing operations; reports to community groups about jobs or company operations; or employee training sessions.

- *To persuade.* Meetings of boards of directors or management to change policies or procedures; reports to change company goals; public statements to clarify company positions on sensitive issues; reports persuading people to interpret facts in a way other than previously done; or reports to consider alternative solutions.

Of course, the purpose of many presentations is a combination of information and persuasion.

Once you have determined a general purpose, you must establish a specific purpose. The following examples illustrate how the general and specific purposes work together:

| ■ **General Purpose** | ■ **Specific Purpose** |
|---|---|
| To inform employees of benefits | To discuss with new employees the various benefits packages available so they can select the benefits that best meet their needs |
| To persuade upper-level management of the benefits of computers | To persuade upper-level management to purchase Macintosh computers for the research and development department |

*The specific purpose of a presentation depends on your purpose and the audience's needs.*

To determine your specific purpose, consider these questions: What do you want your audience to know that they did not know before? How do you want them to feel? What do you want them to believe? What, if anything, do you want them to do?

The way you define your purpose has a noticeable effect on your presentation's content and organization. Imagine that you are to give a speech about the depletion of South American rain forests and its damaging effect on the ozone layer. Here are some examples of how different purposes might be achieved:

Alternative 1—General purpose: To inform.

Specific purpose: To promote general understanding of the problem relating to the depletion of rain forests and the ill effects of such action on the ozone layer.

Approach: If this was your only purpose, you would present the scientific information necessary for the audience to understand that companies are cutting down South American rain forests at a rate that is increasing the size of the hole in the ozone layer. Because the ozone layer protects us from the harmful effects of the sun, projected increases in skin cancer deaths would be part of your presentation.

Alternative 2—General purpose: To persuade.

Specific purpose: To incite the audience to boycott companies that are directly or indirectly involved in depleting the rain forests.

Approach: With persuasion as your sole purpose, you are attempting to persuade your audience to take personal action to stop this depletion. You might be speaking to an audience that does not even believe there is any danger or has not really thought about it. Such an audience's attitude might be: "So what if there's a hole in the ozone layer? Why should I care? I have more important things to worry about!" Your job as a speaker would be to convince the audience that something must be done to prevent further damage to the ozone layer through use of the you attitude. You would have to show them how they will benefit personally if the destruction of the South American rain forests is stopped.

Can you see that the persuasive purpose requires an especially involving approach? Not only must you provide needed information, but you also must entice the audience to accept and act on it.

## CHOOSE A MEDIUM AND CHANNEL

The main advantage of presentations over written messages is the opportunity to get immediate feedback from the recipients.

Robert De Santangelo, the subject of the chapter-opening vignette, chose to give a presentation rather than write a memo for one main reason: Oral communication allows an immediate response from the recipient of the message. The speaker can thus more easily tailor the message to the recipient's needs and interests. In addition, a presentation allows you to present the same message to a number of people simultaneously. By their facial expressions, posture, and gestures, you can judge what parts of your message they are having trouble understanding or accepting and make adjustments as you continue.

Most business presentations are carefully prepared, conversational, delivered to a relatively small group, accompanied by visual aids, and followed by a question-and-answer session.

Oral communication may take many forms. At one extreme is a face-to-face, free-ranging conversation between two individuals; at the other is a highly scripted, glossy motivational speech to an audience of hundreds or thousands. Most business presentations fall somewhere in between: a carefully prepared but conversational speech to a group of 5 to 50, augmented with some simple but effective visual aids and accompanied by an opportunity for the audience to ask questions.

The conversational approach uses one of four presentation styles:

The most common of the four presentation styles is extemporaneous speaking, which is a conversational talk delivered from carefully prepared notes.

Eye contact with the audience helps you build rapport.

- *Extemporaneous.* This is the conversational, natural style preferred in most situations. You carefully prepare notes but do not memorize the entire speech. You do rehearse, however, so you will be thoroughly familiar with the points you wish to make and the order of your presentation. If you lose your place during the presentation or cannot remember the next point, you simply refer to your notes. The chief advantage of this style is that it lets you make eye contact with the audience and, thus, helps you build rapport. (It is assumed in this and the next chapter that this is the style you will be using.)

Although impromptu speaking requires you to think on your feet, with practice you can learn to get your point across intelligently.

- *Impromptu.* This is the "off-the-cuff" style, in which you present your views without advance preparation. The impromptu style is most common in meetings, where you may suddenly be called on to give your opinion of someone else's idea or to provide information needed for making a decision. The prospect of having to give an impromptu "speech" may be daunting, but remember that you are likely to be speaking about a topic you know well. If you are unsure of your facts, you have a legitimate reason to postpone giving the details until later. In addition, impromptu presentations are seldom more than a few minutes long. Believe it or not, you may even apply the planning principles discussed in this chapter to impromptu presentations. With practice, you can learn to use the few seconds it takes to repeat the question or describe the context in order to mentally list a few main points you want to make.

Memorizing or reading a speech may alienate the audience, although either presentation style has its uses.

- *Memorized.* Instead of working from notes, you write out the presentation in full and then memorize each word—perhaps even the gestures. Unless you are a trained actor, this is an extremely difficult way to get your ideas across. For one thing, written language is more stilted and complex than spoken language and thus is more difficult for listeners to comprehend. For another, memorization robs you of the flexibility to explain a point in more detail when you receive signals from the audience that they don't understand what you're saying. Finally, if you lose your place, you are likely to have trouble recovering. Have you ever seen someone struggling for the next words in a memorized speech? The audience squirms while it watches the panic-stricken speaker. However, memorization does have its uses. For example, key phrases of an extemporaneous presentation may be memorized.

- *Read.* Reading an entire presentation is recommended only for carefully prepared statements of policy. This style is used primarily by representatives of companies or governments who must make a formal statement to the press on behalf of their organizations. The carefully worded script ensures that no mistakes or misrepresentations are made. However, most people read in a monotone that can quickly lull an audience to sleep. In addition, the constant need to look at the script prevents the presenter from making eye contact with the audience. Rapport with the audience is further diminished by the lack of gestures (the speaker must use his or her hands to hold and turn the pages of the script).

**Exceeding the allotted time limit is usually considered amateurish or rude.**

The length of your presentation is another important consideration. If you are invited to make a presentation, ask how long it should be. Many a speaker has failed by giving a 20-minute presentation to an audience expecting a 10-minute speech. Besides the length, find out where in the schedule your presentation falls and if there will be a question-and-answer period after it.

## CONSIDER LEGAL AND ETHICAL ISSUES

**Because it is impossible to edit a presentation that has already been delivered, you should try to anticipate and forestall legal and ethical issues beforehand.**

Legal and ethical considerations are as necessary for oral communication activities as they are for written communication activities. In some ways, however, the danger of violating laws is greater. When you write, you can evaluate and edit before sending the message. If you are in doubt about the legalities or the ethics of your message, you can seek advice from company attorneys and other knowledgeable co-workers. When speaking, however, there is seldom a chance to edit what you have already said. Therefore, as you plan a presentation, you must try to anticipate possible problems and think in advance about ways to avoid them.

Imagine that one of your company's ships has leaked 500 gallons of oil into an already polluted harbor. Eighteen months earlier, another of your company's ships had a similar leak and was ordered to install special controls. Now a company spokesperson, when asked by reporters at a press conference to explain why the company did not install the special controls, carelessly answers: "We all know the harbor has been polluted for a long, long time. What real impact would it really have if one small company spent over $2 million for pollution controls when all the other companies around here are conducting business as usual? Would that clean up the bay?" The public would interpret such an answer as: "We didn't spend the money because the harbor isn't really important to us. This company does not feel any responsibility to the society in which it exists."

Once such a statement has been made, it cannot be taken back. The company can release a formal statement clarifying its official position; however, major damage to the company's reputation has already occurred. The spokesperson should have anticipated such a question and rehearsed an appropriate, sincere answer. One such answer might have been: "Consideration of these controls is being made as a part of the company's overall long-term pollution control program. Every attempt it being made to coordinate efforts with other manufacturing facilities in the area. All companies must adopt these controls if they are to be effective in cleaning up the harbor." A statement such as this is less likely to create problems for the company.

The need to communicate with sensitivity is no less important for other types of presentations. The chief dangers of carelessness are damage to the company's reputation (an ethical, or image, problem) and defamation of another person (a legal problem). For a review of the legal and ethical issues that may arise, see Chapter 6.

## ANALYZE YOUR AUDIENCE

To make sure your presentation meets your audience's needs, you must first determine what those needs are. Then you can use the organizational strategy, examples, visual aids, and arguments that are pertinent and interesting to your audience.

Your audience analysis may be based on your own understanding, or you may do some research. An invaluable resource is the person who has invited you to make the presentation. He or she will be happy to answer your questions because doing so helps guarantee that your presentation will serve its purpose and not be a waste of everybody's time.

Here are some questions to ask about the audience for a presentation:

- How many will be present?
- Are they attending the presentation because they have to or because they want to?
- In general, what businesses or jobs do they represent?
- What is their general age range?
- What is their general level of education?
- What do they want to know? Need to know?
- What are their attitudes about the topic?
- What are their expectations of you and the topic?
- What is their familiarity with the subject? With you?
- What objections to your ideas might they have?
- Will your presentation be one of several on the same topic, or will it be unique?
- Have preceding activities made them tired or fidgety, are they preoccupied with what comes next, or are they eager to hear your presentation?
- How might they react to humor?

As an exercise in analyzing an audience, think about the presentation Robert DeSantangelo was planning in the chapter-opening vignette. How do you imagine he would answer these questions?

As with other types of business communication, it is your responsibility to show the audience how they will benefit from the information you are offering or the course of action you are recommending. Follow these steps (described in greater detail in Chapter 6) to define their needs and appropriate motivators:

1. Determine the need level (from Maslow's hierarchy of needs) at which members of the audience are probably operating in terms of your presentation's objectives:

*Ask the person who invited you to make a presentation for information about the audience's needs and interests, or do some research on your own.*

*Use Maslow's hierarchy of needs to determine how you might appeal to the audience members and motivate them to do as you recommend.*

*Level 1—physiological needs.* Will it help them satisfy their basic survival needs for food, water, basic shelter, or reproduction?

*Level 2—safety needs.* Will it help make them feel safer or more secure?

*Level 3—belonging needs.* Will it help them identify with a desirable group; gain social approval; make them sexually attractive; meet their love and affection needs; or make them feel closer to their friends, family, co-workers, or society in general?

*Level 4—esteem needs.* Will it make other people look up to them or make them feel superior to others?

*Level 5—self-actualization needs.* Will it help them be more independent or the best they can be; meet their need to know and understand; or satisfy their desire for truth, beauty, goodness, fairness, or so on?

2. Determine the motivators that can be used to convince your audience that what you want them to know or do will meet the needs identified in step 1.

3. Determine the motivators you will actually use in planning your presentation.

Good you attitude is just as important in presentations as in written messages.

Open, friendly body language helps build rapport with the audience.

Another way to indicate that you are aware of the audience's needs is to frequently use the pronouns *you* and *your*—unless you are telling your audience bad news. Use positive words and phrases, and concentrate on what can be done rather than what cannot be done. Creating rapport with your audience through choice of words is the same for oral presentations as it is for written messages. However, you have one advantage in presentations that is not available to you in writing: body language that indicates you are open, friendly, and sincerely interested in your audience's reaction.

Humor can also be used to build rapport with an audience. Because businesspeople tend to take themselves too seriously, audiences value a sense of humor. When used skillfully and appropriately, humor relieves a solemn atmosphere and makes the speaker seem more human. In a leader, a sense of humor (even in crises) implies control—of both oneself and the crisis. If you decide to use humor, concentrate on the punchline, making sure to deliver it perfectly. Above all, however, humor must be applicable and appropriate to the situation.

The biggest challenge in determining an audience's needs for a presentation is usually to figure out how to deal with their diverse interests. Usually, you will fare best by focusing on the needs of the most important individual or subgroup of individuals. When presenting a progress report to a group of company executives, for instance, focus on the CEO. When presenting new-product information to a group of salespeople and support staff, make a greater effort to meet the salespeople's needs. Sheer numbers may also be the deciding factor. For example, imagine you are speaking about business ethics to a group of teachers, students, and businesspeople. If you determine that approximately 80 percent of the audience will be students and teachers, you should concentrate on giving information about the ethics that students need to succeed in the business world.

## Gather the Necessary Resources

The last step in planning is to gather information, materials, and people you need to prepare the presentation. Do you need to do further library or in-company research, or interview people to support your conclusions and recommendations? Would quotes or evidence from experts in the field add strength to your arguments? What handouts, if any, are needed?

There are times when more than one individual should be involved in the preparation of an oral presentation. Some complex subjects call for the involvement of several specialists. Furthermore, when an individual is speaking on behalf of a company, it is often necessary to get the text approved by company attorneys and/or upper-level executives before delivering it. For fast-moving, interesting presentations, a team of speakers can be used. Careful timing and intensive practice will ensure that there is no lag time between speakers.

## ORGANIZING AND COMPOSING A PRESENTATION

Planning is only the first phase in the process of preparing a presentation. You must then determine the major points of your oral presentation and organize those points into a logical pattern. Freewriting is just as useful for oral presentations as it is for written messages. After freewriting, you must select an appropriate organizational strategy. Then you can develop the main parts of the presentation itself, prepare for the question-and-answer period, and write out your presentation notes.

### FREEWRITE MAJOR POINTS

As you already know, freewriting is a way to get your ideas down on paper. After looking over all your background material, write down in short phrases everything you want to tell the audience. At this time, do not be concerned about the order; just list the main points in your own words as you think of them. This is an excellent way of overcoming writer's block (the psychological barrier that often prevents people from starting or progressing with a communication project).

Once you have thoroughly explored the topic, you should choose approximately three main points you want to make. In this regard, presentations are different from written messages. Because the audience cannot study your message at their own pace, they have a limited capacity for processing information. You are better off presenting fewer points but developing them thoroughly than presenting all the points that occur to you. This rule of thumb applies to presentations of any length. Whether you are speaking for 5 or 45 minutes, you should be able to sum up succinctly at the end. You fill the extra time by presenting more facts, more figures, and more examples—all in support of a few memorable points.

*Regardless of the length of your presentation, focus on approximately three main points so the audience can more easily remember them.*

### CHOOSE AN ORGANIZATIONAL STRATEGY

Select an appropriate organizational strategy for a presentation after analyzing your topic and purpose and predicting the audience's probable reaction to the message.

When you expect the audience to be receptive to you and your message, your presentation can take the most straightforward approach: Tell them what you're going to say, tell them, and then tell them what you told them. However, when you expect your audience to disagree with you or resist your message, you must use different techniques. You might be able to use good you attitude, a positive tone, or other techniques to make them realize their doubts are unfounded. In addition, you could use an indirect organizational strategy to build a case before presenting your main point. For example, suppose you are planning a speech to a group of businesswomen on the differences in how males and females communicate. Your main point, that women often do not communicate effectively, may well meet with some resistance. Thus you would not make the statement directly. Instead, you would provide evidence from research studies that leads the audience members to reach the conclusion on their own.

Depending on your analysis of the audience's probable reaction, you can choose one of three organizational strategies for your presentation: the direct pattern, the indirect pattern, or the persuasive pattern. (These are the same basic organizational strategies used for written business messages.) Use a direct strategy when you expect positive or neutral reactions from an audience. Use an indirect strategy when negative reactions are anticipated. Use a persuasive strategy when your purpose is to get the audience to act or when you want the audience to change its way of thinking on an issue.

These are the basic elements of each strategy:

- *Direct strategy.* Get to the point in the introduction. Support your opening statements with the information they need to know in terms of what it means to them personally. Close with goodwill. Ask your audience to take action, if appropriate.

- *Indirect strategy.* Use a pertinent buffer opening that will not anger or upset your audience; if you have any good news, begin with it. Lead your audience gradually to the negative news or unpleasant conclusions by providing the information they need to know and justification for it. Close with goodwill. Ask your audience to take action, if appropriate.

- *Persuasive strategy.* Do or say something unexpected to get the audience's attention. Use information to create interest in your idea. Explain how audience members will benefit by doing what you want them to do or thinking what you want them to think. Make it easy for them to take the desired action. Directly ask them to do whatever it is you are trying to persuade them to do, and remind them of how they will benefit.

Using the direct and persuasive strategies will help you get your reasons across before the audience decides not to listen, just as indirect and persuasive letters do with readers.

### DEVELOP THE MAIN PARTS

Whatever organizational strategy you decide to use, your presentation will have three main parts: the introduction, the body, and the conclusion. As you read about these elements, think about how Robert DeSantangelo, from the chapter-opening vignette, might organize his presentation to the supervisors at his company.

◗ List the seven ways to introduce oral presentations, and choose the appropriate one for any given presentation.

**INTRODUCTION.**   The introduction is a very important part of a presentation. Although it takes up only 10 to 20 percent of the total time allotted for the presentation, during that time the audience is forming an opinion about your

---

**Organizational strategies for presentations are the same as those for letters and memos.**

**The main point is expressed at the beginning of a direct presentation and in the middle of an indirect or persuasive presentation.**

credibility that will be very hard to change, no matter what you do in the rest of the presentation. To increase your chances of making the best possible impression, plan the introduction carefully, rehearse it thoroughly, and perhaps even memorize it if it is short.

In the introduction, you must accomplish three goals: get your audience's immediate attention, make clear to the audience what your speech is about, and convince your audience that the information you are providing is useful to them. It is your responsibility to establish this rapport. The audience cannot skim ahead, as they can with a letter, memo, or report, to clarify the issues you have left murky.

There are many ways to introduce a topic. Your choice should depend on the nature of your audience and your topic. For instance, you would not want to begin speaking on a deadly serious subject by telling a joke. Here are seven of the more popular ways to introduce a topic (examples follow each introductory technique):

- State the purpose:

    "We are here today to determine a way to make our customers want to remain with us instead of purchasing from low-priced discount warehouses. I will propose a way that should do just that."

    "After my presentation today, you will be able to identify four easy steps you can take immediately to improve the way you relate to people from other cultures."

    "You know why we're here; you know we have a problem. We're here because of management's belief that solutions work best when those who have to implement them are solidly behind them. There is a way to boost our division's lagging sales without cutting jobs. Today I'll concentrate on this plan."

- Use a relevant quote:

    "Since Socrates asked, 'How should one live?,' people and businesses as well have tried to answer his question. By deciding today to adopt the Air Quality Management guidelines for reducing pollution, you will take a bold step toward answering once and for all Socrates' query."

    "Abraham Lincoln said, 'Whatever men do, they do in response to motives. Discover the motives that cause them to act, and you can make them do your bidding.' Lincoln wasn't talking about advertising. However, his advice is as pertinent to those of us in advertising today as it was 160 years ago. Today I'll concentrate on how we can use Lincoln's advice to determine how the American public wants to spend its money."

- Relate an appropriate anecdote or humorous story:

    "There once was an African tribe that required all its public speakers to stand on one leg during a speech. They were allowed to speak only as long as they could stand on the one leg. When the other leg went down, the speech was over. Luckily for me, I've been doing aerobics daily for over a year now. Luckily for you, I've been told I only have 20 minutes. (Read with next paragraph.)

The introduction should get attention, introduce the topic, and explain how the information will benefit the audience.

Choose the technique for opening a presentation that is most consistent with the topic, your purpose, and the audience's needs.

"Even if we don't have the rest of the day to discuss the importance of a physical fitness center program for our staff members, I think you will be able to see within the next 20 minutes the direct, positive benefits to the company of actively promoting the good health of all our employees."

"When I announced that I didn't really need to go to the university after finishing my associate's degree, my mother told me, 'You'll know you're smart when people are willing to drive out of their way and stand in line just to hear what you have to say.' Thank you for making me feel smart.

"But getting a bachelor's degree didn't make me smart. Any intelligence was already there before I started working on the degree. What the degree did do for me, however, is the reason for our being here today. Perhaps you will also see the benefits of, once and for all, being 'smart.' "

- Issue a surprise statement:

  "Women do not communicate effectively in the business world! [Pause until all the shocked eyes in the room are on yours.] Oddly enough, there are still people who believe that statement to be true. [Pause for laughter.] The reason for my being here today is to show you the results of some interesting new studies that show women are effective business communicators."

  "As we sit here today, over 200 small businesses will declare bankruptcy. Why should this matter to you?"

- Refer to the situation or to the audience:

  "I have read often of your organization and the fine work it does in discovering improved treatments for multiple sclerosis. Hundreds of thousands have benefited from your charity. It is an honor to stand before you today, and it is an honor to assist you by delineating a new treatment for children under the age of 12."

  "After working actively to accomplish Delta Pi Epsilon's objectives for the past nine years, I stand before you with pride in the accomplishments of our organization. In our quest to accomplish more and more, it is easy to forget what we have done in the past. Yet remembering the past will actually motivate us to accept the challenges the future presents to us."

- Describe an event that relates to the situation:

  "In our efforts to understand the pain caused by prejudice, it is necessary to put ourselves in someone else's shoes. Close your eyes and imagine yourself a member of the 'green' race. Your skin is moss green, and your hair is a light shade of pea green. All green people, of which there are only a few thousand in your state, have red eyes. You are one of a small number of college-educated greens, yet you are having trouble finding a job.

  "How do you feel when another job applicant sitting out in the waiting room before an interview says, 'I just know they'll hire you instead of me; everyone knows they have to have more greens or they'll lose their government contracts.' Does it make you feel as bad as when the security guard in the parking lot jokingly said, 'How did you manage to get here? I thought all the lights looked red to you guys!' How do you feel when the interviewer says, 'You graduated from college? Wow, that must have been cause for celebration in your neighborhood!'

"These are the same kinds of statements all minority groups must contend with. Sensitivity to other cultures is the topic of our discussion today. Bring your green skin and come along with me—or step out of it if it's too painful."

- Ask questions that build mystery or make the audience start to think about your topic:

"We're here to decide the fate of the Phoenix plant. There are two ways of thinking. One, opposed by the union, would require us to shut down the plant and move all operations to the Nashville facility, leaving 1,600 people out of work. Another, labeled 'impossible' by management, would require the company to spend $4 million to retool the Phoenix plant.

"Which is the right option? In the next 30 minutes, let's try to reach a decision that best meets the needs of both the union and management."

"When was the last time you asked yourself, 'What am I doing in school?' How many times have you said, 'What do I need this for?' Oh, I wish I had a dollar for each time you've thought, 'I should just quit and get a job!'

"Your doubts are not unique; every student has them at one time or another. Sometimes it is hard to see the long-term benefits of finishing school. Yet those rewards are there. I know, because I stayed in school and found a wonderful, satisfying job. That is why your teacher asked me to speak to you today."

**The you attitude is a prime ingredient of the introduction.**

These introductions all have something in common: They create interest in the topic through use of the you attitude. They not only use the words *you* and *your*; they also relate the topic to the audience's concerns, interests, and frames of reference. In addition, each introduction directly states its link to the topic. Even in the examples that introduce potentially sensitive areas (plant closings, racial prejudice, management's directive to solve a department problem), the topic of the presentation is made clear in the introduction.

**Begin confidently so the audience will trust you and your message.**

Notice also that even the introductions dealing with sensitive topics are phrased positively and confidently. Never begin an oral presentation with openings such as these:

"Well, here goes . . . "

"I didn't really have much time to prepare, so bear with me on this."

"I'm sorry; I had hoped to be able to start with a film today, but the airline lost it."

"I'm sorry. Is it me, or is it this microphone that's short? Guess it's just me."

"Most of you know more about this subject than I do."

"Whew! It's really warm in here, isn't it? Perhaps we can get through this fast and get out into the fresh air."

Wishy-washy openings such as these set a negative tone for the entire speech. It is hard enough to get an audience's attention without giving members cause to believe the speaker or the speech itself might not be worthy of their attention.

Develop major and supporting points within the body of an oral presentation.

**BODY.**   The body of your oral presentation takes up between 70 and 80 percent of the speaking time. The purpose presented in the introduction should be developed clearly in the speech's body. For the most part, in the middle portion of your presentation you support your major points with facts, figures, and examples to help your audience understand and reach the same logical conclusions as you did.

*In the body of the presentation, answer all the basic questions about your topic, and provide facts, examples, and expert opinion to support your main point.*

One way to make sure you provide enough support for your main points is to provide answers to all of the following questions: What? Why? How? When? Who? Where? Support may take the form of statistics, quotations, and opinions of authorities; definitions; illustrations; anecdotes; comparisons and analogies; repetition; and restatement of the idea in other words.

*Clearly distinguish between your opinions and the facts, and identify the sources of your information.*

To reassure your audience of your credibility, clearly state when you are moving from your opinion to evidence supported by fact. Tell the audience how you obtained the evidence. As you choose evidence to support your opinions, ask yourself the following questions:

Is the source reliable?

Is the information true?

Is the information up to date?

Are quotes accurate?

When taken out of context, do quotes and other information have the same meaning?

Are the statistics valid?

*Try to explain every point in terms of how it relates to the audience.*

Throughout the body, remember to relate your points directly to the audience's frame of reference. How can they use the information? Of what benefit is it to them? As with any type of message, choose your words carefully. Use positive words and phrases. Select words that express meaning, not those that might impress your listeners. To use the words of Abraham Lincoln again, "Never use two words when one will do; never use a big word where a small one will do."

*Visual aids should be an integral part of most presentations.*

In conjunction with planning your presentation's body, you should prepare visual aids. Consider how they can be used to help improve the audience's understanding of your oral presentation. They should not substitute for your words, but they can supplement, emphasize, and clarify the words. They can be used to break complicated points into easy-to-understand components or to set a mood that enhances the message. As you prepare your presentation, ask yourself these questions:

- Will tables, photos, cartoons, illustrations, charts or graphs, demonstrations, and so on help listeners understand or gain their interest?

- How should the visual aids be presented? (See Chapter 15.) Would it be better to present the visuals as handouts? On the chalkboard? Transparencies for overhead projection? Slides, videos, or films? Posters? Flipcharts? Reports sent to the audience before the speech? Samples?

- Will music or taped commentary help liven up the presentation or establish a mood that makes the audience more receptive to the message?

- What level of professionalism will the audience expect of the visuals? Should the visuals be prepared by professionals, or will casually prepared ones be acceptable?

Remember—when you prepare visual aids for presentations, make sure they can be seen easily by all audience members. Typed or written copy must be easily readable from all parts of the room. Photos or drawings must be large enough for all members of the audience to view. If the audience has to strain to see the visual aids, the visuals will distract more than enhance.

▌Develop appropriate conclusions for a presentation.

**CONCLUSION.**    Like the introduction, the conclusion should take up 10 to 20 percent of the time allotted for your presentation. In general, your goal is to leave the audience with a clear idea of your message and its relevance to them. However, the conclusion is organized somewhat differently for informative and persuasive presentations.

The conclusion of an informative speech should summarize the main points, restate their importance to the audience, and close on a strong, positive note.

If the purpose of your speech is to inform, the conclusion should briefly summarize the major points so your audience will remember them. You should also restate the importance of the information. Then you can close with a strong statement, tied closely to your introduction, that leaves the audience in a receptive and positive frame of mind. For example, the following introduction and conclusion are closely related:

> Introduction: "Women do not communicate effectively in the business world!" [Pause until all the shocked eyes in the room are on yours. ] Oddly enough, there are still people today who believe that statement to be true. [Pause for laughter. ] The reason for my being here today is to give you the results of some interesting new studies showing that women are effective business communicators."

> Conclusion: "In conclusion, women do not communicate in the same way as men: They use more tag questions, different amounts of eye contact and different body language, and have a higher tolerance for interruptions. Nevertheless, research reveals that women are flexible, adaptive communicators. They are able to move freely between the passive communication style society expects of them in their personal lives and the assertive communication style business expects of its leaders. This is encouraging news for women who have struggled against prejudice in the business world. The evidence is clear: Women do communicate effectively."

Notice how this conclusion answers the "hook" used in the introduction: whether women can communicate effectively.

The conclusion of a persuasive speech can also include a summary, as well as quotations, statistics, and stories or other illustrations that tie the major points together. However, even more important in a persuasive speech is one

The conclusion of a persuasive speech should summarize the main points, restate their importance, tie everything together with some sort of illustration, and close with a call to action.

final appeal to your listeners to take action because of the information's importance to them. If your presentation has been well organized, your listeners already know what you want them to do. However, one last appeal adds impact. Here are some examples of how final appeals can be handled in the conclusion of a persuasive presentation:

> Final appeal: "Therefore, it is crucial to the economic health of this city that the naval repair facility be reopened. You can make it happen. Please write to your congressional representative today."

> Final appeal: "The contract negotiated by union leaders and company management is fair. It provides salaries equal to industry standards, protects jobs and benefits, and includes significant improvements in shared decision making between management and labor—all the major gains we wanted before negotiations began. Please support your negotiators by voting yes."

Of course, to end with an appeal to action, you have to know exactly what you want your audience to do. The more practical and doable your recommendation is, the more likely the audience is to act in the desired manner.

End presentations on a strong, confident note.

Beginning speakers often end a presentation by expressing relief, ending abruptly, or hurrying back to their seats. These sorts of endings leave the audience with a negative impression of the entire presentation. "Well, that's all" or "That's it" are poor ways to end a speech. Whether your presentation is informative or persuasive, end with an upbeat, confident statement.

## PREPARE FOR THE QUESTION-AND-ANSWER PERIOD

Prepare for the question-and-answer period after an oral presentation.

Prepare in advance for the question-and-answer period.

In most cases, you will be expected to conduct a brief question-and-answer period after your presentation. An effective speaker anticipates the questions that might be asked and prepares for them ahead of time. Your answers to probable questions and comments should be as well rehearsed as the rest of your speech.

If you are asked a question to which you do not know the answer, it is appropriate to say something such as, "That's an interesting question, but I don't know the answer. My research did not cover the motivational effects of changing job titles. Are there any other questions?"

Think of hostile questions as opportunities to restate your point, and remind the audience of how it can benefit or affect them.

If you anticipate hostile reactions, comments, or questions, be prepared to patiently restate some of the main points of your presentation. When people are upset about what they are hearing, they often do not listen carefully or hear all that is said. Plan to go over some of the details again in different words, using strong you attitude to show listeners how the points brought up in the speech benefit or affect them personally. Explain how you reached your conclusions. Whatever you do, do not lose your temper. Retain control of the presentation. If the person continues to argue with you and it is obvious the rest of the audience is uncomfortable with the confrontation, ask the arguer in a friendly way to meet you later to continue the discussion, or simply agree to disagree. Then ask the audience if there are more questions. Remember that no matter what you do, you will never be able to please everyone.

## PREPARE PRESENTATION NOTES

■ Prepare notes that will help you deliver an oral presentation.

Most extemporaneous speakers take presentation notes (a sort of outline or script) with them to the stage or lectern and use them as a prompt during the presentation. Even extremely well-prepared speakers who have rehearsed their topics at length use notes to make sure they cover all the points they planned to. The notes are also useful as a guide for the nervous speaker who might forget the next point he or she planned to make. By pausing and glancing down at clearly laid-out notes, the speaker can quickly determine what comes next.

*Presentation notes are outlines written in key words or phrases.*

Presentation notes, whether they are on cards or paper, should consist of key words and phrases from the presentation. Complete sentences take longer to read and are, therefore, harder to consult at a glance. There is also the danger that a nervous speaker might resort to reading the speech from the complete sentences. Nothing bores an audience more quickly than forcing them to look at the top of your head while you read a speech!

Some speakers prefer to write out their presentations in full before preparing presentation notes. As they rehearse, they prepare an outline. The outline notes become shorter and shorter as the speaker becomes more familiar with the content. Other speakers write their presentation notes first. They can generally save time by not writing out the presentation in full, and their phrasing is likely to sound more natural and conversational.

*Working from presentation notes allows you to speak more naturally and maintain better rapport with the audience.*

Whether you choose to prepare an outline as you begin or later, you might try the format presented in Exhibit 14.1. Notice how boldfacing is used to highlight the key words. The notes on the right indicate where visual aids fit in. This format helps the speaker remember all the important points without getting bogged down in reading any part of the presentation. The advantage of such presentation notes is an opportunity to build rapport with the audience, which is the secret weapon of accomplished presenters.

## DISCUSSION QUESTIONS

■ Identify instances in which knowing oral presentation skills is useful to businesspeople.

■ Identify the general and specific purposes of formal presentations.

1. Give three examples (other than those mentioned in this chapter) of informative presentations that might be given in the business world. Give three examples of persuasive presentations.

■ Compare the steps for planning oral messages to those for planning written messages, and use these steps in preparing effective oral presentations.

2. Why is an extemporaneous presentation preferred in most situations? Why is memorization not recommended?

■ Compare the steps for planning oral messages to those for planning written messages, and use these steps in preparing effective oral presentations.

■ Select an appropriate organizational strategy for a presentation after analyzing your topic and purpose and predicting the audience's probable reaction to the message.

3. What are the similarities between writing a speech and writing a letter or memo?

**EXHIBIT 14.1**    Sample Presentation Notes

Title:  Marketing Strategies for Small Businesses

General Purpose:  To inform small business owners about marketing strategies

Specific Purpose:  To give small business owners a framework for marketing against bigger competitors and a toolkit of affordable techniques

Organizational Strategy:  Direct

Introduction

I. **Big guys will get you if you don't get smart!**
   A. **Growth** of big chains
   B. Small-business **failure** rate
   C. Anecdote:  **Heartland Business Products**

II. Solution: Don't fight big guys; **capitalize on smallness**

Body

III. Failed approach: compete on price and selection

IV. Successful approach:
   A. Provide **limited product mix**
   B. Provide **excellent service**
   C. Research market

V. Toolkit:
   A. Affordable **market information** sources
      1. Customers/clients
      2. Competitors
   B. Affordable **sales promotion** methods
   C. Affordable **advertising**

Conclusion

VI. **Summary** of above

VII. Anecdote: **Heartland's turnaround**

VIII. Lesson: **Little guys can win if they don't compete head-on with big guys.**

🔖 Identify the general and specific purposes of formal presentations.

4.   What is the difference between a presentation's general purpose and its specific purpose?

🔖 Select an appropriate organizational strategy for a presentation after analyzing your topic and purpose and predicting the audience's probable reaction to the message.

5.   What are the steps in analyzing your audience using Maslow's hierarchy?

🔖 Select an appropriate organizational strategy for a presentation after analyzing your topic and purpose and predicting the audience's probable reaction to the message.

6.   What organizational strategy would be used for a speech to persuade? For a speech to inform? What are the similarities of these patterns to the organizational strategies used for letters and memos?

🔖 Select an appropriate organizational strategy for a presentation after analyzing your topic and purpose and predicting the audience's probable reaction to the message.

🔖 List the seven ways to introduce oral presentations, and choose the appropriate one for any given presentation.

7.   What is rapport? How do you create rapport with an audience?

🔖 List the seven ways to introduce oral presentations, and choose the appropriate one for any given presentation.

8.   Name five effective ways to introduce a presentation. Name five ineffective ways to introduce a presentation.

🔖 List the seven ways to introduce oral presentations, and choose the appropriate one for any given presentation.

🔖 Develop major and supporting points within the body of an oral presentation.

🔖 Develop appropriate conclusions for a presentation.

9.   What percentage of time allocated for a presentation should be devoted to the introduction? The body? The conclusion?

🔖 List the seven ways to introduce oral presentations, and choose the appropriate one for any given presentation.

🔖 Develop appropriate conclusions for a presentation.

10.   How can the conclusion of a speech and the introduction be tied together?

🔖 Develop major and supporting points within the body of an oral presentation.

11.   Name five ways to support your conclusions or major points in the body of an oral presentation.

🔖 Develop appropriate conclusions for a presentation.

12.   Name five effective ways to conclude a speech. Name five ineffective ways to conclude a speech.

🔖 Prepare for the question-and-answer period after an oral presentation.

13.   How can a presenter deal with hostile questions?

🔖 Prepare notes that will help you deliver an oral presentation.

14.   Are phrases or full sentences more effective in presentation notes? Why?

## APPLICATION EXERCISES

🐾 Identify instances in which knowing oral presentation skills is useful to businesspeople.

1. Interview two people in your field. Prepare a memo report to your instructor in which you answer the following questions:
    a. Whom did you interview? Provide names, titles, companies for which they work, length of time with that company and in that position, length of time in the field, and any other information that will establish these individuals' authority.
    b. How important are informal presentation skills in the field or the industry?
    c. How important are formal presentation skills in the field or the industry?
    d. In what types of informal and formal speaking opportunities do they participate?
    e. How has the need for presentation skills changed as they have progressed in their careers?

🐾 Identify instances in which knowing oral presentation skills is useful to businesspeople.
🐾 Compare the steps for planning oral messages to those for planning written messages, and use these steps in preparing effective oral presentations.
🐾 Prepare for the question-and-answer period after an oral presentation.

2. Watch the local and national news or another news program every day for one week. You are looking for a formal statement about a company's position on some issue. Describe one such company statement in your own words; provide the date and time of the broadcast, the channel, the company name, and the name and job title of the spokesperson. Was the statement delivered with good eye contact, or was it read from prepared copy? Was there a question-and-answer period after the statement? What is your opinion of the skill with which the statement was prepared? Submit this information in a memo to your teacher.

🐾 Identify instances in which knowing oral presentation skills is useful to businesspeople.
🐾 Compare the steps for planning oral messages to those for planning written messages, and use these steps in preparing effective oral presentations.
🐾 Identify the general and specific purposes of formal presentations.
🐾 Select an appropriate organizational strategy for a presentation after analyzing your topic and purpose and predicting the audience's probable reaction to the message.
🐾 List the seven ways to introduce oral presentations, and choose the appropriate one for any given presentation.
🐾 Develop major and supporting points within the body of an oral presentation.
🐾 Develop appropriate conclusions for a presentation.
🐾 Prepare notes that will help you deliver an oral presentation.

3. Prepare an informative speech on a business topic (approved by your instructor) to be given to your classmates. Prepare presentation notes, and submit a copy of them to your instructor.

■ Identify instances in which knowing oral presentation skills is useful to businesspeople.

■ Compare the steps for planning oral messages to those for planning written messages, and use these steps in preparing effective oral presentations.

■ Identify the general and specific purposes of formal presentations.

■ Select an appropriate organizational strategy for a presentation after analyzing your topic and purpose and predicting the audience's probable reaction to the message.

■ List the seven ways to introduce oral presentations, and choose the appropriate one for any given presentation.

■ Develop major and supporting points within the body of an oral presentation.

■ Develop appropriate conclusions for a presentation.

■ Prepare notes that will help you deliver an oral presentation.

4. Give your instructor a list of four or five business-related topics you could talk about for two or three minutes. Specify whether each would be an informative talk or a persuasive talk. Your instructor will select one of the topics and give you a few minutes to prepare an impromptu speech to present to your classmates.

■ Compare the steps for planning oral messages to those for planning written messages, and use these steps in preparing effective oral presentations.

5. Using Maslow's hierarchy of needs, go through the three steps necessary to analyze your audience before giving an oral presentation on a topic your teacher assigns.
   *a.* Use your classmates as the intended audience.
   *b.* Use a group of business teachers as the intended audience. Write a one- to two-page memo to your instructor that details the differences between the two audiences.

■ Compare the steps for planning oral messages to those for planning written messages, and use these steps in preparing effective oral presentations.

■ Identify the general and specific purposes of formal presentations.

■ Select an appropriate organizational strategy for a presentation after analyzing your topic and purpose and predicting the audience's probable reaction to the message.

6. Imagine that you are preparing a persuasive talk for one of the following situations. Write a memo report for your instructor detailing all your planning decisions (purpose, length of presentation, audience, and so on) and explaining which organizational strategy you would use and why.
   *a.* You and your classmates are salespersons for the same company. You will be explaining to them why your product (your choice) is better than the competitors' products.
   *b.* You will be speaking to a group of local voters to convince them that the political party currently in power at the state or federal level (your choice) should remain in power.
   *c.* You will be speaking to a group of local voters to convince them of the need to change the political party in power at the state or federal level (your choice).

>   *d.*   What would you change about the city or community in which you live? Prepare a speech to be given to your local governing group convincing them of the need for these changes. How do you want them to make the changes?
>   *e.*   You will be speaking to a group of faculty members and classmates about the need to change the general education requirements for your degree program. How do you want them to effect the changes you recommend?
>   *f.*   You will be speaking to a group of faculty members and classmates about the need for a change in the core requirements of your degree program. How do you want them to effect this change?
>   *g.*   You will be speaking to a group of faculty members and classmates about the need to add another degree program at your institution. How do you want them to effect this change?
>   *h.*   You will be speaking to a group of faculty members and classmates about the need for an advanced business communication class. How do you want them to go about getting this change?

▪ Compare the steps for planning oral messages to those for planning written messages, and use these steps in preparing effective oral presentations.

▪ Select an appropriate organizational strategy for a presentation after analyzing your topic and purpose and predicting the audience's probable reaction to the message.

▪ Prepare notes that will help you deliver an oral presentation.

7.  Imagine that one of your business professors or your boss (your choice) will be making a presentation to your class or to some organization on campus (your choice) on a topic of your choice. Write a two-minute presentation introducing the speaker. Try to explain to the audience the benefit of listening to the speaker. Word your presentation exactly as you would deliver it. Submit the written presentation to your instructor, along with an identification of the speaker, audience, and topic.

▪ Compare the steps for planning oral messages to those for planning written messages, and use these steps in preparing effective oral presentations.

▪ Identify the general and specific purposes of formal presentations.

▪ Select an appropriate organizational strategy for a presentation after analyzing your topic and purpose and predicting the audience's probable reaction to the message.

▪ List the seven ways to introduce oral presentations, and choose the appropriate one for any given presentation.

▪ Develop major and supporting points within the body of an oral presentation.

▪ Develop appropriate conclusions for a presentation.

▪ Prepare notes that will help you deliver an oral presentation.

8.  At your library, consult *Complete Guide to Executive Manners* by Letitia Baldrige. Select a topic from the book that can be discussed in a 10-minute presentation to your classmates. Submit the presentation notes to your instructor.

■ Compare the steps for planning oral messages to those for planning written messages, and use these steps in preparing effective oral presentations.
■ Identify the general and specific purposes of formal presentations.
■ Select an appropriate organizational strategy for a presentation after analyzing your topic and purpose and predicting the audience's probable reaction to the message.
■ List the seven ways to introduce oral presentations, and choose the appropriate one for any given presentation.
■ Develop major and supporting points within the body of an oral presentation.
■ Develop appropriate conclusions for a presentation.
■ Prepare notes that will help you deliver an oral presentation.

9. Review the vignette at the beginning of the chapter. Imagining that you are Robert DeSantangelo, plan a five-minute presentation on the topic of handling employee tardiness. You may find it necessary to consult an article on this topic to come up with supporting details. Be sure to go through all the steps of the planning process. The end product should be one to three pages of presentation notes that you will turn in to your instructor.

■ Compare the steps for planning oral messages to those for planning written messages, and use these steps in preparing effective oral presentations.
■ Identify the general and specific purposes of formal presentations.
■ Select an appropriate organizational strategy for a presentation after analyzing your topic and purpose and predicting the audience's probable reaction to the message.
■ List the seven ways to introduce oral presentations, and choose the appropriate one for any given presentation.
■ Develop major and supporting points within the body of an oral presentation.
■ Develop appropriate conclusions for a presentation.
■ Prepare for the question-and-answer period after an oral presentation.
■ Prepare notes that will help you deliver an oral presentation.

10. Prepare an oral presentation for your class based on the formal report you wrote when studying Chapters 12 and 13. Narrow the topic to a scope you can cover within the time limit specified by your instructor. Thoroughly plan the presentation, and think about how you can use the you attitude to help your audience relate to your topic. Submit complete presentation notes to your instructor.

■ Compare the steps for planning oral messages to those for planning written messages, and use these steps in preparing effective oral presentations.
■ Identify the general and specific purposes of formal presentations.
■ Select an appropriate organizational strategy for a presentation after analyzing your topic and purpose and predicting the audience's probable reaction to the message.
■ List the seven ways to introduce oral presentations, and choose the appropriate one for any given presentation.
■ Develop major and supporting points within the body of an oral presentation.
■ Develop appropriate conclusions for a presentation.

◼ Prepare for the question-and-answer period after an oral presentation.
◼ Prepare notes that will help you deliver an oral presentation.

11. Prepare presentation notes for the following situations. If your instructor wishes, provide a three- or four-page analysis of your audience.

   *a.* A 20-minute after-lunch speech to a local group of businesspeople. The topic is writing effective business letters.

   *b.* A 15-minute presentation on business ethics to be given to your department at your place of work (or to other business students, if you are not currently working).

   *c.* A 10-minute presentation to a group of beginning psychology students on how to use Maslow's hierarchy of needs to motivate people with alcohol- or drug-dependency problems.

   *d.* A 10-minute presentation on how to prepare effective visual aids for presentations and reports, to be given to five middle-level managers of a small business consulting firm.

   *e.* A five-minute presentation to be given to your classmates on one of the topics below. If your instructor does not tell you, you may decide whether the presentation is to be informative or persuasive. All of the following topics are covered in this textbook, so it might not be necessary to do additional research before planning your presentation. If your topic is one that has been covered before by your instructor, you should approach the topic as though it is a review, using examples that were not used before.

   Barriers to communication.

   Criteria for effective business communications.

   Critical thinking.

   Effects of changing technology on the office environment.

   Intercultural communication: age and gender.

   Intercultural communication: decision-making styles.

   Intercultural communication: directness and affection.

   Intercultural communication: eye contact and body language.

   Intercultural communication: gift giving and table etiquette.

   Intercultural communication: impact of religion on business.

   Intercultural communication: individualism versus team or group orientation.

   Intercultural communication: male and female communication styles.

   Intercultural communication: negotiating styles.

   Intercultural communication: race or skin color and social class.

   Intercultural communication: written communication differences.

   Laws relating to business communications.

   Listening skills.

   New computer equipment for the business office.

   New noncomputer equipment for the business office.

   Nonverbal communication: body language.

Nonverbal communication: color choice psychology.

Nonverbal communication: cultural differences.

Nonverbal communication: lying behavior.

Nonverbal communication: object language.

Numbers in business messages.

Paragraph construction.

Parts of formal business reports.

Planning business meetings.

Punctuation: colons and semicolons.

Punctuation: commas.

Punctuation: dashes and hyphens.

Sentence construction.

Visual aids in business messages.

Word choice: clichés and foreign expressions.

Word choice: discriminatory expressions.

Word choice: euphemisms and out-of-date, trite, and roundabout expressions.

Word choice: jargon, slang, and trendy expressions.

- Identify instances in which knowing oral presentation skills is useful to businesspeople.
- Compare the steps for planning oral messages to those for planning written messages, and use these steps in preparing effective oral presentations.
- Identify the general and specific purposes of formal presentations.
- Select an appropriate organizational strategy for a presentation after analyzing your topic and purpose and predicting the audience's probable reaction to the message.
- List the seven ways to introduce oral presentations, and choose the appropriate one for any given presentation.
- Develop major and supporting points within the body of an oral presentation.
- Develop appropriate conclusions for a presentation.
- Prepare for the question-and-answer period after an oral presentation.
- Prepare notes that will help you deliver an oral presentation.

12. Work with a group of students in your class (as assigned by your instructor) to prepare a 30-minute group presentation on a business-related topic that the group chooses. Each member of the group is responsible for an equal portion of the presentation, although the group can decide how to divide the workload. Submit the following to your instructor:

   a. Detailed presentation notes, showing the parts of the presentation to be covered by each member of the group.

   b. Group bibliography, listing the sources used in preparing the presentation.

   c. Group report or set of individual reports by all group members (your instructor will tell you which), showing how the work was divided, analyzing the problems that arose when working as a group, and explaining how your group worked the problems out.

◼ Identify the general and specific purposes of formal presentations.
◼ Select an appropriate organizational strategy for a presentation after analyzing your topic and purpose and predicting the audience's probable reaction to the message.
◼ List the seven ways to introduce oral presentations, and choose the appropriate one for any given presentation.

13. Select a speech from *Vital Speeches of Our Day*, which should be available at your school or local library. Write a memo to your instructor in which you discuss the following:
   a. Clarity of the general and specific purposes.
   b. Appropriateness of the organizational strategy.
   c. Effectiveness of the introduction.
   d. Effectiveness of the body (including the support techniques and visual aids).
   e. Effectiveness of the conclusion.

◼ Identify the general and specific purposes of formal presentations.
◼ Select an appropriate organizational strategy for a presentation after analyzing your topic and purpose and predicting the audience's probable reaction to the message.
◼ Develop major and supporting points within the body of an oral presentation.

14. Attend a speech or presentation on your campus or in your community. Analyze it using the following questions as a guide. Prepare a letter report with the answers for your instructor.
   a. What was the general purpose of the speech? What was the specific purpose?
   b. What was the first major point, and how was it supported? What was the second major point, and how was it supported? What other major points were made, and how were they supported?
   c. Did the speaker clearly distinguish between personal opinion and evidence from other sources?
   d. What is your overall evaluation of the speech and its organization?

◼ List the seven ways to introduce oral presentations, and choose the appropriate one for any given presentation.
◼ Develop appropriate conclusions for a presentation.

15. Choose a presentation topic from the list in Exercise 6. Write out an introduction and a conclusion that will build rapport with the audience, reinforce each other, and help you achieve your purpose in making the presentation.

◼ Prepare for the question-and-answer period after an oral presentation.

16. Choose a presentation topic from the list in exercise 11. Write out five questions the audience is likely to ask, and then give the answers. Be sure to use good you attitude in your responses.

# CHAPTER 15

# DELIVERING BUSINESS PRESENTATIONS

## OBJECTIVES

When you finish studying this chapter, you should be able to:

- List five techniques for practicing a presentation.
- Control your speech anxiety.
- Understand how your voice's tone, volume, and rate affect an audience.
- Understand how body language affects an audience.
- Make the best possible use of the location for a presentation.
- Use visual and audio aids effectively in presentations.
- Use presentation notes and cards effectively.
- Assume a dynamic and poised manner when giving a presentation.
- Evaluate your own presentations and those made by others.

## WHAT WOULD YOU DO IF...?

**GO, TEAM, GO!** Judith Rhodes is the manager of a small branch of a large advertising firm. Her branch has a good record in "pitching" its ideas to clients and has, in fact, designed some of the company's most successful advertising campaigns.

Almost a year ago, Merrill Gubberson was hired by the main office and assigned to Judith's branch. Merrill contributes many unique ideas and is an energetic, hard-working individual. Judith and her supervisor at the main office agree that it is time Merrill had some experience in giving presentations to clients. He will start by backing up Judith at presentations, gradually become a full-fledged copresenter, and make his own presentations only when he has developed some polish.

Judith expected Merrill to be excited about this step forward, but his response was muted. Probing for a reason, Judith discovered that Merrill has considerable anxiety about making presentations. He explained that in college he'd felt queasy and jittery whenever he had to make a presentation to the class, and he would always embarrass himself somehow. For instance, he once turned off the lights in the classroom before turning on the projector, leaving everyone sitting in the dark for what seemed an eternity. His classmates' snickers and sarcastic comments left him even more apprehensive about speaking than he had been before.

Judith hastened to reassure Merrill that he was not a born incompetent and could develop his presentation skills. She promised to help him, and pointed out that advancing in advertising would depend on his ability to make presentations. Although Merrill remained somewhat skeptical, he understood how important presentation skills are for anybody in business and appreciated Judith's offer.

How can Judith deliver on her promise? What sequence of responsibilities would allow Merrill to gradually become a solo presenter? What advice can she give that will help him become more self-confident and poised? As you read this chapter, look for ideas that would help Judith and Merrill accomplish their goals.

## PRACTICING YOUR PRESENTATION

Organizing a good presentation is important, of course, but you must also be able to deliver it well. Even the most interested audience could become bored if you stood like a board at the front of the room and delivered your presentation in a flat voice with a blank facial expression. On the other hand, although delivery style is no substitute for good content and organization, experienced presenters can get an audience's attention for what might otherwise be a boring topic. This chapter outlines delivery principles that can help you make more effective presentations.

As Chapter 14 noted, business presenters commonly use four delivery styles: extemporaneous, impromptu, memorized, and read. An extemporaneous style, which relies on presentation notes instead of a fully written text, is preferred in most situations because it is most natural. However, the extemporaneous style still requires careful preparation, in the form of careful note composition and diligent rehearsal. Each time you practice the presentation, it will change a little, and your notes will become more and more abbreviated.

### PRACTICE TECHNIQUES

List five techniques for practicing a presentation.

Usually, the amount of practice relates directly to the presentation's success. Your goal is to practice enough to feel confident, but not so much that you start sounding as if you've memorized a speech. There are many ways to practice, but one of the following techniques (or a combination) may work well for you:

Practice enough to feel that you have control over the material, but not so much that you know in advance every word you're going to say.

- *Walk-it, talk-it technique.* One of the most effective ways to work from your presentation notes is to "talk" your speech constantly as you move through your daily activities. Keep copies of your notes in your car, your office, your house, and anywhere else you spend time. Your family and co-workers will get used to your talking to yourself as you work. When you find yourself with free time, " talk" your presentation as though you are in front of an audience.

- *Mirror technique.* Some people like to practice in front of a mirror so they can assess their use of gestures, facial expressions, eye contact, and so on as they deliver the speech. One obvious drawback to this technique, however, is the lack of listener feedback.

- *Buddy technique.* Many people prefer to practice their presentation before a friend or co-worker who can provide feedback. It is best to select someone who will provide an honest assessment of your presentation, not simply shower you with praise. If you use this technique, ask your listener for specific information. For example, don't ask, "How was it?" Ask instead, "What can I do to improve the introduction? The ending? My nonverbal communication?"

- *Audio technique.* Many people use tape recorders to evaluate how their oral presentations sound. If you do this, don't be too harsh on yourself. Remember that most people don't like the way their voices sound on audiotape. Have someone else evaluate the sound of your voice; you should listen to the tape to evaluate the length of your presentation, transitions, and other presentation-related details.

- *Video technique.* One of the most effective practice techniques is to videotape the session. In this way, you are able to evaluate your presentation at your leisure. Each time you watch it, you can concentrate on a particular aspect for improvement—for example, transitions from one point to another or use of the lectern or other speaker aids. By making videotapes each time you practice, you are also able to see the improvement that occurs as you become more and more familiar with the topic.

## SPEECH ANXIETY

Control your speech anxiety.

> Speech anxiety is common, and it can be overcome with understanding and practice.

All of these practice methods will help you gain self-confidence and combat speech anxiety—the fear of standing in front of people and making a presentation. Surveys of people's fears usually show speech anxiety near the top of the list, along with fear of spiders, heights, and death. The physical results of such anxiety are a dry mouth, shaky hands, and "butterflies" in the stomach. These are the symptoms that made Merrill Gubberson (in the chapter-opening vignette) so reluctant to present new ideas to clients. It may help you to know that these are the effects of the body's own adrenalin, which can also be channeled into the "edge" that makes you alert to the audience's reactions and speeds up your ability to respond.

Here are some suggestions for getting your speech anxiety under control:

> Use breathing and exercise to rid yourself of nervous tension.

- As you practice, forget for a moment the content of what you are saying and concentrate on your breathing. Think of each breath as a way of expelling your nervous energy. When you are standing before an audience, beware of holding your breath. Take in some extra oxygen to feed your brain and dissipate your tension.

> Use pauses to your advantage—to gather your thoughts and focus the audience's attention.

- You can also release tension before you practice by doing a few stretching exercises. Although such exercises might not be practical as you stand up to give a formal presentation, you can tense and release your shoulder and neck muscles for a few seconds without anyone noticing.

- Don't let pauses bother you. Many presenters use fillers such as "uh," "and uh," "okay?," and "you know?" because they think they should be talking constantly. As you practice, be aware of these fillers and try to avoid them.

Pauses can be a plus—they give you time to gather your thoughts and decide what you are going to say next. They give the audience a chance to absorb what you have just said. In fact, you will seem more authoritative if you learn to pause at the right time in a way that controls the period of silence. Pauses are only noticeable to an audience when they obviously upset the speaker.

- Stand when you practice. Many people say that standing in front of the audience makes them feel self-conscious and vulnerable. Perhaps it's the herd instinct that makes them feel more comfortable in groups. However, the more you practice while standing alone, the more comfortable you will feel when you stand during the actual presentation.

## BUILDING RAPPORT WITH THE AUDIENCE

**Building rapport with the audience is a matter of showing your interest in them, not dazzling them.**

Not only people who have commanded center stage since childhood make good presenters. Many good presenters are the quieter, more thoughtful type who know how to build rapport and link their message to the audience's needs and interests. Moreover, good presenters learn how to get the audience's attention and gain their confidence through skillful use of voice quality, body language, the location of the presentation, visual and audio aids, presentation notes, and a dynamic and poised manner (all of which are discussed in the following sections). Planning and practice will help you acquire these skills and improve your ability to make presentations.

### VOICE QUALITY

Understand how your voice's tone, volume, and rate affect an audience.

**The quality of your voice depends on variations in its tone, volume, and rate.**

A key component of your delivery style is your voice, which conveys the verbal part of your message. The quality of your voice is usually judged by three factors: tone, volume, and rate. Have you ever listened to someone who droned on endlessly, spoke too quietly, or talked too fast? Chances are that you were distracted from the message by these voice qualities. You may have started daydreaming or, worse yet, become annoyed at the effort necessary to understand the presenter. On the other hand, if you analyzed why you liked a certain presentation, you would probably find that the speaker had a pleasant voice with an interesting way of varying its tone, volume, and rate to match the words.

Your goal as a presenter is to keep your voice relaxed, flexible, and natural sounding. You might find it helpful to keep liquid handy while you make a presentation, so you can take a drink of water now and then. The physical act of swallowing helps to relieve tension in the throat. You might also find the following suggestions useful:

**People who speak in a monotone, without any variation in pitch, bore audiences.**

- *Tone.* Tone can be thought of as the musical sound of your voice, the way it falls on other people's ears. In this culture, we like moderate variation in tone of voice. Some words or parts of a sentence are stressed with a higher pitch. Most of us can simply use our normal tone, the one we use when speaking to people with whom we are comfortable. Avoid speaking in a monotone, which means issuing all your words and sentences in the same unvaried key or pitch. Like the constant humming of a fan, a speech delivered in a monotone has a way of putting even the most eager audience to sleep.

- *Volume.* Obviously, your voice should be loud enough to be heard by all members of your audience. However, it should never sound abnormally loud, even to those people sitting in front. In addition, you should vary the volume to match the content of your presentation. When you want to stress a point or show excitement or anger, raise your volume slightly. However, you can also stress things by lowering your voice. If a point is to be considered with reverence, humility, or disappointment, or if you are pretending to tell a secret, lower your volume slightly. What is important is the change; any change in volume helps to focus the audience's attention on what comes next.

- *Rate.* Speak at your normal rate, as long as it is a pace that people can absorb. By this time in your life, you probably already know whether you speak too fast or too slow; our friends have a way of letting us know these things. Keep in mind, however, that nervousness often causes people to pick up the pace. If you speak too fast, your audience will not be able to understand your words, or they might not have enough time to think about each point you make. You may find that you finish the presentation in record time! To combat this common problem, try to pause between sentences and breathe. Such pauses will gain the audience's attention and build suspense for the important points that follow. You can also slow down when you are presenting hard-to-follow, complex information. Increase the speed when you present information or ideas that are easy to understand or with which the audience is already familiar.

If you feel that you need more help with your voice, check your library for books of voice exercises.

## BODY LANGUAGE

Understand how body language affects an audience.

It has often been said that your body speaks louder than your words. Imagine that Merrill Gubberson in the chapter-opening vignette is rehearsing his first advertising presentation. His audience is his boss, Judith Rhodes.

| | |
|---|---|
| His words | "I just want to say first how happy I am to be here presenting to you a proposal for a new ad campaign that will revolutionize the way dog food is marketed." |
| His actions | Eyes flitting to the ceiling and floor, no eye contact with his audience. Grim expression on his face. Hunched posture and motionless stance. Hands jammed into the pockets of his pants. |

*A verbal message can be contradicted by a nonverbal message.*

Merrill's actions make his anxiety obvious. Although Judith is sympathetic to Merrill's discomfort, his eventual audience, the clients, will interpret the discrepancy between his words and his body language as lack of confidence in his own ideas. To help Merrill seem more credible, Judith suggests that he work to improve his eye contact, facial expressions, posture, movement, gestures, and personal appearance, using some of the following techniques.

**EYE CONTACT.**    Eye contact is one of the most important factors in establishing your credibility to an audience. In the majority of American subcultures, people distrust others who do not look them in the eyes. However, there are American subcultures, as well as foreign cultures, in which direct eye contact between people of different classes is frowned on. Therefore, it is important to understand and practice the preferences of the cultural group to which you are delivering your presentation.

With a relatively small audience, you should look each person in the eye for at least a second or two. With a larger audience, however, you should not try to look directly at each individual. Instead, pick out at random individuals in all sections of the seating area. You will be far enough away so that several people around those individuals will feel you are looking at them as well. Don't develop a set pattern and repeat that pattern every time you look up from your notes.

*Good eye contact will help you build rapport, but it should seem natural.*

Beware of the following patterns. If you exhibit these, your audience will focus on the abnormal behavior instead of you and the content of your presentation.

- *Scared rabbit.* Eyes moving abnormally fast, flitting from one person to the next, seeming to jerk all over the room at once. This makes the audience nervous and causes them to watch your eyes rather than listen.

- *Wallflower.* Eyes return constantly to the wall in the back of the room. This makes the audience glance back to see what you're looking at.

- *First grader.* Eyes remain on the notes most of the time. This bores the audience.

- *Love match.* Eyes choose and rest on only two or three people in the audience. This makes the rest of the audience feel left out and causes extreme discomfort for the chosen few.

*As a rule, spend at least half of your presentation time making eye contact with your audience.*

A good rule of thumb is to maintain eye contact with your audience at least 50 percent of the time it takes to give your oral presentation. If you have practiced your presentation as recommended in this chapter, you will not have to look down at your notes excessively. Glancing down at your notes occasionally to prompt your next thought and darting looks toward visuals are the only times you should not be looking into the eyes of the individuals in your audience.

*Most facial expressions, except for your smile, are difficult to control.*

**FACIAL EXPRESSIONS.**    Many subtle changes in your face can convey a great deal of information about the feelings behind your words. The muscles that control your eyebrows, nose, and mouth are particularly expressive. With training and practice, you can develop control over most of these muscles. For the most part, however, they will automatically signal your emotions.

One element of your facial expressions you can control is your smile. A smile helps the audience like you even when they are prepared to dislike your topic. The value of speaking to an audience that likes you is readily apparent; they listen more attentively, and they react more positively to your ideas. However, facial expressions should match the seriousness of the occasion. If you are delivering a eulogy at a funeral, a smile might seem inappropriate unless it is used when fondly relating an occasion in the deceased's past. In most cases, however, you should smile at your audience frequently, particularly when you first greet them.

**POSTURE, MOVEMENT, AND GESTURES.**  The face and eyes are not the only body parts that help convey meaning. The rest of your body also helps you gain the audience's attention, understanding, and goodwill.

To convey competence and involvement, stand up straight.

Your posture—the way you stand—is often the first thing the audience notices about you. A slouching posture makes you appear unsure of yourself or uninterested in your task. To gain credibility, stand erect and walk confidently to the front of the room or the lectern. As you turn to face the audience, plant your feet firmly and survey it with your eyes. Doing so helps establish your right to be listened to.

Have you ever wondered why we usually stand when giving a speech, even to small groups? For a large audience, standing allows everyone to see the speaker. In addition, there is a psychological advantage to height; it helps to establish your authority, and commands the audience's attention.

Feel free to use the space around you to move naturally.

Movement also commands attention and helps you build rapport with the audience. Do not stand rigidly in one place for your entire presentation if it can be avoided. Many beginning speakers are apprehensive about getting too far away from their notes, but you don't have to move far to achieve your goals. A few steps forward, backward, and to the side are as far as you have to go to accomplish a relaxed style of movement. In fact, too much movement—or a repetitive pattern of movement, such as rocking or pacing—is distracting. Many speakers even carry their notes with them to avoid being anchored to a lectern.

Let yourself gesture as you would when talking with someone you know.

Gestures should also be natural and appropriate for the audience and occasion. Avoid using wild or contrived hand and arm gestures to emphasize major points, like a parody of a singer trying to act out the words of a song. In general, you should simply free yourself to gesture in your normal, everyday style. Think about the way you use your hands to emphasize your points when you are engaged in casual conversation with friends and family. Certain gestures are always appropriate. Nod your head slightly and use minor hand and arm gestures to emphasize major points. These gestures help your audience understand which parts of your presentation are important. (Gestures and their meanings are covered more thoroughly in Chapter 3.)

Avoid postures, movements, and gestures that distract the audience.

To avoid distracting the audience from your words, do not overuse the postures, movements, and gestures illustrated in Exhibit 15.1. Take a moment to read the list. These patterns of body language detract from the content of your message only when they are overdone. There is nothing wrong with occasionally putting your hands in your pockets, leaning on the edge of the desk, or clasping your arms in front of you. The audience only focuses on them when they are repeated too often.

**PERSONAL APPEARANCE.**  One of the strongest messages received by your audience is imparted by your personal appearance—your clothing, accessories, and grooming. People automatically make assumptions about your status and credibility based on your appearance. A conservative business suit, for example, usually signals to business audiences competence and stability. A more fashionable, expensive designer suit might help to establish your image as a successful, up-to-date, and fast-rising individual.

**EXHIBIT 15.1**

**Nonverbal Techniques to Avoid**

**Dying Swan.** Leans heavily on the lectern or stands with an air of exhaustion.

**Spineless Wonder.** Clutches the stand as though he or she would melt to the floor without it.

**Trained Dog.** Remains seated on the edge of the desk or table.

**Caged Tiger.** Paces back and forth in front of the audience.

**Pocket Puppeteer.** Leaves hands in pockets too long. Jingles the change in his or her pockets.

**Chained Elephant.** Steps from one foot to another in what seems to be a timed pattern.

**Fig Leaf.** Stands the entire time with hands clasped strategically in front of the lower body.

**Defensive Player.** Folds the arms in front of the body to block out the audience.

**Stern Father.** Waggles an index finger at the audience as if to lecture them.

**Wiggler.** Wiggles one foot or leg constantly.

**Fiddler.** Toys with an object (hair, jewelry, or pen) constantly.

However, some audiences might feel threatened by someone in a suit. For them, casual clothing more in keeping with the way they dress would be better. It might make you seem more like one of the audience; and, for certain types of emotional appeals, it is necessary to establish an emotional bond with the audience. The similarity in dress helps to show the audience you have a right to speak to them about a topic because it affects you in the same way it affects them. An example is the union negotiator who must explain a change in the medical insurance plan to a roomful of union members. Although the negotiator may have worn a suit to meetings with the company's executives, when speaking to union members she might dress more casually in a dress, skirt, or even slacks.

**Be clean and well groomed, and dress the part the audience expects you to play.**

No matter who makes up the audience, you should be clean and well groomed. Beyond that, thoughtful study of your audience should reveal to you what they will expect in terms of clothing and personal appearance.

### LOCATION

Make the best possible use of the location for a presentation.

If you have an opportunity to select a site for your oral presentation, be sure to choose one that is appropriate for the occasion. The room should be large enough to comfortably accommodate the number of people who will attend; it should have adequate lighting and temperature controls; and it should have strategically placed hookups for microphones, projectors, computers, and any other electrical devices you may plan to use. Try to avoid a location with built-in distractions, such as windows looking out on an interesting scene or flimsy walls through which someone else's presentation can be heard.

**Prepare to take advantage of the location of your presentation—or to overcome its disadvantages.**

If you are not able to choose where your presentation will be given, try to look over the facilities ahead of time. You need answers to a number of questions: What provisions have been made for a place to hold your notes—a table, a lectern, a podium? (A lectern is the stand that rests on a table; a podium is the stand that rests on the floor.) Where, in relation to you, will your audience be? How far away from you will they be? Will you be raised above them on a stage or dais or be at their level? How many seats are there, and are they arranged in a wide but shallow pattern or in a narrow but deep pattern? If the room is large, is a microphone provided? If so, how does it turn on and off, and how do you adjust the volume? Will you be able to carry it around the room with you, or is it fixed in place? What types of boards, screens, easels, and so on are provided for displaying visual aids? Should you bring your own audiovisual equipment? If it will be supplied to you, how does it operate? If you need to set up anything in advance, is the room available? Can the lights be turned off and on conveniently when you are using audiovisual aids?

**Move out of "the presenter's space" and into "the audience's space" to break down barriers and build rapport.**

During your presentation, don't be afraid to use the space to your advantage. Avoid standing behind a lectern or a table—or at least to move away from it as much as you can. Anything that comes between you and your audience can become a barrier to effective communication. Move into the audience occasionally instead of remaining in front of them the entire time. This helps keep the audience alert, and it also helps them think of you as being a part of their group—more accessible, more open, and, therefore, more worthy of their trust.

### VISUAL AND AUDIO AIDS

Use visual and audio aids effectively in presentations.

One of the greatest advantages of visual and audio aids is the way they work to involve the audience with your topic, making your points easier to understand and, therefore, more memorable. However, even the most skillfully prepared visual and audio aids will be ineffective unless they are also presented with skill.

When choosing a medium for presenting visual aids to the audience, consider the level of sophistication they expect, your budget, and the need for special equipment.

**DELIVERY MEDIA.** The types of visual aids described in Chapter 10—tables, charts, graphs, and the like—can be presented in many ways. These are the most common delivery media:

- *Handouts.* These visual aids are on pieces of paper and are distributed to the audience. Visual aids delivered via handouts are essentially like the visual aids you would find in reports. They are especially useful when you need to give the audience a great deal of data or some specific data, or when you want them to be able to have the data for future use.

- *Computerized or multimedia presentations.* At the opposite end of the spectrum (in terms of sophistication) is using a computer to present visual and audio aids. Usually, a series of computer screen images is prepared in advance, and a special projector is used to enlarge the images as you call them up on your computer screen. The software for such presentations has become very sophisticated, allowing you to blend pictures and sounds. For example, a professional-looking chart of oil production figures might gradually give way to a video image of an oil rig in operation, with the whole visual being combined with music. The advantages of such a system are that you can prepare the entire program in advance, set it in motion easily from a computer that you control, and stop the program or manipulate it (perhaps by entering new data) whenever you please. Consider, however, the brightness of the projector—many multimedia presentations need darkened rooms.

- *Films, slides, and videos.* These media have excellent clarity but may be difficult to use. Films and videos are expensive to produce, require special equipment, must be viewed in a darkened room, and are somewhat difficult to stop if you need to interject comments. Slides also need special equipment and a darkened room. However, slides are less expensive than films or videos to produce, they can be updated easily by inserting new slides, and they are easy to use if the slides are set up to automatically advance.

- *Transparencies.* Transparencies shown on overhead projectors are easy to use and easy to prepare; and, in most cases, they can be seen without darkening the room. Transparencies can be made by photocopying onto a piece of film an image that you produce first on paper. At most copy shops, black and white transparencies cost approximately $1; color transparencies vary from about $2 to $5. Although transparencies require extra equipment (the overhead projector and a screen), the equipment is usually easy to operate and is more portable than most film and computer equipment. Transparencies are also fast and easy to produce, but often lack sophistication. However, desktop publishing and presentation software programs have helped to improve the appearance of transparencies. Exhibit 15.2 shows an example of an interesting transparency prepared with the software program PowerPoint. Such programs contain a variety of backgrounds, colors, typefaces, artwork, and borders you can choose from to liven up your transparencies.

- *Flipcharts.* Flipcharts are large pads of paper bound at the top. You draw each visual aid on a piece of paper ahead of time, and at the appropriate time during your presentation, you flip the page to reveal your graphic. You can also sketch diagrams or list ideas on flipchart pages as you make the presentation. Flipcharts require no high-tech equipment (only an easel or wall clips) and are handy if you do not have very many. However, turning

EXHIBIT 15.2  Computer-Prepared Visual Aid

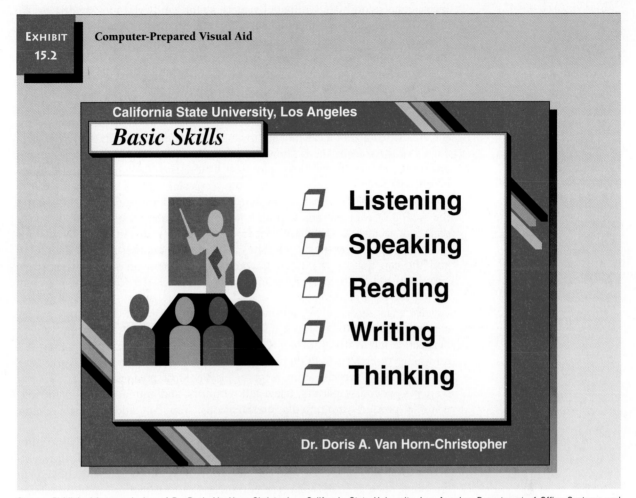

Source: Published by permission of Dr. Doris VanHorn-Christopher, California State University, Los Angeles, Department of Office Systems and Business Education.

the large pages is sometimes awkward. In addition, the appearance of the graphics is limited to the drawing skill of the presenter.

- *Boards.* Chalkboards and whiteboards may also be used to sketch graphic messages. Although boards are available in many locations, they allow very little advance preparation and, like flipcharts, depend on the drawing skill of the presenter. In addition, board use should be limited to presenting short, quickly sketched or written material, because eye contact is lost while a presenter is drawing on the board. They should be used only when informality is acceptable.

## MULTIMEDIA TECHNOLOGY

Multimedia presentations are rapidly becoming the standard by which business presentations are judged. Microcomputers and even laptop computers using multimedia software can be used to prepare unique presentations that incorporate smoothly coordinated visuals, sound, and even moving images. An array of additional equipment allows the production of even more sophisticated presentations. The frequently changing images get and hold the attention of an audience more than most canned presentations.

A multimedia presentation might work something like this: As your potential client watches a sales presentation on a big computer screen on the wall, she is entertained by kaleidoscopic images. The client hears commentary about the quality of the automobiles you are selling while viewing in the center of the screen a videotape of a car moving through an assembly line. In the upper right corner of the screen, she is shown a quick succession of photos of the models and colors of cars available for purchase. Before the client has a chance to get bored, she sees a cartoon of a person staggering out of a crashed auto (a competitor's model) with stars around his head; this animated sequence begins the section of your presentation on how your car's safety features can lessen the danger of accidents. The client can choose what she wants to watch by pushing a button or touching the screen. She can change to another topic at any point, and she can quit at any time. If you have a camera on site, you can even surprise the client by projecting an image of her onto the screen at some point during the presentation.

The main drawback to multimedia presentations is that they require special equipment and software. At a minimum, you will need a fast computer with between 2 and 4 MB of RAM and a 30-160 MB hard disk, memory, a mouse, a mid-range or better CD-ROM drive, an audio sound board, a music synthesizer, and a digitized speech audio recorder/player. Most businesses also use color scanners, videodisk players, television monitors, and animation and paint software to produce multimedia presentations. You can add a touch screen, camcorder/VCR, motion cards, and audio cards.

Multimedia presentations are attractive because of their cost, flexibility, and quick production times. They are particularly useful not only for presenting information to clients but also for providing information in convenient locations, such as kiosks near the entrances of government or medical offices. They are also good for training employees. For example, factory workers who need more information about a new procedure can walk over to a computer, punch a button and view the procedure as it is performed on the screen, complete with voice annotations. If the worker desires more information, sketches of the product or the part can be shown to illustrate why a procedure is performed as recommended. The presentations can be updated frequently and, when compared to other visual technology, easily. All it takes is someone trained in computers who is interested enough to learn a little about animation, sound, and film.

The first rule of displaying visual and audio aids is to make sure the audience can see and hear the information.

**DELIVERY TECHNIQUES.**   Regardless of the medium you are using to present visual and audio aids, you should make sure the audience can see and hear everything clearly. With written material, be concise so that the information can be absorbed quickly. Use lettering large enough to be read from the back of the room. Stand to the side of your visuals and use a pointer or your hand to direct the audience's attention to appropriate areas. Once you have made your points, turn off the equipment, remove the visual from sight, or walk away from the visual to regain your audience's attention. Otherwise, they will tend to remain focused on the visual rather than on you.

Put each visual and audio aid in context.

For each visual and audio aid, prepare your audience for what they are about to see or hear. Tell the audience why you are presenting the information to them—why it will be useful to them and how it fits into the rest of your presentation—and what they should look for. It is usually best to paraphrase the information or to point out the most important passages rather than reading the material to your audience word for word. Afterward, debrief the audience by summarizing the key points or questioning them about what they learned. For example, when giving a speech to persuade environmentally conscious people to invest their funds in your company, you might use a 10-minute film to emphasize the message. Tell your audience the film will show the unusual nature of your company's approach to its environmental responsibilities. Tell them they will be shown some unique programs that might change their attitudes about a corporation's ability to care about the world they live in. When the film is over, summarize the conclusions you wanted the audience to reach. Knowing the importance of audience involvement, you might decide to ask your listeners to make the conclusions verbally. Audience involvement, however, requires more time and must be considered during the planning stage of the presentation.

When using visual and audio aids, prepare for the worst.

Make sure all the equipment you need is in place and actually works before you give your presentation. Because equipment tends to act up whenever you need it most, always take backups with you—in a different medium, if need be. Keep extra bulbs handy for projectors. When you prepare for and rehearse your speech, plan what you will do if all your visuals are destroyed or cannot be used. One advertising executive attributes her success to one such disastrous occurrence. None of the four 3′×6′ full-color advertising layouts she wanted to show arrived at the airport with her. Afraid that canceling the meeting would offend the potential clients, she asked them to close their eyes and envision their products as depicted on the advertising layouts. Fortunately, her descriptive verbal skills and their imaginations saved what could have been a disaster. They liked what they heard and agreed to wait for the layouts to arrive before making a decision.

Rehearse the use of visual aids so they are an enhancement, not a distraction.

If you are using any kind of equipment, rehearse its use so the transition from your spoken words to the visual and audio aids is smooth. Imagine the embarrassment of a new corporate president who had interwoven his first-day speech to the workers with numerous short segments of inspirational music intended to lighten the mood. Because he and the person in charge of turning on the music had not rehearsed adequately, the president had to point to his helper each time he was ready for a new musical interlude, and the audience was forced to wait a few uncomfortable seconds each time before the music began. Adequate practice would have enabled the helper to turn on the tape after hearing certain predetermined cues in the speaker's presentation. The music would have had the desired effect if there had been no time lag before it was heard.

Exhibit 15.3 outlines other principles to consider when using audio and visual aids. Although they present some pitfalls, visual and audio aids can add power to your spoken message, when used properly.

## PRESENTATION NOTES

Use presentation notes and cards effectively.

Generally, you should not try to memorize an entire presentation unless you have a great deal of speaking experience or your presentation is very short (one or two minutes in length). Instead, you should work from presentation notes.

**EXHIBIT 15.3**    **Tips for Using Audio and Visual Aids**

| Audio and Visual Aids | Principles for Use |
|---|---|
| <br>Transparency | Lay transparency on deck of overhead projector so you can read it as you face audience. For visibility, make sure no other lights shine directly on screen. Use pointer or finger to draw attention to parts of transparency as you discuss them. Turn off projector when finished, unless you are immediately showing another transparency. Choose the brightest projector you can afford. |
| <br>Films, slides, videotapes, and CD-ROM discs | Darken room. Prepare automatic advance cues for slides used with prerecorded sound. If working with assistant, practice beforehand. |
| <br>Handouts | Distribute handouts before your presentation begins or after it is over to avoid losing audience's attention. Paraphrase most important information; do not read entire handout. |
| <br>Chalkboards and whiteboards | Keep writing and sketches to a minimum. As you write on board, with your back to audience, look back and forth to audience as you talk. Erase board as soon as discussion of points on board is finished. |

| Audio and Visual Aids | Principles for Use |
|---|---|
| <br>Flip charts | Use blank pages between visuals so audience can focus on you, not previous visual. |
| <br>Music | Select music that sets mood and appeals to audience's tastes. Control volume and length to meet audience's expectations. |
| <br>Product samples | Distribute samples before or after presentation so they do not distract audience. |
| <br>Scale models | Give audience close-up view of model before or after presentation to avoid loss of their attention. |
| <br>Computer multimedia presentations | Rehearse thoroughly. Arrive early to set up equipment. If possible, run through entire presentation immediately before presenting to an audience. Keep a technical specialist on hand to assist with equipment and software malfunctions. |

Referring infrequently to a carefully planned outline will help to ensure that you maintain rapport with the audience while presenting a logical message and making all your major points clear.

Some people prefer to have all their notes on one neatly typed page, such as that illustrated in Chapter 14. Placing such notes on a lectern or podium would make it easy for you to glance down at your notes to guide your presentation. It is best not to hold paper notes in your hands while you speak if you are somewhat nervous. Empty shaking hands often go unnoticed; however, when shaking hands are holding a sheet of paper, the paper makes the shaking more visible.

> Presentation notes may be written on pieces of paper or on notecards.

The use of notecards is also acceptable. If held in the hand, cards should be small, no larger than 3 x 5 inches; large notecards are too noticeable to an audience. Keep the number of cards you hold to a minimum to avoid having the audience anticipate the end of your speech by mentally tabulating how many cards are left in your hand.

> It is more distracting to apologize for losing your place than to pause briefly and return to your notes.

For most presentations, you should try to move away from the lectern or podium so it does not become a barrier between you and your audience. However, moving to the side means you will not be able to glance down quickly at your notes if you forget the next point you planned to make. If this happens, think nothing of it. Don't introduce a negative tone by apologizing to your audience. Just walk back to your notes, look at your outline, and proceed to the next point. No one expects any speaker to fill up every second with sound. Natural-sounding presentations include pauses.

> Every member of a presentation team should have a full copy of the notes.

If you are giving a team presentation, it is important for each member of the team to have the notes for the entire presentation. Team members can then prompt a speaker who forgets the next point he or she planned to make.

## DYNAMISM AND POISE

Assume a dynamic and poised manner when giving a presentation.
It is often difficult to define just what separates a good presenter from a mediocre one. Two presenters working from the same material and observing all the same rules of good presentations may still elicit very different responses from the audience. Why? The answer is often one presenter's manner. A presenter who seems both dynamic and poised can win the audience's attention and confidence.

> A dynamic, poised manner helps a presenter keep audience members' attention and win their trust.

These qualities are tough to pin down, because they are not so much techniques as reflections of the presenter's attitude. **Dynamism,** for instance, is an aura of energy and enthusiasm. It may appear in the freedom with which a presenter moves and the variability of his or her voice. You can, of course, practice these techniques, but your delivery technique is likely to appear somewhat mechanical if you don't also feel a real enthusiasm for your topic and a real desire to relate it to the audience's needs. The payoff for a dynamic delivery style is an audience that stays tuned in to your presentation and, in the end, responds to your ideas.

> A dynamic speaker demonstrates his or her enthusiasm for the topic and interest in the audience.

> A poised speaker demonstrates self-confidence.

**Poise,** which is an easy, self-assured manner, is also difficult to project if you don't have the right attitude. You can perhaps conceal your nervousness by using some of the techniques presented in this chapter, but your best bet is to thoroughly prepare for your presentation. If you know your topic, have planned effectively, and have practiced thoroughly, you should feel confident about your presentation.

You should also learn how to throw off the negative thoughts that wreck self-confidence. The most dangerous time is the few hours or minutes just before the presentation. Close your eyes and imagine yourself delivering the talk calmly and confidently. Refuse to think of failure or all the embarrassing things that might happen. As you gain experience, you will find that poise comes more naturally. As an incentive, remember that poise can help your audience believe in you and what you have to say.

## EVALUATING YOUR PRESENTATION

Evaluate your own presentations and those made by others.

**Use the audience's feedback and your own powers of analysis to evaluate your presentations.**

As with written communication, each oral presentation should be evaluated for its effectiveness in achieving its intended objectives. If you make it a practice to evaluate objectively all your presentations, you will find that your speaking ability improves.

Feedback from the audience is one way to evaluate a presentation. Audiences provide two kinds of feedback: verbal and nonverbal. Verbal feedback is given during the question-and-answer period at the end of the talk. An audience interested in and enthusiastic about your talk will ask questions if adequate time has been set aside. You should be able to tell from their questions if the audience's needs were met.

**Observe the audience members carefully for their verbal and nonverbal feedback.**

Audiences usually provide more nonverbal feedback than they do verbal. When people agree with you, they nod their heads up and down. When they're interested in what you are saying, they lean forward in their seats. If their eyes glaze over or they frequently look away, your audience is either bored or uncomfortable with what you are saying. If they cock their heads to one side, they're either having trouble hearing you, or they're confused. As you go through your presentation, assess the nonverbal feedback and make changes as necessary to keep the audience's attention and clarify information. Try to take note, for later analysis, of what in your presentation causes the most trouble. If your talk is part of a team presentation, when team members are not speaking they can watch for the audience's reaction.

**Each presentation should be followed by an evaluation session that specifies the things you did well and those you should work to improve.**

Following each presentation, make it a practice to set aside a few quiet moments to go back over the speech and consider the audience's reactions as well as your own feelings about your delivery. One way to get a more accurate evaluation is to videotape your presentation. You can also use the checklist in Exhibit 15.4. If you know someone who will be completely honest with you, ask him or her to also complete a checklist. If your presentation was part of a group effort, other group members should be involved in the evaluation process. Wherever anyone indicates a need for improvement, determine the specific things you can do to improve. For example, if you check "Improvement Needed" for the first question on the checklist, write down how you can better show your audience that the information you are going to provide will be useful to them.

An honest, in-depth analysis of each presentation you make will enable you to focus on the specific items you need to improve, and continue the techniques that are working. The result will be a marked improvement in your ability to make effective presentations.

| EXHIBIT 15.4 | **Evaluation Checklist for Oral Presentations** | | | |
|---|---|---|---|---|
| | | ■ Yes | ■ Not Sure | ■ Improvement Needed |

### ■ Introduction

| | Yes | Not Sure | Improvement Needed |
|---|---|---|---|
| Did it get the attention of the audience by appealing to their needs or interests? | ___ | ___ | ___ |
| Was it interesting? | ___ | ___ | ___ |
| Was it appropriate for the topic? | ___ | ___ | ___ |
| Was it an appropriate length? | ___ | ___ | ___ |
| Was it delivered forcefully and confidently? | ___ | ___ | ___ |
| Was its purpose clear? | ___ | ___ | ___ |
| Was there a smooth transition to the body of the speech? | ___ | ___ | ___ |

### ■ Body

| | Yes | Not Sure | Improvement Needed |
|---|---|---|---|
| Did it hold the attention of the audience by appealing to their needs? | ___ | ___ | ___ |
| Was it an appropriate length? | ___ | ___ | ___ |
| Were points made clearly? | ___ | ___ | ___ |
| Was it clear that the speaker knows his or her topic? | ___ | ___ | ___ |
| Were the conclusions justified? | ___ | ___ | ___ |
| Were there smooth transitions from one point to another? | ___ | ___ | ___ |
| Was there a smooth transition to the conclusion? | ___ | ___ | ___ |

### ■ Conclusion

| | Yes | Not Sure | Improvement Needed |
|---|---|---|---|
| Did it appeal to the audience's needs? | ___ | ___ | ___ |
| Was it an appropriate length? | ___ | ___ | ___ |
| Was it delivered forcefully and confidently? | ___ | ___ | ___ |
| Did it summarize adequately? | ___ | ___ | ___ |
| Was it tied to the introductory statements? | ___ | ___ | ___ |

### ■ Question-and-Answer Period

| | Yes | Not Sure | Improvement Needed |
|---|---|---|---|
| Was it clear that the speaker was eager for questions? | ___ | ___ | ___ |
| Was adequate time allowed for questions? | ___ | ___ | ___ |
| Were difficult questions, if any, handled skillfully and patiently? | ___ | ___ | ___ |
| Was the speaker friendly? | ___ | ___ | ___ |
| Did the speaker demonstrate confidence? | ___ | ___ | ___ |
| Did the speaker demonstrate knowledge of the topic? | ___ | ___ | ___ |

### ■ Organization and Practice

| | Yes | Not Sure | Improvement Needed |
|---|---|---|---|
| Was the presentation well organized? | ___ | ___ | ___ |
| Was it evident that the speaker had practiced adequately beforehand? | ___ | ___ | ___ |

### ■ Voice

| | Yes | Not Sure | Improvement Needed |
|---|---|---|---|
| Was the tone appropriate? | ___ | ___ | ___ |
| Was the volume appropriate? | ___ | ___ | ___ |
| Was the rate of speech appropriate? | ___ | ___ | ___ |
| Was each syllable enunciated clearly and distinctly? | ___ | ___ | ___ |

| EXHIBIT 15.4 | Continued | ■ Yes | ■ Not Sure | ■ Improvement Needed |
|---|---|---|---|---|

**■ Audio and Visual Aids***

| | | | |
|---|---|---|---|
| Was the quality appropriate? | ___ | ___ | ___ |
| Were aids used skillfully? | ___ | ___ | ___ |
| Was the number of aids appropriate? | ___ | ___ | ___ |
| Did the aids help the presentation? | ___ | ___ | ___ |

**■ Notes and Cards**

| | | | |
|---|---|---|---|
| Did the speaker avoid reading, except when appropriate? | ___ | ___ | ___ |
| Did the speaker's notes seem to provide the guidance that he or she needed? | ___ | ___ | ___ |
| Were notes and cards used in such a way as to be inconspicuous? | ___ | ___ | ___ |

**■ Body Language**

| | | | |
|---|---|---|---|
| Was eye contact appropriate? | ___ | ___ | ___ |
| Was the speaker's way of moving appropriate and natural? | ___ | ___ | ___ |
| Were the speaker's gestures appropriate and natural? | ___ | ___ | ___ |
| Did the speaker use body language to emphasize his or her points? | ___ | ___ | ___ |
| Was the speaker's posture appropriate? | ___ | ___ | ___ |
| Did the speaker seem poised and confident? | ___ | ___ | ___ |
| Were the speaker's facial expressions appropriate? | ___ | ___ | ___ |
| Did the speaker's overall appearance and dress help the presentation? | ___ | ___ | ___ |

*Audio and visual aids are not an essential component of every oral presentation. Evaluate this area if audio and visual aids were used. If no aids were used and you believe they would have added to the presentation, check "Improvement Needed" for each question.

## DISCUSSION QUESTIONS

◆ List five techniques for practicing a presentation.

1. What are the five techniques for practicing a presentation? Which of the five do you think will work best for you? Why?

◆ Control your speech anxiety.

2. How does focusing on breathing and doing stretching exercises relieve speech anxiety?

◆ Understand how your voice's tone, volume, and rate affect an audience.

3. What is a monotone, and why is it not recommended for presentations?

◆ Understand how body language affects an audience.

4. What is the minimum amount of time for which you should maintain eye contact with your audience?

◆ Understand how body language affects an audience.

5. Why is it not advisable to use repetitive gestures?

■ Make the best possible use of the location for a presentation.

6. Why is it not advisable to remain standing behind a lectern or table for the majority of a presentation?

■ Use visual and audio aids effectively in presentations.

7. List one disadvantage of each of the following delivery media for visual aids: films, slides, transparencies, flipcharts, boards, and multimedia computer presentations.

■ Use visual and audio aids effectively in presentations.

8. Name five principles for using visual and audio aids effectively.

■ Use presentation notes and cards effectively.

9. When using presentation notes, what should you do if you have moved away from the lectern and don't remember what comes next?

■ Assume a dynamic and poised manner when giving a presentation.

10. How can you develop the dynamism and poise necessary to make effective presentations?

■ Evaluate your own presentations and those made by others.

11. List the types of positive nonverbal feedback an audience might give a speaker.

■ Evaluate your own presentations and those made by others.

12. How should a team of three speakers go about evaluating the results of their presentation?

## APPLICATION EXERCISES

■ List five techniques for practicing a presentation.

1. Working with the presentation notes you prepared for one of the application exercises in Chapter 14 (exercises 3, 8, 9, 10, or 11), experiment with one of the five practice techniques described in this chapter. Write a two- to three-page memo report to your instructor that describes in detail how you conducted this practice (e.g., where did you practice, how much time did you devote overall, how many times did you repeat the rehearsal, and who or what helped you?). Include an analysis of this method's suitability for future practice. Would you use this method again, or would you try something else? What, specifically, were the difficulties you encountered? What further suggestions could you make to people who might want to try this method?

■ Control your speech anxiety.
■ Use presentation notes and cards effectively.

2. In the library, do some research on adrenaline and the physiological aspects of anxiety. Prepare a five-minute presentation for the class on what anxiety

is and how it can be dissipated. This is a very brief presentation, so be sure to limit your scope. Avoid repeating the information presented in this chapter.

◼ Understand how your voice's tone, volume, and rate affect an audience.

3. Check out a book of voice exercises from your local or school library. In a memo report to your teacher, explain two exercises that would help presenters improve the tone, volume, or rate of their speaking. Be prepared to demonstrate these voice exercises to your class if so directed by your instructor.

◼ Understand how body language affects an audience.
◼ Evaluate your own presentations and those made by others.

4. Attend a presentation on campus or in your community, and observe carefully the speaker's body language. Write a memo report to your instructor giving your overall impressions of the presenter's dynamism, poise, and rapport with the audience. Then specify the things the presenter did to contribute to those impressions. The last section of your report should be a list of suggestions that you and your classmates could follow to make more effective presentations.

◼ Make the best possible use of the location for a presentation.

5. Prepare a checklist you and other presenters could use to ensure that a presentation's location is adequate.

◼ Use visual and audio aids effectively in presentations.
◼ Evaluate your own presentations and those made by others.

6. In a memo report to your instructor, evaluate your classmates' quality and use of audio and visual aids as they give presentations. Give specific examples of effective and ineffective use of audio and visual aids.

◼ Use presentation notes and cards effectively.

7. Transfer the presentation notes you prepared for one of the application exercises in Chapter 14 (exercise 3, 8, 9, 10, or 11) to notecards. Submit the cards to your instructor, along with a brief memo explaining how they differ from the original notes.

◼ Evaluate your own presentations and those made by others.

8. As your class members give presentations, complete an evaluation checklist (Exhibit 15.4) for each of them. Be honest, so your classmates can improve their delivery skills.

◼ Evaluate your own presentations and those made by others.

9. As your classmates make presentations, take notes about the techniques they use to appeal to your needs or those of other audience members. Write a memo report to your instructor listing specific instances of good you attitude. Be sure to identify the presenter in each instance. Your instructor will inform you of the number of presenters you are responsible for evaluating.

◾ Evaluate your own presentations and those made by others.

10. Attend a presentation in your community or at your school. Complete an evaluation checklist for the individual who gave the presentation, and turn it in with a letter report to your teacher. (The letter report should spell out how the individual could have improved the presentation.)

◾ List five techniques for practicing a presentation.
◾ Control your speech anxiety.
◾ Understand how your voice's tone, volume, and rate affect an audience.
◾ Understand how body language affects an audience.
◾ Make the best possible use of the location for a presentation.
◾ Use visual and audio aids effectively in presentations.
◾ Use presentation notes and cards effectively.
◾ Assume a dynamic and poised manner when giving a presentation.
◾ Evaluate your own presentations and those made by others.

11. Give an individual presentation to your class; the length of the presentation and the topic will be determined by your instructor. (Many of the topics suggested in the application exercises for Chapter 14 would be of interest to your classmates.) On the class day after your presentation, submit to your instructor an evaluation checklist evaluating the effectiveness of your presentation. In a memo report to your instructor, give specific information about how the presentation could have been improved.

◾ List five techniques for practicing a presentation.
◾ Control your speech anxiety.
◾ Understand how your voice's tone, volume, and rate affect an audience.
◾ Understand how body language affects an audience.
◾ Make the best possible use of the location for a presentation.
◾ Use visual and audio aids effectively in presentations.
◾ Use presentation notes and cards effectively.
◾ Assume a dynamic and poised manner when giving a presentation.
◾ Evaluate your own presentations and those made by others.

12. Give a team presentation to your class. Your instructor will provide more information about the group's composition, the length of the presentation, and the topic. (The topics suggested in the application exercises in Chapter 14 can be used for this assignment.) On the class day after your presentation, submit to your instructor evaluation checklists for yourself and each of your team members. In a letter report to your instructor, give specific suggestions for improving the team presentation.

# EMPLOYMENT COMMUNICATION

# CHAPTER 16

# RESEARCHING JOBS AND WRITING RESUMES AND APPLICATION LETTERS

## OBJECTIVES

When you finish studying this chapter, you should be able to do the following:

- Look for job opportunities by checking all possible sources.
- Fill out application forms so that a potential employer has all the necessary information about your background and skills.
- Highlight in a resume the most attractive information about your education.
- Explain in a resume your work experience so that your achievements and skills are emphasized.
- Present five or more acceptable references to potential employers.
- Write a resume with optional information that will appeal to potential employers.
- Write a resume that does not include information that is no longer required or allowed.
- Use a resume format that will draw attention to your most desirable features and will make important information accessible to potential employers.
- Apply the message formulation process to application letters.
- Write an ethical application letter.
- Understand the needs of people who read application letters.
- Collect information about the company to which you are applying for a job.
- Know what type of strategy to use for an application letter.
- Evaluate an application letter before sending it.

## WHAT WOULD YOU DO IF...?

**DYNAMIC DUO.**    Kevin MacGilvray is not the typical college student. He's a little bit older, for one thing. For another, he has dual interests that he wants to pursue when he graduates in a couple of months.

Kevin has always struggled to reconcile his competing interests. He went to college right after high school, but left after a year and a half because he didn't feel ready to commit to a major. Instead, he got a job in an office-supply warehouse during the week and played synthesizer in a band on weekends. The only thing these two pursuits had in common was their use of electronic equipment. In the warehouse, Kevin learned to use a computerized inventory system to track deliveries and shipments; in the band, he learned to program and repair his own synthesizer.

After a couple of years, Kevin realized that neither playing in a band nor working in a warehouse would allow him to achieve his life's goals: a good job with status and benefits, a nice car, and his own home. Therefore, he returned to college. Again, however, he found himself pursuing two interests at once. He will graduate in about a month with a dual major in business administration and computer information systems.

Kevin feels that he has chosen a good combination, but he isn't sure where he can find an entry-level job that will allow him to eventually achieve his goals. He could look for either a technical job with advancement potential or a management trainee position in a company that manufactures or sells computer equipment. He also harbors a secret desire to maintain a link to the music business. He has to make some kind of decision now, however, because he wants to have a good start on the job-search process by the time he graduates.

What kinds of jobs do you think Kevin should investigate? Where could he find out about such jobs? How can he construct a resume that will make him seem like a reliable employment prospect and not just a guy who can't make up his mind? The information in this chapter will help you answer these questions.

## IDENTIFYING JOB SOURCES

▶ Look for job opportunities by checking all possible sources.

As Kevin MacGilvray is learning, it is not enough to obtain job skills and knowledge; you must also develop a plan for getting a suitable job. Too many job hunters never realize why they are not being offered the jobs they want. People who are successful in getting the best jobs—those that pay well, make optimum use of your education and skills, and offer opportunity for advancement—usually follow the suggestions outlined in this chapter and the next.

The first step in finding the ideal job is a thorough search of all possible sources of information about job openings:

**Begin your job search with the six most popular sources of leads.**

- *Newspaper classified ads.* This is the best-known source, but be aware that many good jobs are not advertised in the newspaper. In fact, only about 2 percent of the jobs available are advertised in the want ads.

- *Professional publications.* The more experience and education you have in your field, the more likely it is you can find work by answering job advertisements in professional publications. Your college library probably carries many publications aimed at experts in your field. Even when job advertisements are not included, professional publications can help you narrow your job search to companies that are mentioned in the articles or that advertise in the periodical.

- *City, county, or state employment agencies.* These sources list many entry-level positions as a way to link employers and workers. Once an employer notifies a government employment agency of a specific job opening, the agency sends qualified applicants to interview. Depending on the type of job in which you are interested and the regulations in your area, the agency might require you to take tests to determine your skill level. For example, if you are looking for a word processing position, you might be given a test to determine your typing speed or a proofreading test requiring you to compare sets of numbers or words. However, the same agency might not require testing for a management or accounting opening. Call your local or state employment agency to determine its application and testing procedures for the kind of job you are seeking.

Beware of private employment agencies that require you to pay a fee before you get a job.

- *Private employment agencies.* Private agencies work very much like government employment agencies, but with one important difference—they charge for their services. A private employment agency charges either the employer who has advertised a job opening through the agency or the applicant who accepts a job after passing an agency-arranged interview. Obviously, it would be to your advantage to register with an agency that requires employers to pay the fee. If you decide to work with an agency that requires you to pay, you should know that the maximum fee is regulated in some states. However, the fees vary tremendously. Typical fees for lower-level jobs may range from 13 to 50 percent of the first month's gross wages (before taxes are deducted). Some contracts specify that part of the fee is due when a job offer is accepted—even before you receive a paycheck. Be sure to read carefully any contract you are asked to sign. Compare the contracts of several agencies before selecting one. Avoid agencies that require you to pay anything before you get a job; reputable agencies usually do not charge an applicant until employment is actually obtained.

- *College placement offices.* Employers often like to hire graduates of local colleges and universities; therefore, school placement offices are usually good sources of entry-level openings. If your school has a placement office, visit it to determine any services they offer that can make your job hunt easier.

- *Computer job banks.* Electronic bulletin boards accessible through the Internet and on-line computer services, such as Prodigy and CompuServe, offer job postings, especially for computer-related positions. They also offer the opportunity to exchange information with others in your field about the job-search process. Some job seekers even publish their resumes electronically.

- *Unions, religious groups, and civic groups.* These sources often have formal and informal ways of advertising job openings. The yellow pages of the telephone book will tell you whom to call for information about registering with these groups.

The people you know may be your best source of information about job openings.

- *Friends, relatives, and acquaintances.* This is one of the most effective sources of information about job openings. Employers often prefer to hire someone who has been recommended by a trusted employee rather than risking an unknown. Tell everyone you know about the type of job in which you are interested. Clubs and organizations are also likely sources. The networks developed through membership in community, professional, and social organizations can be invaluable.

- *Medium- and large-size companies.* Many experts cite "walk-ins" as the most successful way to find a job. Employers with human resources departments usually maintain files of job applicants for specific jobs, and they do not always wait for openings to occur before interviewing. You can visit these

"Walk-ins"—visits to medium- and large-size employers to pick up job descriptions and application forms—are highly effective.

human resources departments to pick up job descriptions and application forms, but go prepared to talk to an interviewer. Some personnel departments interview everyone who walks in the door to avoid having to schedule return appointments. Applicants who are not properly dressed or who do not have their resumes and reference lists with them are at a definite disadvantage. If you do not already know the specific company or type of company or industry in which you would like to work, a review of the yellow pages can help focus your job hunt. Employers admire initiative, so don't hesitate to go from door to door or to call human resource departments to ask about openings and to get detailed job descriptions for positions in which you are interested.

- *Executive search firms.* Often called "head hunters," these employment agencies specialize in top management positions. Although it is possible for them to be approached by an individual looking for a job, head hunters usually contract with employers to narrow the search for key personnel by contacting a few highly placed executives. The fees for the services of executive search firms can easily run into thousands of dollars.

If you start feeling overwhelmed by the task of identifying potential employers, remember that the more places you check, the more likely you are to find a good job.

## FILLING OUT APPLICATION FORMS

Fill out application forms so that a potential employer has all the necessary information about your background and skills.

Whatever method you use to find job openings, you are likely to be asked to fill out application forms. Even if you also submit a resume, you will have to fill out an application so the company can easily compare job applicants. As much as you might dislike filling out forms, do so with care. You will be judged on the way you perform this first task.

Application forms can be frustrating, but try to answer the questions in a serious, businesslike manner. For instance, one applicant filled in the "Salary expected" blank with the word "Yes!" instead of a dollar amount. Her response got a chuckle, but her attitude toward the application process raised questions about her attitude toward work. Another job seeker, answering the question "Are you a natural-born citizen of the United States?", wrote "No. Caesarean." His flippant answer to that one question put all his other qualifications in doubt.

Neatly fill in all the blanks on an application form so the employer knows you are conscientious and thorough.

Application forms do not have to be typed, but if they are not, they must be printed neatly. Use black ink, because blue ink does not always photocopy well. Read through the entire application before filling in any of the blanks. Do not leave any of the areas of the application blank. If requested information does not pertain to you, write "N/A" (not applicable) or a dash in the area to show the employer you did not just ignore the question. Don't ever write "See attached resume" instead of filling in requested information. Most companies throw away all resumes after a position has been filled; however, they usually keep the application forms in the files.

A new trend is to feed applications or resumes into a computer scanner that searches them for key words, such as computer names and models, software names, degrees, job titles, and so on. Therefore, it is important you include as much detailed information as possible and that you avoid abbreviating information.

If you make an error that cannot be erased easily, draw one neat line through it and print the correct information above it. Correction fluid should be used sparingly and never for more than one or two short words.

To prevent these problems, the ideal way to fill out an application form is in the quiet and comfort of your own home. If you photocopy the form, you can use the copy as a worksheet and then transfer the information to the original form.

**The safest response to a question on an application form about expected salary is usually "open" or "negotiable."**

There will probably be a question on the application form asking you to state the salary you expect to make. If you choose to state a salary figure, make sure it is a reasonable amount. This question is often used as a way of excluding applicants who ask for salaries higher than the company is willing to pay. On the other hand, if the figure is too low, there is also a sense that the individual might not be adequately qualified for the job. It can also put you at a disadvantage once you are offered the job and must negotiate for the highest salary you can get. Instead of a specific amount, you might choose to state a salary range (for example, $1,500 to $1,900 per month); however, even this is not a good negotiating tactic. An employer is likely to think of your lowest figure as a maximum, rather than as a minimum. Writing "open" or "negotiable" in the blank will allow you to negotiate salary later.

## WRITING THE RESUME

**A resume should be a brief review of your qualifications; save the details for an interview.**

A **resume,** sometimes called a *personal data sheet,* is a one- or two-page summary of your background as it pertains to the position for which you are applying. Employers—or their computers—will glance at your resume to determine your qualifications for a specific job. If your resume is easy to read, looks professional, and contains the information the employer wants to see in the format he or she expects, you will be called to interview for the position. Remember: The purpose of the resume is to get you an interview, at which time you can convey your interest in the job and explain your qualifications in greater detail. Developing your resume according to the information presented in this section will help you get interviews.

### REQUIRED SECTIONS

**Describe your education first if you have relatively little work experience; put your work experience first if it outweighs your education.**

Four sections, containing four different types of information, should be included in all resumes: a heading, an education section, a work experience section (unless you have never worked), and references. The heading is at the top of the page, and the references are usually at the bottom. Whether it is best to type the education section or the work experience section first will vary from one individual to another. An individual with little education but a good record of employment should list work experience before education. Another individual with a degree but very little work experience would emphasize education by placing it before work experience.

**HEADING.**   You can think of the heading as the ID portion of your resume, which tells the employer who is the subject of the resume and how to get in touch with that person. Therefore, at the top of the page display your name, address, and telephone number (with area code). If you are currently working and it is all right for potential employers to telephone you at work, include your work telephone number in the heading. A title (e.g., "Resume" or "Personal Data Sheet") is not necessary but may be included if you have the space. Exhibit 16.1 shows examples of acceptable resume headings.

■ Highlight in a resume the most attractive information about your education.

**Listings of your educational and work experience should be in reverse chronological order—most recent experience first.**

**EDUCATION.**   Because potential employers are most interested in what you have been doing recently, within the education section of your resume list first your most recent or current educational experience (an arrangement referred to as **reverse chronological order).** Specify the month and year you graduated or, if you have not yet completed your schooling, the month and year you will graduate. Even if you are not sure when you will finish, you should estimate the date to show the employer you have set a goal. The ability to set and reach goals is an important part of any business career.

**Emphasize the degrees and courses that are relevant to the job you wish to obtain.**

Specify the complete name of the school and of the degree, diploma, or certificate you earned or are in the process of earning. A grade point average (GPA) may be included if it is good but should be left out if it is below a "B" average. If you attended a school but did not graduate from it, you may, if you wish, specify the number of credits, units, courses, semesters, months, or hours attended. In this section, you may also include any other courses you have taken that are relevant to the job.

Kevin MacGilvray, from the vignette at the beginning of the chapter, might list the following in the education section of his resume:

Graduated May 1995, Hartford College, 3.45 GPA

　　Major Business Management Courses Completed:

　　　　Purchasing (2 courses)

　　　　Inventory and Materials Management

　　　　Managerial Accounting

　　　　Managerial Communications

　　Major Computer Information Systems Courses Completed:

　　　Digital Logic Design

　　　Computer Languages (5 courses in Fortran, UNIX, and C++)

　　　Multimedia Software and Applications

　　　　Word processing programs (Word, WordPerfect)

　　　　Desktop publishing programs (QuarkXPress, PageMaker, Adobe Illustrator)

Whether or not to include information about your high school diploma (or GED—General Education Diploma) on a resume is debatable. If you have received degrees or certificates from other schools since high school, you may want to leave off the information about your high school education. However, some companies require a high school diploma or a GED as a minimum requirement for employment. Therefore, if you have only been out of high school

**EXHIBIT 16.1**

**Sample Resume Headings**

Example 1

*Include your work telephone number in the heading of your resume only if your current employer won't mind your receiving calls from prospective employers.*

**PAMELA LEWIS**
3342 East 63rd Street, No. 13
New York, NY 10185

(212) 441-4325 (Home)
(212) 797-3637 (Work)

Example 2

# Richard Moore

268 North Ridgewood Drive
Atlanta, GA 30307
404-661-1120 (home)
404-343-4862, Ext. 961 (work)

Example 3

**Personal Data Sheet**

**MICHAEL CAPELLINI**
11267 Chandler Boulevard
Jonesboro, LA 71251
(Home) 318-797-8742
(Pager) 318-797-5212
(Business) 318-442-4607

Example 4

**Resume of
JANET MCKAY**

*Include in the heading whatever information potential employers will need to get in touch with you during your job hunt.*

Current Address:
4780 NE Mason Street, Apt. 2A
Portland, OR 97217
(503) 445-3462

Address After June 1:
369-A Polymer Street
Denver, CO 80206
(303) 366-8063

a few years and have not yet finished your college or professional education, it might be to your advantage to show that you have achieved your high school diploma or GED. (The resume in Exhibit 16.7 illustrates one way to present information about high school. Note that it emphasizes special training that is applicable to the job for which the individual is applying.)

▟ Explain in a resume your work experience so that your achievements and skills are emphasized.

**WORK EXPERIENCE.**    The work experience section of your resume should describe not only any paid experience you have had, but also responsible volunteer positions (community offices, etc.). Do not assume that only work experience in the field for which you are applying should be listed. Employers are well aware that all jobs, no matter what level, are important and teach people skills relevant to any position. For example, have you ever worked as a babysitter? Mowed lawns? Cleaned houses? Worked the counter at a fast-food restaurant? Some of the skills you learned from these jobs would be important in any position—such as responsibility, dependability, time management, money management, bookkeeping and scheduling, and the ability to get along with others (superiors, co-workers, customers). List such positions on your resume until you have had enough work experience in your field to begin excluding some of these less important jobs.

> If you are just beginning your career, interpret "work experience" broadly—it may include both responsible volunteer experience and paid work in which you learned good work habits and attitudes.

If you have been in the workforce a number of years, you might not want to include all your work experience on a resume. You could use a heading, such as "Relevant Work Experience" or "Selected Employment Experience," and include only those positions related to the field in which you are now working. For example, someone who is applying for a midlevel accounting position might list only two or three previous accounting jobs that cover the last seven or eight years.

> If you have been working for a while, focus on the work experience most relevant to the job you wish to obtain.

If you have served in the armed forces, you can list this information under work experience as merely another job, or you may emphasize it by creating a separate heading called "Military Experience." Because many employers give hiring preference to veterans, it is to your benefit to include military experience, if applicable. Be sure to include the dates you were in the military, your rank, the duties of your last rank (and others if they apply to the job), special schools you attended, certificates you earned, your security clearance level (if applicable), and any special commendations you received.

> Military service can be a valuable addition to your resume.

As with the education section of the resume, what you are currently doing or have done most recently is most important to an employer. Therefore, the first job listed on the resume should be your current or most recent work experience. The remainder should be listed in reverse chronological order.

The employer expects to see certain things about each job. There is no set order for listing them, but you should emphasize the most important or most attractive points. The resume examples in this chapter illustrate different ways of combining the following components: dates of employment, job title, job duties, and company name and location. Each is covered in detail below:

> For each job that you list on your resume, you should provide four kinds of information.

- *Dates of employment.* Employers are interested in the length of employment for various reasons—some obvious (how much work experience, in general, you have and how long you actually worked at a particular job) and some not so obvious (do you hop from job to job, or do you stick with one). A consistent record of short-term employment (job hopping) might indicate an individual who does not get along with others, who quits when the going gets rough,

> To avoid giving the impression that you are a "job hopper," you may want to note which jobs were part-time, temporary, or seasonal employment.

who has been fired frequently, or who is simply irresponsible and unreliable. Because there are acceptable reasons for short-term employment, and some job hopping might even be excused for a young entry-level employee, it might be to your benefit to explain such periods on the resume. For example, you might note in parentheses next to the dates of employment any summer employment, seasonal employment, or temporary jobs (see Exhibit 16.6). It is also helpful, although not absolutely necessary, to let a potential employer know which of your jobs were part-time positions, especially when you have held more than one at a time. Because employers will probably scan the dates of your work experience for periods of unemployment, they will also notice overlapping dates and may be confused. Most of all, make sure the dates of employment are accurate. Most companies will call or write former employers to verify employment information, and you might seem dishonest if the information you have given is inconsistent with that which the employer has given.

- *Company name and location.* Although it is not necessary to give complete addresses on the resume, it is helpful to include at least the city in which you worked. If a job was outside the country in which you are applying, specify the country. It can add interest to your resume, thereby making you stand out from other applicants. Anyone who has had little or no work experience and who is concerned that the resume will not fill a page might also include the complete addresses. If it is important for the employer to know what department you worked in, you might also include that information.

| |
|---|
| **Dates of employment and job titles are easily verified, so avoid the temptation to inflate the facts.** |

- *Job title.* If you do not remember your job title for a specific job, call the company's human resources department. If you cannot get the information by calling, use a title that is indicative of the work you did. However, avoid the temptation to make your work seem more important than it really was by giving yourself a misleading title. The prospective employer is likely to verify your previous employment, and the discrepancy could knock you out of contention for a job you really want. However, you should stress the positive: If you have ever been promoted from one position to another, say so. The fact that someone liked your work well enough to promote you to a more responsible position will impress a potential employer. (Exhibits 16.7 and 16.8 illustrate two ways to emphasize a promotion. Note that the latest position is still listed first in both cases.)

| |
|---|
| **Describe your job duties in active terms. Do not use inactive constructions like these to describe your job responsibilities: "responsible for," "in charge of," "use of," "demonstration of," or "typing of."** |

- *Job duties.* This is the information that shows potential employers how your work experience relates to a job opening. It can also reveal the pride you have in your work. Avoid using weak phrases such as "responsible for" and "duties included." A good job description uses active verbs in the correct tense to draw the reader into the action. Past-tense active verbs should be used to describe the duties of past jobs; present-tense active verbs should be used to describe positions in which you are currently working. A list of active verbs is provided in Exhibit 16.2. Here are some examples of job descriptions that demonstrate the importance of active verbs:

> Past job description: "Case Management Specialist. Verified information for accident reports, analyzed caseloads of 14 agents for scheduling of investigations, testified before juries in complex cases."

> Analysis: This is a good description of the job this individual held. It uses active past-tense verbs (verified, analyzed, testified) so the reader

**EXHIBIT 16.2**

**Active Verbs for Job Descriptions**

Use present tense active verbs for current jobs and past tense active verbs for past jobs.

| | | |
|---|---|---|
| acquire | delegate | maintain |
| adjust | deliver | manage |
| administer | demonstrate | modify |
| advise | design | monitor |
| analyze | determine | open |
| apply | develop | organize |
| appraise | devise | plan |
| arrange | direct | prepare |
| assess | draft | present |
| assist | drive | process |
| assure | edit | program |
| brief | enlist | prohibit |
| bring | ensure | project |
| budget | establish | purchase |
| buy | estimate | rate |
| call | evaluate | recommend |
| catalog | expand | relate |
| chair | expedite | report |
| change | explain | research |
| classify | file | review |
| close | finance | revise |
| communicate | forecast | schedule |
| compare | formulate | search |
| compile | gather | select |
| complete | grade | set |
| conceive | guide | solve |
| conclude | implement | specify |
| conduct | initiate | study |
| contact | input | suggest |
| continue | inspect | summarize |
| control | instruct | supervise |
| coordinate | interpret | teach |
| correct | interview | test |
| counsel | introduce | train |
| critique | investigate | treat |
| deal | keep | type |

can visualize the action being performed. The word *complex* reveals the individual's pride in the work he performed.

Result: He was invited to interview for a higher-level position in the insurance field.

Current job description: "Market researcher. Extensive consumer research. Responsible for some pilot projects. Occasional use of computers and software. Some supervision. Run errands for others as needed."

Analysis: This is a poor description of a current job. The only present-tense active verb (*run*) is used to describe something only low-level employees are asked to do—run errands for other people. The phrase "'extensive consumer research" is ambiguous. Did he do the research himself? What kind of consumer research? Other questions left unanswered: What computers and software did he use? Who and how many did he supervise? What were his supervisory responsibilities? The language used gives the impression that this individual's job is low level and boring. He also does not give the interviewer the information needed to determine how his current job relates to the marketing research position for which he is applying.

Result: This applicant was not invited to interview for the position.

Be as specific as possible when you describe your duties. For example, don't type "computer literate." Instead, list the computers, software courses, and so on that make you computer literate. Computers that scan resumes look only for specific information. Therefore, someone who says only that he or she is computer literate will not be listed in the database as having any computer skills unless they appear elsewhere on the resume.

🔩 Present five or more acceptable references to potential employers.

**REFERENCES.**   Most employers expect you to give the names, addresses, and telephone numbers of five or more people who are willing to attest to such things as your character, your attitude toward work, and your ability to perform the duties of the job you are applying for. Some employers contact all the references listed by job applicants. However, some will not communicate with any of your references because they assume these people have been chosen because they have only good things to say about you.

If you have worked before, most of your references should be people with whom you have worked (supervisors, co-workers, subordinates, clients, customers). However, other acceptable references include teachers (especially those who teach skills related to the position for which you are applying) and members of the community who can assess your personality or character. Make sure you ask permission to use a person as a reference; it is considered a serious breach of business etiquette to use an individual's name without permission. From those who have indicated their willingness to serve as references, select the most prominent individuals. Generally speaking, the higher the title (president, chief executive officer, manager) or the more recognizable the name, the better.

Even though the reference section is a vital part of any resume, detailed information about each of your references does not have to be included on the resume itself, as shown in Exhibit 16.3. If you wish, you may simply specify "References available on request" or some other appropriate phrase on the resume (see Exhibit 16.6). You must then type a separate sheet, like the one in Exhibit 16.4, to give to employers who request a copy of your references. The choice to list your references on the resume or to put them on a separate sheet is yours. Whichever you choose, you should include the following information for each reference:

Name.
Business title.
Company name.
Complete company address.
Company telephone number, with area code and extension.

*For references, choose five or more people, preferably prominent, who can attest to your ability, character, and potential. Get their permission before using their names.*

**EXHIBIT 16.3**   **Detailed References as a Section of the Resume**

| | |
|---|---|
| **References** | Leon Singleton, Senator, State of Louisiana |
| |    Senate Offices, Suite 347, Washington, DC 20510 |
| |    202-331-1227 (Washington), 318-744-1987 (Louisiana) |
| | Christine Roche, DVM |
| |    33567 Benning Road, NW, Washington, DC 20520 |
| |    202-555-9988 |

*A separate reference sheet may be furnished on request, or references can be listed on the resume.*

Consuelo Madrid, Special Auditor, General Services
   Administration, General Services Headquarters
   1625 K NW, Washington, DC 20405
   202-705-4387, Ext. 301
Richard Hassim, District Chairperson, Republican Party
   836 Columbia Drive, Apple Grove, WV 25502
   304-441-5028
Russell Colburn, Office Products Inc.
   290 Lincoln Blvd., Apple Grove, WV 25502
   304-441-1111

## OPTIONAL SECTIONS

▪ Write a resume with optional information that will appeal to potential employers.

In addition to the four required resume sections, you may also include optional sections that present your unique qualifications for work in a positive light. Such optional sections might describe your career objective, job skills, relevant coursework, personal interests, special activities and honors, and languages. Some of these optional sections are illustrated in the resume samples in this chapter (Exhibits 16.7 and 16.8).

**CAREER OBJECTIVE.**   A career objective, sometimes called a *job objective* or *occupational goal,* is usually typed at the top of the resume, immediately following the heading. The career objective indicates a specific job or field for which the applicant is applying. Here are two examples:

> For a position as a court advocate for children: "A position within a social service organization in the area of child advocacy."

> For a computer programming position: "Programmer/A position as a programmer with a special interest in marketing and financial applications."

**EXHIBIT 16.4**  References as a Separate Sheet

**References Of**

**MARCEY G. LEONARD**
243 North Colgate Road
Boston, MA 02184

*Include all the information that a potential employer will need to call or write to your references.*

| | |
|---|---|
| Ms. Alyssa Uno<br>Personnel Specialist | Hughes Aircraft<br>543 East Wright Street<br>Mesa, AZ 85264<br>(602) 335-2217 |
| Ms. Jacqueline Harless<br>Vice President | GTI International<br>34 East First Street, Suite 12<br>Agana, Guam 96910<br>(809) 226-1990 |
| Dr. Linda Beamer, Dept. Chair<br>Office Systems and Business<br>Education | California State University, L.A.<br>4500 College Boulevard<br>Los Angeles, CA 90032<br>(213) 343-2908 |
| Mr. Alan George<br>Senior Analyst | BDM Corporation<br>1801 Randolph Road<br>Farmington, NM 88130<br>(505) 326-7356 |
| Ms. Clover Pinion<br>Owner/Consultant | Administrative Center<br>1934 East 20th Street<br>Farmington, NM 88130<br>(505) 326-4889 |
| Mr. Arek Arbanian<br>Administrative Assistant | Paramount Studios<br>10009 Wilshire Blvd.<br>Los Angeles, CA 94528<br>(213) 789-1011 |

In determining whether or not to use a career objective on your own resume, consider the pros and cons:

| ■ Pros. | ■ Cons |
|---|---|
| Helps the busy resume reader by clearly revealing the position being sought. | Limits use of the resume to only one position, so a new resume must be prepared for any other position. |
| Helps those with little experience and education to fill the resume page with meaningful and relevant information. | Includes information that is not needed when an application form or application letter, which will prominently display the same information, accompanies the resume. |
| Helps the clerk reading the resume for the first time decide where to file it. | Takes up space that may be needed for other information. |

**You may wish to include, at the top of your resume, a career objective that is specific and reader oriented.**

If you decide to use a career objective, be specific. Some applicants use career objectives so general that they provide no information to the reader; other objectives go on and on about nothing in particular, thereby branding their writers as unprofessional or immature. Anyone who is potentially interested in two different kinds of jobs (like Kevin MacGilvray in the chapter-opening vignette) must either write two different career objectives (and resumes) or carefully phrase a single objective to cover both possibilities. For example, Kevin might write "Management trainee with technical responsibilities for producing multimedia presentations." In addition, you should write a career objective with good you attitude. Some career objectives emphasize only what the applicant wants to get out of a job, rather than what he or she can do for the employer. Consider the following example:

> Poor career objective: "Seeking a challenging position with opportunity for advancement that will provide an opportunity for me to use my skills and knowledge and to develop further understanding of the field."

> Analysis: This objective provides no useful information. It doesn't reveal the job or the field for which the applicant is applying. It stresses only what the applicant wants in a job, yet the potential employer's primary concern in determining who to interview is what the applicant can do for the company. Two phrases—"challenging position" and "opportunity for advancement"—have been overused. The writer should come up with something more original.

Acceptable career objectives for selected fields appear in Exhibit 16.5. With a little imagination, you can substitute other words to make these objectives suitable for many other types of jobs or fields.

**You may wish to list the specific skills that will make you a desirable employee.**

**SKILLS.**    If you have job-related skills and abilities you would like to emphasize, such as the ability to fluently speak a foreign language, consider setting them off in a separate section labeled "Skills" or some other appropriate term (see Exhibits 16.7 and 16.8). When these specific skills are a product of only the education an individual has received, they are sometimes listed as a subheading under the educational section.

Here are some examples of skills that might be listed in this optional section:

Computers and other equipment you can operate (makes and models).

Software programs (specify version numbers) you are able to use.

Programming languages you know.

**EXHIBIT 16.5**

**Sample Career Objectives**

Accounting/Bookkeeping:
  An accounting position in which knowledge of spreadsheet programs can be applied
  Accounts receivable/payable clerk
  A position within a multinational corporation in which in-depth knowledge of international
    finance can be applied to the preparation and interpretation of accounting documents
  A CPA position within a public accounting firm with the eventual goal of progressing to
    partnership level
  Tax accounting
  Entertainment accounting
  Full-charge bookkeeper
Auditing:
  An internal auditing position for a government agency
  On-site auditor/consultant
Banking:
  A bank management training program in which a positive contribution to branch
    management, credit analysis, and commercial lending can be made
  Customer service representative
  Branch manager
Computers:
  Programmer
  Systems analyst
  Data entry
  A position as a programmer, with special emphasis on marketing and financial
    applications; long-range goal is to manage a large management information systems
    installation
  A position as a programmer or systems analyst to make use of quantitative and
    mathematics training
  Software designer
Fashion/design:
  Fashion designer
  Buyer
  A position as buyer for a large American retail organization; able to travel; have personal
    knowledge of the fashion industry in Italy and France
  Creative fabric design
  Innovative designer of fashions for men
Human resources:
  A position within the personnel management training program of a firm where knowledge
    of wage administration, benefit programs, safety, and labor relations can be applied;
    eventual goal is full management responsibilities
  Human resource management
  A position in an employee training department that requires thorough knowledge of needs
    assessment, strong teaching skills, and superior organizational skills
Insurance:
  Insurance sales
  A position as a claims adjustor within the insurance industry, with the eventual goal of
    progressing into management responsibilities
Journalism:
  Copywriter within a large advertising firm, with the eventual goal of editor
  Copywriter
  Reporter for a large metropolitan newspaper
  Sports writer

**EXHIBIT 16.5** **Continued**

Management:
An entry-level management position with potential for promotion within the retail industry
Manufacturing/electronics:
Computer numerical control
A computer numerical control posit8ion in which hands-on experience with EDM machines can be applied
Electronics technician
Computer-assisted drafting
A welding position with a multinational construction firm; willing and able to travel for extended periods on short notice
Telecommunications specialist
Marketing/sales management:
A marketing and sales management position with an organization interested in growth, solid profits, and having a team member who can produce results
Pharmaceutical sales representative
Marketing
Sales
Real Estate:
Real estate sales
A sales position with a progressive real estate firm in which strong people skills can be applied
Secretarial/clerical/word processing/desktop publishing:
A responsible position as an administrative assistant, involving strong secretarial and word processing skills, in which abilities and experience will have valuable applications
Word processing specialist
Clerk typist
A legal secretarial position, in which knowledge of WordPerfect, Microsoft Word, Lotus 1-2-3, and Excel can be applied to create error-free documents
Desktop publisher
Graphics designer
Small business management:
Operate a fast-food outlet, with emphasis on efficiency, limited expenses, and increased profits
Teaching:
Business administration instructor
Banking operations teacher for a regional occupational program

Your typing and shorthand speeds (only if required for the job).

Foreign languages you are able to use.

Other skills pertinent to the job (e.g., people skills, management skills, communication skills, creative skills, debating skills, decision-making skills, labor-relations skills, leadership skills, organizational skills, sales skills, and/or public relations skills).

When you list your skills, be as specific as possible. For instance, specify all the software you can use and, if you know the latest version, list that as well. The degree of fluency in foreign languages should be made clear. For instance, you might list the following:

Foreign languages:   English (fluent), Spanish (fluent), German (reading only)

Some resumes, sometimes referred to as *functional resumes,* emphasize qualifications and skills more than they do work experience and education. This format (see Exhibit 16.8) is good for applicants who are changing fields and want employers to notice the close match between the open position and an applicant's background. It is also good for applicants who have finished their education but who have little or no job experience in their chosen field. In a functional resume, a skills section, listed first on the resume, focuses attention on the qualifications and away from actual work experience (strategically placed either on the second page or lower on the same page). In this way, there is time to build interest in the reader's mind before he or she can categorically reject an applicant whose experience does not, at first glance, seem to fit a job opening.

**RELEVANT COURSEWORK.**   You may stress any job-related courses you have completed in a section called "Relevant Courses" or "Major Coursework," either as a separate section or as a subsection under "Education." The courses listed in this section should be only those that pertain to the job for which you are applying; general education courses are usually not placed in this section.

Use the correct names of the courses only if the titles clearly reveal the courses' contents. For example, Accounting I, II, and III and Beginning Accounting mean nothing to an employer who is not familiar with the program at your school. If the course names are not self-explanatory, you can describe the courses in more detail:

> "Word Processing: Three classes stressing high-speed, error-free production of letters, reports, memos, and newsletters."

> "Accounting: One semester covering the complete accounting cycle, from journal and ledger entries through financial statement preparation and analysis."

> "Economics: Five courses ranging from monetary theory and policy to sampling techniques and econometrics. Heavy emphasis on advanced mathematics."

**List your personal interests only if they relate to the job you wish to obtain.**

**INTERESTS.**   Employers aren't just looking for people who are competent in a particular skill area; they also like to hire individuals who are enthusiastic about what the company does. Thus, you may include a section in your resume describing the personal interests that make you stand out—but only if they are related to the job. For example, indicating an interest in classical music would be a benefit to someone applying for any position with a symphony orchestra but not to a person applying for a position in the aerospace industry.

**ACTIVITIES AND HONORS.**   Another section of the resume that can make an individual look more qualified to a potential employer is a section that may be called "Activities and Honors" (or "Extracurricular Activities," "Professional Affiliations," or something similar). These types of activities and honors reveal the social side of an applicant's character and are often indicative of his or her leadership potential. The single most-cited reason people are fired is for not getting along with others. Listing club memberships and leadership activities on your resume proves that you do get along with and are looked up to by others.

**Your extracurricular and social activities may indicate a potential for leadership on the job.**

This section may list any clubs of which you are a member, particularly those related to your chosen career; leadership positions to which you have been appointed or elected; committee work you have been involved in; special honors and awards (e.g., scholarships, sports awards, and employee competitions); and any community or school-related volunteer experience you have had. The resume in Exhibit 16.6 includes this information within the education section of the resume; the resume in Exhibit 16.7 lists it under a separate heading.

Do not include long-ago awards or honors. It would be ridiculous for a 35-year-old to mention she was elected homecoming queen in high school. However, there is no standard for determining when awards and activities are out of date and should, therefore, not be included, so use your best judgment. Put yourself in the position of the person reading your resume.

## OUTDATED RESUME INFORMATION

◼ Write a resume that does not include information that is no longer required or allowed.

> Personal information not related to the job—such as race, age, gender, marital status, and health—may not be considered in making hiring decisions.

In the past, job applicants were expected to give personal, non-job-related information on their resumes (e.g., age, birthdate, sex, height, weight, marital status, number of children, and health status). However, such information should now be excluded. The Civil Rights Act of 1964 (Title VII) and its 1972 and 1978 amendments prohibit employment discrimination based on factors unrelated to the job. The hiring decision must be made on the basis of job qualifications rather than personal characteristics.

For the same reason, it is now also illegal to require an applicant to include a photograph. The only exceptions are such careers as modeling or acting, where one's looks may be essential to a particular job. In fact, actors often type their resumes on the backs of 8 × 10-inch photographs of themselves.

## RESUME FORMAT

◼ Use a resume format that will draw attention to your most desirable features and will make important information accessible to potential employers.

Resumes don't all look alike, but they typically use headings and lists to conveniently display the necessary information about a person's qualifications for a job. Exhibits 16.6, 16.7, and 16.8 are only a sampling of the many ways resumes can be laid out. None of these formats is more acceptable than another; however, some are more creative than others.

> Your resume should look and be easy to read, with similar information treated consistently.

In addition, certain factors make some resume formats more effective than others. People looking for new employees spend many hours scanning stacks of resumes for qualified individuals to interview. Resumes that look easy to read are more likely to be scrutinized more carefully. If the reader's initial perception of the resume holds true, the content and the layout of the items on the page will keep him or her interested long enough for the applicant's qualifications to be given full consideration. A sloppy, unprofessional, and poorly formatted resume will probably never even be read. Although fills (background shading) in boxes are attractive, they cannot be scanned by computers; therefore, it is probably best not to use them unless you know a company does not use computers to process resumes.

Here are some basic guidelines you can follow to ensure that your resume not only looks easy to read, but actually *is* easy to read:

**EXHIBIT 16.6**

Sample Resume (one page with emphasis on education)

**GLENDA A. PEABODY**
1019 East Mission
Oklahoma City, OK 73160
(405) 441-4324 (home)
(405) 790-2766, Ext. 3388 (work)

**OCCUPATIONAL GOAL:**
Pharmaceutical Sales
Representative

---

**EDUCATION**

*Information about Glenda's activities while in school are a natural part of the education system.*

**Bachelor of Science in Business Administration, Marketing Option.** University of Oklahoma.
Will graduate August 1996. 3.7 GPA in major.
Extracurricular activities: Phi Beta Lambda, national business society—Vice President and Membership Chair.

**Associate of Arts in Chemistry and Physics**, 7/94
Houston Community College. 3.1 GPA

**EXPERIENCE**

9/94 to present

**Produce Sales Representative**
Kraeger Farms, Oklahoma City
Solicit large-scale contracts to buy farm products. Accounts include large grocery chains and specialty stores.
   **Achievements:** Increased sales to special accounts by 38 percent within first year of employment. Steady increases since that time. Work 20–30 hr./week during school and full time during holidays and summers.

1/90 to 5/94

Johnson and Johnson Pharmaceutical, Houston

*Glenda emphasizes her promotions to show how well her supervisors thought of her.*

**Inventory Manager** (promoted—full time), 12/92–5/94
Supervised 4 warehouse employees. Ordered, cataloged, and distributed drugs and supplies to regional outlets. Devised and maintained computer inventory program.

**Inventory Control Clerk II** (promoted), 1/91–12/92
Maintained inventory related to addictive and experimental drugs.

*To avoid giving the wrong impression about her tenure at Unitech, Glenda points out that the job was for the summer only.*

**Inventory Control Clerk I**, 1/90–1/91
   **Achievements:** Promoted twice. Maintained inventory control clerk positions 20 hours a week or more while attending high school and college full time.

5/89 to 9/89
(summer only)

**Purchasing Clerk**
Unitech Dental Appliances, Houston
Ordered and distributed drugs and precious metals for use in research and development projects.

**REFERENCES**

Will be furnished upon request.

*By offering to provide references on request, Glenda can keep her resume to a single page.*

**EXHIBIT
16.7**

Sample Resume (two pages with emphasis on experience)

# SHARON RAMOS

3405 Richmond Street
Jacksonville, FL 32216
(904) 584-2438 (residence)
(904) 584-6940, Ext. 2124 (work)

**Career
Objective**

**Human Resources Management**

**Employment
Experience**

**Human Resources Specialist II**, 10/93 to present.
Holiday Inns International, Jacksonville.
Interview and recommend hiring of hotel employees of all levels.
Counsel problem employees. Conduct exit interviews of terminated
employees. Maintain personnel files of 87 percent of hotel
employees—middle-level management and below.

**Business Center Coordinator**, 5/92 to 9/93.
Miami–Dade Community College, Miami.
Managed computer instructional laboratory; worked with students
and faculty to demonstrate software features and to troubleshoot
problems; hired and supervised 11–14 student employees; handled
payroll and scheduling of all employees. Proposed, negotiated, and
maintained Center budgets.
  Promoted to Coordinator position from a student employee
  position (9/91-5/92).

*Sharon's note about her part-time
work demonstrates her drive and
responsibility.*

Various part-time positions while attending high school and
community college, 11/87 to 9/91.
Self-financed 60 percent of personal expenses in high school and
100 percent during college.

**Academic
Background**

**Bachelor of Science in Business Administration, Human
Resources Management Major, Hotel & Restaurant
Management Minor.**
University of North Florida, Jacksonville.
Estimated date of completion: May 1996.

Transfer courses—Miami–Dade Community College.
Completed all general education courses and 18 units of computer
and software applications courses.

*To point out her specialized
training, Sharon includes
information about her high
school education.*

High School Diploma, 5/91. Specialized in Regional Occupational
Program taught by Thomas Kelly, retired Chairman of the Board
of Hilton International Hotels. Jacksonville High School.

**EXHIBIT 16.7** Continued

# SHARON RAMOS
**Page 2**

**Major Courses and Skills**
Human resources management, introduction to management, marketing management, accounting (four courses), economics and statistics (three courses).
Excellent decision-making and problem-solving skills.
Superior management and communication skills.
Computers: IBM, Compaq, and Macintosh computers.
Software: Microsoft Word, WordPerfect, Adobe Illustrator, QuarkXPress, PageMaker, Lotus 1-2-3, Excel, Microsoft Works, EmpTrak (a Holiday Inn personnel tracking program).

**Honors and Achievements**
Holiday Inn National Employee of the Year, 1994.
Holiday Inn local Employee of the Month, 4 times.
President and Secretary, Jacksonville Young Republicans.
Unocal Presidential Scholarship.

**Languages**
Bilingual—English/Spanish.

*Sharon's bilingualism could be a big advantage.*

**References**
Available on request.

**EXHIBIT 16.8**   Sample Functional Resume (two pages with emphasis on skills)

### HERMAN L. CHANG

| 85 Boxwood Lane, Hicksville, NY 11801        (303) 336-9498 or (303) 336-2213, Ext. 9631 |

*A separate section highlights the technical and personal skills that Herman wishes to stress.*

### SKILLS

Accounting—Used computer-aided accounting program. Maintained accounts payable and receivable and payroll records. Balanced monthly bank statement and prepared statements of receipt and disbursement. Made adjusting entries.

Sales—Received employee-of-the-month sales awards three months in a row. Identified new clients through personal and telephone contacts. Planned, organized, and wrote telephone marketing presentations that immediately increased company sales by 9 percent. *The note about sales awards, combined with active and specific words describing his job duties, makes Herman look like a real go-getter.*

Personal—Strong people skills, leadership skills, and organizational skills.

### EDUCATION

Bachelor of Business Administration in Accounting, Winston–Salem State University. Accepted for September 1994 entry. Graduation date: June 1998.

Certificate of Completion, Accounting Program, June 1994.
Bryer School of Business, Queens, New York.
   Courses completed: Six months of intensive training in accounting principles and practices, hands-on computer applications in accounting, spreadsheets (Excel and Lotus 1-2-3), business English, business communications (letter and report writing), computer keyboarding (37 wpm), electronic calculators (181 strokes a minute), and business math and finance.
   Activities: Treasurer, Beta Alpha Psi, national accounting club.
      Chaired Big Brother/Big Sister Committee—organized and participated in volunteer program to help orphaned and abandoned children in area.

*Herman uses underlining to draw attention to his promotions.*

### EMPLOYMENT

Bookkeeper—NBU Computer Software, Hicksville, New York. September 1987 to present (part-time).
   Oversee 5 night staff in accounts receivable/accounts payable section. Operate IBM computer and train new employees in computer accounting. Began in telephone sales, promoted to counter sales, then promoted to payroll section of accounting department, and most recently promoted to current position.

### REFERENCES

Will be furnished at interviewer's request.

- Keep descriptions short. Use phrases, not complete sentences.

- Limit your resume to a maximum of two pages. Use a second-page heading, as in Exhibit 16.7.

- Emphasize important phrases with underlining, boldface, and capital letters (but use such devices consistently).

- Use consistent indentions and spacing between sections and items.

- Use equal side margins and equal top and bottom margins—approximately three-quarters to one inch in width.

- If possible, prepare an original resume on good paper for each interview. If you cannot, use a top-quality copy machine and good paper so it is difficult to tell whether your resume has been photocopied. If you must type your resume on a typewriter, do not use erasable bond paper; it has a slick finish that does not photocopy well and is too flimsy for an original resume.

- Use white, cream, ivory, or light gray bond paper only. Other colors appear unprofessional and might not be computer readable.

- Use a dark ribbon, preferably a carbon ribbon, on your typewriter. If you use a dot matrix printer, set it at the highest resolution possible. If you use a laser or laser-quality printer, make sure it is inking properly, so you don't end up with streaks or light areas on your copies.

- Proofread carefully and make skillful corrections; the final copy should be error free.

In preparing your resume, your goal is to use a format that will get busy resume readers to focus on your qualifications. Effective layout and active, reader-centered phrasing should do the job. From that point on, your qualifications will stand on their own.

## KEEPING TRACK OF A JOB SEARCH

*To save time and to project an organized image, keep careful records of where you have sent resumes and what the responses were.*

Even the simplest job search is likely to require that you send a resume to several potential employers. If you are like Kevin MacGilvray in the chapter-opening vignette, you may plan to prepare more than one resume and seek more than one type of job. In either case, you will want to keep track of the people and companies you contact and the results of your contacts. Setting up a form like that in Exhibit 16.9 will help keep you organized from the beginning. By writing down the names, addresses, and telephone numbers of companies to whom you send resumes, you will be able to follow up later. You can use the same form to keep track of the interviews you go to and the results of all your job-search efforts. Taking an organized, businesslike approach to the task is the best way to ensure that you get a good job.

## PLANNING YOUR MESSAGE

*An application letter is a cover letter for the resume; it merely highlights the more detailed information in the resume.*

Apply the message formulation process to application letters.
If you are sending your resume to a potential employer, you must write a letter to accompany it. This letter is called an **application letter** or *cover letter*. It introduces the resume to the reader but does not repeat everything printed on

| | | | | |
|---|---|---|---|---|
| **EXHIBIT 16.9** | **Job Search Contact Sheet** | | | |

| Date | Company and Person Contacted | Action Taken | Follow-Up/Date | Comments |
|---|---|---|---|---|
| | | | | |

the resume. Exhibit 16.10 illustrates an application letter that could accompany the resume presented in Exhibit 16.7.

The process of formulating an application letter is the same as the process of formulating any type of business message. You begin by planning, and then you organize, compose, and evaluate. Careful planning is crucial for application letters. You are trying to communicate with someone you don't know well—the employer—about a matter of critical personal importance—your future. The time you spend planning is, therefore, well worthwhile.

## ESTABLISH YOUR PURPOSE

*Your ultimate goal in writing an application letter is to get a job interview.*

The ultimate purpose of the application letter and the accompanying resume is to get you a job interview. To achieve that goal, you must convince the reader that you are a qualified applicant.

Your specific purpose is to draw attention to some aspect of your qualifications that will win you further consideration. Here are some examples of specific purposes:

- To convince the recruiter for Mega Tek that the electronic courses I have taken will enable me to troubleshoot their product line.

- To convince Ms. Hazelton that I have the "in-depth knowledge" of spreadsheet software and systems analysis experience that she is seeking.

3405 Richmond Street
Jacksonville, FL 32216
April 15, 1996

Ms. Willa Slumberjay
Human Resources Director
Clarion Hotels
1880 Arlington
Orlando, FL 32839

Dear Ms. Slumberjay:

**Application for Position of Site Director, Human Resources**
Please consider this the first step in my application for the human resources position advertised in the June issue of *Hotel Management*. The following narrative highlights my qualifications for this position.

*Excellent you attitude shows how hiring Sharon will be good for the company.* You will see from the enclosed resume that I will complete in May a Bachelor of Science in Human Resources Management with a minor in Hotel and Restaurant Management. This degree, combined with my experience in the field, makes me a logical choice to head the human resources team at any of your hotels worldwide. Fluency in Spanish will make me particularly useful in your Florida hotels as well as in many other areas of the world. Having full knowledge of the responsibilities of this position and an understanding of Hilton's expectations, you will find that I am able to lead human resource employees toward the attainment of one of a hotel's most important objectives—maintaining a staff of caring professionals who work together to further the comfort and satisfaction of visitors.

The enclosed resume shows that all my education (even my high school education) and my recent work experience have been directed toward a career in hotel management. By hiring me, you can by sure you are getting someone committed to meeting the high standards of excellence for which Hilton hotels are known.

**EXHIBIT 16.10**    Concluded

Ms. Willa Slumberjay                    2                    April 15, 1996

Please call me at (904) 584-2438 or (904) 584-6940, Ext. 2124, to
arrange a time when we can get together to talk about this position. I
look forward to hearing from you soon.

Sincerely,

*Sharon Ramos*

Sharon Ramos

Enclosure

- To provide a brief overview of the accomplishments that make me the self-motivated, people-oriented training director being sought.

The more precisely you can define your purpose and link it to the reader's needs, the more likely you are to write a concise application letter that has real impact.

### CHOOSE A MEDIUM AND CHANNEL

> An application memo may be written for openings within the company you currently work for, but otherwise, a letter is the correct format.

If you are required to mail a resume to be considered for a job opening, a letter is the appropriate medium and channel for the message you wish to communicate. If you are applying for another job or a promotion within the company you are currently working for, you could write either a memo (see Exhibit 16.11) or a letter. Whichever you write, remember that you are likely to be competing with other applicants—sometimes many other applicants. You will have the reader's attention only briefly, so you must be able to deliver your message clearly and concisely.

### CONSIDER LEGAL AND ETHICAL ISSUES

Write an ethical application letter.

It is tempting to overstate your qualifications and experience when an important job is at stake. If an otherwise suitable job requires certain experience you do not have, you face a difficult decision—either lie about your experience and run the risk of not being able to do the job if hired, or tell the truth and risk not even being considered for the job. You will probably be faced with this type of dilemma sometime during your working life.

> The unpleasant consequences of lying in an application letter should motivate you to acquire the qualifications needed for the job you aspire to.

The consequences of lying are unpleasant. In most companies, lying about qualifications is considered grounds for firing an employee, no matter how well he or she has performed on the job. Imagine how hard it would be to explain in later job interviews why you were terminated. At the very least, an employee who lies about qualifications will severely damage his or her reputation within the company. It is human nature to mistrust someone who has lied to you in the past. The employer may not feel comfortable assigning a position of responsibility to an untrustworthy person—even a position for which the person is qualified.

Honesty really is the best policy. You should resist the temptation to overstate your qualifications. Instead, consider taking a class to acquire the knowledge you lack, or hunt for another job that will give you the experience you need to eventually get the job you want. When you do, you will perform well from the beginning because you will know what to do and you will have more confidence in your abilities.

### ANALYZE YOUR AUDIENCE

Understand the needs of people who read application letters.

> First-person pronouns are acceptable in an application letter, as long as you focus on the reader's needs when explaining your qualifications. However, keep them to a minimum.

It is just as important to incorporate the you attitude in an application letter as it is to be you-oriented in any other type of business message. However, because an application letter requires you to discuss your personal qualities and background, you might find it difficult to completely avoid first-person pronouns (*I, me, my*) and use second-person pronouns (*you, your*). First-person

**EXHIBIT 16.11**     Sample Memo Applying for a Promotion

**To:**     Darroch Young

**From:**     Dorothy Gelvin *DG*

**Date:**     March 3, 1996

**Subject:**     Application for Position of Recruitment and Employee Relations Administrative Aide

*The opening refers to the writer's source of information about the job.*

In response to your advertisement in the *Weekly Employment Opportunities* bulletin, I am applying for the position specified above.

*Dorothy points out the advantages of hiring her because she is familiar with the company, its procedures, and its people.*

For the past four years, I have been employed by JPL as a secretary in the procurement division. My procurement and secretarial experience at the Laboratory has familiarized me with JPL policies and operating procedures. My current assignment to the Mars Observer Project has given me insight and exposure to the interactions among technical, managerial, and clerical employees. This experience would serve as an excellent background for your position and would enable me to adapt quickly and effectively with a minimum of supervision.

Successful experience at JPL is only a portion of what I have to offer you. I am currently studying human resource management at California State University, Los Angeles, and will finish a degree in less than a year. Specific courses in my major that will be helpful as a recruitment and employee relations administrative aide have included research and practice in recruiting, interviewing, evaluating performance, and training.

*Dorothy reveals her eagerness to travel, a factor of the job many people might find uninviting.*

In addition, extensive travel throughout the United States, Europe, and Japan as a member of a military family has made me adaptable, self-assured, and eager to continue traveling and meeting people. The high level of travel required of your recruitment aide will be welcome.

**EXHIBIT 16.11**  Concluded

Darroch Young
Page 2
March 3, 1996

*Reference to the resume is woven smoothly into the body of the memo.*

The attached resume will provide you with additional background information and work-related experience. A letter of recommendation from Johnie Merrit, my current supervisor, is also enclosed. I will be happy to provide you with the names of other JPL co-workers and CSLA faculty members who will give you good references.

*The letter of recommendation from a current supervisor could be a real plus.*

Please call me at (818) 441-0000 or at Extension 2314 to arrange an interview to discuss the advantages of hiring me as JPL's new Recruitment and Employee Relations Administrative Aide.

Attachments

pronouns are acceptable in an application letter; however, they should be kept to a minimum.

Nevertheless, the you attitude is still crucial to the success of the letter. Instead of being a matter of using the right pronouns, however, it is a matter of showing how you can meet the employer's needs. The needs of most employers revolve around the desire to increase profits, maintain a good reputation, and have a productive team. If you can relate your skills, education, and experience to these needs, you will have a better chance of getting hired. Think in these terms:

This is what I can do for you and for your organization:

- Make the organization, my supervisor, and my co-workers look good.
- Make life easier for my supervisor and co-workers.
- Help the organization meet its goals.
- Help to increase profits and productivity, and decrease expenses.
- Help to improve products, services, and operations.

To communicate your value to an employer, be specific in explaining how your qualifications and the employer's concerns overlap. For example:

Your firm's goal of producing fine furniture at affordable prices can be better realized by hiring me for the position of accountant. Completing five semesters of an intensive accounting program has given me the theoretical and practical hands-on experience you need. This background and a positive work attitude would enable me to become a contributing member of your accounting team with a minimum of time and expense.

As your research and development technician, I will be able to apply years of experience using and selling your products. While attending college, I am working at an outlet that sells and rents in-line skates. Because of the frequent complaints about the lack of brakes (because these skates were originally designed for hockey players who do not need them), I designed a functional front brake that allows skaters coming from regular roller or figure skating backgrounds to feel more comfortable on in-line skates. As you might guess, the word got out, and our sales increased dramatically. You may be sure that I will bring this same innovative spirit to work for you if hired for this position.

The you attitude—in the form of an understanding of what employers are trying to accomplish—will help you relate your own qualifications to a specific employer's needs. Exhibit 16.12 shows how someone with no experience directly related to an advertised job used good you attitude to show that she would be a good person to hire.

## GATHER NECESSARY RESOURCES

Collect information about the company to which you are applying for a job. Because each application letter you write should be tailored to a particular position at a particular company, you will often have to do some research before doing any writing. To learn about the job, telephone or visit to obtain a copy of the job description (if one has been written). A formal job description listing the specific duties and responsibilities of a position will give you the information you need to discuss your skills in terms of the job's requirements.

In addition to the specific responsibilities of the job, you should also know something about the company itself so you can explain how you can benefit it. If you want to interview for a corporate communications position with a major

---

*Show how you can help employers achieve their overriding needs: to operate profitably, present a good image, and have good working relationships among their employees.*

*Your application letter should explain exactly how your qualifications will help the employer meet specific needs.*

*By demonstrating a deep understanding of an employer's particular needs, applicants who feel qualified for a job although they lack the specific background or skills listed in a job description may, nevertheless, be able to persuade the employer to interview them.*

*Write a new application letter for each position you apply for, so you can link your qualifications to the requirements of a particular job and a particular employer's unique needs.*

106 N. Grove Street
Newark, NJ 07106
November 2, 1995

Good Faith Publishing
ATTN: Personnel Department
550 N. Oak Street
Newark, NJ 07110

<u>Application Letter for Position of Proofreader</u>  *The subject line helps those who are evaluating applications sort them accurately.*

Please consider this the first step in my application for the proofreading position advertised in the December 4 *Newark Courier*. The following narrative highlights my qualifications for this position.

*Although the writer of this letter has not worked for pay as a proofreader, she has relevant training and experience.*

You will see from the enclosed resume that I am completing classes leading toward an associate degree. Two classes in English grammar and composition, two classes in typing (62 words per minute), and one I am currently taking in journalism have required extensive proofreading and editing of both my own and others' work. A strong background in basic English skills and the ability to work diligently and methodically will enable me to carry out your proofreading responsibilities effectively.

As the publisher of religious materials, you are probably also looking for someone who shares your beliefs. A lifetime of active participation in church activities and a commitment to live my life according to the church's precepts give me the background necessary to relate on common ground with my supervisors and co-workers.

*Beacuse she is not directly qualified, she needs to point out some compensating qualities—in this case, beliefs consistent with those of the prospective employer.*

You can reach me at (201) 537-1137 to schedule a time to discuss my career with your firm. Please call me soon.

Sincerely yours,

*Julie Christensen*

Julie Christensen

Enclosure

oil company, for example, you could explain how your skills could help them get through an oil embargo or environmental crisis or could help spread the word about the company's plans to employees and the community.

Before you write an application letter, you might want to find answers to these questions:

What is the company's major line of business?

How old is the company?

How is the company viewed by employees? By the community?

What has the company's top management said publicly about its plans for a particular division, product, or service?

Does the company promote from within?

Is in-company training available to employees?

Does the company pay for job-related schooling?

Where does the company rank within its industry?

Has the company or its products, services, or employees been featured lately in newspapers or magazines, or on television or radio?

Who are the company's major competitors?

Where are the company's main offices and its branches, plants, stores, and other facilities located?

What are its short-term and long-term profit trends?

Is the company a local, regional, national, or multinational organization?

What are the names and ages of the company's top management people?

What kind of emphasis does the company place on research and development of new products?

How will the company be affected by economic developments in its home country? In foreign markets?

You will have a head start on such research if you regularly read the business section of your local newspaper and listen to or watch business news programs. You can also find information about specific companies in your school's job placement office, at your state employment agency, and in libraries. Exhibit 16.13 suggests some commonly available sources of information about the business world.

The time you spend researching a company will be well invested. Not only will you have a good foundation for your application letter, but you will also impress those with whom you interview later. Most interviewees know little or nothing about the company for which they hope to work. Your knowledge of the company, its products, its services, and its problems will mark you as an above-average job candidate.

*Find out everything you can about a prospective employer's history, reputation, products, operations, finances, employees, and corporate culture.*

## ORGANIZING YOUR MESSAGE

The second phase in writing an application letter, after the planning phase, is to organize your message. As with any other type of business letter, in this phase you begin by freewriting the major points you want to make and then choose an organizational strategy for presenting those points.

**EXHIBIT 16.13**

**Sources of Information about Potential Employers**

Business Periodicals Index
Company annual reports/10K forms
*Dun & Bradstreet Million Dollar Directory*
*Moody's* Manuals
Standard & Poor's Industry Survey
Standard & Poor's Stock Reports
State, county, and city directories
*Thomas Register of Corporations, Directors and Executives*
*U.S. Industrial Outlook*
*Value Line*
*The Wall Street Journal*
*The Wall Street Transcript*

## FREEWRITE MAJOR POINTS

The easiest way to begin is by jotting down the points you want to get across, with no concern for order. For an idea of how one might freewrite in the preparation of an application letter, look at Exhibit 16.14. After seeing the following advertisement for an entry-level accounting position, Richard Doan avoided writer's block by first freewriting his thoughts about the match between his background and the job's requirements:

> ACCOUNTING ASSISTANT. Accounts payable/receivable, financial statement preparation. Assist in conversion to computerized accounting. Opportunity for advancement with fast-growing mortgage brokering firm. Send resume to Kathleen Horton, Vice President, Douglas E. Horton, Inc., 12294 North Olympic Avenue, No. 24-B, Hicksville, NY 11801.

The job description in the ad helped Richard analyze how his qualifications might help the employer achieve its goals. The result was the set of freewritten notes in Exhibit 16.14.

## CHOOSE AN ORGANIZATIONAL STRATEGY

▪ Know what type of strategy to use for an application letter.

When applying for an advertised job opening, use the direct organizational strategy.

Exhibit 16.14 also shows how Richard Doan decided to organize his points, using numbers and letters to indicate their sequence. As he reviewed his freewritten notes, he decided to leave some things out and to put the remainder in direct order. He can begin with the main point because he is responding to an advertisement for a particular job opening that he is qualified to fill. This is a message that the reader expects to see and wants to see. In the middle Richard can summarize the relevant details of his resume—namely, his skills and experience as they relate to the requirements listed in the job description. He can then close with a specific request for an interview. See Exhibit 16.15 for Richard's completed application letter.

All letters of application for jobs that have been advertised can use this sort of direct strategy. The basic pattern for messages that will be received positively or neutrally is as follows:

1. Direct statement indicating the purpose of the correspondence.

2. Necessary details to carry through the purpose.

**EXHIBIT 16.14**

**Freewritten Notes for Application Letter**

① Job - mention it

③ computer experience—accounting-related
   school
   at NBU

   Software and equipment—write out

② accounting courses—6 months
   a. accounts payable and receivable
      posting, journals, ledgers
   b. financial statements—balance sheets and income
        statements
      analysis
      ~~income tax~~
      ~~government accounting~~
      corporate accounting

Work in
somewhere > dependability, responsibility, etc.

( RELATE TO COMPANY'S NEEDS!!!!!!!! )

④ phone number—ask for interview

3.  Goodwill statement that brings the correspondence to a close and, if necessary, a request for specific action.

In the first sentence, mention what position you are interested in and how you learned of it.

If you want your application letter to be read, get to the point in the first sentence. Exhibit 16.16 summarizes the information that should be included in the various parts of an application letter that uses the direct approach.

When seeking a position that does not yet exist or has not been advertised, you may use the persuasive organizational strategy.

Sometimes, however, you can anticipate that the reader of your application letter will need to be persuaded. If you are interested in working for a particular company that is not currently advertising any suitable job openings, you can't begin by saying you are responding to an ad. Although your ultimate purpose is the same as with a direct strategy, you have a better chance of getting the reader to consider your application if you use a persuasive strategy. These are the main elements:

1.  *Interest stage:* Attention-getting yet relevant statement that can serve as a theme.

2.  *Desire stage:* Reader benefit of considering your proposal.

3.  *Conviction stage:* Specific request, along with reader benefit.

85 Boxwood Lane
Hicksville, NY 11801
January 15, 1996

Ms. Kathleen Horton
Vice President
Douglas E. Horton, Inc.
12294 North Olympic Avenue, No. 24-B
Hicksville, NY 11801

Dear Ms. Horton:    *The confident tone of the opening enhances a clear statement of the position being discussed and the source of information about that position.*

Enclosed is my resume to be considered in filling the position of accounting assistant advertised in the January 14 edition of *The New York Times*. You will see that my experience and training make me well qualified for this position.

*The body of the letter begins with a general statement of Richard's qualifications and then reviews, one by one, how they meet the job's requirements.*

Completing a six-month-long intensive accounting program and experience as a bookkeeper have given me a thorough background in the handling of accounts payable and receivable. My education emphasized effective preparation and interpretation of income and expense statements, balance sheets, and other financial reports.

*Richard sets himself off from other applicants by stressing his preparation for a distinctive element of this particular job.*

In addition to having the experience and educational background required for your position, I will also be able to assist you in converting your manual system of accounting to computerized accounting. My enthusiasm for computer accounting and skill in the use of computers, which were the major reasons my current employer promoted me to my current position, would help you make your changeover quickly and smoothly. My experience in training people to use computers should also be of benefit as you update the skills of your employees, some of whom might not yet be "sold" on the idea of changing the system. In my current position, I have found enthusiasm, patience, and close initial supervision to be the keys to a successful changeover.

**EXHIBIT 16.15**  Concluded

Ms. Kathleen Horton
Page 2
January 15, 1996


Please call me at (303) 336-9498 or (303) 336-2213, Ext. 9631,
for an interview. I am eager to discuss how my solid technical
background and computer expertise will help you update your
operations.

Sincerely,

*Richard Doan*

Richard Doan

Enclosure

*A specific request for an interview, with phone numbers for easy access, and a final reference to the benefits of hiring him end Richard's letter on a strong note.*

**EXHIBIT 16.16**

**Direct Organizational Strategy for Application Letters**

**Your street or box number**
**Your city, state, and zip code**

Date


Name and Title of Person Doing Hiring (or Human Resources Manager)
Business Name
Street Address
City, State, and Zip Code

Salutation:

<u>Subject Line</u> (optional)

The first sentence should come right to the point. It (or the preceding subject line) should specify the position for which application is being made and should identify the source of information about the job (e.g., a newspaper advertisement or the school placement office). If someone told you about the job and his or her name might help you get the position, mention it.

If specific qualifications have been advertised for the job, each item in the job description should be addressed in the middle of the letter. Underlined headings are sometimes used to make the letter more pleasing to the eye and to make it easier to read. These headings would be separate areas of responsibility as advertised (e.g., "Programming Languages," "Software Experience," "Equipment Used," "Experience").

Stress your qualifications for the position in terms of your value to the employer. Information about all training, experience, and personal qualities should be worded in terms of how they will benefit the prospective employer.

Closing paragraphs should summarize your qualifications and stress your enthusiasm for the job. Mention must be made of the enclosed resume at some point in the letter. If letters of reference or other documents are included, these must also be referred to somewhere in the letter.

**EXHIBIT 16.16**

Concluded

Name of recipient                    2                         Date

The final paragraph should ask courteously for a personal interview to further discuss your qualifications for the position. Make it easy for the reader to set up an interview by providing your phone number and area code. If you are applying for a position in a town other than where you are currently living, suggest a date when you will be available to go to their offices.

Complimentary closing,


Your name

Enclosure notation

4.  *Action stage:* Request for next action (an interview) related to theme and reader benefit.

The most difficult part of the persuasive strategy for application letters is writing an attention-getter that strikes the appropriate tone. In some industries, such as advertising or public relations, you can be clever and dramatic, but in more subdued industries you should be more businesslike. Contrast these two openings:

> "New Year's Eve, Mardi Gras, and the Fourth of July all rolled into one"—that's how the local press reporter characterized last fall's Hinsdale centennial celebration. With your company's reputation for outstanding special events coordination, wouldn't it be nice to have the person behind Hinsdale's celebration on staff?

> A recent press release from your company mentioned that more clients than ever are asking about Internet. You may be interested, therefore, in having an Internet expert on hand to answer their questions.

One thing about using the persuasive strategy in application letters should be abundantly obvious: You must clearly point out the benefits of reading the letter and resume, interviewing you, and hiring you. Furthermore, to make a convincing case about these benefits, you must know something significant about the potential employer.

*The main pitfall of using the persuasive strategy for an application letter is that the attention-getting opening may seem unbusinesslike to the reader.*

*If you are using the persuasive strategy, it is more important than ever to point out how the employer will benefit by hiring you.*

## COMPOSING YOUR MESSAGE

Composing an application letter is a relatively routine task if you have already freewritten your basic ideas and chosen an appropriate organizational strategy. Then you need only to draft the message and put it into the accepted format.

With the job advertisement, his list of freewritten points, and a direct organizational strategy, Richard Doan drafted the application letter shown in Exhibit 16.15. If you read the letter and then compare it to the freewritten notes in Exhibit 16.14, you will see that some of the items that Richard originally thought to mention were not included in the letter. The drafting process frequently generates new ideas about what to say and how to say it. Freewritten notes are meant to serve only as a guide.

As far as the format is concerned, any acceptable business letter style (see Appendix C) may be used for application letters. However, because the letter is usually typed on plain paper and not on printed letterhead, the complete address of the writer must be typed above the date. This format is referred to as a **personal business letter**. All of the examples included in this chapter are personal business letters. However, you may also create a letterhead of your own. The second resume heading shown in Exhibit 16.1 would make a nice letterhead for an application letter.

An application letter is, in essence, you on paper, so it is important that it be perfect in every way. Typographical corrections should be undetectable, and careful attention must be paid to ensure that grammar, spelling, and sentence structure are correct. Use the same medium- to heavyweight bond paper for the letter that you use for the resume. If you are working on a computer, use a laser or laser-quality printer. A well-written letter that also looks professional will make you seem like the type of conscientious person employers like to hire.

*For application letters, use the personal business letter format, with a complete address typed above the date instead of preprinted onto letterhead.*

*Make sure your application letter is perfect in every detail so the prospective employer gets the best possible impression of your pride and professionalism.*

## EVALUATING YOUR MESSAGE

Before sending out an application letter, evaluate its content, organization, use of language, and appearance.

Evaluate an application letter before sending it.

Before you send an application letter, read it carefully and ask a few basic questions:

- Is it organized and written to achieve your purpose?
- Is the content correct in every detail, and clear, concise, complete, and courteous?
- Have you used the you attitude to show how your qualifications can meet the reader's needs?
- Is the message sincere?
- Have you used up-to-date, positive words and phrases?
- Are the spelling, grammar, sentence and paragraph structure, punctuation, and other language elements correct?
- Have you neatly made all needed corrections?
- Is the format correct?
- Does the letter look good?

You can also evaluate application letters by the results they produce: If they get you an interview, they are effective.

If you can say "yes" to each of these questions, your letter has a good chance of getting you a job interview—which is, of course, the ultimate goal of an application letter. However, before you send your letters, evaluate them by answering the questions in Exhibit 16.17. The few minutes it takes to evaluate your application letters thoroughly and honestly might make a real difference in your search for a satisfying job.

## DISCUSSION QUESTIONS

Look for job opportunities by checking all possible sources.

1. What is the major difference between a state employment agency and a private employment agency?

Look for job opportunities by checking all possible sources.

2. List four sources of information about current job openings in your field.

Look for job opportunities by checking all possible sources.

3. What is a job description? How does having one help you apply for a job? How can you get one for a job opening for which you want to apply?

Fill out application forms so that a potential employer has all the necessary information about your background and skills.

4. If you make a mistake when filling out an application form, how should you correct it?

Fill out application forms so that a potential employer has all the necessary information about your background and skills.

5. Why isn't it acceptable to write "See attached resume" instead of filling in a portion of the application form?

| | |
|---|---|
| **EXHIBIT 16.17** | **Checklist for Direct Application Letters** |

Answer the following yes/no questions. If a point does not apply, put N/A (not applicable) in the blank.

■ **The opening and the closing**

___ Does the first sentence (or the subject line) state the job for which you are applying?

___ Did you state where you found out about the opening, if appropriate?

___ Is effective you attitude used in the opening paragraph?

___ If the names of people who referred you are mentioned, is it done professionally—without obvious name dropping?

___ Is goodwill in the closing relevant to the situation?

___ Does the closing paragraph avoid trite, overused words and phrases?

___ Does the closing paragraph request an interview, making it easy for the reader by providing the telephone number (the number may be in the letterhead if a letterhead is used)?

___ Does the closing avoid thanking the reader in advance?

___ In the closing, is gratitude, if used, tied to the action the reader should perform?

■ **The Message**

___ Have all the employer's announced job requirements been addressed?

___ Have you said how your abilities and background can benefit the employer?

___ Have you shown by discussing the specific job requirements that you know what the job entails and that you can handle the job?

___ Have you avoided repeating the same wording used in the resume?

___ Have you disclosed clearly and completely everything that should be communicated?

___ Does the message you composed accomplish the purpose(s) established during freewriting?

___ Did you use positive words?

___ Did you mention the enclosed resume (and letters of reference if they are to be included)?

■ **The Tone**

___ Did you avoid overuse of *I, me,* and *my?*

___ Did you emphasize *you* and *your?*

___ Is goodwill sincere and appropriate to the situation?

___ Has the reader been treated with courtesy and respect?

___ Have you shown confidence in your abilities without sounding boastful?

___ Does your letter show enthusiasm for the job?

■ **The Mechanics**

___ Are the reader's name and title spelled and used correctly?

___ Have all words been spelled correctly?

___ Is correct sentence structure used for all sentences?

___ Is correct paragraph structure used for all paragraphs?

___ Are there transitions between each paragraph?

___ Is punctuation, etc., correct?

■ **The Readability**

___ Is the reading level appropriate for intended reader(s)?

___ Are subheadings used, if appropriate?

■ **The Format and Appearance**

___ Did you use a personal business letter style with the address typed above the date? (A personal letterhead with the same information may also be used.)

___ Are side margins equal?

___ Are corrections undetectable?

___ Has the letter or memorandum been folded correctly?

___ Is your signature readable?

___ Did you use an enclosure notation for the resume and, if included, letters of reference?

■ **Other**

___ Is the entire message truthful?

___ Have you been fair to the employer?

___ Would you be proud if everyone you know were aware of all the details in this letter?

___ Did you reply to the job announcement promptly?

___ Have deliberate distortions, slang, discriminatory language, clichés, redundancies, roundabout expressions, and confusing foreign expressions been avoided?

___ Did you research the company and its needs?

___ Did the letter result in an interview?

🔻Highlight in a resume the most attractive information about your education.

🔻Explain in a resume your work experience so that your achievements and skills are emphasized.

6. What one factor determines whether the education section or the work experience section of a resume should be listed first?

🐾 Highlight in a resume the most attractive information about your education.
🐾 Explain in a resume your work experience so that your achievements and skills are emphasized.

7. What is reverse chronological order? How does it pertain to the education and work experience sections of a resume?

🐾 Highlight in a resume the most attractive information about your education.
🐾 Write a resume with optional information that will appeal to potential employers.

8. Does the section "Major Courses Completed," if used, have to be a separate section of the resume with its own subheading? If so, why? If not, where else can this information go?

🐾 Explain in a resume your work experience so that your achievements and skills are emphasized.

9. Name the five items of information about an applicant's current and previous jobs that an employer expects to see on a resume.

🐾 Explain in a resume your work experience so that your achievements and skills are emphasized.

10. In the work experience section of a resume, is it permissible to include jobs for which you were not paid (e.g., volunteer positions or jobs where you received, instead of money, college credit)? If not, why? If so, where should these types of work experience be listed?

🐾 Explain in a resume your work experience so that your achievements and skills are emphasized.

11. What is an active verb? Give three examples of active present-tense verbs and three examples of active past-tense verbs. How does using active verbs improve the description of a job's duties?

🐾 Present five or more acceptable references to potential employers.

12. On what basis should you choose which references to list on a resume?

🐾 Write a resume that does not include information that is no longer required or allowed.

13. Why is it no longer necessary to include information about one's race, age, and gender on a resume?

🐾 Use a resume format that will draw attention to your most desirable features and will make important information accessible to potential employers.

14. What is the maximum number of pages for a resume? What is the rationale for that length?

🐾 Use a resume format that will draw attention to your most desirable features and will make important information accessible to potential employers.

15. If a second page is used for a resume, what should its heading include?

🐾 Apply the message formulation process to application letters.

16. What is involved in applying the message formulation process to application letters?

▖ Apply the message formulation process to application letters.

17. What is the ultimate purpose of an application letter?

▖ Understand the needs of people who read application letters.

18. What are the basic needs of the person who reads an application letter?

▖ Collect information about the company to which you are applying for a job.

19. Under what circumstances is it important to do research on a company before writing the application letter?

▖ Know what type of strategy to use for an application letter.

20. Why is it important to let the reader know you are applying for a job in the first sentence of an application letter?

▖ Know what type of strategy to use for an application letter.

21. When would it be appropriate for you to reveal in an application letter the name of someone who told you about a job opening in her or his company?

▖ Know what type of strategy to use for an application letter.

22. What is the role of persuasion in an application letter?

▖ Know what type of strategy to use for an application letter.

23. What are the components of the last paragraph of an effective application letter?

## APPLICATION EXERCISES

▖ Look for job opportunities by checking all possible sources.

1. Call your state employment agency to determine the application and testing procedures for the type of position in which you are interested. Write a memo report for your instructor that completely describes the process and any tests that may be required.

▖ Look for job opportunities by checking all possible sources.

2. Visit or call a private employment agency to determine its application and testing procedures for the type of position in which you are interested. Write a memo report to your instructor that includes complete descriptions of the process and any tests that may be required. Other information to include: How are their fees computed? Who pays the fee? When is it due? Do the fees vary? Copies of the application form and the contract should be included with your report.

▖ Look for job opportunities by checking all possible sources.

3. Use your telephone book and telephone to track down this information: How do you go about applying for a job in your chosen field if you want to work for the civil service? The state? The county? The city? What are the application and testing procedures of each? What do these jobs pay? Can

you get job descriptions? Write a memo report for your instructor that details your findings.

■ Look for job opportunities by checking all possible sources.

4. Using the yellow pages of your local telephone book, list three companies or individuals, if any, that are involved in these fields:

Oil and gas exploration and/or production.

International construction.

Advertising.

Secretarial services.

Law.

Medicine.

Aerospace/aircraft manufacturing and design.

■ Look for job opportunities by checking all possible sources.
■ Fill out application forms so that a potential employer has all the necessary information about your background and skills.

5. Obtain an application form from a large employer in your area, preferably one that you might like to work for. Fill out the form as neatly and completely as possible, and submit a copy of it to your instructor.

■ Highlight in a resume the most attractive information about your education.
■ Explain in a resume your work experience so that your achievements and skills are emphasized.
■ Use a resume format that will draw attention to your most desirable features and will make important information accessible to potential employers.

6. Prepare, as if for a resume, a draft display of your educational qualifications and work experience for a job that would meet your career objective at this point. Be sure to present the most significant section first, and arrange the information within each section in reverse chronological order. At the top of the page, describe your career objective.

■ Explain in a resume your work experience so that your achievements and skills are emphasized.

7. Analyze the strengths and weaknesses of the following descriptions of work experience:
   a. For a current position as a machine transcriber: "Often asked to transcribe long legal documents, type on a computer with a Dictaphone transcriber, responsible for doing work for as many as five individuals, trained new employees."
   b. For a previous position as a bookkeeper: "Reported directly to chief accountant, made daily journal and ledger entries, balanced checkbook, prepared rough draft balance sheets and income and expense statements, operated an IBM-compatible computer with both Quicken software and software designed specifically for this company's use, assisted in conversion from manual to computer accounting."
   c. For a former position as a hostess at a prestigious restaurant: "My duties were to greet customers by phone and in person, make

reservations, sort and seat customers according to size and number depending on parties already scheduled for on-floor servers. Received two $50 bonuses."

🔖 Present five or more acceptable references to potential employers.

8. Prepare a separate reference sheet for yourself according to the principles presented in this chapter. Include at least five people who have given you permission to use their names.

🔖 Write a resume with optional information that will appeal to potential employers.

9. Make a complete list of all your skills, coursework, interests, activities, and honors that might possibly interest an employer in the field in which you are interested. At the top of the list, specify your career objective.

🔖 Write a resume that does not include information that is no longer required or allowed.

10. At the library, research some aspect of the topic of employment discrimination that interests you (e.g., discrimination on the basis of age, gender, sexual preference, race, or disability). Write a three- to five-page report, complete with references.

🔖 Use a resume format that will draw attention to your most desirable features and will make important information accessible to potential employers.

11. Prepare and type an effective resume for yourself using the principles presented in this chapter. Be honest about your background; do not include incorrect or misleading information.

🔖 Apply the message formulation process to application letters.
🔖 Write an ethical application letter.
🔖 Understand the needs of people who read application letters.
🔖 Collect information about the company to which you are applying for a job.
🔖 Know what type of strategy to use for an application letter.

12. Write an application memo for a promotion within the company where you now work or an application letter for a job advertised in the local newspaper or your school placement office. Choose a job for which you are now qualified. If you have not already done so, prepare a resume for this type of job. Submit both the application memo or letter and the resume to your instructor.

🔖 Apply the message formulation process to application letters.
🔖 Write an ethical application letter.
🔖 Understand the needs of people who read application letters.
🔖 Know what type of strategy to use for an application letter.

13. Find a job opening that you are now qualified to fill by consulting the advertisements in the local newspaper or the postings at the school placement office. Freewrite a list of the major points you should cover in writing an application letter for this job. Be honest about your qualifications; do not include incorrect information. Prioritize the items in the list, and submit it in rough form to your instructor, along with a copy of the advertisement.

◤ Apply the message formulation process to application letters.
◤ Write an ethical application letter.
◤ Understand the needs of people who read application letters.
◤ Collect information about the company to which you are applying for a job.
◤ Know what type of strategy to use for an application letter.
◤ Evaluate an application letter before sending it.

14. Find an appealing job listing in a newspaper or at your school placement office for which you have most but not all the stated qualifications. It may be a job related indirectly to your qualifications (e.g., an outside sales job for a person with public relations experience) or a job a rung or two up your chosen career ladder (e.g., a job as a sales representative for someone who has worked in sales support). Write a persuasive application letter that ethically presents your true qualifications but makes a strong case for hiring you despite the discrepancy between the job description and your qualifications.

◤ Apply the message formulation process to application letters.
◤ Understand the needs of people who read application letters.

15. From the job advertisements in a local newspaper or at your school placement office, select three jobs for which you are now qualified. (If you cannot find three such jobs, devise hypothetical jobs.) Write a specific purpose statement for an application letter for each job. Prepare a brief memo report for your instructor that includes the three purpose statements and explains how and why they differ; attach copies of the job descriptions or advertisements.

◤ Understand the needs of people who read application letters.
◤ Evaluate an application letter before sending it.

16. In a group of three of four students assigned by your instructor, do the following:
    a. Analyze each group member's application letter prepared in exercise 12 to determine if the you attitude has been used to reveal how the applicant's qualifications meet the employer's needs.
    b. Evaluate each letter according to the list of basic questions presented at the end of this chapter (see Exhibit 16.17).
    c. Compare the letters with the resumes they are intended to accompany. Do the letters simply restate what is already typed on the resumes, or do they highlight the important parts of the resume that are pertinent to the job sought?
    d. Make suggestions for improving both the application letters and the resumes.

◤ Understand the needs of people who read application letters.
◤ Evaluate an application letter before sending it.

17. Analyze how the you attitude is used in each of the sample application letters in this chapter (Exhibits 16.10, 16.11, 16.12, and 16.16). For each one, point out specific passages that reveal how the applicant's background, skills, personal qualities, and so on meet the reader's needs. Note where the use of I, me, and my has been avoided. Can you suggest any improvements in how the you attitude has been used?

■ Collect information about the company to which you are applying for a job.

18. Go to your school or local library to consult the sources of company information that are listed in Exhibit 16.13. Focusing on two major companies in your area, determine answers to at least four of the questions about companies posed in this chapter (in the section titled "Gather Necessary Resources"). Copy the pages from these sources that you use to answer these questions, and submit them along with a memo report on your findings.

■ Collect information about the company to which you are applying for a job.

19. Call or visit a major company in your area to ask for a copy of its annual report. What kinds of information from this annual report could you use to write a reader-oriented application letter for the career for which you are training? Prepare a brief memo report, and submit it with the annual report.

■ Know what type of strategy to use for an application letter.
■ Evaluate an application letter before sending it.

20. Evaluate in a memo report to your instructor the following openings to application letters:
    a. "It has long been a dream of mine to work for . . . "
    b. "inclosed is my aplication for the pposition of proofreader. You will see that Im well qualified for the job advertised in yesterday's newspaper."
    c. "You will see from reading the enclosed resume that I am a well-qualified applicant for the sales associate position you advertised with the Crenshaw College placement office."
    d. "My research into the ethnic makeup of the upper-level management of your company reveals you are in violation of the law requiring minorities to be represented in numbers approximately equal to the local population. Hiring me will help you meet this goal."

# CHAPTER 17

# INTERVIEWING FOR JOBS AND FOLLOWING UP

## OBJECTIVES

After studying this chapter, you should be able to do the following:

◆ Use three methods to secure job interviews.

◆ Progress comfortably through the four phases of a job interview.

◆ Convey a professional image through your clothing, grooming, and body language.

◆ Frame responses to likely interview questions before the interview takes place.

◆ Respond confidently to typical interview questions.

◆ Handle inappropriate interview questions.

◆ Ask questions that demonstrate your interest in the job and reinforce your strengths.

◆ Write follow-up correspondence that is appropriate to the circumstances and enhances your prospects of getting a good job.

### WHAT WOULD YOU DO IF...?

**DIFFICULT CHOICES.**   Lip Yeon Gow came to the United States from Malaysia seven years ago and is now a U.S. citizen. His strong accent makes it obvious that Lip's native language is not English; however, he has a bachelor's degree in accounting from a U.S. college. Lip is married and has three children, one who is now in college and one who will be starting college next year.

Applying for a job as an accountant with Wilkinson-Scopes, a major manufacturing firm, Lip interviewed successfully with a personnel department employee. Lip was convinced after the interview that he would like to work for Wilkinson-Sharpes. The salary was significantly more than that for his current job, the company has a better retirement program, and he will have the opportunity to use all his accounting skills and knowledge. Lip was very pleased when he was called to come for a final interview with the head of the accounting department, John Clark.

However, now, during the interview with Mr. Clark, Lip has become disturbed by the nature of the questions, many of which have nothing to do with Lip's ability to do the job. Mr. Clark obviously appreciates Lip's skills and experience, but he also has made a number of biased comments, among them the following:

"I can't even tell which is your first name and which is your last name! Have you ever thought about changing your name?"

"Are you Chinese or Japanese? What about your wife?"

"I hear you people are good with numbers."

"You're a lot older than most of the people who work for me. Would that bother you?"

"How do you feel about living in the United States? Did you bring all your relatives over with you?"

"With that accent, do you think you'll have any trouble communicating with the rest of us?"

Lip is torn between his desire for the job and his wish to challenge Mr. Clark. He wants to tell Mr. Clark that some of his questions are discriminatory, because they would not be asked of all applicants for the job and because they do not focus on the skills and qualities necessary to perform the job. However, Lip is afraid of losing the job if he stands up to Mr. Clark in the interview.

Put yourself in Lip's shoes. What would you do if something similar happened to you? What are Lip's options? Should he challenge Mr. Clark and risk losing the job offer, or just answer the questions pleasantly? Is there anything else he can do during the interview to protect his rights? What do you think these questions might indicate about the working relationship that would exist between Lip and John Clark? Then consider this situation from Mr. Clark's point of view. Should employers have the right to ask anything to ensure they hire people who will benefit their companies? How can the rights of individuals and those of employers be balanced? The information presented in this chapter will help you answer these questions.

A job interview doesn't have to be torture if you're well prepared!

"Have you ever been fired from a job? How many children do you have? Do you work well with younger people? Tell me everything you know!"

## INTERVIEW ESSENTIALS

A job interview is a chance for the employer to get a better look at you and for you to get a better look at the employer and the company.

The job interview is the goal of all the tasks discussed in Chapter 16: identifying sources of jobs, writing a resume, and writing an application letter. If you are successful in getting an interview and then convincing the interviewer that you are qualified for the job, have the personality to get along with other employees, and fit the company's image, you will probably be offered the job. At the same time, the interview gives you a chance to determine if the job, the conditions of employment, and the company itself actually provide what you are looking for. To help you approach this important event with confidence, this section explains how to secure an interview, when to schedule it for greatest advantage, and what will happen as an interview proceeds. With forethought and preparation, job interviews can become positive experiences. Although all interviews will not result in job offers, you can still learn to interview better with each job search experience.

### SECURING AN INTERVIEW

▶ Use three methods to secure job interviews.

You may already know how hard it is to get a job interview these days. Most jobs, especially entry-level jobs, seem to have hordes of applicants. Unfortunately, of all those who send resumes and application letters or submit application forms, only a few get a chance to meet face-to-face with someone who has hiring authority. You may have to be creative, confident, and persistent to get an appointment. However, if you are willing to try the following techniques, you should get your share of the available slots.

One way to get a job interview is by mail, but this method gives you the least opportunity to persuade an interviewer to see you.

**BY MAIL.**   One way to secure an interview is to send a letter with a resume. An effective application letter, written to explain how your qualifications can meet the employer's needs, may convince the person scheduling interviews that you are a likely candidate for the job. On the other hand, an application letter is easy to ignore. A more active approach may work better in some cases.

When you visit a medium- or large-sized company, you may be able to secure an interview through courtesy and persistence.

**BY WALK-IN.**   Chapter 16 described the technique of visiting a medium- or large-sized company in your area, without an appointment, to get information about job openings. This "walk-in" technique may also get you a job interview. Instead of just asking for an application form, tell the receptionist the type of position for which you are applying and ask for an interview. If it is not possible to interview on that day, you can try to set an appointment for another day.

Don't allow yourself to be discouraged by statements such as "Leave your name and number; Ms. Kelly is too busy to see you now" or "We don't have any openings." It is the receptionist's job to protect busy co-workers from unwanted interruptions. However, you may be able to get what you want with a friendly, nonthreatening, but persistent response:

"Oh, I'm sorry she's not available now. I'd be happy to wait here to see if she can, perhaps, work me in."

"Oh, I'm sorry there aren't any current openings. You're lucky to work for Hughes. Ever since I took my first helicopter ride, I've wanted to work for the company that makes them. I'd like to talk to your boss today if it's humanly possible—just to see if I can convince her I'm the one she needs for the next job that comes up. Could you arrange it? I'd really appreciate the favor."

If this approach doesn't work, try to get the receptionist to set an interview for another day. A courteous, upbeat attitude might encourage the receptionist to help you secure that all-important interview. Most working people identify with a person looking for a good job.

> A phone call may get you an interview or at least some important information: descriptions of jobs currently open, application forms, or best of all, the name of the person in charge of the department in which you'd like to work.

**By Telephone.**   The same sort of approach can be used if you telephone to request an interview. Practice beforehand how you will begin the conversation because, for many people, the beginning is the most difficult part of a telephone call. If you are calling about a current job opening, you might begin as follows:

"Hello, my name is Juan Gutierrez. I'm calling to schedule an interview for the purchasing position you advertised."

While you're on the phone, you could also ask for the name of the person for whom you would be working, even if someone else will be conducting the interview. Then ask to speak to that person, or call him or her later. If you get a chance to talk with the supervisor, this telephone conversation could be extremely important. In fact, you should view it as an extension of the interview. If you can convince your potential boss that you are qualified for the job and that you will be an interesting, pleasant person to work with, she or he might put in a good word for you with the interviewer. You might also get valuable inside information that could be used to your advantage during the interview.

When you don't know if the company is currently hiring for the type of position you want, you should ask for someone in the personnel department and then try an opening along these lines:

"Hello, my name is Juan Gutierrez. I'd like to schedule an interview for a position in your purchasing department."

Even if the person says there are no openings currently, you can make your phone call count. Ask the person you talk with to send an application by mail. Ask for the name, and its correct spelling, of the person who is in charge of the department in which you hope to work. Then send this individual the completed application form, along with an application letter and a resume. You could also deliver the completed application form yourself, and try to get an interview at that time.

### Scheduling the Interview

> Try to be one of the last people interviewed for a job.

If you are given a choice of interview dates, consider whether you would prefer to be one of the first individuals to interview for a job opening or whether there might be a psychological advantage to being one of the last. If a lot of people are scheduled over a period of several days, those who are interviewed toward the end are more likely to remain fresh in the minds of the interviewers. As long as you make a good impression during the interview, having one of the last appointments might increase your chances of being selected for the job.

Schedule an interview for a day and time when the interviewer will be able to concentrate on you.

In addition, try to avoid the days and times when people may be distracted by other concerns. People are not usually at their best on Monday mornings, Friday afternoons, or right before and after lunch.

Once an interview has been scheduled, ask that an application form and a written job description for the position be mailed to you in advance (if you didn't get them earlier). You can then bring the necessary forms with you to the interview, and the job description will help you think ahead of time about how your qualifications and the job requirements match.

## UNDERSTANDING THE PROCESS

In the typical interview, one applicant and one interviewer meet face to face, although you may encounter variations.

Most job interviews are the standard format: Each job applicant is interviewed face-to-face for perhaps 15 minutes to an hour by one person who makes a decision about whom to hire after all the applicants have been interviewed. However, you may encounter one of these variations:

- *Multistage interview.* A series of interviews gradually narrows the field of applicants. You must "pass" each stage to move on to the next interviewer, who is usually someone higher up in the organization. Typically, someone from the personnel department will narrow the number of candidates to three or four, who are then interviewed by the supervisor for whom the new employee will work. It is usually the supervisor who makes the final decision.

- *Group interview.* You are invited to meet with a group, usually composed of people who are familiar with the job for which you are being interviewed or who work in the same department. Any member of the group may have questions for you; all will participate in making the hiring decision. However, one or more people may be included for other reasons—for example, to ensure that the interview is conducted legally and in accordance with affirmative action guidelines.

- *Telephone interview.* An out-of-town applicant may be interviewed by one person over the phone or by a group of individuals in a conference call. A telephone interview is often used as the first stage in a multistage interview. It takes less time to narrow down the number of applicants by telephone than to interview them in person.

- *Computer interview.* In the latest variation on the traditional job interview, you read questions on a computer screen and type answers into the computer. No interviewer is present. The computer then prints out a summary of the information you have provided. Like the telephone interview, the computer interview is often used to screen applicants. Desirable candidates are telephoned to return for a second interview, this time with a person.

- *Video interview.* Another high-tech variation of the interview is one in which an applicant responds to questions printed on a sheet of paper while being video-taped—somewhat like a video dating service! Videos are then scanned by human resources professionals who quickly determine who will be invited back for a face-to-face interview.

Progress comfortably through the four phases of a job interview.

Most of these interview types (except possibly the computer and the video interviews) usually proceed through four phases: preinterview, warmup, discussion of the candidate's background, and conclusion and candidate summary. During each phase, you have special opportunities to prove that you are qualified and have the personal characteristics that will make you a good employee.

**PREINTERVIEW PHASE.** From the moment you walk through the company's front door, you are being evaluated. Therefore, you should smile and introduce yourself cordially to the receptionist, extend your hand for a handshake, and explain the purpose of your visit. People who will participate in the hiring decision could be passing by, so even at this early stage, you want to display good manners. In addition, making a good impression on the receptionist could be important later if you need special help.

Before the interview even begins, you are being evaluated on your appearance and manners. Even the lower-level employees you encounter may influence the hiring decision.

As with any business appointment, promptness is important. You should plan to arrive at the office 5 to 10 minutes early. Being late is a poor way to demonstrate your reliability. However, if being late is unavoidable, be sure to call the interviewer ahead of time.

Of course, you should be prepared to prove your qualifications. In a new file folder or, preferably, a nice briefcase, you should have copies of your resume, a list of your references with their telephone numbers and addresses, and detailed information about your former jobs. You may be asked to complete an application form, which may ask for facts not included on your resume. Other items that might make it easier for the interviewer to judge your ability to perform the job are photocopies of diplomas or certificates, samples of work you have done similar to the kind of work the job requires, and copies of reference letters not sent previously with your resume.

If you are not immediately escorted to another office for the interview, take advantage of this time to look through your supporting documents. Think positive thoughts, and imagine yourself in the position for which you are applying. If annual reports or other company literature are lying on the tables, read them. You might glean some valuable information that will help you during the interview.

**WARMUP.** The warmup phase begins when you are escorted to the interviewer. Cordial greetings, smiles, and a handshake break the ice. Usually, you and the interviewer will spend a few moments exchanging small talk about such things as the weather or recent sporting events. Small talk is a good way for the interviewer to see how you relate to people in general. You can prepare for this phase by keeping abreast of local events, especially by reading the sports pages of your local newspaper, before interviewing for a job.

The warmup phase gives the interviewer a chance to evaluate your social skills.

**CANDIDATE'S BACKGROUND DISCUSSION.** During this phase of the interview, the interviewer discusses your resume or application form or asks you to provide an overview of your background. At this stage, the interviewer is usually verifying his or her initial impression of you. The emphasis is often on your career goals and whether they are consistent, realistic, positive, and compatible with what the organization can offer.

Most of the interview time is spent on a review of your qualifications, but the interviewer will also be evaluating your career goals and your enthusiasm for the job and the company.

Your goal is to provide information that proves you are qualified as well as to convey your enthusiasm for the job and the company. You should, therefore, answer questions with more than a simple "yes" or "no." Phrase all your answers in terms of how your knowledge, skills, and personal characteristics will benefit the company and match the requirements for the job. "Sell" yourself—subtly, but without hesitation.

A note of caution here—if you are the kind of person who tends to be overly enthusiastic or dominate conversations, remember to concentrate more on listening to the interviewer. Be sure your natural tendency to control the conversation doesn't lead the interviewer to conclude you are overbearing.

Carefully observe the interviewer's body language, and adjust your manner and your answers if signs indicate that the interviewer disapproves.

How the interviewer perceives you and your answers can often be determined by observing his or her body language. When people agree with you or are interested in what you are saying, they usually lean forward in their seats and do not cross their arms in front of their bodies. Other encouraging signs from the interviewer include maintaining good eye contact, nodding his or her head, and saying "yes" and "uh-huh" to reassure you. If the interviewer is not exhibiting these sorts of behaviors, adjust what you are saying or how you are saying it.

Toward the end of the interview, you may want to probe the interviewer for possible misgivings about your qualifications so you can refute them and reinforce your strengths.

**CONCLUSION AND CANDIDATE SUMMARY.** Toward the end of the interview, you should be able to tell if the interviewer is interested in you. If he or she seems to be trying to convince you the company is a good firm for which to work, a job offer is likely to follow. Sometimes, in contrast, the interviewer will let you know that you do not meet the requirements. However, you might have to ask for this feedback if you are not getting clear signals. You can then try to overcome the objections. First, agree that the requirement is an important one. Then communicate your confidence that you can fill the need. Relate an example or two from your prior experience that shows how you addressed a similar situation or how you learned a new skill and were able to apply it when needed.

A good interviewer will usually conclude by asking if you have questions. Always ask questions, but don't ask only about what the company can do for you. Imagine the impression the following response would make?

> Questions? Oh yes! How many weeks of vacation would I get, and how flexible are you about working hours? You said raises are considered only once a year? Is there any way that can be changed? Doesn't the company have any plans to add vision care to its dental and medical insurance package?

When the interviewer's body language indicates it is time to leave, it is your responsibility to summarize your key qualifications and your understanding of what is to happen next.

If the interviewer doesn't tell you when the interview is over, you will probably be able to tell by his or her nonverbal cues: shifting posture, stacking papers up neatly on the desk, and/or aligning pencils and pens beside the folders. At this point, it is your responsibility to begin the candidate summary. This is an important part of the interview, although it often takes place as you are both standing, ready to part. Summarize very briefly what you understand to be the significant points covered in the interview and the key events that are to follow. Make sure you and the interviewer understand each other completely. For example, during the parting handshake, while making good eye contact with the interviewer, you might say:

> I understand, Ms. Salardino, that you feel I am well qualified for the position, and I will be considered further. (Pause for a split second for a comment or a nod from the interviewer.) Would it be alright if I call you on Thursday after you finish your interviews if I haven't already heard from you? (Pause again for a response.) Thank you again, Ms. Salardino, for talking to me about the job. I would like to work for CNC Industries. I have a lot to offer you and the company, so I hope to hear from you soon.

This is a confident and sensible wrapup that can only work to your advantage.

## A PROFESSIONAL IMAGE

■ Convey a professional image through your clothing, grooming, and body language.

As you can see from the illustrations below, the impression you make in an interview depends on what you do *and* say. A later section will give you some hints about making a good verbal impression; this section deals with the nonverbal impression. In general, you want to appear professional, competent, responsible, and confident. You want your clothes, grooming, and body language to help convince a potential employer that you are the best person for the job.

**There is a right way to dress for business!**

**And a wrong way too!**

### CLOTHING AND GROOMING

You will be evaluated on the way you look from the minute you walk in the door, so be sure your clothing and grooming are suitable for business.

First impressions are important, and a large part of what the interviewer will first see is your clothes and grooming. If you look like a mature, confident professional who knows what the business world expects, your chances of being offered a good job will increase significantly. People who look professional are usually treated more professionally in the interview and often wind up with higher salaries.

The safest outfit for both female and male applicants is a conservatively styled business suit.

The guiding principle is to dress in clothing appropriate for the job for which you are applying. For most career positions, a simple business suit is appropriate interview garb for both men and women. However, if you are applying for a job in, say, the fashion or film industries, trendier garb might be more acceptable. In either case, your clothing should be relatively conservative, giving an impression of quiet confidence and mature self-assurance.

For women, the standard business suit has a skirt hemmed just below or above the knee. The suit you wear to the interview should be navy blue, gray, or some other neutral color; save your more colorful suits for later, when you have actually won the job. The suit should also be conservatively styled; indeed, a suit that remains in fashion from year to year is a good investment for a businesswoman. The blouse you wear with the suit should have a modest neckline and little ornamentation (no frilly details). You may wear a simple necklace, a small ribbon tie, or an expertly tied scarf with the blouse. Your shoes should have closed toes and heels and should be polished and in good repair. Wear low heels, never spikes. Keep jewelry small and to a minimum—at the very most, small earrings, a small watch, one ring on each hand, and perhaps a simple necklace or bracelet.

Acceptable business clothing for men is much like that suggested for women. Navy blue and gray suits with tasteful, conservative ties are considered standard. Although in some businesses only long-sleeved white shirts are acceptable, light blue and other pastel colors are now fairly common. You should wear dark-colored socks that match the suit and conservative loafers or dress shoes made of smooth leather (black for navy blue and gray suits). Keep your jewelry to a minimum: no more than a watch, one ring on each hand, and, possibly, a tie tack.

If you carry a briefcase, make sure it is simple and well maintained. Leather is nice, but there are also acceptable imitation leather briefcases. Women should not carry both a purse and a briefcase; instead, they can slip their wallets and other supplies into the briefcase.

Grooming is as important as your clothing. Wearing an expensive suit won't overcome the dismal impression you'll make if your clothes are grimy, your fingernails are dirty, and your hair is greasy. Make sure you smell good too, but don't overdo the cologne—your interviewer may have allergies. As for your hair, choose a conservative style and a natural color. Short, off-the-collar hairstyles are preferred for men in conservative businesses; however, longer hair is perfectly acceptable in some fields, such as the entertainment industry. Women's hair may be long or short, but make sure it is not too bushy or wild and does not require constant fiddling. Poor grooming brings unwanted attention to your looks; good grooming will help the interviewer focus on your qualifications.

Good grooming—cleanliness and neatness—is a sign that you respect yourself and the standards of the business world.

The interviewer will be sensitive to nonverbal signs that you are confident, enthusiastic, and sincere.

**BODY LANGUAGE.** Another important aspect of the nonverbal message you convey to an interviewer is your body language. Here are a few things you can do to appear professional, confident, enthusiastic, and sincere:

- Never smoke or chew gum, even while you are sitting in a waiting area.
- Use a firm handshake, smile, and look the interviewer in the eye when being introduced and concluding the interview.
- If you are able to choose a chair to sit in during the interview, choose one at the side of the interviewer's desk instead of across it. (You want to avoid having a barrier between you and the interviewer.)
- Sit comfortably, not stiffly, but fairly erect. Lean forward slightly to show you are attentive. Avoid leaning back with arms folded across your chest,

because this posture is often interpreted as an unconscious attempt to block out the interviewer.

- During the interview, maintain good eye contact. The applicant who seldom looks the interviewer in the eye might simply be shy; however, poor eye contact is often interpreted as a sign that the person is lying.

- Be an attentive and eager listener. Reinforce the interviewer's comments with nods and approving "ahs."

- Let your feelings show on your face; facial expressions that show warmth and enthusiasm are especially winning. Gesture when you emphasize points, but squelch any tendency you may have to be overly dramatic.

- If you are a woman, cross your legs at the ankles. Crossing them at the knee is often perceived as an attempt to draw attention to the legs.

- Keep your hands away from your mouth, neck, and ears when answering questions, because this sort of touching is often interpreted as a sign of lying.

- Avoid annoying speech mannerisms that people often use to fill in the spaces while they search for words to say. Peppering sentences with "you know," "like," "ah," or "um" is interpreted by others as a sign of insecurity, immaturity, lack of professionalism, or lying behavior.

- Let your enthusiasm show in a voice that varies naturally in tone and rate; a monotone will make you seem dull and bored. Emphasize major points by raising your voice's volume slightly.

## INTERVIEW QUESTIONS AND ANSWERS

Frame responses to likely interview questions before the interview takes place.

**The questions you will be asked concern your qualifications, attitudes, and technical knowledge.**

Questions and answers consume the largest part of a job interview. Although no two interviews are the same, they generally cover many of the same questions. Some of the questions will be asked by the interviewer, and some will be asked by the applicant. Of course, you will be asked questions about your background, many of them covering points you have already made in your application letter and on your resume. Other questions that are typically asked in job interviews concern your attitudes toward work and your feelings about your own competence. You must also be prepared for technical questions about equipment, programs, procedures, and other things that are unique to each job.

Listen carefully to questions as they are asked. If a question asked of you is not clear, you may ask the interviewer to restate it, or you may put what you think he or she meant into your own words. The interviewer will restate the question if your interpretation is not correct.

**You can overcome anxiety about answering the interviewer's questions if you think of the interview as an opportunity to sell yourself and get more information, and if you prepare answers ahead of time for some of the most likely questions.**

Many people are intimidated by the thought that they will have to answer the interviewer's probing questions. You can overcome your anxiety if you think of those questions as opportunities to talk about your good points. Remember, too, that you are actually evaluating the interviewer and the company to decide if you even want to work there. The interview gives you a chance to find out more about the job and the company. Use this three-step process to predetermine responses to the questions you are most likely to be asked:

**As you prepare your answers, explore these three questions.**

1. *Why would the employer want to know this information?* One of the reasons for asking some questions is obvious—the information is needed. An example is the question "What do you do in your current job?" The motives are less obvious for a question like "Is your grasp of English sufficient to allow you to communicate effectively with customers and co-workers?" The interviewer who asks you this question might be trying to get you to reveal information about your national origin that cannot legally be requested. Other types of inquiries that are questionable are discussed later in this chapter.

2. *What would the interviewer probably like to hear as a response?* Once you have determined the probable motive(s) for a question, you must then ask yourself what a desirable answer would be. You shouldn't lie, of course, but you should try to meet the interviewer's expectations.

**Your answers should emphasize your strengths and point out the benefits of hiring you.**

3. *How will I respond to the question?* Frame your answer to each question in terms of your strengths and their value to the employer. Point out how you can help the employer do the following: increase profits, decrease risk, make life better or easier for other employees or for the public, save time, and enhance the company's or supervisor's prestige or image. Just remember that there is no one correct response for each question. Each job, each company, and each individual bring new factors to bear on any response. Whatever your answers, however, they should be truthful and sincere.

Here's an example of how you can apply the three-step process in formulating a response to the first question in Exhibit 17.1: "What are your long-range career objectives, and how do you plan to achieve these goals?"

1. *Why would the employer want to know this information?* Your answer to this question about career objectives reveals how serious you are about the job. It also shows whether you have goals and a plan for achieving them and how this job relates to your long-term goals. If the company hires you, what is the likelihood you will remain on the job and with the company for a significant length of time?

2. *What would the interviewer probably like to hear as a response?* The interviewer would probably like to hear that this job is a logical step in achieving your long-term career goals. If your immediate job objective and your long-term career objective are related, you are more likely to remain with the company for a long time. Such an answer also demonstrates the ability to set reasonable goals and devise a plan to reach them.

3. *How will I respond to the question?* A good response to this question in an interview for a job as a fire department dispatcher might be as follows:

> My long-term career objective is to be an emergency medical technician. I plan to achieve that goal by taking courses to become certified. This job as a dispatcher will enable me to be actively involved in the field while I am attending school. I grew up in a boating family, so I'm familiar with radio communications. I should need little training for the job. Daily association with your EMTs would be a rewarding learning experience for me, and my obvious interest in the field and my training will enable me to serve you much better than someone who sees this job only as a means to a paycheck.

Notice that this response not only directly answers the question but also leads into a discussion of the applicant's strengths.

---

**EXHIBIT 17.1**

**Frequently Asked Interview Questions**

1. "What are your long-range career objectives, and how do you plan to achieve these goals?"
2. "What do you expect to be doing 5 (or 10) years from now?"
3. "Why did you choose this career?"
4. "Why do you want this job?"
5. "In what type of position are you most interested?"
6. "Why do you want to work for us? What do you know about our company?"
7. "What do you think about what is happening in our industry today?"
8. "What do you consider to be your greatest strengths?"
9. "What do you consider to be your greatest weaknesses?" (Also: "In your last job, did you get any clue as to your development needs? In what areas were/are you weakest? For example, have you found you don't work as hard as the average person, get along poorly with certain people, or need to be better organized?")
10. "How would you describe yourself? Tell me something about your background."
11. "Why should I hire you?"
12. "What have you accomplished that would show us you are the right person for this job?" (Also: "What two or three accomplishments have given you the most satisfaction? Why?")
13. "What must a job have to give you satisfaction?"
14. "What criteria are you using to evaluate the company for which you hope to work?"
15. "What changes would you make in the last company you worked for (or the last school you attended)?"
16. "What major problems did you encounter in your last job? How did you handle them?"
17. "Why are you leaving your current job? Previous jobs?"
18. "Have you ever had difficulty getting along with other students? Teachers? Supervisors? Co-workers?"
19. "Do you have any serious illness, injury, or disability (mental, physical, or sensory) that might affect your work performance?"
20. "Tell me something about your education and your school(s)."
21. "What duties did you like least (or best) in your last (or current) job?"
22. "Do you think a company should consider a person's grades when hiring a person?"
23. "Do you prefer working by yourself or with others?"
24. "What are your ideas on salary?" (Also: "What are you worth?")
25. "If X (some sort of problem) happened to you on the job, what would you do?" (case study)

Think if you have ever come away from an interview saying, "Oh, no, I forgot to say . . . " The stress of an interview may understandably cause you to forget the important points you wanted to make. However, by preparing thoughtful answers to the most likely questions in advance—writing down your answers and practicing them—you will be more likely to have the words you need to convince the interviewer that you are a good prospect.

## TYPICAL QUESTIONS AND ANSWERS

Respond confidently to typical interview questions.

The questions most typically asked in job interviews fall into five major categories: those to which you will respond with technical information about your specific field, those to which you will respond by stressing your strengths, those that address your weaknesses, those dealing with your reasons for leaving current and prior jobs, and those dealing with your beginning salary. The following suggestions will give you some ideas about how to answer each type of question.

Prepare for technical questions by keeping abreast of developments in your area of specialty and in your industry.

**TECHNICAL INFORMATION.** Technical information is, of course, different for each job and each company. Commonly used equipment, procedures, problems, and outlook for the industry and the company are likely to be the subjects of this category.

The best way to prepare for this type of question, besides accumulating personal experience and education, is to read magazines and newspapers in your field. The same research sources recommended in Chapter 16 for planning an application letter can be used to prepare for an interview.

In answering questions about your strengths, provide concrete examples.

**STRENGTHS.** Applicants whose strengths match employers' needs are usually the people hired to fill job openings. Besides technical knowledge, interviewers admire dependability, responsibility, friendliness, ability to work well with others, loyalty, and enthusiasm for the job.

The question "What do you consider to be your greatest strengths?" is the most obvious question in this category. However, the following can also be answered in terms of your strengths:

"How would you describe yourself? Tell me about your background."

"Why should I hire you?"

"What must a job have to give you satisfaction?"

Whenever you claim a strength, be sure you give an example or two to show how you reached that conclusion. For example, here are two good responses to the question "What are your greatest strengths?" asked during an interview for an accounting position:

Besides the fact that I am thoroughly trained as an accountant, you will find me to be dependable and responsible. In my current job, my supervisor usually leaves me in charge when he is out of town or away from the office, because he knows I will be able to do my job and his as well as seeing that the other 17 people in the department are taken care of.

My greatest strength in terms of benefiting you would be the fact that I am an exceptional accountant. My work is accurate and neat, and I am able to foresee the significance of accounting actions. Another strength that should come in handy when you open your Tokyo subsidiary is my knowledge of Japanese accounting methods. One of my major professors was Japanese, so he made sure we were aware of how accounting is handled in Japan—in addition to teaching us the standard American methods.

Transform questions about your weaknesses into opportunities to mention your strengths and show that you are good at identifying problems, planning ways to overcome them, and accomplishing your goals.

**WEAKNESSES.** The ability to handle questions dealing with one's weaknesses is the major difference between skilled and unskilled job applicants. Examples of this type of question are:

"What do you consider to be your greatest weaknesses?"

"In your last job, in what areas were you weakest?"

"If you were to enroll in one course today that would help you most in your job, what would it be?"

Other questions designed to ferret out your weaknesses are less obvious:

"What major problems did you encounter in your last job? How did you handle them?"

"Have you ever had difficulty getting along with other students? Teachers? Supervisors? Co-workers?"

"What do/did you like least about your current (or last) job?"

"Do you think a company should consider grades when hiring someone for a job?"

Although honesty is important in a job interview, no one really expects you to make a detailed confession in response to this type of question. Yet, some respondents give far too much information. Consider the following:

I guess you could say one of my biggest weaknesses is that I sometimes have trouble relating to people who don't agree with me. Sometimes people think I'm not friendly, but it's not that; I'm just shy, and I don't like to argue with people, even when they're wrong.

This overwhelmingly negative response will leave the interviewer with a bad impression. The candidate has offered more weaknesses than the interviewer probably expected, and everything was stated too firmly. The applicant failed to indicate what he or she is doing to overcome the weaknesses.

When you explain a weakness, make sure it is a weakness that is not too closely related to the job, and explain how you are handling the problem. Your task is to show the interviewer how your experience with the particular problem will turn out to be an asset for you. For example:

Major weakness? . . . I can't really think of a major weakness that would apply to this job, but I guess you could say I used to be too shy to handle difficult clients and salespeople. I realized, though, that my shyness was due to a lack of experience and was keeping me from conducting business effectively. Therefore, I forced myself to maintain good eye contact; speak directly and assertively; and, in general, stand up to people and do what I knew was right. I find now I can handle all kinds of difficult people in all kinds of difficult situations. Somewhere along the way, my shyness disappeared!

This applicant turned a question about weaknesses into a response about strengths. The answer also made clear that the applicant is goal oriented and capable of recognizing problems and then solving them.

**CURRENT AND PRIOR JOBS.** Most information you give about your current and previous jobs should be framed in terms of your strengths and the responsibilities relating to the job for which you are applying. However, a couple of questions in this category may trip you up if you're not careful.

In responding to questions about previous or current jobs, focus on the positive and the personal; do not criticize or gossip about other employers.

One of the most sensitive questions is "Why are you leaving your current job?" By all means, avoid condemning your current employer. Be as honest and direct as you can without revealing information that might make it seem as though there are problems. Among the acceptable reasons for leaving jobs are desiring to relocate, have greater responsibility, more money, a promotion or better opportunities for advancement, or the opportunity to use all one's skills and abilities. A good answer to this question might, therefore, be as follows:

In a lot of ways I will regret leaving Taylor Productions. The people are great, and so is my supervisor. However, no matter how much I like my job, I'm not able to use my design skills. All the company's design work is done in Korea, and upper-level management doesn't want to make a change. The position you are offering appears to provide the same type of congenial work environment, and it would give me an opportunity to implement some of the designs I've been working on since my first design class.

Another question that deserves forethought is "What changes would you make in the company for which you are now working?" Avoid giving an exceedingly negative or bitter answer, and do not gossip about your current employer. No matter how tempting it is, "Fire everyone and start all over again" is not a good answer! If possible, present solutions to a problem that is well known, such as upheavals in the airline industry or management changes following a takeover or a merger of two businesses.

**STARTING SALARY.**  Success in achieving your salary goals is largely a function of how well you negotiate. If you discuss this issue skillfully, you will get what you want, and the interviewer will feel that he or she is getting a competent employee at a reasonable salary. In other words, both sides will feel they have won.

The best time to negotiate salary is when you are sure the company wants to hire you for the job. You will know if the interviewer says something like "This is a great company to work for" or "You would like working in the developmental materials department; your supervisor is the best in the field." Most interviewers, however, will probably not be so obvious.

Typically, salary negotiations run something like this:

Interviewer  What salary do you expect to make if you're hired for this position?

Applicant  Well, with my background, I should be making about $35,000.

Interviewer  Whew! Unfortunately, that's quite a bit more than I'm authorized to pay. We couldn't possibly pay that much, or we'd have a revolt on our hands from our other employees. We anticipated bringing someone in for about $29,000.

Applicant  I can understand what your problem is, but there has to be a way we can get these two figures closer together. I like what I see here, and I know there's a lot I can do for your company. [*Persuasively restates major qualifications.*] How do you think we can convince the people who decide on salary to get the figure up? [*Switches from individual action to team effort to convince someone else to raise the figure.*]

Interviewer  Well, I might—and I emphasize *might*—be able to get them to go as high as $31,000, but they aren't likely to give me any more.

Applicant  Perhaps if we emphasized my computer skills and explained to them how I was able to save my current employer thousands of dollars by making some simple, inexpensive changes in procedures . . . With the kind of initiative I can bring to the job, you can be sure I'll save you far more than the cost of my paycheck. I suppose I could go as low as $33,500, but it just wouldn't pay for me to make a change for any less—no matter how much I'd like to work for your company.

Questions about starting salary are really a signal to begin negotiating; aim for a win–win solution to discrepancies between your desires and the employer's desires.

| Interviewer | I understand what you're saying, but we just can't pay our people that much as a starting salary. If I could get them to agree to $32,500, would you be willing to take the job? |
|---|---|
| Applicant | Well, even though it's awfully low, I do think I would like working for your company. I like the people I've met so far, and I like what you've told me. Yes, I will take the job at $32,500 if you're positive you can't get a higher salary authorized. |
| Interviewer | Great! You're going to like it here! |
| Applicant | I think I will too. [*Pause*] However, could we say that, instead of the usual one-year evaluation period, I could be evaluated and considered for a raise at the end of six months? [*Takes advantage of the interviewer's feeling of having "won" to seek a way of achieving the original salary goal.*] |
| Interviewer | Well, sure; that's a reasonable request. Even though we usually only evaluate people yearly, I don't see why we can't make a change in your case. |

Although every salary discussion is unique, you can use these guidelines to prepare for assertive negotiations:

- Use confident body language. A nervous negotiator is an obvious victim.

- Think before you speak, and don't lose control of your emotions. If you reveal your emotions, the other person will know how to manipulate you.

- Don't be afraid to keep talking just because the other person says negotiations are closed.

- Use silence as a response to an unacceptable position. The other person will feel pressured to come up with an alternative.

- Really listen to the other person. He or she may give away valuable information that will help you get what you want.

- Use a win–win approach. In the end, each person should feel a sense of victory.

### IMPERMISSIBLE INQUIRIES

▶ Handle inappropriate interview questions.

It's the law: Employers cannot ask applicants for information that is not directly related to their job performance, and they must ask all applicants the same questions.

In this country, equal employment opportunity laws and affirmative action provisos forbid prospective employers to ask questions that do not pertain to the job. Such questions must be avoided because they can be used to discriminate intentionally or unintentionally against people on the basis of race, age, religion, gender, ancestry, disability, or arrest and court record. Instead, questions must be directly related to qualifications that are absolutely necessary to perform a job. They must be asked of all applicants for a particular job, not just a few applicants who exhibit certain characteristics.

In the vignette at the beginning of the chapter, a number of the interviewer's questions were impermissible. They may have been no more sinister than an awkward curiosity about someone noticeably different from others interviewed in the past. At the worst, however, they indicate potential bias on the basis of race, national origin, family status, age, and language.

Particular regulations about impermissible questions vary from state to state, but they generally fall into the following categories:

- *Race or color:* "You people are usually good at math. Are you?"

- *Gender, marital status, or sexual preference:* "Are you married?" "Do you have any children?"

- *National origin, ancestry, or birthplace:* "Of what country are you a citizen?" "That's an interesting name. Where are you from?" "Do you have any relatives in the area?"

- *Age:* "How do you feel about working for someone younger than you?"

- *Type of military discharge:* "Did you receive an honorable discharge?"

- *Disabilities that do not affect work performance:* "You walk with a limp. How did that happen?"

- *Religion:* "We need people with strong moral values. Do you go to church on Sundays?"

- *Arrest or court record:* "We need honest people. You've never been arrested, have you?"

Asking for a photograph is not allowed either, because a photograph may legally bias the person making the hiring decision. It must be pointed out, however, that an inquiry is acceptable if it is substantially related to one's ability to perform a particular job and if it is asked of all applicants for the job. For example, it is permissible to ask all applicants to provide photographs for modeling or acting jobs, because a certain look is considered to be substantially related to job performance. It is also acceptable to ask if someone is a U.S. citizen for jobs in the defense industry that involve access to sensitive or secret information.

Most interviewers are aware of the law and respect individuals' rights, but some do not. If you should be asked questions that are not permissible, you have three choices:

- *Ask in an unchallenging way how the information is related to the job.* Realize, however, that although the interviewer might appreciate your knowledge of the law and the tactful way you asked the question, he or she might interpret your response as a challenge.

- *Answer the question directly and honestly.* This is usually the best option when you know your answer is what the interviewer wants to hear. When your answer may result in discrimination, you have the option of trying to turn your "weakness" into a strength or of showing that it is outweighed by qualities relevant to the job.

- *Tell the interviewer what he or she wants to hear even though it is not the truth.* Some people feel their lying is justified by the interviewer's asking impermissible questions. However, if you choose this response, you will probably have to deal with the truth sometime during your employment, and the employer's reaction to your lying may be negative.

In the chapter-opening vignette, the middle option may have been the best choice for Lip Yeon Gow. He could have assumed the interviewer was simply curious about someone from a different culture and graciously answered the questions about his name, language, and family. He could have good-naturedly mentioned that, as an immigrant, he has learned how to adjust to new circumstances and is similarly flexible in work environments. In response to the question about

| **EXHIBIT 17.2** | **Thought-Provoking Questions to Ask during the Employment Interview** |
|---|---|

1. "Do you have a training or orientation program for new employees?"
2. "Where is your research and development emphasis being placed?"
3. "Will I have an opportunity to use my training in X?"
4. "What are the specific responsibilities of this job?"
5. "What percentage of your management openings are filled from within?"
6. "In this position, how much contact will I have with senior management?"
7. "What is the cost of living and the housing situation where I will be employed?" (for out-of-town applicants)
8. "Does the company pay for job-related college courses?"
9. "Does the company have any additional benefits, such as cost-of-living adjustments, group life and medical insurance, or a company-paid retirement plan?"
10. "Who would be my immediate supervisor? Can you tell me a little bit about him or her? To whom does he or she report?"
11. "What is the salary for this position?" (if not mentioned previously)
12. "How frequently are performance evaluations given? Are raises and promotions tied to these evaluations?"
13. "Is the current sales growth in the new product line sustainable?"
14. "Is it possible to move through the training program faster?"
15. "What is the average age of top management? Middle-level management?"
16. "What is the single largest problem facing the company (or the department) now?"
17. "Recently, I read about recent developments in the area of X. How does this affect your company?"
18. "I really appreciate your offer. How soon do you need a decision?"
19. "Questions? No, I think you covered everything. However, I just want to clarify one point you made earlier." (Follow this up with a clarification question, e.g., "You did say the job will be filled by the end of the week, didn't you? Would it be okay if I telephone you on Friday?")

*If you are asked an illegal question during an interview, your best option may be to answer the question in a positive, upbeat, confident way; explain that your "weakness" is really a strength or that your qualifications are far more important than any superficial, unrelated characteristics.*

his age, Lip could have pointed out that his years have given him additional accounting and business experience that other applicants might not have; in addition, his family responsibilities make him a stable, reliable employee. The question about his communication skills might have been answered with this sort of statement: "In the job I currently hold, I have had no trouble communicating with co-workers or clients. In fact, my knowledge of a foreign language was even valuable to my employer one time, when a Malaysian client was seeking information." Self-confidence and a positive outlook are likely to win points with any interviewer.

If a positive approach doesn't work and you feel you were not offered a job because of discrimination, contact your local Equal Employment Opportunity Commission. Employers that are found to have violated the law will be fined. The process takes a long time, but you will have the satisfaction of knowing that your experience will help prevent discrimination in the future.

### APPLICANT INQUIRIES

Ask questions that demonstrate your interest in the job and reinforce your strengths.

*When given the chance to ask your own questions, show that you are interested in the job or the company, not just interested in your own welfare.*

At the conclusion of the interview, the interviewer will usually ask if you have questions. Show your interest in the position by asking two or three intelligent questions, but do not focus unnecessarily on the employment benefits or your own needs. Try to ask questions that subtly emphasize your strengths. Exhibit 17.2 contains examples of some good questions to ask if the information has not already been covered.

## FOLLOW-UP CORRESPONDENCE

🔖 Write follow-up correspondence that is appropriate to the circumstances and enhances your prospects of getting a good job.

After the interview, you should contact the interviewer at least once more, usually in writing. A follow-up letter shows you are interested in the job and brings your name to the interviewer's attention again. The most common forms of follow-up correspondence are the thank you letter and the inquiry letter; others are the acceptance letter and the refusal letter.

### THANK YOU LETTER

*Writing a thank you letter to the interviewer further demonstrates your professionalism and gives you one last chance to "sell" yourself.*

The first follow-up contact should be a thank you letter to the person who interviewed you. It should be written within a day or two of the interview. Although you can express your gratitude by telephone if the hiring decision is being made right away, a letter lends a touch of professionalism to the job search. Because most job applicants do not take the time to write or telephone after the interview, your competence and your courtesy will stand out.

Exhibit 17.3 is a typical thank you letter. It uses a direct organizational strategy and begins by thanking the interviewer and specifying the position. In letters to interviewers who interview for more than one job opening at a time, you should also include the date of the interview. Because the purpose of this letter is to convince the employer once and for all of your suitability for the job, in the body of the letter you should reemphasize your key qualifications in terms of their benefit to the reader. The closing should contain a telephone number to make it easy for the interviewer to call you—ideally, with a job offer.

### INQUIRY LETTERS

*An inquiry letter keeps communication channels open and shows that you remain interested in the job.*

If you have not heard from the interviewer within a reasonable length of time or if the hiring decision date has passed without your being contacted, you may wish to write an inquiry letter. This type of letter may also be used whenever you have not heard from a company after sending in your resume and application letter.

In the letter, do not give the impression you are disappointed about their not contacting you. Just assume a simple oversight has caused the delay, and write the letter accordingly. An example appears in Exhibit 17.4.

### ACCEPTANCE LETTER

*If you write an acceptance letter, use it to document any understanding you and the interviewer reached about salary and other conditions of employment.*

One of the most enjoyable letters to write is one accepting a job. Jobs are accepted more often by telephone than by letter; however, if a letter is expected, make sure you reply within a few days of the offer.

Using a direct organizational strategy, begin an acceptance letter by enthusiastically accepting the job (see Exhibit 17.5). The middle of the letter should contain additional information the company may need, as well as any questions you may have. If a salary has already been discussed, it is a good idea to mention it, as well as any special conditions discussed and agreed to during the interview. As with any written correspondence, the acceptance letter serves as a legally binding contract, so it is a good idea to put in writing any unusual conditions agreed to during the interview. Such special conditions might include a shorter evaluation

**EXHIBIT 17.3**

Sample Thank You Letter

10 East Second Street
Anchorage, AK 97330
January 15, 1995

Mr. Randy Lielsen
Office Manager
Gordon, Cooper & Liebrand
165 Main Street
Anchorage, AK 97330

Dear Mr. Lielsen:

Thank you for taking the time yesterday to speak with me about your desktop publishing position. You were very candid in your assessment of this position, and I appreciate the time you took to show me your facilities.

After talking with you, I am convinced I can make a significant contribution to Gordon, Cooper & Liebrand. Not only am I well trained in the use of PageMaker and Microsoft Word, but my expertise in page layout and design should make the production of your monthly magazine far easier than it has been in the past. Strong people skills will help me to work directly with your customers in developing professional advertising copy that meets their needs.

Please call me at (915) 832-7878 or 832-1329 if you have additional questions. I look forward to hearing from you soon.

Sincerely,

*Chester Ryan*

Chester Ryan

**EXHIBIT 17.4**

**Sample Inquiry Letter**

741 Olivas Road, Apt. No. 201
Albuquerque, NM 87411
January 25, 1995

Mr. George Begay, Vice President
Sunflower Products, Inc.
10095 West Montana Road
Albuquerque, NM 87411

Dear Mr. Begay:

During our visit on January 12 concerning the research assistant
position, you indicated a probable hiring date of January 18. I am
eager to work for your firm, because the job we discussed would
provide the opportunity to combine my chemistry and business
expertise in developing and testing an exciting range of new
products for your firm.

To help you make your decision, enclosed are two examples of
laboratory write ups I have done recently. You will see the work
is similar to that done in your Research and Development
Department. The second write up contains a particularly
innovative approach to shortening the amount of time needed for
testing cooking oils.

Please call (505) 325-7256 to let me know your decision. I look
forward to hearing from you.

Sincerely,

Tiffany O'Nan

Tiffany O'Nan

Enclosures

**EXHIBIT 17.5**

Sample Acceptance Letter

4627 Dixie Highway
Louisville, KY 40216
February 5, 1995

Mrs. Dorit Yañez
Executive Vice President
Bank of the Far East
9068 East Valley Boulevard
Louisville, KY 40218

Dear Mrs. Yañez:

I enthusiastically accept the position of Cosupervisor of Teller Operations and look forward to starting on Monday, March 2.

As we discussed, I will be sharing the job with a cosupervisor, and my work schedule will be Monday, Tuesday, and Wednesday from 9 AM to 7 PM at a monthly salary of $2,412. I appreciate the opportunity you are giving me to participate in this innovative work arrangement. You may be sure I will work closely with your current supervisor to ensure continuity.

In the meantime, please send me copies of the bank's policies and procedures manuals and any other information you feel would be helpful in familiarizing me with the specifics of employment at Bank of the Far East.

Sincerely,

*Stacey Leonard*

Stacey Leonard

period necessary for consideration of a pay raise, unusual working conditions not given to other employees (e.g., a condensed four-day week or a split schedule), or hours and times of shared employment.

## REFUSAL LETTER

Using the indirect organizational strategy and good you attitude in a refusal letter will help you maintain a good relationship with the employer, just in case your paths cross again in the future.

Sometime in your career, you might have to write a letter declining a job offer. An indirect organizational strategy should be used for this type of letter, because the reader will be disappointed in your decision. Exhibit 17.6 is an example of such a letter. Be careful to maintain goodwill, because you might want to work for the company in the future.

## DISCUSSION QUESTIONS

Use three methods to secure job interviews.

1. What are the three methods of securing a job interview, and what are the advantages of each?

Use three methods to secure job interviews.

2. In all likelihood, the receptionist in the waiting room will not be making the hiring decision. Why is it important to treat this individual in a professional and friendly manner?

Progress comfortably through the four phases of a job interview.

3. How do the five types of interviews differ?

Progress comfortably through the four phases of a job interview.

4. What are the four phases of a typical interview? What is the main significance of each phase?

Progress comfortably through the four phases of a job interview.

5. How should you prepare for the small talk that often occurs in the warmup phase of the interview?

Progress comfortably through the four phases of a job interview.

6. What nonverbal cues tell you the interviewer likes and agrees with what you are saying? What nonverbal cues tell you when the interview is coming to an end?

Convey a professional image through your clothing, grooming, and body language.

7. What clothing and accessories are recommended for men who are interviewing for most business career positions? For women?

**EXHIBIT 17.6**   **Sample Refusal Letter**

5713 Que Street
Central Islip, NY 11760
December 13, 1996

Mr. Conrad McVey, President
MJC Industries
12787 Central Boulevard, Suite 178
Flushing, NY 11715-1278

Dear Mr. McVey:

Thank you for offering me the position as your Chief of
Operations.

When we interviewed, I was particularly excited about the
opportunity to work for a firm that makes such high-caliber
environmental products. However, since our meeting, I received a
similar job offer from Benson and Mills, which is located 60 miles
closer to my home. Because of a deep commitment to protecting
the environment, I must accept the position that keeps my driving
to a minimum.

I regret our relationship did not work out, but I am confident you
will find someone equally qualified who also has a strong belief in
saving the environment. Best wishes to you and your firm.

Sincerely,

*Robert Hosea*

Robert Hosea

◤ Convey a professional image through your clothing, grooming, and body language.

8. If you are able to choose a chair to sit in during the interview, which one should you choose?

◤ Frame responses to likely interview questions before the interview takes place.

9. What three questions should you ask yourself when preparing appropriate responses to likely interview questions?

◤ Respond confidently to typical interview questions.

10. How can silence be used during salary negotiations? Why does it work?

◤ Handle inappropriate interview questions.

11. What kinds of information should not be asked for in a job interview?

◤ Ask questions that demonstrate your interest in the job and reinforce your strengths.

12. What are the three goals behind the questions you ask at the end of an interview?

◤ Write follow-up correspondence that is appropriate to the circumstances and enhances your prospects of getting a good job.

13. What are the four types of follow-up correspondence? Briefly explain when each would be appropriate.

## APPLICATION EXERCISES

◤ Use three methods to secure job interviews.
◤ Convey a professional image through your clothing, grooming, and body language.
◤ Write follow-up correspondence that is appropriate to the circumstances and enhances your prospects of getting a good job

1. Make an appointment to meet with someone who interviews job applicants on a regular basis, and ask the following questions. Following your interview, write to the interviewer and thank him or her for meeting with you. In a memo report to your instructor, describe what happened in each of the four phases of your interview, and summarize the answers you received to your questions. Include a copy of the thank you letter.
   a. "What is your job title?"
   b. "How long have you been interviewing applicants for jobs?"
   c. "Approximately how many applicants do you interview a month?"
   d. "For what types of jobs do you interview applicants?"
   e. "How do most of your applicants get an interview appointment? As the result of a letter and a resume? As the result of a walk-in visit? As the result of an applicant-initiated telephone call? In response to an advertisement? As the result of an employment agency relationship? Any other methods?"

f. "How important is it for an applicant to provide letters of recommendation at or before the interview?"

g. "Do you always contact applicants' references? Do you contact them by telephone, or do you have a written form? What kind of information about applicants do the references provide? How useful is this information to you in making your decision?"

h. "How does your company expect job applicants to dress? Is a suit recommended? Do your dress expectations change from one job classification to another? Do you have any pet peeves about applicants and their outfits?"

i. "How can you tell if applicants are lying to you? Are there any nonverbal cues that give them away?"

j. "What is good nonverbal communication in the job interview?"

k. "What is the most difficult question for applicants to answer?"

l. "Do you have a standard list of questions you ask of all applicants for all jobs? A standard list for all applicants for a particular job opening? If so, what are some of those questions? If not, how do you determine what to ask of each applicant?"

m. "Do you have an evaluation form you fill out for each applicant after an interview?"

n. "What advice do you have to help my classmates perform better in job interviews?"

o. "Recall the worst candidate you've ever interviewed. What did he or she do to create earn this dubious reputation?"

🔲 Convey a professional image through your clothing, grooming, and body language.

2. Go to your local or school library to research the subject of lying behavior. Write a report that describes the nonverbal cues people use to determine when another person might be lying. Do good liars exhibit the same nonverbal behavior as bad liars? Be prepared to present your report orally if your instructor asks you to do so.

🔲 Frame responses to likely interview questions before the interview takes place.
🔲 Respond confidently to typical interview questions.

3. Evaluate the following answers to interview questions:
a. In an interview for a position as a film production assistant: "What are your long-range career objectives?"
Response: "Some day I'd like to be a pharmacist, but I don't know if I'll ever be able to get the money to go to school."

b. In an interview for a position as a registered nurse: "How would you describe yourself? Tell me something about your background."
Response: Well, I was born into a typical American family in a small town in Georgia. I had three brothers and one sister and went to college in Mississippi. I guess you could say I have a very typical background."

c. In an interview for a position as a manager trainee in the defense industry: "What do you think about Congress's recent decision to increase spending for weapons technology?"

Response: "I think it's great! We've been waiting too long for Congress to realize the American people's commitment to ensuring we are viewed by others in the world as a strong and powerful nation. I'm particularly pleased, as I know you must be, about the increase in funding for your fighter plane. Your company developed a unique plane that produced remarkable results in the recent conflict in the Middle East. I'd like to be a part of its continued success."

▪ Frame responses to likely interview questions before the interview takes place.
▪ Respond confidently to typical interview questions.

4. Imagine that you work for the office of your academic department at your school. The department needs to hire a new secretary. The person hired will type many letters, course outlines, tests, forms, and the like. The department has a computer, an electric typewriter, a 10-key calculator, and a photocopy machine. The secretary will be required to use the telephone extensively and act as a receptionist for all visitors to the office, including faculty, students, administrators, and people in the community. He or she will handle the department chair's appointment schedule and answer inquiries about faculty and courses in the department. The qualifications needed are word processing skills, some relevant on-the-job experience, telephone skills, and communication skills. As part of a team made up of four faculty members, two students, and the department chair, you will be screening about 10 applicants. Prepare a list of five to seven questions to ask all applicants. Prepare a list of acceptable answers to those questions.

▪ Frame responses to likely interview questions before the interview takes place.
▪ Respond confidently to typical interview questions.

5. Divide a page in half lengthwise. On the left side of the page, list the strengths you would want an interviewer to know about you. On the right side of the page, list your weaknesses. Submit this list to your instructor in a memo report that identifies the job for which you are applying and tells how you would explain each of the weaknesses to an interviewer. Is there a way to minimize them or make them seem less important? Are there any that should not be mentioned at all in an interview? If you have weaknesses you believe should not be brought up in an interview, is there something you can do to eliminate them altogether?

▪ Respond confidently to typical interview questions.

6. Compose answers to the frequently asked interview questions in Exhibit 17.1. Your answers should be truthful and reflect your current education and experience.

▪ Respond confidently to typical interview questions.

7. Practice your interviewing techniques in a group of four students (assigned by your instructor). Designate one student as the applicant; the other three students then decide on four or five questions to ask from the list in Exhibit 17.1. The applicant will respond truthfully with real information about his or her background. During the interview, one student will be the interviewer, one will take notes about the applicant's and interviewer's nonverbal

communication, and one will take notes about the answers' effectiveness. If possible, videotape the interview as well.

After the interview, the two observers should share their notes with the students who acted as applicant and interviewer. What should they do to improve?

Repeat the process, giving each student a chance to play each role.

🔳 Handle inappropriate interview questions.

8. Imagine that the interview team mentioned in exercise 4 is to select the top two applicants, who will then be interviewed by the dean. The dean will make the final decision. Your team agreed unanimously on one applicant but is having trouble choosing one of the following to recommend to the dean. Which one would you choose? In a memo report addressed to the dean, explain your decision. Point out in your memo which information provided here is relevant and which should not be considered at all.

a.   Cesar Bustamente, 23, is a graduate of a local school's two-year secretarial program but has no previous secretarial experience. He has worked for the last five years as a roof layer for a local construction company. Cesar has good letters of recommendation from teachers at his school and from his current employer. His grade point average is 2.6, and he specialized in word processing and other computer application courses. Cesar has a thick accent, and he was sometimes difficult to understand during the interview. He is Hispanic.

b.   Susan Collins, 31, has been working for the last seven years as the secretary for your school's science department. She wants to transfer because business was her major in college, and she is thinking about finishing her bachelor's degree in office systems. She has used word processing software and was able to answer all your questions about the software your department uses. However, she says she prefers to do her work on a typewriter. She has an excellent letter of recommendation from her current department chairperson. Besides mentioning her excellent secretarial skills, the letter also mentions her ability to relate well to students and to faculty. Although this point didn't come up during the interview, you know Susan has three children and is divorced. She is Caucasian.

c.   Jim Carter is a 27-year-old African-American applicant. He is currently employed as a travel agent. In this job, which he has held for two years, he uses computers to make travel reservations. He also uses the telephone extensively. Although Jim has not used the word processing software your department has, he is familiar with other word processing programs. Jim is at least 50 pounds overweight, and he did not dress appropriately for the interview. He brought a letter of recommendation from his previous employer but did not bring one from his current employer. When asked why he did not bring a letter from his current employer, he said he forgot it. One of the team members called to verify his employment. The manager at the travel agency verified that Jim does work there; however, he said he was prevented by company policy from saying anything other than the dates of employment and the position held.

■ Write follow-up correspondence that is appropriate to the circumstances and enhances your prospects of getting a good job.

9. Evaluate the following letter openings to follow-up messages. Do they use the correct organizational strategy? Are they worded effectively?
   a. From a thank you letter: "It has long been a dream of mine to work for your firm. Now that the interview is over, I feel I am getting even closer to fulfilling that dream."
   b. From an inquiry letter: "You said you were going to notify all applicants by mail of your decision on April 5. However, it is now April 10, and I haven't received anything. Please give me the courtesy of a response."
   c. From an acceptance letter: "Thank you for offering me the job as manufacturing engineer at your Los Angeles facility. I am happy to accept the position."
   d. From a refusal letter: "I regret to inform you that circumstances prevent me from accepting your job offer."

■ Write follow-up correspondence that is appropriate to the circumstances and enhances your prospects of getting a good job.

10. Analyze how the you attitude is used in each of the sample letters in this chapter (Exhibits 17.3–17.6). For each letter, point out specific reader benefit passages. Do you recommend any improvements in the you attitude?

■ Write follow-up correspondence that is appropriate to the circumstances and enhances your prospects of getting a good job.

11. After reading the following documents, analyze their strengths and weaknesses. Revise them so they follow the guidelines within this chapter, and submit the revisions to your instructor.
    a. "Thank you, Ms. Cooper, for taking the time yesterday to speak with me regarding the Development Coordinator position. The opportunity to speak with you was a once-in-a-lifetime experience, and I am enthusiastically awaiting your call to let me know I've been hired."

    "Even though I don't have much experience, I'm sure I can handle the challenges this job presents. You won't find me lacking in any way. I have long awaited the opportunity to do fundraising and public relations."

    "You mentioned that one of the drawbacks of the job is that I would have to do most of my own clerical tasks. You don't have to worry about me on that account! With a professional staff of five and only one secretary in my current job, I often find myself executing a project from conception of the ideas to typing of the finished copy."

    "It was a pleasure speaking with you. I look forward to your telephone call."

    b. "Life is so unpredictable. Yesterday I had no job; today I have two!"

    "Thanks for the job offer. However, the other company is willing to pay me $2,000 a year more than you are. Therefore, I think I'll take the other job—unless you're willing to beat their offer, that is! Please let me know immediately. I'll hold them off as long as I can."

# PUNCTUATION

To understand punctuation, you must first understand what makes a sentence a sentence. A **sentence** contains at least one independent clause although it might also contain dependent clauses and phrases.

An **independent clause**, also known as a main clause, contains a subject and a verb and can stand alone as a sentence. These are examples of independent clauses. In each example, the subject is underlined once, and the verb is underlined twice.

The interior decorator recommended brighter colors for the office.

The office is painted in ivory tones.

The vice president prefers shades of blue.

A **dependent clause** is a group of words that may contain a subject and a verb but cannot stand alone as a sentence. The following examples of dependent, or subordinate, clauses show the subjects and verbs. However, each independent clause is missing something—the main point of the statement. Therefore, none of the following examples can stand alone as a sentence.

if you choose the paint yourself

because the decorator is trained in color psychology

since the color green exerts a calming influence on people

Dependent clauses usually begin with words such as these:

| | |
|---|---|
| if | while |
| when, whenever | since |
| because | though, although |
| before, after | until |
| as | |

A **phrase** is a group of words that does not contain both a subject and a verb. dependent clauses already mentioned, they also begin with words that make them dent on the rest of the sentence for meaning.

However, phrases are different from clauses in that they do not contain both and a verb, as shown by the following examples:

As a consequence of your decision

After consulting with the interior decorator

If necessary

It is easy to see that these phrases do not express a complete thought; therefore cannot stand on their own as sentences. However, it is primarily the words they be that make them phrases instead of clauses.

Once you can identify the differences in independent and dependent clauses and phrases, you are ready to study how to punctuate sentences.

## END-OF-SENTENCE PUNCTUATION

End-of-sentence punctuation consists of periods, question marks, and exclamation points. Since using these punctuation marks is almost second nature to most college students, only the finer points are covered in this section. Take the self-check in Exhibit A.1 now to determine how well you understand end-of-sentence punctuation.

The self-check should have given you some indication of whether you need further instruction in punctuating the ends of sentences. Other than the obvious rules concerning the use of periods, exclamation points, and question marks, this will help you deal with the finer rules concerning the use of these punctuation marks:

**EXHIBIT A.1**

**Self-Check**
End-of-Sentence Punctuation

First, cover up the answers at the bottom of the self-check. Then determine if each of the following items can stand alone as a sentence in a letter or a memorandum. If it can, decide if a period, a question mark, or an exclamation point is the appropriate mark of punctuation for the end of the sentence. Check your answers with the fine print at the bottom.

1. When do you expect me to have the report done
2. (Supervisor to employee) Will you please bring me the PrimeCo file
3. Please let me know when you want the painting of the office to be completed
4. I wonder how soon it will be before the budget for redecorating exceeds the figure budgeted for employee salaries
5. If it is necessary to complete the redecorating before negotiating the duMaurier contract
6. You are to be commended for doing an excellent job on the duMaurier project
7. Will you please take a moment to write out a check for the overdue bill today
8. Let the ProKay Lawncruiser do the work for you
9. Because the chief business officer considers it feasible
10. Once you understand clauses and phrases, you are ready to determine when to use commas and semicolons

Answers:
1. done?
2. file.
3. completed.
4. salaries.
5. (dependent clause—no end-of-sentence punctuation)
6. project. (An exclamation point might be considered unnecessarily emotional in tone.)
7. today.
8. you. (An exclamation point might be appropriate if this is a sales message, and only if the use of exclamation points has not been overdone.)
9. (dependent clause—no end-of-sentence punctuation)
10. semicolons.

- Use a period instead of a question mark when expressing polite requests.
- Avoid the use of exclamation points that add an unnecessarily emotional tone to business messages.

A **polite request** is a request that sounds like a question but really is a declarative statement telling the reader what to do. For example, a boss might use these words to ask a subordinate who has been taking too much time for lunch to be on time in the future: "Will you please make sure you're at your desk at 1 PM after lunch." Both the boss and the subordinate know this *is* an order; however, because it is worded politely, it is less threatening than the direct order, "Be at your desk from now on," would be.

In deciding whether to use a period or a question mark in these circumstances, ask yourself whether you expect a yes or no answer from the reader. If you do, then use a question mark; if not, use a period. The following example is not a polite request; therefore, a question mark is used. In this case, the writer really wants to know if it is possible for the reader to finish the study by Friday.

Can you complete the study by next Friday?

If the writer was giving an order *telling* the reader to finish if by Friday, a polite way to get the idea across would be to use this polite request: Will you please complete the study by Friday, June 3.

Polite requests, however, are risky because some people do not understand the distinction between the period and the question mark. In the interest of clarity, your writing might be improved by stating the following clearly:

Please complete the study by Friday, June 3.

## COMMAS AND SEMICOLONS

Take a minute now to take the self-check in Exhibit A.2. If your answers show that you need a review of commas and semicolons, proceed by reading the rest of this section and doing the exercises at the end of the appendix.

The following rules are the most important points you need to know to understand when to use a semicolon and a comma, the most frequently used punctuation mark.

Before you read these rules, however, take this advice to heart—when you are in doubt about whether to use a comma, leave it out. Commas should not be placed everywhere you pause, although many people mistakenly believe this to be true. People from different areas of the world and from different cultures learn to pause at different places in sentences, and it would certainly be confusing if the rules for using punctuation were applied inconsistently. Although it is better to know and apply the following guidelines for using commas, it is better to leave them out than to run the risk of using too many in your writing.

### When Two Independent Clauses Are Joined by a Coordinating Conjunction, Use a Comma before the Conjunction.   When you see a coordinating conjunction (*and, but, or, nor, for, yet,* and *so*) in a sentence, it should have a comma before it if the clauses on both sides of it are independent

EXHIBIT
A.2

**Self-Check**
Commas and Semicolons

First, cover up the answers at the bottom of this self-check. Then indicate where commas and semicolons should be placed in each of the sentences. If any of the sentences is correct as printed, write a C in the margin before the number. Finally, check your answers with the fine print at the bottom.

1. You must act soon the sale ends next week.
2. Crimes the lawyer said are wrongs that interfere with the fundamental rights of the community.
3. You were correct in sending the larger sizes however the order specified the Norton collection rather than the Probe series.
4. "Common stock" Riersen tells us "is a class of corporate ownership that has no special privilege or claim against earnings."
5. No one person is responsible for the losses we have experienced everyone in the company must be held accountable.
6. It was a genuine pleasure to assist you Ms. Adelante.
7. Send 44 copies in red blue and green as soon as possible.
8. The trips are planned for senior citizens nevertheless a few younger people often make reservations.
9. Orders were placed by the Quicker Supply Service on February 23 1994 November 17 1994 and February 2 1995.
10. Some of the sales staff have been late turning in their reports for example Sun Deialle and Amelia Knack.
11. In addition to my January 21 letter overdue notices were sent four and six weeks later.
12. By Friday the photographs will be developed.
13. The memorandum announced the laying off of over 5000 employees.
14. Last year we hired 43 new employees the year before only 11.
15. It is however not necessary to send payment immediately.
16. Mr. Byers stressed that it is important all key personnel attend the annual stockholders' meeting and that they arrive ahead of time to greet the stockholders.
17. This year's United Way Campaign was nevertheless successful and I hope your firm will approve the reappointment of John Gonzales to head next year's efforts.
18. Perry Winslow the Vice President of Manufacturing took over in April of last year never has any one person done more to increase profits in such a short time.
19. No one saw her leave the office or use the newly minted key to the service elevator.
20. Taylor Kensington MD performs the physicals for all new personnel.

Answers:

1. soon; (*or* soon. The)
2. Crimes, said,
3. sizes; however, (*or* sizes. However,)
4. "Common stock," us,
5. experienced; (*or* experienced. Everyone)
6. you, Ms.
7. red, blue, (second comma is optional)
8. citizens; nevertheless, (*or* citizens. Nevertheless,)
9. February 23, 1994; November 17, 1994; and February 2, 1995.
10. reports; for example,
11. letter,

12. C
13. 5,000
14. employees; before,
15. is, however,
16. C
17. was, nevertheless, successful;
18. Winslow, Manufacturing, year; (*or* year. Never)
19. C
20. Kensington, MD,

(contain both a subject and a verb and can stand alone as a sentence). A comma before the conjunction helps avoid confusion and provides a clear indication of where one clause ends and another begins. Some examples:

> I searched for the files, and I found them buried on the desk.

> It takes time to set up a mail merge on the computer, but the time saved makes it worth it.

> The tone in your letter is too negative, yet it has a certain strength that Terry's letter lacks.

One exception to this rule occurs when a sentence is short. Because short sentences do not need a break to make them clear, no comma is needed. For example:

> I searched and I found it.

> It takes time but it saves time too.

> Terry spoke out so I laughed.

Make sure you understand what an independent clause is, however, because when one of the clauses is dependent, no comma is used before the conjunction—no matter how long the sentence is. Clauses are dependent when they do not contain a subject. Compare the clauses in the following examples to those in the previous sentences until you are sure you can tell the difference between independent and dependent clauses:

> Complex regulations were provided and must be followed to prevent penalty. (Second clause is dependent—no subject.)

> When programming decisions are made only by executives, the general public is usually disappointed and, as a result, switches channels. (Second clause is dependent—no subject.)

**When Two Independent Clauses Are Joined with a Coordinating Conjunction or a Conjunctive Adverb and One or More of the Clauses Contains Commas, Use a Semicolon before the Conjunction or the Conjunctive Adverb.**    Sentences with too many commas are hard to read, so it is sometimes necessary to provide a bigger break at the conjunction. The semicolon provides such a break. Notice how it is used in these sentences consisting of two independent clauses, at least one of which contains commas:

> Studies show that men, as you might guess, typically smile less than women; and, instead of making women seem more open, some say it has the effect of making women seem weak and subservient. (Two independent clauses, both of which contain commas.)

> An understanding of proxemics, the study of how people relate to the space around them, is important if you want to manage people effectively; and you must also know how to interpret other forms of nonverbal communication. (Two independent clauses, one of which contains a comma.)

Try it yourself. Is the punctuation in this sentence correct?

> As you learned in your study of indirect letters, they should begin with a buffer paragraph; and should be followed by statements explaining the negative action.

If you said no, this sentence is not correct as punctuated, you are right. The clauses on both sides of the conjunction *and* must be independent (able to stand alone as a sentence) before any punctuation goes before the conjunction. Since the second clause is dependent on the first clause (that's where the subject is), the sentence should be punctuated as follows:

> As you learned in your study of indirect letters, they should begin with a buffer paragraph and should be followed by statements explaining the negative action. (No comma or semicolon before the conjunction because the second clause is dependent.)

Try another one:

> The last paragraph of a sales letter should show the reader how easy it is to acquire the product, but, before you can get the order, you will have to use an interesting, creative opening to get the reader to read the whole letter.

This sentence is correct as punctuated. Both the clauses are independent, and the second one has commas in it. Therefore, the reader needs a larger breather than normal at the conjunction. To provide that extra break, a semicolon is used in place of what would normally be a comma.

Semicolons and commas are always used with conjunctive adverbs (adverbs used as conjunctions to join two independent clauses into a single sentence). These are conjunctive adverbs: *however, therefore, furthermore, thus, accordingly, consequently, hence, in fact, likewise, moreover, nevertheless, notwithstanding, otherwise, so, still, then,* and *yet*. Note how semicolons and commas are used in the following sentences:

> You must hurry; in fact, I don't see how you can possibly complete the job by Friday. (Two independent clauses joined by a conjunctive adverb.)

> Specifications were submitted by the customer; therefore, they must be followed to the letter. (Two independent clauses joined by a conjunctive adverb.)

> You will, nevertheless, want to attend the grand opening, won't you? (*Nevertheless* is not used as a conjunctive adverb in this case; it is merely a parenthetical expression [covered later], so set it off from the rest of the sentence by commas.)

**Use a Semicolon between Two Independent Clauses when the Conjunction is Omitted.**   Closely related independent clauses (those that can contain both a subject and a verb and can, therefore, stand alone as a sentence) may be joined without a conjunction as long as a semicolon is used in place of the conjunction. Study the following sentences to see how the semicolon is used:

> The Kira is the most economical sprinkler on the market; it can be purchased for only $49.95. (Two closely related independent clauses joined by a semicolon.)

> Many dignitaries came to honor us on the tenth anniversary of our company's founding; your presence, however, meant more to me than all the others put together. (Two closely related independent clauses joined by a semicolon.)

Both of the previous examples would have also been correct had the clauses been separated into two separate sentences with periods in between. When you use semicolons to join sentences, however, make sure the independent clauses are closely related. This would not be correct:

> The Kira is the most economical sprinkler on the market; you may want to look at our automotive products as well. (Two unrelated independent clauses. Should be two separate sentences.)

**Set Off Long Introductory Words, Phrases, and Clauses from the Rest of the Sentence by Commas.**   Introductory elements are those that precede the subject of the sentence and its verb. A comma after introductory elements helps the reader see where the main clause containing the subject and the verb begin. However, when introductory elements are short (four words or less) and there is no danger of misreading, the comma may be omitted.
Some examples:

> At the end of the fiscal year, the appropriate IRS forms must be completed.
>
> When you decide the script is finally finished, the production team is ready to take over.
>
> In 1994 two plants will be added in our Canadian division.

An exception to this rule occurs when the verb comes before its subject. For example:

> Out of the printer came a high-pitched squeal. (Note that the subject, *squeal,* follows *came,* its verb.)

**Set Off Nonessential Clauses with Commas; Do Not Separate Essential Clauses from the Rest of the Sentence.**   Nonessential clauses, also known as nonrestrictive clauses, are not essential to the meaning of a sentence; therefore, they should be separated from the rest of the sentence. Setting nonessential clauses off from the essential part of a sentence helps readers pick out only the parts of the sentence that make the meaning clear.
Nonessential clauses simply provide additional information; that is why they are considered unnecessary. For example:

> Tom Beaudre, the only person who knows what's going on, is on vacation this week.
>
> The attorney, who had never tried a criminal case, succeeded in getting her client acquitted.

To determine if a clause is essential to the meaning, try reading the sentence without it. If the sentence still makes sense and nothing essential to the main point has been omitted, use commas to set off the nonessential clause. Try this technique on the two sentences above this paragraph, and you'll see that they make sense without the clauses set off by commas. The major point of each sentence is clear without the information in the commas. Without the nonessential clauses, the sentences read as follows:

> Tom Baudre is on vacation this week.
>
> The attorney succeeded in getting her client acquitted.

Contrast the sentences above with the following sentences in which the clauses are essential to the meaning. Because the meaning of each sentence would be changed without the clauses, they are considered essential and, therefore, should not be separated from the rest of the sentence.

> The administrative assistant who was in charge of the Thompson investigation was promoted to a higher level. (This distinguishes this particular administrative assistant from other administrative assistants.)

> The bank officers who were convicted of perjury were removed from the board. (This makes it clear that only some of the bank officers were convicted of perjury, not all of them.)

**Use Commas to Set Off a Parenthetical Expression that Interrupts the Flow of a Sentence.**   Parenthetical words, phrases, and clauses are used to create transitions between thoughts. If you think of parenthetical expressions as not being essential to the meaning of a sentence, you can see why commas are used to set them off by themselves. Parenthetical expressions do not supply information needed for the grammatical completeness of a sentence. Here is a list of some of the most commonly used parentheticals:

| | | |
|---|---|---|
| accordingly | however | therefore |
| as well as | as a result | in addition |
| at the same time | in fact | in my opinion |
| for example | furthermore | by the way |
| otherwise | in the meantime | nevertheless |

Note how the parenthetical expressions are used in the following examples:

> As a result, no new procedures will be added.

> An increase in the number of vacation days for all employees, as you can well understand, would add considerably to our cost of doing business.

> The result, however, will be that no hiring is done until the new fiscal year.

> We will, of course, send a representative to the sales meeting in Atlanta.

However, in sentences containing other punctuation marks, some people prefer to omit the commas around parenthetical expressions to avoid over punctuation. For example, the following sentence might be confusing if the parenthetical were set off by commas:

> It is therefore too early to judge, but it is also too late to plan.

As a general rule, set parenthetical expressions off from the rest of the sentence unless clarity suffers. Use your judgment on this one.

**Separate Appositives from the Rest of the Sentence by Commas.**   An appositive is a noun or a noun phrase that immediately follows a noun and that provides additional information about the noun. Because it contains extra information and could be omitted from the sentence, it is set off from the rest of the sentence by commas. Also use commas to separate appositive expressions introduced by *or, like,* and *such as.*
Some examples:

> Ralph Villaseñor, the employee we fired last week, filed a charge against the company with the state labor authorities.

His ad campaign, a very graphic one, was not approved by the client.

Scientists all over the world, like those in California, must confine their control of earthquakes to worry.

Marginal word changes, such as *human resources* rather than *personnel*, may be requested.

However, when the noun or noun phrase is used as an adjective as in the following sentences, it should not be set off from the rest of the sentence:

The little-known writer Hillary Goins is responsible for our current theories on expense reduction.

My predecessor James Mobasherian preferred to use a separate set of programming instructions for each database.

**Separate Elements in a Series with Commas. A Comma before the Conjunction Is Optional, But Its Use or Exclusion Should Be Consistent throughout a Document. Use Semicolons between the Items in a Series When One or More of the Items Contains Internal Commas.** Commas are used to separate three or more equally ranked words, phrases, or short clauses in a series. Note how the commas are used in the following sentences:

Before writing a report, you must develop the questionnaire, survey the population, and analyze the results.

Terry is the team leader, John is the motivator, Bernice is the negotiator, and Sean is the aggressor.

The sentences above would have also been correct without the commas before the conjunctions; however, to avoid confusing the reader of a document, pick one method and use it consistently.

When items in a series contain commas as in the examples below, keep confusion to a minimum by separating the series items with semicolons. They help the reader see where each element in the series begins and ends.

Your travel itinerary places you in Wilmington, Delaware; Houston, Texas; and Honolulu, Hawaii, during the next month. (Three items containing internal commas.)

You will be traveling with Charles O'Nan, chief of maintenance, El Paso Natural Gas Company; Jerry Southland, vice president of operations, Berlington Northern; and Mary Miller, training coordinator, Los Alamos Laboratories.

**Set Off Words or Phrases of Direct Address, Titles, Degrees, and Abbreviations with Commas.**   This principle is best illustrated by example. Notice how commas are used in these sentences:

Sir, you are the best person for the job. (Direct address)

You must agree, Ms. Walsh, that our performance has exceeded that of Lexington, Inc., over the past year. (The first is direct address; the abbreviation *Inc.* should be set off by commas unless the company's legal name does not include the comma.)

Harvey Stromberg, MD, is on the board of directors of a major pharmaceutical firm. (The Abbreviated title *Dr. Harvey Stromberg* would have also been correct if the abbreviation following the name were not used.)

**Use Commas to Set Off Contrasting or Opposing Expressions.**    Commas should be used to separate contrasting expressions from the part of the sentence they oppose. Often, not always, these expressions are introduced with words such as *not, never, but,* and *yet.* Study the following examples:

The lower the interest rate you offer, the more sales you will make.

The negotiating council recommends a one-year contract, not a two-year contract.

She stated adamantly, yet inaccurately, that she is innocent.

**Separate Most Elements in Addresses, Dates, Measurements, and Geographical Items with Commas.**    Tradition, not logic, determines comma usage in this area. However, generally speaking, when addresses, dates, measurements, and geographical items contains more than one element, the elements are usually separated by commas. The key, however, is determining what an element is. Study the following examples:

The meeting will be held on Tuesday, January 28, 1995, at 3:30 PM. (Three elements set off by commas. Like an appositive, the year is separated on both sides by commas because it explains exactly which January 28 you mean.)

Set aside January 1995 for interviews. (It is considered modern usage to omit the commas around the year when no date is used.)

The building joists were set two feet, eleven inches apart. (Two elements separated by a comma.)

The claims office will be moved to 8239 East Seventh Avenue, Suite 6516, Denver, CO 80201-6516. (Four elements separated by commas. The state and zip code are considered one element.)

Susan was transferred first to Homewood, Illinois, and then to Rochester, New York. (Two elements.)

Glenn Jones II was president from 1988 to 1992 during the time that Alan Bacon, Jr., was the board chairperson. (No comma is used when numerals follow a name, but both *Jr.* and *Sr.* are set off by commas.)

According to the specifications, $6,375,677 will be needed to furnish only 1,220 offices. (Commas used in numbers of three or more digits. Rule excludes the use of commas in telephone numbers, house numbers, decimals, page numbers, etc.)

**Set Off a Short Quote from the Rest of the Sentence with a Comma; Use Two Commas If the Quotation Is Divided into Two Parts.**    Direct quotes taken from other sources must be skillfully blended into your own writing. To do this, it is usually necessary to add your own words such as is done in the following examples:

As Mrs. Pagett says, "Don't beat a dead horse; form a committee and bury it."

"Don't beat a dead horse," says Mrs. Pagett, "form a committee and bury it." (Note the placement of the comma and the period inside the quotation marks.)

**Use a Comma in Place of an Omitted Verb.** Just as an apostrophe can be used to replace a letter in contractions (*don't, can't, you'll*), a comma can replace a word. For example:

Fran prefers the Macintosh; Bill, the IBM. (The second verb, *prefers,* was omitted.)

Some contracts contain hundreds of clauses; others, only two or three. (The second verb, *contain,* was omitted.)

**Separate Two or More Adjectives Modifying the Same Noun with Commas.** When two or more adjectives of equal importance precede a noun that they modify and when they are not separated by a conjunction, the adjectives should be separated by a comma. The hard part, however, is determining if both the adjectives are really independent. For example:

A good contract results in a happy, productive staff. (Both adjectives modify the noun equally. The comma actually substitutes for *and.*)

Recent layoffs did not result in increased productivity; they merely left us with unhappy major stockholders. (*Unhappy* modifies *major stockholders,* not just *stockholders.*)

**Use a Comma When Necessary for Clarity.** There are cases when commas are used just to increase the readability of difficult constructions. One example of this is when two identical words appear together for emphasis. Some examples:

Whichever gambler rolls, rolls at his or her own risk. (Repeated words.)

Whatever is, is good. (Repeated words.)

You said that that book was preferable to the one you used to use. (The convention is to omit the comma when two *thats* appear together. Suggestion—just leave out the first *that* to make the sentence easier to read.)

The more, the merrier. (For clarity.)

The less you have, the more they want. (For clarity.)

**Use a Semicolon to Precede a Word or an Abbreviation Used to Introduce an Illustration or a Series. Follow It with a Comma.** Words normally used to introduce are *namely, that is, i.e., as, for example, e.g.,* and *for instance.* The following sentences show how they are preceded by a semicolon.

A profitable corporation benefits many; namely, its stockholders, its employees, its executives, its customers, and the general public as well. (Word introducing a series.)

Many of the people you will meet are key players in the stock market; for example, Jason Deal of NewMarket Industries, Cynthia Walker of Beryle Cinch, and Cecila Tung of AA Alliances.

However, when these words are used parenthetically as in the following example, substitute a comma for the semicolon:

A dying industry, namely, machine tool manufacturing, often requires government intervention to bolster it against foreign competition.

If you want to find out how well you understand commas and semicolons, do the exercise at the end of this appendix. Then proceed to the next section.

## OTHER PUNCTUATION MARKS

Probably the least understood punctuation marks in the English language are colons, dashes, hyphens, and parentheses. However, most people also find it necessary to review occasionally when they use underlining, italics, and quotation marks. To find out if you need a review of these punctuation marks, take the self-check in Exhibit A.3.

How did you do on the self-check? If you found that you need to review the rules for using colons, dashes, parentheses, hyphens, underlining, quotation marks, and italics, study the following principles and complete the exercises at the end of the appendix.

**Use a Colon after a Salutation in a Business Letter.**    It is also correct to use no punctuation at all in this area, but a comma is never correct. Examples showing salutations in business letters are included in Appendix C.

**Use a Colon after an Independent Clause that Introduces a Formal List of Items. A Dash May Be Used to Indicate an Informal List.**    The list is usually introduced with words such as *the following, as follows,* and *these*; however, these words may be implied rather than stated. Some examples:

The most commonly ordered products in our spring catalog include these: jackets, shoes, belts, and jewelry. (List with introductory word specified.)

Programming executives have listed new shows for next year: Credible Edibles, Star Watch, and Kari. (List with introductory word implied.)

The following new computer games will be included in the next catalog:

1.   Shanghai Dragon's Tail

2.   Solitaire Rummy Style

3.   Victoria's Revenge

She was a great boss—understanding, clear, direct, and fair. (Dash indicating an informal list.)

**EXHIBIT**
**A.3**

**Self-Check**
Colons, Dashes, Parentheses, Hyphens, Underlining, Quotation Marks, and Italics

First, cover up the answers at the bottom of this self-check. Then indicate where colons, dashes, parentheses, hyphens, underlining, quotation marks, and italic punctuation marks should be placed in each of the sentences. If any of the sentences are correct as printed, write a C in the margin before the number. Finally, check your answers with the fine print at the bottom.

1. The program is informative, enlightening, educational, and comprehensive in summary, it's perfect for its intended audience.

2. Mothers in law are not considered immediate family and, therefore, may not be included in an employee's medical coverage.

3. An article entitled A Tough Wall to Tear Down will appear in the next issue of Black Entrepreneur.

4. A main feature of the seminar will be a debate featuring two experts who are pro business and two who are not.

5. Directions to the newest PWS Health Club
   a. From the 210 Freeway, take the Lake Street exit and turn left.
   b. Turn right on Colorado Boulevard about three blocks.
   c. Turn left on Oak Knoll, and park in the first parking lot on your right.

6. Our team exhibits all the qualities of good management and runs around so called leaders, no respect for teammates, and failure to prepare a game plan. (Assume you are writing this statement in a sarcastic tone.)

7. The four panelists who will be included are John Steinberg, Pamela Dills, Conchita Prospect, and Don Robidoux.

8. A graphics portfolio should include the finest in depth examples of your work (color separation samples, newsletters with graphics and text columns, and brochures).

9. New York, Los Angeles, Brownsville, and Boston—these are the only ports receiving government funds for expansion.

10. "Effective nonverbal communication", according to Sisneros, . . . "is of primary importance to the successful salesperson in clinching the final sale."

Answers:
1. comprehensive—
2. Mothers-in-law
3. "A Tough Wall to Tear Down" Black Entrepreneur or *Black Entrepreneur*
4. pro-business
5. Club:
   (about three blocks).
6. "team"
   management—(might also be a colon)
   so-called
7. C
8. in-depth
   (color separation samples, newsletters with graphics and text columns, and brochures).
9. C
10. communication,"
    ". . . is of primary importance to the successful salesperson in clinching the final sale."

Colons are not used to introduce lists:

1. When the list follows a being verb (*is, am, are, was, were, has, been,* etc.). For example: The three models featured in this issue *are* Stacey Leonard, Susan Mushinski, and Linda Horning.

2. When another sentence comes between the list's introduction and the list itself. For example: Maintenance painted the following offices with lead-based paint. This paint will have to be removed before the offices can be occupied safely.

> B241
>
> A123
>
> LS24
>
> Adm24

3. When the list immediately follows a preposition (*to, in, on, by,* etc.). For example: Water coolers should be located by large lecture halls, restrooms, cafeterias, and snack bars.

**Parenthetical Expressions and Other Interrupters May Be Set Off with Dashes or Parentheses When More Emphasis Is Needed Than Commas Would Provide.**    As you learned when you reviewed the rules for commas, parenthetical words, phrases, and clauses are used to create transitions between thoughts. Most of the time, these are set off from the rest of the sentence by commas. However, it is also all right to set them off as illustrated in the following sentences when you want to emphasize them. Notice how the dashes emphasize the most amount of emphasis, the parentheses a little less emphasis, and the commas, the least amount of emphasis. When you write, you will determine how much emphasis is appropriate.

> Illegal copies of designer fashions, as you might have guessed, have a serious impact on sales and profits. (Least emphasis.)
>
> Illegal copies of designer fashions (as you might have guessed) have a serious impact on sales and profits. (Moderate emphasis.)
>
> Illegal copies of designer fashions—as you might have guessed—have a serious impact on sales and profits. (Most emphasis.)

**A Dash Follows a Listing When It Is Summarized.**    An example illustrates this rule best:

> She was demanding, rude, and uncommunicative—in short, a lousy supervisor. (A comma would also be correct in place of the dash; however, it would provide less emphasis.)

**Use Parentheses to Set Off Explanatory Material.**    To indicate that explanatory or extra information can be omitted from a sentence, put it in parentheses. For example:

> The most-used internal punctuation marks (commas and semicolons) are covered in this chapter.
>
> Your report should include exhibits (charts, graphs, photographs, etc.).

In the first example, commas would have been fine because the information within the parentheses is used as an appositive to further explain exactly what punctuation marks are being discussed. However, in the second example, the three types of exhibits are simply provided as examples of many that might be added to a report. Therefore, they must be included within parentheses.

Parentheses are also used in legal documents to prevent misunderstanding or alteration of dollar figures. However, this use of parentheses should be confined to legal documents only, not to business correspondence or reports.

To my four daughters I leave four hundred thousand dollars ($400,000) each in addition to that stated above.

**Use a Hyphen to Join a Compound Expression That Singly Modifies a Noun; No Punctuation Appears in Compound Expressions When They Are Not Placed before a Noun.**   When two or more words appear before a noun and modify that noun, they are usually joined by hyphens. For example:

An up-to-date schedule is needed. (*Up-to-date* modifies the noun *schedule* and appears before the noun so hyphens are needed.)

Is your schedule up to date? (The noun *schedule* does not follow the compound expression; therefore, no hyphens are used.)

The report was done in a first-rate manner. (*First-rate* modifies *manner* and appears before it.)

The report was first rate. (No noun appears after *first rate* so no hyphen is needed.)

**Use a Hyphen to Separate the Parts of Compound Words Beginning with Prefixes Such as *Self, Ex, All*, and *Quasi*; Normally Words with Prefixes Such as *Pro, Inter*, and *Non* Are Not Hyphenated although a Dictionary Should Be the Final Authority.**   Words such as these should be hyphenated:

self-check       all-encompassing
ex-manager      quasi-official

Words such as these should not be hyphenated:

proactive       interactive
nonessential

Often, especially when words are new to the language and when the vowel at the beginning of the word is the same as the vowel at the end of the prefix, the hyphen is required.

pro-choice (Relatively new compound phrase.)

anti-inflammatory (Matching vowels.)

If you find yourself confused about whether to hyphenate words with other prefixes, consult a dictionary.

**Use a Hyphen When It Is Considered Part of the Accepted Spelling of Words.**   Certain words, such as *mother-in-law, step-child*, and *self-addressed*, are required by convention to have hyphens. Consult a dictionary if you are unsure of when to use a hyphen.

**Use a Hyphen to Divide Words between Syllables at the End of a Line of Type.**   Most good word processing programs are able to divide words according to the following principles—if you know how to tell the program to do so. Words are divided at the ends of lines for the sole purpose of keeping the right and left margins as equal as possible. Word processing programs can be set to justify the margins, adding extra spaces between words and letters to keep the margins exactly equal. However, word division is preferable if your printer leaves perceptible gaps between words. When you decide to divide words to maintain even margins, follow these principles:

1.  Divide only between syllables.

2.  Do not divide words of fewer than seven letters.

3.  Divide hyphenated words only at the hyphen (e.g., pro-Democrat).

4.  Divide words only when at least three characters will appear on the second line and two appear on the first line (e.g., do not divide *aggressively* before the *ly* suffix; do not divide *wouldn't*).

5.  When a one-letter syllable appears in the middle of a word, do not divide before the one-letter syllable (e.g., *punc-tu-a-tion* may be divided in these two ways only: *punc-tuation* or *punctua-tion*)

6.  Avoid dividing proper names and numbers even between elements (For example, all three elements of the name *Frances G. Chandler* should appear on one line if at all possible. However, if it must be divided, the least readability is lost if it is divided after the middle initial. The number $1,367,802 would become almost unreadable if it were divided onto two lines.)

**Underline or Italicize Words that Deserve Unusual Emphasis, although this Technique Should Be Used Sparingly.**    Underlining and italicizing words for emphasis can result in a message that yells at its reader. Therefore, don't overdo it. However, these examples illustrate how this technique can be used:

> You were told to make calls to clients only *after* you had completed your training.

> Why didn't you complete the assignments *before* the final exam?

**Underline or Italicize the Titles of Books, Newspapers, and Magazines.** Because most typewriters could not type in italics, underscoring was used in the past for the titles of books, newspapers, and magazines. However, use italics if you are using a word processing program to compose your messages and reports.

**Use Quotation Marks (a.) Around Words that Are Quoted Exactly as Stated or Written, (b.) To Indicate that a Word Should Be Treated in a Special Way, and (c.) Around Titles of Newspaper and Magazine Articles and Book Chapters.**    When you use the words of others, put quotation marks around those words to avoid plagiarism. Use quotation marks as follows:

> According to Hightower, "This is the last of three major discoveries in the field of metallurgy." (Ending quotation after the period. Capitalized first letter since quotation is a complete sentence.)

When ellipses ( . . . ) are used to indicate material has been left out of a quotation, include the three dots inside the quotation marks at the exact point the words were omitted.

Harriman apparently agrees with this analysis, as indicated by her identification of "heightened growth from increased productivity . . . and a decrease in business inventory" as being two major differences between the 1994–95 slow recovery and economic recoveries of the past. (The original and complete quotation reads as follows: "Six factors indicate why this economic rebound is so different from previous economic recoveries: declining employment in the manufacturing sector, heightened growth from increased productivity, reduced investment in nonresidential structures, disappointing growth in wages and salaries, keeping inflation under control, curbing the rate of government spending, and a decrease in business inventory.")

Quotation marks may be used to indicate when a word should be read in an unusual or ironic way, such as:

"Win–win" negotiations have gotten us nothing more than lost benefits, lost wages, and lost respect.

Some examples of magazine and newspaper titles and chapter titles in sentences:

Be sure to read "How to Succeed in Business without Really Crying" in the next issue.

"English the Easy Way" is a chapter everyone should read before writing another word.

## APPLICATION EXERCISES

To test your understanding of the principles taught within this appendix, complete the following exercise. If you find that you need even more help, investigate your school's tutoring and learning assistance services. They might have tutors who will work with you personally; or they might have tapes, software, and other materials that will improve your ability to use punctuation effectively.

### PART ONE—END-OF-SENTENCE PUNCTUATION AND INDEPENDENT AND DEPENDENT CLAUSES

In each sentence, underline the dependent clauses once and the independent clauses twice. Punctuate the sentences with appropriate end-of-sentence punctuation.

1. Presenting numerical data effectively and ethically requires knowledge of graphics, statistics, and a sense of what is right and wrong

2. ElectroMart has 55 electronics stores in the United States and 5 in Mexico

3. Our survey indicates that 42 percent of Anchorage customers are in the $45,000 to $54,000 income range and that they are likely to purchase high-end stereo and television equipment within the next year.

4. Will you please make sure the figures are accurate and are expressed in the simplest terms possible

5. Not to belabor a point too long

6. Our human need to be surrounded by a specific amount of space is strong and, thus, can't be ignored when planning offices

7. It is one thing to construct graphics poorly or to use numbers ineffectively and another to deliberately misuse them so the data will be misinterpreted

8. The mean is the total of all figures divided by the number of figures; the median, the number that appears in the middle when the numbers are arranged from low to high; the mode, the number that appears most often

9. To increase the accuracy rate, we should demand better performance and, while we're at it, test applicants before hiring them

10. Meaning is interpreted according to experience; therefore, people from different cultures may interpret the same event in completely different ways

## PART TWO—INTERNAL PUNCTUATION.

All the internal punctuation in Part One is correct. Using the principles presented in this appendix, write down the reason for each mark of punctuation in each sentence. You do not need to cover end-of-sentence punctuation in this exercise.

## PART THREE—COMMAS AND SEMICOLONS.

Correct the use of commas and semicolons in the following sentences, adding them where necessary and deleting them when they appear where they should not be. If any of the sentences are correct as printed, write "correct" by the sentence. Do not change the periods, question marks, and exclamation points at the ends of the sentences.

1. According to John Ortiz Product Development Specialist the initial product must first be tested in supermarkets, drug stores, and discount outlets.

2. It has been a very very hard campaign.

3. The negotiators settled for a 4 percent raise not the 7 percent raise they had hoped for.

4. Most of the contract will take effect on January 1, 1995 nevertheless the most important provisions will not be effective until July 1995.

5. You will be glad to know, Ms. Sabatello that your proposal has been approved and that your company will be the recipient of the $250000 grant.

6. His election to the chairmanship was achieved as you might have guessed through nothing more than old-fashioned intense politics.

7. Nonverbal communication includes body language as well as object language and sign language.

8. When using the full block letter format you may not indent paragraphs; with modified block format however you may indent the paragraphs, if you wish to do so.

9. Correcting your boss requires diplomacy and tact.

10. "Sweat equity" says Realtor Linda Webster "can be more valuable to a homeowner than a rich uncle."

11. Whoever pays, pays with the understanding that he/she will receive no public recognition or thanks for such an admirable deed.

12. Lying behavior may be demonstrated by a combination of nonverbal actions namely ear pulling neck rubbing, no eye contact, fidgeting and a weak handshake.

13. Eagles we are not but with our imaginations we can still fly.

14. There is no limit to what we can accomplish if it doesn't matter who gets the credit.

15. Using sophisticated laser scanning to capture the vibrancy of the original photography the posters are printed on the purest premium heavyweight paper available.

16. According to the landscapist's specifications the trees must be planted 14 feet 9 inches from one another.

17. The well-known columnist, Abbey Goins, has consented to speak at the president's retirement dinner.

18. The seminar program includes Barbara Kupper engineer, Thomas Ramos landscape architect, and John Cupertino interior designer.

19. The U.S. Postal Service or *snail mail* as it is sometimes called is experiencing increased competition from electronic mail services.

20. For example when exclamation points are used excessively in a letter there is a danger the reader will tire and stop reading.

## PART FOUR—OTHER PUNCTUATION

Correct the internal punctuation in the following sentences, adding punctuation where necessary and deleting punctuation that appears where it should not be. If any of the sentences is correct as printed, write "correct" by the sentence. Do not change the periods, question marks, and exclamation points at the end of the sentences.

1. An employer has a right to expect certain things quality work, regular attendance, high productivity, good manners, and loyalty.

2. (Direct quote.) The deadline for the scholarship application, said the counselor, was last Tuesday.

3. (Use maximum emphasis for the parenthetical expression.) The architect's plans call for the following condominiums, apartments, single family homes, schools, parks, and the biggest advantage of all electronic surveillance.

4. You could choose either alternative—to increase your salary by that amount or to add a week to your yearly vacation allowance.

5. If Fundamentals of Business Communication is well received, a second edition will be printed soon.

6. Ship these by second-day air
   The proposed contract (two copies)
   The previous contract
   Business plan
   Prospectus

7. The following classic cars pictured in the enclosed brochure are now available. Sealed bids must be received by 5 p.m. on Friday, January 4:
     1957 Chevrolet
     1965 Mustang
     1962 Corvette

8. To create organization out of confusion, our motto became "First come, first served."

9. One chapter, "Communicating with Diverse Cultures (including both ethnic and gender differences)," was added to the original plan; and the chapter "Business Communication Technology" was incorporated into another chapter.

10. *Cooperate* means *to operate together.*

11. (Written sarcastically) Just exactly what is *revenue enhancement* money that grows when watered?

12. (Use a moderate degree of emphasis for the parenthetical expression.) The committee members both ethnic minorities and whites approved the plan to improve diversity by advertising jobs in non traditional publications; namely, *The Black Register,* the *Hispanic Quarterly,* and the *Chinese Times.*

13. The repairman was ignorant, incompetent, dishonest, and rude to sum it up, a real prince!

14. Extra security guards should be stationed in every branch that: has been robbed in the past six months, has received threats by mail or telephone, takes in more than $500,000 in daily receipts, or is located near major freeways and highways.

15. (Punctuate this salutation) Dear Mr. Cruise

16. (Use maximum emphasis for the parenthetical expression.) The Request for Qualifications requires so why am I not surprised a professionally certified audit and an above average level of governmental intervention in company operations.

17. The ad specified a need for a well-informed production supervisor, but most of the people interviewed today are definitely not well informed.

18. (Punctuate this quotation showing where information has been omitted. The entire quotation as it originally appeared is printed after the following sentence.) Krugman disagrees with these findings, stating, "Economists list many reasons why wages have become more unequal since the energy crisis of 1973: the spread of technology and its resultant need for more well-educated workers as well as an escalating business tax, resulting in fewer lower-level jobs.

    Original quotation without omission: Economists list many reasons why wages have become more unequal since the energy crisis of 1973: the spread of technology and the globalization of world trade and its resultant need for more well-educated workers as well as an escalating business tax, resulting in fewer lower-level jobs.

# EDITING AND PROOFREADING SYMBOLS

These editing symbols are used by most people in business to indicate changes that should be made in typed manuscripts. Most teachers use these proofreading marks so you have probably already learned many of them. The use of common editing symbols is particularly important for work done by collaborative writing groups. They allow for quick, easy understanding of recommendations for changing written text.

| ■ Symbol and meaning | ■ Example | ■ Corrected copy |
|---|---|---|
| ∧   Insert | the process of *and writing* researching business reports | the process of researching and writing business reports |
| #   Insert space | body language | body language |
| ∧   Insert punctuation mark | the presidents wishes | the president's wishes |
| | result however, it is | result; however, it is |
| ∧̿   Insert hyphen | well written memos | well-written memos |
| ◡   Close up space | 18 per cent | 18 percent |
| ◯   Spell out | 18% | 18 percent |
| ℓ   Delete | the process of researching ~~and writing~~ business reports | the process of researching business reports |
| • • •   Leave as it was originally; do not make the correction | the process of *and writing* researching business reports | the process of researching business reports |
| stet   Leave as it was originally; do not make the correction | the process of researching *and writing* business reports | the process of researching business reports |
| ≡   Capitalize | The Effects of Salary on Productivity | THE EFFECTS OF SALARY ON PRODUCTIVITY |
|   Lower case | Sincerely Yours, | Sincerely yours, |
| ¶   Start a new paragraph | the end of the discussion. Before the meeting, | the end of the discussion.<br>   Before the meeting, |

| ■ Symbol and meaning | ■ Example | ■ Corrected copy |
|---|---|---|
| *no* ¶ Do not begin the paragraph here (combine this paragraph with the previous one) | the end of the discussion. *no*¶ Before the meeting, | the end of the discussion. Before the meeting, |
| ___ Underline or italicize | the style manual <u>A Manual for Writers</u> | the style manual <u>A Manual for Writers</u> or |
| | | the style manual *A Manual for Writers* |
| ∿∿ Use boldface for emphasis | the key is <u>ethical behavior</u> | the key is **ethical behavior** |
| (rom) Use regular type (Roman type—no bold, no italics, no underline) | the key is **ethical** (rom) **behavior** (rom) | the key is ethical behavior |
| (ss) Single space | Gender differences in the use of (ss) language | Gender differences in the use of language |
| (ds) Double space | (ds) Gender differences in the use of language | Gender differences in the use of language |
| (ts) Triple space | (ts) BALANCE SHEET J. Robinson, Inc. | BALANCE SHEET J. Robinson, Inc. |
| ⌐ Move right | ⌐ Indent paragraphs one-half inch. |    Indent paragraphs one-half inch. |
| ⌐ Move left | ⌐ Full block style is flush left. | Full block style is flush left. |
| ⌐⌐ Center | ⌐BIBLIOGRAPHY⌐ | BIBLIOGRAPHY |
| ⊓ Move up | ⌐Sincerely,⌐ | Sincerely, |
| ⊔ Move down | ⌐Very truly yours,⌐ | Very truly yours, |
| = Align horizontally | <u>Name:</u> John Jones | Name: John Jones |
| // Align vertically | $125.89 // 39.36 // | $125.89   39.36 |
| ∾ Transpose letters | recieve | receive |
| ⊋ Transpose words | to vertically align the figures | to align vertically the figures |
| ⊋ Run lines together | Chairperson, Staff Resources Ctte. | Chairperson, Staff Resource Ctte. |
| Z Start new line | Marcey Leonard Data Entry Specialist | Marcey Leonard Data Entry Specialist |

# LETTER AND MEMORANDUM FORMAT

Letter format is used for messages mailed to people who do not work for the same firm. Messages to people who work for the same firm are generally done in memorandum format. However, if a company sends messages to an employee's home rather than through company mail, a letter would be the appropriate format.

Besides formatting your messages correctly, make sure everything else meets the reader's expectation. The letter should look good; and looking good means that it should appear easy to read, corrections must be undetectable, and it should be folded correctly. The following sections of this appendix explain in detail what you need to know to lay out your messages on a page.

## MARGINS

To look good, a letter or memorandum should be centered on the page with the left and right margins appearing approximately the same. This is sometimes referred to as *framing*. It is recommended that you use a ragged right margin instead of justifying if you are using a computer. Justified lines are those that all end on the same space (like those on this page). Justified lines look good and do ensure perfectly balanced left and right margins; however, many people believe justified lines make a letter look as though it has been printed for mass consumption (like a published book). Anything that might take away from the personal tone a writer works so hard to create is, of course, not recommended. In addition, unless you have a good printer–computer interface that is able to handle justification properly, your printer might add large extra spaces between words and letters to force the shorter lines to end at the same point as longer lines. These extra spaces tend to form rivers of white space on a page that are noticeable to the reader, a negative distraction from the message.

Side margins may vary, depending on the length of a letter or memorandum. For letters, anything from approximately three-fourths of an inch to an inch and one-half, is acceptable in today's business world as long as the letter is balanced on the page and does not appear cluttered or crowded. The side margins of memorandums are usually determined by the printed information at the top of the memo (see Exhibit C.6 and C.7). Maintain the following principles when deciding on the margins:

Leave plenty of white space on the page; to appear readable at least 50 percent of a page should be uncovered by words and/or graphics.

To conserve paper, attempt to get letters on one page unless it makes the page appear crowded, thus hindering readability.

Without making the letter appear to be forced too low on the page, leave a bottom margin that is approximately one inch if possible (the eye compares the bottom margin to the white space above the printed letterhead).

When a letter or memorandum takes more than one page, the side margins should match the margins on the first page. However, the top margin is not the same. Continuation pages should be typed on plain paper of the same quality as the letterhead. Create a heading consisting of the addressee's name, the date, and the page number placed one inch from the top of the page. Two types of headings are acceptable: block headings and horizontal headings.

Block heading typed at the left margin:

Mrs. Cynthia                    Tynbar Industries Incorporated
July 30, 1995                    March 18, 1996
Page 2                          Page 2

Horizontal heading spread across the top of the page:

Mrs. Cynthia O'Lane                    2                    July 30, 1995

The body of the letter or memorandum should begin three lines below the continuation page heading. When deciding where to divide a message onto two different pages, take the following into consideration:

At least two lines of a paragraph must be typed on each page.

The last word on a page should not be divided.

Tables should not be split onto two different pages.

In addition to setting the margins properly and handling multiple pages, there are other things you can do to help frame your letter on the page. These are discussed in the following sections.

## LETTER STYLES

The letter style a company or an individual prefers is usually a combination of tradition and image. Some like unusual letter styles, such as the simplified for functional styles, believing that they project an up-to-date image. However, others prefer styles that are more common, such as the modified block or full block styles. Whichever you choose, make sure you use all the letter parts correctly so your readers can focus on what you have to say, not on mistakes in format.

Take a minute now to compare the business letter styles in Exhibits C.1 through C.5. Be sure to read each of the letters since they contain suggestions for using letter styles. Then read the following information about the parts of a business letter. The most common business letter styles contain these parts:

Letterhead          Body
Date                Complimentary closing
Inside address      Writer's name and title
Salutation          Reference initials

Clint, Whiton & Walsh

October 31, 1995

Mr. James Bruce, Superintendent
Kirtland Manufacturing Inc.
1674 East Donan Street, Suite 331
El Paso, TX 79922

Dear Mr. Bruce:

   This is an example of the modified block letter with indented paragraphs.
This letter style is the most common in U.S. businesses, and it is sometimes
referred to as semiblocked.

   This letter style is unique in that it is the only one that uses indented
paragraphs. The indentions should be one-half inch, although some law offices
prefer one-inch indentions. The date and closing lines of this letter must begin
at the exact center of the page, not be centered or typed on the right margin.
At the bottom of the letter are all the special letter parts that might be used in
a letter. Of course, they would only be typed at the bottom when appropriate.

   Modified block letters with indented paragraphs project a conservative
image; but, because they are familiar to all people in business, this letter style
will always be a safe choice for any situation.

                              Sincerely,

                              *Wanda Thomason*

                              Wanda Thomason
                              Lead Consultant

mgl

Enclosure

c: Michael Ryan

Please let me know if there is more information I can provide to you before we
meet next month.

Street Address, Memphis, TN 38152    (901) 555-5555   Fax: (901) 555-5555

Clint, Whiton & Walsh

October 31, 1995

Mr. James Bruce, Superintendent
Kirtland Manufacturing Inc.
1674 East Donan Street, Suite 331
El Paso, TX 79922

Dear Mr. Bruce

**Letter Samples for Training Seminar**

This is an example of the modified block letter without indented paragraphs. This letter style is the second most common in U.S. businesses. The subject line used above is optional and may be used with any letter style to identify immediately what the letter is about.

This letter style is exactly like Exhibit C.1 except for the lack of indented paragraphs. The date and closing lines of this letter must begin at the exact center of the page, not be centered or typed on the right margin. With the letter styles in C.1 through C.3, a company name may be included in the signature area as indicated below. At the bottom of the letter are all the special letter parts that might be used in a letter. To save space, these letter parts may be single-spaced. Of course, they would only be typed at the bottom when they apply.

Modified block letters without indented paragraphs project a conservative image; but, because they are so common, this letter style will always be a safe choice for any situation.

Sincerely

CLINT, WHITON, & WALSH

*Wanda Thomason*

Wanda Thomason
Lead Consultant

mgl
Enclosure
pc: Michael Ryan
Please let me know if there is more information I can provide to you before we meet next month.

Street Address, Memphis, TN 38152   (901) 555-5555   Fax: (901) 555-5555

**EXHIBIT C.3**

**Block Letter Style (Mixed Punctuation)**

Clint, Whiton & Walsh

November 3, 1995

Mr. James Bruce, Superintendent
Kirtland Manufacturing Inc.
1674 East Donan Street, Suite 331
El Paso, TX 79922

Dear Mr. Bruce:

This is an example of the block letter (also known as a fullblock). Many people consider this letter style the most efficient because everything begins on the left margin. The typist would not have to set a tab at the center point so it is ideal for those with minimal keyboarding skills.

At the bottom of the letter are all the special letter parts that might be used in any letter. Of course, they would only be typed at the bottom when appropriate.

This letter style is still considered conservative because it has been used for so many years; however, it is not used as frequently as the modified block styles. Nevertheless, a block letter is still a safe choice for any situation.

Sincerely yours,

*Tiffany Chester*

Tiffany Chester, Executive Assistant

mgl

Enclosure

c: Michael Ryan

Please let me know if there is more information I can provide to you before we meet next month.

**EXHIBIT C.4**

**Simplified Letter Style**

Clint, Whiton & Walsh

November 5, 1995

Ms. Amy Guylo
Director of Training
Kirtland Manufacturing Inc.
1674 East Donan Street, Suite 331
El Paso, TX 79922

SIMPLIFIED LETTER SAMPLE FOR USE IN TRAINING SEMINAR

This is an example of the simplified letter style. While this style is not new, it is not as popular as the other letter styles. Because it does not contain a salutation or complimentary closing, some people feel it is cold and impersonal.

However, this letter style has distinct advantages. If you think about it, salutations and complimentary closings are somewhat trite simply because people hardly ever really read them.

Simplified letters always begin with a capitalized subject line; and, as long as there is space on the page, there should be a triple space above and below the subject line. After the message, drop down three to five lines and type your name and title in capital letters.

After the writer's name and title, type whatever special letter parts are appropriate—exactly as illustrated on the other letter styles shown in Exhibits C.1 through C.3. Just as with other styles, the special letter parts may be single-spaced if there is little room left on the page.

The employees attending your training session should like this letter style; it is particularly useful for routine business letters that do not require a strong personal touch.

*Tiffany Chester*

TIFFANY CHESTER, EXECUTIVE ASSISTANT

mgl
Enclosure
c Michael Ryan

Street Address, Memphis, TN 38152   (901) 555-5555   Fax: (901) 555-5555

**EXHIBIT C.5**

**Functional Letter Style**

Clint, Whiton & Walsh

November 5, 1995

Mr. James Bruce
Superintendent
Kirtland Manufacturing Inc.
1674 East Donan Street, Suite 331
El Paso, TX 79922

The functional letter style is a relatively new style that is considered efficient by some
and impersonal by others. Of all the letter styles in this chapter, the functional style is
the least used. However, it is new and might gain in popularity as people get used to
seeing it.

Like the simplified format, the functional style does not have a salutation or a
complimentary closing. Unlike the simplified style, however, the functional style does not
require a subject line. Another major difference is the fact that the name and title of the
writer are not typed in all capital letters. Many people prefer this because the capital
letters of the simplified style place an unnecessary emphasis on the writer—questionable
you attitude. All lines of a letter formatted in the functional style must begin on the left
margin.

At the bottom of the letter are some of the special letter parts that might be used in a
letter. Of course, they would only be typed at the bottom when appropriate, and their
spacing depends on the amount of space available.

This is the last of the letter styles you will be receiving for your training session.
However, samples of memorandums should be arriving soon.

*Tiffany Chester*
Tiffany Chester
Executive Assistant

mgl

Enclosure

Copy to Michael Ryan

However, as you know from reading the exhibits in this appendix, the salutation and the complimentary closing are omitted when the functional and simplified styles (Exhibits C.4 and C.5) are used. The reference initials should be omitted when you compose, type, and sign your own letters. Optional letter parts that are included only when desired or when necessary include

Attention line

Subject line

Company name in closing lines

Enclosure notation

Copy notation

Postscript

**Letterhead.**  To create a professional image, business letters should be printed on high-quality letterhead stationery. Engraved letterheads are commonly used for important clients, major stockholders, and others with whom company representatives want to promote a successful company image. The same letterhead on cheaper stationery is commonly used for other purposes.

Smart business owners know that a letterhead goes a long way toward promoting the image of a company. Therefore, considerable planning normally goes into designing a letterhead that creates exactly the image a company wants to project.

Letterheads typically contain a company symbol, the company name, company address, telephone number, and facsimile number. For organizations and government agencies, it is common to list the names of people in office at the time; for example, the officers of a club, the mayor and city council members of a city, and so on. This information may all be included at the top of the stationery, at the bottom, at the left side, or a combination of all three. To allow adequate room for messages, it is recommended a letterhead occupy no more than two inches at the top of a page.

**Date.**  The date of a letter should be at least a double space (one blank line) away from the letterhead. Approximately two and one-half inches from the top of the page works for an average length letter. However, the placement of the date depends upon the length of the letter and the depth of the letterhead. Dates for long letters would naturally be higher than dates for short letters. To help balance the letter on the page better, the date for a short letter should be typed a line or two lower, say approximately two and three-fourths inches from the top of the page.

In business letters, write dates out in full without abbreviating them. For example:

Use September 7, 1995—not 9/7/95 or Sept. 7, 1995.

The U.S. military and many European countries use what is called the *international style* (7 September 1995); however, this is not recommended for U.S. business letters.

**Inside Address.**  The inside address contains the complete name and address of the letter's recipient. It should be typed four to eight lines below the date (four lines for long letters, up to eight lines for short letters). Inside addresses should contain the following:

| **Components** | **Example** |
|---|---|
| Courtesy title and name | Mrs. Gina Corcini |
| Business title (if appropriate) | Vice President of Operations |
| Department, branch, or unit (if necessary) | Ferrell Branch |
| Company name (if appropriate) | First National Bank |
| Street or post office box, suite | 1463 NE 29th Street |
| City, state zip code | Cape Coral, FL 33904-1463 |

When your letter is going to an individual, always use a courtesy title unless another title, such as Professor or Doctor, precedes the person's name. Acceptable courtesy titles are Mr., Ms., Mrs., and Miss. The newest courtesy title is M., which would only be used in very specific circumstances. M. works well for (a) gender nonspecific names (Terry, Frances, Lynn, and Chris); (b) names foreign to you (Kang Duang), and (c) initials (L. T. Washington). In circumstances such as these, it is also acceptable to omit the courtesy title in the address.

After the courtesy title, type the first and last name of the recipient. The person's business title may go on a line by itself or, if it is not too long, on the same line as the name separated by a comma (see Exhibits C.1 and C.3).

If the company name is long, it may be typed on two lines with the second line indented two or three spaces. Many authorities believe that Boulevard, Street, Drive, and so on should not be abbreviated. Always spell the city name in full; for example, type *Los Angeles* instead of *L.A.* However, don't spell out the names of states. Instead, use the two-letter state abbreviations recommended by the post office. These are included in Exhibit C.8 at the end of this appendix. It is considered old-fashioned to use the out-of-date, longer state abbreviations (e.g., Kent. for Kentucky).

For international addresses, type the name of the country in all capital letters on the last line. For example, a Canadian letter would be addressed as follows:

Ms. Josette Prevost

Cameron International

2025 Quebec Avenue

Selkirk, Manitoba

R1A 1B9

CANADA

Attention lines are optional and may be included within the inside address itself or two lines below the inside address. An attention line is used to direct the letter to a specific person, position, or department for processing when the letter is addressed to a company or an organization. It is used when you do not know the name of the person to whom the letter should be addressed or when you want the letter to be opened and handled by someone—even if the addressee is gone. For example:

| Name not known—letter to be directed to the service manager (if there is one) or to the person who normally handles that type of work. | TVP Enterprises<br>ATTN: Service Manager<br>342 Buehller Boulevard, Suite 202<br>Rockwood, PA 15557 |
|---|---|

| | |
|---|---|
| Letter to be opened by another company representative if the addressee is not available. | TVP Enterprises<br>Attention: Mr. Stephen Kendall<br>352 Buehller Boulevard, Suite 202<br>Rockwood, PA 15557<br><br>or<br><br>TVP Enterprises<br>352 Buehller Boulevard, Suite 202<br>Rockwood, PA 15557<br>Attention: Mr. Stephen Kendall |

**Salutation.**    Two lines below the inside address (or the attention line if it is used), type the salutation. These salutations should meet the majority of situations you will encounter:

| | |
|---|---|
| Individual, normal business situation | Dear Mr. Gollohon |
| Individual, have done business on a first-name basis | Dear Jim |
| Individual, gender unknown | Dear A. K. Hamlin<br>or Dear M. Hamlin |
| Company or organization | Ladies and Gentlemen<br>Dear Personnel Manager<br>Dear Home Medical Supplier<br>or<br>Use the functional or simplified letter styles that do not have salutations. |
| Recipient, not addressed to a specific person | Dear Customer |
| Husband and wife | Dear Mr. and Mrs. Holyoke |
| Two men | Dear Mr. Jarvis and Mr. LeVake<br>or<br>Dear Messrs. Jarvis and LeVake |
| Two women | Dear Ms. Faber and Ms. Ewing<br>or<br>Dear Mses. Faber and Ewing<br>(use *Mesdames* for married women, and *Misses* for unmarried women, if it is important to specify such information) |
| Attention line used in inside address | (Do not use the name of the person on the attention line.)<br>Dear TVP Enterprises<br>or<br>Dear Service Department |

Salutations for business letters may be punctuated with a colon, or they may have no punctuation at all following them. However, they must match the complimentary closing. When a colon is used after the salutation, a comma must follow the complimentary closing; this is referred to as *mixed punctuation.* If you prefer open punctuation, use nothing after the salutation or the complimentary closing. Either punctuation style is equally acceptable in business. However, under no circumstances should you use a comma after the salutation, a punctuation style used only for casual letters to friends and relatives.

**Subject Line.** Considered part of the body, a subject line is optional. However, subject lines help the writer get to the point immediately, and they help the reader identify immediately the topic of the message. For example, an account clerk who sees an account number in a subject line can look up that account before reading the rest of the letter. Referring to both the company files and the letter should improve the clerk's ability to handle the situation discussed in the letter. When a subject line is used, it should appear two lines below the salutation or as illustrated in Exhibit C.4 (simplified letter style). Subject lines may be typed in boldface type, or they may be underlined. The major words in a subject line should be capitalized. You may use *Subject:* or *RE:* before the subject; however, it is also correct to leave them out. Note these examples:

Dear Mr. Echols:

**Subject: Correlation of Account No. 24576-B-129**

or

Dear Ms. Hartunian

Final Report on Communication Audit

**Complimentary Closing.** The complimentary closing should be typed two lines below the body of the letter. Its inclusion in a letter and its placement on the page depends upon the letter style used, so consult the examples in this appendix for more information. These closings are the most used:

Sincerely

Sincerely yours

Cordially

Cordially yours

These complimentary closings are considered more formal and old-fashioned. Therefore, they are used less frequently.

Yours truly

Yours very truly

Very truly yours

Respectfully

Respectfully yours

Closings such as the following are seldom used, and many people would argue that they should not be used at all. Therefore, use them with caution.

Best wishes

As always

With regards

**Company Name in Closing Lines.**   Some companies like to emphasize the company name in the closing lines. To do this, type the company name in capital letters two lines below the complimentary closing. Follow the company name by three to five lines before typing the name and title of the writer. For example:

Sincerely,


RITGER PRODUCTIONS

*Francisco De la Joya*

Francisco De la Joya
Executive Producer


**Signature Lines.**   The signature lines consist of the handwritten signature, the typed name of the sender, and the sender's title. It may also include a department name, if necessary, beneath the sender's title. Letters should be signed in black ink, and the signature should be clear and readable. Readable signatures communicate openness; readers often interpret unreadable signatures to mean the writer is either sloppy or arrogant. Leave three to five lines for the signature, depending upon the size of your signature and the length of the letter. If the letter is getting close to the bottom of the page, leave only three lines; if the letter is short, you may leave as many as five lines to help center the letter on the page better.

Unless the title of the writer is printed in the letterhead, the title should be typed either on the same line as the writer's name (separated by a comma) or on the next line. If the letter is short, put the title on the line below the name. However, if the letter is long and the name and title together will not look excessively long, put them on the same line.

When someone authorized to sign for the writer does so, his or her initials should be placed under the handwritten signature such as in this example:

Sincerely yours

*Francisco De la Joya*

Francisco De la Joya
Executive Producer

In the past, women were expected to type *Mrs.* or *Miss* in parentheses before their names. Doing so let the reader know what to call the writer (this was before *Ms.* did for women what *Mr.* did for men—married or unmarried). It is not wrong to type these courtesy titles today; however, it is considered old-fashioned.


**Reference Initials.**   The term *reference initials* refers to the writer of the letter—if the writer is not the same person who signed the letter—and the typist. When the writer's name appears in the signature area, there is no need to repeat his or her initials next to the typist's; therefore, only the typist's initials would be included. When you compose, keyboard, and sign the letter yourself, omit the reference initials.

When appropriate, reference initials should be typed at the left margin two lines below the signature area. The typist's initials should be lower case. However, if the writer and the signer are not the same, the writer's initials should be uppercase; and they should be separated by a colon or a slash (/). Some examples:

When the signer is the writer:         Susan F. Keiser
                                        City Planner

                                        snl

When the signer did not compose the letter:    Susan F. Keiser
                                        City Planner

                                        RTM:snl

On the same line as the reference initials, or sometimes beneath them, many companies also include the name of the stored document. This enables the document to be retrieved easily from its computer file. Document names should be kept short (up to eight characters long with an optional three-letter extension). This extension is often the typist's initials. An example of a code indicating where a memorandum would be filed is
   snl/Kirt.Bru
This code tells anyone looking at the hard copy that the document was typed by a typist with the initials *S.N.L.,* it is filed in the Kirtland folder or file, and it is addressed to someone whose last name starts with *Bru.*

**Enclosure Notation.**   An enclosure notation should be used when other documents are to be enclosed with a letter or memorandum. The term *attachment* may also be used when the enclosure is to physically attached to the document by stapling or some other method. Whether an attachment or an enclosure, the notation is normally typed two lines below the reference initials; however, if space is a problem, it may be on the line immediately below. Because it is normally the last thing printed on the page, an enclosure notation serves as a last-minute reminder to the person mailing a letter to make certain the enclosure is included before inserting the document into an envelope.

Enclosure notations may be itemized if necessary. Commonly used examples are

Enc.

Enclosure

Enclosures: (2)

Attachments (2)

Attachments: Sample letter
             Invoice

**Copy Notation.**   When copies of a letter are to be sent to someone in addition to the recipient, that should be indicated in a copy notation at the bottom of the page. It appears at the left margin two lines below the enclosure notation (or the reference initials if there is no enclosure notation). As usual, these components may be single spaced if the letter is getting close to the bottom of the page.

Type the word *Copy* or *Copies* and follow it with the name or names of the people to whom a copy will be distributed. It is also correct to use the letters *c* (for copy), *xc* (for extra copy), or *pc* (for photocopy). For example:

c Samuel Olayinka

Copy to S. Olayinka, Director of Human Resources

Copies to: Samuel Olayinka
           Rena Parks

pc: Samuel Olayinka
    Director of Human Resources

xc Mr. Arlo Neilsen
   Star Rt., Box 23
   Jemez Springs, NM 87024

When you do not want the addressee to know you are sending a copy of a letter or memorandum to someone else, use a blind copy notation. This should be the last notation on the page and should, of course, not be typed on the addressee's copy. Something like the following would be indicated at the bottom of the file copy and the copy of the person receiving the "blind" document:

bc Anna Parminter

Blind copy to Anna Parminter

**Postscript.**    Although it should never be an excuse for poor planning, a postscript appears to be an afterthought that is added to the bottom of the page. However, the use of postscripts should be confined to information that needs to be emphasized. Keyboard the postscript two lines below the last notation on the page. A postscript such as this might appear at the bottom of a collection letter:

By the way, if our letters have crossed in the mail, please accept our thanks for your payment.

It is no longer necessary to include the abbreviation *P.S.* before a postscript. Such a note's placement on the page makes it obvious what it is.

## MEMORANDUM STYLES

Many companies use preprinted forms for their interoffice correspondence. These forms usually contain a simple letterhead or merely the word *Memorandum* or *Interoffice Memorandum* centered at the top of the page. Some companies use no label at all, preferring to begin memorandums with only the heading information.

Take a minute to look at and read the two sample memorandums illustrated in Exhibits C.6 and C.7. The styles illustrated are two of the most used in

**EXHIBIT C.6**     Sample Memorandum Format

## INTEROFFICE MEMORANDUM

**TO:**       Richard Candleria, Training Director

**FROM:**     Linda Russell, Aztec Branch Manager

**DATE:**     April 23, 1996

**SUBJECT:**    Sample Memos for Business Communication Seminar

As you requested, this and the attached are copies of typical interoffice memorandums written by Aztec Branch staff. These should be useful to you in planning next month's seminar.

Like letters, the typical memo is single-spaced with two lines between paragraphs. The paragraphs should begin on the left margin, three lines down from the subject line. The side margins are usually set to align with the heading, but side margins of one inch are most common. As with letters, use a ragged right margin; do not justify the margins.

Memorandums that extend beyond a single page use a continuation-page heading just like letters. One inch from the top of the page, type the name of the recipient, the date, and the page number. The heading may be blocked or horizontal, and it should be followed by three blank lines before the body of the memo is continued.

Memorandums are typically signed or initialed after the name as you can see above. Although some people do not sign memos, it is recommended you do so to protect yourself.

After the body of the memo (two lines below it), type the reference initials and, if appropriate, an enclosure notation, a copy notation, and a postscript. These should be double-spaced if there is room and single-spaced if the memo is getting close to the bottom of the page.

snl

Attachment

c Virginia Nordstrom

**EXHIBIT C.7**

**Sample Memorandum Format**

February 18, 1996

**TO:**        Richard Candleria

**FROM:**     Linda Russell

**COPIES TO:** Virginia Nordstrom

**SUBJECT:**  Sample Memos for Business Communication Seminar

Many of the Aztec Branch staff prefer this memorandum style; therefore, it should be included in next month's seminar, Richard.

The differences in this format and the one in Exhibit C.6 are the placement of the date (four to seven lines above the recipient's name) and the inclusion of the copy notation in the heading rather than at the end of the memo. The date may also begin at the exact center of the page.

Although longer memorandum reports are often double-spaced, the average memorandum should be single-spaced with two lines between paragraphs. The paragraphs are blocked. The side margins are usually set to align with the heading, but side margins of one inch are most common. As with letters, use a ragged right margin.

These sample memos should help you prepare for the seminar. I am certainly looking forward to seeing you again; your sessions are always helpful. Whatever you can do to help us get our messages across clearly and correctly will be welcome.

snl

If you need more samples, please let me know. I'm sure I can find lots of good examples and probably a few bad ones too!

| EXHIBIT C.8 | **U.S. Two-Letter State, District, & Territory Abbreviations** | | | |
|---|---|---|---|---|
| | Alaska | AK | Montana | MT |
| | Alabama | AL | Nebraska | NB |
| | Arizona | AZ | Nevada | NV |
| | Arkansas | AR | New Hampshire | NH |
| | California | CA | New Jersey | NJ |
| | Canal Zone | CZ | New Mexico | NM |
| | Colorado | CO | New York | NY |
| | Connecticut | CT | North Carolina | NC |
| | Delaware | DE | North Dakota | ND |
| | District of Columbia | DC | Ohio | OH |
| | Florida | FL | Oklahoma | OK |
| | Georgia | GA | Oregon | OR |
| | Guam | GU | Pennsylvania | PA |
| | Hawaii | HI | Puerto Rico | PR |
| | Idaho | ID | Rhode Island | RI |
| | Illinois | IL | South Carolina | SC |
| | Indiana | IN | South Dakota | SD |
| | Iowa | IA | Tennessee | TN |
| | Kansas | KS | Texas | TX |
| | Kentucky | KY | Utah | UT |
| | Louisiana | LA | Vermont | VT |
| | Maine | ME | Virginia | VA |
| | Maryland | MD | Virgin Islands | VI |
| | Massachusetts | MA | Washington | WA |
| | Michigan | MI | West Virginia | WV |
| | Minnesota | MN | Wisconsin | WI |
| | Mississippi | MS | Wyoming | WY |
| | Missouri | MO | | |

the United States. However, there are others that are equally effective. Since memorandums are for internal correspondence, companies and individuals tend to develop their own unique formats.

**Heading.**   No matter what format you choose to use, all memorandums should contain the following information. These guide words should be printed on the memo in the heading; however, the date may be included elsewhere. Whether you use preprinted stationery or keyboard your memos on plain paper, include these in the double-spaced heading:

To:

From:

Date:

Subject:

Many companies also include *Copies To:* in the heading beneath the *From:* line rather than using copy notations at the bottom of the page (see Exhibit C.7). Other differences include the position of the date line. Sometimes the date is typed four to seven lines above the name of the recipient, much like what is done for letters. Some style manuals show the date typed two lines above the *To:* line; however, that placement is not recommended. Positioning the date directly above the name of the recipient is poor you attitude because the date should not compete for attention with the name of the recipient.

Sign or initial the memorandum on the right side immediately following your typed name. Some individuals do not sign their memorandums; however, this practice is not recommended. There may be a time when you need to prove you either did or did not write a memorandum that has gone out in your name. A signature or initials can provide such proof.

The guide words may be typed in boldface type, and a tab stop should be set two spaces away from the colon on the longest line (*Subject:*). See the exhibits for an example of how the information should line up. The guide words are normally double spaced; however, the information on those lines may take up more than one line when necessary. The first example below includes a mail code that would be repeated on the envelope. The second example would be used on a form memo sent to two groups of people.

TO: Mona Martin, Research Coordinator
　　　Koester Law Library 3462-2

TO: Sales Representatives
　　　Market Survey Statisticians

On the subject line, type the topic of the memo, keeping it concise; but make sure it contains enough information to identify for the reader the major point of the memorandum. Type the subject line in either all caps or initial caps only.

Follow the heading by three blank lines before typing the body of the message. Like letters, memorandums are single-spaced with two lines between paragraphs.

**Closing Notations.**　The notations that may be used at the bottom of a memorandum are exactly the same as those for letters: reference initials, enclosure (or attachment) notation, copy notation (if not included in the heading), and postscript. Each of these letter parts is covered in detail in preceding sections of this appendix. Reread them if you need to do so.

## BUSINESS ENVELOPES

For external mailing, most companies use printed envelopes that match their letterhead stationery. For interoffice correspondence, most companies use envelopes that can be reused. Exhibits C.9 through C.11 show examples of No. 10 (9½″ × 4⅛″) envelopes, the size used most often in the business world. However, the spacing of the addresses can easily be adapted for use on other envelope sizes if necessary.

To save paper and money, many companies use an envelope like that in Exhibit C.12. Envelopes such as these can be reused because they are not glued shut. Often they have a string fastener on the back side; but, unless there is a need for confidentiality, mail can usually be sent through interoffice systems with the envelope flap open.

**Envelope with Preprinted Return Address**

**PBJ Productions**
**303 York Avenue**
**St. Paul, MN 55101**

Ms. Lynette Shishido
Decision Support Specialist
Stone & Lambert
420 Fairview Lane, No. 287
St. Paul, MN 55101

**Envelope with Keyboarded Return Address**

P. A. Stezaker, Vice President
Stewart's of London
18110 NE 34th Street
Camas, WA 98607

Mr. Russell Colburn
Operations Manager
Staples Office Products
180 Westridge Drive
Watsonville, CA 95076-9910

**EXHIBIT C.11**   Envelope with Postal and Addressee Notations

**PBJ Productions**
303 York Avenue
St. Paul, MN 55101

PERSONAL                                                    SPECIAL DELIVERY

                          Dr. Susan Leslie
                          MBO Enterprises
                          1588 Kerper Boulevard
                          Dubuque, IA 52001

---

**EXHIBIT C.12**   Interoffice Envelope

| INTEROFFICE MAIL | | | | | |
|---|---|---|---|---|---|
| **Name** | **Location** | **Name** | **Location** | **Name** | **Location** |
| Marjorie Black | B 231 | | | | |
| John Bishop | K 43 | | | | |
| PURCHASING DEPT. | A 102 | | | | |
| Melvoona Boren | F 60 | | | | |
| Judi Smith | Adm 192 | | | | |
| Ed Yanez | 15 87 | | | | |
| | | | | | |
| | | | | | |

EXHIBIT
C.13
**Folding Standard Stationery for No. 10 Envelopes**

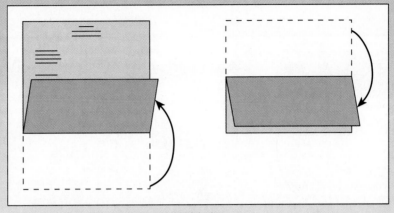

1. Fold up and crease the bottom one-third of the letter.
2. Fold down the top of the letter to approximately one-third to one-half inch from the first crease.

Exhibit C.11 illustrates the placement of special handling instructions on business envelopes. Unusual mailing instructions should be typed two or three lines below the stamp area on the right margin, and they should be in capital letters. Instructions to the addressee should also be in capital letters two or three lines below the inside address on the left margin. Common postal notations include these: Priority Mail, Airmail, Registered Mail, Certified Mail, Special Delivery, and Return Receipt Requested. These are the most common addressee notations:

| | |
|---|---|
| Attention | Directs the letter to a specific person but lets the company know that, should that person not be available, someone else should open the letter. |
| Personal or Confidential | Indicates that the letter is to be opened only by the addressee, not by a secretary or clerk. |
| Hold for arrival | Directs those at the address to hold the letter, which will be picked up by the addressee upon his or her arrival. Often a date is indicated to show when the addressee will arrive. |
| Please forward | Directs those at the address to forward the letter to the addressee's new address if it is known. |

**Folding and Inserting Correspondence.** Exhibits C.13 through C.15 show how to fold letters for insertion into various envelope sizes. Folding letters is not as easy as it looks so you might want to practice on scrap paper before folding documents you intend to mail.

**EXHIBIT C.14**

**Folding Standard Stationery for a No. 6 3/4 (6 1/2" x 3 5/8") Envelope**

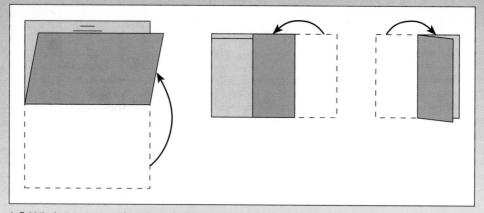

1. Fold the bottom to approximately one-half inch of the top of the letter, and crease it.
2. Fold the right side of the letter approximately one-third to the left, and crease it.
3. Fold the left side over the right side, stopping one-third to one-half inch short of the crease on the right. Crease it.

**EXHIBIT C.15**

**Folding Standard Stationery for a Window Envelope**

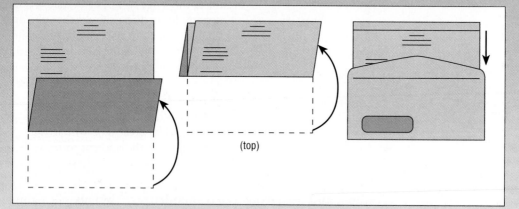

(top)

1. Type the inside address on the letter so it will align with the window on the envelope.
2. Fold up the bottom third of the letter, and crease it.
3. At that crease, fold the top third back and down to about one-third to one-half inch from the bottom fold. Crease it.

# INDEX